RETAIL STORE PLANNING & DESIGN MANUAL

Second Edition

The National Retail Federation Series

The National Retail Federation Series comprises books on retail store management, for stores of all sizes and for all management responsibilities. The National Retail Federation is the world's largest retail trade association, with membership that includes the leading department, specialty, discount, mass merchandise, and independent stores, as well as 30 national and 50 state associations. NRF members represent an industry that encompasses more than 1.4 million U.S. retail establishments and employs nearly 20 million people—1 in 5 American workers. The NRF's international members operate stores in more than 50 nations.

The National Retail Federation Series includes the following books:

Published Books:

FOR 1994: Financial & Operating Results of Retail Stores in 1993
     National Retail Federation

MOR 1994: Merchandising & Operating Results of Retail Stores in 1993
     National Retail Federation

Competing with the Retail Giants: How to Survive in the New Retail Landscape
     Kenneth E. Stone

Value Retailing in the 1990s: Off-Pricers, Factory Outlets, and Closeout Stores
     Packaged Facts, Inc.

Credit Card Marketing
     Bill Grady

Loss Prevention Guide for Retail Businesses
     Rudolph C. Kimiecik

Management of Retail Buying, Third Edition
     R. Patrick Cash, John W. Wingate, and Joseph S. Friedlander

Retail Store Planning & Design Manual, 2nd Edition
     Michael J. Lopez

Forthcoming Books:

Practical Merchandising Math
     Leo Gafney

RETAIL STORE PLANNING & DESIGN MANUAL

Second Edition

MICHAEL J. LOPEZ, A.S.I.D, I.S.P.

John Wiley & Sons, Inc.

New York • Chichester • Brisbane • Toronto • Singapore

Library of Congress Cataloging-in-Publication Data:

Lopez, Michael J.
    Retail store planning & design manual / Michael J. Lopez.—2nd ed.
      P. cm.—(The National Retail Federation series)
    Includes index.
    ISBN 0-471-07629-5 (cloth)
    1. Stores, Retail—Planning—Handbooks, manuals, etc. 2. Stores,
  Retail—Design and construction—Handbooks, manuals, etc.
  I. Title. II. Title: Retail store planning and design manual.
  III. Series.
  HF5429.L59 1995
  725'.21—dc20   94-42640

This manual is dedicated to the next generation of retailers, store planners, and educators in this dynamic industry.

I am indebted to Marilyn Lopez and my numerous associates, colleagues, retail clients, and friends who have encouraged me throughout my gratifying career.

Special thanks to the National Retail Merchants Association, New York, for originally recognizing the need for this manual as an educational tool, and to the National Retail Federation for its continued endorsement of this manual.

CONTENTS

FOREWORD

The National Retail Federation is pleased to have assisted in the completion of the *Retail Store Planning & Design Manual, Second Edition*, written by Michael Lopez. This up-to-date edition will serve as the reference standard for members of the retail, design, construction, and educational communities. Written from the store planner's perspective, it contains comprehensive illustrations and will be useful to professionals and novices alike.

The store environment, particularly as it reflects a firm's merchandising philosophy, is critical to establishing an identity and an awareness among shoppers. The positive impact that store renovations as well as new store designs and concepts have on sales volume has been demonstrated repeatedly in all segments of the industry. The emergence of retail as an entertainment form has further challenged store designers and merchants to present the goods in the most productive manner possible. Using the proven techniques addressed in this book, along with the right mix of creativity, should make for successful results.

We trust that you will find the *Retail Store Planning & Design Manual* to be among your most productive tools and look forward to bringing you additional publications to enhance your retail library.

John A. Ronzetti
National Retail Federation

ACKNOWLEDGMENTS

This book could not have been written without the assistance of many people. It includes the comments and contributions of countless industry professionals who have helped guide my efforts over the past thirty years. My thanks to the senior executives and store-planning staff of Allied Stores Corporation during the early concept days and to the National Retail Federation for its encouragement and support.

I salute the American Society of Interior Designers, the Institute of Store Planners, the National Association of Display Industries, and the National Association of Store Fixture Manufacturers for their dedication and commitment in promoting educational opportunities within the industry.

M.J.L.

INTRODUCTION

This book should serve as the vehicle for demystifying the store-planning function and the related merchandising process. It is intended to outline to novices, experienced merchants, store managers, and store planners the fundamentals of planning and design—and to put the fundamentals into an understandable format.

When I entered the retail-store-planning field over thirty years ago, I was amazed to find that it offered such a diverse palette of opportunities and career options. I started as an apprentice draftsman and then progressed on to become a coordinator, estimator, project supervisor, field supervisor, and installer. The art of merchandising was passed on to me through on-the-job training. It took many, many years before I was qualified to form my own firm and share my knowledge with others.

The development of a design plan that is both cost-effective and sales-effective demands the ability to clearly interpret the thoughts and ideas of at least the merchant, store manager, and planner. The unique compilation of narrative and illustrations that is in this manual should serve as a most valuable source in better understanding the complexities of planning either a department or an entire store.

The first edition of the book has been exceptionally well received by the retail industry. It has been rewarding to receive the positive comments of professional planners, retail executives, and educators. I hope that you, too, will find your copy of *Retail Store Planning & Design Manual* of significant value.

Michael J. Lopez

Michael J. Lopez Designs, Inc.
P.O. Box 1690
McHenry, IL 60051-1690

RETAIL STORE PLANNING & DESIGN MANUAL

Second Edition

Chapter 1

THE COMPLEX ROLE
OF STORE PLANNERS

What Is a Store Planner?

What is a *store planner*? Ask ten different people and you will get ten different answers. Store planners are individuals with specialized talents in presenting merchandise so that it will be purchased by customers. The leaders in the store planning and design industry have a special zest for knowledge. The majority of these talented professionals have had mentors who have influenced the development of their careers.

Professional store planners have learned to use their talents to help retailers in effectively marketing their goods and services. Store planners work on a variety of projects and designs and are always concerned about maximizing their creative abilities to ensure that merchandise is presented in the most effective manner in a given store. Store planners are highly regarded artists, technicians, and business people. They are also individuals who are willing to share their ability and knowledge with others. Many are generous enough to instruct and guide the next generation of potential store planners and prepare them for the future. Some of the most successful store planers are, in fact, teachers. They often give

lectures to the new and upcoming talent entering the industry. Many professional store planners are recognized as leaders within the community. Why? Because so many merchants look to them for help and direction.

To be a success in the store planning industry today requires foresight, awareness, and the ability to "wear many hats." Store planners are constantly challenged to maximize the utilization of space. They bring theater into retailing and offer the customer a new shopping experience. Their lives touch upon every element in the presentation of merchandise in the store. The lighting, colors, and ambiance present a backdrop that allows the merchandise to tell a story. The talents of store planners cause shoppers to take notice of the mood, taste, environment, and, most of all, the merchandise within the store.

Store planners, along with management, are responsible for the evolution presently taking place in retailing. Today, more than ever before, stores are under great pressure to develop the type of sales environment that not only reduces the sales help and time spent with the customer, but also encourages personalized self-selection whenever possible. Store

1

planners are most important to the success of a store. In many ways, when they plan and design a store, they are acting as a salesperson. They attempt to create an atmosphere with maximum appeal while working within a budget that is sometimes unrealistic. They are called on to use their talents time and time again during this age of increased productivity to simplify and expedite the process of a sales transaction in the shortest possible time. Creativity helps to encourage sales, trade-ups, and impulse buying. Doing all of these things, while creating a special atmosphere that will distinguish one store from another, will make the shopper want to return again and again. The store planner must also consider accommodation for handicap accessibility in retail stores.

Store planners are recognized as a vital part of a store's marketing strategy. They are people with unparalleled talents and creativity. Two of the main ingredients of successful store planners are maintaining leadership and giving service to both the customers and merchants.

Opening new stores, designing shops, creating new environments, working with the staff—all keep store planners abreast of merchandise and help management develop and run their business. Store planners must have a rare combination of acquired talents. They must constantly ask, "Why?" They must continue to develop new concepts. Frequently, during the creative process, assumptions are challenged, patterns are recognized, and new ways are shown to make connections by taking risks and by taking advantage of change. Planners see new ways to transform the familiar, revealing complexity and beauty. Creativity is a special ability to make connections by bringing together unrelated ideas in ways that relate to new concepts. Store planners are challenged daily by the economy, interest rates, and tight money, constantly testing not only their abilities but the environment they have developed.

Store planning firms that employ store planners and designers who have advanced training, who use modern methodology and possess astute marketing ability, and who are able to efficiently utilize human resources, will not only grow but also prosper. Store planning is truly the backbone of the dynamic field of modern retail merchandising and design.

What Does a Store Planner Do?

There are literally hundreds of individual tasks that must be performed by store planners. Perhaps the most important task is to fully understand and carefully interpret what is in the best interest of clients. Once this is accomplished, planners begin what is often the long process of collecting the "nitty gritty" of information on details such as the conceptual plan, elevations, construction details, work schedules, and color palettes. At later stages, planners prepare bid documents, conduct bidding procedures, and award contracts. They will supervise construction and will likely become immersed in activities such as promoting the services of the planning firm and taking part in negotiations.

Among other duties, planners must direct the budget aspects of the project and supervise implementation of the production timetable from start to finish. This requires planning and managing such factors as (a) preparing the scope-of-work criteria, (b) coping with the limitations imposed by the shape of the space and taking proper action, and (c) analyzing the availability of building materials, perimeter wall requirements, placement of freestanding fixtures, and the proper housing for merchandise to be displayed, signed, and sold.

Yes, store planners do wear many hats. They constantly are challenged to be knowledgeable about the intricacies of many trades. Planners are often asked for opinions. In fact, planners usually spend more time explaining the "whys" and "hows" of each question.

It can take years for the store planner to acquire the knowledge and skills necessary to fully understand the most complex client needs, to learn how to live within budgets, and to master other fine arts such as matching designs to marketing environments and creating the best overall images for merchandising outlets.

Communication

Flow of Information

At the onset of a project, the principle players—planner and merchants—may not be aware of the full extent of the information that they must exchange before one line is drawn on paper. Planners sometimes are blamed for incorrectly interpreting client needs, when it has been the merchants who have improperly prepared themselves with necessary information. Of course, the reverse can also be the case.

Correctly communicating the scope-of-work criteria, the budget figures, and the required timetables are keys to the successful implementation of any size project. Store planners who develop comprehensive checklists and guidelines to help facilitate this information sharing are invaluable as the work progresses.

Communication Is the Key

Even though communicating clearly and cheerfully with clients will always be one of the most important attributes of any store planning firm, it is a facet of office operations that is often neglected. There is no aspect of store planning more crucial than for employees to communicate effectively and pleasantly with clients. Every telephone call should be answered with professionalism and appropriate concern for the client's needs. Employees also should be well versed on what to say when they are describing the firm's services.

Management has the responsibility to coach all staff members on what items of information should be collected when a prospective client makes an inquiry.

The following are examples of items of information that should be gathered regarding projects being discussed: (1) name of store and principal, (2) address, (3) name of facility, (4) square footage to be processed, and (5) projected completion date. It is generally a good idea to follow the conversation with a prompt letter to show appreciation to the caller for showing an interest in the services of the company. The letter also provides an opportunity to describe the full scope of services. Promotional literature should also be enclosed.

Once prospective clients have received the correspondence, it is wise to call again to see if there is a desire for still more information. This is the time to dispel any misunderstandings arising from correspondence or proposal.

Clients should have the courtesy to promptly notify planners of their decisions, either positive or negative, and not leave planners hanging. By the same token, planners should have the courtesy to promptly notify potential clients if the firm cannot deliver drawings as requested.

When possible, a request for the scope-of-work outline should be made early so that the particulars of the facility under consideration can be carefully studied.

No two projects are exactly alike, even though they may be products of the same design. Before arriving at the cost of doing the project, it is essential that all conditions that will influence the production costs and margins of profit are reviewed and analyzed.

Client and Planner Correspondence

Once the initial meeting has taken place between planner and client, much can be done to improve chances of a harmonious relationship. Correspondence plays a critical role. Follow-up letters to a client might include an outline of the scope-of-work criteria, a contract, a letter of agreement, or just a note of thanks for the client's time and attention.

Balancing the Workload

From a financial standpoint, it generally is healthy for store planners to be working on both short- and long-range projects simultaneously. However, care must be exercised not to take on additional jobs if there is a danger they will not be delivered on schedule or if it is clear that the staff will not have the time to keep up the close communications.

Reworking Means Delays

Keep firmly in mind that markups and profit margins generally are slim where finished drawing work is concerned. When working drawings have to be reworked because of misunderstandings or poor communication, the margins that were originally thought adequate can quickly disappear. Put another way, inadequate drawings almost always delay projects and can escalate bid prices.

Reworking has a domino effect. When the contractor's completion dates are delayed, it costs money for everyone in the chain of implementation. The result usually is that the planner's credibility suffers, and prospects for future business with the client are jeopardized.

Setting the Fee

Long-range projects and multiple projects of like design should be examined from the standpoint of investment of production time. Negotiated fees should be arrived at very carefully. The fee structure should be derived by using a sliding scale contingent on what the actual square footage is of the retail space to be processed.

It is important to realize that the square-foot fee for smaller projects normally should be higher than for larger projects due to the disproportionate amount of work required. Whether the project is large or smaller, essentially the same process must be followed. When negotiating price, remember that if completion dates for drawings are required sooner than normal, overtime work will be necessary and the square-foot fee must be reviewed accordingly.

There are times when it is possible, for various reasons, to draw a project out over a longer period than was first envisioned. Others can be produced profitably at less-than-prime rates. Such projects are candidates for filling voids between projects with normal production schedules.

Achieving Internal Organization

Attentive store planners periodically review all in-house work to see if there are any out-of-sequence projects, so they can alert staff members about new projects that will be phased into the existing schedule. This will also allow for the assessment of finances to be sure that the money supply is adequate to support normal office expenses. Payments on accounts receivable should closely approximate proceeds from work in progress. Another routine duty for planners is to check on accumulated expenditures for production, including fees for outside contract services.

The New Assignment

Assume all the initial steps have been taken and a new assignment has been landed. Now is the time to negotiate any terms and conditions that remain unsettled and prepare a contract for signing. A warning is required here: Don't fall for the temptation to begin a project out of eagerness until all legal authorization has been finalized. Even signed contracts can be terminated by a landlord, retailer, or planner under certain circumstances. Make sure all contracts clearly spell out the responsibilities of all parties involved. The contracts should also include a payment schedule because clients do not appreciate any unexpected invoices.

Once the new job is posted and the number of project hours has been accurately estimated for each project phase, it is time to begin keeping track of progress. Too often, costly hours are eaten up by trying to "reinvent the wheel." Planners and designers sooner or later must learn the discipline of working within time frames allocated for preliminary drawings, plans elevations, color pallets, and so on.

The Rendering Task

In the typical planning office, renderings are handled by one or two draftspersons. Not everyone who draws needs to have the ability to render, even though rendering is a subject heavily stressed in many schools of design. Planners need to be better draftspersons than renderers, although the ability to render is certainly convenient to have for those times when that skill is needed. As a useful talent, the mechanics of drafting usually outweigh the ability to render in most planning firms.

In order to present an interpretation of the client's ideas in a format that can be understood by all, the planner must translate thoughts accurately on paper. Since many retailers have difficulty reading blueprints and drawings, the planner must find a way to guarantee that there will be no misunderstandings of the concepts. If thoughts are translated more clearly on paper, there will be fewer problems encountered on the job. There will also be less chance for criticism caused by the client having a confused notion of what was planned.

New Production Schedule

Before launching a new production schedule, there is a need to assign a *job captain*, the person who will be responsible for coordinating the drawing of the project. Working from the scope-of-work criteria that was developed jointly with the client and from the rough drawings from each meeting, it is time to ask certain questions.

Each project is unique by nature and scope, even though typical details are repeated from job to job. Requirements for hardware, finish, and so on, almost always change, even if two buildings are commonly owned, are used for the same purpose, and appear to be cut out of the same mold.

Achieving Quality Control

No matter which phases of a project the store planner, job captain, or engineer may be responsible for, drawing and details will be required for each phase, along with a careful check for errors and omissions. In order to keep the drafting room operation running smoothly, frequent inspection of drawings may be necessary. Working from sketches, the job captain should check on freestanding fixtures and decor to see if there have been any misinterpretations of the preliminary sketches and to see if the designs are likely to result in a waste of materials.

Ideally, fixtures should be designed to get the maximum amount of product from a given amount of stock. A wise job captain will check the flow of production periodically in order to spot any problems.

Quality Control Checks

Not all staff members will work at full capacity all of the time—there will be good and bad days. Mistakes, caused by inattention and lack of knowledge, are inevitable. The lesson to be learned here is that these mistakes should be caught in the preparatory stages, not while bidding, construction, or installation is taking place. Therein lies the value of frequent quality control checks.

The best planners carefully monitor and guide a project from start to finish, preventing as many mistakes and omissions as possible.

Job Captain's Function

Another key part of the job captain's function is to review the work of the staff with respect to the capabilities and limitations and individuals. Just one detailer who does not understand the fundamentals of store fixturing and construction can cost a firm dearly in terms of lost time and "aggravation." When job captains have a clear idea of what is required and a dedication to the task, they can deliver a comprehensive set of drawings of which they can be proud and that reflect the correct image of the company. To meet these conditions, the job captain must properly adjust for changes demanded by shifting field conditions or revisions to orders requested by the client. The job captain must also keep records of all hours worked that go beyond those that were originally contracted.

Once a project has cleared the drafting room, management should be in a position to review the actual costs of producing all the drawings and fix a realistic profit margin, taking into account estimates of the time required for following the project to its completion. This should give management an accurate idea of problems with either the project or the personnel who worked on it. This is the right time to take action to improve production time, or, failing that, to adjust fees upward to compensate.

Pricing Services and Negotiating the Contract

Profit margins are affected by a number of variables. Among these variables are a fee, the type of facility planned, the type of drawings required, the availability of typical building details, the project criteria, the value of the planner's reputation, and the number of production hours available to complete the job on time.

When negotiating a price for services, keep a figure in mind with which to begin bargaining and another that is rock bottom. Any contract should clearly spell out the responsibilities of all parties. The contract must also make provisions for adequate compensation for any overruns for extra work not negotiated. And when and if the planner can find an opportunity to give the client a price break, it may turn out to be of value in terms of good will.

Once there has been agreement on the price of services, stick to that price. After that, there may be only a slim possibility of increasing the fee unless a substantial difference develops between the actual project conditions and the given contract terms.

Prior to signing the contract, give it very close scrutiny. Try to determine whether there is a possibility that the fee is so low that no profit will be realized from the job, take a stand, establish the bottom-line price, live with it, and then live within it!

Once a new work assignment has been landed, try discreetly to learn why your firm was chosen over the competitors. This can help to build a better understanding of true market conditions and the realities of price competition. Also, try to learn whether budget numbers compared realistically with those projected by the competition.

When a job has been lost, try to learn why the other company was selected and, if possible, what was agreed to in terms of fee and projected overall costs. This information will help in negotiating future projects and in working with other retailers in the same or similar categories of trade. In case it was discovered legitimately that mistakes were made in estimates and fee structure, notify the client as promptly as possible. Don't feel embarrassed about doing this because in the end it may actually improve credibility with clients. Many times, an opportunity will arise to submit another bid under terms that are more favorable. In any event, every contract should accurately spell out the terms and conditions under which the planner will be working, and the schedule of payments expected or services.

It is wise to reread the entire contract when it is returned to see if there are new provisions that did not appear in the original proposal. Once satisfied with the contract as signed, make sure to live up to the provisions to which you have agreed—your professional reputation depends on it, and you do not want to set yourself up for legal difficulties down the road for noncompliance.

The Drawings

When it is possible, the client should send the store planner a complete set of building drawings once the contract is signed. As the drawings are reviewed, look for obstructions that could cause problems and delays. Advise the client of these possible trouble spots as soon as possible. A preliminary building-plan outline drawn prior to the first working meeting should acquaint the planner with the limitations imposed by the space. Advise the client of existing or potential problems once the drawings of the building have been carefully analyzed. If the building already exists, a field survey exposes conditions not indicated in drawings. The plan may also give a more realistic idea of how the space can best be utilized.

Buildings were not always built exactly as indicated on plans and drawings. In addition, plans and drawings seldom seem to be updated. When the facility is inspected, try to identify even minor renovations made in recent years that may not be reflected in blueprints. Make careful notations of architectural, mechanical, or electrical locations, and transfer this information to the new building plan.

These preliminary steps will save extra work in the long run. If plans have to be reworked later, the cost will seriously affect your profit margins. See if a better approach can be found to relocate equipment if it appears to be potentially obstructive. Make sure, as the drawings are reviewed, that the planner responsible is including any line of walls or merchandising hardware systems that can be reused repetitively. Also look for existing equipment and materials that can be reused to help economize on overall cost.

New vs. Old Materials

Today there are many innovative construction methods and materials constantly being offered that produce savings with added cosmetic benefits. Every wall system and finish will impact on the budget in a different way, but usually will be more costly when a new product is used, rather than a conventional one that has been available for many years. Finding ways to use existing building materials and

equipment that were bought at cost lower than newer replacements is an excellent means to increase value to the client. Merchants always appreciate the reuse of an existing wall or satisfactory equipment if it represents a significant savings.

Watch for the point of no return. Planners love to rip out and start fresh. Don't fall into this trap. If, instead of a total revamp, a savings can be realized by reworking walls or materials into the plans, do so as long as they are compatible with the overall finish and presentation format.

Realistic Specifications

Planners often will call for a point of design that the customer never, or rarely, sees. An added expenditure may be a waste if the design concept turns out to be a "nightmare" or quickly becomes dated. In such circumstances, the client must either live with the mishap or discard it. Before walking away from a completed project, try to consider what is really in the client's best interest. The services provided should fully satisfy the client. The design should not be achieved to provide the planner with an ego trip.

As drawing progresses, frequently refer to the scope-of-work guidelines and budget. This will help make sure that the client's intent has been fully understood.

Be as sensible and frugal as possible in allocating materials, while at the same time not sacrificing good taste and quality design.

A special color, textured paint, or inexpensive wallcovering may be found that can achieve the desired effect even though the planner first intended to use a more expensive surface material. Another example is that a planner may call for a heavy textured surface at merchandise level that may be expensive and can snag, scratch, or damage merchandise.

It is absolutely crucial to remember that it is the merchandise, not the decor, that is always emphasized by good store planning. Sometimes wallcoverings conflict with the presentation of merchandise by clashing with the patterns or colors of the products being sold. Choosing a neutral background usually reduces the risks of such mismatches.

Consistently applying colors, textures, and materials that are harmonious with the surroundings is a thoughtful way to insure the best presentation of merchandise.

If there is a need to propose an out-of-the-ordinary building material that is new to the client, discuss the cost and practical side of the application with the client first. Clever planners always have a second recourse in mind (perhaps a similar product) in case the first idea is ill-received.

Having Second Options Ready

In some cases, a planner will work conscientiously to get a single product specified, only to discover that in the course of building the project, it cannot be delivered on schedule. Again, such setbacks argue for having alternatives in mind.

Planners often are insistent on using a particular material or in achieving a special effect. In their eagerness, they may not even bother to consider alternatives or compare costs.

Planners who are tempted to specify a particularly rich building material or expensive fixture should ask themselves, "What are the chances that this detail may hardly be noticed?" Common-sense judgment should be used when tempted to specify anything extravagant. Instead, it is better to settle on something that is appropriate for the circumstances.

When clients insist on using a product that will create problems, find a diplomatic way to get them to change their mind. This is especially necessary when there may be a delivery problem. Any materials that may require a long delivery time should be ordered and shipped as early as possible to the successful contractor so last-minute substitutes are not required.

Ordering Materials

All material purchases should be covered with purchase orders. This will help coordinate drawings with purchases. You should indicate items to be supplied by your client to the contractor for incorporation in the project. The early arrival of materials is always preferable to waiting for them unless, by coming early, an obstruction is created.

The store planner shoulders the responsibility to ensure materials arrive on time. It is helpful to develop a materials list—as often as weekly—to help update each project and keep track of particular items.

Making Drawings Specific

Make sure that all materials are clearly specified in the drawings; for example, the drawing might indi-

cate that a laminate plastic is the desired finish. This should be done even though the base price for the finish varies as many as four times, depending on differences in color, texture, and finish. Clients respect planners more when directions are specific enough to prevent confusion over similar, but unequal, materials. Clients will also appreciate it when they can choose alternates that give the same general appearance but cost less.

Management, planners, engineers, job captains, designers, and detailers must keep a close watch on all appropriate aspects of the project as it progresses. There is no margin for error in a complicated project.

If they plan carefully and then work their plan, they will be much more likely to catch oversights in engineering, drawings, and drafting that require immediate correction. The contractor, if notified early, will be in a position to deliver the project faster. *It is the job of the store planner to anticipate questions before they are asked and to provide answers in advance.*

Controlling Costs

Administrators of planning companies must be aware of the importance of controlling overhead costs. If the gross margin of profit is too low due to unforeseen production costs, they must come to a clear understanding of how the underestimation occurred and then execute a plan to prevent recurrence.

The need to coordinate closely with the accounting department during each project phase is essential to provide better control over production costs and avoid cost overruns.

Ideally, no project should be robbed of the time required to produce it efficiently and correctly. Although detailing of a project can be the most important part of the drawings, planners often treat detailing too lightly, hoping that the contractor will cover for their shortcomings.

Once in a while, administration must ask questions such as, "Is our profit too high, enough to make us uncompetitive? Is our gross margin too low? Have we taken this project at below cost just to fill a production void?" When venturing into a new type of retail design with little or no experience, be especially cautious. Projects often prove to be more expensive to produce than they first appear. With each new project, look at the staff's background and capabilities and decide if each is experienced and mature enough to handle the project successfully. When negotiating to get the job, make sure to do a little extra homework before signing a contract. When competing with recognized planners in an area with prior experience, keep in mind that startup cost may be an extra liability that your firm may need to recover. If, on the other hand, sales and margins look profitable and staff are capable of delivering a successful project, don't be hesitant.

Information Processing

With any new project, processing information is crucial, but it can also be costly. Information needs include plans, elevations, and details, plus the specifying of materials that will perform as intended under normal conditions.

Lay out and plan every necessary phase of the project carefully; then proceed with developing plans, elevations, and details. Construction details should indicate not only the application of materials, but the size, application method, the color, the finish, and even the manufacturer's telephone number. This body of information is essential both for bidding and purchasing. If the materials are new to the draftsperson or the contractor, there will be a need to explain.

Complete Details

Details should be produced on time, of course, but should not be rushed unnecessarily. Although detailing is an important ingredient in the overall production scenario, rushing often causes aspects of a project to be overlooked. If a firm is forced to redo the drawings, the resulting delays will surely impact on the profit margins. Missing information will cause a delay in the arrival of material that, in turn, will cause other manufacturers a delay.

Once all of the drawings are complete, the planner will proceed with the normal bidding procedures as outlined in this manual.

Summary

There are numerous job responsibilities continuously overlapping during all phases of the project. It is the store planner's job to be constantly alert and to recognize any potential problems that might crop up in any phase due to inattention.

At this time, it is virtually impossible to fully describe the entire, very complex role of the store planner. The process of collecting and analyzing the information may be different with each new project. After several projects, the planner will begin to establish his or her own method of dealing with specific problems and thus, a unique "Complex Role of a Store Planner."

Chapter 2

ACCOMMODATION FOR HANDICAPPED
ACCESSIBILITY IN RETAIL STORES

Americans with Disabilities Act

When planning or designing a retail store, store planners must comply with the Americans with Disabilities Act (ADA) that was enacted into law on July 28, 1990. This federal law prohibits discrimination on the basis of certain disabilities and mandates access for the handicapped to public accommodations, including retail store environments. New retail stores, as well as remodeled facilities, require accommodations to be useable by both handicapped customers and employees.

From a project's outset, considerations must be given on how the disabled gain store access. Handicapped parking spaces and ramps are part of the exterior planned design of the store and should be located near or adjacent to the front of the store.

Other considerations include, but are not limited to, entrances, actual store emergency exits, aisle widths, counter heights, rack heights, fitting rooms, toilet facilities, elevators, telephones, and drinking fountains. These are, however, just a few of the many technical requirements that are included in planning retail space.

It is strongly suggested that the planner acquire the uniform code and current standards for handicapped users. A copy can be obtained from the *American National Standard*, published by the Council of American Building Officials, 5203 Leesburg Pike, #708, Falls Church, VA 22041, which illustrates in detail all required specifications and standards. The planner should also be aware of state and municipal codes, which occasionally are stricter than the federal regulations. Many times when existing retail facilities undergo major renovations, it will be necessary to bring several areas of the store up to these codes.

Exterior and Interior Ramps and Parking Spaces

Exterior courtesy ramps for wheelchairs and mobile individuals who cannot negotiate regular step elevations are designed to minimize the effort necessary to access the store. The length and slope of the ramp are determined by the incline level that a wheelchair has to travel.

Interior ramps within a store are required when the level of the floor plane changes. The length of

9

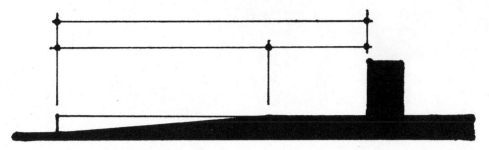

This cross section illustrates a ramp connecting the sidewalk.

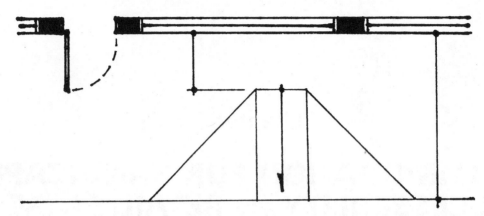

This plan illustrates ramp sidewalk and store entrances.

the ramp is determined by the height of the rise.

Parking spaces for the handicapped should be designed to be in close proximity to the entrance allowing the handicapped person to easily make his or her way from the vehicle without the obstruction of closely parked vehicles in adjoining spots. The handicapped parking lot spaces are to be striped and identified by special signage.

The federal minimum of handicapped-accessible parking spaces is determined by the total number of spaces at a 1:25 ratio for the first 100 spaces, 1:50 for the next 100, with an additional space for each additional 100 spaces or fraction thereof.

Entrances

Clear access must be provided for both handicapped and nonhandicapped customers approaching the store. Easy access should be visible from the approaching thoroughfare and parking lot to encourage handicapped customers from afar. At least one entrance must be dedicated to handicapped customers/employees. Handicapped entrance access includes the width clearances for the door entrance and traveling distances within a vestibule between doors. Motion detectors to open doors are often installed as an added convenience. Floor surfaces

must be on a level plane to minimize hindrance of the disabled's locomotion. It is important to verify the distance allocated between the door plate (handles) and adjacent walls or glass partitions and the federal ADA standards.

Aisles and Merchandising Racks

The majority of handicapped customers and employees are independently mobile. If they are not, the disabled will often shop with an ambulatory friend. Aisles should be designed to accommodate all types of handicapped customers, whether they use a wheelchair, crutches, or a walker. The main entrance aisles to a retail store are always larger to help invite and funnel customers into a store. Main aisle widths of 5 feet to 12 feet are considered normal, depending on the space's square footage and configuration. The widths of the aisles diminish as they progress into deeper areas of the store, but the minimal aisle width of 48 inches should be maintained.

Consideration should be given to aisle widths between clothing racks or other merchandise and to the height at which merchandise is hung on the racks. In the case of long clothing, such as coats, dresses, and intimate apparel, there is not much

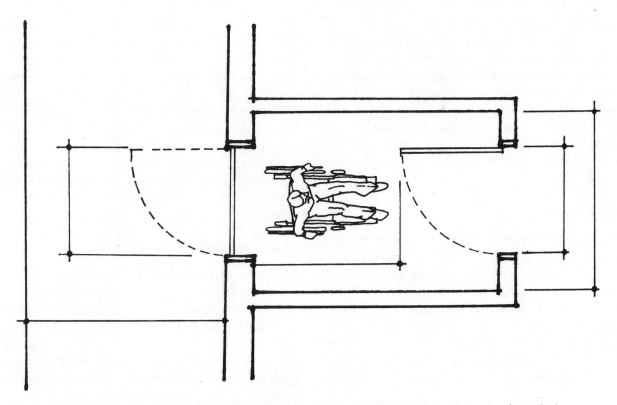

This illustration depicts minimum clear width for single wheelchairs and depth of vestibule.

choice as to the height at which they can be hung. In these instances retail sales assistance should be available for shoppers who are not able to reach high merchandise.

Counter Heights and Showcases

When planning and designing the merchandising layout of the store, the planner must give thorough consideration to handicapped customers and employees. Showcase islands, cash-and-wraps, counters, and customer service counter areas must be closely scrutinized to insure proper design, manufacturing, installation, and usage of the store fixtures with the handicapped in mind. The dimensions of counters must be correctly accommodated to handicapped persons' special needs. The height, length, and width of these special fixtures are dif-

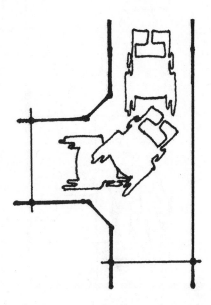

At any point that aisles intersect, turning space is required by a wheelchair.

ferent from the dimensions of other similar merchandise-presentation fixtures used in the store. In special cases, auxiliary counters may be added to fulfill these needs. Regard must be given to the design of these fixtures for clear floor space, parallel approach, and high/low side-reach limits and maximum side-reach over obstructions. Attention should be given to any checkout area that will be elevated or on a platform since an accessibility ramp will be required.

Fitting Rooms

Handicapped fitting rooms are frequently designed to be incorporated into the bank of standard fitting-room partitions, or they can be located in a convenience area. Corridors to a handicapped fitting room usually are 42 inches wide with either a swinging 36-inch door, which must open outwardly, or a sliding door. Within the fitting room, ample space must be provided so that a wheelchair could have a clear floor space of 180 degrees including

space for benches, grab bars, mirrors, and hooks. With the exception of certain accessories and grab bars and a bench, the handicapped fitting room interior is finished like all other fitting rooms within the store. The height of the bench is important for persons who wish to transfer from a wheelchair to the bench. The bench itself should be structurally strong with rounded edges. Mirrors should be installed to accommodate both wheelchair-bound and standing persons using the room. The handicapped fitting room should be marked with identification signage.

Toilet Rooms

The store planner should always verify the exact installed location of the rough plumbing and whether one unisex toilet room is acceptable per floor. Each unisex toilet room shall contain one wash basin, one lavatory, and one wheelchair-accessible entrance door with privacy latch. Grab bars, along with other standard toilet-room accessories, should

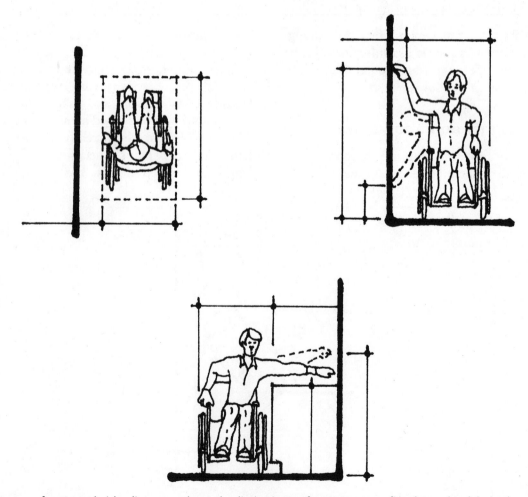

These top, front, and side diagrams show the limitations of a person confined to wheelchair shopping.

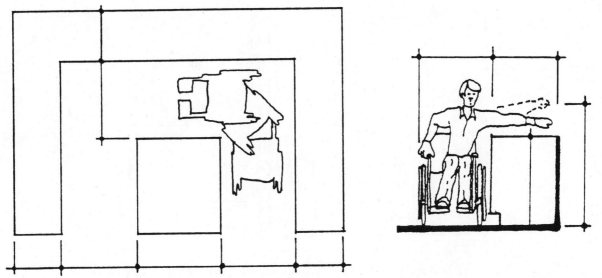

This plan illustrates maneuverability within a showcase island.

be included. Increasingly, a wall-mounted "baby changer fold-down platform" will be added to a toilet room as a customer convenience. However, additional square footage is required.

This room must be designed for wheelchair maneuvering clearance within the space. Items such as forward reach, side reach, and general space usage must be considered.

Drinking Fountains and Telephones

Fountains

It is recommended that if a single drinking fountain be installed within a retail store, this should be accomplished by using a two-level or high/low fountain that provides fountain accessibility for both wheelchair/child user height, as well as customers/employees who have trouble bending. The planner should be wary of painted wall finishes around

fountains since water splattering can damage or discolor the surface over time. Either heavy-duty wall coverings or a vinyl wall-surfacing system should be used around fountains.

Telephones

In some cases, public telephones may be considered a convenience in a retail store and will be installed in areas adjacent to offices or toilet rooms. The installed height of these phones should meet governing regulations.

Elevators

If the retail store is multilevel, an elevator may be necessary. The store planner should work closely with the architect to verify exact elevator locations and to ascertain that all requirements are reviewed and met before the planning of the space.

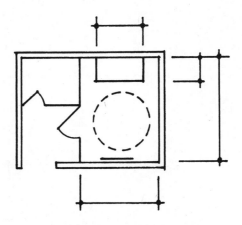

This diagram indicates a plain view of a handicapped fitting room.

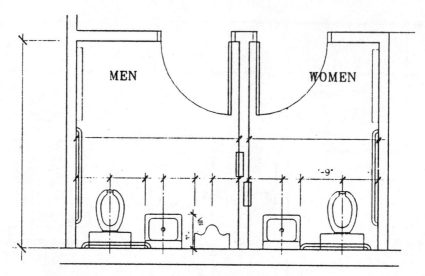

This diagram suggests a typical layout of toilet room fixtures.

The elevator cab interior should be designed to facilitate easy operations by handicapped persons.

Needless to say, there are many obstacles to be overcome by the physically challenged customer or employee. Careful store planning with an eye to the new ADA regulations can alleviate many store hindrances for the handicapped. In most cases, the planning board will review the drawings and will bring to the attention of store planner and owner any regulatory misinterpretations or oversights; yet the responsibility lies with the planner for compliance with occupancy codes.

Chapter 3

A STORE-PLANNING BUSINESS SEQUENCE (IN BRIEF)

This manual presents a detailed 26-step procedure that serves as a guide through the various steps involved in store planning. This guide begins with the earliest collection of critical information and follows through until the final punchlist is established by planner and job captain before the project work is finally approved.

Below is an index to those stages, arranged more or less in the sequence in which the tasks are logically performed. Following this index, there is a detailing of each of the steps of the full procedure.

Business Sequence Index

1. Client-Collected Information
2. Scope-of-Work Outline
3. Negotiating the Contract
4. Project Meeting
5. Project Schedules
6. Budget Discussions
7. Project Communications
8. Final Review of Program Guidelines
9. Planning the Allocation of Merchandising Space
10. Planning the Allocation of Nonselling Space
11. Preliminary Review of Lease and Building Documents
12. Preliminary Review of Merchandising Plan by Client
13. Preliminary Review of Block Merchandising Plan
14. Development of Preliminary Merchandising Plan
15. Conceptual Design Discussions
16. Conceptual Reflected Ceiling/Power Plan
17. Conceptual Flooring Plan
18. Final Design Presentation
19. Development of Plan/Elevations/Drawings/Details/Sections
20. Color and Material Books
21. Incorporating Architectural, Mechanical, and Interior Documents and Specifications into Drawings
22. Collecting and Awarding of Contracts
23. Shop Drawings
24. Progressive Payment Schedules
25. Coordination
26. Final Punchlist Review

1.   Client-Collected Information

Even before the so-called "initial" meeting with new clients or prospects, planners can make a big contribution to the ultimate success of a project by preparing guidelines to store owners, managers, and store personnel for the collection of data. The careful collection of necessary data can help staff to fulfill their responsibilities.

Conversely, there may be a need to encourage the store management to contact knowledgeable principals of the store-planning firm for recommendations. Discussion might involve how to arrive at a consensus regarding budget, how to plan facilities to help insure only minimum future reinvestment, how to project the desired store image, what competitors are up to, and other similar matters.

2.   Scope-of-Work Outline

The scope-of-work outline lists in writing for the client the services required of all parties to the contract, describes those services in sufficient detail, itemizes the extras required, gives a budget projection, and establishes the store-planning fee.

3.   Negotiating the Contract

Once the scope-of-work has been agreed upon, it is time to draft the contract and negotiate the final terms with the appropriate representatives of the building owner or lessee. Negotiated terms and conditions can include the precise services to be rendered, responsibilities of the parties to the contract, and schedules of payment to the planner.

4.   Project Meeting

Organizational charts are drafted during a project meeting involving both the planner and client. The chart will list the client team, design team, architects, engineers, developers, contractors, and consultants. The chart outlines design concepts and merchandising criteria, assigned responsibilities, job descriptions, interrelationships of job functions, scope of the project's work, and the methods for conveying information.

Responsibilities of the building owner/lessee at this point usually include attendance at important meetings and supervisory involvement as the project progresses.

5.   Project Schedules

Project schedules are carefully developed that include an outline of steps 1, 2, 3, and 4. The schedule also includes estimated deadlines for drawing/design, bidding, construction, reviews, decor and fixturing, installation, promotional events, and the official opening of the store.

6.   Budget Discussions

Budget discussions involve per-square-foot costs in relation to general requirements, the specific objectives of management, type of image envisioned, and scope of design and coordination required. Planners have the responsibility to negotiate a working agreement that is realistic in terms of the services desired by clients. This agreement—called a Design Agreement—may be largely an assimilation of language in previous contracts and will include the following: (a) a Letter of Intent, (b) a Letter of Agreement, and (c) the Contract.

7.   Project Communications

Once all necessary revisions have been made to the work schedule, it is time to communicate to staff members their responsibilities. This is done by putting together a "prestart" list to help organize the information to be passed along to staff members. It is helpful to make a list of answers to questions that are most frequently asked. When possible, also assemble any information received from the client that can be duplicated and distributed to staff as an aid to their understanding of the project scope and design requirements.

Finally, explain to staff members what has been assembled. Materials should include an outline of program criteria, assignments of internal responsibilities, requirements for direct contact with client personnel, and the project timetables and work schedules.

8.   Final Review of Program Guidelines

At any "final" review with the client before construction begins, it is time for any last-minute reworking of project programming, criteria, objectives, estimates, and schedules. It is also the time to resolve any unsettled issues such as how to design to reflect corporate philosophy, how to capture the overall "look and feel" required to appeal to targeted customers, and how to match merchandise to the customer profile dictated by the store's location. Marketing strategies should concern competition within a given radius, long-term outlook on conversion of existing space, and how the current plan can best be devised to provide for growth and expansion.

9. Planning the Allocation of Merchandising Space

Usually it will be the function of the store manager to develop a list of department names and numbers; square footages of each existing department; amount of space to be expanded, decreased, eliminated, or moved elsewhere (by department); specific department locations and adjacencies; aisle exposures; and other specifically chosen placements of nonselling areas.

10. Planning the Allocation of Nonselling Space

Usually it will also be the responsibility of the manager to determine the percentage of the overall space to be devoted to stock and where nonselling support areas will be located. Examples of nonselling areas include show windows, entrances, receiving areas, customer service/credit, gift wrap, layaways, marking, executive offices, store manager's office, general offices, money room, computer areas, security areas, lockers, rest rooms (employee and public), and electrical and mechanical areas.

11. Preliminary Review of Lease and Building Documents

The following is a list of the 10 documents that should be reviewed in designing newly built merchandising space before construction begins:

1. Lease exhibits
2. Site plans
3. Building (or mall) criteria
4. Architectural/structural details, column spacing (bays)
5. Mechanical locations (electrical, HVAC, plumbing)
6. Receiving areas
7. Shape of building
8. Storefront design and store signing
9. Exterior building design
10. The plan for exterior parking lot entrances

Care should also be taken to examine any evidence of signing limitations, such as building/design/architectural details/power sources, budget limitations, preliminary schedules, and photographs or perspectives.

When planning merchandising space in a remodeled building, the following recommended list of items should be reviewed with the contractor or store management:

1. Existing building and highwall plan
2. Architectural details
3. Existing reflected ceiling grid and lamping
4. Condition and location of wall hardware systems
5. Aisle and department lines
6. Existing adjacencies and locations of stock or nonselling areas
7. The relationship of interselling spaces
8. Any photographs of informational value

12. Preliminary Review of Merchandising Plan by Client

The preliminary review of the merchandising plan by clients is the ideal time for store planners to present additional plan ideas for discussion, revisions, and resubmission.

Included in this review will be a building plan ($1/16$", $1/8$", or $1/4$" scales) indicating the positions of the following:

1. Building site and overall size
2. Column spacing
3. Entrances for customers and flow of traffic
4. Sales-support and nonselling areas, receiving

This is the best time to present the block merchandise department adjacency plan for review, revision, and approval. This plan will show the store entrances, the plan for the overall interior, and the escalators, elevators, and conveyor systems.

Once the preliminary plan has been approved and any misinterpretations by the planner or others have been resolved, it is time to review the following items with the contractor: special architectural requirements to support load-bearing areas and the placement of electrical panels, mechanical elements, or roof-top (HVAC) sprinkler grids layout.

The preliminary plans to be reviewed by the clients include merchandise adjacency and sequence of classification of merchandise type; placement of fitting-room banks, stockrooms, sales-supportive or nonselling areas; location of cash/wrap desks in relation to fitting-room entrances; and floor stock requirements.

Clients are required to give their approval to the general concept of the overall program once it has been reviewed.

13. Preliminary Review of Block Merchandising Plan

Prior to placement of loose fixtures, clients are shown department layouts and size, center-of-aisle lines, and widths of the following: fitting rooms, stockrooms, sales-supportive areas, nonselling areas, escalators, elevators, and so on, that are in a semi-state of acceptance and incorporate all ideas. Finally, at this phase, clients should also be given an opportunity to critique the latest storefront design, to question specific details, and to hear any other presentation necessary before approving (or disapproving) the general merchandising and design concepts.

14. Development of Preliminary Merchandising Plan

Prior to the first meeting between a planner and management, copies of the preliminary merchandising plan should be distributed to general merchandising managers/buyers. This plan will familiarize them with various locations, square footages, aisle exposures, and department adjacencies. The plan should aid those who later will be responsible for generating exacting merchandise requirements, such as perimeter linear hangings or shelving requirements, loose fixture placement, type and quantity of merchandise, visual merchandising, and display.

This is the time to further refine the plan by bringing to the attention of management any significant changes that are anticipated or recommended. It is another opportunity to discuss the recommended design approach or to offer a final review of the merchandising or fixture-density layout.

15. Conceptual Design Discussions

Conceptual designs should be presented in the form of perspective drawings or flat elevations. The drawings must reflect an accurate understanding of earlier discussions regarding the image to be projected, budgets, interior architectural features, the highwall plan, fixture placement, lighting requirements, color selections, and material concept boards. The con-

ceptual design should include price information for carpeting and wall coverings plus all other decorative elements and materials of decor.

16. Conceptual Reflected Ceiling/Power Plan

The conceptual reflected ceiling/power plan will illustrate the exact placement of light fixtures and give the desired data regarding illumination (e.g., foot-candles/sq. ft., watts/sq. ft.). It will show power locations for showcase lines, registers, telephones, computers, and so on. These plans are essential in establishing electrical panel requirements, heat loads, and other budgetary considerations.

17. Conceptual Flooring Plan

As shown in the approved merchandising plans, all hard- and soft-surface materials for aisle and flooring lines are locked into place. An alternate schedule should be included.

18. Final Design Presentation

The final design presentation is, as the name implies, a showing of all the major elements of the overall plan, including the merchandising plan, fixture layout, color perspective renderings, percentage of color to be used, and so on. Note: Client approval of these items is required before hard-line drawing begins.

19. Development of Plan/Elevations/ Drawings/Details/Sections

During this developmental store-planning stage, initiate the elevations, sections, and details to implement perimeter decor, merchandising, and fixture concepts. The documents produced will include the graphic package, logos and signage, final refinements, and the management's signed approval prior to beginning the hard-line drawing.

20. Color and Material Books

While drawings are out for bid, the material and color books should be assembled for distribution later to contractors who are successful in landing the project.

Various symbols, indicating the recommended material and color applications, are drawn on the elevations. These symbols allow the contractor to estimate costs and square footages of materials.

As for color books, a series of at least seven to ten should be compiled with pages in an orderly and logical sequence. Each must include an index that gives the names, addresses, and phone numbers of all manufacturers whose products are shown in the books along with cost.

The color books will be used as a close reference by planners and designers, store owners, general contractors, perimeter fixture contractors, freestanding fixture contractors, and painting contractor. Others will serve as file copies and for use elsewhere as necessary.

21. Incorporating Architectural, Mechanical, and Interior Documents and Specifications into Drawings

The following is a checklist of miscellaneous tasks for incorporating the necessary documents and specifications into the finalized drawings and for properly exchanging information during the bidding process. These tasks have been arranged in a sequence that is most commonly followed. These drawings will be rendered by other members of the team but must correspond with the planner's drawings.

- Review building drawings
- Incorporate revisions to drawings
- Finalize building drawings
- Prepare invitations to bid
- Prepare bidding guidelines
- Prepare specifications guidelines
- Make final review of drawings (prior to releasing to bidders)
- Notify client of bidding dates
- Notify client that bidding document is prepared
- Present client with a copy of the bidding document
- Notify client of contractors who have expressed an interest in bidding
- Prepare letter of transmittal that lists all documents and data being transmitted to bidders (e.g., blueprints of completed drawings, guidelines for bidding, specifications, and bid-submission forms)
- Have letter of intent signed by bidders for forwarding to store planner
- Deliver all documents to the contractors that must be circulated to bidders and subtrades

22. Collecting and Awarding of Contracts

During the bidding, store planners should prepare themselves to answer contractors' questions as they arise and to help clear up any misinterpretations of drawings or discrepancies in them.

Bids from contractors must always be submitted to planners, with copies to store owners. Store planners are obligated to register the time that bids were received, reviewed, and recorded. Following the bid review, contracts are awarded to those contractors who have best satisfied the bid criteria.

23. Shop Drawings

Shop drawings that have been submitted by contractors must also be reviewed to determine if there were areas of misinterpretation having to do with joinery, assembly techniques, and finished appearance.

24. Progressive Payment Schedules

Approved progressive billing should follow the payment schedule outlined in the payment-to-contractors section. Developing a progressive punchlist will aid this payment process and should help planners and merchants assure the completion of work on designated dates.

25. Coordination

Store planners and their job captains coordinate all work schedules, authorize changes in the schedules, and authorize payments to contractors. Again, it helps to develop and work from a progressive punchlist.

26. Final Punchlist Review

Once work is in a semifinal stage of completion, it must be inspected to detect any unacceptable work and to order necessary corrections before final payments to contractors are authorized.

Chapter 4

GENERAL GUIDELINES FOR OFFICE ADMINISTRATION

Administrative Procedures

Planners sometimes feel it is more advantageous to their careers to start their own firm. Basic knowledge of how to administer a business is essential. The better the preparation in the beginning, the easier it is to handle growth of the business. Good administrative procedures are crucial to financial success.

Listed here are general guidelines that successful planners should be aware of in setting up their own firm:

1. Billing: Invoices should be issued as soon as a phase of work has been completed. Invoices for reimbursables should be sent immediately upon receipt.

2. Accounts Receivable: Payment received should be deposited immediately. A system should be established, keeping tight control over the open balances that will show at a glance the status of client accounts. Delinquent customers should be reminded in a friendly but firm manner to fulfill their obligations according to the terms set forth in the contract.

3. Accounts Payable: Control of all incoming in-voices as to accuracy, date due, and possible discount should be maintained. It is advisable to make use of given terms before remittance is sent.

4. Bank Reports: A report in regard to all movements in the bank account should be maintained daily and reviewed.

5. Taxes: The federal as well as the local government requires payment of all taxes at specific deadlines. It is important that all taxes and moneys due are deposited on time.

6. Payroll and Employee Administration: A payroll cycle must be established to accommodate both company and employee needs. Weekly, biweekly, or semimonthly is the usual formula.

7. Administration: Part of the responsibilities of a business owner is to maintain accurate files. An orderly system helps everyone in their respective job requirements.

These points can only be general since the managing of a business requires a much more in-depth approach. Further administrative function information is contained in various chapters. It is very important to maintain a high standard of administration within a given profession. Each individual firm should develop a system that best suits its needs.

Example of Standard Introductory Letter

Any Company
Any Street
Any Place

Dear Mr./Mrs./Ms. _____

As a follow-up to our recent meeting, I'd like to better acquaint you with the store-planning services we provide.

Regarding price, our fee structure for projects of _____ square feet to _____ square feet ranges between $_____ and $_____ per square foot.

In our proposal for each project, we include:

—developing/reviewing scope-of-work, timetable, budget
—preliminary merchandising adjacency studies (block plan)
—approved adjacency plan and revisions
—design and color concept
—merchandising plan indicating department size, fixtures, etc.
—high-wall plan (indicating wall and hardware placement)
—reflected ceiling plan (indicating ceiling and perimeter lighting)
—floorcovering plan (indicating hard aisles and floorcovering)
—elevations (indicating perimeter design, construction,
    sections, and details)
—loose-fixture detail drawings (keyed to merchandise plan)
—color boards and color books
—final review prior to bidding
—overviewing of bidding
—review of quotations, evaluation, and awarding of
    construction and fixturing contracts
—field trips and inspections

When color renderings of departments or design are required, there will be a direct billing of $_____ for each 24" x 36" rendering. Should you decide to eliminate any of the above items, a percentage discount will be reflected in the fee.

Our store-planning service does not include alterations to the existing structure or removal of structural walls. However, our drawings will include areas needing special attention, coordinated with a local architect or engineer of your choosing. We can, if requested, supply and coordinate supportive architectural or engineering services at a separate rate. We do not include any mechanical, HVAC, or architectural seals or permits. If they are necessary, it will be the responsibility of the general contractor to secure seals and permits, as well as to coordinate necessary trades.

All documents forwarded from this office will be blueprints or sepia of our original drawings. Any documents of the existing facilities that are necessary, such as existing high-wall, reflected ceiling, or power and signal, will be photographically transferred to sepia mylars (with your permission) for incorporation and will be used as part of the demolition drawing. Upon completion of the job, we will forward all original 24" x 36" documents to you for your permanent file.

Our payment schedule is based on the percentage of work completed. We will invoice our fee in four to seven phases:

Phase I   Preliminary Studies and Deposit   _____%

Phase II   Merchandising Development   _____%
Phase III   Design   _____%
Phase IV   Detaining   _____%
Phase V   Fixture, Decor, and Color   _____%
Phase VI   Power and Signal, Reflected Ceiling _____%
Phase VII   Completion of Bidding Schedule   _____%

                                     100 %

Standard reimbursable expenses, billed separately, will include outside blueprinting, long-distance tele-phone charges, postage, overnight express charges, transportation, plus other out-of-pocket expenses. Copies of all billable expenses will be submitted under the terms of the agreement and shall become due upon presentation. You will be billed for any direct services not included in a specific contract at the following rates: $_____ per hour for principal/owner time; $_____ per hour for drafting and coordination; and $_____ per hour for color coordination. No deductions will be made from the planner compensation on account of penalty, liquidated damages, or other sums withheld from payment to the contractors. Phase VIII will be billed 30 days prior to the completion date of construction.

If the project is terminated by either party prior to completion, you will be charged only for the work completed by _____(the planner)_____ on a direct percentage in relation to the total drawings required, plus a percentage of the amount of design work contracted for. This will include all reimbursables through and including the date of termination.

We are very interested in developing a working relationship with your company. We can assure you of a strong capability of delivering the store-planning services and design that you require. Thank you for giving consideration to our firm. We look forward to hearing from you.

                             Very truly yours,

                             (Name) _____
                             (Company Name)_____
                             (Title) _____

Enclosures

Example of Short-Form Introductory or Cover Letter

Date

Name
Company
Street Address
City, State ZIP

Dear _____:

When retailers across the country look to increase their sales and profits through departmental changes, major renovations, or an overall visual merchandising program, they retain _____(Store Planning Firm)_____ for assistance and direction.

The focus of _____(Store Planning Firm)_____ is to provide cost-effective and creative ideas designed to increase market share. The attached portfolio describes how_____ _____ coordinates the merchants' perspectives with professional store-planning services.

_____ has proven its abilities in every type of retail operation. Performing within established budgets and stringent timetables is our specialty. Please let us know how we can help you improve your company's bottom line.

I look forward to hearing from you.

Sincerely,

Very truly yours,

(Name) _____

(Company Name)_____

(Title) _____

Enclosures

Example of Draft Proposal

A contract like this should follow the introductory letter once all phases of the introductory letter have been worked out. It should be written on company letterhead.

Date

Name
Company
Street Address
City, State ZIP

Dear _____ :

The following draft proposal shall serve as our outline to plan and design the _____(store name)_____.
_____(Store planner's name)_____ will hereinafter be referred to as _____(SPN) (abbreviation)_____ .

Our concept reflects new marketing strategies within a decor-and-fixturing package of flexible and transferable elements. Additionally, our concept includes new graphic communication devices developed to reflect merchandise quality, features and benefits, assortment and price, and value image. Designed within a modular format, our concept affords easy application to the footprint shape of _____(store name)_____ .

Using our store-planning layout and design expertise, we will provide analysis and evaluation of _____(store name)_____ operational and facility configuration, operating policies, customer profile, demographics, merchandise, and stock assortment in order to recommend and develop the most advantageous retail store image. In the course of arriving at a suitable image, _____(SPN)_____ will examine, analyze, and evaluate the following specific elements with regard to present operational and facility configurations existing at _____(store name)_____ . Using our store-planning layout and design expertise, we will provide you with recommendations on each of the following:

A) Store Layout
1. Departmental space allocation, location, and adjacency is to be provided by _____ _____ .
2. Checkout System—develop and locate check-out system to control and expedite transactions of merchandise.
3. Layout and types of fixtures within each department.
4. Location, size, and layout of storage, nonselling, and administrative offices.

5. Customer Service Areas—layaway, special orders, and merchandise return. Cashiers—locations and relationship to customer.

B) **Operating Costs—Effective of Layout and Design on Cost Of**
1. Personnel productivity
2. Utilities
3. Maintenance

C) **Interior Design**
1. Selling
2. Wall, floor, and ceiling finishes
3. Carpeting areas/aisles
4. Lighting—general and highlighting
5. Colors and textures

D) **Fixture Design**
1. Selling fixtures—self-service type, clerk-service type, showcases, modular fixtures, racks, specialty fixtures, vendor fixtures
2. Cash wrap/customer service counters—wrap stands, check-out counters, service counters
3. _____

E) **Interior Store Signing—Department Identification**

F) During the evaluation and analysis, (SPN) will coordinate and discuss with management team, as required by various options, decision points, and tradeoff factors required in the development of store image.

G) Using the results of A, B, C, D, E, and F, we will provide the most advantageous retail store image for review.

Based upon the decision reached during our first meeting, (SPN) will develop layouts and a design for _____. The layouts and design will include the following specific elements:

_____

H) We will provide one (1) floor-plan layout for floors _____ .
First-floor layout to include _____ .
Est. sq. ft. @ _____ per sq. ft. _____ .

The merchandising plan will include:
1. Department and fixture layout of sq. ft. (estimated)
2. Merchandise categories to be indicated on fixture designations
3. Entrance and exits
4. Customer service areas
5. Back stockroom areas
6. Traffic aisles

The store design plans will include:
1. Departmental signing
2. Cornice/curtainwall treatment
3. Color correlations
4. Lighting
5. Decor package
6. Wall treatment
7. Floor treatment
8. Ceiling treatment
9. Merchandising sections

10. Freestanding fixture details
11. Supplemental and accent lighting plan
12. Floor power plan

It is _____'s responsibility to provide one (1) set of dimensioned "as is" drawings provided by the owner.

It is our understanding that we will prepare a concise set of retail store plans, and it will be the responsibility of the owner to coordinate with the general contractor for engineer or architectural seal for building permit. If architectural or engineering drawings are required for structural or electrical work, it will be the responsibility of the owner/general contractor to provide those services on a direct fee basis.

If changes to previously approved directions and drawings are required by the management of _____ , a separate letter will be provided and will outline changes being made and additional fees will reflect any adjustment to the drawings.

Performance Time Frame

Trip 1: One day meeting in _____ to review program with _____ and management team of _____ _____: 1 day—1 person—principal, store planner.

Trip 2: To review program primary plan: 1 day—1 person—principal: Store planner and board members of _____ and _____ .

Trip 3: Develop merchandising plan and discuss entire scope and determine timetable, inventory of loose fixtures for reuse. Approval to proceed required: 2 day—1 person—principal, store planner.

Trip 4: Presentation in _____ to include merchandising plan concept, design concept, perimeter elevations, lighting, flooring, freestanding fixture approval: 1 day—1 person—principal, store planner.

Compensation

_____(SPN)_____ for providing the aforementioned services, fee will be approximately _____ per sq. ft. gross areas.

Store Planning and Design Fee Schedule

Our billing schedule is based on the same percentage and will invoice you for each phase of the project upon commencement. Our invoices are due immediately upon receipt.

1. Block plan and adjacencies .... %
2. Merchandise requirement and fixture plans .... %
3. Working drawings, bid documents, and specifications ...... %
4. Interior design/color .... %
5. Reflected ceiling and power and signal .... %
6. Bidding and/or negotiating with contractors .... %
   TOTAL .... ____

Reimbursable Expenses
In addition to the fee set forth previously, the undersigned shall be entitled to reimbursement for expenditures made for or in the interests of the project including transportation, long distance calls, FAX, mailing expenses, Federal Express, document reproduction, and printing or blueprinting services. The undersigned shall be paid at currently prevailing rates with no markup for

handling. _____ will be responsible for all _____(SPN)_____ living expenses while in _____.

If any of _____(SPN)_____ invoices remain unpaid for a period of ten (10) days, _____(SPN)_____ shall, without liability and without affecting any of its rights under the agreement, suspend work on the project until all amounts are paid.

Extra Services
The owner and (SPN) agree that:

A. If changes are required by the owner or consultant to previously approved frozen plans, designs, and criteria, or for special studies, acceleration of schedules, or for services not specifically outlined in this agreement, such will be considered extra services and shall be billed as additions to the basic contract.
B. Such additional services shall be billed at the prevailing rate of the department involved in the additional work.

Department Charges:

Principal/Owner _____ per hour
Drafting Coordinator _____ per hour
Color and Coordination _____ per hour

No deductions shall be made from the designer's compensations on account of penalty liquidation damages or other sums withheld from payment to the contractors.

Signed and Accepted:

_____
(Store Planning Firm)

_____   _____
(Owner)   (Store Planner)

_____   _____
(Date)   (Date)

Example of Typical Project Schedule Description

1. Prepare Department Areas Store

Management prepares departmental areas based on the available selling area. The Store Operations department also prepares required areas for the service facilities.

2. Phase I Planning (Building Facilities and Department Adjacencies)

Store Planning prepares $1/16$" scale plans indicating the building fixed facilities, service facilities and the selling department adjacencies-plan flow.

These plans are then issued to the Project Architect for the building development drawings, code compliance, etc.

3. Exterior Design

Project Architect to develop exterior building designs for management's review and approval.

4. Preliminary Fixture Plan and Merchandising

The project Designer prepares conceptual plan

designs indicating departmental layouts. The Designer then reviews these plans with store planning and store management for merchandise requirements input. Merchandise meetings are conducted at this point.

5. Phase II Planning (Partition Plans)

Project Designer prepares the plan layout and preliminary design elements. The first issue of the partition plans is executed during this phase to the Project Architect.

It should be noted that this issue is a progress issue and should not be interpreted as a final issue.

6. Phase III-A Planning Preliminary Lighting and Electrical

Project Designer prepares *Preliminary* floor and ceiling electrical plans. These plans are issued for electrical *load only*. They are not to be used by the Architect as final drawings.

7. Interior Design Working Drawings

Project Designer completes plans, designs, and working drawings in preparation for the Fixturing Bid issue package.

8. Construction Working Drawings

Project Architect prepares set of drawings for the building Construction Bid issue package. This package is to include all pertinent Interior Design information from the Project Designer.

9. Phase III-B Planning (Frozen Drawings)

Project Designer prepares final floor and ceiling electrical plans and final dimensioned high-wall plans indicating all curtain walls and fixture work at the ceiling.

These drawings are issued to the Project Architect for use in assembling the Construction Bid package. The project Architect has 4 to 6 weeks to include this final information in the bid package.

10. Construction Bid and Award

Self-Explanatory

11. Fixture Bid and Award

Self-Explanatory

12. Construction

Period required for construction of the building.

13. Fixturing

Period required for the installation of the Interior.

Project Schedule

Store Name _____   Today's Date _____

Location _____

Item	Start Date	Finish Date	Responsible Party
1. Prepare Departmental Areas	_____	_____	Store Manager
2. Phase I Planning (Bldg. Facilities & Dept. Adjacencies)	_____	_____	Designer/Store Manager
3. Exterior Design	_____	_____	Designer/Store Manager
4. Preliminary Fixture Plan & Merchandising	_____	_____	Designer
5. Phase II Planning (Partition Plans)	_____	_____	Designer
6. Phase III-A Planning (Prelim. Lighting & Elec. Plan)	_____	_____	Designer
7. Int. Design Working Draw.	_____	_____	Designer
8. Const. Working Drawings	_____	_____	Architect
9. Phase III-B Planning (Frozen Drawings) (Partitions & Elec.)	_____	_____	Designer
10. Const. Bid & Award Pre-Bid Steel & Foundation	_____	_____	Designer/Store Manager
11. Fixturing Bid & Award	_____	_____	Designer/Store Manager
12. Construction	_____	_____	Designer/Store Manager
13. Fixturing	_____	_____	Designer/Store Manager
14. Merchandising	_____	_____	Designer/Store Manager
15. Open Store	_____	_____	Store Manager

Transmittal Letter

PHONE _____ FAX _____

Store Planner's Name
Address
City
State

Project: **Job No.:**

To: **Date:**

We transmit herewith the following via:

By:_____   **Copies to:**

A transmittal letter is a cover sheet which serves as a document to list the contents of the package or fax transmission.

Chapter 5

THE INTERVIEW OF A STORE PLANNER

A Word about Competition

Some companies looking at store-planning firms will base their hiring decisions solely on such simple considerations as the quality of the correspondence from the firms and the prices quoted. Most retailers, however, make their decisions based on several factors, including the capabilities of individual store planners and the compatibility of their ideas with those of the owners. Many owners want a complete review of qualifications, including ample documentation of quality work. Some owners may even want to visit the offices to see how well the planner's business is operated. Because it is impossible to have all work samples available in the client's office, an invitation to review in the planner's office will give the owner a broader overview of the planner's talents, qualifications, and operations.

The owners may also want to discuss industry trends and issues, costs for individual items, upgrading formats and images, and security. They may ask how new fixtures and techniques can cut or reduce costs without sacrificing standards.

Not all planners and retailers were meant to work together. Zealous planners who stubbornly insist that there is only one way to execute a job usually are eliminated. On the other hand, planners who are capable of formulating sound merchandising advice consistent with the budgets, schedules, and owner's viewpoint always seem to have the best chance of landing jobs.

Retailers look for concept flexibility and up-to-date presentation of ideas that they are confident will not look dated quickly. When making presentations, store planners should assure clients that they have an accomplished staff that will be drawing on a broad knowledge of merchandising materials and store-planning principles.

Store planners who can deliver an effective sales presentation and demonstrate that they are also confident, management-level decision makers are at a distinct advantage. Effective selling also requires careful listening. Positive personal relationships built upon trust and confidence go a long way in establishing long-term mutual store planner and retailer respect.

The Initial Interview

The first and second orders of business when planning an initial interview/presentation with prospective clients are (1) to identify the appropriate persons with whom to meet and (2) to structure interviews/presentations for the best possible result.

The major purposes of the first meeting with prospective clients are to open channels of communication with primary contacts at the company, to learn the roles each will have, and to begin to gain an understanding of the parameters of the pending assignment. Usually it is the store owners who make the final determination about which store-planning firm will be hired to design the store.

If a project is comparatively large, the planners should be prepared to meet first with a member (or members) of an in-house staff for preliminary discussions, even though the decision about whom to hire will rest with the store owner.

When the owner does not have an in-house staff, the planner ordinarily will meet with the owner and general merchandise manager. No matter who is present, the initial interview is of paramount importance, and careful preparation is essential.

The Basis for Judgment

In most cases, the selection will be based on a firm's credentials for handling the scope-of-work involved, the planning firm's fee structure, its success in handling similar projects, and the firm's standing within the planning/merchandising fraternity. Always be prepared with answers on all those key points.

Even though each prospect will have a different set of selling and merchandising priorities and will be looking for a certain set of answers, it is the store planner's job to anticipate as completely as possible the points for which the decision maker will be looking.

Most clients will expect to see more than just typical fixture designs. The planner must be primed to discuss the format and presentation of merchandise, the way the store design will coordinate with and highlight the merchandise to be presented, the ability of the store-planning firm to help attract new customers from competing stores, and a number of other considerations.

Fact-Finding

In the initial meeting, a number of key items of importance in guiding the staff in their preparation of an appropriate plan must be learned, for example, the demographics and lifestyles in the area, the retailer's personal view of the image to be projected, and key budget considerations. Each store design must differ in accordance with the makeup of the market it serves.

Proper preparation for the first meeting will require some prior knowledge of the departments within the store that will have the greatest customer appeal and prospects for profit. Most retailers have fairly concrete notions about what form they want their new or redesigned store to take; but all will be looking to the planner for some guidance in this respect. Store planners who can bring enough experience and understanding to the task will be able to recommend a combination of elements to create a selling entity in which sales will grow and satisfactory profits will be realized in the shortest possible time.

As has been emphasized—and it surely bears repeating—no two stores should ever be alike. That is why it is so important for planners to do as much market research as possible in the early stages so their recommendations will best serve the needs and wants of the customers in the region served by the store.

Effective store planning requires taking all of these factors into account and planning accordingly. Why should individuals be hired to perform a store-planning function when they are not able to assist retailers in finding the most profitable markets and the most attractive ways to use the space?

Other Retailer Considerations

What are some of the other important things that retailers will be looking for in the presentation? Perhaps the most significant is evidence that the store-planning firm has consistently provided its clients with dependable service and that they deliver design products that "weather" well—designs that do not become obsolete with the next passing trend.

The more time and money that owners invest, the more assurance they will want that the selection can be justified with specific experience, professional credentials, and fee.

To be effective, store planners need have not only in-depth knowledge about plans, drawings, and pallets, but also a command of the vocabulary that goes with them. Merchants are careful to appraise the store planner's knowledge of planning and design closely. They are also well aware of personal appearance. They are particularly concerned about how the follow-up communications are handled after the meeting is over.

The interview is both a learning and teaching process. Listen closely! Only when a good grasp of the project parameters and client needs and desires are assessed are store planners in a position to effectively interpret them in the desired format. Take notes! Give feedback! If possible, show knowledge by demonstrating handling tasks during various stages of development.

Other factors that retailers will likely consider in evaluating a given plan/design are:

1. How many other stores of similar size and type has the firm designed?
2. How does this retailer's project compare with similar projects completed recently?
3. How capable of working within the time frame established for completion is the store-planning firm?
4. What is the store planner's record for completing jobs on time?
5. Does the firm have a progressive work schedule established?
6. How responsive is the firm in developing a new merchandise presentation format at the owner's request?
7. How many full-time employees does the firm have? Part-time? Back-ups?
8. Are the firm's business affairs conducted efficiently? Is it on a sound financial footing?
9. What economies can be expected in the production of documents that will help make the firm competitive in producing and pricing?

Presentation Techniques

Presentation techniques should be customized to serve the needs of particular clients that fit a given situation. In other words, the medium should be suited to the message.

Audiovisual presentations can be effective in showing design concepts that have been executed in previous applications. They also can be useful in showing closeups of interior features that best illustrate the talents and expertise of the store planner.

At the initial meeting, the planner should be prepared with an exciting portfolio of photographs that show representative samples of the firm's best work. The planner should also bring a list of projects completed to date, identified by name, location, size, type, and photographs. A listing of professional

references, with current address and telephone numbers, should be at the ready.

After the Meeting

Immediately after the meeting, while ideas are still fresh, the planner should organize the information collected, check instructions carefully, and put them into printed form for future reference by those individuals who may be involved in planning and designing the project.

A client will be impressed when he or she sees concrete evidence that shows that a particular store planner is capable of expediting quickly. A practice that many professional planners have found valuable (*invaluable* at times) is having ready-made forms and schedules at the initial meeting that guide them through the information-gathering process (see sample at end of chapter). If the planners have anticipated all or most of what they need to know, they will have the correct forms for collecting all the information needed. If the time allowed for the meeting doesn't permit collecting all the information needed, then it will be necessary to follow up by telephone calls or letters to collect the rest.

The Quotation

Obviously, this efficiency will help cut down on the time required to submit the quotation. Planners have everything to gain by getting their quotation to clients as quickly as possible. Only in the most unusual circumstances should a bid arrive any later than one to two weeks after the initial meeting.

If the store planners have been well organized from the start, then quotations can be determined quickly, and the correspondence will arrive on the prospect's desk within a few days—the earlier the better, from the standpoint of a good impression, since it will be another mark of efficiency. Certainly, ample time should be allowed for compiling, comparing, checking, and changing, but the quotation process should not drag on. Delay only sends a message to the client that the planning firm may be less than enthusiastic about landing the assignment.

The planner should start early, anticipate carefully just what must be known to bid intelligently, organize forms in an efficient manner, and then act with dispatch after the right information is collated and digested. All quotations must be signed by the appropriate company officer or representative.

Store-Planner Questionnaire to Interview Merchant

These questions will provide both the designer and the store planner with enough information to negotiate or outline the project, scope, and fee.

Example of Interview for Scope-of-Work and Contract Development

1. Name of project and location: _____

_____

2. Owner's name and phone/fax numbers: _____

3. Name and title of business contact: _____

_____

4. Location, city, zip code: _____

_____

5. Phone number and extension: _____

6. Starting date of project: _____

7. Bid date: _____

8. Name and address of developer or landlord: _____

_____

9. Opening date of project: _____

10. Space number (if any): _____

11. Approximate square footage to be processed: _____

12. Company name of any other consultants or engineers working on the project (consultants, engineers, mechanical engineers, electrical engineers, architectural engineers): _____

_____

_____

_____

13. Name of the house operation contact: _____

_____

14. Department names, size, adjacency, dollar volume, and problems: _____

_____

_____

_____

15. Store's size and quality of merchandise compared with neighboring competition: _____

_____

_____

16. How is the store accessible: Short car drive? Long car drive? Public transportation? _____

 Is the store in a mall? A strip center? A downtown location? _____

 _____

17. In what segment of the market is the store operating? _____

 _____

18. What departments need to grow or be initiated, and what departments cut back or eliminated?

 _____

 _____

19. What is the projected budget for the project and does it match the image? _____

 _____

20. How soon after the contract is signed can the planner begin the project? _____

21. When was the last time the store was remodeled? _____

22. How long from the initial meeting and signing of the contract will the first adjacency plan be presented?

 _____

23. How will the planner work and with what level of management? _____

 _____

 _____

24. What is expected as bid documents? _____

 _____

25. How much time will be allowed for last-minute changes in merchandising or design at owner's request?

 _____

26. How much time will be allowed to complete the bid documents? _____

 _____

27. With which suppliers have they worked, and were all contractors notified of upcoming work?

 _____

28. How will the perimeter be handled? How long will it take to install? What materials will be used? What will be preassembled in a shop to save installation time in the field? _____

 _____

 _____

 _____

29. What type of lighting is to be used and foot-candle leveled? _____

 _____

30. What type of electrical service is provided? _____

 _____

31. What type of ceiling, drops, curtain walls, elevations? _____

_____

_____

32. What will hard and soft surfaces be? _____

33. Is a scope of work or outline available? _____

34. Has the retailer projected the square-foot construction cost? _____

35. Has the retailer projected its square-foot fixture and decor cost? _____

_____

36. What is the actual starting date of the planner's drawing? _____

_____

37. Has there been an outline and schedule set for the project? _____

_____

38. Is the owner aware of a designer's flowchart and the process of each phase? (This will be most helpful in assuring your client organization.) _____

_____

39. Are there any special or unusual problems? _____

40. Is the retailer aware of A.D.A. requirements or is the building up to code? _____

_____

Chapter 6

OPINION QUESTIONNAIRES

On succeeding pages, there are a variety of sample questionnaires that store owners, store managers, and store planners will find useful in sampling opinions about the state of such daily management concerns as housekeeping, inspections, staff training, fixturing needs, presentation of merchandise, management responsibilities, security, and advertising. Successful store planners will encourage internal research of this kind since, in the case of remodeling of retail space, planners can use the results to detect needs for change. In the case of new construction, opinions about conditions at other company-owned outlets may give valuable insight into how a new facility can be designed to avoid repeats of past mistakes.

The information provided will be used to evaluate fixturing requirements and to revise the block merchandising adjacency plan prior to the first actual working meeting with management.

The planners will analyze, evaluate, and recommend square footage, depth, location, shape, and aisle exposure of each department.

Based on the information given and the density of new store fixtures (and prior to submitting plan for preliminary review), the planners will confirm in writing the square footage of the department.

Example of Store Profile and Evaluation

Project _____	Location _____
Store Contact _____	
Dept. Names _____	Dept. No. _____
CLASSIFICATIONS OF STORE	
Dept. Name _____	Sq. Ft. _____
Dept. Name _____	Sq. Ft. _____

Dept. Name _____   Sq. Ft. _____

Dept. Name _____   Sq. Ft. _____

Dept. Name _____   Sq. Ft. _____

Dept. Name _____   Sq. Ft. _____

Dept. Name _____   Sq. Ft. _____

Dept. Name _____   Sq. Ft. _____

Dollar volume per square foot _____

Percent of sales (dept. vs. total)_____

New square footage of department _____

Staff minimum _____

Number of cash-and-wraps _____

Existing Type of Fixtures Used:

Walls _____   Glass cubes _____

Showcases _____   Wraps _____

Tables _____   Miscellaneous _____

Gondolas _____   Round racks _____

Display bases _____   4-Way racks _____

Shelves _____   T-Stands _____

Number of fitting rooms used in store_____

Locations of fitting rooms _____

_____

Length of the showcase glass line _____

_____

Department depth from aisle lines (aisle to back wall) _____

_____

Desired type and number of new fixtures for the following:

	Type	Number		Type	Number
Walls			Hanging racks		
Wraps			Glass cubes		
Tables			Display platforms		
Gondolas			Fitting rooms		
Bases			Miscellaneous		

Example of Store Inspection Report
(To Be Conducted by Store Management)

Store Name _____

Store Number _____

Store Manager's Name _____

Date of Inspection _____

Date of Last Inspection _____

Inspected by _____

Retailing Section

1. Merchandise presentation— comments:

   _____

   _____

   _____

	Excellent	Adequate	Inadequate
a. Departmental setup	_____	_____	_____
b. Appearance of merchandise	_____	_____	_____
c. Special prom setup	_____	_____	_____
d. Advertised items setup	_____	_____	_____
e. Stock filled in	_____	_____	_____
f. Displays	_____	_____	_____
g. Signing	_____	_____	_____
h. Old season merchandise	_____	_____	_____

2. Store cleanliness— comments:

   _____

   _____

   _____

	Excellent	Adequate	Inadequate
a. Selling floor	_____	_____	_____
b. Stock areas	_____	_____	_____
c. Receiving room	_____	_____	_____
d. Rest rooms	_____	_____	_____
e. Office and utility	_____	_____	_____

f. Employee lounge _____ _____ _____

g. Store exterior _____ _____ _____

h. Fitting rooms _____ _____ _____

i. Alterations _____ _____ _____

3. Store orderliness— comments:

_____

_____

_____

	Excellent	Adequate	Inadequate
a. Selling floor	_____	_____	_____
b. Stock areas	_____	_____	_____
c. Receiving room	_____	_____	_____
d. Office and utility	_____	_____	_____
e. Employee lounge	_____	_____	_____
f. Alteration room	_____	_____	_____

4. Store staffing— comments:

_____

_____

_____

	Excellent	Adequate	Inadequate
a. Selling floor	_____	_____	_____
1) Adherence to schedules	_____	_____	_____
2) Store performance report	_____	_____	_____
b. Office and Utility	_____	_____	_____
c. Fitting room	_____	_____	_____
d. Receiving rooms	_____	_____	_____

5. Store personnel— comments:

_____

_____

_____

	Excellent	Adequate	Inadequate
a. Appearance	_____	_____	_____
b. Productivity	_____	_____	_____

c. Attitude _____ _____ _____

d. Morale _____ _____ _____

e. Job knowledge _____ _____ _____

f. Adherence to store policies by personnel _____ _____ _____

6. Security— comments:

_____

_____

_____

	Excellent	Adequate	Inadequate
a. Merchandise holds	_____	_____	_____
b. Doors	_____	_____	_____
c. Cash Office	_____	_____	_____
d. Receiving room	_____	_____	_____
e. Stockroom	_____	_____	_____
f. Package check	_____	_____	_____
g. Fitting rooms	_____	_____	_____
h. Terminal area	_____	_____	_____

7. Awareness of sales trends, merchandise needs, departmental events, competition, etc.— comments:

_____

_____

_____

	Excellent	Adequate	Inadequate
a. Manager	_____	_____	_____
b. Assistant Manager	_____	_____	_____
c. Supervisor	_____	_____	_____
d. Sales Associate	_____	_____	_____

Maintenance Section

If any of the following show a poor rating, the solution to the problem rests in the office of the vice president of operations.

1. Electrical: Excellent Adequate Inadequate

   Comments: _____

_____

_____

2. Aisle Floor   Excellent   Adequate   Inadequate

   Comments: _____

   _____

   _____

3. Carpet: Excellent   Adequate   Inadequate

   Comments: _____

   _____

   _____

4. Paint/wallcoverings: Excellent   Adequate   Inadequate

   Comments: _____

   _____

   _____

5. Ceiling/tile: Excellent   Adequate   Inadequate

   Comments: _____

   _____

   _____

6. H.V.A.C.:   Excellent   Adequate   Inadequate

   Comments: _____

   _____

   _____

7. Wall hardware: Excellent   Adequate   Inadequate

   Comments: _____

   _____

   _____

8. Floor racks: Excellent   Adequate   Inadequate

   Comments: _____

   _____

   _____

9. Floor fixtures: Excellent   Adequate   Inadequate

   Comments: _____

   _____

10. Floor wrap desks: Excellent Adequate Inadequate

Comments: _____

_____

_____

11. Store equipment: Excellent Adequate Inadequate

Comments: _____

_____

_____

Excellent ratings in: _____

_____

_____

Inadequate ratings in: _____

_____

_____

Signed: Inspector _____

              Manager _____

Overall inspector's comments: _____

_____

_____

_____

Manager's comments:

_____

_____

_____

_____

Example of 50 Questions to be Asked in a Store Inspection
(To Be Conducted by Store Management and Store Planner)

1. Who conducted the field survey with the planner. _____

2. How many levels are there in the store?   _____

3. What is the square footage of the store?   _____

4. What is the square footage (or approximation) of each department?   _____

5. How many fitting rooms service each department? (Attach list if necessary.)   _____

6. What is the general condition of the fitting rooms?   _____

7. Can they be reused?   Yes ☐   No ☐
   If yes, how?   _____

8. What is the general condition of the entrance to the store?   _____

9. Are show windows used?   Yes ☐   No ☐

   Of what type is the show-window floor?   _____

   Of what type is the background?   _____

10. Is the lighting satisfactory in the show windows?   Yes ☐   No ☐

11. What are the conditions of the wall and hardware to be reused?

    Wall _____

    Hardware_____

12. What is the color and condition of the carpeting in each area?

	Color	Condition
Women's ready to wear	_____	_____
Intimate apparel	_____	_____
Men's	_____	_____
Children's	_____	_____
Accessories	_____	_____
Shoes	_____	_____
Housewares	_____	_____
Domestics	_____	_____
Budget	_____	_____
Other	_____	_____

13. What is the width and type of material used for aisles?

_____   _____
Width   Material

14. Are stockrooms easily accessible to sales floor?   Yes ☐   No ☐

15. What is the condition of existing ceiling tile?

_____   _____   _____
Damaged   Adequate   Replacement
                                   Needed

16. Are there any obstructions to the line of the ceiling? If yes, describe.   Yes ☐   No ☐

17. Which type of lighting system (and lens) illuminates the general sales area?

_____

_____

_____

18. Does the perimeter cornice have single-tube or double-tube fluorescent lights?   Single ☐   Double ☐

19. In general, how is the merchandise highlighted throughout the store?

_____

_____

_____

20. Are spotlights used effectively or ineffectively throughout the store? Explain shortcomings in some detail.   Effectively ☐   Ineffectively ☐

_____

_____

_____

_____

_____

21. How is any accent lighting used in the store?

_____

_____

_____

22. Is the visual presentation of merchandise simple or elaborate?   Simple ☐   Elaborate ☐

Executed tastefully?   Yes ☐   No ☐

23. Are mannequins used?   Yes ☐   No ☐

24. Are mannequins used on platforms adjacent to featured merchandise?   Yes ☐   No ☐

25. How often are mannequins changed?   _____

26. How often are windows changed?   _____

27. Are display platforms used effectively?   Yes ☐   No ☐

28. Are transparencies used as feature displays? If yes, describe.   Yes ☐   No ☐

_____

_____

29. Is the area above the cornice line used for display?

Yes ☐   No ☐

30. Is seasonal trim (or foliage) used throughout the store?

Yes ☐   No ☐

31. Are there other types of display presentations used throughout the store? If yes, please describe.

Yes ☐   No ☐

_____

_____

32. What is the age and theme of existing decor?

_____   _____
Age   Theme

33. Are mirrors used effectively throughout the store? Please comment.

Yes ☐   No ☐

_____

_____

34. What type of signage system is used for each department?

Department   Sinage System
_____

_____

_____

35. What is the most obvious feature about the general presentation of merchandise throughout the store?

_____

_____

_____

36. Which departments present merchandise most successfully?

_____

_____

_____

    Least successfully?

_____

_____

_____

37. What type of shelving is used for perimeter wall merchandise?

_____
Glass / Wood / Laminate / Plastic / Metal

38. Is binning required for the presentation of merchandise?

Yes ☐   No ☐

39. What is the condition of showcases?

Full Vision _____

$1/3$ Vision _____

Open _____

40. Are pads used in showcases?   Yes ☐   No ☐

41. What types of racks are used throughout the store?

_____	_____	_____
Straight	Round	3-way round
_____	_____	_____
T-stands	4-way	Others

42. Do the present racks present merchandise to the optimum?   Yes ☐   No ☐

43. What is the condition of the tables?   Drawered   Parson's   Decorative

_____

_____

_____

44. What is the condition of columns?   _____

_____

45. Are columns used effectively for mirror placement?   Yes ☐   No ☐

Merchandise presentation devices?   Yes ☐   No ☐

46. What is most obvious about the general housekeeping of the store?

_____

_____

_____

47. Is there a security system used throughout the store? If yes, identify type.   Yes ☐   No ☐

_____

_____

48. Are shoplifting notices posted at fitting-room banks?   Yes ☐   No ☐

49. How many display personnel are employed at the store?   _____

How regularly do they work?   _____

_____

_____

50. How many personnel are required to staff store for opening?   _____

For closing?   _____

Example of In-Store Evaluations

Evaluation of Store Inspections

Do you feel your store has been inspected often enough? Yes _____ No _____

If no, please explain: _____

_____

What is your general feeling about store inspections?

_____

_____

Are the inspections comprehensive enough? Yes _____ No _____

How often should the store be inspected? _____

Do branch store inspections offer a consistently fair method of evaluation? Yes _____ No _____

If no, please explain: _____

_____

_____

_____

Evaluation of Store Managers' Knowledge

The collective answers to the following questions should help us determine some strengths and weaknesses in manager training.

Do you feel that store procedures and merchandise-presentation format responsibilities have been spelled out in a clear, concise manner? Yes _____ No _____

Should a procedure manual be prepared by management? Yes _____ No _____

What, in your opinion, is the best way to evaluate the performance of a store manager? _____

_____

_____

_____

Evaluation of Manager Training

Have you, as manager, had the training necessary to allow you to do your job effectively in the following?

Store-cleaning techniques	Yes_____	No_____
Store inventory	Yes_____	No_____
Correct-line floor-fixture merchandising	Yes_____	No_____
Rack-and-line floor-fixture arrangement	Yes_____	No_____
Correct wall merchandising (shelving, hanging)	Yes_____	No_____
Personnel staffing	Yes_____	No_____

Correct use of wall hardware	Yes_____	No_____
Correct merchandise signage	Yes_____	No_____
Separate stock system (paperwork and procedure)	Yes_____	No_____
Markdown system (paperwork and procedure)	Yes_____	No_____

Store-Fixture and Maintenance Needs

Please grade the needs of your store in the following categories:

	Good	Adequate	Poor	Explain Poor Rating
Electrical/Lighting	_____	_____	_____	_____
Plumbing/Rest Rooms	_____	_____	_____	_____
Flooring/Aisles/Carpets	_____	_____	_____	_____
Floor fixtures	_____	_____	_____	_____
Paint	_____	_____	_____	_____
Air conditioning	_____	_____	_____	_____
Heating	_____	_____	_____	_____
Glass shelves	_____	_____	_____	_____
Receiving room equipment	_____	_____	_____	_____
Cleaning/maintenance equipment	_____	_____	_____	_____
Wall hardware	_____	_____	_____	_____
Store signs	_____	_____	_____	_____

Merchandise Presentation

Do you feel your merchandise presentation is:

Good _____   Adequate _____   Poor _____

Do you feel that housekeeping (store appearance) generally is as good (or better) that the competition's?

Yes _____   No _____

Is your store overstocked with more merchandise than necessary?

Yes _____   No _____

Should there be additional training for managers on proper merchandise presentation?

Yes _____   No _____

Evaluation of Merchandise

Do you feel you and your store personnel have enough input into the types of merchandise that are bought and displayed?   Yes _____   No _____

Are the needs of customers fulfilled with the types of merchandise you sell? Yes _____   No _____

Does the store do a good job on "basics"? Yes _____   No _____

Should the store try to trade up? Yes _____   No _____

If yes, in what areas? _____

If no, why not? _____

Are the customers offered a wide enough selection of merchandise? Yes _____   No _____

List what you consider to be the store's strengths in merchandise selection/presentation. _____

_____

List what you consider to be the store's weaknesses in merchandise selection/presentation. _____

_____

Do you have enough lead time and information to display merchandise properly? Yes _____   No _____

Do you feel markdowns are timely? Yes _____   No _____

Do you get seasonal merchandise on time? Yes _____   No _____

Evaluation of Security

Is there adequate security in the store? Yes _____   No _____

Is there adequate nighttime supervision in the store? Yes _____   No _____

Is there adequate supervision in the store on Sundays? Yes _____   No _____

Rank (1, 2, 3) where you feel the greatest shortages in security are in your store:

Internal loss _____

Shoplifting _____

Paperwork _____

Evaluation of Advertising

Do you feel that you, as a manager, have enough input as to the type, quantity, and timing of advertising for your store? Yes _____   No _____

If no, please explain: _____

_____

Is notification regarding advertising adequate under the existing system? Yes _____   No _____

If no, please explain: _____

_____

Do you feel that the manager should have the responsibility for evaluating the success of ads within his or her store area? _____ Yes _____   No _____

Please rate the following advertising elements that affect your store:

	Good	Adequate	Poor
Type of advertising	_____	_____	_____
Overall amount of advertising	_____	_____	_____
Frequency of "local" advertising	_____	_____	_____

Timeliness of advertising   ____ ____ ____

Adequate lead time   ____ ____ ____

Amount of stock to cover advertising response   ____ ____ ____

Managerial participation in advertising decisions   ____ ____ ____

Type of merchandise delivered   ____ ____ ____

Cooperation from advertising department   ____ ____ ____

If you have answered "poor" on any of the preceding, please comment on the reasons for this grade:

_____

_____

_____

_____

Miscellaneous Evaluation

Based on surveys, rank (1, 2, 3, 4, 5) the factors that you feel most influence women to purchase apparel merchandise:

    Newspaper ads   _____

    In-store presentation   _____

    Observing dress of people in magazines   _____

    Observing dress of people on TV   _____

    Watching what other people wear   _____

    Other (fashion magazines, etc.)   _____

What are the first five things you do at the store in the morning?

1. _____

2. _____

3. _____

4. _____

5. _____

List some of the things you expect your night supervisor to do:

_____

_____

_____

_____

_____

_____

Example of Memorandum

TO: All Store Managers

RE: Questionnaire

DATE: _____

The following confidential questionnaire will be considered part of the agenda at the Managers'

Meeting at the _____ on _____, 19___. Please do not sign this

questionnaire. Be as objective and fair as possible in answering the questions so the results will

have maximum value in the discussions. Please send the completed form to _____

by _____.

Example of Questionnaire

Is there adequate security in the stores? Yes _____   No _____

Is there adequate supervision of night operations? Yes _____   No _____

Is the maintenance schedule completed by staff on a timely basis? Yes _____   No _____

Is there adequate supervision of Sunday operations? Yes _____   No _____

Is your store overstocked with more merchandise than necessary? Yes _____   No _____

Do you feel that your ideas on merchandising (i.e., customer sentiments, hot-selling items) are understood and appreciated at the home office? Yes _____   No _____

Is our advertising effective? Yes _____   No _____

Is the scope and direction of our advertising communicated to you on a timely basis? Yes _____   No _____

Compared to our competitors, do you feel that our housekeeping is as good? _____   Better? _____   Not as good? _____

Should store audits and branch store inspections be conducted more often? _____

Less often? _____

Please feel free to comment here and/or on the reverse on any of the above subject or other matters you feel need to be addressed.

_____

_____

_____

_____

_____

Chapter 7

DEPARTMENTAL SQUARE-FOOT
ALLOCATION SCHEDULES

In order to plan, merchandise, and design any store, the store planner must have a clear understanding of all departments, the existing square footage of each, the current departmental dollars generated per square foot, the proposed square footage of each redesigned department, and the projected dollar volume per square foot of each redesigned department.

The following schedules will be of value in assuring that no department or classification is overlooked. The schedules will be filled out by management and are given to the store planner for review and processing. Once the store planner has reviewed the square-foot allocation schedule, a plan will be developed based on this information.

Store Name _____

Store No./Location _____

Completion Date _____

Job Telephone _____

Job FAX _____

Store Planner _____

Address _____

City, State _____

Telephone _____

FAX _____

DEPARTMENTAL SQUARE FOOT ALLOCATION SCHEDULE		Job # _____		Date _____		
				Sheet _____		
	DEPARTMENT NAME	EXISTING SQ. FT.	CURRENT $/SQ. FT.	REQUESTED SQ. FT.	PROJECTED $/SQ. FT.	ACTUAL SQ. FT.
	WOMEN'S & MISSES' COATS AND SUITS					
	• Women's & Misses' Jackets—Casual					
	• Women's & Misses' Jackets—Tailored					
	• Women's & Misses' Coats—Casual					
	• Women's & Misses' Coats—Tailored					
	• Women's & Misses' Suits					
	FURS AND FUR GARMENTS					
	ALL DRESSES (EXCEPT JUNIOR)					
	• Bridal and Formal					
	• All Women's Dresses					
	• All Misses' Dresses					
	• Daytime Dresses, Uniforms, Aprons					
	• Maternity Clothing and Accessories					

Store Name _____
Store No./Location _____
Completion Date _____
Job Telephone _____
Job FAX _____

Store Planner _____
Address _____
City, State _____
Telephone _____
FAX _____

DEPARTMENTAL SQUARE FOOT ALLOCATION SCHEDULE	Job # _____ Date _____ Sheet _____				
DEPARTMENT NAME	EXISTING SQ. FT.	CURRENT $/SQ. FT.	REQUESTED SQ. FT.	PROJECTED $/SQ. FT.	ACTUAL SQ. FT.
WOMEN'S & MISSES' SPORTSWEAR					
• Women's & Misses' Spectator Sportswear					
• Women's & Misses' Active Sportswear*					
JUNIOR COATS AND SUITS					
• Junior Jackets— Casual					
• Junior Jackets— Tailored					
• Junior Coats—Casual					
• Junior Coats— Tailored					
• Junior Suits					
ALL JUNIOR DRESSES					
JUNIOR SPORTSWEAR					
• Junior Spectator Sportswear					
• Junior Active Sportswear*					

* Includes swimwear, beachwear, and accessories; all other summer playwear; ski jackets, pants, and other winter sports playwear.

Store Name _____
Store No./Location _____
Completion Date _____
Job Telephone _____
Job FAX _____

Store Planner _____
Address _____
City, State _____
Telephone _____
FAX _____

DEPARTMENTAL SQUARE FOOT ALLOCATION SCHEDULE	Job # _____ Date _____ Sheet _____				
DEPARTMENT NAME	EXISTING SQ. FT.	CURRENT $/SQ. FT.	REQUESTED SQ. FT.	PROJECTED $/SQ. FT.	ACTUAL SQ. FT.
BRAS, CORSETS, AND GIRDLES					
• Bras					
• Corsets and Girdles					
INTIMATE APPAREL, SLEEPWEAR, & ROBES					
• All Intimate Apparel					
• All Sleepwear					
• All Robes and Loungewear					
ALL JEWELRY AND WATCHES					
• Fine Jewelry and Watches					
• Costume Jewelry*					
HOSIERY AND GLOVES					
• Women's Hosiery					
• Women's Gloves					

*   Includes synthetic and imitation pearls.

Store Name _____

Store No./Location _____

Completion Date _____

Job Telephone _____

Job FAX _____

Store Planner _____

Address _____

City, State _____

Telephone _____

FAX _____

DEPARTMENTAL SQUARE FOOT ALLOCATION SCHEDULE	Job # _____		Date _____		
			Sheet _____		

	DEPARTMENT NAME	EXISTING SQ. FT.	CURRENT $/SQ. FT.	REQUESTED SQ. FT.	PROJECTED $/SQ. FT.	ACTUAL SQ. FT.
	WOMEN'S LEATHER GOODS					
	• Women's Handbags					
	• Women's Small Leather Goods					
	HATS, HAIRPIECES, AND TRIMMINGS					
	MISCELLANEOUS APPAREL AND ACCESSORIES					
	• Neckwear and Scarves					
	• Handkerchiefs					
	• Umbrellas, Folded Rain Accessories					
	• Belts and Other Accessories					

Store Name _____
Store No./Location _____
Completion Date _____
Job Telephone _____
Job FAX _____

Store Planner _____
Address _____
City, State _____
Telephone _____
FAX _____

DEPARTMENTAL SQUARE FOOT ALLOCATION SCHEDULE		Job # _____	Date _____		
			Sheet _____		
DEPARTMENT NAME	EXISTING SQ. FT.	CURRENT $/SQ. FT.	REQUESTED SQ. FT.	PROJECTED $/SQ. FT.	ACTUAL SQ. FT.
MEN'S CLOTHING					
• Overcoats*					
• Suits and Formal Wear					
• Casual Jackets and Slacks					
• Uniforms and Occupational Clothing					
• Men's Furnishings					
• Sports Shirts					
• Dress Shirts					
• Sweaters and Vests					
• Hosiery					
• Pajamas and Robes					
• Underwear					
MEN'S HATS AND CAPS					

*   Includes topcoats, raincoats, stormcoats, and dual-purpose coats.

Store Name _____

Store No./Location _____

Completion Date _____

Job Telephone _____

Job FAX _____

Store Planner _____

Address _____

City, State _____

Telephone _____

FAX _____

DEPARTMENTAL SQUARE FOOT ALLOCATION SCHEDULE	Job # _____ Date _____ Sheet _____					
	DEPARTMENT NAME	EXISTING SQ. FT.	CURRENT $/SQ. FT.	REQUESTED SQ. FT.	PROJECTED $/SQ. FT.	ACTUAL SQ. FT.
	ACCESSORIES					
	• Ties					
	• Handkerchiefs					
	• Jewelry and Small Leather Goods					
	• Toiletries, Umbrellas, & Other Accessories					
	• Gloves and Mufflers					
	ACTIVE SPORTSWEAR					
	• Beach and Swimwear*					
	• Ski Clothes**					

*   Includes all other summer-type playwear.
**   Includes all other winter-type sportswear.

Store Name _____

Store No./Location _____

Completion Date _____

Job Telephone _____

Job FAX _____

Store Planner _____

Address _____

City, State _____

Telephone _____

FAX _____

DEPARTMENTAL SQUARE FOOT ALLOCATION SCHEDULE		Job # _____ Date _____ Sheet _____				
	DEPARTMENT NAME	EXISTING SQ. FT.	CURRENT $/SQ. FT.	REQUESTED SQ. FT.	PROJECTED $/SQ. FT.	ACTUAL SQ. FT.
	INFANTS AND TODDLERS					
	• Apparel and Accessories					
	• Furniture*					
	GIRLS					
	• Little Girls' Clothing Sizes 3–6x					
	• Girls' Clothing Sizes 7–14					
	• Subteen Clothing Sizes 6–16 or 8–14					
	• Girl Scout Uniforms					
	• Apparel Accessories**					
	• Intimate Apparel					

*   Includes room furnishings, appliances, wheel goods, domestics, toys, miscellaneous.

**   Includes little girls, girls, and subteens.

Store Name _____
Store No./Location _____
Completion Date _____
Job Telephone _____
Job FAX _____

Store Planner _____
Address _____
City, State _____
Telephone _____
FAX _____

| DEPARTMENTAL SQUARE FOOT ALLOCATION SCHEDULE | Job # _____ | Date _____ |
| Sheet _____ |

	DEPARTMENT NAME	EXISTING SQ. FT.	CURRENT $/SQ. FT.	REQUESTED SQ. FT.	PROJECTED $/SQ. FT.	ACTUAL SQ. FT.
	BOYS					
	• Little Boys' Clothing Sizes 2–6x or 8					
	• Boys' Clothing Sizes 4–12 or 4–16					
	• Young Men's Clothing Sizes 13–20, 32–44					
	• Boy Scout Uniforms					
	• Boys' Furnishings (all age groups)					
	PERSONAL NEEDS					
	• Beauty Salon					
	• Barber Shop					
	• Photo Studio					
	• Optical					
	• Hearing Aids					
	• Prescription Drugs					

Store Name _____

Store No./Location _____

Completion Date _____

Job Telephone _____

Job FAX _____

Store Planner _____

Address _____

City, State _____

Telephone _____

FAX _____

DEPARTMENTAL SQUARE FOOT ALLOCATION SCHEDULE	Job # _____ Date _____ Sheet _____				
DEPARTMENT NAME	**EXISTING SQ. FT.**	**CURRENT $/SQ. FT.**	**REQUESTED SQ. FT.**	**PROJECTED $/SQ. FT.**	**ACTUAL SQ. FT.**
REPAIRS AND RENTALS					
• Fur Storage and Repair					
• Jewelry and Watch Repair					
• Shoe Repair					
• Tuxedo Rental					
STATIONERY, OFFICE EQUIPMENT & SUPPLIES					
• Stationery, Greeting Cards*					
• Office Equipment, Wrapping Supplies					
RESTAURANT, SNACK BAR, AND CANDY					
• Restaurant**					
• Snack Bar					
• Candy					

 *   Includes writing and school implements and supplies.

**   Includes Coffee Shop (waitress service).

Store Name _____
Store No./Location _____
Completion Date _____
Job Telephone _____
Job FAX _____

Store Planner _____
Address _____
City, State _____
Telephone _____
FAX _____

	DEPARTMENTAL SQUARE FOOT ALLOCATION SCHEDULE	Job # _____	Date _____		
			Sheet _____		
	DEPARTMENT NAME	EXISTING SQ. FT.	CURRENT $/SQ. FT.	REQUESTED SQ. FT.	PROJECTED $/SQ. FT.	ACTUAL SQ. FT.
	GROCERIES					
	• General Groceries					
	• Meats, Fish, and Poultry*					
	• Baked Goods and Confections					
	• Alcoholic Beverages					
	• Tobaccos and Smoking Goods					
	COSMETICS, DRUGS, AND TOILETRIES**					
	• Cosmetics, Fragrances, Toiletries					
	• Personal Hygiene, Grooming Supplies					
	• Drugs and Pharmaceuticals					
	• General Supplies and Sickroom Equipment					

*   Includes produce and dairy products, and delicatessen.
**   Includes sickroom supplies.

Store Name _____
Store No./Location _____
Completion Date _____
Job Telephone _____
Job FAX _____

Store Planner _____
Address _____
City, State _____
Telephone _____
FAX _____

DEPARTMENTAL SQUARE FOOT ALLOCATION SCHEDULE   Job # _____   Date _____   Sheet _____

	DEPARTMENT NAME	EXISTING SQ. FT.	CURRENT $/SQ. FT.	REQUESTED SQ. FT.	PROJECTED $/SQ. FT.	ACTUAL SQ. FT.
	HOBBIES AND OTHERS					
	• Pet Shop					
	• Stamps and Coins					
	• Travel Agency					
	• Magazines					
	• Radio, TV*					
	• Driving School					
	ELECTRONIC AUDIOVISUAL APPLIANCES**					
	• Radio, Audio Appliances & Supplies					
	• Television					
	• Musical Instruments***					

    *   Includes audio repair.
   **   Includes musical instruments, records, and sheet music.
  *** Includes records and sheet music.

Store Name _____
Store No./Location _____
Completion Date _____
Job Telephone _____
Job FAX _____

Store Planner _____
Address _____
City, State _____
Telephone _____
FAX _____

DEPARTMENTAL SQUARE FOOT ALLOCATION SCHEDULE   Job # _____   Date _____
Sheet _____

	DEPARTMENT NAME	EXISTING SQ. FT.	CURRENT $/SQ. FT.	REQUESTED SQ. FT.	PROJECTED $/SQ. FT.	ACTUAL SQ. FT.
	TOYS					
	BOOKS, ART, PHOTOGRAPHIC SUPPLIES					
	• Books, Periodicals, Maps, References					
	• General Arts and Crafts					
	• Photo Equipment & Supplies, Optical Goods					
	• Art, Drafting, Modeling Equipment*					
	LUGGAGE					
	SPORTING GOODS					
	STATIONERY					

*   Includes sculpting equipment and supplies.

Store Name _____
Store No./Location _____
Completion Date _____
Job Telephone _____
Job FAX _____

Store Planner _____
Address _____
City, State _____
Telephone _____
FAX _____

DEPARTMENTAL SQUARE FOOT ALLOCATION SCHEDULE   Job # _____   Date _____

Sheet _____

	DEPARTMENT NAME	EXISTING SQ. FT.	CURRENT $/SQ. FT.	REQUESTED SQ. FT.	PROJECTED $/SQ. FT.	ACTUAL SQ. FT.
	AUTOS, TRUCKS, TRAILER PARTS*					
	• Vehicles, Power Plant**					
	• Tires					
	• Chassis, Body Accessories, Fuel					
	• Motorcycles, Motorbikes***					
	BOATS, BOAT TRAILERS****					
	CLEANING AND UPHOLSTERY					
	• In-Home Cleaning					
	• Rug and Upholstery Cleaning					
	• Reupholstery					

    *   Including equipment and accessories, and not including boat trailer parts.
   **   Including transmission systems.
  ***   Including scooters, motorized carts, and sleds (replacement parts and accessories).
****   Including marine accessories.

Store Name _____

Store No./Location _____

Completion Date _____

Job Telephone _____

Job FAX _____

Store Planner _____

Address _____

City, State _____

Telephone _____

FAX _____

| DEPARTMENTAL SQUARE FOOT ALLOCATION SCHEDULE | | Job # _____ Date _____ |
| | | Sheet _____ |

	DEPARTMENT NAME	EXISTING SQ. FT.	CURRENT $/SQ. FT.	REQUESTED SQ. FT.	PROJECTED $/SQ. FT.	ACTUAL SQ. FT.
	FURNITURE AND BEDDING					
	• Upholstered					
	• Case Goods; Dining, Bedroom Furniture					
	• Mattress and Springs					
	• Dual Sleep & Other Sleep Furniture					
	• All Other Occasional Furniture					
	FLOOR COVERINGS					
	• Broadloom and Paddings					
	• Area and Room-Size Rugs					
	• Hard Floor Coverings*					

*   Including floor coverings, accessories, and supplies.

Store Name _____
Store No./Location _____
Completion Date _____
Job Telephone _____
Job FAX _____

Store Planner _____
Address _____
City, State _____
Telephone _____
FAX _____

DEPARTMENTAL SQUARE FOOT ALLOCATION SCHEDULE

Job # _____   Date _____

Sheet _____

DEPARTMENT NAME	EXISTING SQ. FT.	CURRENT $/SQ. FT.	REQUESTED SQ. FT.	PROJECTED $/SQ. FT.	ACTUAL SQ. FT.
CHINA AND GLASSWARE					
• China					
• Glassware					
SILVERWARE					
LAMPS AND LIGHTING FIXTURES					
PICTURES, MIRRORS, CLOCKS, & MISCELLANEOUS					
• Pictures, Mirrors, Wall Decorations					
• Clocks, Timers, Door Bells*					
GIFT SHOP & CHRISTMAS DECORATIONS					
• Gift Shop					
• Candles, Religious Articles					
• Christmas Decorations					
FLORIST**					

*   Includes chimes and weather indicators.
**   Includes artificial flowers.

Store Name _____

Store No./Location _____

Completion Date _____

Job Telephone _____

Job FAX _____

Store Planner _____

Address _____

City, State _____

Telephone _____

FAX _____

DEPARTMENTAL SQUARE FOOT ALLOCATION SCHEDULE   Job # _____   Date _____

Sheet _____

DEPARTMENT NAME	EXISTING SQ. FT.	CURRENT $/SQ. FT.	REQUESTED SQ. FT.	PROJECTED $/SQ. FT.	ACTUAL SQ. FT.
HOME IMPROVEMENT					
• Storm Doors and Windows					
• Home Improvement Supplies					
MAJOR APPLIANCES					
• Kitchen Appliances					
• Laundry Appliances					
• Air Conditioning					
• Vacuums, Floor Polishes					
SMALL ELECTRICAL APPLIANCES					
HOUSEWARES					
• Kitchen Utensils and Pantry Tools					
• Laundry and Cleaning Supplies					
HEARTH AND FIREPLACE EQUIPMENT					
PAINTS, WALLPAPER, RELATED SUPPLIES					

Store Name _____

Store No./Location _____

Completion Date _____

Job Telephone _____

Job FAX _____

Store Planner _____

Address _____

City, State _____

Telephone _____

FAX _____

DEPARTMENTAL SQUARE FOOT ALLOCATION SCHEDULE	Job # _____ Date _____ Sheet _____				
DEPARTMENT NAME	EXISTING SQ. FT.	CURRENT $/SQ. FT.	REQUESTED SQ. FT.	PROJECTED $/SQ. FT.	ACTUAL SQ. FT.
HARDWARE, TOOLS, & ELECTRICAL EQUIPMENT					
LAWN, GARDEN, & OUTDOOR EQUIPMENT					
• Lawn Mowers and Snow Throwers					
• Hand Tools and Power Tools					
• Seed, Fertilizer, Bulbs, Etc.					
• Barbecue and Picnic Equipment					

Store Name _____

Store No./Location _____

Completion Date _____

Job Telephone _____

Job FAX _____

Store Planner _____

Address _____

City, State _____

Telephone _____

FAX _____

DEPARTMENTAL SQUARE FOOT ALLOCATION SCHEDULE	Job # _____ Date _____ Sheet _____				
DEPARTMENT NAME	EXISTING SQ. FT.	CURRENT $/SQ. FT.	REQUESTED SQ. FT.	PROJECTED $/SQ. FT.	ACTUAL SQ. FT.
CUSTOM DRAPERIES					
AND SLIPCOVERS					
CLOSET EQUIPMENT, BATH SHOP*					
• Closet Shop					
• Bath Shop					
• Mattress Pads and Covers**					
LINENS AND DOMESTICS					
• Towels					
• Sheets and Pillowcases					
• Blankets, Comforters, Pillows					
• Table Coverings					
WINDOW & FURNITURE COVERINGS					
• Ready-Made Draperies***					
• Ready-Made Curtains****					
• Bedspreads and Ensembles					

*   Includes mattress pads and covers.

**   Includes other miscellaneous related textiles.

***   Includes slipcovers, supplies, and accessories.

****   Includes shades, blinds, and all hardware and trim.

Store Name _____

Store No./Location _____

Completion Date _____

Job Telephone _____

Job FAX _____

Store Planner _____

Address _____

City, State _____

Telephone _____

FAX _____

DEPARTMENTAL SQUARE FOOT ALLOCATION SCHEDULE

Job # _____   Date _____

Sheet _____

	DEPARTMENT NAME	EXISTING SQ. FT.	CURRENT $/SQ. FT.	REQUESTED SQ. FT.	PROJECTED $/SQ. FT.	ACTUAL SQ. FT.
	SEWING*					
	• Apparel Fabrics					
	• Home Decorative Fabrics					
	• Patterns					
	• Sewing Notions					
	• Sewing Machines and Accessories					
	ART NEEDLEWORK**					

*   Includes fabrics, notions, patterns, and sewing machines.
**   Includes knitting and embroidery.

Chapter 8

DEVELOPING DEPARTMENTAL ADJACENCIES AND FIXTURING THROUGH THE USE OF A BUBBLE PLAN

One of the major challenges facing store planners is the supervision of the preparation of a practical plan that pulls together the visual merchandising ideas for merchants. This plan also complements the supportive architectural and mechanical drawing prepared by others and results in a "blueprint" for the proper guidance of those charged with implementation.

The planner's approach must be honest and direct. They key aspects of the project—such as sales criteria, image desired, customer base, and building conditions—must be discussed with candor and realism.

The plan should encompass all major merchandising and operational requirements and should anticipate the entire physical environment of the store and the uses to which each section of the store are to be put as dictated by the shape and size of the building and its interior space.

Purpose of the Bubble Plan

One hallmark of successful planning is the careful examination of the scope-of-work that takes place before the development of a *bubble merchandising adjacency plan* begins. In the scope-of-work, planners indicate all entrances to sales and operational areas and then determine the positioning of departments. This determination is based on sales-volume estimates and square-footage calculations.

The freehand shapes shown on the plan—known as *bubbles*—can be round, square, or rectangular, or variations of those configurations. They are used to indicate the size of spacing of the various retail departments and to show department locations and adjacencies.

The principal purpose of bubble (or block) plans is to carefully pinpoint departments and to take every advantage for showing merchandise at its best, as it relates to customer lifestyles or home environments. The proper plan will reflect the personality of the store and its selling philosophy. The bubble plans are reviewed and adjusted as required until all arrangements are agreed upon by store management.

Bubble plans should at least roughly indicate departmental function and form. They are functional tools that ultimately help entice, steer, and satisfy customers. The good bubble plan is a thoughtful approach to setting walls, fixtures, and sales support areas that do more than just help retailers maintain business; they subconsciously induce impulse buying. A good plan will stand the test of time. A bad plan usually will show problems from opening day.

Department stores—especially high-end specialty stores—tend to be frequently upgraded. Discount stores more often seem to be transforming themselves into budget operations. Industrial factories regularly are being converted into discount warehouses. The layout of all store types begins with the bubble plan.

The size and shape of fitting rooms are determined by the number of rooms required and their placement within a department. Control and wrap areas should have clear views into fitting-room entrances and to store entrances and exits.

In order to establish showcase lines and points of control, tracing paper should be placed over the bubble plan with lines and control points clearly indicated. Showcase lines are determined by the number of linear feet of glass required to show products. Any rooms that project from the perimeter walls should be carefully positioned to avoid shop-lifting pockets.

Bubble plans help to pull together a wide assortment of information. During the early stages, the planners transform known numbers into two-dimensional drawings. As the adjacent space is planned, planners incorporate all requirements dictated by the path customers are expected to follow through the store. Planners must be especially perceptive about what customers will actually see and remember.

Several bubble plans may be developed and refined until each department is assigned proper adjacencies on all sides and across the aisles. Each bubble diagram should include sufficient aisle exposure and should indicate exact shapes, sizes, and depths.

Planners, working within a framework of key principles, guidelines, and rules, follow this plan with as much continuity as possible. One of the best ways to do this is to take advantage of normal visual sightlines to focus attention on design elements to which shoppers respond. The plan will only be successful when customers find comfort and satisfaction in the store.

Basic Bubble Plans

There are three basic types of bubble plan: open, core, and cluster. The *open plan* focuses interest on perimeter walls and brings attention to various departments without blocking views elsewhere in the store. The open plan must have continuity of design so as not to detract from or overwhelm adjacent departments. Supportive areas (fitting rooms, stockrooms, etc.) are best tucked into perimeter walls so customers' views are unobstructed.

The *core plan* purposely uses walls to obstruct vision across the store, using wall decor to give special identification to certain departments. Both floor-to-ceiling walls and freestanding walls are used for this purpose.

The *cluster plan* employs various types of fixtures or walls to subdivide classifications and departments in the center of the space. This plan gives maximum flexibility in altering the size of departments. Merchandise of various departments or classifications encompasses the wall or fixtures, giving an open appearance while focusing on a given type of classification.

The Preliminary High-Wall Line Plan

Once the basic bubble (or block) plan concept is approved, the next step is to refine presentation requirements, including the type and density of fixtures required. Finally, the *preliminary high-wall line plan* is developed for review.

The preliminary high-wall plan defines the shapes and sizes of the building and departments and establishes the ceiling or decor break lines. The perimeter wall, with proper supportive hardware systems, supports the weight of the merchandise presentation and backdrop.

These are typical questions that are answered in the details of the preliminary high-wall line plan:

- What type of merchandise presentation is required?
- What types of hang rods are needed: single, double, triple, faceout, staggered?
- Will waterfalls or faceouts be needed to show the face of the merchandise?

Special classifications or groupings can be highlighted by coordinating them with the plan and design. Once wall locations have been determined, a hard-line wall plan can be drawn that finalizes the size of departments and nonselling areas.

Proper placement of supportive hardware on the walls or interior partitioning is most important to the overall presentation. The hardware should be fairly evenly proportioned, both in placement and function. Choice of hardware type and its placement depends on the image desired, usage planned, size of slotting involved, and gauge of steel necessary. The high-wall plan must indicate the central measurement and placement of supportive hardware to be attached or incorporated into the wall.

Hardware systems usually are placed on two-foot or four-foot centers. Both systems accommodate shelves and hangrods. Supportive merchandise hardware, vertically mounted on two-foot or four-foot centers, can be elevated by one or two feet above the floor line.

Perimeter walls can be planned to create fitting or stock space. In allowing for a fitting room or stockroom, the most desirable finish depth is seven feet. These areas should be planned so as not to obstruct the department or create shoplifting opportunities.

Dividing walls that separate classifications should not be overpowering, nor should they narrow the overall view. In reviewing the various wall systems, the planner should be sure that the decision is based on actual needs and budget.

Selecting the Hardware

Supportive merchandise hardware systems help present goods to their best advantage and accommodate inventory fluctuations. All new hardware should be coordinated with any standard wall hardware already in place, if possible, and with the particular merchandise being sold. Modular hardware, for example, can be used to vary presentation ideas and can be adjusted as inventories change. Waterfall and faceout brackets are used principally for color-presentation stories. Staggered, straight, or shaped hangrods allow for greater stocking capacities on walls.

Walls must always look neat, organized, and well stocked. When inventories are low, displays can be introduced to fill the void. A second option is to convert sold-down classifications from hangrods to face-out presentations. Staggered hangrods (single or double) give the merchandise the appearance of being fuller.

Continuous straight hangrods can be boring and offer little imagination in the presentation of merchandise in active or ready-to-wear areas. Continuous hangrods generally are used to display men's clothing and coats, but sometimes are used in other special areas.

Faceout Presentations

Waterfall or faceout brackets, when used correctly, will attract more than casual attention. Depending on wall length and the number of classifications involved, these brackets visually divide sections and help introduce new classifications.

The return wall, which ends a perimeter (or dividing) wall, is known as a *wing wall*. The wing wall adds strength to the perimeter wall. When dividing walls project toward the center of the store and two wing walls are placed back to back, a display focal point is created. These two wing walls that support a dividing wall are also known as an *endcap wall*. When a dividing wall ends below the ceiling, it should have a height of at least eight feet. This allows a one-foot cornice at seven feet—an excellent height for lighting merchandise classifications. Wall heights of eight and ten feet may be used since these are standard lengths in building materials.

When dividing walls are used, they should be placed on department break lines. Freestanding dividing walls often allow vision beyond the wall (if not to ceiling) and are less apt to interfere with HVAC, mechanical, and sprinklers.

When planning the wall, questions involving decor must be considered, such as: Will a cornice or overhead drop (such as a curtain wall) be used? *Cornices* are projecting ornamental boards above the height of merchandise that are used, among other things, for attachment of strip lighting and to provide an element of decor.

Curtain walls are overhead walls that drop from the ceiling line in front of back or perimeter walls. They can be used to hide lighting strips and also add decor. However, they can narrow a small space.

Cornices and curtain walls both can add character to overall design. Remember that curtain walls generally cost more than cornices.

Retail stores use full-height walls to subdivide selling areas from nonselling areas. The combination of full-height walls and lower dividing walls can add interest to a store presentation and contribute to the selling atmosphere. Full-height dividing walls may limit the expansion or contraction of a department due to renovation costs.

In setting walls, local codes should be checked for ceiling height requirements. When stock mezzanine areas are being considered, the planner should verify with local code the minimum ceiling clearance both above and below.

Soffits are underhanging walls that can be incorporated into the wall plans. They are used to conceal mechanical equipment, hide unsightly surface conditions, and add in other ways to the decor.

In the final wall plan, the accessory hardware should be coordinated with the merchandise of each department to interact with the supporting wall-hardware system. It is important in the planning process to know when and when not to use cornices, curtain walls, soffits, and the like.

When developing the portion of the bubble plan that pertains to freestanding fixtures (showcase lines, wrap counters, and racks), provision should be made for the necessary quantities and densities of merchandise. Freestanding fixtures are considered mobile, even when they require electrical hookups. They should be placed so as to maximize selling space. Whether fixtures are selected from catalogs or are custom-designed, each must be judged from the standpoints of practicality, life expectancy, and the ability to house, display, and sell merchandise to the optimum.

Customers should be able to see wall-displayed merchandise from the aisle line, so the height of each fixture is an important consideration. Heights over 54 inches can provide enough concealment to cause security problems. A fixture's design should conform with all other design criteria and should not be more conspicuous than the walls and merchandise.

Final Notes

Planning should include any racks and fixtures that can be used creatively to present goods at various interesting levels and angles. The fixture plan should be flexible enough to allow the easy removal of fixtures from the selling floor when merchandise sells down. The finish of all freestanding fixtures and perimeter decor should coordinate well with the department's design, including finish, colors, and textures.

A Case Study

The following case study is an example of the steps a store planner would take when approaching the remodeling of a store. However, similar steps would also be taken when planning and designing a new store. This example illustrates how the merchant and store planner must jointly review the existing conditions and discuss the new merchandising requirements. Items such as existing lighting and department size are reviewed.

It is important to remember that the merchant will have significant input and suggestions. It is the responsibility of the store planner to help the merchant walk through all phases of the project until a plan is agreed upon. Many times, the first plan will be reworked several times until an acceptable plan is established. Once a plan has been approved, plans will be developed that will incorporate additional information. Once all of the additional information has been reviewed, studied, and approved, it is time to begin to develop a complete set of working drawings.

Although the store in the case study is 40,000 square feet, similar steps must be taken regardless of the size and shape of the actual project.

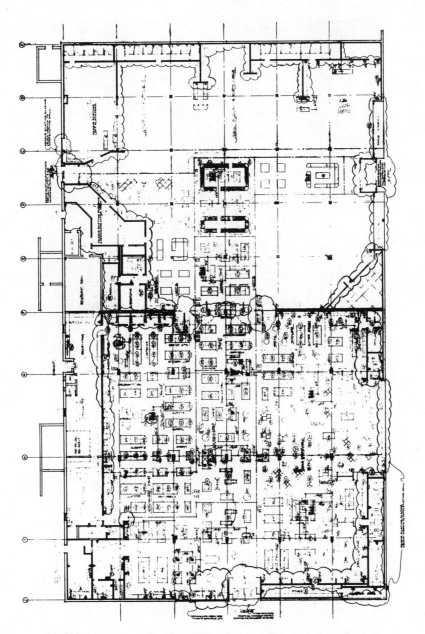

Here is an example of an existing merchandise plan. The merchant and store planner must review the existing conditions and discuss new merchandising requirements.

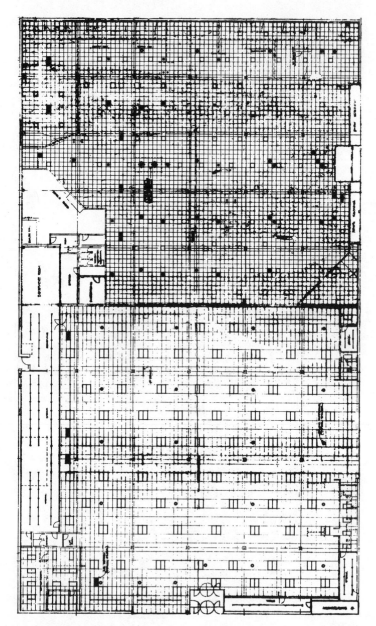

The existing ceiling and lighting plan must also be evaluated to check how the new plan will affect the existing distribution of light.

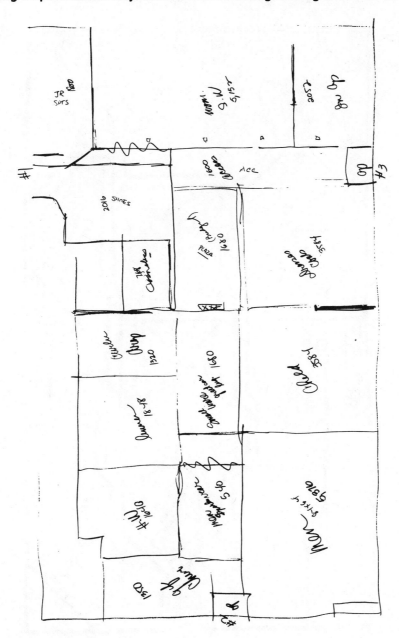

A quick and freehand overlay of the existing departments will help the planner verify department locations, adjacencies, and relative square footages.

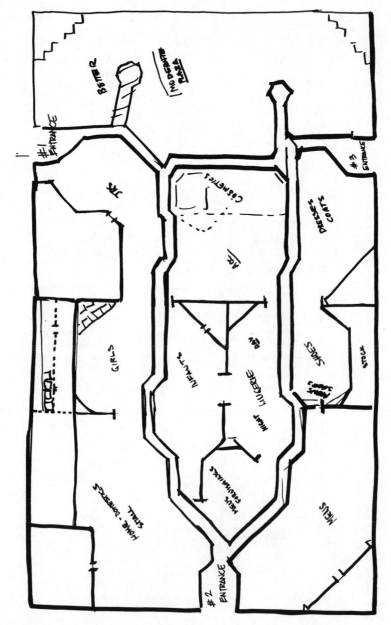

Sometimes the merchant will submit to the planner a preliminary sketch that indicates preferred adjacencies, department locations, and other suggestions.

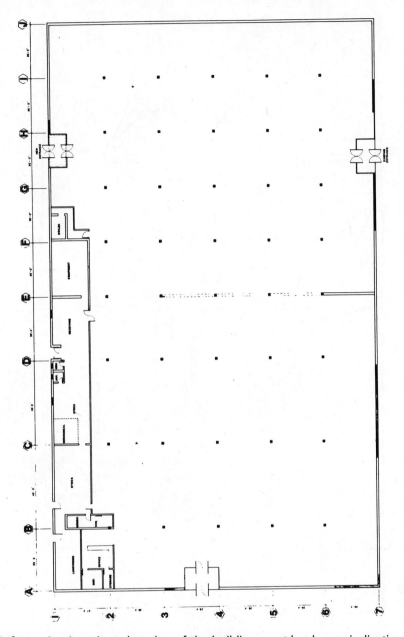

Once all this information is reviewed, a plan of the building must be drawn, indicating building, walls, selling and nonselling areas, windows, and entrances.

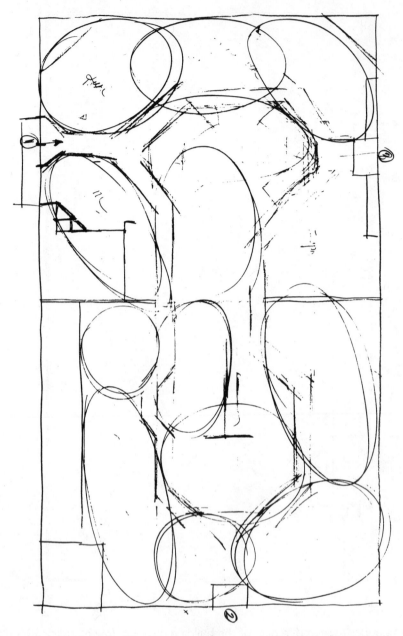

A bubble plan will be developed with all current information, including departments, square footages, and adjacencies.

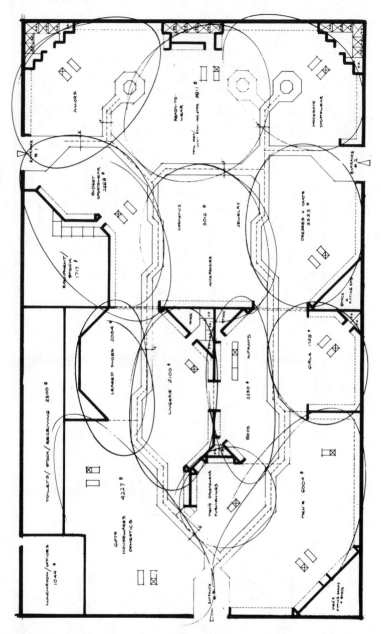

A preliminary Bubble, Wall, and Traffic Plan will suggest departments, square footages, adjacencies, entrances, and aisles.

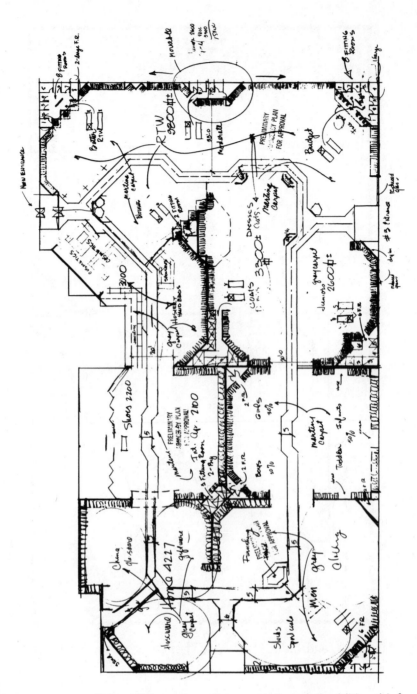

Many times, a space will be refigured, based on a meeting and additional information.

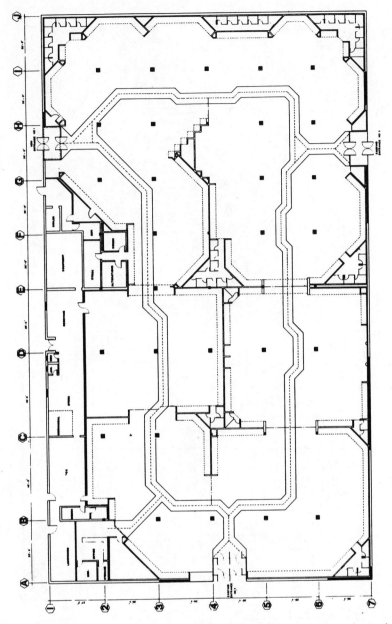

A hard-line plan is drawn, clearly indicating walls, aisles, and traffic movement through the space. At this stage, the merchant has reviewed the plan and may suggest an additional study.

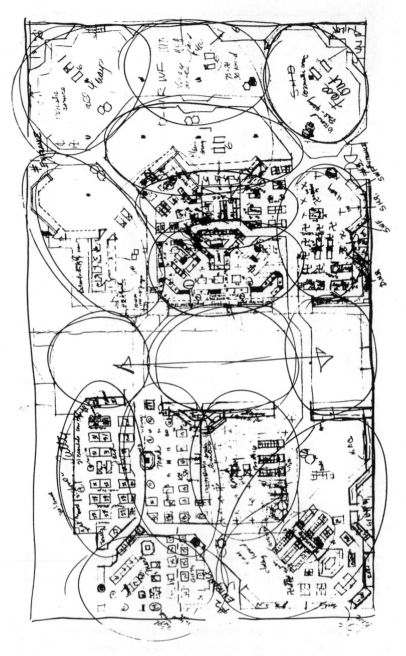

The additional study may suggest wall reconfiguration and fixture-density studies.

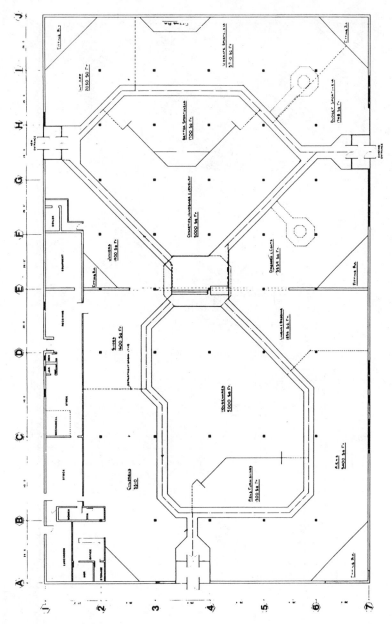

As a result of the additional studies, a new plan and concept of layout may evolve. Once again, this plan must be studied, reviewed, and adjusted.

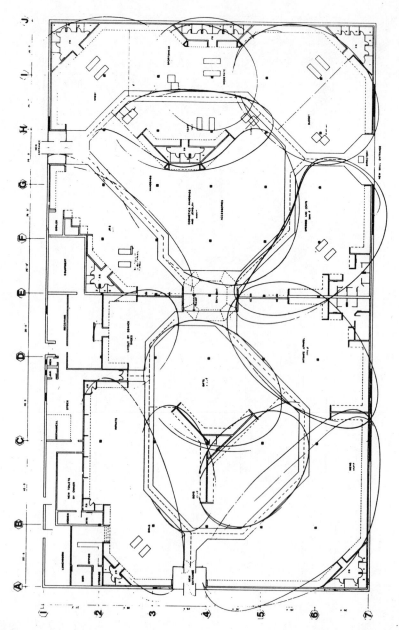

The final layout of the plan, both hard-line and bubble, allows the merchant to closely examine, adjust, and eliminate any potential problems.

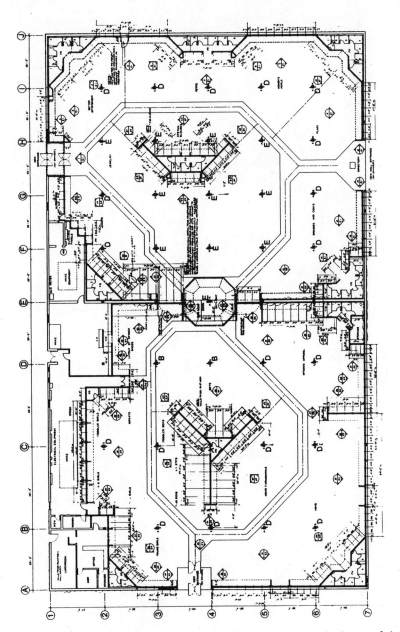

The high wall plan is frozen, and merchandising hardware is indicated. The balance of drawing can now begin.

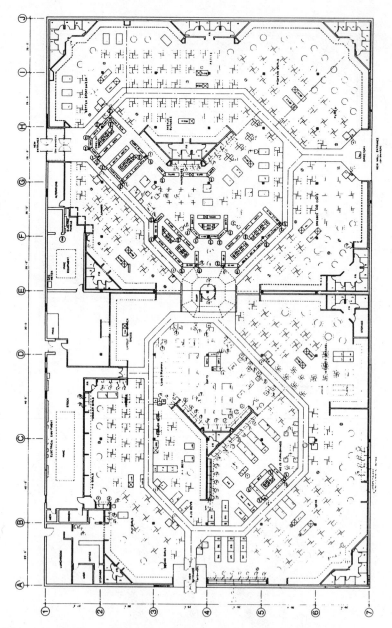

The merchandising plan indicates department placement, selling and nonselling areas, fitting rooms, and control areas, along with traffic movement and fixture placement.

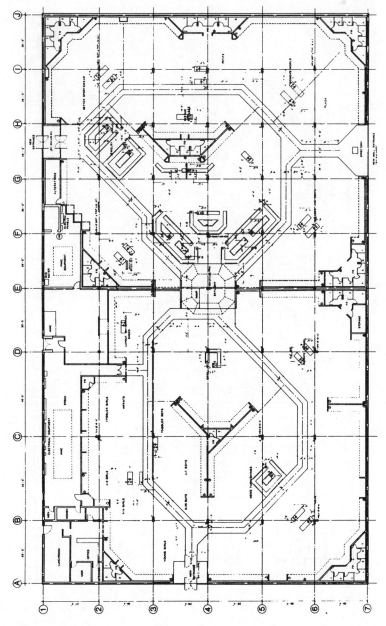

The power and signal plan helps to establish all the floor electrical requirements to bring electrification to freestanding fixtures, showcases, P.O.S. systems, telephones, and so on.

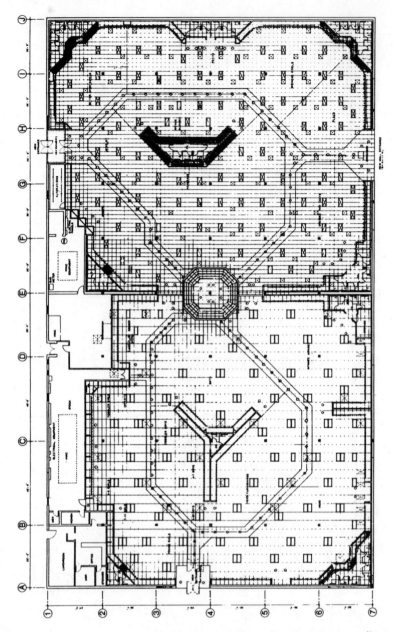

The reflected ceiling and lighting plans for both the ceiling and perimeter are adjusted to coordinate with the new plan.

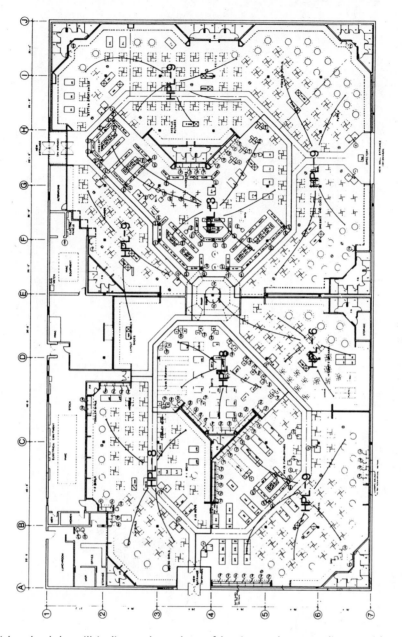

The fixture-finish schedule will indicate the colors of laminate that coordinate with each department.

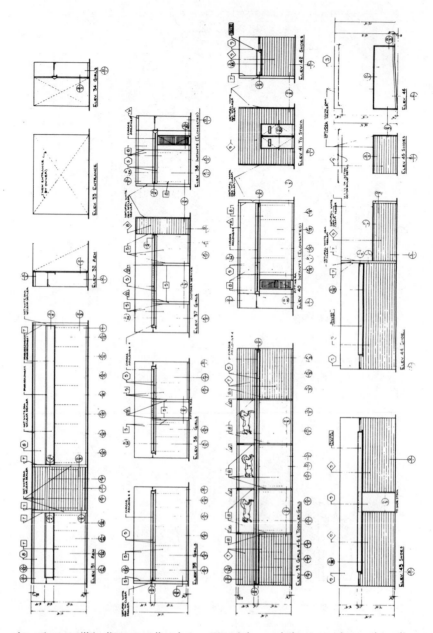

The perimeter elevations will indicate wall colors, materials, and decor and merchandise applications.

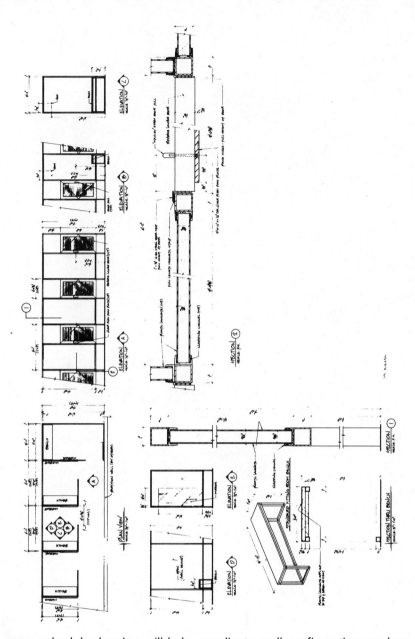

The fitting-room schedule drawing will help coordinate wall configurations and requirements.

Chapter 9

STORE LAYOUTS

The following 17 store layouts illustrate the shape of the building, department locations, and traffic patterns. Many of the projects a store planner will design will not be rectangular boxes but variable sizes and shapes. They can be located in a mall, a strip center, or a freestanding building. Many times a store will have a selling or a nonselling mezzanine area. No matter what size or configuration the building is, all of the plans will illustrate how the customer will travel through the space into each department.

Each merchant will have different ideas about the setup of a store. Some of the plans will illustrate fixture placement, selling and nonselling areas, fitting rooms, customer service area, and so on.

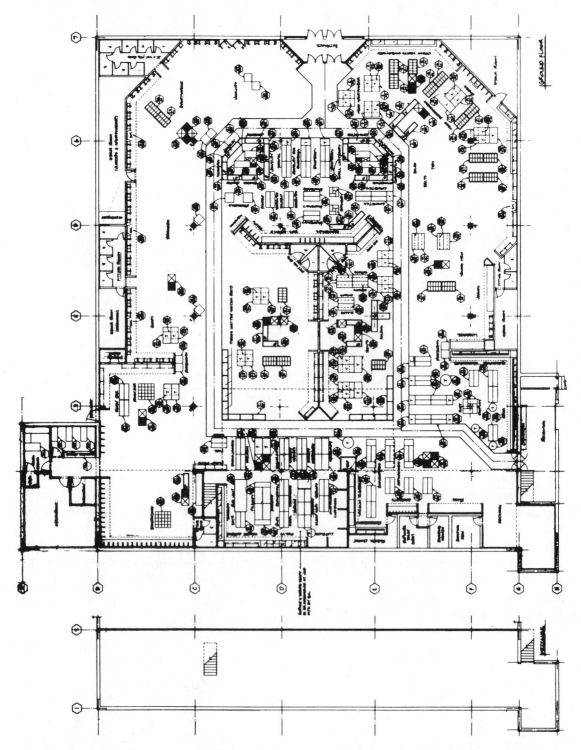

As an anchor store at a strip center, this 25,000 sq. ft. building sat at the center of the strip and was formerly occupied by a grocer. The redevelopment of this space included addition of HVAC and mechanicals. The traffic aisles help generate customer movement to the rear of the store. This specialty store includes Women's, Cosmetics, Jewelry, Accessories, Men's, Children's, and Home Departments. An 8-foot wall partition is used to develop wall and department identification in the center of the store. This is a core plan.

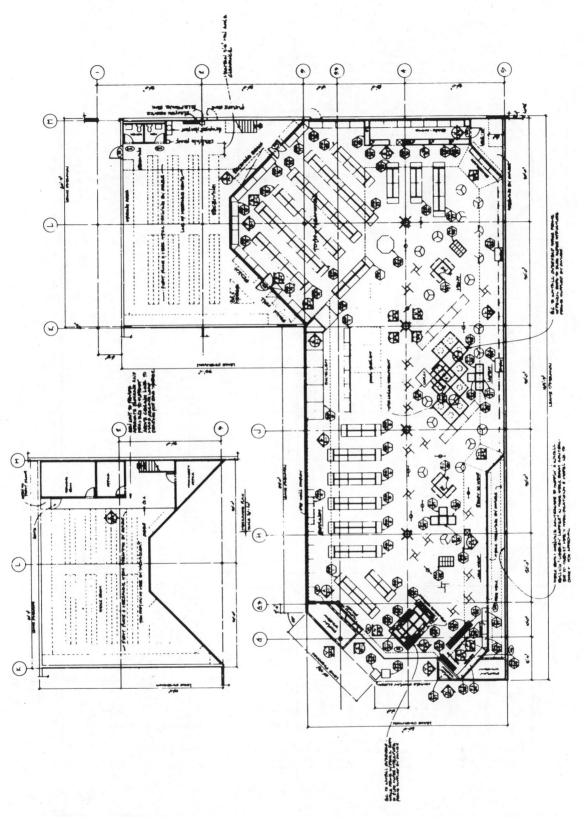

This open-plan sporting goods store is in a mall and accessed by two corridors. A stock mezzanine was added to accommodate backup merchandise. The hard-line store incorporated complete sports-oriented ready-to-wear clothing for women, men, and children. The shoe department is located at the front of the store. This concept allows for the customer to view and enter this space with no obstructions.

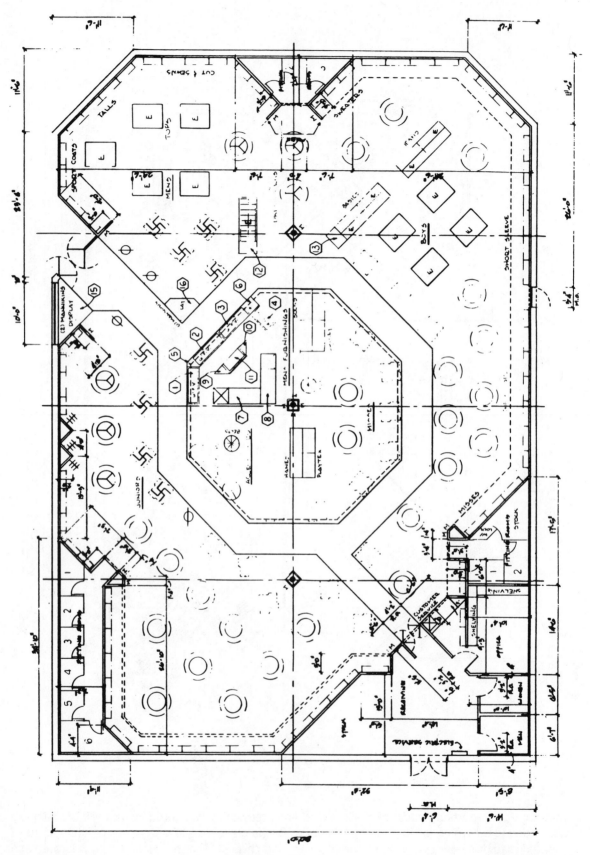

This open-plan freestanding building focuses its attention on the plan and on the movement and control of customers. This plan allows maximum exposure to the aisle. The showcase and wrap counters help control the entrances.

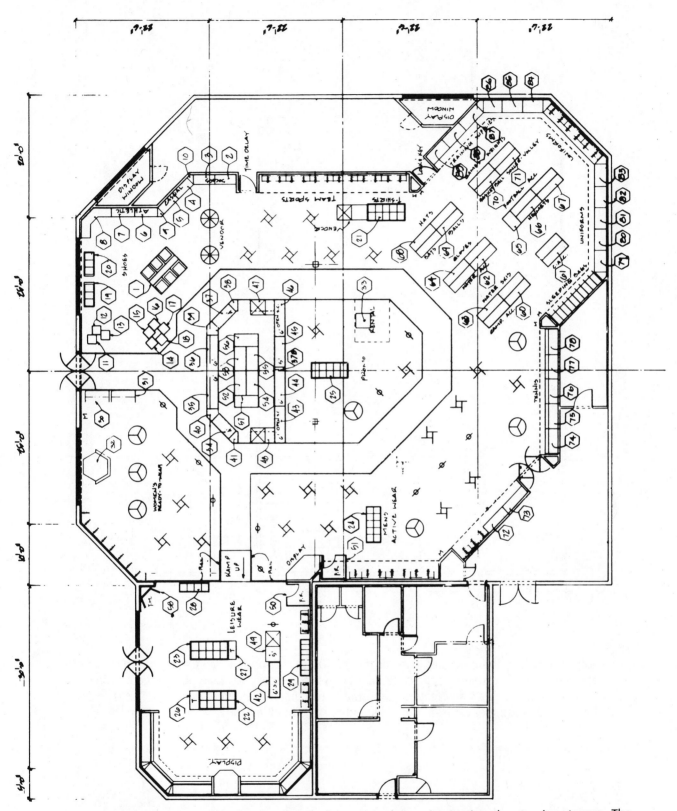

This open-plan sporting goods store has its shoe department dominating the store's entrance. The active-sportswear areas accent the balance of the storefront. A smaller area with featured merchandise has a separate entrance. The doors were planned to be open only during high-traffic times of day.

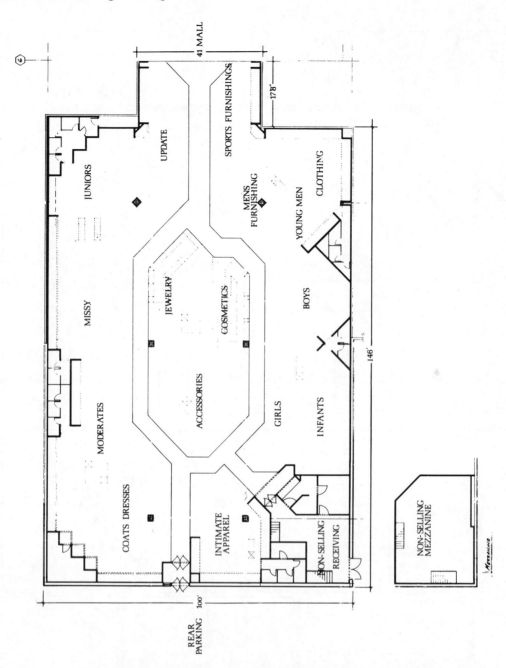

This open plan allows the customer to enter the 15,000-sq.-ft. specialty store from the mall or from the rear parking lot. Customers appreciate easy access to a store. This plan allows the customer to choose the direction to walk and features exposure to merchandise in either direction. This is an open plan because the customer can see across the entire store at all times.

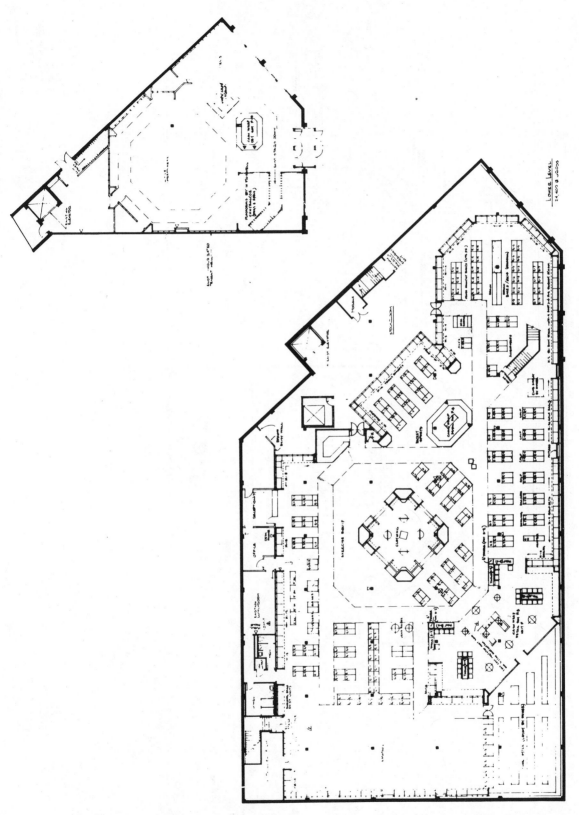

This 25,000-sq.-ft. sporting goods store is located at the end of a strip center in a suburban community. The 5,000-sq.-ft. ground-entrance level features fashion sporting goods and ready-to-wear for both men and women. This space, which was formerly occupied by a furniture store, boasted a large inviting stairwell to a lower level of 20,000 sq. ft. At the store entrance, hard-line departments border the perimeter walls. A platform for selective selling and promotional display creates interest in this lower level.

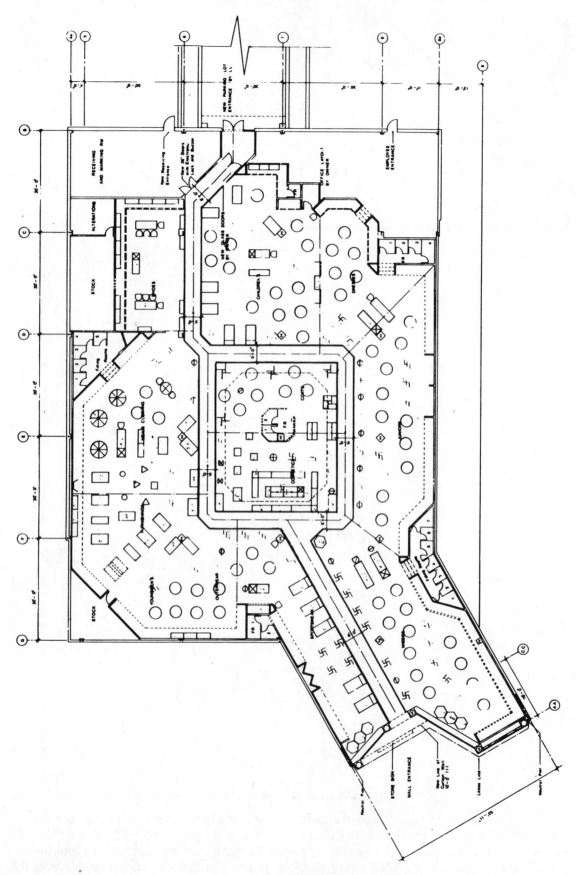

This open plan generates traffic through an unusually configured space. Each department has maximum exposure to the aisle. Wrap counters control the fitting-room entrances.

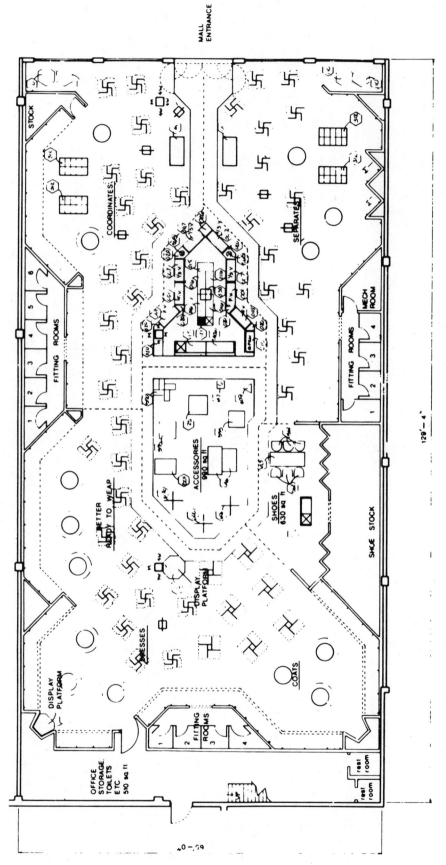

The reworking of this women's special ready-to-wear store included the storefront and relaying of interior departments and adjacencies. A commanding center island helps control fitting-room entrances.

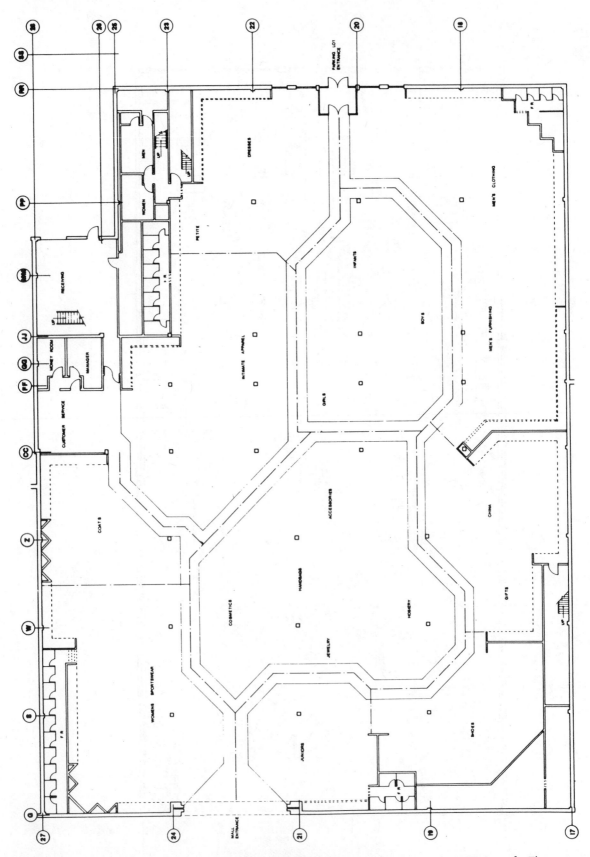

The remodeling of this 35,000-sq.-ft. anchor store increased its selling space by 4,000 sq. ft. The store features excellent circulation because of its parking-lot and mall entrances. It also has maximum aisle exposure for each department, and no department is deeper than 40 feet.

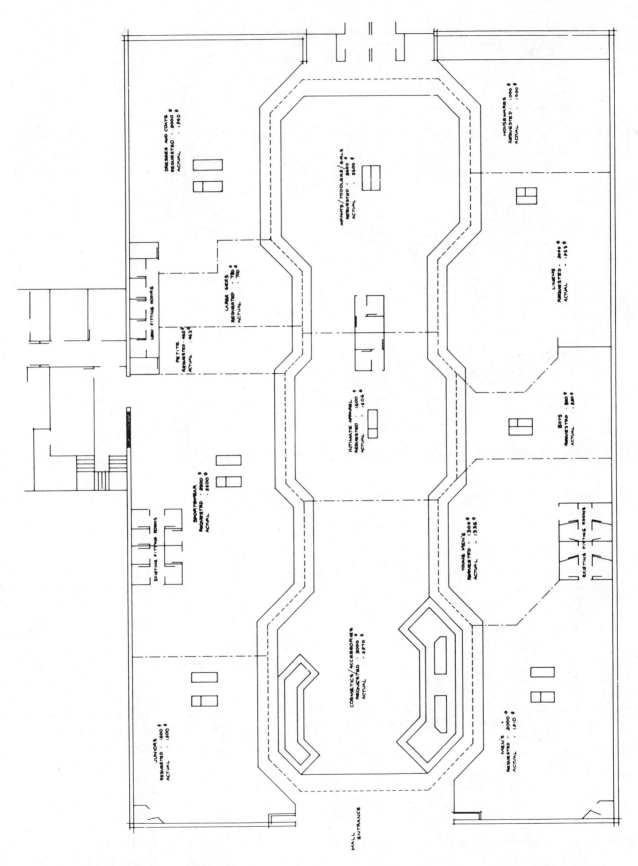

This is an example of a quick preliminary department-size-and-adjacency study. In this 22,000-sq.-ft. location, departments were relocated and two cross aisles in the center core were eliminated, thus creating the option of easy expansion or contraction of the departments within this core.

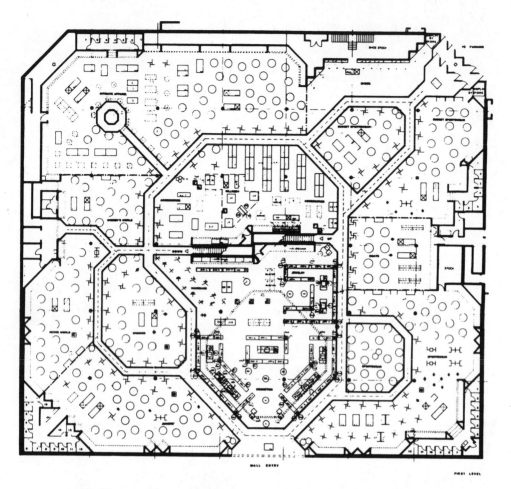

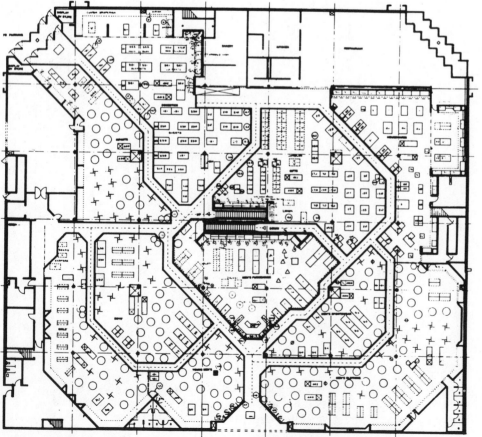

The configuration of the traffic aisles in this 80,000-sq.-ft. anchor department store allows for maximum aisle access to all departments. In the case of a large floor area, secondary aisles were introduced to keep the maximum department depth at 40 feet. The first level, which has mall and parking-lot entrances, has Cosmetic, Jewelry, and Accessory cores, along with all Women's Ready-to-Wear and Shoe Departments. The second level, which also has mall and parking-lot entrances, includes the Men's, Young Men's, Boys', Infants', Gifts, Domestics, and Houseware Departments as well as a Bakery and Restaurant.

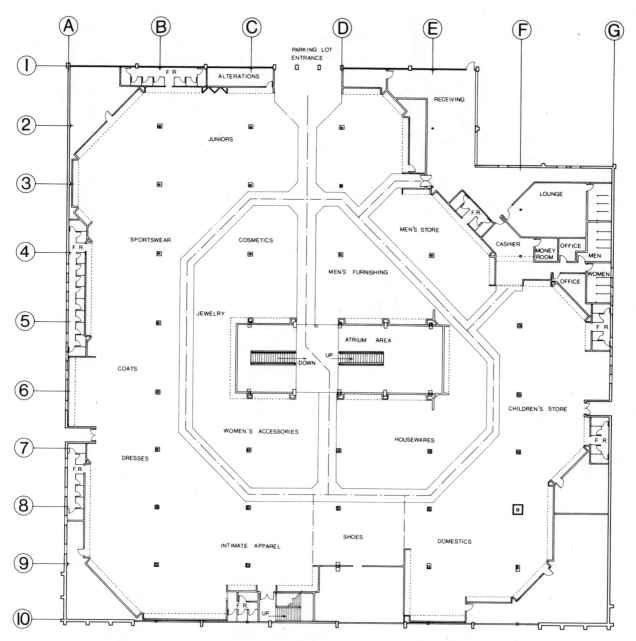

This unusual space, which was originally designed for offices on the second level of a mall, was re-planned as retail space. A bridge and escalators were added to bring vertical transportation to this level. The main entrance to this department store is on an upper level of an inclining terrain.

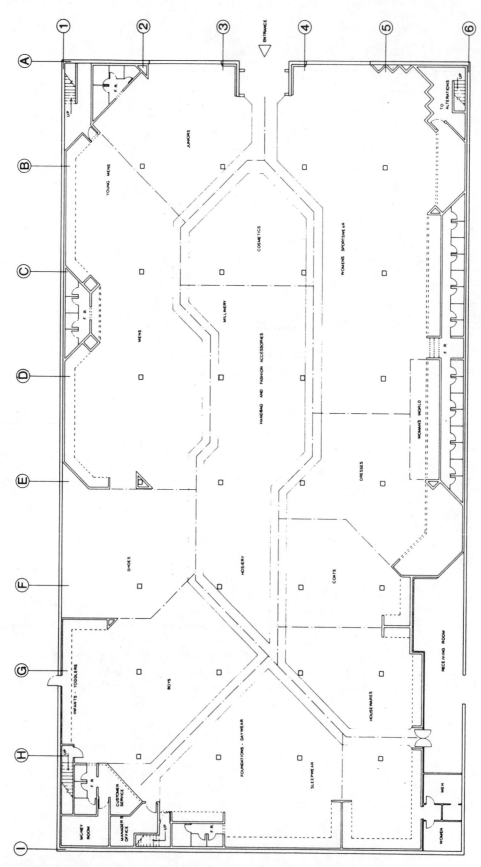

The remodeling of this 35,000-sq.-ft. specialty store located in a strip center included the addition of perimeter stock mezzanines. In relaying this store, the department location and size was based on the dollar volume of previous sales.

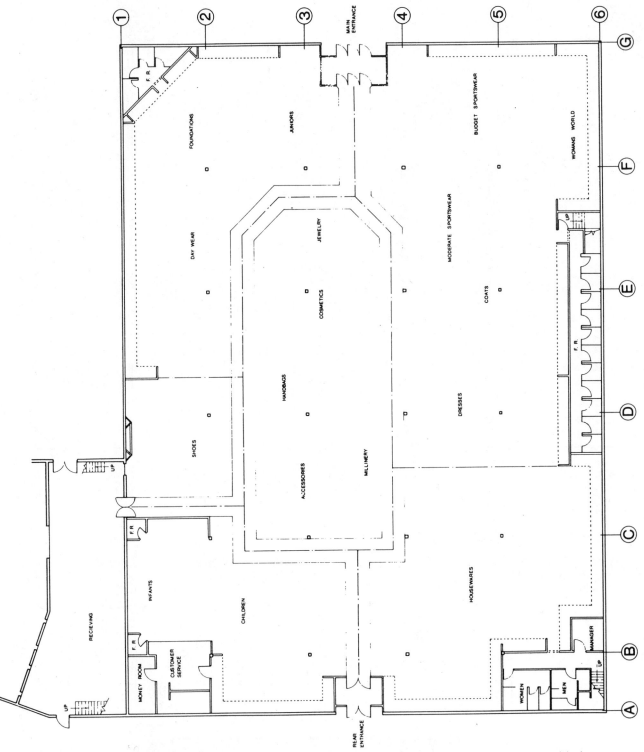

When remodeling this 27,000-sq.-ft. store, a new 2,500-sq.-ft. first-floor receiving area was added to the present facility, along with a 2,500-sq.-ft. stock mezzanine. New entrances and hard-surface aisles were introduced to establish a definite traffic flow.

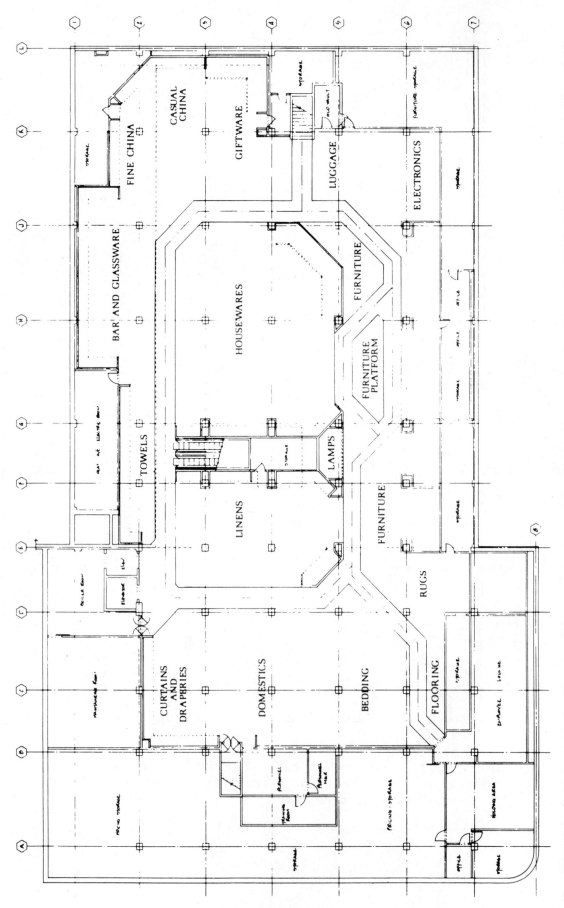

This 27,000-sq.-ft. lower level of a downtown department store was transformed into a store for the home. This facility is serviced by a street entrance, escalators, and elevators, and the hard-surface aisle configuration allows for maximum exposure to each department.

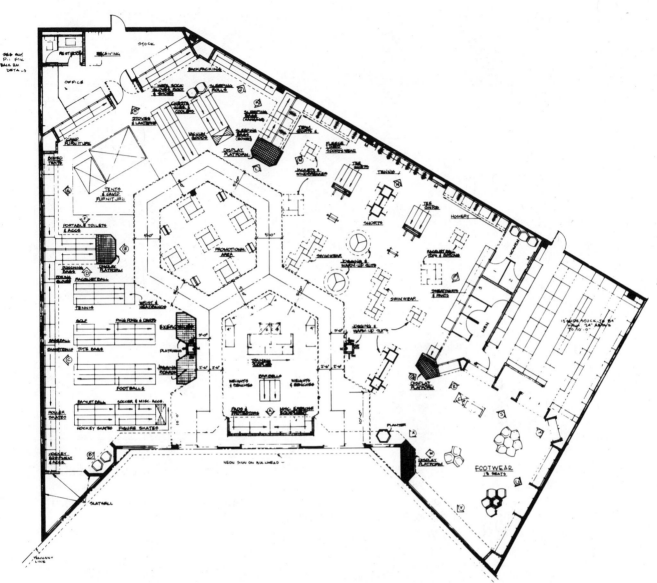

This 12,000-sq.-ft. irregular store configuration allowed the merchant 87 linear feet of mall storefront exposure. The departments were segregated through the use of wing walls with feature display platforms at the endcaps. The promotional area, encompassed by a hard aisle, allows this sporting goods retailer to feature seasonal displays and to accentuate promotional merchandise.

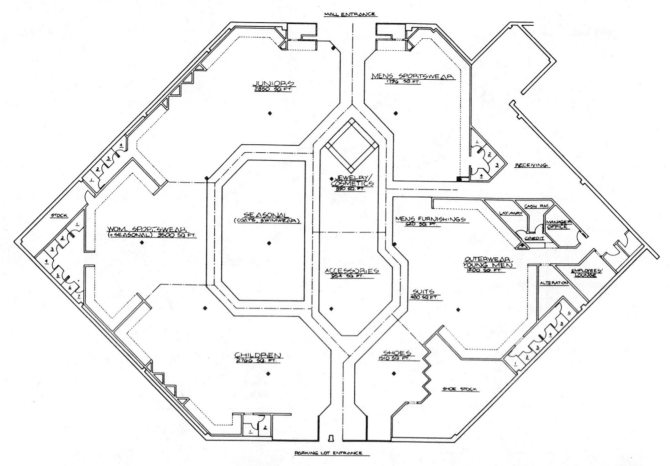

This preliminary study exemplifies not only that all stores are not square boxes, but also that traffic patterns can be designated to accommodate the size of each department as well as to work within the confines of the building shape. This example of a 25,000-sq.-ft. facility in a mall indicates how each department, with its curious shape, has maximum aisle exposure, while nonselling areas are neatly tucked away into one of the corners.

Chapter 10

BUDGETING

Aligning Budgets with Scope of Work

One of the many tasks the store planner must perform is the establishment of a realistic budget that aligns with the scope of the work. Often the retailer's scope of work will far exceed the constraints of the budget. Therefore, it is vital for the store planner to have a working knowledge of cost per square foot and how that cost will be divided over the entire project.

As an example, a retailer could say, "I would like to remodel my store (or build a new store) that is approximately X thousand square feet, and I want to spend Y dollars." The store planner must be able to sit down with the client and frankly explain, "Yes, we can do it within this budget" or "No, the budget is unrealistic for the scope of work."

There are many factors involved in determining exactly what the store will cost per square foot. These factors are the cost of each individual building material and its applicable labor. Some of these materials include ceiling systems, lighting, wall construction, wall hardware, aisle materials, carpeting, freestanding fixtures, showcases, back islands and back wraps, painting, wallcovering, decor, and

signage. The store planner must have an active list of estimated or projected costs per square foot and be able to quickly calculate the amount of square footage and project an estimated cost based on processed square feet.

This chapter is designed to help the novice become aware of the many factors involved and possible pitfalls encountered during the process of preliminary planning and budgeting. After preparing a preliminary plan and analysis of the area to be processed—a plan that reflects the desired scope of work—the store planner must be able to confer with management and advise whether or not the scope of work must be adjusted to align with the budget.

Budget Items

The items discussed in this chapter apply to store remodeling as well as to the design of the new stores. Exceptions include demolition and/or moving of electrical or plumbing services or entrances to the facility, and the removal of existing aisles, carpets, walls, freestanding fixtures, electrical wiring, hardware, and other associated items that reflect the merchandising and design concept of the new plan.

Also discussed are the advantages and disadvantages, as well as options that can be taken to maximize the value of the investment without compromising the overall design.

In this chapter are briefly discussed each of the items mentioned, how they will impact the budget, and what modifications can be suggested to help reduce the budget or to apply the dollars to another portion of this project.

Concrete

Within all stores there are electrical requirements in the floor to bring power to showcases, cash and wraps, point-of-sale areas (POS), computers, telephones, security devices, visual merchandising areas, and any other special needs. In most cases, during the remodel of the store, it will be necessary to relocate many of the floor electrical outlets. The store planner must evaluate the locations of existing floor outlets and locate them on the plan for possible reuse. Moving floor outlets is very expensive since the concrete floor must be cut and channeled and new conduit laid for the running of electrical, telephone, POS, and computer cables. Once these conduits are laid, the concrete trenches must be filled to align with the existing floor surface. If a store planner can use the existing location of a checkout, it is to the merchant's and budget's advantage.

Other suggestions for placement of electrical services would include abutting a checkout next to a column where the electrical lines could be hidden within the column enclosure. Another option would be to drop power poles from the ceiling. Power poles are not considered desirable as they can interrupt the departmental concept but are considered within the industry an inexpensive way of electrifying a fixture. Many times, power poles from the ceiling will be dropped only in discount or budget areas, or as a temporary measure.

Masonry

Masonry is any work involving brick or block work for the construction of the store. This work can include, but is not limited to, the exterior building walls and store fronts. *In some cases, the developer may have placed the receiving door in an area that is not workable with the new plan.* New openings must be cut in the masonry to provide openings for the new location of the header, doorjamb, and door. In the case of a storefront, if brick, marble, or other similar material is to be used, masonry work will be required to support the weight of those materials.

Miscellaneous or Structural Steel

In some cases, miscellaneous steel or structural steel may be needed to carry the weight load of floors if penetrations are to be cut in the floor or ceiling. Of course, the structural engineer or architect would be involved to determine the use of steel that is the most economical yet sufficient to carry the weight loads. This could occur in areas where new stairwells, skylights, expanded openings, and so on, are desired.

If new mechanical systems (heat, ventilation, air conditioning) units are to be installed on the roof, new openings must be made that will require steel for the support of those units. Steel may also be required if new openings are to be cut into the building to create show windows or windows looking into the space, or to comply with mandated access for the handicapped. These are just some of the examples of how the budget can be affected by the use of steel within a store remodeling project.

Roof

During the inspection of the building, it may be deemed necessary to replace the roof to protect the investment. This responsibility is normally coordinated with the owner of the property or the developer who will bring in independent consultants to ensure that a proper roofing system has been installed to guarantee a tight and dry interior.

Fire-Proofing and Asbestos Removal

All the finished building materials used within the retail space must carry a Class A fire rating, Ratings are designed to ensure that in the event of fire, the building materials will minimize their contribution to flammability. The building owner or developer is responsible for fire-proofing the structure and will work with their consultants and insurers to ensure that the fire-proofing meets all local and national codes.

Asbestos abatement must be carried out and must meet all state and federal regulations for removal and disposal. It is the store planner's responsibility to work with the owners to ensure a phased program for the removal of any asbestos.

Rough Carpentry

The term *rough carpentry* is used for any new fire retardant woodblocking that will be installed within walls for the anchoring of decor, fitting rooms, stock, or freestanding merchandising walls. This blocking is installed and is coordinated with the drawings to ensure attachment of the equipment for stability. If a store planner should fail to take this factor into consideration, it could result in expensive sheetrock removal, installing the blocking and new sheetrock, and preparing the wall for finish. Lost time, as well as expense, is a major hazard if rough carpentry requirements are neglected by the planner.

Miscellaneous Insulation

Within a retail store, there are areas that require insulation. The insulation may be required between the building wall and fixture wall, depending on the store's geographic area. Other insulation for soundproofing within the retail store may be installed within the business or office areas where privacy is required. These areas might include the offices of executives, managers, and buyers; personnel offices; training areas; or any retail walls that abut these areas.

Doors and Windows

Most doors within a retail store are used as entrances into stock rooms, offices, security areas, and so on. These doors are commonly key locked and are specified in either a paint-grade wood or hollow *metal* door. There are advantages and disadvantages of using both paint-grade wood doors or hollow metal doors. Successful contractors, when submitting bids, will specify their door of preference and any cost savings that could be passed on.

Windows within a retail space are primarily used as show windows. In most cases, these windows are supported by the use of prefinished aluminium extrusions. These extrusions, in most cases, provide the support for the glass and any entrance or exit doors to the space. Aluminum extrusions are one of the most cost-effective ways of installing exterior windows.

Exterior Entrances

Depending on its shape, size, and location, a store may have one or more entrances from a parking lot, an arcade, or a street. Usually, the exterior entrances will be built with extruded aluminium channels, glass, and doors. There are many metal finishes available, including anodized and color-coded finishes.

These extruded systems are practical and hold up under many years of hard use. Depending on the location of the entrance, tinted glass may be required to help diffuse the sunlight into the retail space. In the case of stores built in cooler climates, vestibules must be built to meet local codes. It is not necessary to use tinted windows in the vestibule glazing. Tinted windows can also have an impact on the cost of the glass.

Mall Entrances

The mall entrance to any facility is the number-one entrance to the retail space and should be designed to be open and inviting to encourage easy flow of traffic into the store. The mall storefront, entrance, and signage should be designed to attract maximum attention. Often an existing mall entrance can be cosmetically treated for updating along with the reuse of the existing overhead or sliding-glass-door system.

The store planner should work closely with management in reviewing the existing mall entrance and discuss the possibilities of how it can be remodeled without replacing the overhead or sliding-glass-door system. Many mall enclosure door systems are manufactured in stock sizes and variable finishes. In most cases, the door closure system will be concealed and out of sight of the customer while the store is open.

Many standard mill finishes will be used on these closures in order to help reduce the cost of the system. Other items that are applied to the mall storefront will have an impact on the cost of the mall storefront.

High Walls

High walls is a term that is used for walls that are to be constructed within the retail space and that separate retail from nonretail or fitting rooms. Where required, these walls are usually built of metal studs with plasterboard, and either recessed or surface-mounted standards. It is important when designing these walls that the centers of the studs are spelled out (*indicated*) where surface-mounted standards will be applied.

Surface-mounted standards will support the *faceout* hardware, which in turn will be used as a vehicle to support the merchandise. Standards and hangrods cannot be supported from plasterboard alone; they must have the backing of studs or blocking.

In some cases where heavy equipment or other weighty items will be displayed on a wall, extra woodblocking will be installed in conjunction with the steel studs in order to provide maximum support. The finishing of high walls will be discussed later in this chapter.

In the case of remodeling, it is to the great advantage of the store planner and merchant to retain as many of the existing walls as possible and to modify those walls as necessary. This will not only help save time during the demolition and construction phase, but will slash costs. Once the new high walls are built in conjunction with the existing high walls and they are painted or finished with the decor elements to create the new environment, the existing walls will blend into the new high walls.

Ceilings and Coves

Most retail stores today are built with lay-in two-by-four ceilings. These ceilings are designed to be suspended from the overhead building structure. They are also designed so that lay-in panels can be easily inserted and removed for service to the mechanical areas above the ceiling.

Most ceiling T-bar systems are installed in white with a complementary lay-in ceiling tile or pad. These pads come in an array of finishes, colors, and textures. The ceiling pads have an impact on the cost per square foot based on the density of texture and any design or regular reliefs designed into the ceiling pad. A tegular pad is designed so that it drops below the line of the grid to help give the ceiling additional dimension. A flat lay-in two-by-four ceiling pad will be less expensive than a tegular two-by-four ceiling pad. Flat lay-in ceiling pads give a very plain and uniform look to the ceiling plane, whereas tegular pads can add dimension and visual interest.

Coves are plasterboard structures designed into the ceilings in order to give upward illumination of the ceiling. These coves can be internally lit with neon or fluorescent lamps. Cove lighting can be ambient to a space; however, this can add significantly to the cost of the ceiling. Coves must be structurally built and hung from the overhead structure with studs and plasterboard. They need to be properly designed and executed to allow for easy main-

tenance or changing of lamps, along with ensuring the proper reflection onto the ceiling plane. Coves are used to bring drama and attention to a designated area of the store. The store budget and design concept should dictate the extent to which coves are used within a space. The design of the cove lighting should ensure that no light breaks occur within the cove that could distract from the overall intent of the cove.

Other Dry Wall

The term *other dry wall* refers to any decorative wall relief, such as soffits, baffles, curtain walls, wing walls, or T-walls. These design elements are used to create merchandising designs or light baffles on existing or new walls to highlight perimeter merchandise.

Other dry wall can also refer to a new wall surface that is required for the painting or application of decorative materials where old decorative materials have been removed. This term can also be used for the patching and repairing of any door openings that have been previously removed and have now become part of a selling or visual wall.

Floor Aisle Material

There is a wide array of flooring materials, that can be used for traffic aisles. The products include vinyl composition tile, marble, slate, prefinished wood parquet, terrazzo, carpet, ceramic tile, and others. Each distinctive material will require its own maintenance. The maintenance of these aisles must be discussed with the store management to ensure that servicing of these aisles will not be an operational problem for the retail facility.

Each material has its advantages and shortcomings. Traffic aisles are a high-maintenance area and need to be tended to on a daily basis and sometimes throughout the day. The maintenance and upkeep of these aisles is a key factor to consider when designing the store. Each material can vary greatly in price and will have a heavy impact on the final cost, design concept, and image of the store.

Vinyl Composition Tile

Vinyl composition tiles that are glued directly to a concrete floor will require some floor preparation and are easily washed and waxed. These aisles, by far, are the most cost effective installation of all other alternatives.

Marble Tile Aisles

Marble tile aisles must be set in a mortar bed and leveled and plumbed in order to ensure a flat and level surface. Once the mortar has set, lines between the tiles must be grouted. It is desirable to use grout that is the same color as the marble finish since the grout will tend to darken over a period of time with traffic dirt. The grout lines will becomes less obvious. Marble aisles are by far the most expensive to maintain because they require not only washing and waxing, but also buffing to maintain their appearance.

Ceramic Tile Aisles

Ceramic tile aisles are an economical alternative to marble aisles; however, they will create a different image. Ceramic tiles, like marble tiles, must be set in a mortar bed and must be grouted. Ceramic aisles require normal maintenance and do not require buffing as marble does.

Wood Parquet Aisles

Wood parquet aisles come in range of colors, finishes, and dimensions. Many of the wood parquet products used in retail stores today are designed to have the finish entirely throughout the material itself. This helps ensure durability and ease of maintenance. The products are directly glued to the concrete floor with adhesives. Parquet floor must be maintained as directed by the manufacturer and should be buffed occasionally.

Carpet Aisles

In some cases, a retailer will suggest the use of a carpet aisle as an economical way to move traffic through the store and designate the aisle space from the selling space. Sometimes, carpet will be used for the aisle that contrasts with the field carpet. In some instances, the same carpet color will be used for the field and the aisle; however, the aisle carpet will be of a higher density and pile height to ensure wearablity.

Aisle carpet takes a lot of abuse and can wear out at wrap or showcase lines. The quality of the material should be a major consideration. Carpet aisles are easily picked up and replaced when necessary.

The store planner must take the total square footage of the traffic aisles within the space; evaluate the square footage with a percentage for overage, breakage, and cutting; then establish the square footage of aisle material needed for the installation of the traffic aisles.

Carpet

The carpet selected for use in the retail store will have marked influence on the design and decor of the facility. The store planner must make a decision and advise management whether tufted or woven carpets will be used. Tufted carpets are less expensive than woven carpets, and nylon carpets will be less expensive than wool carpets. Pile height and weight of the carpet also determine the price.

When all these factors are reviewed, a ceiling cost per yard should be determined based on the highest quality carpet available for a given budget. The cost of the carpet will be the main factor in determining the total cost and, thus, the quality of the carpet chosen, but other factors that affect the total cost are carpet removal, pad removal, floor preparation, and type of installation.

In preparing a budget, the installation of carpet can be based on local labor charges times the number of yards to be installed. This equation helps to determine the exact carpet price for a store.

Many times when discussing carpets with management, decisions will be made to use one grade of carpet throughout the store with higher grades of carpet reserved for specialty areas. This, again, will have an impact on the cost of the carpet.

Painting

Paint, by far, is the most economical wall finish for plasterboard and trim. Painting walls can update a store image for the smallest investment. Painting includes:

- Walls
- Doors
- Jambs
- Casings
- Trims
- Moldings
- Soffits
- Curtain walls
- Baffles and coves

Often in the course of a remodeling, one coat of

eggshell enamel flat paint will be figured into the budget. However, sometimes a primer is needed to cover up trendy colors that were previously used. In some cases, if management wants to reuse the ceiling grid system, they also will require painting. (Ceiling pads should not be painted as they will loose their soundproofing qualities and can sag. The painting of the grid can be labor-intensive if not sprayed with an airless sprayer.) When contractors are preparing bids for painting, all necessary repairs to the wall should be included.

Wallcovering

All wallcoverings that are installed in a retail store must be of a Class A fire rating. This rating helps minimize smoke in case of fire. Wallcoverings can sharply increase the cost of a retail store, but they should be used in high traffic or surface areas or where the public is in contact with walls.

A wallcovering in a nondescript pattern that is used above a cornice or a baffle and is not readable as a wallcovering from eye level is not an economical decor item. A paint color of equal value to the wallcovering could achieve the same effect. Wallcoverings installed on perimeter walls of the fitting room bank are very economical from the standpoint of wearabilty and cleanability. Decorative pattern wallcovering can be used in areas to highlight or bring attention to a department.

Heavily patterned wallcoverings should not be used behind merchandise since they compete with the merchandise. Avoid using foil or reflective wallcoverings that can produce glare. Contract commercial 54-inch-wide wallcovering is more economical to install than 27-inch-wide wallcovering. A budget for the wallcoverings should be established up front and maintained.

Sprinkler Systems

Store remodeling often requires relocation of store sprinklers to accommodate new walls. All local and state codes governing sprinklers must be inspected. Once the wall plan has been developed, the store planner can verify at the location how many heads will have to be moved or relocated. There is considerable cost involved in the moving of sprinkler heads, and it is to the advantage of the store planner and management to try to establish a plan to work around existing heads.

HVAC (Heating, Ventilation, Air Conditioning)

In most cases, if the ceiling in the retail store is untouched, a minimal amount of work will have to be done with the HVAC. However, if new fitting-room banks are built out in a new location, new runs may be required for air distribution. It is important to have adequate air flow in the fitting rooms to ensure customer comfort. There are many ways a store planner can work around existing diffusers in the ceiling of the retail store by adjusting the lighting. It is far more economical to relocate a fluorescent or incandescent light than to relocate an air diffuser or sprinkler head.

Electrical

Electrical is a term used for but not limited to new floor outlets for cosmetic islands, checkouts, perimeter lighting, accent lighting, and perimeter convenience outlets where required. Power will also be needed for any new or supplementary lighting, including fluorescent, tracks, spots, and accents. Electrical service is required for floor, perimeter walls, freestanding walls, and any new electrified sinage or neon requirements.

It is the store planner's responsibility to reuse and relocate, wherever possible, existing lighting fixtures that match the overall system in the ceiling.

Merchandising Fixtures

Merchandising fixtures include items such as showcases, back islands, and cash and wraps. These fixtures require electrical hookup and should be planned with electrical service in the floor where required. It is an expensive mistake on the store planner's part to locate any of this equipment on the sales floor without considering its electrical hookup.

Many times, after carpet or tile is installed, it becomes obvious that a costly error has been made, carpet or hard surface flooring material must be ripped up, the concrete floor trenched, conduit installed, and the floor filled and resurfaced. Such an expensive rectification undermines the planner's profit margin, causes unfortunate delays, and embarrasses the planner—and is entirely avoidable through careful integration of planning.

Loose Fixtures

Loose fixtures are fixtures requiring nonelectrical hookup and are considered moveable within the retail space. These fixtures could include four-way as well as round racks, T-stands, tables, bases, gap tables, visual merchandising tables, display fixtures, laminate cubes, glass cubes, shoe cubes, special fixtures, towers, armoires, drawer units, and gondolas. These items are planned to be mobile and to be changed seasonally to accommodate various levels of merchandise within the store. Once the store planner has developed a merchandising plan, he or she can recommend to management various grades of quality of fixtures. Imported racks many times are more economical than those domestically produced. Considerable cost savings can be achieved without compromising the overall image of the store.

Perimeter Fixturing

Perimeter fixturing includes high-pressure laminate bases, visual merchandising shelves, new faceout perimeter hardware (such as hangrods, brackets, or prongs), bins, (plexiglass, glass, or wood) slat wall, light boxes, and special decor or fixturing units for designer shops.

It is important for the store planner to sit down with the management and thoroughly discuss the merchandising requirement and faceout hardware for perimeter walls. Many times, inexperienced buyers will ask for store-fixturing equipment to be placed on the perimeter walls that can accomplish only one task. Fixtures for the perimeter walls should be designed to ensure multiuse flexibility to accommodate seasonal changes in merchandise capacities.

Frequently, money is spent on fixtures for perimeter walls to store inventory, such as base cabinets, drawers, sliding cabinet bases, that are duplicated in the stockroom. Casework is an expensive item to build for a retail store, and each area should be reviewed with management to ensure that the request matches the operation of the department and that casework built for the retail selling floor does not end up in the stockroom.

Glass Walls

Within the course of a design project, the store planner will often be asked to include glass walls that could create a featured-display area or a surround for an escalator or stairwell, or at the corner or entrance to a designer shop. These glass walls must be planned well in advance to the material arriving at the job site. Structural blocking at the ceiling line must be preinstalled to ensure stability

and ease of installation. If these measures have not been taken in advance, cost overruns can occur.

Perimeter Lighting

Perimeter lighting is a term used to describe how merchandise on perimeter walls will be illuminated. There are many economical systems used to illuminate perimeter walls, for example, overhead wall washers, continuous troffer wall washers, cornice boards, baffles, track lighting, and spotlighting. Each of these items has significant impact on the cost and the decor concept of the space.

Relamping (Overhead and Perimeter)

All overall store remodeling projects should include the relamping (replacing the bulbs) of existing overhead fluorescents and perimeter lighting. Initially, after relamping the store, the store will have a brighter appearance since all lamps will be new. *Once the lamps have been in operation, the established foot-candles, as recommended by the manufacturers, should be maintained.*

The relamping of an existing store and the cleaning of all existing light fixtures is an economical way to improve both image and lighting of the store. It is important that lamp tubes are removed and fixtures and lenses are cleaned before relamping takes place. This ensures the best reflective value for both the tube and fixture.

Fitting Rooms

The cost of an individual fitting room can vary depending on the system and the finish materials. The experienced store planner can inform his client of the approximate cost of a fitting room.

When designing a fitting room, the store planner must consider the panel and wall finish; the framing system that will support the panels; the use of doors or curtains, flat mirrors or triple mirror; seat, bench, or chair; purse shelf; clothing hooks; and the illumination. Custom fitting-room designs are more expensive than stock, modular, prefabricated fitting-room systems. These prefabricated fitting-room systems can be purchased with custom laminates and/or colors and may offer a significant cost savings to the retailer. A fitting-room system that has been well planned and designed with quality materials should endure the life of the remodeling. The design of fitting rooms today must also take into account security and the ease of accessibility for handicapped shoppers.

Special Vendors, Shops, or Concepts

Many designers offer fixture designs that help reflect the attitude or the image of the shop. These companies offer drawings or prefabricated fixtures that can be purchased from a source to help identify the department. In many cases, the management of the store will supply these fixtures. Their cost, however, must be included within the budgetary constraints.

Shoe Department Chairs

Shoe chairs represent a significant investment and should be selected from companies who supply chairs specifically designed for the shoe industry. Shoe chairs are designed to take long-term abuse while the customer is being fitted. Strain is placed on the backs, arms, and rear legs of the chair, and therefore, the chair can become weakened it not properly constructed.

The store planner should select durable upholsteries that will work within the decor of the department and hold up over the life of the chair. Trendy chair designs or deep cushions many times make it awkward for the customer to try on shoes and stand up. Compare and shop for the best value that reflects the image of the department.

Interior Signage

Interior store signage are the signs placed throughout the store to bring attention to a department or a classification of merchandise. These signs can be worked into walls, cornices, and fixtures, and in most cases are nonelectrified.

These signs are made of various materials, including plastic, laminates, mirrors, and painted surfaces. After the drawings for signs are developed, sign packages are assembled and bid out separately to various sign manufacturers. Due to the competitive nature of signage, the cost-savings impact is thus minimized.

Store Visual Display

Many times in the planning and designing of a retail store, the visual budget will be placed within the store remodeling budget. Each company has a director for a visual design and merchandise presentation. This individual will present to management and the store planner a package of selected visual merchandise display items for incorporation into the space. It is management's responsibility to determine any cost savings that can be achieved since management is more actively involved with the visual department.

Special Equipment

Other items to consider when determining the store budget could include neon signs, TV monitors, ADT, closed-circuit TV, stockroom storage fixtures, conveyors, and audio/video equipment. This list of items many times is not brought to the attention of the store planner at the onset of the project and can have significant impact on the cost. It is important that these items be reviewed and discussed to establish the estimated budget up front.

Summary

The store planner is expected to have a great working knowledge of all the intricacies, cost factors, installation factors, and wearablity factors, and functional information of the many items and materials needed for a store. He or she should be able to sit down with the management team and authoritatively discuss how each material will impact not only the image of the space but also the budget. The education of a store planner is an ongoing process in which new industry standards change rapidly.

Chapter 11

STORE PLANNER'S ESTIMATED
STORE-FIXTURE BUDGET

In order for the store planner to totally understand what is in the best interest of the client and project, each category and type of building material that will be used to complete the interior must be determined. It is the responsibility of the store planner to review with the client items such as wall materials, ceilings, flooring, freestanding fixtures, electrical supplies, stockrooms, stockroom equipment, and so on.

Various types of materials will have either a square foot, linear, or unit price. There are many products that will serve the same purpose; however, cost will play the biggest part in determining what will be selected.

The estimated store-fixture budget will serve as a basis for helping the store planner to stay within budget and prepare specifications.

Store Name _____
Store No./Location _____
Completion Date _____
Job Telephone _____
Job FAX _____

Store Planner _____
Address _____
City, State _____
Telephone _____
FAX _____

ESTIMATED STORE-FIXTURE BUDGET

Job # _____   Date _____

Sheet _____

NO.	CATEGORY/DESCRIPTION/TYPE	SQ. FT. PRICE	LIN. FT. PRICE	UNIT PRICE	QUAN.	TOTAL COST
	FREESTANDING, PERIMETER WALL, CORNICES, COLUMNS					
	• Fire-rated wood stud partition w/ ⅝" plasterboard: 1 side taped and spackled.	X				
	• Fire-rated wood stud partition w/ ⅝" plasterboard: 2 sides taped and spackled.	X				
	• 6'0" surface-mounted heavy duty wall standard: 1 side			X		
	• Metal stud partition with ⅝" plasterboard: 1 side taped and spackled.	X				
	• Metal stud partition with ⅝" plasterboard: 2 sides taped and spackled.	X				
	• Recessed display stud with 8'0" insert slotted wall partitioning system with ⅝" plasterboard: 1 side (11'0") taped and spackled.	X				
	• Recessed display stud with 8'0" insert slotted wall partitioning system with ⅝" plasterboard: 2 sides taped and spackled.	X				
	• Cut and finish 3'0" x 6'8" opening into existing wall.			X		

Store Name _____

Store No./Location _____

Completion Date _____

Job Telephone _____

Job FAX _____

Store Planner _____

Address _____

City, State _____

Telephone _____

FAX _____

ESTIMATED STORE-FIXTURE BUDGET	Job # _____ Date _____ Sheet _____

NO.	CATEGORY/DESCRIPTION/TYPE	SQ. FT. PRICE	LIN. FT. PRICE	UNIT PRICE	QUAN.	TOTAL COST
	FREESTANDING, PERIMETER WALL, CORNICES, COLUMNS					
	• Supply and install 3'0" x 6'8" door with jamb and passage hardware.			X		
	DOOR TYPE:					
	Wood Hollow Core					
	Metal Hollow Core					
	Wood Solid Door					
	Metal Insulated Door					
	Louver Door					
	• Cut and finish 5'0" x 6'8" opening into existing wall.			X		

Store Name _____
Store No./Location _____
Completion Date _____
Job Telephone _____
Job FAX _____

Store Planner _____
Address _____
City, State _____
Telephone _____
FAX _____

		Job # _____ Date _____				
ESTIMATED STORE-FIXTURE BUDGET		Sheet _____				
NO.	CATEGORY/DESCRIPTION/TYPE	SQ. FT. PRICE	LIN. FT. PRICE	UNIT PRICE	QUAN.	TOTAL COST
	FREESTANDING, PERIMETER WALL, CORNICES, COLUMNS					
	• Supply and install 1 pair of 3'0" x 6'8" doors with jambs and passage hardware.			X		
	DOOR TYPE:					
	Wood Hollow Core					
	Metal Hollow Core					
	Wood Solid Door					
	Metal Insulated Door					
	Louver Door					
	• Supply and install 5½" ceiling trim.		X			

Store Name _____

Store No./Location _____

Completion Date _____

Job Telephone _____

Job FAX _____

Store Planner _____

Address _____

City, State _____

Telephone _____

FAX _____

ESTIMATED STORE-FIXTURE BUDGET						
		Job # _____ Date _____				
		Sheet _____				
NO.	CATEGORY/DESCRIPTION/TYPE	SQ. FT. PRICE	LIN. FT. PRICE	UNIT PRICE	QUAN.	TOTAL COST
	FREESTANDING, PERIMETER WALL, CORNICES, COLUMNS					
	• Supply and install ³/₄" x 4' x 8' horizontal solid core slatwall with paint as per elevation on perimeter wall.			X		
	• Supply and install ³/₄" x 4' x 8' horizontal fiber core or vertical slatwall with paint as per elevation on perimeter wall.			X		
	• Wall Cornice Application:					
	1'0" wide plain colored lacquer finish with cornice brackets.		X			
	1'6" wide plain colored lacquer finish with cornice brackets.		X			
	1'0" wide plain plastic laminate finish with 36" cornice brackets.		X			
	1'6" wide plain plastic laminate finish with 36" cornice brackets.		X			
	1'0" wide plain wood finish with 36" cornice brackets.		X			
	1'6" wide plain wood finish with 36" cornice brackets.		X			
	One application of ¹/₄" polished plate silver or bronze mirror cornice; verify width with elevation.		X			
	4" continuous plastic trim at top or bottom on face of cornice.		X			
	3" continuous wood trim at top or bottom on face of cornice.		X			
	3", 4", or 6" continuous plastic laminate accent band.		X			

Store Name _____
Store No./Location _____
Completion Date _____
Job Telephone _____
Job FAX _____

Store Planner _____
Address _____
City, State _____
Telephone _____
FAX _____

		SQ. FT. PRICE	LIN. FT. PRICE	UNIT PRICE	QUAN.	TOTAL COST
ESTIMATED STORE-FIXTURE BUDGET	Job # _____ Date _____ Sheet _____					
NO.	CATEGORY/DESCRIPTION/TYPE					
	FREESTANDING, PERIMETER WALL, CORNICES, COLUMNS					
	1'0" slatwall cornice colored lacquer finish with 36" cornice brackets.		X			
	1'6" slatwall cornice colored lacquer finish with 36" cornice brackets.		X			
	1'0" slatwall cornice wood finish with 36" cornice brackets.		X			
	1'6" slatwall cornice wood finish with 36" cornice brackets.		X			
	2'0" stepped cornice with decorative face material with 26" cornice brackets and extra support brackets.		X			
	1'0" half round cornice (fabric cov'd) with 36" cornice brackets.		X			
	2'0" double tube, round cornice (fabric cov'd) with 36" cornice brackets.		X			
	4'0" curtain wall with ⅝" plasterboard face, bottom return, and underside of soffit.	X				
	• Painted plasterboard column.	X				
	• Wallcovering on column.	X				

Store Name _____
Store No./Location _____
Completion Date _____
Job Telephone _____
Job FAX _____

Store Planner _____
Address _____
City, State _____
Telephone _____
FAX _____

ESTIMATED STORE-FIXTURE BUDGET			Job # _____	Date _____		
				Sheet _____		
NO.	CATEGORY/DESCRIPTION/TYPE	SQ. FT. PRICE	LIN. FT. PRICE	UNIT PRICE	QUAN.	TOTAL COST
	FREESTANDING, PERIMETER WALL, CORNICES, COLUMNS					
	• Supply and install colored lacquer, wood finish, or laminate plastic slatwall column enclosure: 4 sides as per detail.	X				
	• Supply and install colored lacquer, wood finish, or laminate plastic slatwall column enclosure: 3 sides; 1/4" polished plate mirror 1 side.	X				
	• Supply and install colored lacquer, wood finish, or laminate plastic slatwall column enclosure: 2 sides; 1/4" polished plate mirror 2 sides.	X				
	• Supply and install 1/4" polished plate mirror column enclosure: 4 sides; with polished metal trim.	X				

Store Name _____
Store No./Location _____
Completion Date _____
Job Telephone _____
Job FAX _____

Store Planner _____
Address _____
City, State _____
Telephone _____
FAX _____

NO.	CATEGORY/DESCRIPTION/TYPE	SQ. FT. PRICE	LIN. FT. PRICE	UNIT PRICE	QUAN.	TOTAL COST
	ESTIMATED STORE-FIXTURE BUDGET Job # _____ Date _____ Sheet _____					
	OVERHEAD CEILING LIGHTING, WALL AND FLOOR ELECTRICAL					
	• New ⁵/₈" plasterboard ceiling: taped and spackled.	X				
	• Reuse existing ceiling grid, supply and install new 2' x 2' ceiling pads (fire-rated).	X				
	• Reuse existing ceiling grid, supply and install new 2' x 4' ceiling pads (fire-rated).	X				
	• New ceiling grid and 2' x 2' ceiling pads (fire-rated).	X				
	• New ceiling grid and 2' x 4' ceiling pads (fire-rated).	X				
	• New metal accent ceiling system (fire-rated).	X				
	• Replacement of 2' x 2' prismatic lens in existing fixture.			X		
	• Remove and relocate 2' x 2' existing ceiling fixture.			X		
	• Remove and relocate 2' x 4' existing ceiling fixture.			X		
	• Install new 2' x 2' fluorescent curved tube light with energy-saving ballast and prismatic lens.			X		
	• Install new 2' x 4' fluorescent fixture with 4 lights, energy-saving ballast and prismatic lens.			X		
	• Install new 2' x 2' fluorescent fixture with energy-saving ballast, and chrome or brass lens (open cell).			X		
	• Install new 2' x 4' fluorescent fixture with energy-saving ballast, and chrome or brass lens (open cell).			X		

| Store Name _____ |
| Store No./Location _____ |
| Completion Date _____ |
| Job Telephone _____ |
| Job FAX _____ |

| Store Planner _____ |
| Address _____ |
| City, State _____ |
| Telephone _____ |
| FAX _____ |

ESTIMATED STORE-FIXTURE BUDGET					

Job # _____ Date _____
Sheet _____

NO.	CATEGORY/DESCRIPTION/TYPE	SQ. FT. PRICE	LIN. FT. PRICE	UNIT PRICE	QUAN.	TOTAL COST
	OVERHEAD CEILING LIGHTING, WALL AND FLOOR ELECTRICAL					
	• Continuous, single-lamp, rapid-start fluorescent fixture with energy-saving ballast.			X		
	• Continuous, double-lamp, rapid-start fluorescent fixture with energy-saving ballast.			X		
	• Industrial decorative incandescent fixture as per elevation.			X		
	• Overhead directional spot fixture concealed in ceiling.			X		
	• Overhead low-voltage directional spot fixture concealed in ceiling.			X		
	• Overhead down light fixture.			X		
	• Ceiling-mounted track with insert and canister.		X			
	• Special light fixture.			X		
	• Supply and install new electrical wall box 18" from finished floor.			X		
	• Supply and install new electrical wall box 4" above cornice height. (Verify with elevation.)			X		
	• Supply, cut, and install new floor electrical box. (Verify with power and signal plan.)			X		
	• Fixture plug-in connection (electrical and hookup).			X		
	• Permanent electrical connection and hookup.			X		

Store Name _____
Store No./Location _____
Completion Date _____
Job Telephone _____
Job FAX _____

Store Planner _____
Address _____
City, State _____
Telephone _____
FAX _____

ESTIMATED STORE-FIXTURE BUDGET			Job # _____ Date _____ Sheet _____				
NO.	CATEGORY/DESCRIPTION/TYPE		SQ. FT. PRICE	LIN. FT. PRICE	UNIT PRICE	QUAN.	TOTAL COST
	OVERHEAD CEILING LIGHTING, WALL AND FLOOR ELECTRICAL						
	• Continuous wall-mounted plug strip with outlets 12" on center (o.c.).			X			

Store Name _____
Store No./Location _____
Completion Date _____
Job Telephone _____
Job FAX _____

Store Planner _____
Address _____
City, State _____
Telephone _____
FAX _____

ESTIMATED STORE-FIXTURE BUDGET	Job # _____ Date _____ Sheet _____					

NO.	CATEGORY/DESCRIPTION/TYPE	SQ. FT. PRICE	LIN. FT. PRICE	UNIT PRICE	QUAN.	TOTAL COST
	FLOORCOVERING—SOFT/HARD					
	• Removal and disposal of tackless carpet and pad.		X			
	• Removal and disposal of gluedown carpet.		X			
	• New 3/8" plywood underlayment.	X				
	• New 28 oz. woven nylon carpet, glue down, freight included.		X			
	• New 30 oz. plush nylon carpet, freight included.		X			
	• New foam pad (commercial).		X			
	• Installation of new gluedown carpet.		X			
	• Installation of tackless carpet.		X			
	• Removal of existing tile.	X				
	• New vinyl composition tile.	X				
	• New parquet tile.	X				
	• New marble tile.	X				
	• New ceramic tile.	X				

Store Name _____

Store No./Location _____

Completion Date _____

Job Telephone _____

Job FAX _____

Store Planner _____

Address _____

City, State _____

Telephone _____

FAX _____

ESTIMATED STORE-FIXTURE BUDGET	Job # _____ Date _____ Sheet _____				

NO.	CATEGORY/DESCRIPTION/TYPE	SQ. FT. PRICE	LIN. FT. PRICE	UNIT PRICE	QUAN.	TOTAL COST
	PAINT AND WALLCOVERING					
	• Wallcovering removal and wall preparation.	X				
	• Sanding and wall preparation.	X				
	• One coat prime, one coat finish paint color.	X				
	• Furnish and install vinyl wallcovering per sq. ft.	X				

| Store Name _____ |
| Store No./Location _____ |
| Completion Date _____ |
| Job Telephone _____ |
| Job FAX _____ |

| Store Planner _____ |
| Address _____ |
| City, State _____ |
| Telephone _____ |
| FAX _____ |

ESTIMATED STORE-FIXTURE BUDGET

Job # _____   Date _____

Sheet _____

NO.	CATEGORY/DESCRIPTION/TYPE	SQ. FT. PRICE	LIN. FT. PRICE	UNIT PRICE	QUAN.	TOTAL COST
	INTERIOR SIGNAGE					
	• Departmental interior signage (perimeter).			X		
	• Electrified store directory: floor model.			X		
	• Electrified store directory: wall model.			X		
	• Nonelectrified store directory: wall model.			X		
	STOCKROOM					
	• 96" x 48" x 12" (H x W x D) with base and 6 adjustable shelves (for shoes).			X		
	• 96" x 48" x 18" with 2 adjustable hangrods.			X		
	• 96" x 48" x 24" with base and 4 adjustable shelves (for stock).			X		
	• 30" x 96" x 48" receiving table.			X		

Store Name _____
Store No./Location _____
Completion Date _____
Job Telephone _____
Job FAX _____

Store Planner _____
Address _____
City, State _____
Telephone _____
FAX _____

NO.	CATEGORY/DESCRIPTION/TYPE	SIZE (H X W X D)	UNIT PRICE	QUAN.	TOTAL COST
	ESTIMATED STORE-FIXTURE BUDGET Job # _____ Date _____ Sheet _____				
	RACKS/ÉTAGÈRES				
	• T-stand with two arms.		X		
	• 36" or 42" round rack (continuous).		X		
	• 36" or 42" 3-way adjustable rack.		X		
	• 4-way adjustable star rack with four 21" arms.		X		
	• Heavy duty 4-way rack.		X		
	• 4-way adjustable straight hangrod rack.		X		
	• 6-way adjustable slant and straight hangrod rack.		X		
	• Adjustable handbag rack.		X		
	• Adjustable double hanging étagère.		X		
	• Adjustable 3-shelf étagère.		X		

| Store Name _____ |
| Store No./Location _____ |
| Completion Date _____ |
| Job Telephone _____ |
| Job FAX _____ |

| Store Planner _____ |
| Address _____ |
| City, State _____ |
| Telephone _____ |
| FAX _____ |

ESTIMATED STORE-FIXTURE BUDGET

Job # _____   Date _____

Sheet _____

NO.	CATEGORY/DESCRIPTION/TYPE	SIZE (H X W X D)	UNIT PRICE	QUAN.	TOTAL COST
	FREESTANDING FIXTURES				
	• Full-vision showcase (modular tube frame).	38" x 48" x 21"			
	• Full-vision showcase (modular tube frame).	38" x 72" x 21"			
	• $\frac{1}{3}$-vision showcase (modular tube frame).	38" x 48" x 21"			
	• $\frac{1}{3}$-vision showcase (modular tube frame).	38" x 72" x 21"			
	• Open showcase (modular tube frame).	38" x 48" x 21"			
	• Open showcase (modular tube frame).	38" x 72" x 21"			
	• Showcase fills.				
	• Full-vision showcase (laminate plastic covered).	38" x 48" x 21"			
	• Full-vision showcase (laminate plastic covered).	38" x 72" x 21"			
	• $\frac{1}{3}$-vision showcase (laminate plastic covered).	38" x 48" x 21"			
	• $\frac{1}{3}$-vision showcase (laminate plastic covered).	38" x 72" x 21"			
	• Open showcase (laminate plastic covered).	38" x 48" x 21"			
	• Open showcase (laminate plastic covered).	38" x 72" x 21"			

| Store Name _____ |
| Store No./Location _____ |
| Completion Date _____ |
| Job Telephone _____ |
| Job FAX _____ |

| Store Planner _____ |
| Address _____ |
| City, State _____ |
| Telephone _____ |
| FAX _____ |

| ESTIMATED STORE-FIXTURE BUDGET | Job # _____ Date _____ Sheet _____ |

NO.	CATEGORY/DESCRIPTION/TYPE	SIZE (H X W X D)	UNIT PRICE	QUAN.	TOTAL COST
	FREESTANDING FIXTURES				
	• Back island with drawers.	54" x 36" x 18"			
	• Back island with doors.	54" x 36" x 18"			
	• Back island with drawers.	54" x 48" x 18"			
	• Triangular back island.				
	• Back island wrap counter.	54" x 36" x 24"			
	• Back island fills.				
	• Cash-and-wrap at showcase line.				
	• Cash-and-wrap at showcase line.				
	• Museum or display cube.				
	• Museum or display cube.				
	• Reversible-rim drawered table.	30" x 48" x 24"			
	• Reversible-rim drawered table.	30" x 48" x 30"			
	• Reversible-rim drawered table.	30" x 60" x 30"			

Store Name _____
Store No./Location _____
Completion Date _____
Job Telephone _____
Job FAX _____

Store Planner _____
Address _____
City, State _____
Telephone _____
FAX _____

ESTIMATED STORE-FIXTURE BUDGET		Job # _____ Date _____ Sheet _____			
NO.	CATEGORY/DESCRIPTION/TYPE	SIZE (H X W X D)	UNIT PRICE	QUAN.	TOTAL COST
	FREESTANDING FIXTURES				
	• Display platform: hexagonal.				
	• Display platform: hexagonal.				
	• Display platform: hexagonal.				
	• Display platform: half hexagonal.				
	• Display platform: cube.				
	• Display platform: cube.				
	• Display platform: cube.				
	• Display cube with mirrored top.				
	• Display cube with mirrored top.				
	• Display cube with mirrored top.				
	• Parsons table.	30" x 48" x 24"			
	• Parsons table.	30" x 48" x 30"			
	• Parsons table.	30" x 60" x 30"			

Store Name _____
Store No./Location _____
Completion Date _____
Job Telephone _____
Job FAX _____

Store Planner _____
Address _____
City, State _____
Telephone _____
FAX _____

	ESTIMATED STORE-FIXTURE BUDGET				
		Job # _____ Date _____ Sheet _____			
NO.	CATEGORY/DESCRIPTION/TYPE	SIZE (H X W X D)	UNIT PRICE	QUAN.	TOTAL COST
	FREESTANDING FIXTURES				
	• Fixed-rim Parsons table.	30" x 48" x 24"			
	• Fixed-rim Parsons table.	30" x 48" x 30"			
	• Fixed-rim Parsons table.	30" x 60" x 30"			
	• Closed-end Parsons table.	30" x 48" x 24"			
	• Closed-end Parsons table.	30" x 48" x 30"			
	• Closed-end Parsons table.	30" x 60" x 30"			
	• Closed-end Parsons table (carpet covered).	30" x 60" x 30"			
	• Closed-end Parsons table (carpet covered).	24" x 52" x 30"			
	• Closed-end Parsons table (carpet insert).	30" x 48" x 24"			
	• Closed-end Parsons table (carpet insert).	30" x 48" x 30"			
	• Closed-end Parsons table (carpet insert).	30" x 60" x 30"			
	• Round display table.				
	• Round stack display table.				

Store Name _____

Store No./Location _____

Completion Date _____

Job Telephone _____

Job FAX _____

Store Planner _____

Address _____

City, State _____

Telephone _____

FAX _____

ESTIMATED STORE-FIXTURE BUDGET				
Job # _____ Date _____				
Sheet _____				

NO.	CATEGORY/DESCRIPTION/TYPE	SIZE (H X W X D)	UNIT PRICE	QUAN.	TOTAL COST
	FREESTANDING FIXTURES				
	• Round stack display table.				
	• Sit-down desk.				
	• Write-up desk.				
	• Millinery table.				
	• Mug tree.				
	• Rug displayer.				
	• Open base with riser.				
	• Drawered base with riser.				
	• Drawered base with star riser.				
	• Star riser with base.				
	• Security star riser with base.				
	• Risers with base.				

Store Name _____
Store No./Location _____
Completion Date _____
Job Telephone _____
Job FAX _____

Store Planner _____
Address _____
City, State _____
Telephone _____
FAX _____

ESTIMATED STORE-FIXTURE BUDGET		Job # _____ Date _____ Sheet _____			
NO.	CATEGORY/DESCRIPTION/TYPE	SIZE (H X W X D)	UNIT PRICE	QUAN.	TOTAL COST
	FREESTANDING FIXTURES				
	• Étagère riser with insert base.				
	• Étagère riser with drawered base.				
	• Display riser.				
	• Display riser.				
	• Gondola with 9" prongs.				
	• Gondola—two 10", 12", 14" glass shelves.				
	• Gondola—6" prongs and two 16" glass shelves.				
	• Gondola—three 16" glass shelves.				
	• 10" x 10" x 16" glass-cube assembly on base.	6" x 54" x 36"			
	• 10" x 10" x 16" glass-cube assembly with endcap on base.	6" x 72" x 36"			
	• 12" x 12" x 12" glass-cube assembly on base.	6" x 66" x 30"			
	• 18" x 18" x 18" glass-cube assembly on base.	6" x 60" x 42"			
	• 17" x 22" x 24" glass-cube assembly on base.	6" x 72" x 54"			

Store Name _____
Store No./Location _____
Completion Date _____
Job Telephone _____
Job FAX _____

Store Planner _____
Address _____
City, State _____
Telephone _____
FAX _____

	ESTIMATED STORE-FIXTURE BUDGET				

Job # _____ Date _____
Sheet _____

NO.	CATEGORY/DESCRIPTION/TYPE	SIZE (H X W X D)	UNIT PRICE	QUAN.	TOTAL COST
	FREESTANDING FIXTURES				
	• Cash-and-wrap.	42" x 72" x 30"			
	• Cash-and-wrap.	42" x 96" x 30"			
	• Freestanding cash stand.				
	• Support of cash-and-wrap.				
	• Foundations back bar.				
	• Receiving table.	36" x 96" x 48"			
	• Demonstration unit.				
	• Curtain and bedspread display.				
	• Hosiery fixture.	54" x 60" x 24"			
	• Hosiery unit.				
	• Sheet fixture.				
	• Feature display pedestal.				
	• Feature display unit.				

Store Name _____
Store No./Location _____
Completion Date _____
Job Telephone _____
Job FAX _____

Store Planner _____
Address _____
City, State _____
Telephone _____
FAX _____

ESTIMATED STORE-FIXTURE BUDGET	Job # _____ Date _____
	Sheet _____

NO.	CATEGORY/DESCRIPTION/TYPE	SIZE (H X W X D)	UNIT PRICE	QUAN.	TOTAL COST
	FREESTANDING FIXTURES				
	• Triple mirror.				
	• Feature gift displayer.				
	• Perimeter platform.				
	• Perimeter base.				
	• Perimeter drawered base.				
	• Perimeter sliding-door base.				

Store Name _____
Store No./Location _____
Completion Date _____
Job Telephone _____
Job FAX _____

Store Planner _____
Address _____
City, State _____
Telephone _____
FAX _____

ESTIMATED STORE-FIXTURE BUDGET		Job # _____ Date _____ Sheet _____			
NO.	CATEGORY/DESCRIPTION/TYPE	SIZE (H X W X D)	UNIT PRICE	QUAN.	TOTAL COST
	FREESTANDING FIXTURES				
	• Perimeter walls partition for fitting room.				
	• Freestanding fitting room.				
	• Fitting room—wood.				
	• Fitting room—1' modular tube frame.				
	• Fitting room—extruded aluminum.				
	• Fitting room—drywall.				
	• Fitting room—drywall—freestanding.				

Store Name _____
Store No./Location _____
Completion Date _____
Job Telephone _____
Job FAX _____

Store Planner _____
Address _____
City, State _____
Telephone _____
FAX _____

ESTIMATED STORE-FIXTURE BUDGET					
Job # _____ Date _____					
Sheet _____					

NO.	CATEGORY/DESCRIPTION/TYPE	SQ. FT. PRICE	LIN. FT. PRICE	UNIT PRICE	QUAN.	TOTAL COST
	SEATING/TABLES					
	• Occasional seating.			X		
	• Cosmetic makeup chair.			X		
	• Shoe chairs.			X		
	• Shoe stool.			X		
	• Restaurant side chair.			X		
	• Double booth (four seats).			X		
	• Single booth (two seats).			X		
	• Continuous wall bench with finished ends.			X		
	• 24" x 30" pedestal base tabletop.			X		
	• 36" x 36" pedestal base tabletop.			X		
	• 36" x 36" table with four 7" wide drop leaves to convert table to 50" round.			X		

Chapter 12

BASIC LIGHTING TECHNIQUES

Introduction

The importance of lighting in the retail setting cannot be overemphasized. Lighting is one of the prime tools that create the overall store concept. The store planner must have a fine working knowledge of lighting and appreciate the varied effects lighting will have on the merchandise. He or she must consider reflective qualities and how the lighting plan will interact with the color scheme and merchandise within the store—neutral, jewel-toned, and pastel colors on walls and carpets help reflect light, dark carpets and walls absorb light. Other considerations in designing an effective lighting plan are the quality of the light (which includes color, brightness, and intensity), energy usage, initial cost, and maintenance.

The intent of this chapter is to assist the novice store planner in developing a comprehensive and effective lighting, or reflected ceiling, plan—a plan that shows the exact location of each electrical lighting fixture. The lighting plan also indicates curtain walls, soffits, any changes of ceiling-light heights, and any decorative drops that appear on a ceiling plan.

Ceiling Systems

The lighting system is supported by the ceiling system, which can be sheetrock ceilings, louvered ceilings, concealed spline ceiling systems, open construction, and the two-by-four or two-by-two lay-in ceiling system. This metal T-bar system is installed in a grid configuration suspended by wires from the overhead building structure and accommodates both lay-in acoustical ceiling tiles and electrical lighting fixtures. Each ceiling system has advantages and disadvantages. When designing a retail store, the store planner must discuss the various types of ceiling systems available. The ceiling system and lighting will not only enhance the overall image of the store and bring attention to the merchandise, but is actually part of the store design.

The most popular, economical, and widely used ceiling system is the T-bar system. T-bar systems are offered in white, black, and custom colors. Custom-color T-bar systems are available at higher cost. The object of the ceiling is to create a plane that will be used as a system to support the lighting system and yet not detract from the atmosphere of the merchandise space. In most cases, retailers will request a white ceiling grid with white lay-in ceiling pads. A white ceiling best reflects light, creates an inviting atmosphere, and also gives the illusion of a higher space.

Ceiling pads come in an assortment of textures and finishes. Standard ceiling lay-in pads are designed to fit within the grid. Tegular ceiling pads are designed to drop below the surface of the T-bar grid while suspended within the grid. These tegular tiles add dimension and texture to a ceiling finish. These lay-in ceiling tiles will vary tremendously in cost per square foot. The greater the density of the texture, the greater the cost per square foot of the ceiling lay-in pads.

Reflected Ceiling/Lighting Legend

Symbol	Description
	Typical 2' X 4' ceiling grid with lay-in ceiling
	Typical 2' X 2' ceiling grid with lay-in ceiling
	2' X 4' fluorescent fixture with prismatic lens
	2' X 4' fluorescent fixture with paracube lens
	2' X 4' fluorescent fixture with deep cell parabolic lens
	1' X 4' fluorescent fixture with prismatic lens
	2' X 2' fluorescent fixture with paracube lens
	Wall-mounted fixture with opal acrylic diffuser
	Double-lamp fluorescent strip light
	Single-lamp fluorescent strip light
	Surface-mounted fluorescent light
	Surface-mounted tract light fixture
	Recessed track mounted light fixture
	Recessed incandescent down light
	Recessed adjustable accent light (spot)
	Recessed adjustable accent light (flood)
	Shallow recessed down light
	Ceiling outlet for pendant fixture
	Standard double lamp fluorescent fixture
	Exit sign with battery standby
	Open cell (1/2' X 1/2" x 1/2") plastic eggcrate

The electrical light fixtures that are installed in the T-bar system may include, but are not limited to:

1. Two-by-two lay-in fluorescent fixtures
2. Two-by-four lay-in fluorescent fixtures
3. Track lighting
4. Perimeter lighting
5. Cornice or soffit lighting
6. Accent lighting
7. Visual merchandising lighting
8. Down lights
9. Wall-washing systems
10. Strip lighting for stock rooms
11. Emergency lighting
12. EXIT signs

Mechanical Interruptions

When developing an effective lighting plan, the store planner must be aware of all mechanical interruptions within the ceiling plane. These projections could include sprinklers, HVAC (heating, ventilation, air conditioning) locations, ceiling interruptions, stairwell openings, escalator openings, skylights, changes in ceiling heights or plane, entrances and exits, floor-to-ceiling walls, freestanding walls, fitting rooms, stockrooms, receiving, and customer service areas, rest room facilities, and all sales support offices and nonselling areas.

Illumination

Each area of the store will require different foot-candles of illumination. A foot candle is a unit for measuring illumination: It is equal to the amount of direct light thrown by one candle on a surface one foot away.

The following table may be used as a guide to determine illumination for various areas:

Illumination Levels

Area	Foot-Candles
General light/Ambient lighting	40 to 55
Accent lighting	150 to 250
Fitting rooms	50 to 70
Cornice or wall lighting	80 to 100
Sales/Transaction areas	50 to 70
Corridors/Aisles	10 to 20
Stockrooms	20 to 30
Receiving rooms	70 to 100
Offices	60 to 70

(Foot-candle readings are measured 30 inches above the floor.)

Incandescent lamps.

Lamps

Various kinds of lamps need to be considered.

Incandescent Lamps

Incandescent lamps are manufactured in various shapes, sizes, coatings, wattage, and voltages. The most common lamps that are used are "PAR," parabolic illuminized reflector. "R" reflector lamps are no longer manufactured because of federal energy legislation.

Fluorescent Lamps

Fluorescent lamps are manufactured in lengths from 6 inches to 96 inches and in various diameters, from five-eighths inch (T-5) to two and one-eighth inches (T-17). (The letter "T" indicates the tubular shape, and the number indicates the diameter in eighths of an inch.)

Fluorescent lighting features more light for the watts consumed and longer lamp life. Although more costly, the premium-colored triphosphorus lamps are most popular. This type of fluorescent lamp provides excellent color rendition for all merchandising and is more compatible with incandescent and quartz lamps. However, standard warm white lamps are still the most widely used because of their lower cost, but the energy code will affect availability of these lamps soon.

Energy Use

The store planner must also consider the cost of operating and maintaining the designed lighting

Fluorescent lamp.

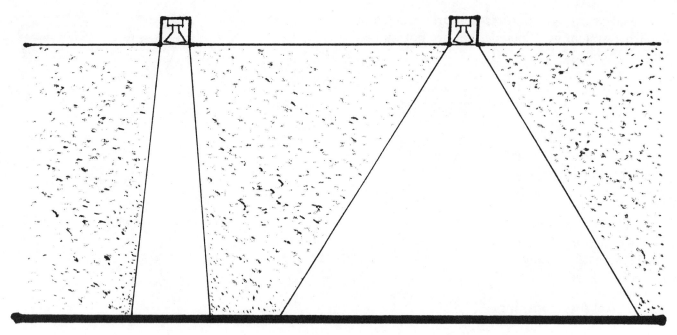

This illustration shows the comparative beam spread between a spotlight and a floodlight. The spotlight emits a narrow beam. The floodlight floods the display with light.

system. Certain municipalities and states enforce limitations on allowable energy usage for illumination. Local codes and regulations must be reviewed to prevent costly design revamps. Many stores tend to be overilluminated, generating higher than necessary electric bills. This can result in the store's total electrical consumption being over the recommended standard, which in most states is 2.5 watts per square foot. It is the store planner's responsibility to advise the client how to achieve efficient, cost-effective lighting with minimum wattage.

Here are just a few examples of ideas to use when planning a lighting layout to help save the initial cost of the light fixture, installation, lamps, maintenance, and energy consumption.

- If possible, never install fluorescent lighting over traffic aisles. Never use down lighting in aisles.
- Only spotlights should be used in aisles placed to highlight merchandise at the aisle line.
- Use down lights for transaction areas and above customer service counters where surface brightness is important for the exchanging of money or writing of checks.
- The primarily goal of retail-store lighting is to sell merchandise and achieve an effective mix between merchandising and energy efficiency.

Laying Out the Lighting System

Once all this information has been compiled and a preliminary plan established, the store planner will often work with a lighting consultant. A lighting consultant will help the store planner and retailer achieve their goals while maintaining the estimated budget for lighting. The store planner is now ready to begin laying out a lighting system that will interact successfully with the merchandising, design, and image of the store. First, general lighting will be considered and then the lighting of various elements of the store.

Working with the base merchandising plan, the store planner can determine where accent lighting is needed to highlight featured goods at aisle lines and perimeter walls. There are many types of lighting systems used to illuminate a retail store. For simplicity, this chapter will focus on the most common lighting systems used today.

General Lighting

General lighting is a term used when referring to the overall lighting system; for example, most stores today with a two-by-four lay-in ceiling system will use fluorescent light fixtures, arranged and placed in a grid configuration. These fixtures are arranged above merchandising areas and help

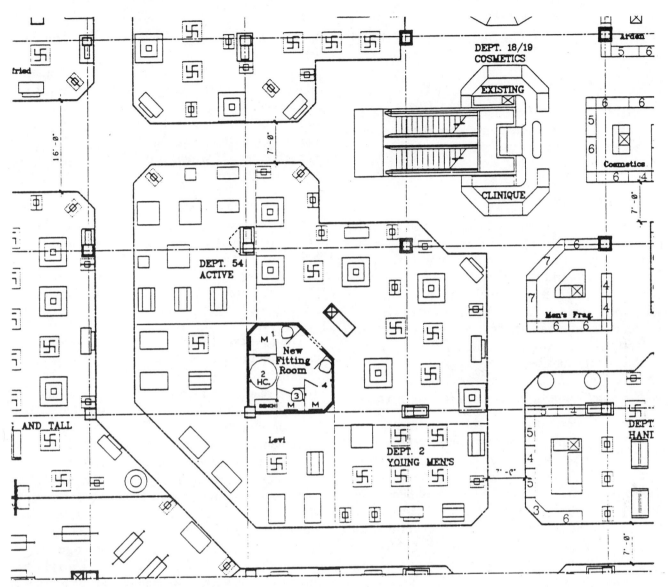

The lighting plan must be designed to enhance the merchandise.

to maintain a uniform level of lighting throughout the area.

Light Fixtures

There are several types of light fixtures used for general lighting:

1. Fluorescent Lighting Fixtures

General fluorescent lighting is usually the best and most economical source to effectively illuminate retail space. It provides a long lamp life and an even output of light. There are several choices of fluorescent lamps available for color rendition and energy consumption. Energy-saving lamps and ballasts make fluorescent lighting very appealing.

Three types of fluorescent light fixtures are commonly used to create general lighting: two-by-two fixtures, two-by-four fixtures, and round compact fluorescent fixtures. These fixtures can be fitted with prismatic lenses or parabolic louvers.

A large variety of fluorescent lamp colors are available; lamps of different colors should not be used within the same space. For retail lighting, triphosphor lamps with warm color produce the best effect.

Note: As with any element used within a retail store, maintenance of the lighting fixtures is a key factor in the selection process. Fluorescent light fixtures need periodic maintenance. Servicing includes opening a door, removing the tubes, wiping down the interior of the fixture, and removing surface dust and dirt from the lens.

2. *Prismatic Light Fixtures*

Prismatic fixtures diffuse light at the ceiling line. These lights on the ceiling are more obvious than parabolic light fixtures because the eye is drawn to the light.

3. *Parabolic Light Fixtures*

Parabolic light fixtures are designed with a reflective cell grid lens to redirect higher angle light to the merchandise area. The ceiling brightness is significantly reduced and the light is not as obvious as a prismatic fixture. Both light fixtures are manufactured with three or four light tubes with energy-saving electronic ballast. Two-by-two prismatic or parabolic light fixtures are designed with single, double, or triple tubes.

4. *Compact Fluorescent Down Lighting Fixtures*

Compact fluorescent down lighting consists of one or two single-ended compact fluorescent lamps, generally in a recessed fixture design. Small fixture trim diameters and good glare control make the ceiling appear uncluttered and subdued. The light tube has been designed for maximum efficiency and reflective qualities. Different color temperatures are available in this series of lamps. This type of fixture can also have an electronic ballast.

Preliminary Plan

With all this general information, the store planner can begin developing a preliminary lighting reflected ceiling plan. Working with the merchandising plan that indicates the building shape, walls, aisles, and merchandise placement, the store planner will establish a grid line within the plan and begin to lay out the placement of the electrical lighting fixtures that will create the general ambient light.

The foot-candles, or general lighting, will be established by the center-to-center line of the placement of the lay-in of the two-by-four three-lamp fixtures. Working with a 10-foot ceiling, for example, two-by-four fluorescent light fixtures that are placed on 8-foot-by-10-foot centers will establish approximately 60 foot-candles. Two-by-four fluorescent light fixtures placed on a 10-foot ceiling on 10-foot-by-12-foot centers will generate approximately 40 foot-candles of luminosity.

As the diagrams show, the spacing and quantity of the light fixtures will determine the foot-candles in a given area. The foot-candle level required for any store is determined by the type of merchandise sold. Listed here are types of stores or departments for which foot-candle requirements would vary:

Clothing and associated merchandise	50 foot-candles
Housewares and domestics	50 foot-candles
Specialty stores	50 foot-candles
Bookstore	60–70 foot-candles
Discount stores	75 foot-candles
Drugstores	75 foot-candles

The foot-candles for bookstores and drugstores would be greater than that for ready-to-wear or clothing stores because in the former, the shopper will be reading, which requires higher lumens, or light. So the store planner and lighting consultant must develop an effective plan to meet lighting requirements that fit the marketing and merchandising scheme of a given store.

It is sometimes very helpful for the store planner to have a drawing or grid the same scale as the plan so that the grid can be moved around and adjusted for placement. This grid can be drawn on vellum or onion skin or can be computer-generated. Within the grid, an X can fill in where a light fixture would be within the ceiling, and whether it is on 8-by-10 centers, 10-by-12 centers, or any other center.

By placing this grid pattern over the merchandising plan, the store planner will be able to easily adjust the grid pattern over the plan to ensure the lighting plan interacts with the merchandising plan. Once this plan has been established, the store planner can then start laying in perimeter lighting, decorative lighting, and visual merchandising lighting.

Perimeter Lighting

Now that the general lighting has established a uniform lighting pattern, the store planner must consider the method of perimeter-walls illumination.

The object of perimeter wall lighting is to focus attention to the merchandise arrayed on

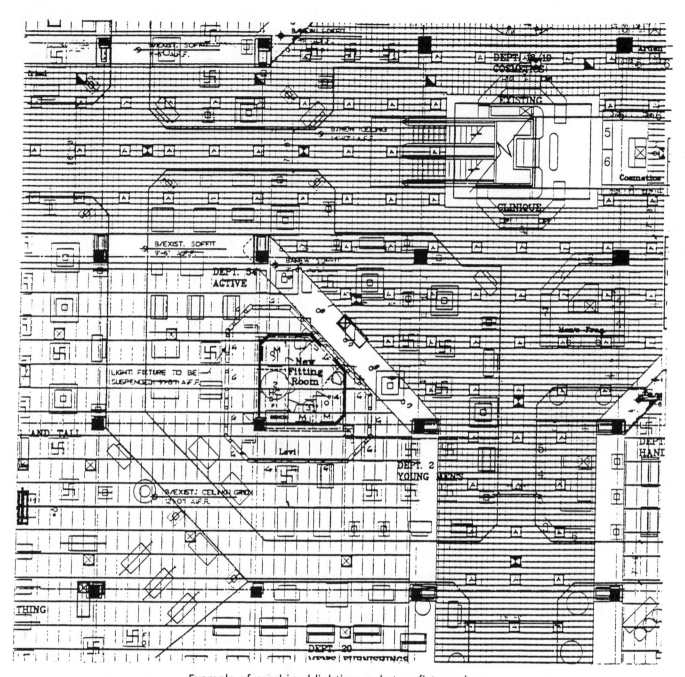

Example of combined lighting and store fixture plan.

the perimeter walls. The perimeter wall of a department is one of the most effective tools in the selling environment. From a distance, the merchandise on the wall above the line of racks or case goods signals attention to various classifications of merchandise.

Perimeter walls are considered some of the most valuable real estate within a retail environment because the sight line on the merchandise is higher than that of the merchandise on the floor and, therefore, wields a commanding dominance.

In order to bring attention to these perimeter walls, effective lighting must be designed. Successful methods of lighting perimeter walls are as follows:

1. Incandescent recessed or track lighting
2. Fluorescent single or double tube behind cornice or valance boards
3. Recessed fluorescent wall washers
4. Recessed fluorescent ceiling troffers
5. Compact fluorescent wall washers

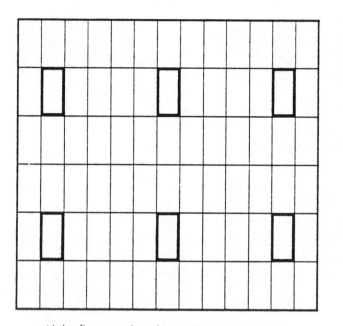

Light fixtures placed on 10' x 12' centers.

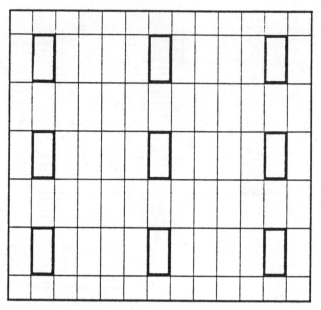

Light fixtures placed on 8' x 10' centers.

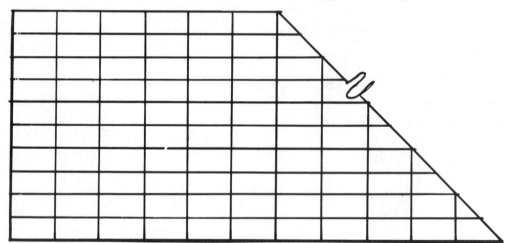

Plan view.

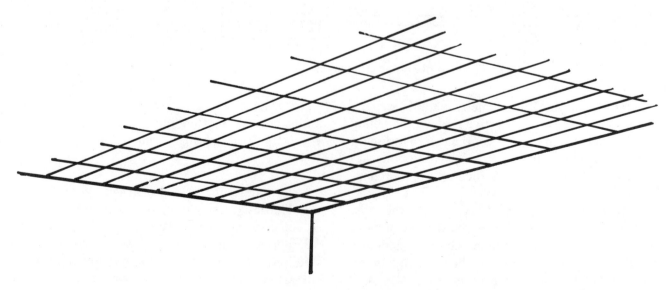

Here is an isometric view and a plan view of what a two-by-four ceiling grid looks like.

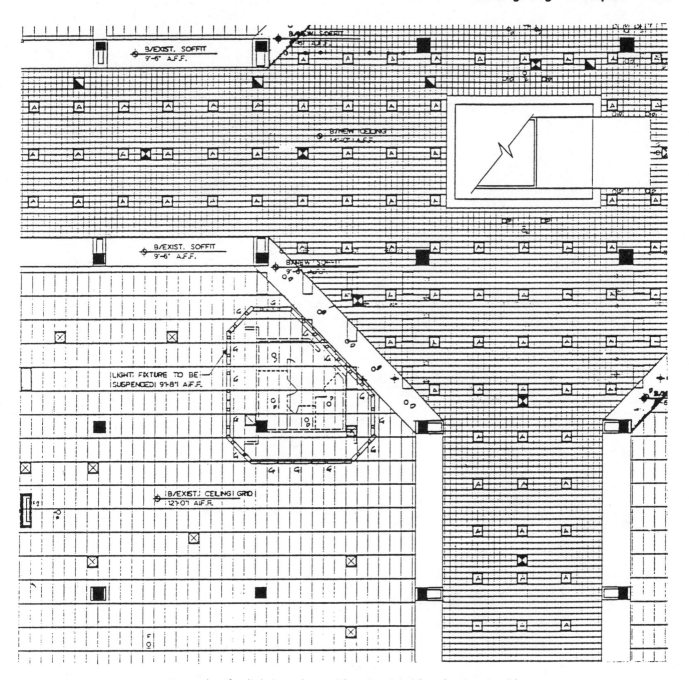

Example of a lighting plan; with a 2 x 2 grid and a 2 x 4 grid.

6. Continuos parabolic wall-washing systems
7. Single- or double-tube fluorescent strip-lighting systems
8. Track lighting systems, track mounted or suspended on cables
9. Down Lighting
10. Incandescent wall washers (these do not provide enough light to use for merchandise.)
11. Hanging decorative lighting, such as warehouse lamps, others

Each of the listed light fixtures will produce different lighting effects:

Compact Fluorescent Wall Washers

Energy conservationists call on store planners and architects to lower ceilings and reduce the interior space. Thus, conventional wall cornices have given way to new concepts of lighting perimeter walls. One of the most successful ways to illuminate perimeter merchandising walls is the use of

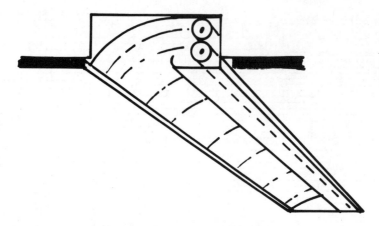

Recessed fluorescent ceiling troffer.

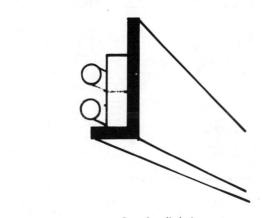

Cornice lighting.

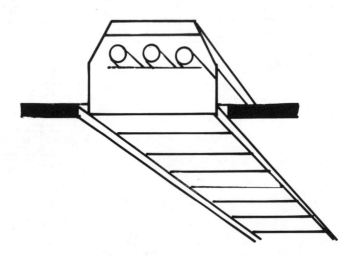

Recessed fluorescent troffer.

recessed single-lamp compact-fluorescent wall washers.

Working with the manufacturer's recommendations and guidelines, the compact fluorescent light fixtures are located on the ceiling plan approximately three to four feet from the perimeter wall at the ceiling line. In most cases these compact fixtures of 1-foot-by-2-foot are placed on 4-foot centers and

will give an even line of lighting along the perimeter wall. Illumination of 70 foot-candles will be achieved.

The fixture is designed to focus below the ceiling line and spread light evenly to the floor. The lighting level or foot-candles will decrease as the light travels to the floor line. The type of tube used in these fixtures will determine the color of the lighting.

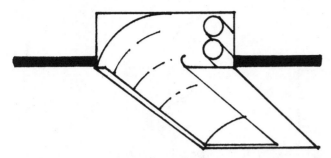

Recessed double-lamp compact-fluorescent wall washer.

Continuous Parabolic 1-Foot-by-4-Foot Lighting Fixtures

These fixtures are similar to the 2-foot-by-four-foot parabolic fixtures used throughout the store. Recessed and placed at an exact distance from the wall, per manufacturer's recommendations, they create an even wash of light on the wall.

This type of lighting will also provide an even line of light above the merchandise, which will decrease as it travels the distance to the floor. These fixtures are designed with double-fluorescent tubes.

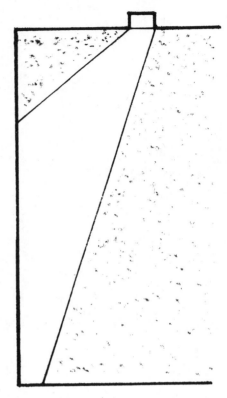

Ilumination path of compact-fluorescent light fixture.

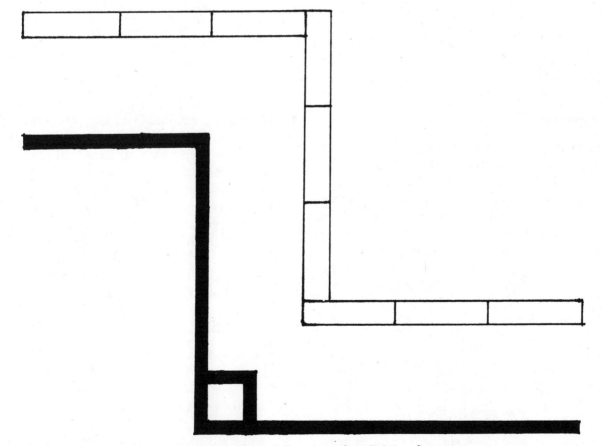

Continuous parabolic 1-foot by 4-foot lighting fixtures.

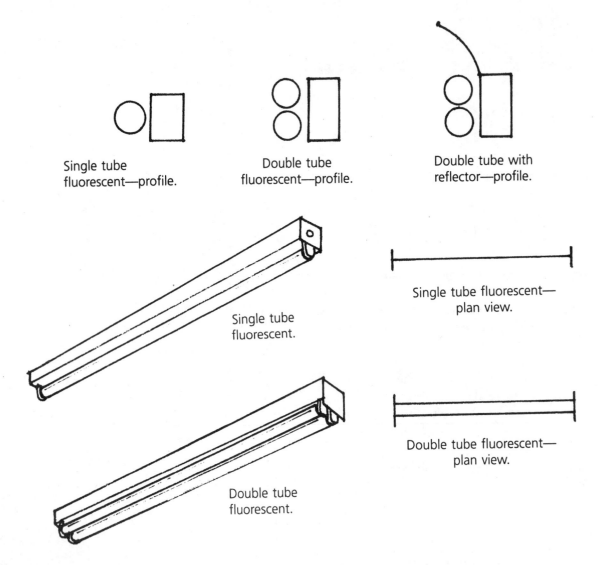

Single tube
fluorescent—profile.

Double tube
fluorescent—profile.

Double tube with
reflector—profile.

Single tube
fluorescent.

Single tube fluorescent—
plan view.

Double tube
fluorescent.

Double tube fluorescent—
plan view.

Strip Lighting

Perimeter strip lighting is also used to illuminate perimeter merchandising walls. Often, these fixtures will be used in single or double tubes, although double tubes will usually be required to provide sufficient light. Double-tube fixtures are usually required to achieve the level of light desired.

Many times, reflectors are used with this type of light to redirect light which otherwise would be wasted. The backside of the cornice or curtain wall, along with ceilings, should be painted white to enhance the reflective value of this type of lighting. These fixtures are also available with an electronic energy-saving ballast.

Fluorescent lamp strips generally take on three forms: cornices, valances, and coves.

Cornice lighting should be located at least 36 inches from the wall and at a height of 6 feet 4 inches from the floor to maximize the efficiency of the lamp.

Strip lights installed in cornices should be made up of 3-, 4-, and 8-foot lengths. Anything over 5 feet in length can be constructed with a combination of these tubes. Two-foot lamps will reduce lumen output and are less cost efficient.

Reflectors on the strip lighting will help focus light on the merchandise. There are some areas within a store in which single-tube lighting can be used. When merchandise is light-colored and a wall surface is bright, a single row of lamps with a reflector will sufficiently illuminate the wall.

Track Lighting

Track lighting is one of the most commonly used wall-washing systems to bring attention to or highlight an area. Track lighting can be installed at the ceiling line or can be suspended by cables. Energy consumption of track lighting is high and needs to be evaluated in terms of merchandise displayed, color, and energy cost-effectiveness.

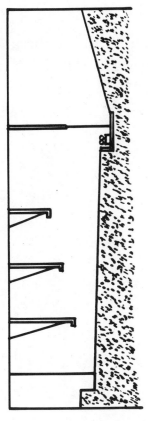

Cornice lighting.

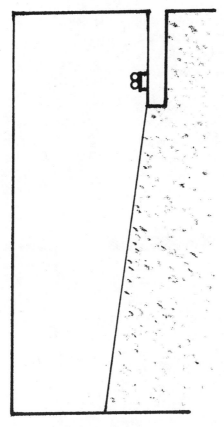

Valance lighting.

Cove lighting.

Tracks and lighting canisters come in white, black, and custom colors. White tracks and lighting canisters placed on a white ceiling help to minimize the visibility of the fixtures.

Black tracks and lighting canisters on a white ceiling will be quite obvious. Custom-colored tracks and light canisters can be colored to match any colored ceiling and minimize visibility. When track

canisters are repositioned, they should be removed from the track and reinstalled at the desired location. The canisters must be reconnected properly to ensure maximum illumination.

One problem in using track lighting is that employees responsible for readjusting the lamps may not be aware that using too many canisters might dangerously overload the circuits. It is, therefore,

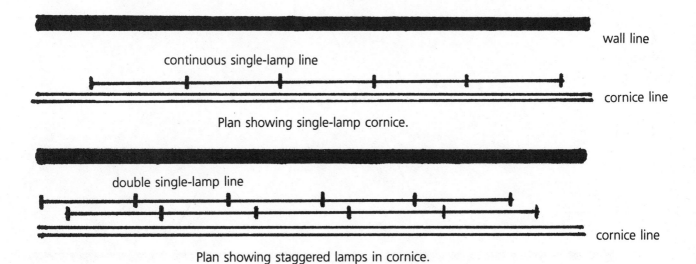

wall line

continuous single-lamp line

cornice line

Plan showing single-lamp cornice.

double single-lamp line

cornice line

Plan showing staggered lamps in cornice.

recommended that those responsible for adjusting any ceiling track lighting be educated as to system limitations and the maximum number of canisters that can safely be installed within a 4-foot or 8-foot section of track.

Standard household bulbs should be avoided in track-canister fixtures as they lose their effectiveness; only par lamps should be used. The track lamp should not face downward to the floor. The purpose of track lighting is to highlight the merchandise—never the floor.

Down Lighting

Down Lighting means that the light in the ceiling is directed downward to the floor. Various areas benefiting from down lighting are:

1. Entrances
2. Escalator wells
3. Under-store entrances and canopies
4. Vestibules, etc.
5. Showcase lines

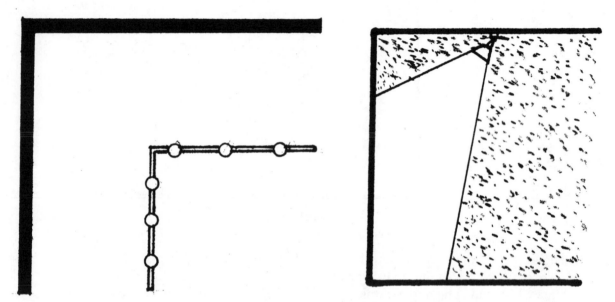

This illustration shows placement of track lighting to illuminate a wall. The isometric diagram on the right shows the track and canister interacting with merchandise on the wall.

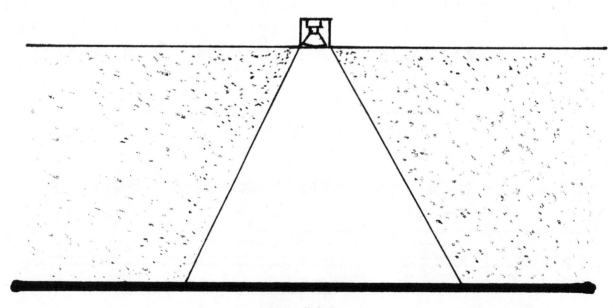

Down lighting.

Down lighting helps create a surface brightness. Down lighting at store entrances helps to create a warm and welcoming environment, while down lighting above cosmetics, accessories, or jewelry showcase lines brings foot-candles higher than that of the general lighting, adding sparkle to the merchandise.

Adjustable Incandescent Wall Washers

These recessed fixtures are concealed in the ceiling and are located in a direct line, at the manufacturer's recommended distance from the wall, to achieve maximum coverage. These types of fixtures direct the light downward. The distance these are placed from the wall is determined by the ceiling height, the type of merchandise, and the desired brightness (without blinding the customers when they turn around).

This type of fixture is normally placed on 4-foot centers, and the type of lamp will determine the brightness. Lamps used in these fixtures are designed for maximum reflectivity with minimum energy consumption. However, they consume much more energy than fluorescent fixtures.

Decorative Lighting

There is a wide array of decorative and accent lighting that can be profitably used in a retail store; however, decorative lighting illuminates perimeter walls effectively. Decorative lighting can add a decor element to a wall; however, supplemental lighting may be required. Decorative lighting in a store may include a chandelier or a type of decorative lighting drop from the ceiling.

Interior Wall Lighting

The height of the ceiling and the height of the merchandise presentation are important factors when wall lighting with incandescent lamps. Lighting fixtures must be adjustable in order to focus the light on repositioned merchandise. Assuming that the wall merchandise is 7 feet high, spacing should be as follows:

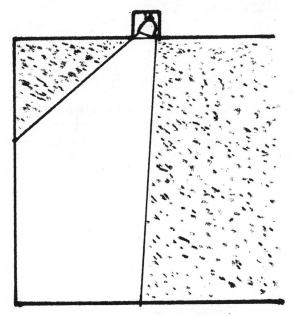

Adjustable wall washer.

Decorative or chandelier drop.

Decorative wall lamp.

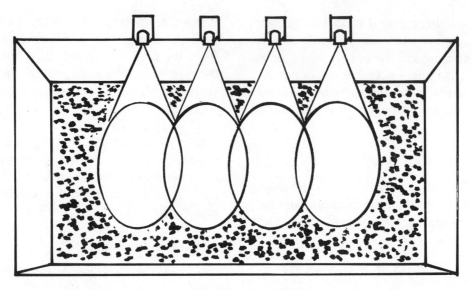

Elevation view.

- For 10- to 12-foot ceiling heights, fixtures should be placed approximately 2 feet 6 inches to 3 feet on center and 36 inches from the wall.
- Crisscross patterns are especially useful in creating highlights and shadow effects on merchandise.

Visual Merchandising Lighting

Working with the merchandising plan, visual merchandising lighting is designed within the ceiling to highlight mannequins or displays at the aisle line; decor or decorative elements atop cosmetics, acces-

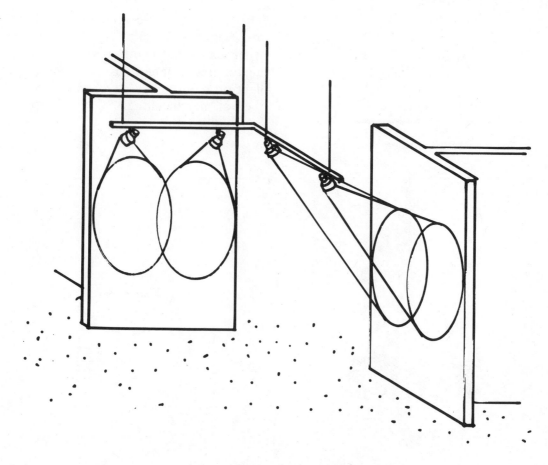

Isometric view.

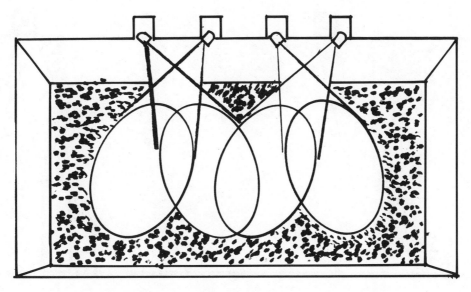

Crisscross patterns.

sories, or jewelry back islands; aisle islands; and other special store areas in which highlighting is required.

This type of fixture is normally a recessed adjustable canister that will use an incandescent spotlight. These fixtures are placed within the ceiling grid to interact with the mannequin or display and wash the face of the display. These lamps should not be placed directly above the designated area because they create undesirable shadows on the goods.

Incandescent lighting is the least efficient lighting source, but because of its excellent color properties, it is often selected for areas displaying quality merchandise. When using incandescent lighting, the height of the ceiling is very important and will determine the type of the lamp to be used. Floodlights are chosen when there is a need to spread the light.

The purpose of merchandising lighting is to increase the general foot-candles over that of the general lighting and to bring special attention to a display; for example, if the general lighting was established at 50 foot-candles, the visual merchandising lighting would be at least three times greater, or 150 foot-candles. This increased candle power gives a brighter appearance to which the eye is naturally drawn.

The most attractive displays have little appeal or vibrancy without visual merchandising lighting. A thoughtfully lighted display creates a dramatic and effective sales tool. Recessed internally adjustable

Flood lights.

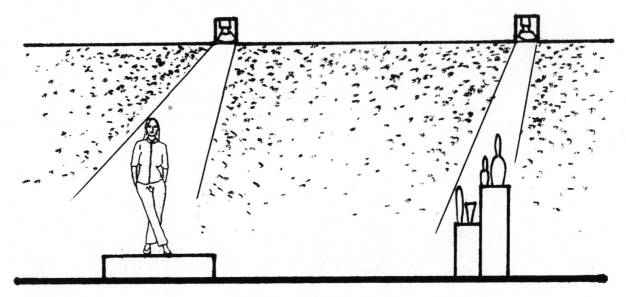

Visual merchandise lighting.

fixtures are capable of approximately 30-degree adjustability. These types of fixtures are inefficient when angled due to the loss of light within the housing.

Recessed internally adjustable light fixtures with approximately 45-degree adjustability are more effective in disbursing a greater beam of light but do so at premium cost. Recessed pull-down adjustable fixtures with 90-degree adjustability and 355-degree rotation capability are by far the best recessed-type fixture.

Surface-mounted adjustable fixtures with 355-degree rotation and 90-degree adjustability are also an excellent source of visual merchandising light. The canisters can, however, create ceiling clutter.

Using Track Lighting

Track-mounted adjustable fixtures with 355-degree rotation and 90-degree adjustablity allow for greater flexibility. Lighting tracks that are surface-mounted to the ceiling are available in standard 4-foot and 8-foot sections. It is recommended that no more than three canister fixtures be installed on a 4-foot track

Visual merchandise lighting.

and no more than five fixtures on an 8-foot track. If additional fixtures are installed, they could cause a circuit overload.

Targeting

In order to simplify lighting-beam locations, use the term targeting, as in aiming at the center of a target. As the fixture is adjusted, the light beam is directed to the target. Targeting spotlights on a lighting plan ensures the beam of light will be where it is desired. This concentrated light will be targeted onto a mannequin or other type of merchandise to create striking visual impact. Remember: When laying out this spotlighting, the main objective is to bring attention to a specific point within a department layout. The use of too many spotlights can totally defeat the purpose.

The design and installation of an effective lighting system is only half the job. Whenever displays are moved, changed, or replaced, the spotlights should be redirected to accommodate the change in the merchandise presentation for optimal lighting effectiveness.

Low-Voltage Lighting

Low-voltage lamps and fixtures are not widely used for major visual merchandising lighting; however, they are an excellent source for lighting small items such as jewelry. Low-voltage lamps are available in various beam patterns from narrow pinpoints to wide beams. The spotlights will have concentrated light spreads.

Use of wider beam spread is effective for applications where merchandise is close to the lamp. These lamps can be very effective, they add sparkle and color, and are considered essential for jewelry, china, and silverware departments. Because of the low wattage and the design of the reflectors, these lamps also minimize heat output.

Low-voltage lamps are most popular in 20, 50, and 75 watts. Low-voltage lighting requires step-down transformers, which can be a potential maintenance problem. They also add substantially to the cost of the fixture. The preferred application is one transformer for each lamp.

A word about low voltage spots: There are many innovative types of low-voltage spots now available. Low-voltage spotlights are an effective tool in visual merchandise presentation; however, in designing a light system, the cost of the fixture and the lamp must be a prime consideration due to the fixture's higher price and the short life span of the lamp. Using low-voltage lamps is an energy-efficient method of providing accent lighting. It requires careful planning because the beam produced is very tight compared with spotlights. It can take two or three lamps to accomplish what one spotlight will do. This, then, is no longer economical.

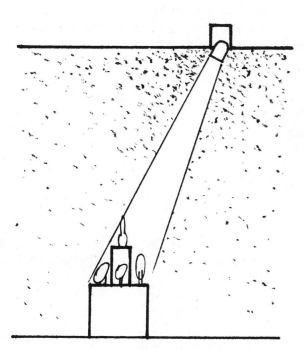

Targeting.

Adustable ceiling light fixture.

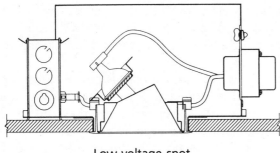

Low-voltage spot.

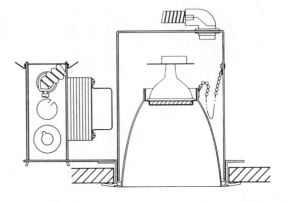

Low-voltage down light.

Rules for Visual Merchandising Lighting

1. Select the proper lamp and beam pattern that will best highlight the merchandise and attract customer attention.
2. Dramatic highlights can be achieved by targeting the light beam off center. The light and shadows can add drama to the display. Lamps should not be angled more than 45 degrees off the vertical surface. Extreme angles glare into customers' eyes and can be distracting. Minimize the distance between the light source and the display.
3. Light beams spread over a long area tend to weaken the principal highlighting purpose and lose effectiveness. Use spotlights on displays, not flood lights. Flood lights fill an area with light but no focus. Do not waste energy or light by illuminating ceilings, aisles, or bare walls. Target light to enhance the merchandise or display.
4. Never use track lighting or adjustable lamps on mirrored walls or columns; these lamps will reflect on mirrors and create distracting glare. If merchandise on mirrored walls requires accent lighting, louvers should be used. Do not waste energy or lighting by directing a lamp to light the floor. Reangle the fixture to illuminate merchandise.
5. Estimate the amount of lighting that will be required for the display. Remember: Dark colors require more wattage. Minimize the use of track lights as it adds clutter to the ceiling.
6. Incandescent lamps are designed to achieve different effects for various lighting techniques. The type of bulb and the distance the light will have to span as well as the type of merchandise will best determine the type of lamp that is selected. Keep lamp selections to a minimum to avoid maintenance problems.

Miscellaneous Lighting

Emergency Lighting

Emergency lighting is placed in coordination with the general lighting. The emergency lighting is designed to be battery operated and to be activated by a power failure. This lighting helps customers and employees evacuate the retail space in case of fire, or other emergency. Local codes dictate the amount of emergency lighting required.

EXIT Lights

EXIT lights are strategically placed throughout the store and at all entrances, exits, and stairwells within the space. These EXIT lights are illuminated around the clock to provide an easily distinguishable sign at the ceiling. They are battery powered to ensure independent illumination during power outages. Again, local codes must be consulted as to requirements. EXIT lights are part of the store signage system and do not contribute to lighting levels.

Night Lights

Night lights are fluorescent fixtures that are placed within the plan to provide after-hour lighting for stocking, cleaning, or security purposes. Usually these are normal fixtures controlled separately from other lighting.

Stockroom Lighting

Stockroom lighting is designed to minimize electrical consumption while adequately illuminating

Emergency light.

Exit light.

the space. Strip lighting installed on the ceiling should run parallel to shelving, between aisles. This ensures ample lighting on the stock. Sometimes stockroom lighting will be put on a timer if the stockroom is not in continuous use, as in a shoe stockroom.

New Sources for the Future

New metal halide lamps are now becoming available which will have many applications for merchandising. Metal halide has not been an acceptable source in the past because of poor color and unacceptable color shift. This new series of lamps have excellent color, efficiency, and stability. They will be available in several configurations; PAR and E.E. shapes being best suited for ambient lighting. The color of these lamps will be slightly cooler than incandescent but very acceptable for most applications. Much less energy will be required to accomplish an equal or better lighting design. Costs for these products will be higher and designers will have to evaluate the savings in energy and lamp replacement against the added cost.

Conclusion

A well-designed and disciplined lighting plan will bring years of cost-effective lighting to a retail store.

In many cases, when the store receives a cosmetic remodeling, the general lighting will remain untouched, and modifications to perimeter or visual merchandising lighting will be made to fit the new plan.

It is the responsibility of the store planner to lay out the best possible lighting plan that can accommodate modifications, yet endure for the life of the retail space.

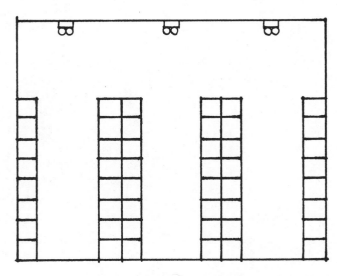

Example of stockroom lighting.

Chapter 13

THE PERSPECTIVE: AN ILLUSTRATIVE SELLING TOOL

Definition of the Perspective

The *perspective* is a three-dimensional representation of the design concepts. It is a drafting technique for presenting exterior or interior composition in a point of view approximating that of the human eye. A rendered perspective can illustrate almost anything in a store—from a complete interior to a single fixture. It can convey hundreds of separate thoughts, if necessary.

Since a good perspective is a valuable selling tool, it should be prepared to look as professional as possible. A perspective aids clients in understanding the planner's thoughts, helps them envision the ultimate appearance of the store, elicits important dialogue and precipitates key decisions, and can be invaluable in inspiring merchants and planners to make appropriate design statements. The perspective can also be used to emphasize special areas and departments.

The backgrounds of perspectives can be illustrated as larger or smaller than actual size, with structural barriers shown or excluded, depending on what helps explaining the concepts.

There are several stages in the development of perspectives, beginning with the rough sketch and ending in the final drawing. Since different vantage points project different points of view, scales must be in proportion to that normally seen by the eye so points of view are not distorted. The perspective helps the viewer look over or through an object at eye level and can fairly accurately illustrate distant views of decor lines. Perspectives should be drawn from the edge of a department, just as a person would view the area or decor from natural sight lines.

The perspective is best when its format is simple. It should provide clues about the "philosophy" of the design.

The rough ideas are first illustrated in preliminary drafts, which later evolve into hardline stages. Typically, these are drawn by one draftsperson.

Perspectives drawn to a scale ordinarily will differ from preliminary sketches. The finished perspective indicates sight lines, textures, or reflective surfaces in more literal terms, that is, more like the eye actually sees it.

Steps in a Perspective

There are four basic steps to rendering a perspective:

1. Vanishing points.
2. Basic perspective.
3. Preliminary perspective.
4. Simple format perspective.

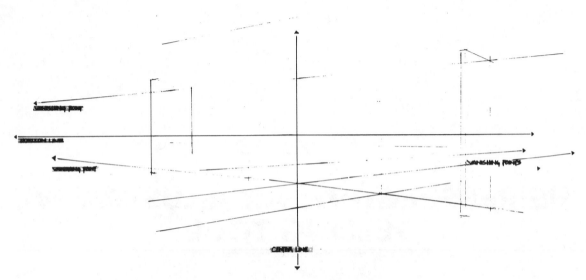

Vanishing points: Establishing your vanishing points determines the angle at which an area will be viewed. The horizon line should relate to the human eye so that it indicates the actual view of a customer.

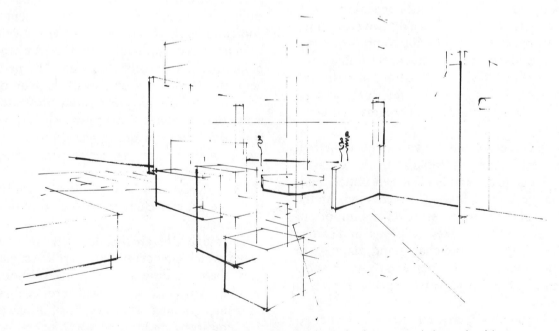

Basic perspective: The perspective helps the viewer to look over and through objects.

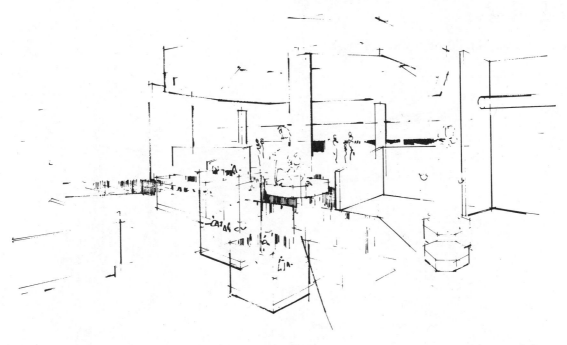

Preliminary perspective: At this stage, shapes and objects begin to take form. Design ideas and decor in the background are introduced into the perspective.

Simple format perspective: The perspective should be of a simple format that suggests how the customer will view an area of the store.

Mall Entrances

The mall entrance should be open and inviting.

Angular aisles help funnel and direct traffic into the store.

Various types of durable materials—such as wood, marble, brick, metal, and glass—promote the image and tone of a store.

Mall Doors

Overhead metal grill doors used at store entrances are concealed above the entrance opening.

Sliding glass and metal doors require a pocket to hide the doors while the store is open.

Entrance Design Concepts

The design concept of a storefront should be applicable to any configuration.

The same design concept as applied to a linear elevation.

Store Entrances

The dynamic concept helps the merchant to present the same image at both street (shown above) and mall entrance (shown below).

The mall entrance uses overhead grill doors, eliminating glass windows and doors.

Shoe Store Entrance and Interior

This perspective allows the merchant to see through the storefront and into the retail space.

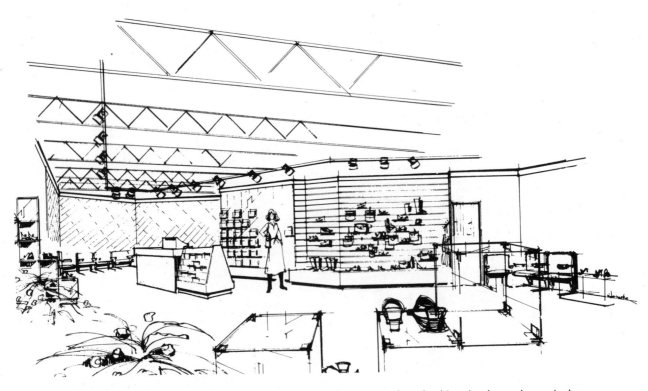

This view suggests how the customer may see the store when looking in through a window.

Shop Concepts at Store Entrances

The customer should have clear vision into a store. Lifestyle merchandise in windows relates to the customer.

The merchandise displayed at entrances should attract attention and encourage the customer to come in and browse.

Freestanding Fixtures

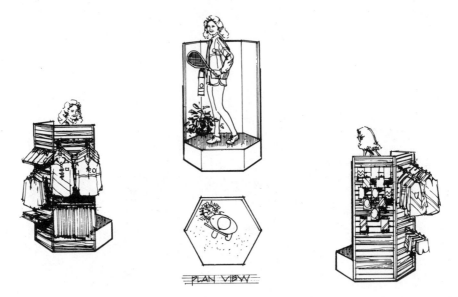

PLAN VIEW

Freestanding fixtures for window displays can incorporate selling on the reverse side.

Vignettes and displays bring attention to selective merchandise classifications. The wrap counter helps control the store's entrance.

Glass Store Entrances

Glass wall systems allow full visibility of the space.

Sliding glass door panels helps control merchandise at store entrances.

Store Entrances

Open displays at store entrances attract customers, but are more susceptible to vandalism.

Show windows at store entrances can attractively display merchandise, while at the same time providing protection for the display.

Store Entrances

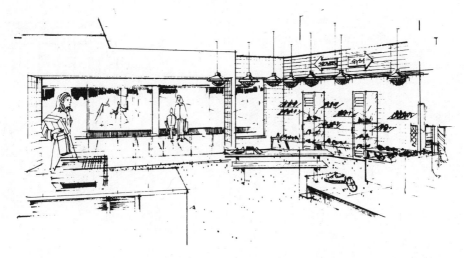

The customer should be able to quickly identify featured departments and merchandise at mall entrances.

Special shop concepts at mall or street entrances help to generate additional traffic and sales.

Shop Concepts

Attention can be brought to a small classification of merchandise through the use of a specialty shop concept.

Shop concepts help to bring identity to various vendors or classifications of merchandise.

Shop Concepts

Designer fur and gown areas may require a special shop concept or entrance.

Shop concepts can be used to bring identity within a department.

Use of Aisles

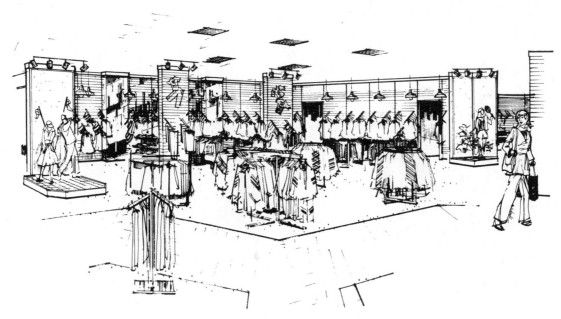

Aisles direct traffic movement through a store and provide easy access to various departments.

The customer should always be able to view more than one type of merchandise while walking through aisles.

Four-foot-wide secondary aisles help to draw traffic into large departments. They also help in developing an area for special classification.

A display and simulated skylight effect can bring attention to other merchandise classifications within the area.

Secondary aisles provide access to deeper portions of a department.

Displays at intersecting aisles channel attention to a department and classes of merchandise.

Showcases at aisle lines help display the product and create service areas.

Mannequins at aisle lines help to feature merchandise within the department.

Merchandise attractively displayed at the aisle line helps promote impulse sales.

Freestanding decor elements can be used at aisle lines to separate departments and create alluring focal points.

Department Concepts

Various types of decor elements are used to create the departmental design and theme.

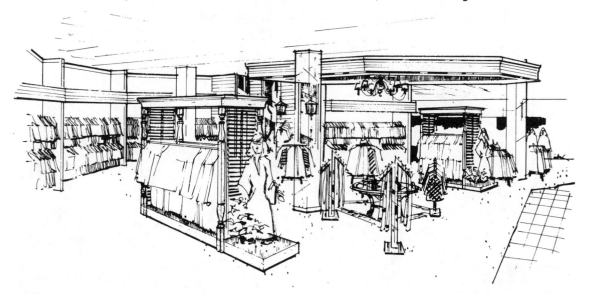

Overhead beams can visually define an area of selected merchandise. Open, freestanding fixtures help to create a shop feeling.

Casual seating areas can add much to the overall decor and design concept of a department.

The perimeter decor backdrop can visually define separare merchandise classifications and helps break the line of departments.

Custom cabinetry can help create a break in decor and focus attention on selected merchandise.

Custom mill work and antique furniture helps to distinguish divisions of merchandise within a department.

Decor and fixturing can present a feel of formality and elegance.

Modern fixturing and decor presents a contemporary or casual ambience.

Cove Lighting

Cove lighting above showcases can add drama and depth to an area.

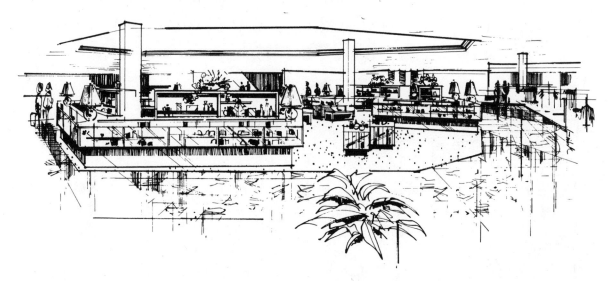

Recessed cove ceiling lighting pulls attention and definition to a department. Showcases at wide aisle lines entice customers to concentrate their attention on the products.

Merchandise Presentation

Interesting displays within a department help reinforce the adjacent merchandise.

Alternating merchandising and display panels helps to create a department theme and heightens attention on the merchandise.

Creating Focal Points

A break in the design of perimeter decor can help visually divide a department.

A centered sawtooth wall configuration helps to break up long monotonous runs of perimeter decor. It can also help bring attention to a selected classification of merchandise.

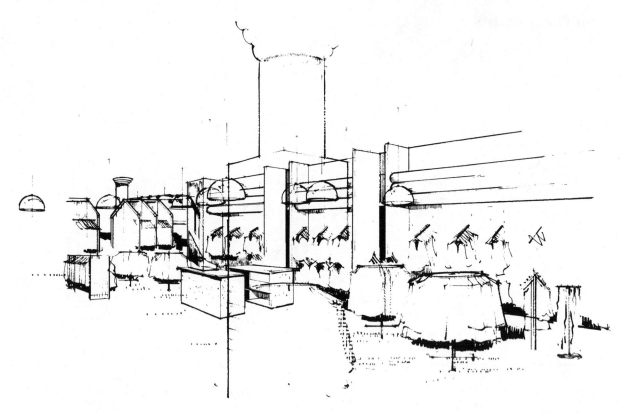

When remodeling older structures, it is unnecessary for perimeter walls to run full ceiling height. The ceiling and the space between the ceiling and wall height can be painted the same color, thus visually dropping the ceiling height.

Heavy perimeter decor, such as backdrops, require additional wall-blocking and support hardware.

Focal Points

Angular sawtooth wall configurations with light boxes help produce focal points for special classifications.

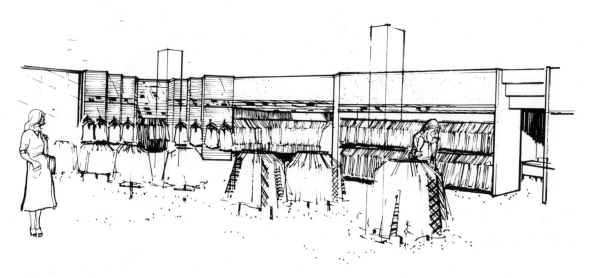

Trim elements can be incorporated into sawtooth walls and curtain walls to create a unified design concept.

Signage

Imaginative interior store signage can capture attention to a classification of merchandise or department.

The integration of innovative graphics into the decor brings immediate identification to a department.

All types of merchandise classifications should be visually displayed to attract attention.

Signage and graphics help the customer to quickly locate merchandise.

Perimeter Cornices

Cornice or valance lines help to illuminate perimeter walls.

Vertical fins can help stop a cornice line. Additional vertical fins form a new design element.

Store Image

Merchandise and samples of merchandise for customer viewing should have easy access. The theme of the store must appealingly relate to the type of merchandise it sells.

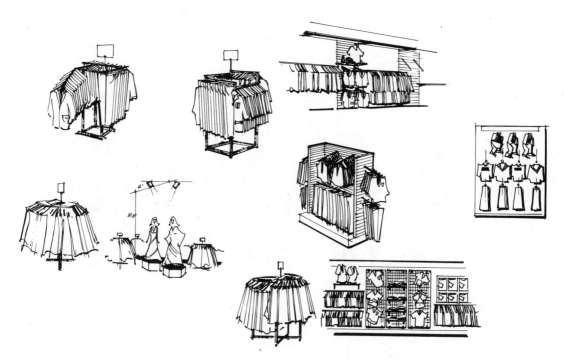

Freestanding fixtures and perimeter merchandising presentation techniques help create the image of the store.

Decor Cutouts

An 8-foot departmental dividing wall helps the customer to see that the store continues beyond the wall. Cutouts further reinforce the effect.

Cutouts help the customer see through a wall and into additional merchandised areas.

Merchandise Presentation Systems

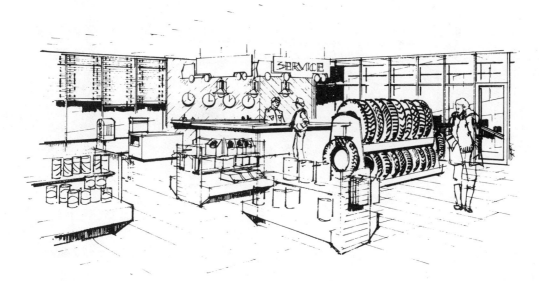

Certain specialty areas of the store may require heavy duty store fixtures and hardware to support heavy merchandise.

Various dynamic decor and merchandising effects can be achieved by spacing and by alternating wall panels and staggered faceout hardware.

Cosmetics Department

Cosmetics departments are planned and designed to focus on specific vendor lines.

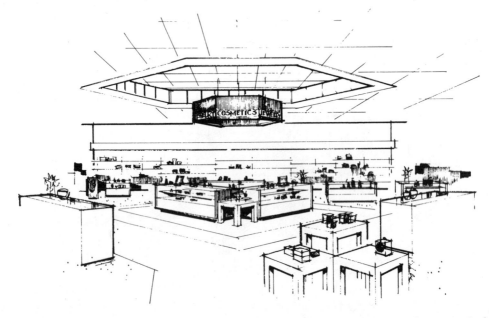

Here is an example of an overhead treatment used in a cosmetics and accessories area. A simulated skylight provides a pleasant and unexpected break to the ceiling plane and visually encloses the feature area.

Shop Concepts

Custom boutique areas within a store are designed to highlight better merchandise.

Custom casework and decor emphasize better jewelry and accessory departments.

Merchandise Presentation Techniques

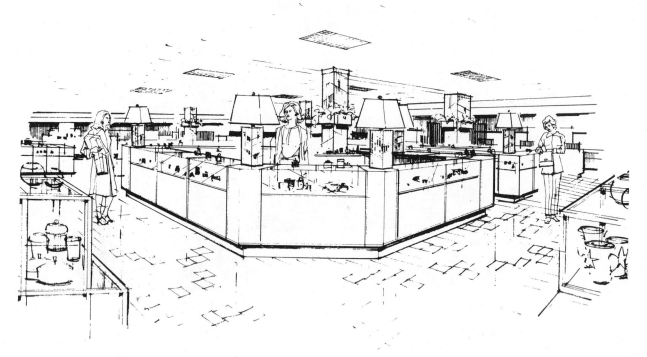

Illuminated, a ⅓-vision showcases display cosmetics or jewelry to its optimum.

Narrow merchandising spaces can be utilized for vertical presentation of merchandise.

Security Showcases and Cabinets

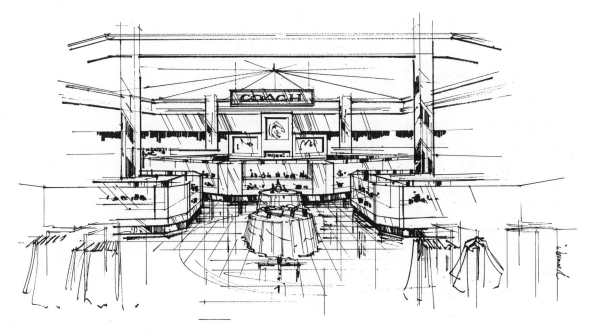

Better merchandise can also be displayed within showcases.

Merchandise can be displayed in vertical secured cabinets where security may be an issue.

Security Showcases and Cabinets

Higher-ticket merchandise can be secured behind case lines.

Merchandise that tempts theft should be locked. Both wallcases and showcases are commonly used to secure target items.

Linens and Domestics

Displays of featured merchandise on perimeter walls of linen and domestics departments help create colorful, visual excitement.

Freestanding drapery and curtain display windows help the customer to envision the merchandise as it will be seen in the home environment.

Shoes

The planning and design of a shoe department should provide for readily divided classifications of footwear.

Flexible display fixtures at aisle lines promote featured or sale merchandise.

Shoes

A feature display wall dividing two departments helps to separate different categories of merchandise.

A shoe department design should visually divide women's, men's, and children's shoes while still allowing for service to be conducted from one area of the department.

Merchandise Presentation Systems

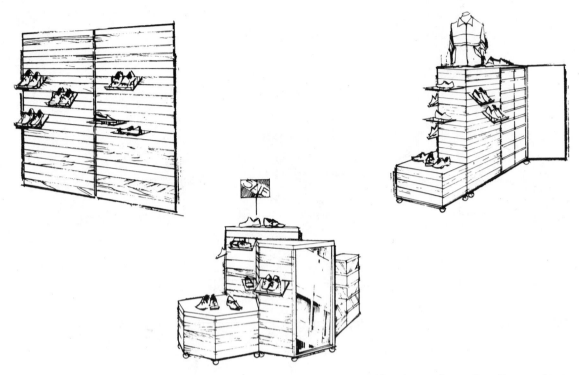

Freestanding special fixtures are designed to display various classifications of merchandise, such as shoes, handbags, and accessories.

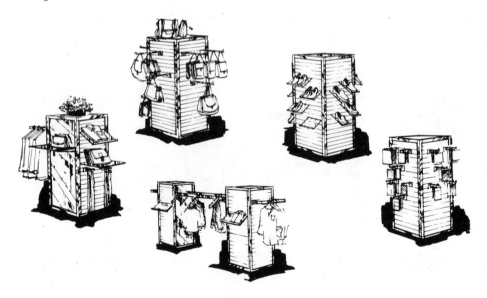

Stairwells

An engaging display area above an open and appealing stairwell should spark attention and interest to classifications of merchandise on the lower level.

Stairwells to mezzanine selling areas must encourage upward physical movement. The openness gives full visibility of departments. Avoid cramped, low ceilings under mezzanines.

Fitting Rooms

The cash-and-wrap counter should have a clear view into the fitting room area and should be accessible, neat, and clean.

Additional specialty merchandise is featured on faceouts at fitting-room entrances. The showcase and wrap counter helps service and control the fitting room.

Customer Service Areas

Customer service areas are conveniently located within the store for easy access.

Customer service areas are located adjacent to receiving and service areas within a store.

Kiosks

A kiosk is a freestanding shop located in high traffic areas in malls.

The decor elements of a kiosk can be modified to change with the merchandising concept.

Minimalls

The design theme of this minimall suggests an Old World theme.

A classic storefront design tends to weather well over a period of years.

Chapter 14

THE PRELIMINARY PLAN—GENERAL NOTES AND SPECIFICATION REVIEW

Presentation of Preliminary Plans

The importance of satisfying specifications of landlords is almost on par with having the whole project approved. Part of this investigatory process is the preliminary screening of plans and drawings by landlords, or their agents, to be sure that areas of conflict and misunderstanding are discovered and that all of the requirements of landlords are otherwise being met. This also is the time to review the lease and tenant's criteria package to be sure the planner, the landlord, and tenants are aware of each other's responsibilities.

First, ascertain how much time is allocated for submission of drawings, then schedule the presentation early enough to meet the deadline spelled out in the lease. It is also a good idea to find out how many sets of plans will be needed for submission and approval, and whether transparencies or sepias are required.

The documents that should be discussed during this review are:

1. The reflected ceiling plan.
2. A profile section of the storefront, delineating shape and height of windows, entrances, and signs.
3. The color palettes of interior and exterior finishes.

If the landlord finds the drawings incomplete, he or she will return them for revision, indicating the so-called "gray areas" that necessitate changes. It is often acceptable to exchange these documents by mail without a formal, in-person presentation to the landlord.

It is always a good idea to prepare a punchlist, or checklist, to help keep track of the myriad details involved. Also, be sure to record names, addresses, and telephone numbers of all people who may be sources of valuable information.

All of the plans must be dimensionally accurate, with actual field conditions indicated. Sometimes the spaces are not built precisely to dimensions on the drawings because complications in the field made changes necessary.

Instructions/Specifications

1. **Scheduling and Procedures**
   A. All work will be performed while store is in operation. Work will be phased in specific areas. OWNER shall determine sequence of work and will furnish instructions to CONTRACTOR prior to start of construction.
   B. ALL BIDDERS shall visit the site at the designated time to inspect conditions under which work will be performed.
   C. CONTRACTOR shall obtain all required permits, engineering seals, and certifications required for the work immediately upon contract award.
   D. It is the OWNER'S intent to award the following contracts to complete all work shown and specified herein.
      (1) General Contract: to include all items shown on perimeter wall strip elevations except free-standing fixtures, floorcoverings, and items specified to be provided by the OWNER.
      (2) Freestanding Fixture Contract: to include removal or modification of existing, and furnishing and installation of, new freestanding fixtures and associated items as itemized in Division 001 to 699 with Divisions 800 to 899 in "Legend of Store Fixtures"; also includes work itemized in Divisions 700, 800, 900 and 951 to 999 (wood items only) in the "Legend of Store Fixtures"; verify with STORE PLANNER whether Divisions 001 to 099 will be furnished by OWNER.
      (3) Floorcovering Contract: to include all floorcoverings (carpet, tile, marble, terrazzo, wood, etc.) shown on drawings.
      (4) Verify whether the electrical work will be performed by the OWNER.
      E. Where the term "CONTRACTOR" is used on these drawings and specifications, it shall refer to items provided under the "General Contract" as defined in 1 D (1).

2. **Demolition and Removals**
   A. CONTRACTOR shall remove and legally dispose of all partitions and other items shown on plans and all partitions that do not appear on new high-wall partition plan.
   B. Remove existing fixturing as required to accomplish required demolition. Existing fix-tures indicated to be reused shall be reinstalled in the new work by this CONTRACTOR. Existing fixtures not reused shall be disposed of, off the premises, by this CONTRACTOR. OWNER reserves the right to remove and save any unused existing fixtures, at the OWNER'S EXPENSE.
   C. The term "fixturing" reefers to all items abutting or fastened to existing columns, partitions, and ceilings. Fixturing includes, but is not limited to, items such as hardware, platforms, hangrods, shelves, cabinets, wallcoverings, slatwall base, etc.
   D. Verify with drawings where existing ceilings are to be removed and/or replaced by new grid system. Verify all ceiling conditions in field and coordinate to provide installation of new ceiling where required.
   E. The removal of all electrical, mechanical, plumbing, and similar items required to be removed to accomplish the required demolition shall be included in the work of this CONTRACTOR.
   F. Provide temporary dust partitions of 4 mil polyethylene, with appropriate supports, to separate construction areas from store operations areas. Mask off grilles, registers, and other openings to prevent dust entry into existing ventilation systems.
   G. Provide all repairs, patching, etc., to existing surfaces due to removal of partitions, ceilings, hardware, and fixtures.
   H. All debris shall be removed from the premises daily. Work areas shall be left broom clean at the end of each working day.
   I. The removal and demolition of freestanding fixtures shall be done by others under a separate contract.

3. **New Partition Work**
   A. See technical specifications for detailed material requirements for new partitions. Work includes freestanding partitions, furring, doors and frames, cased openings, and end trim caps and associated items shown or specified herein.
   B. CONTRACTOR shall prepare shop drawings at a scale of $1/2" = 1'0"$ showing elevations of all walls to receive merchandising hardware, fixtures, or special decor. Drawings shall be fully detailed and dimensional to show exact locations of standards, brack-

ets, and other hardware, as well as locations of all required backup studs and blocking.

C. Merchandising hardware shall be furnished by OWNER and installed by the CONTRACTOR. Special metal studs shown are part of merchandising hardware. All required backup studs and blocking for fastening brackets, fixtures, shelving, decor, etc., shall be furnished and installed by the CONTRACTOR.

D. When metal studs are used as backup for surface-mounted standards, provide minimum of 3 molly-tape fasteners in top 3 holes of all standards.

E. All surface-mounted merchandising hardware shall be attached with fasteners appropriate for the substrate encountered. All partitions shall be reinforced, cross-braced to ceilings, etc., as required to support all attached fixturing loads.

F. All partitions shall be taped, finished, and sanded as specified herein for application of finishes. All verticals shall be finished so as to prevent "telegraphing" of joint defects through foil-type wall coverings or other gloss finishings. When such defects occur, the wall surface will be rejected by the store-planning firm and will be retaped, sanded, and finished at no additional expense to the OWNER.

G. All hardwood jambs shall be machined from clear poplar to the shapes, sizes, and dimensions shown on drawings. All fasteners shall be set, filled, and sanded. See detailed specifications below for shop-finished wood door requirements.

4. Fixturing

A. CONTRACTOR shall provide all fixturing shown or specified herein except that defined as "Freestanding Fixturing."

B. Materials

(1) All painted plywood shall be paint grade birch. All laquer-colored or plastic-laminate-faced shelves supported at 4-foot intervals, or greater, shall be $^3/_4$-inch-thick plywood.

(2) Detail drawings of showcases, tables, gondolas, back-islands, risers, and fixtures in nonselling areas indicate where particle board construction will be allowed. Particle board may also be used for column enclosures, corner fillers, dividers or vertical fins and special wall fixtures and low plastic-laminate-covered partitions. Colored-lacquer or laminate-covered shelves supported at intervals of less than 4 feet may be constructed of particle board.

(3) All $^3/_4$-inch slatwall shall be solid core construction source as specified. Substitutes to be approved.

(4) Light cornice, hanging curtain wall, soffits, and light boxes may be constructed of birch plywood, or filled particle board, at the CONTRACTOR'S option.

(5) All natural-finish veneers shall be (_____ type of wood _____) and must be of a matched grain at least $^1/_{30}$-inch thick. Veneers in connection with enameled surfaces shall be birch.

(6) Store-planning firm will furnish color chips for color indications on all painted surfaces and samples of natural-wood finish required. In turn, samples of all wood finishes must be submitted for the store-planning firm's approval by the CONTRACTOR. These samples are to be on plywood or solid wood.

(7) Where moldings must be nailed on, all nail holes are to be puttied, sanded, and sponged before finishing. Unexposed backs and bottoms of fixtures must be painted one heavy coat of lacquer enamel. Interiors of drawers to be sandpapered smooth, sealed, and finished with one coat of clear lacquer.

(8) Natural-wood surfaces shall be bleached as necessary in order to obtain the desired tone and uniformity of color, then sanded to remove all raised grain and machine marks. Apply filler, sealer, and stain as necessary. Apply three coats of clear lacquer; sand lightly between each operation. Allow three hours for drying between coats of lacquer. Final coat to be rubbed to a dull eggshell with pumice stone and oil. CONTRACTOR to note instances where detailed drawings specifically call for wood finishes. The information as called for on detailed drawings is to

take precedence over these specifications.

(9) All open-grain wood is to be properly filled and wiped across grain. All filler is to be removed from surfaces. Apply two coats of undercoating and two coats of enamel. Allow sufficient time between all coats to dry hard; sand lightly between all coats; and rub last coat to an eggshell finish unless otherwise specified or instructed by the store-planning firm. The CONTRACTOR shall assume enamel surfaces being finished in a variety of colors as directed by the store-planning firm.

(10) All plastic laminate shall be as specified in the store-planning firm's standard color book. All shelves shall be laminated on both faces and all edges.

(11) Glass shelves shall be 3/8-inch polished plate with polished edges, or as specified.

C. CONTRACTOR shall submit shop drawings for all fixturing. Shop drawings shall show all details, finishes, and materials, including where particle board is proposed for use.

D. Carpet and carpet base on fixtures and partitions will be furnished and installed by others under separate floor-coverings contract.

E. Stock shelving in stockrooms will be furnished and installed by OWNER. This CONTRACTOR shall furnish and install standards and hangrods in stockrooms, where indicated on plans.

5. **Merchandising Hardware and Accessories**
   A. All merchandising hardware shall be furnished by the OWNER and installed by this CONTRACTOR. See high-wall plans, elevations, and merchandising sections for quantities of hardware. See hardware accessories list for type of items required.
   B. Verify spacing of standards or struts as indicated on high-wall plan. Hangrods shall be 4 feet long with two endcaps. When hangrod is longer than 4 feet and continuous, splicers shall be used. All hangrods shorter than 4 feet shall be cut to fit on job site.
   C. If existing hardware is to be reused, the OWNER will provide a complete hardware inventory and new locations for hardware prior to bidding.
   D. All straight and up-slant brackets shall be 2 inches shorter than the shelves.
   E. Down-slanted and adjustable angle brackets for glass shelves are to be the same size as the shelf and have front clip. Plastic laminate, carpet-covered, etc., shelves shall have brackets 2 inches shorter than the shelf and have front clip. Provide groove in shelf to receive the clip.
   F. For shelves 18 inches wide and over, use heavy duty brackets. Pull-out rods for ready-to-wear and clothing areas shall be furnished at one level (top) of hangrail where indicated on the drawing. When pullout rods are not indicated, they are to be furnished 12 feet on center.

6. **Vendor Units/Merchandising Racks**
   In proposal form, submit hourly rates for unloading, unpacking, assembling, and setup of vender-or OWNER-supplied merchandising racks.

7. **Column Treatments**
   A. Column types are indicated on drawings with the following legend:
      Type A: Vinyl-covered gypsum board (verify location of mirrors)
      Type B: Slatwall on all four sides
      Type C: Slatwall on two sides; mirror on two sides
      Type D: Slatwall on three sides, mirror on one side
      Type E: Mirror on all four sides
   B. CONTRACTOR shall furnish and install all gypsum-board column enclosures, vinyl, slatwall, and mirrors.
   C. Mirror frame assemblies shall be shop fabricated and installed by others (Freestanding Fixture Contract).
   D. All shimming of mirrors and frame assemblies to make mirrors plumb and square shall be done by this CONTRACTOR.
   E. Hardwood base at columns will be furnished and installed by others (Freestanding Fixture Contract).

8. **Fitting Rooms**
   A. All new metal prefabricated fitting rooms

shown on plans will be furnished and installed by OWNER.

B. If existing fitting rooms are to be reused, this CONTRACTOR shall rework existing walls and other components as shown on drawings.

C. This CONTRACTOR shall supply final finished field dimensions of fitting-room bank to fitting-room manufacturer, as directed by store-planning firm.

D. Fitting-room bank shall receive vinyl wall-covering throughout, floor to ceiling.

E. All new wood, plastic laminate, or vinyl fitting rooms with louvered door will be furnished and installed by this CONTRACTOR.

9. **Perimeter Signs**
Provide 8-inch-high uppercase (style of letters) where shown on plans. Letters shall be ¼-inch thick, mirror Plexiglas on ¾-inch-thick foam equal to those manufactured by (_____vendor name_____). Paint sides of letters to match wall.

Chapter 15

THE DEVELOPMENT OF CONSTRUCTION AND STORE-FIXTURING PLANS

Once a wall-line plan has been established, it is time to begin preparing a comprehensive set of drawings with specifications.

The High-Wall Plan

One of the most important drawings is the high-wall plan. A *high-wall plan* (see page 231) delineates the internal shape and space of the building, in which interior partitions, mezzanines, and ceiling heights are fully dimensioned. This plan will include entrances to the building, weather doors, overhead grills, or fire exits. All walls should be identified as new or existing. Walls that do not run to the ceiling should be so indicated. The high-wall plan should be accompanied by a legend that shows clear identification of wall type. Drawings should note the location of escalator and elevator areas, nonselling and sales-support areas, receiving rooms, and any display or stockrooms and windows.

A high-wall plan shows the centers of all vertical stud supports (this aids in the placement of merchandising hardware), and any special wood cross-blocking required for support of special equipment of decor. Each high wall is keyed with symbols that give the elevation and sheet reference numbers. Normally, planners will begin the drawing with the elevation at the main entrance and move around the interior perimeter walls in a clockwise rotation.

The Reflected Ceiling Plan

Another of the essential sets of drawings is the reflected ceiling plan (see page 232), which indicates types of ceilings being used and their exact height from the floor. The plan will show the placement of the grid system, all mechanical diffusers, grills, and decor items (such as curtain-wall drops) that hang from the ceiling or cornice lines. It serves as a layout for all attached materials that run the full height of the walls. The plan will indicate the exact placement of any skylight areas, escalator wells, openings, and so on.

The plan will help establish the placement of light fixtures in relation to sprinkler heads and other mechanical obstructions, with notations of power sources and electrical hookups to assist the engineer when diagraming the wiring.

The plan will indicate illumination requirements (in foot-candles). An estimation of actual hours of usage, electrical load requirements, and all other electrical support information will help serve as a basis for estimating the electrical cost, based on local rates.

The reflected ceiling plan should indicate every type of lighting fixture to be used and its placement. The various types may include low-voltage fixtures, 2-feet x 4-feet fluorescent fixtures, track lighting, incandescent spots/floods, cornice strip lighting, and fitting-room lighting.

Important—The planner should check lease documents to learn of any types of light fixtures that are prohibited and should be familiar with the type of service provided in the building.

The placement of ceiling fixtures should coincide with any perimeter decor lighting in order to avoid wasteful duplication of illumination and to reduce the possibility of "hot spots" on walls or curtain walls.

The placement of ceiling fixtures should be keyed to a legend that is the same shape, size, and designation, and specification as indicated on the plan. The legend, or schedule, will specify manufacturer, type, style, and model number. If possible, it should include the name and telephone number of the contact at the manufacturer or distributor. The complete reflected ceiling plan will also be used to lay out the sprinkler plan and show the location of emergency and exit lights.

One of the store planner's duties is to check local codes and ordinances to learn the type of battery-operated emergency lights required, as well as installation and mounting instructions and hookup.

The Electrical Ceiling Plan

The electrical plan of the ceiling includes layouts and scheduling of outlets and fixtures, and provides answers to a variety of questions: What types of conduits will be used? Where is the main service panel? Are panels, meters, and fuse-disconnection points located in other areas? What electrical load is calculated for accommodating freestanding electrified store equipment? What is the type of overload system to be built into the electrical system to protect store equipment and fixtures? What is the wire size? Who is responsible for arranging telephone and electrical installation? What types of conduits will the utility company service? What types of conduits are not allowed? What types of galvanized steel and weather-proofing will exposed equipment have? What type of independent fuse is re-

quired for fluorescent fixture ballasts? Will all work indicated on the plans be performed to meet state and local codes? Are the plans in accord with the National Electrical Code?

The planner should check the local code regarding use of the flexible conduit to be attached to interior electrified store fixtures. This plan is supplied by others but must coordinate with the planner's drawings.

The Electrical Floor Plan (Or Power and Signal Plan)

What is included in the electrical floor plan? First, the plan should clearly indicate floor and wall outlets, dimensioned from wall or center-of-column lines. Outlets must be coordinated with the merchandising-fixture plan. The type of underground conduit should be indicated, along with circulation patterns.

Every electrified freestanding store fixture will require power from the floor. Freestanding fixtures sometimes have a power-pole drop from the ceiling, but their appearance can be distracting. All special conditions for store electronic and telephone lines should be coordinated closely with the equipment and store management.

The electrical floor plan (see page 233) will indicate hookup requirements and locations of perimeter wall lighting, registers, showcases, electrified fixtures, computers, phones, plugmolds, and TV antenna locations. This plan is supplied by others but must coordinate with the planner's drawings.

The Mezzanine or Double-Deck Plan

A mezzanine plan indicates permanent construction of selling, stock, or sales-support space above the floor level.

A double-deck plan indicates a system with elevated walkways for stocking at the second level.

Prior to developing plans, the planning firms should check local codes on mezzanine and double-deck stockroom requirements. The following are some of the questions that should be answered:

- Will the mezzanine attach to the building or will it be self-standing?
- Will the existing construction properly support the mezzanine?
- Is the mezzanine or double-deck stock space part of the selling or sales-support plan?

- What types of construction materials will be used for mezzanine or double-deck areas?

This plan is supplied by others but must coordinate with the planner's drawings.

The Interior Elevation

The interior elevation is a two-dimensional representation of an interior wall that gives floor and ceiling heights and wall lengths, which correspond (and are keyed) to the high-wall plan, showing the same lengths or shapes. The drawing gives the height lines of the doors and ceilings and the overall dimensioned height of the elevation. All mechanical elements, grills, and door openings should be elevated and keyed to a schedule. The exact location of wall-merchandising hardware systems must be indicated on the interior elevation (again, corresponding to the high-wall plan, the installed height of the standard from finish floor line, decor, trim, and merchandising hardware).

All backdrop or decor treatments should be clearly indicated as to design, materials, and colors, with any special notes required to make the elevation understood. Colors, finishes, and wallcoverings, must be keyed. All required cuts through the decor, backdrop, and merchandising area must be shown for the benefit of the estimator, builder, and contractor. The planner should be prepared to provide a section drawing that includes other essential information.

The following are some of the questions that should be answered by the interior elevation:

- What is the ceiling height?
- What is the underside height of cornice or curtain wall?
- What is the height of the cornice and finish?
- Is there any trim on cornice or wall?
- Is there any wallcovering? If so, what type?
- What is the pain color above or below the cornice?
- Are signage or graphics required?
- What is the hardware or case goods requirement? Any special requirements?
- What must be included in construction notes?
- What information should be supplied with regard to closing off the building from the selling space?
- What is the exact condition of floor, wall, and ceiling areas that separate actual selling areas from nonselling areas.

- Are all sections for merchandising construction and details keyed?
- Are all the color symbols keyed with information?

The elevation and section should include clear directions for the partitioning of selling areas from nonselling or stock areas, with notations. Plans for entrances and glazing should be carefully reviewed prior to the development of drawings.

The Merchandise Plan

A merchandise plan (see page 234) delineates the shape and space of a store or department within the building. The plan will include the placement of fitting rooms or supportive nonselling areas, showcase lines, racks, cash-and-wraps, displays, and any other type of fixture on which merchandise is housed, signed, and sold. Each fixture on the plan should be identified as new, existing, or vendor. The fixtures must be keyed with symbols and numbers that coordinate with a legend and a supplemental manual illustrating fixture types and details. The drawings indicate the exact location and position of each fixture. The merchandising plan is usually developed in a freehand concept that would roughly indicate the shape and type of fixture; later, it is refined, drawn, and adjusted. These fixtures help to define the type of merchandise and use of fixtures. This plan provides a traffic pattern for the desired movement of merchandise and people throughout the space.

The Key Plan

There are two types of key plans: interior-wall-elevation plans 9see page 231) and freestanding-fixture plans. The interior-wall key plan normally starts at the main entrance of a store, works its way around the peri-meter of the building in a clockwise fashion, and in-corporates perimeter and freestanding walls in the core or center of the space. It will indicate assigned numbers and is coordinated with a list and drawing of various fixture types. The free-standing-fixture plan will be keyed to the merchandising plan and a number or symbol will coordinate the item to a ref-erence book that will identify type of fixture and size.

The Demolition Plan

A demolition plan indicates all areas of the project to be removed before new construction begins. The plan can involve floors, walls, ceilings, electrical, plumbing equipment, HVAC, and freestanding fixtures. The plan should clearly indicate everything that must be removed, with sufficient notes and specifications to ensure that the job is done properly.

These notes should identify the parties responsible for various parts of the work among the landlord, developer, and lessee, as necessary, and should cover dust barriers, daily removal and cleanup procedures, and areas needing special attention.

The Floorcovering Plan

A floorcovering plan indicates the various floor finishes required throughout the store. This plan will delineate all hard-surface or carpet aisles, carpeted areas, and sealed floors. It will indicate the width of aisles and any special conditions for ramps or stairs. The plan must be fully dimensioned.

A schedule of all product specifications and installation methods should be included to help assure ease of estimation and installation. A flooring plan also will indicate any areas needing new flooring or floor repair. Each type of flooring material must have a legend and keying system.

One caution about carpeting: Neutral and tweed coloration of carpeting usually will complement a wide variety of merchandise and decor. Pattern carpeting often will be in distracting conflict with merchandise. Carpet border can, by itself, draw attention to a department but, of course, will add to the cost.

Aisle Material

There is almost an endless choice of materials for aisles and walkways—tile, marble, parquet, ceramic, terrazo, carpet, and so on. The costs of these materials, which fluctuate widely, invariably will influence your selection because of budgetary considerations.

The widths of main aisles from mall entrance vary, but normally will narrow to direct traffic flow: for example, the carpeting at a 40-foot-wide entrance narrows toward a point that funnels customers onto an aisle that is variable in width.

At the heaviest traffic area, the main aisles are established at 5 feet, 6 feet, or 7 feet wide, with secondary aisles into deeper departments at 4 feet or 5 feet wide. A minimum of 5 feet should be allowed for service entrances. If a secondary aisle is required into a deep department, it is best to have it match the finish of the main aisle; it can be limited to 4 feet wide.

A Warning about Wallcoverings

There is a note of caution for anyone designing the decor of a retail store. Every ingredient in that decor must be treated with careful respect. Designers should be particular about their choice of style, texture, and type, and should take pride in those choices; they should remember that wallcoverings are *backgrounds*—nothing more. Many times a wallcovering makes a great contribution to the overall decor, yet never seems to distract the customers. This is the mark of a successful wallcovering choice. The difference between a textured wallcovering and paint, for example, may be striking. It should be remembered that durable wallcoverings usually are easy to maintain and tend to wear well over a period of years. They can create a nice, if unobtrusive, texture (or self-pattern) at a distance. They should never be strong enough to dominate a department or overwhelm the merchandise. A wallcovering should be used at customer level where servicing is a problem. All wallcoverings in stores should be fire rated.

Perimeter Decor

The perimeter decor, as a background, should be a tasteful design. Obviously the selection of finished materials will greatly affect overall appearance. Each curtain-wall backdrop or cornice will need a finish and possibly some type of trim, such as wood, metal, wallcovering, paint, or color. Remember to plan for any columns, overhead beams, curtain walls, and even mechanical equipment that might interrupt a department's design.

The Merchandising Section

A merchandising section is a cross-section or profile of various interior walls, indicating placement of merchandising hardware systems with brackets, hangrods, shelves, casegoods, and other secondary merchandising systems.

The merchandising section, which is coordinated with the interior strip elevation, also includes bases, prongs, faceouts, waterfalls, hangrods, casegoods, and any other special fixtures required for merchandise presentation.

Since every type of merchandise can be presented

in a multitude of ways, the presentation method will depend on factors such as budget, type of store, and client preferences, as well as the "idiosyncrasies" of the merchandise itself.

The Decor Section

Decor sections are cross-sections or profiles indicating such things as size, construction methods, materials, and trims. They include, but are not limited to, walls, cornices, curtain walls, decorative drops, and installation methods. Decor sections are coordinated with the fixture-finish schedule and color book of finished material. Decor finishes should also be found on the color materials plan.

The Loose-Fixture Details

Loose-fixture details are coordinated with the merchandising plan and are keyed to the merchandising plan through the use of symbols. These symbols, which coordinate with a legend of loose-fixture drawings, indicate the type, shape, size, hardware, construction material, finish, and usage of fixtures. In many cases, the same fixture may be used in different areas of the store and house different classifications of merchandise. Though some fixtures are reconstructed to the type of merchandise that can be displayed for sale (such as hanging or shelved), loose fixtures should be designed with the maximum amount of flexibility to insure longevity and multiuse applications. A freestanding-fixture detail illustrates the shape, size, and type of various store-fixturing furniture components. The illustration and section accommodates the merchandise and provides the manufacturer with the pertinent information on the construction, accessory hardware, finishes, and any other element that encompasses the finished product, appearance, and usage. Each type of fixture will require different assembly methods and hardware.

The Water and Sanitary Plan

The water and sanitary plan includes drawings for all special areas requiring plumbing or drainage (i.e., toilets, kitchenettes, food-preparation areas, water fountains, service areas, etc.) and are provided by other contractors.

Local codes must be examined to determine toilet room requirements, such as whether "rough-in" plumbing is mandatory when only one room is required. Certain federal requirements, such as special facilities for the handicapped, must also be met. These drawings will be supplied by others but will coordinate with the planner's drawings.

The Sanitary Line Layout Plan

In the sanitary line layout plan, the specification and details should clearly indicate the size of the sanitary line, the location of cleanout spots, and all ventilation through ceiling roof lines.

Some questions to answer are:

- What is included in the water heaters or tailor/alterations shop?
- At what point does the service enter the building?
- Who is responsible for arrangements with local utilities?

Factored into the plan should be a schedule of all fixtures (including plumbing fixtures) with specifications that give full details as to style, type, and model number. Is the service existing? If not, who will provide it? Is there a suggested location for toilets and food-preparation areas? Is more than one room required? Are air gaps necessary on waste lines from food-service equipment? This plan is supplied by others but will integrate with the planner's drawings.

The Sprinkler Plan

The sprinkler plan (see page 236) is a layout that coordinates sprinkler heads with ceiling electrical and HVAC requirements in both sales-related and nonselling areas. Sprinkler heads are designed so as to maximize spacing, and their density is partly a function of ceiling height. Additional sprinkler heads may be required in exposed-construction stock areas (the local fire code must be checked). Local codes will dictate the spacing of sprinkler heads. Sprinkler heads are installed throughout the entire store, including selling areas, nonselling areas, toilet rooms, below and above mezzanine areas, at show windows, behind curtain walls, and so on. It is good to note who will supply and service fire extinguishers. Will special sprinkler systems be required for food-preparation areas? These drawings will be supplied by others but will coordinate with the planner's drawings.

The Heating/Ventilation/Air-Conditioning (HVAC) Plan

The HVAC plan (see page 237) is a layout plan that indicates types of systems, sizes, heights, and elevations above the finished floor line and damper locations.

The plan must coincide with the reflected ceiling plan and with locations of all ceiling lighting fixtures. Capacities for grills, registers, and diffusers should be specified. Local codes should be reviewed with regard to exhaust systems for food-preparation areas, toilet rooms, show windows, and tailoring areas. The method of installation and specifications for each should be summarized in the general notes.

The HVAC plan should indicate the exact locations of all roof openings. Details on mounting the system may be included, along with sources of heating and cooling and the specifying and operating procedures. The plan should show whether extra steel will be required to support roof-mounted equipment.

The design plan should indicate the heating and cooling capacities of equipment. It should also identify any fresh-air direct or indirect intakes, or indirect return air grills. Any special heating requirements, such as supplemental base heating, or special cooling for electronic equipment rooms, should be identified with their locations shown. This plan will be supplied by others but will coordinate with that of the planner.

Here are some typical questions to consider:

- Is a particular air-conditioning system recommended?
- Are roof-top units acceptable?
- Is a combination roof-top/split system acceptable?

This plan will be supplied by others but will coordinate with the planner's drawings.

Plan Examples

HIGH-WALL & KEY PLAN

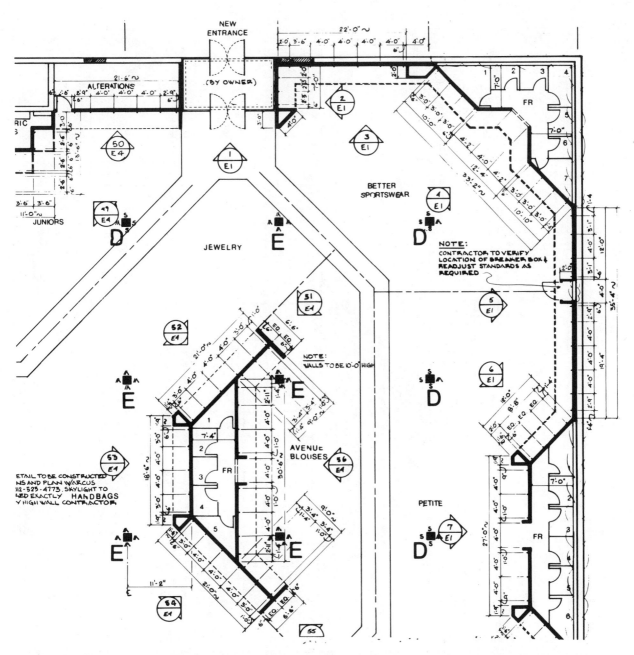

The high-wall plan is primarily used to indicate dimensions of all wall lengths and hardware spacing. These dimensions are used for the actual construction, so they must be accurate. The plan is also used to key all elevations and indicate the number of the street on which the elevation will be found. Lastly, the plan should include column treatments, decor concepts, and general notes to contractors.

REFLECTED CEILING PLAN

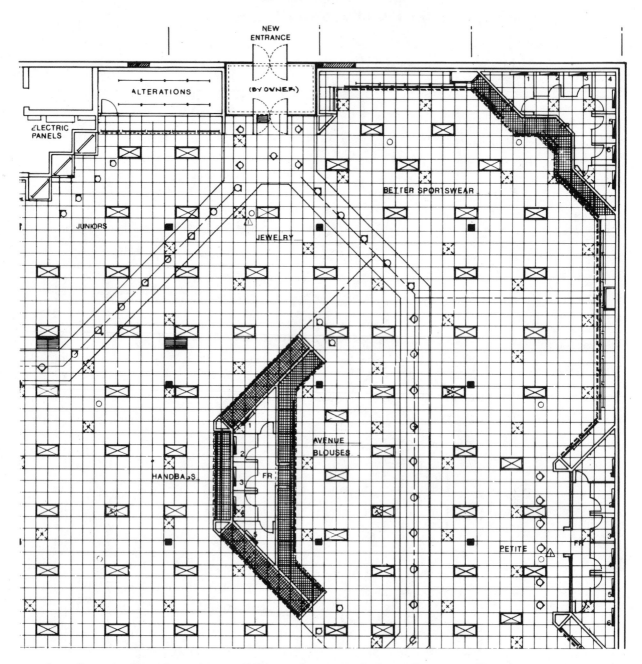

The reflected ceiling plan indicates all lighting fixtures, including selling, nonselling, fitting room, cornice, and accent lighting. Note the fixtures that are dotted in. These represent existing fixtures that are to be removed. This plan also shows areas where eggcrate will be used under the cornice. These areas are indicated by the cross-hatching.

POWER AND SIGNAL FLOOR PLAN

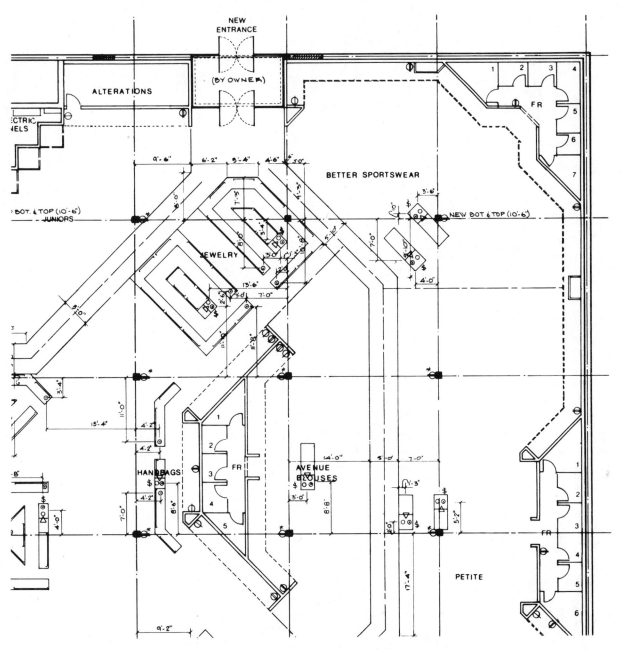

The power and signal floor plan must indicate all electrical wall and floor outlets. It should also include any telephone and communication outlets, along with lighting and power requirements for showcases. The most important item to include in this plan is the dimensioning. All floor outlets are dimensioned to center lines. This allows the electrical contractor to install these outlets in the proper locations to coordinate with the merchandising plan.

MERCHANDISING PLAN

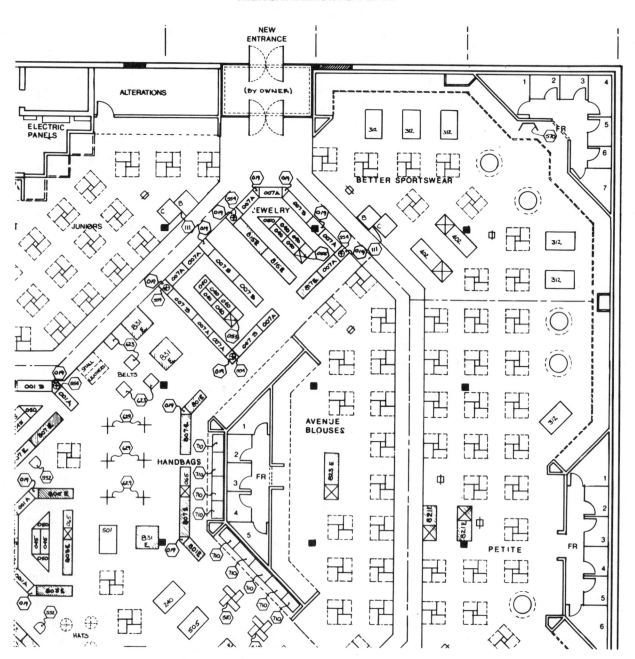

The merchandise plan indicates exact placement of every rack, showcase, display cube, cash and wrap, freestanding fixture, vendor fixture, and perimeter casework. All these items are keyed to a handbook that illustrates each fixture and includes general notes and details.

FIXTURE FINISH SCHEDULE

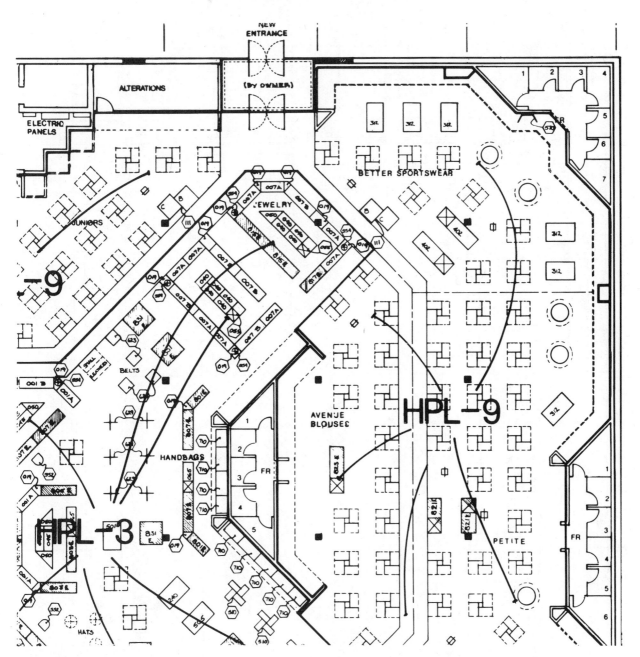

The fixture finish schedule designates which high-pressure laminate (HPL) is used in each area. The laminate is usually used on perimeter casework, cash and wraps, showcases, display cubes, or any other freestanding fixture in the respective area.

SPRINKLER PLAN

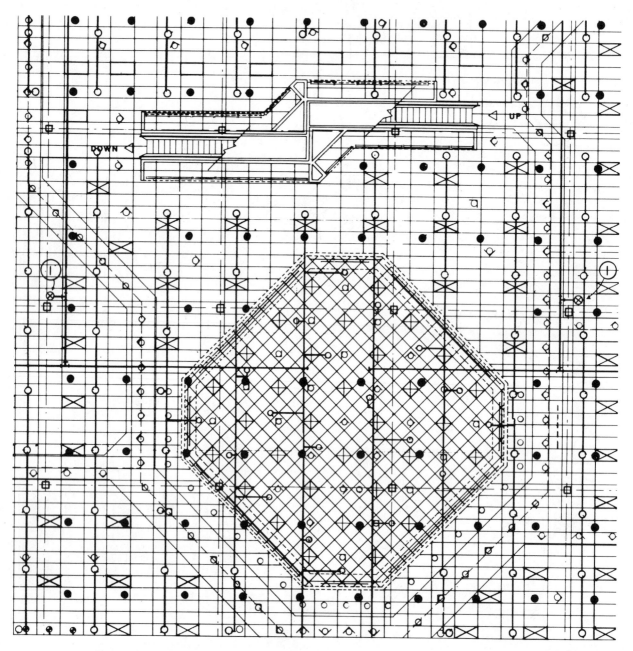

The sprinkler plan coordinates sprinkler heads with the ceiling, electrical and HVAC equipment. Local codes play a crucial role in determining the type of system and spacing required. The sprinkler plan should include general notes, specifications, and methods of installation.

HVAC PLAN

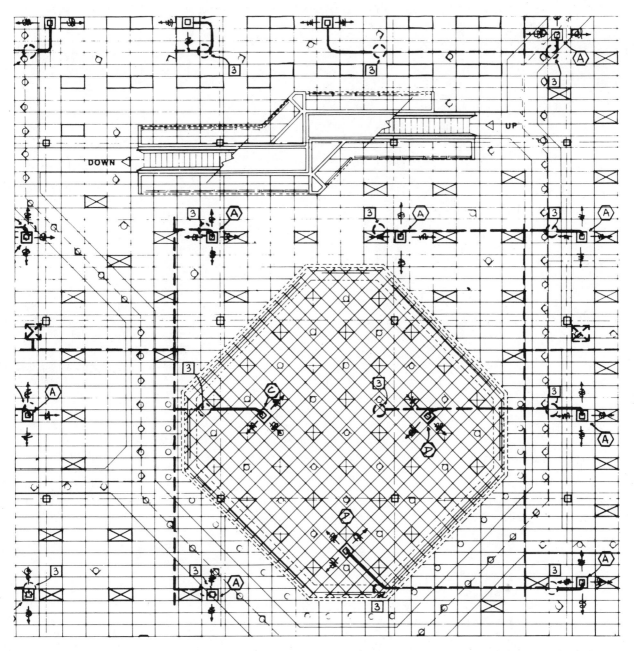

The HVAC plan should indicate all exhaust systems, grills, registers, and diffusers, along with their locations and capacities. It is very important that local codes are checked to verify which systems are allowable. The plan should also include general notes, specifications, and methods of installation.

Chapter 16

LEGENDS

In order to produce a comprehensive set of understandable drawings, the store planner must refer to a set of legends. Every store-planning office will have its own type of legends to which the entire company will adhere in order to prevent confusion.

- Line legend symbols (see page 240) are used to draw the building, interior walls, and decor.
- Reflected ceiling and lighting legend symbols (see pages 241 and 242) are used to indicate the direction of the ceiling grid and the types of lighting fixtures that will illuminate the interior.
- The symbols in the power/electrical legend (see pages 243–244) indicate what type of electrical outlets, services, capacities, and locations are required for the electrification of equipment.
- Plumbing legend symbols (see page 245) indicate water-related service.
- Color legend symbols (see pages 246) help to indicate the finishes within the interior space.
- The symbols in the legend of the freestanding store fixtures (see pages 247–249) indicate placement and type of equipment.
- The rack legend symbols (see pages 249–250) indicate typically used shapes to identify fixture type or usage.

Store Name _____
Store No./Location _____
Completion Date _____
Job Telephone _____
Job FAX _____

Store Planner _____
Address _____
City, State _____
Telephone _____
FAX _____

LINE LEGEND

Job # _____   Date _____

Sheet _____

SYMBOL	DESCRIPTION
	Existing building wall
	New building wall
	Existing interior partition / with slatwall
	New interior partition / with slatwall
	Low wall—verify height and elevations
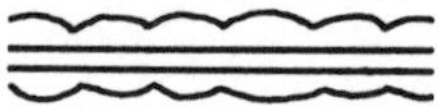	Existing wall removal
	Mezzanine line
	Curtain wall
	Single cornice
	Double cornice
	Fitting-room partition system
	Floorcovering break line
	Aisle center line / departmental break line
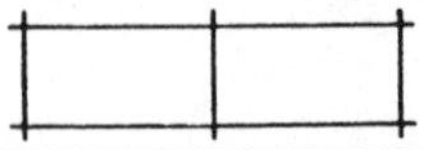	Typical 2' x 4' ceiling grid with designer's specified lay-in ceiling

Store Name _____

Store No./Location _____

Completion Date _____

Job Telephone _____

Job FAX _____

Store Planner _____

Address _____

City, State _____

Telephone _____

FAX _____

REFLECTED CEILING/LIGHTING LEGEND

Job # _____   Date _____

Sheet _____

SYMBOL	DESCRIPTION
	Typical 2' x 2' ceiling grid with designer's specified lay-in ceiling
	2' x 4' recessed fluorescent framed-door troffer with acrylic prismatic lens*
	2' x 4' recessed fluorescent with paracube lens*
	2' x 4' recessed fluorescent with deep-cell parabolic lens—verify number of cells with reflected ceiling plan
	1' x 4' recessed fluorescent framed-door troffer with acrylic prismatic lens*
	2' x 2' recessed fluorescent with paracube lens*
	Wall-mounted low-contrast illumination fixture with opal acrylic diffuser; length as indicated*
	Surface-mounted (horizontally) double-lamp fluorescent strip light*
	Surface-mounted (horizontally) single-lamp fluorescent strip light*
	Surface-mounted (vertically) fluorescent strip light*
	Surface-mounted track with track-mount converter fixture
	Recessed track with track-mount converter fixture
O	Recessed incandescent downlight; to include floodlamp and bar hangers

*   Lights to include energy-saving ballast and fluorescent tube lamps as required by designer's specifications.

Store Name _____
Store No./Location _____
Completion Date _____
Job Telephone _____
Job FAX _____

Store Planner _____
Address _____
City, State _____
Telephone _____
FAX _____

REFLECTED CEILING/LIGHTING LEGEND	Job # _____ Date _____ Sheet _____

SYMBOL	DESCRIPTION
⬦	Recessed, adjustable, incandescent accent light; to include spotlamp and bar hangers
⬦→	Recessed, adjustable, incandescent accent light; to include floodlamp and bar hangers
▣	Shallow recessed downlight furnished with bar hangers
 ☀	Ceiling outlet for chandelier light to be determined by owner's choice
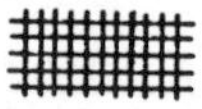 ▦	Standard industrial double-lamp fluorescent fixture*
⊗	Exit sign with battery standby, stencil face type, red on white, dual voltage, universal mount**
▭	Open-cell (1/2" x 1/2" x 1/2") plastic eggcrate

*   Lights to include energy-saving ballast and fluorescent tube lamps as required by designer's specifications.
** With directional arrows as indicated on plan.

Store Name _____

Store No./Location _____

Completion Date _____

Job Telephone _____

Job FAX _____

Store Planner _____

Address _____

City, State _____

Telephone _____

FAX _____

POWER/ELECTRICAL LEGEND

Job # _____   Date _____

Sheet _____

SYMBOL	DESCRIPTION
⊙	Floor outlet; 110V with ground
 ⊖	Wall outlet; 110V with ground
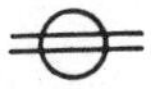 ⊜	Duplex wall outlet; 110V with ground
 ⟨○⟩	Outlet by fixture contractor; with ground (mounted as part of fixture)
 ⟨⊜⟩	Duplex outlet by fixture contractor; with ground (mounted as part of fixture)
○	Communication outlet
Ⓙ	Junction box; floor mounted
 Ⓙ̄	Junction box; mounted above ceiling
 Ⓙ⊢	Junction box; wall mounted
Ⓙ	Junction box by fixture contractor (mounted as part of fixture)
△	Telephone outlet
$	Cash register
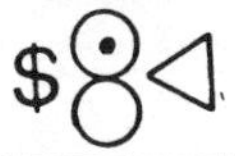 $⊙◁	Cash-and-wrap location
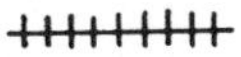 ++++++++	Horizontally mounted plugmold with outlets 6" on center; (mount as indicated above finished floor)

Store Name _____
Store No./Location _____
Completion Date _____
Job Telephone _____
Job FAX _____

Store Planner _____
Address _____
City, State _____
Telephone _____
FAX _____

POWER/ELECTRICAL LEGEND	Job # _____ Date _____ Sheet _____

SYMBOL	DESCRIPTION
+	Vertically mounted plugmold
Ⓐ	Antenna floor outlet
Ⓐ⊣	Antenna wall outlet
[A]	Vertically mounted antenna track
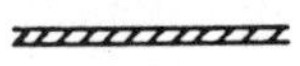 /////////	Horizontally mounted antenna track
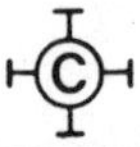 ⊢©⊣	Ceiling-mounted clock
©⊣	Wall-mounted clock
[S]	Security system device
AFF	Above finished floor
FM	Antenna used for radios
P	Public pay telephone
TV	Antenna used for television (VHF and UHF)

PLUMBING LEGEND   Job # _____   Date _____

Sheet _____

SYMBOL	DESCRIPTION
(wh)	Water heater; see plans for specifications
(D)	Waste drain with vent
(H)	Hot water supply
(C)	Cold water supply
[EWF]	Electrical water fountain
[D]	Floor drain
[S]	Sink; see plans for specifications
(□)	Other special requirements

Store Name _____

Store No./Location _____

Completion Date _____

Job Telephone _____

Job FAX _____

Store Planner _____

Address _____

City, State _____

Telephone _____

FAX _____

COLOR LEGEND

Job # _____   Date _____

Sheet _____

SYMBOL	DESCRIPTION
☐	Paint
 △	Colored lacquer
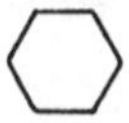 ⬡	Wallcovering
 ◇	High–pressure laminate
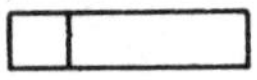 ▭	Special finish
 ○	Floorcovering

Store Name _____
Store No./Location _____
Completion Date _____
Job Telephone _____
Job FAX _____

Store Planner _____
Address _____
City, State _____
Telephone _____
FAX _____

LEGEND OF FREESTANDING STORE FIXTURES	Job # _____ Date _____ Sheet _____

SYMBOL	DESCRIPTION
	DIVISION 001–099 SHOWCASES AND ACCESSORIES
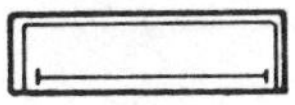	001–039 Showcases and fills
	040–059 Back islands and fills
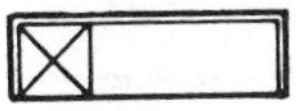	060–079 In-line cash-and wraps
	080–099 Miscellaneous fixtures
	DIVISION 100–199 HIGH-PRESSURE LAMINATE CASEWORK
	100–109 Drawered tables / variations of shapes
	110–119 Display platforms / variations of shapes
	120–139 Tables / variations of shapes or configuration
	140–149 Round tables / variations
	150–159 Desks

Store Name _____
Store No./Location _____
Completion Date _____
Job Telephone _____
Job FAX _____

Store Planner _____
Address _____
City, State _____
Telephone _____
FAX _____

LEGEND OF FREESTANDING STORE FIXTURES

Job # _____   Date _____

Sheet _____

SYMBOL	DESCRIPTION
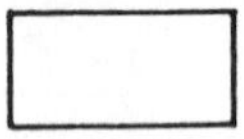	160–179 Miscellaneous fixtures
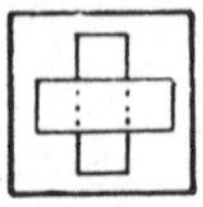	180–199 Bases with risers
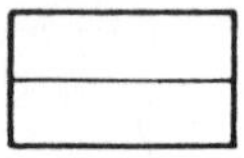	**DIVISION 200–299 GONDOLAS, SUPERSTRUCTURES, AND FRAMES**
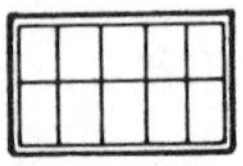	**DIVISION 300–399 GLASS CUBE ASSEMBLIES**
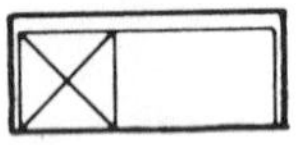	**DIVISION 400–499 CASH-AND-WRAPS AND CUSTOMER SERVICE COUNTERS**
	DIVISION 500–599 MISCELLANEOUS CUSTOM FIXTURES
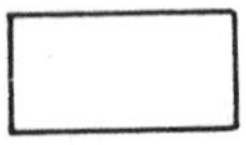	500–549 Custom-designed fixtures
	550–599 Manufacturer's fixtures (see accessory spec)

Store Name _____
Store No./Location _____
Completion Date _____
Job Telephone _____
Job FAX _____

Store Planner _____
Address _____
City, State _____
Telephone _____
FAX _____

LEGEND OF FREESTANDING STORE FIXTURES	Job # _____ Date _____ Sheet _____

SYMBOL	DESCRIPTION
	DIVISION 600–699 GARMENT AND VENDOR RACKS
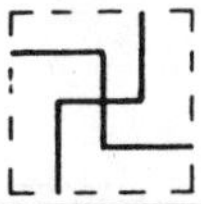	600–649 Garment racks (see rack legend)
	650–699 Vendor racks (verify size)
	**DIVISION 700–799 PERIMETER CASEWORK**
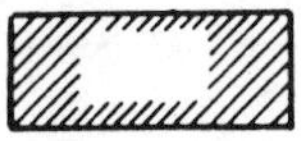	**DIVISION 800–899 REFURBISHED EXISTING FIXTURES**
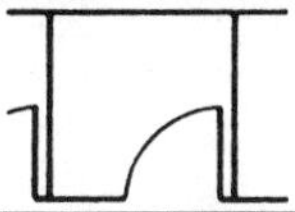	**DIVISION 900–999 FITTING ROOMS**

Store Name _____
Store No./Location _____
Completion Date _____
Job Telephone _____
Job FAX _____

Store Planner _____
Address _____
City, State _____
Telephone _____
FAX _____

RACK LEGEND

Job # _____   Date _____
Sheet _____

SYMBOL	DESCRIPTION
	36" Round rack
	36" Three-level rack
	36" x 60" Straight gondola rack
	36" x 60" 6-way rack
	4-way rack with 21" arms
	4-way rack with 16" arms
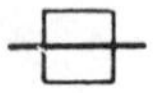	30" T-stand
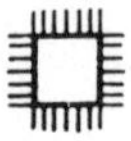	24" x 24" Pronged rack

Chapter 17

MERCHANDISE PRESENTATION TECHNIQUES

Presentation Plan

In order to effectively present merchandise and stimulate sales, there must be a well-thought-out presentation plan. Part of this plan should give attention to theme departments, simulated "shops," and departments singled out for special attention.

The plan should categorize the stock supporting each department by stock classification, subclassification, type, and coloring. And it should make suggestions like the following:

• When presenting goods on surfaces such as cubes, bins, showcases, tables, and shelves, both composition and color should be taken into consideration in the arrangement of the goods.

• Vertical hanging of merchandise on perimeter walls and floor racks should be attractively displayed and neat in appearance. Extra interest can be created by alternating faceout and staggered shoulder arrangements on hangrods.

• Merchandise at the aisle line should be appealingly arranged to invite the customer into the department. A view unobstructed to the perimeter walls will bring attention to merchandise deeper into the department.

• The placement of fixture types and sizes should be planned so that small-scale fixtures start at the aisle line, with fixtures getting progressively larger toward the center and back of the department; racks graduate in height without blocking the view of goods at the perimeter walls.

• Advertised and other featured merchandise should be displayed as prominently as appropriate.

• Special creative displays can be focal points within departments by using build-ups, forms, mannequins, platforms, and other devices. Any fixture design or color that calls more attention to itself than the merchandise it holds should be avoided, with the exception of special vendor-supplied fixtures.

• Control points and sight lines should be clearly established so good visibility, along with control, is assured for each classification.

• Sales personnel should be well trained in the critical task of keeping the merchandise neat, rack to rack, along with dusting the showcases and glass daily.

Making the Best Use of Showcases

The principle purpose of a showcase is to present small items as attractively as possible and to provide security for valuables and better-quality items. Most showcases are used for cosmetics, better jewelry, costume jewelry, crystal, handbags, accessories, men's furnishings, and electronics. Sit-down showcases are sometimes required for cosmetics, layette, bridal, silver, or stationery counters.

Full-vision, one-third-vision, and two-thirds-vision showcases usually are used in cosmetics and jewelry areas, with the type depending on density of merchandise and store type.

When placed at the aisle, the showcase line can help direct traffic, add atmosphere, and help establish a "transaction area." Showcases usually are placed in heavy-traffic sections.

Customers can be expected to ask for service whenever showcase merchandise is displayed; that is why sales personnel should always be assigned to showcase areas. Each showcase island or case line should have sales transaction capability. Trundling customers to a second location to complete a sale is an inconvenience that is not always satisfactory.

Special tips to remember when choosing and using showcases:

• Decide which are the high-risk items from a security standpoint, and act accordingly (i.e., don't use an open-front showcase for expensive items).
• Better jewelry should be sold in one-third-vision showcases with drawers on clerk's side for back stock.
• If full-vision showcases are used for costume jewelry, limit the number of shelves to three.
• When full-vision showcases are used to display cosmetics, the products should be well stocked and arranged in organized fashion. Mirrored end panels and sliding doors help this merchandise to look more tempting.
• If one-third- or two-thirds-vision showcases are used, stock should be placed in drawers, not behind sliding doors.
• Showcases requiring locks should have like keys or be keyed to the back island. There is hardly

anything more bothersome than needing different keys for every showcase.
• Showcase top glass should be fastened to the frame.
• A simple clean-design showcase will stand the test of time.
• Fabric pad installed (loosely) in a showcase helps to bring attention to merchandise on lower shelves.
• Each showcase should be electrified and illuminated.
• The interior should be neutral in color so as not to conflict with merchandise.
• Showcase fills help to complete the configuration on the plan.
• Showcase length should be 3, 4, 5, or 6 feet. Showcases larger than 6 feet are difficult to relocate and expensive to manufacture and ship.

Fitting Rooms

Fitting rooms are an integral part of the selling environment and are silent salespeople. Changes in design have been made for the convenience of the customer and as an aid to salespeople monitoring rooms and merchandise.

Planning the Fitting Room

There are several considerations in keeping fitting rooms functional. The size of the standard modular room is 4' x 4' or 4' x 5'. The finish should be a high-pressure laminate, heavy-duty vinyl, chrome, or baked enamel, each of which is easy to clean. (Painted surfaces clean less well and must be frequently repainted.) Carpeting is a must. Tile floors are rarely free of dust and shoe scuffs.

Fitting rooms should be equipped with a bench worked into the frame. (Chairs wear out, can be moved, or can hinder a cleaning crew.) A full-length mirror (2' x 5') and a shelf for purses and packages should be included. The mirror should be attached to the wall with a silicon seal to thwart shoplifters who remove sales tags from unsold merchandise and hide them behind mirrors. Ceiling tiles should be secured if they are in reach. Louvered doors sometimes deter shoplifters.

When fitting rooms are of neutral color, they are less distracting and less likely to conflict with the clothing being tried on. A wall-mounted fluorescent fixture placed 8 feet above the finished floor will illuminate both the fitting-room interior and the aisle, providing a softer level of illumination. A white ceiling will give maximum light reflection. Sometimes a lower ceiling is used (9 feet) to call less attention to the ceiling.

Standard doors are 4 feet high and 2 feet wide and should be attached 1 foot from the floor to permit the legs and head of customers to be seen. A continuous magnetic-strip lock or catch is best for securing the door. Draperies are costly and constantly need cleaning and replacement.

Locating Fitting Rooms

Placement of the fitting rooms within a space requires careful planning. Locating fitting rooms near cash-and-wrap stations means benefits for both customer and retailer. Retailers accomplish several things with this arrangement: First, close proximity of fitting rooms to cash-and-wrap centers helps control shoplifting because thieves are less bold with clerks nearby; second, clerks can better observe the number of customers who need attention while still attending to the cash-and-wrap station. Customers are more likely to make their purchases quickly without having to wander through the department looking for help. Customers are always delighted with a system that improves service and makes their shopping experience easier.

Once the system is in place, it is important to train the staff to use the system to its best advantage. Clerks at cash-and-wraps obviously cannot see through fitting rooms, so special monitoring of the fitting room is needed to maximize service and minimize shoplifting.

If possible, alteration shops should be located near fitting rooms complete with a service bell at the point of fitting to alert the tailor or seamstress that a visitor is present. (For security reasons, altered garments should be stored in a separate stock area adjacent to the service counter.)

Fitting-Room Systems

There are several fitting-room systems:

1. Modular prefabricated tandem system (metal and laminate board)
2. Freestanding (4 feet x 4 feet movable unit)
3. Wood post-and-panel system

Tandem fitting rooms are tied together using a common metal dividing post and panel to separate fitting rooms. Wood post-and-panel systems are also installed in tandem. Tandem metal- or wood-post fitting rooms offer a cost savings due to common dividing walls or partitions.

An individual 4-foot movable fitting-room module can accommodate shifts in merchandise requirements, serve more than one area, and act to separate classifications or departments. This type is excellent for swing-shop areas in ready-to-wear, children's, and sporting goods department.

Among the arrangements for fitting rooms is a corner-fitting setup, which can add design interest and solve the problem of a deep corner, but wasting floor space should be avoided.

If a bank of fitting rooms is located behind a 7 foot partition, an inviting 3-foot-wide entrance should be planned, allowing a 4-foot depth for the fitting and 3 feet for the aisle. The opposite end will serve as a larger fitting room. If the entrance is centered, two oversized fitting rooms can be had at no extra cost.

Fitting-room banks can be designed to accommodate more than one department. A movable divider, for example, allows the number of fitting rooms serving an area to be contracted or expanded.

Outfitting the Stockroom

The following tips are valuable in planning stockroom areas:

- Stockrooms should be adjacent to selling space whenever possible.
- If the stockroom is used for higher-priced items, holds, or will-call items, doors should be key-locked from two sides.
- When stockrooms are shared by more than one department, panels can be used to subdivide spaces so they can be separately locked.
- If the code permits using the same slotting on movable wall partitions, the systems can be slotted on two sides, making the wall system a better investment.
- A 7-foot-wide stock space will allow double- or triple-hanging space on both walls or a combination of hanging space and shelving.
- Fire-treated wood studs, with heavy-duty surface-mounted hardware 3 feet from the finish floor in a 6-foot length, will allow triple hanging or a maximum of 9 feet of vertical stock space with a 12 foot ceiling.
- A sealed stockroom floor will serve as well as a tile floor, at the same time cutting costs.

- Entrances to stockrooms through fitting rooms should be discouraged because they increase the risk of shoplifting.
- Stockrooms can serve as expansion areas for fitting room expansion if planned 7 feet wide.

Making the Best Use of Racks

Every clothing or ready-to-wear department has racks for hanging and displaying merchandise. Store owners usually are interested in knowing about the new styles of racks and will have opinions about racks with which they have had good experiences. Sturdy racks are the best buy for the long haul.

Many retailers still use 36-inch or 48-inch round-track racks, but three-way adjustable models are more commonly used today. Round racks limit the display of merchandise to the shoulder of the garment, but they are still the most reliable staple in many retail operations. Three-way racks are useful for distinguishing colors, groupings, and collections in ready-to-wear departments. The choice of four-way racks, with either straight arms and/or waterfall brackets, depends on the density of merchandise and the kind of presentation desired. T-stands many times are placed next to four-way racks, along the aisle, to display smaller groupings of merchandise. Six-way racks are useful for showing a variety of coordinates.

Straight racks are an old format, yet some retailers still prefer them. All hanging racks should be fully adjustable. The planner should be concerned with the amount of flexibility available with adjustable racks and should learn to take advantage of all the benefits that have been designed.

Questions worth asking are: What is the maximum length of the merchandise that will hang on each rack? Will the rack accommodate more than one type of merchandise? What is the type of tubing and gauge of the steel? What type of rack should be used for featured merchandise? Will the customer notice the difference in rack designs? Will the rack overpower the merchandise? Are the racks designed to be easily folded for removal when the inventory is low? Have enough racks been selected to merchandise small groupings? How many levels of display can be viewed?

The four-way (or quad) rack, the three-way round rack, and T-stands are the most commonly used in ready-to-wear departments. Before placing an order the planner should find out whether the racks are in stock and when delivery can be expected.

Ten Rules for Selecting Racks

The following rules for rack selection should be followed in finding the right racks for the requirements:

1. See the fixture with merchandise on it (or photos of it) prior to ordering.
2. Remember retailers are selling merchandise, not fixtures. The right fixture will not upstage, or obscure, the merchandise.
3. Buy the type of quality fixtures that will be in service for a long time.
4. Buy the fixture best designed to present the item to be sold, not just to fill a space on the floor. Remember: Fixtures are silent salespeople.
5. Buy fixtures that are compatible with each other and with existing fixtures or finishes.
6. Make sure the fixtures help to clearly identify the merchandise. The better the fixture, the less the signage required.
7. Choose fixtures that are simple to clean and that do not have to be maintained frequently.
8. Choose well-designed fixtures—they are usually safe fixtures that will not bruise ankles and shins, for example, and that are sturdy and steady.
9. Critique fixtures one by one: Will they help sell merchandise? Why? Why not?
10. Review the checklist on the following page before you select or purchase a rack.

Specialty Shops

Store areas such as designer, bridal, juniors, and young men's departments need to be especially distinctive in the overall design, yet all must flow together and have a coordinated look. Such specialty shops need an individual character that sets them apart from adjacent departments but does not make them look like an uncoordinated part of the whole.

The degree of sophistication of the design should be based on the classification of merchandise and trends in the industry. The atmosphere also should reflect the tastes of the customer. Specialty shops require extra staffing at all times, whether open or enclosed.

Speciality shops can require design changes as quickly as the merchandise can. Major efforts expended to maintain flexibility of design will pay continuing dividends. Built-in concepts are costly to build, maintain, and staff.

CHROME RACK SPECIFICATION GUIDELINES

1. Size of Tubing _____ X _____
2. Gauge of Rack Steel Tubing (16 Ga.) _____
3. Gauge of Steel Rods _____
4. Gauge of Extenders (16 Ga.) _____
5. Gauge of Base Stock _____
6. Finish of Raw Tubing (Polished) _____
7. Type of Finish (Polished Mirror Chrome) _____
8. Type of Spring and Button Mechanism and Spacing _____
9. Type of Mechanical Fittings (Mfg.) _____
10. Type of Spring-Load Mechanism _____
11. Type of ElectroPlating on Plastic or Metal Caps _____
12. Type of Stretchers _____
13. Type of Spotwelds, Grinding, and Finishing _____
14. Lengths of Extenders (Hangrods or Arms) _____
15. Lengths of Waterfall and Spacing of Pins _____
16. Metal Lugs Welded into Tube Gauge _____
17. Type of Screw, Thread, and Head Type _____
    Allen _____ Phillips _____ Straight _____
18. Type and Manufacturer of Bolts _____
19. Type of Leveler _____
20. Type of Ball Caster _____
21. Type of Set Screws _____
22. Type of Clamp or Arm _____
23. Thickness of Glass Top _____
24. Type of Rubber Pads to Rest Glass on _____
25. Adjustable Heights from _____" to _____"
26. Type of Sign Fitting _____
27. Thickness of Plastic Accessories _____
28. Metal or Plastic Caps _____

Speciality areas are valuable for drawing the shopper's attention to a particular segment of a department, even though they require additional coverage and expense. Walk-in concepts can be valued in helping to set these entities apart from the rest of the store.

Store design concepts today put more stress on economy and value than in the recent past. This seems to have led to a more relaxed, if not less sophisticated, approach to retailing. Shoppers, in particular, want shopping to be a comfortable, unhurried experience in a sophisticated setting. The key to creating this pleasant, quality environment in a specialty area is the proper choice of decor, both for the space and the perimeter walls. This means no trendy or outdated fixtures and decor that spoil the mood or detract from the quality image of the merchandise.

Such walls and partitions should not hide merchandise on the opposite side. When additional wall space is needed (if less than ceiling height), flexibility can be gained with double-sided fixture systems that allow merchandising from both sides.

Fashion-Story Presentations

In ready-to-wear departments, loose casework and properly fixtured walls can be used to heighten awareness of special fashion lines, in other words, to present "a fashion story." Staggered rods with faceouts create a fuller view for ready-to-wear goods. Hangrods should have a minimum of five to seven garments per foot of length. A glass cube should have a minimum of three to ten shirts.

When well-displayed merchandise sells down, you can establish a more prominent focal point of display and reduce congestion by eliminating floor fixtures and racks to reclaim the space for new promotional merchandise.

Cash-and-Wrap

A well-designed cash-and-wrap station should be placed strategically to control fitting-room entrances, near the center of the department's general space, if possible. When not used within a case line, cash-and-wraps should be placed in pairs within ready-to-wear areas. It should be planned to provide all the basic functions of transacting business.

Tables

Tables with drawers used in the presentation of merchandise are enclosed fixtures that generally contain stock reserves underneath, either in drawers or behind sliding doors, while utilizing the upper horizontal surface for flat merchandise presentation. Drawered tables should only be used when constant restocking is necessary.

Tables are still in widespread use, even though they are being replaced in many instances by new merchandising and fixture concepts that house and display goods more effectively.

Laminate plastic finishes used on tables should match carpet colors. Tables can serve as efficient fixtures for self-servicing of flat goods; a minimum of 3 to 4 feet should be kept between tables. No more than two 30-inch x 60-inch modules should be placed together. If a third is added, it should face out on the aisle line and be used for sales promotion. This is known as an endcap display.

With a standard height of 28 to 30 inches, each pair of tables should incorporate a riser bringing attention to the merchandise on the table. Reversible rimmed tops add flexibility. Drawers, even though more expensive than sliding doors, are more effective. Sliding doors never seem to get closed by the clerk and the interior stock always looks messy.

Presentation (or Parsons) tables are useful, singly or in a grouping, for featuring new classifications. The size of a table used for display promotions should be 30 inches wide and 28 inches high and either 48 or 60 inches long. It should have a high-pressure laminate covering or a wood finish. Carpet inserts that match the department carpeting can be incorporated at staggered heights into table designs for shoes, luggage, lamps, and electronics.

Perimeter Shams and Case Goods

Perimeter shams and case goods should be (1) covered in high-pressure laminate (in the same color as the carpet); (2) a maximum of 28 inches high, 24 inches deep, and 48 inches long; and (3) finished on four sides.

Modular shelf units can be used against a wall to create room for added flat stock. They should not be used with hanging merchandise. When relocated from the wall to floor space, they can be turned into a base for a superstructure. A superstructure is a frame in which shelves can be added. Built-up wall shams without drawers are movable, more economical, and simpler to use.

Display Cubes

Display cubes—hollow, square, hexagonal, or wood—are used in clusters to show item stores in departments such as housewares, giftware, china, shoes, and electronics. Cubes usually vary in height from 15 inches to 30 inches. Widths can be variable. High-pressure laminates, mirrors, and carpets all make strong and lasting finishes for such multiple uses. Mirrors (gray, silver, and bronze) are good for displaying glassware, giftware, and china. Carpet works better for heavier goods, such as lamps, electronics, and luggage, where scratching occurs. Carpeting also works as a soft background for shoes. Carpet inserts should match the color of laminate plastics.

Grouped display cubes do more to attract the

casual impulse buyer than cubes placed individually. Display cubes need spots of incandescent light that are brighter than those for surrounding areas.

Museum Cubes

Museum cubes are excellent for displaying a variety of items, including cosmetics, better accessories, and electronics. When cubes are placed at mall entrances or at the center of aisles, they alert the shopper to a featured item. Cubes can be used successfully in pairs by varying the height of the 18-inch cube on a high-pressure laminate base.

Glass Cubes

Systems of glass cubes are offered in both plate or tempered glass, with connectors that are metal, transparent, or wood. They are effective for showing shirts, sweaters, linens, domestics, and giftware and should be placed on a base that is a minimum of 6 to 18 inches high. Some retailers like to add ball casters for ease of movement.

Accent Fixtures

Accent fixtures can be introduced into specialty areas to facilitate viewing of different groupings, enhance otherwise routine fixture designs, and help bring contracting differences to items of merchandise.

Gondola Displays

Next to the showcases, tables, and platforms, gondolas are among the oldest and most reliable fixture types in use by merchants today. Gondolas are island-type self-serve fixtures with back-to-back tiered shelves or hangings. Gondolas have taken different shapes over the years but still provide the same basic function: elevating merchandise to be displayed, signed, and sold.

It is best not to use more than one or two units in line or more than 10 feet of fixture. Gondolas can be designed with end panels added to accommodate additional goods.

Frames can be altered in many ways through the creative use of hardware accessories such as brackets, hangrods, angular shelves, metal shelves, bases, glass, and prongs. This flexibility is especially useful when displaying housewares, stationery, gifts, auto accessories, toys, sport goods, and so on. The fixture designs of today are especially innovative for housewares, stationery, and domestics.

Reworking of used frames can be both economical and expensive, depending on requirements and approach. Gondolas with plexi-center panels or endcaps give special attention to featured items, yet permit easy viewing of the other classifications as well. The fixture end panel helps detract from the sameness of the stereotype gondolas and can add an element of function or decor.

Plexi

Plexi shelves and case goods are most durable when fabricated at a thickness of 3/8 inch and are less likely to sag and crack; however, they will scratch.

Reflective plexi (silver, bronze, or colored) on cornices and slatwalls can be used to accent an area.

Fixtures manufactured from standard sheet sizes are economical since there is less scrap. These fixtures can have limited durability, so invest wisely.

Display Platforms

Display platforms are expensive to build and maintain and are difficult to move. Show-window platforms, which tend to be more flexible and movable, make better alternatives. They can be covered with a carpet, high-pressure laminate, or wood that matches or complements the floor. They can be used in groupings of various heights to add visual impact. Platform heights of 12 inches, 18 inches, 24 inches, and 30 inches are recommended.

The idea of a display platform, of course, is to highlight featured items. The platforms can be used at aisle lines, behind the first row of merchandise on the aisle, at the end of a secondary aisle, or next to a stairway. At rear walls, they should be used in special circumstances only.

Display platforms differ in size and shape, but all, regardless of height, should be 36 inches across. Smaller ones (of 30 inches or less) can be used, but they must be large enough to accommodate a mannequin base. Platforms that people can trip over and bump into easily should be avoided as should very large or high platforms unless they are needed to solve a particular problem or create a special effect. Access panels to floor power help to electrify seasonal trim. Built-in display areas tend to be expensive to maintain and can limit flexibility.

Mannequins should be placed on platforms for two reasons:

- Platforms help maximize the mannequin's visibility.
- They help protect an expensive investment.

In general, it is best to avoid overpowering displays that may interfere with viewing of any department.

Corners should be square or radial. Radial corners cost more to make and are desirable where carpet coverings are involved. Remember, the client must have an adequate staff to maintain the number of display platforms they are requesting.

The plan should also provide a sound answer to one final question, which is, "What type of lighting will accent the merchandise on the platform in the display area?" Incandescent spots (five times the foot-candle level of general lighting) bring extra attention to merchandise.

Freestanding Fixtures

Any racks selected should conform to rigid manufacturing and design specifications. Simple designs are best since they are less likely to compete with merchandise for customer attention.

Specially designed fixtures made in small quantities cost far more than standard items. Frame systems often can be found that will serve more than one merchandising function to cut costs. It is best to forget about homemade fixtures unless they can be fabricated with the appearance of quality.

Ceilings and Lighting

Ceilings often attract more attention than they should. The trend today is to make them less obvious by using toned colors, textures, and lighting. The main purpose of lighting is not to illuminate the ceiling but to flatteringly illuminate the goods being sold.

The choice of ceiling colors should vary with the space available and the type of store involved. Lighter ceilings reflect more light; darker ceilings absorb more light. In larger open spaces, neutral or taupe tones suggest a softer, longer-lasting effect. Most ready-to-wear specialty stores have neutral, taupe, or off-white ceilings, although accent colors often are added to call extra attention to a department. Track lighting fixtures can be painted in a color that is the same or close to the color of the ceiling so less attention is diverted to the fixtures.

The lay-in, T-grid, ceiling tile system is perhaps the most common ceiling system for merchandising applications. Some store designs incorporate more than one ceiling system into a large space including metal, plasterboard, open grids, and so on.

The 2' x 2' or 2' x 4' grid accommodates standard light reflectors and fixture housings. Several ceiling systems in use today are suspended from the structure of the building. Other effects, such as skylighting, can be incorporated to add drama to the lighting environment. After examining all requirements, the plan should be developed by a lighting engineer competent to judge the lighting specifications and recommend sound improvements.

Continuous strip lighting can be located behind a cornice or curtain wall to illuminate the perimeter. Other options are track lighting, lamps recessed in soffit, tracks, and spotlights. All can be used effectively to add visibility, improve color rendition, attract attention, and deliver cosmetic results.

The lighting plan for the ceilings must complement and reinforce the overall design concept. Each fixture should be chosen to satisfy a particular need: to improve ambient lighting conditions, to add "seeability," to wash a wall with light, or to spotlight a featured product. A well-planned lighting system is a silent salesperson that helps stimulate impulse buying. Properly designed ceiling lighting creates an inviting atmosphere that interacts with the merchandise, walls, freestanding fixtures, and displays.

It is important that both lighting and floor plans correlate well with the final high-wall and freestanding-fixture plans.

Customer Seating

One of the most appreciated amenities that a retailer can provide for customers is an ample supply of chairs for those weary times when they must await service or a shopping companion.

The most logical departments for special seating are the shoe department, men's clothing, fashions, bridal registry, specialty shop, and custom drapery. Special seating also may be required in demonstration, cosmetics, and general customer service areas. The finish of the seating should be easy to maintain, and the fabrics should be of commercial quality.

Signage

Interior store signage brings immediate identification to a department or an individual classification of merchandise. The signage package for the perimeter of a store should have continuity in size, style, placement, and height and must be presented in an attractive manner. Signage can be installed on perimeter walls, curtain walls, cornices, columns, and so on. Smaller signage is also used with fixtures, such as interior showcase signage. Accent signage of different material and size can be used to draw attention to a specialty shop or department. Many times, the signage will be one of the final items that will be reviewed and established in the sequence of the project. The style, shape, and size, along with the finish of the signage, are important in capturing customers' attention.

Chapter 18

PRESENTATION TECHNIQUES FOR
PERIMETER MERCHANDISE

Introduction

In order to develop a concept to present merchandise on the perimeter walls of the store, a store planner must understand how the merchandise will look from the aisle line or the edge of the aisle. The visibility of the perimeter walls will be interrupted with various sorts of floor racks and case good items. Therefore, it is important to create a concept that will draw keen attention to merchandise on the walls. Perimeter walls are considered some of the most valuable real estate within a retail store because they act as the backdrop for the merchandise presentation and help the customer immediately identify what classification of merchandise is represented in each area of the store.

Merchandising-presentation systems—hangrods, faceouts, prongs, shelves, binning, and so on—are used to provide mechanics to support the merchandise presentation. Each type of merchandise will require a different format of presentation. Sportswear and clothing, for example, are hung on hangrods, either rectangular or oval. A hangrod system displays the profile of the merchandise, whereas a waterfall or faceout bracket displays the face or front of the merchandise. Within one section of a store, it may be desirable to use hangrods and waterfall or faceout brackets in interesting combinations. In another area of the store, shelves or bins may be required to display other merchandise.

Retail stores are designed with mechanical systems—known as "surface-mounted" or "recessed-standard"—that are incorporated into the wall-finish system and allow for the weight of the brackets and hardware, as well as the merchandise to be displayed, to be properly supported by the wall system.

In the planning and designing of a retail store, the merchandise presentation of the perimeter walls is used to draw the customer into the department and to the back wall. Visual displays are also incorporated into the merchandising of some perimeter walls to help create a story or a theme.

These displays are placed upon the visual merchandising shelves and help focus in on a specific classification of merchandise. Too many displays incorporated into a department are distracting and will not concentrate attention on the center point of the department.

Perimeter-merchandising wall systems should be designed to be moveable and interchangeable throughout the entire store. It is not recommended that more than one mechanical system be used for the support of brackets and hangrods as this will add significant cost to the hardware inventory and future labor, and will limit any single system's usage throughout the store.

When placing any of the faceout hardware on the perimeter walls of the store, the store planner and merchant must be aware of how customers shop, examine, and handle merchandise presented from perimeter walls. The presentation must be simple enough for a customer to readily and easily remove and replace items on hangrods or shelves while at the same time avoiding a perpetual housekeeping problem.

The sales staff is responsible for constantly monitoring these walls to keep them in neat and organized order, which insures consistency in presentation. The illustrative examples in this chapter are intended to give the reader an idea of the advantages and limitations of each presentation technique.

Examples of Perimeter-Merchandise Presentation

Hanging—Single

Merchandise "paraded" on a single hangrod has advantages and disadvantages. The advantage is that you can display a greater quantity of merchandise hanging on a single hangrod; however, the disadvantage is that customers see the shoulders or color of the garment only. Single staggered hangrods should be placed on the wall to create visual interest.

Continuous straight hangrods placed on a wall in long runs are visually tedious and show little imagination in the presentation of merchandise. Single hangrods are used for long garments such as coats, dresses, nightgowns, and any garment where double hanging is not practical.

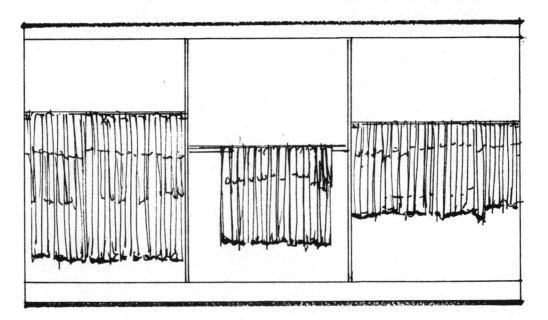

Hanging—Double

Double hangrods suspend shorter merchandise where high capacity is necessary. Double hangrods support merchandise such as shirts, blouses, skirts, shorts, tops, and bottoms.

Double hangrods of 4-foot lengths should be staggered on the wall to create visual interest. Long continuous rows of double hangrods present a dull and static approach to merchandise presentation that actually inhibits sales.

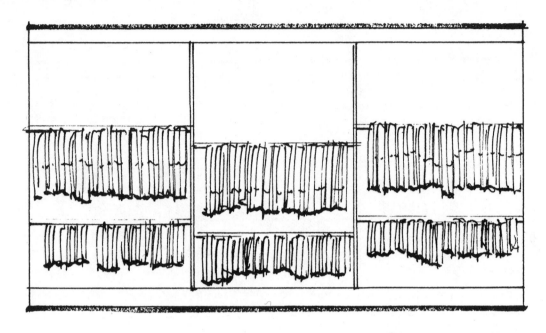

Hanging—Triple

Triple hangrods of staggered 4-foot lengths are placed on a wall to accommodate merchandise of smaller size where large-selection capacity is impor-

tant. Triple hangrods can be used for infants, swimsuits, shorts, and similarly related short merchandise. Monotonously long triple hangrods create an unengaging and "assembly-line" presentation of merchandise that shows scant creativity.

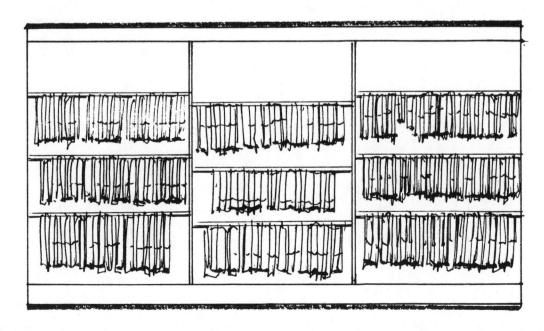

Hanging—Single Faceout, Waterfall

There are two types of single hanging, faceout brackets: waterfall and straight. A waterfall faceout is designed to thrust the merchandise forward. It allows the customer to see the color or pattern of similarly related merchandise. The capacity will be limited to the number of balls, prongs, or pegs on the bracket, which allow for the stepping of the merchandise on anchors.

Single waterfall brackets can be installed in wall standards, on crossbars, or on hangrods and are adjusted to the height of the garment, such as coats, dresses, and shirts.

Hanging—Straight Faceout

The advantage of a straight faceout is that the capacity is usually greater than a waterfall faceout. The drawback is that all the garments are hung on the same plane, which precludes stepped presentation of merchandise. Another drawback of a straight faceout is that you only see the lead garment. Single faceouts can feature long items such as coats, dresses, skirts, and pants.

Hanging—Double Faceout Waterfall

Double waterfall faceouts may be used on a perimeter wall to cascade the stepped presentation of hanging merchandise. Merchandise that can be cascaded in this fashion includes blouses, shirts, skirts, and shorts. Again, the amount of merchandise that can be shown on a waterfall faceout is limited to the number of balls or prongs.

In most cases, a waterfall bracket will be used on the top row with straight faceout brackets on a lower row. The advantage is the ability to see the face of the garment placed on the waterfall.

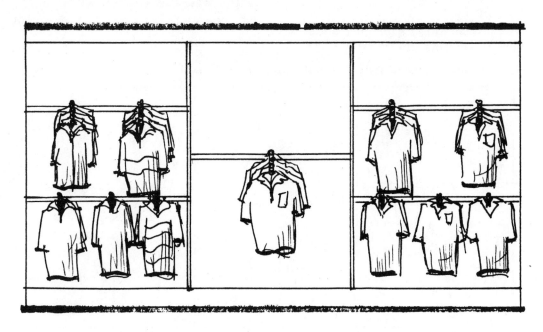

Hanging—Double Straight Faceouts

Double straight faceouts can be installed on a wall where capacity is necessary. These are used for blouses, shirts, skirts, tops, bottoms, and so forth.

The advantage of double faceouts is increased merchandise volume. A shortcoming is that only the facing garment is seen.

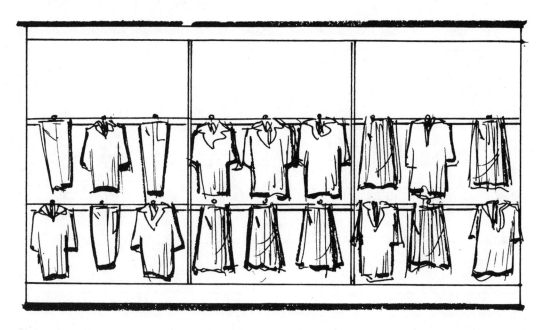

Hanging—Triple Waterfalls or Straight Faceouts

Triple waterfall faceouts are displayed in areas such as infants, swimsuits, and intimate apparel. The height of the waterfall is adjusted to accommodate the size of the merchandise. The number of units on a waterfall is limited to the number of balls or prongs on the waterfall bracket.

This waterfall presentation highlights the colors or detailing within a given garment array.

Triple straight faceouts are used on a wall to show small items such as infants, swimsuits, and intimate apparel. The benefit of a straight faceout is that a greater quantity of merchandise can be hung. The disadvantage is that only the face of the garment is seen. Be sure that the garments on each bracket are all the same size. Uniform sizing on brackets make selection more convenient to the customer.

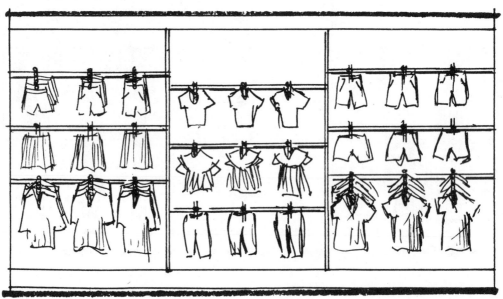

Hanging—Triple Faceouts—Handbags

Handbag faceouts are designed with J-hooks on the underside of the bracket in order to hang the strap of the handbag. The quantity of handbags that can be displayed is limited to the number of hooks. Only one handbag should be hung on each hook. Often

the straps of the handbags are too long and must be adjusted to eliminate overhang or the obstruction of the visibility of the handbag hanging below. Handbags should not be slung on straight faceout brackets, which impede the easy removal of the handbags for customer inspection.

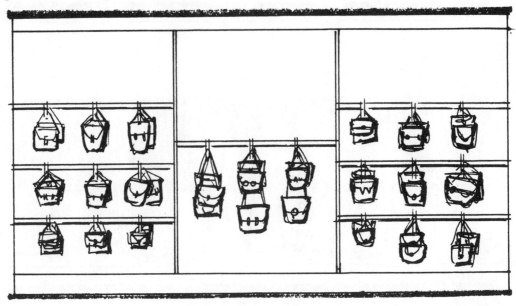

Hanging—Single Hangrod with Waterfall Faceout

This hardware combination has the advantage of allowing the retailer to display the face of the garment and color with high capacity below. Within a 4-foot section, two faceouts can be used above with a single 4-foot hangrod below. This combination can be used in 8- to 12-foot runs or can be staggered on 4-foot sections.

Hanging—Hangrod and Shelf

Hangrods and shelves are often used to hang capacity merchandise with a visual display on the shelf above.

Hanging—Prongs

Prongs are used to face out merchandise such as intimate apparel, housewares, and packaged goods. Prongs should be used for display of merchandise on hangers or merchandise that has been prepack-aged and designed to hang on prongs. The weight of merchandise should be proportionate to the prong size to keep the prong and merchandise from sagging forward.

Hanging—Prongs—Socks

Prongs are also used for the display of socks. Prongs placed in rows create a convenient presentation for the easy selection of color and/or size. The number of rows of prongs on a wall will be determined by the height of the sock and the number of stocking units to be arrayed.

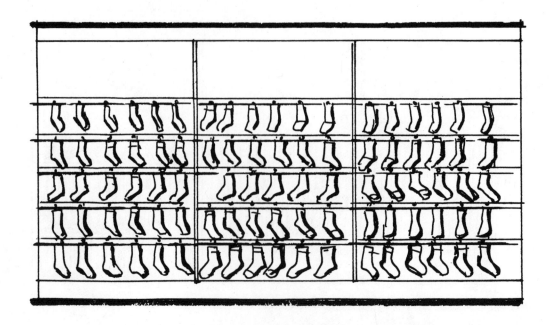

Hanging—Prongs with Base Cabinet Below

Prongs with base cabinets below are used to show merchandise selections such as housewares, prepackaged merchandise, and notions. The base cabinets below, with either doors or drawers, can be used to house back stock of merchandise. The length and diameter of the prongs selected should accommodate merchandise weight and size. When placing prongs on walls, shorter prongs should be used on the top rows with longer prongs on the lower rows.

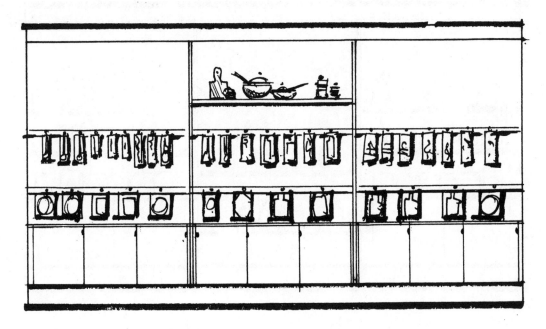

Prongs, Shelves, and Bases

Prongs, shelves and bases can be fixed in areas such as infants' or housewares. Prongs of variable depth can be used to display smaller prepackaged or blister-packed items, while a shelf with glass binning is used to divide segments of merchandise, with a base for larger or boxed items.

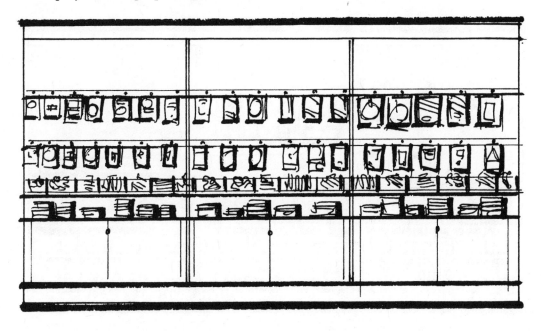

Glass Shelves with Base Cabinet

Shelves with base cabinets can be used in areas such as gifts, housewares, and folded merchandise. These shelves are normally graduated on a wall with depths of 10 to 16 inches. Shelves are placed on the wall to accommodate the vertical height of the merchandise. Bases are used to elevate the merchandise and to prevent damage to merchandise at the floor line.

Shelves with base cabinets can also be used in furnishings, home accessories, or gift areas. These shelves can be graduated in width to accommodate merchandise. The base cabinets can be open with drawers or sliding doors. The base cabinets can be used to store extra merchandise not displayed on the shelves.

Glass Shelves with Laminate Ledge

Glass shelves with laminate ledges can be used in furnishings and gift areas. Glass shelves used in furnishing areas should be a minimum of 16 inches deep to accommodate the width of a folded sweater or dress shirt with a laminate ledge of 20 inches deep. The laminate ledge helps bring weight to the appearance of the wall and safeguards merchandise from floor-line damage.

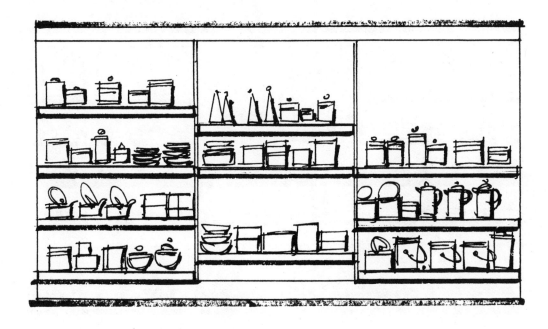

Shelves with Glass Binning and Base Cabinet

Glass shelves with binning are used in housewares and gadget areas. Shelves with glass binning help separate various classifications of merchandise and bring organization to the department where order is essential. Base cabinets below can have drawers or doors and can house back stock of merchandise.

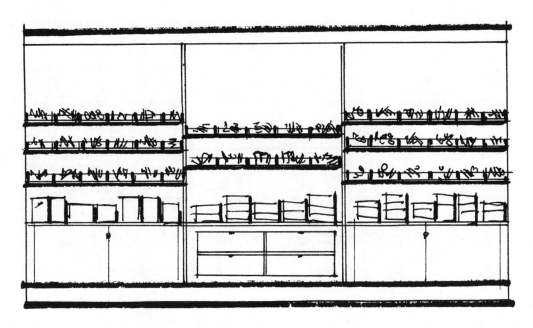

Glass Shelves—Men's Furnishings

Shelves can be used in a men's furnishings area to present dress shirts and sweaters. However, spring-loaded plexiglass dividers must be used on shelves in order to divide the merchandise. If dividers are not used, a shirt wall quickly can become very disorganized and unattractive.

Angular shelves can be used above the shelves that house the shirts to display or model a shirt and tie. Base cabinets can be used with doors or drawers for back stock if needed.

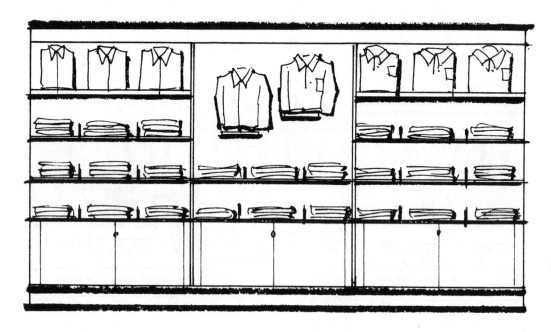

Shelves—High-Pressure Laminate or Metal

High-pressure laminate plastic shelves can be used in any department to exhibit merchandise. However, these shelves do not allow light to penetrate and should be limited to those areas only where heavy merchandise is to be displayed on a wall. These types of shelves should be used only when weight is a factor and when the merchandise will be featured on the front edge of the shelf.

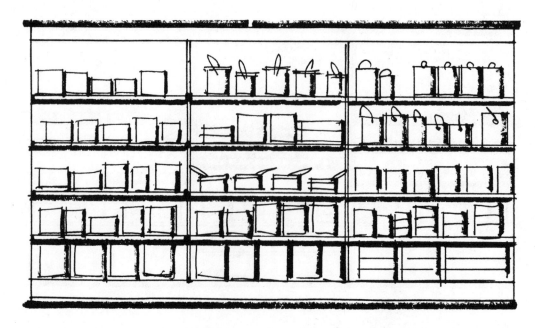

Shelves—Wood or Laminate Plastic

These types of shelves are used in jeans or pants areas. The shelves fabricated out of wood or laminate plastic should be a minimum of 18 to 22 inches deep to accommodate the folded pants. They are installed on a wall in straight runs to insure maximal unit capacity.

Many times, these shelves will be incorporated with a low base fixture that will also house the same merchandise. Pants should be folded so sizes can be easily read from the front of the shelf.

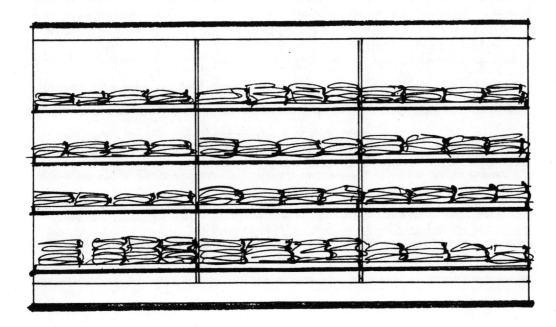

Shelves—Carpet-Covered

Carpet-covered shelves are used in areas such as TVs or electronics. These shelves are built out of wood with rounded edges so the carpet can be wrapped around the shelf's face edge. Since this merchandise is heavy and bulky in size, the carpet allows the merchandise to be moved on and off the shelf with minimal damage to the shelf or item.

Many times, a continuous plugmold strip and cable will be installed on the wall behind the shelf to electrify the component. Optional bases are occasionally used to elevate the merchandise off the floor.

Plexiglass Shelves—Comforters, Quilts, and Spreads

This type of plexiglass shelf is angled upward in order to keep the merchandise erect and supported by the wall surface. These angular shelves bring attention to large, bulky, prepackaged merchandise.

Plexiglass Shelves—Pillows

Angular plexiglass shelves are used to display decorative pillows. These angular shelves help to support the pillow against the rear wall while highlighting colors, sizes, or patterns.

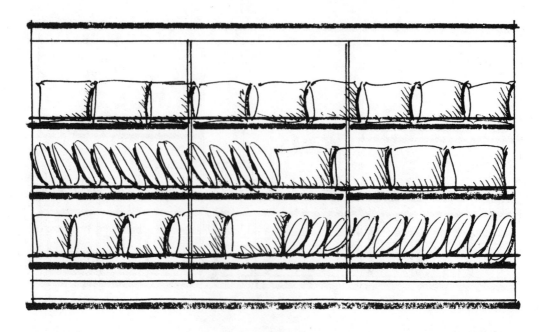

Glass Shelves—Kitchen, Linens, Gifts, or Accessories

Glass shelves of varying depths help to neatly organize linens and other associated merchandise. Shelves bring organization and capacity to areas of the store where flat presentation is desirable. Frequently a base cabinet, outfitted with drawers or doors, will be placed below the shelves for back storage.

Angular Carpet-Covered Wood Shelves—Luggage

Angular wood shelves covered with carpet or laminate plastic can be used to display luggage or related merchandise. The depth of the shelf will be determined by merchandise size. It is important that the underside of the shelves be illuminated with a continuous fluorescent strip light to emphasize the merchandise below. Track lighting or supplemental lighting is suggested to illuminate the face of this merchandise since the shelves are typically deep.

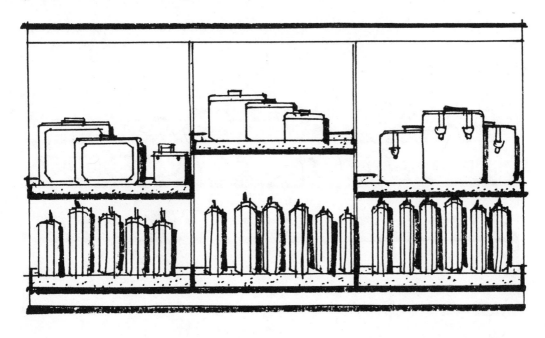

Angular Carpet-Covered Wood Shelves—Men's Shoes

Angular carpet-covered wood shelves are also used in areas for better men's shoes. This type of shelf arrangement helps to show off better shoes; however, they must be illuminated from the underside to pull attention to the next row of shoes below the shelf. Typically, an angular carpet-covered base will also be incorporated.

Fixed Electrified Shelves

Fixed electrified shelves are used in areas such as china, crystal, or gifts. These shelves are designed with a return to hide a continuous fluorescent strip light. This shelf design helps to throw light on the face of the product featured on each shelf.

Glass inserts can also be cut into the top surface of the shelf in order for light to pass through the shelf. It is important to verify the merchandise height before the permanent setting of any shelf.

Glass Cubes—Men's Dress Shirts and Sweaters

Glass cubes are designed to accommodate various types of merchandise. Glass cubes used for men's dress shirts help a retailer organize size, style, and color. Cubes should be designed with a back glass to eliminate the racking, provide stability, and to align the cubes.

These glass-cube systems are joined by a lexon clip or metal screw-type connector. Both tempered and nontempered glass is used for cube construction; however, tempered is highly recommended. Glass cubes should always be situated on a base fixture or cabinet. Bases should provide firm anchoring for the weight and stability of the glass. The glass cube should be sized to accommodate merchandise size. Back glass pieces are recommended to insure stability and eliminate rocking.

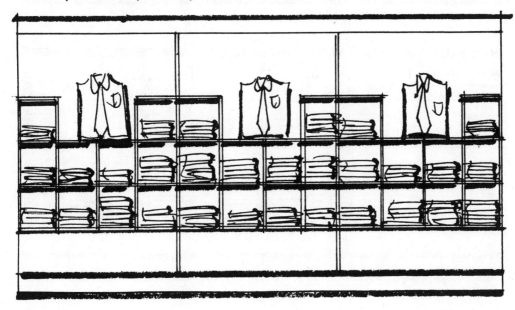

Glass Shelves—Towels

Glass shelves can be used to inventory towels. Shelves are 16 inches deep to accommodate a folded towel. Base cabinets with drawers or doors can be used for back stock; however, this is not recommended.

Shelves above the merchandise line can also be installed to incorporate a foam sham towel display. These shams are designed to focus attention on the merchandise below. The towel is inserted into the foam sham and from a distance appears as multiple towels on display. These towel shams are placed above the merchandise line for display purposes only.

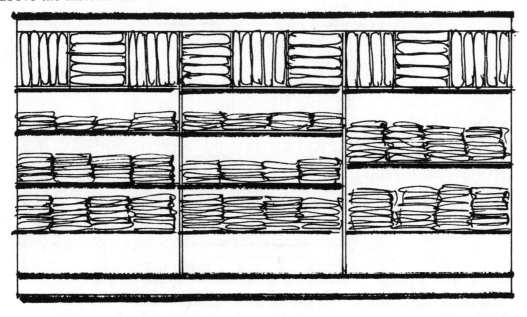

Glass Cubes—Towels

Glass cubes for towels are commonly used today for the hormonious presentation of this type of easily jumbled merchandise. The cube must be sized in order to accommodate the folded towel. Glass cubes help to bring organization and color separation to a towel wall.

Many times, foam sham towel displays will be used above the cubes to attract attention to the towel wall from the aisle line. Glass towel cubes can also be used in the design of freestanding fixtures to house inventory. It is recommended that cubes be firmly stationed on a base or cabinet. Back glass pieces are recommended to insure stability and eliminate rocking.

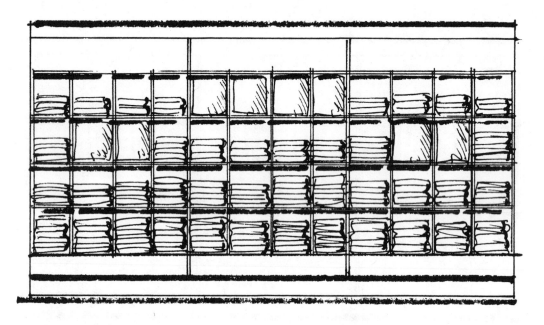

Shelves and Hangrods—Shower Curtains

Shelves with hangrods are used in areas such as shower curtains. The hangrod makes it easy to display the various styles, colors, and patterns of the shower curtains while allowing easy accessibility to stock behind the curtains. The wood shelves are spaced on the wall to accommodate the height of the boxed or packaged merchandise, and the hangrod is supported by a bracket in front of the shelves.

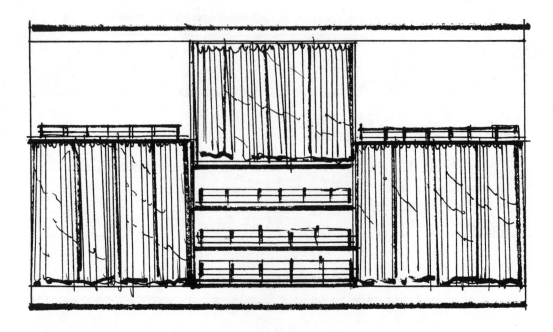

Light Box Windows with Shelves—Curtains

Light boxes can be used above shelves in order to simulate an exterior window for curtains and higher priced shades. Illuminated light boxes help the customer visualize the appearance of the curtains on a window. The shelves below the windows help organize the inventory of merchandise shown above. The depth and size of the shelf is determined by the package size of the merchandise.

Binning–Comforters, Pillows

Wall binning for comforters or pillows is designed to accommodate merchandise size. This binning, in most cases, is built of plywood and painted in a neutral color in order not to compete with its displayed merchandise. The binning is designed as large, vertical boxes with recessed adjustable shelves to accommodate any size or change in the packaging of the merchandise.

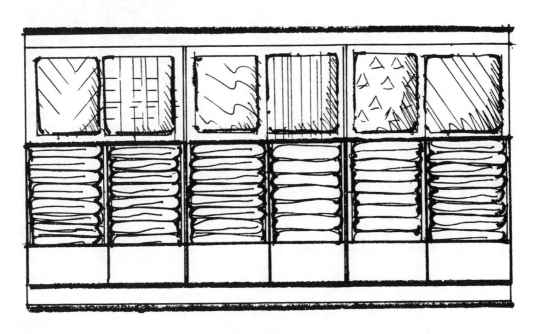

Slatwall or Slotwall

Slatwall has become one of the key building blocks of retail stores. It is used in the design of merchandise presentation systems for both perimeter walls and freestanding fixtures. The overuse of this building material has diminished its popularity with some retailers; however, slatwall is still considered the backbone of many visual presentation formats.

Slatwall can be used to present any type of merchandise. It is commonly used for the presentation of shoes, pronged merchandise presentations, socks, sportswear, housewears, giftware, and so on. Various standard finishes as well as custom-face finishes are available. Inserts of both plastic and metal are used to further strengthen and upgrade the appearance of this material.

This building material is available in both 4-by-8-foot and 4-by-10-foot sheets, with either vertical or horizontal grooving. The spacing of the grooves is typically 3 inches; however, custom spacing of grooves is available through various manufacturers.

When selecting or ordering slatwall, consideration should be given to the core construction, as the core construction will determine the strength and life expectancy of this material. Slatwall is not recommended to support heavy items, as it is not structurally designed to hold excessive weight. Slatwall with metal inserts will support heavier items. Slatwall with plastic inserts is only decorative. This material has the same adjustability and flexibility as perforated-board systems; however, slatwall's overall appearance is more desirable.

Slatwall/Slotwall—Shoes

Brackets are designed to show either the face or side view of a shoe. These brackets are typically fabricated of clear plexiglass to fit into the slot and to support the merchandise adequately. The brackets can be arranged to attractively display the merchandise in an organized manner.

Slatwall/Slotwall—Socks

Metal prongs are inserted in rows to achieve linear display of merchandise. Varying lengths of prongs can be installed from top to bottom of the panel, with shorter prongs at the top and longer prongs at the bottom. Prong length will vary from 4 to 8 inches.

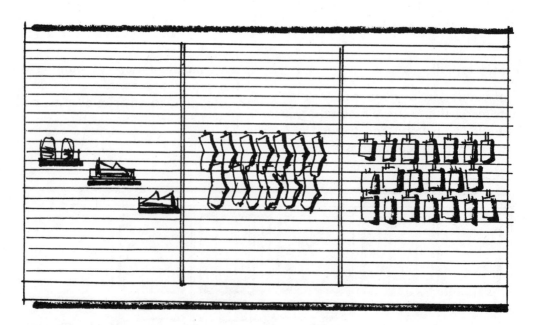

Slatwall/Slotwall—Gadgets and Packaged Goods

Prongs can be arranged on this panel for an attractive display of gadgets and packaged goods. The prongs should be sized accordingly to accommodate the merchandise size and weight.

Chapter 19

METHODS OF DIVIDING STORE INTERIOR CLASSIFICATIONS

Owners and retailers understandably want the best products at the best prices. In preparing the store-planning project for bid, it is wise to divide the bid package into several categories because it helps achieve the best prices possible for clients. The planner and owner can review alternatives in bid pricing from each of several contractors in order to achieve the portion of the project at the best price.

Explaining to contractors how the bid package is broken down aids in getting the most favorable prices from several competitive sources. Projects can be delivered faster when contractors do not have to subcontract any more work than necessary at marked-up prices. Manufacturers tend to carry out their responsibilities more quickly when the planner deals with them directly.

There should be a limit on the number of contractors bidding each portion. When it is apparent that there are more than the usual number of contractors involved, the extent of the competition may cause some companies to decline to bid.

Store fixturing is a specialty. Planners who are qualified in this specialty should recommend which contractors should be asked to bid on which portions of a project. When owners suggest contractors of their own choosing, they are probably planning to buy items (such as racks, showcases, fitting rooms) directly. Some companies that open many new locations annually have standing contracts for the production of store fixtures with contractors whose finished products are acceptable both in quality and price.

By splitting the bidding, burdens put on one manufacturer by project size, density of fixtures, and delivery schedules can be reduced. However, more coordination is required upon installation. Planners should explain to owners that dividing classifications improves chances of a good price while keeping the fixture contractor on his toes.

These are classifications that can be subdivided: showcase line, back island, freestanding laminates, gondolas, glass cube assemblies, metal racks, fitting rooms, and reworking of existing equipment.

Alternate bids should be given when any portion of a project is deleted, such as:

1. Work undertaken by the owner
2. Reworking or demolition

3. New wall work
4. Painting
5. Perimeter decor
6. Glass shelving
7. Perimeter casework
8. Ceiling electrical (and related) work
9. Floorcovering and aisle material

Within freestanding categories, complete bidding instructions may be required.

Legend of Store Fixtures

(See Legend of Freestanding Store Fixtures, Chapter 16, for numerical listing of all fixtures.)

Division 001—050

Full-vision showcases and back islands, one-third-vision showcases, open showcases, self-selection showcases, corner fills, angular fills, counter-height column fills, pedestal cash-and-wrap at case line, miscellaneous fixturing at case line or at perimeter walls, back islands with sliding doors, back island cash-and-wrap, $3/8$" glass shelves, mirrored fronts, mirrored sliding doors, mirrored sides, lexon shelf-edging strip, binning, trays, hardware, brackets, light rails, and miscellaneous items necessary for the installation. All reflectors, light rails, balast, and wiring are installed as per local code and destination.

Division 051—099

Same as above, except wood-case construction covered with plastic laminate.

Division 100—199

Freestanding high-pressure plastic laminate fixtures

All modular and fixed-base platforms, shams, base cabinet with drawers, base cabinet with sliding doors, freestanding base platforms, modular bunkers, continuous perimeter bunkers, drawered tables, sliding door tables, Parsons tables, rimmed tables, risers, build-ups, plastic laminate and wood shelves, and similar fixtures of production runs. Included are build-ups constructed of wood, laminate plastic, metal, glass, plastic slotted hardware, electrical hookups where required, and $3/8$" glass shelves.

Division 200—299
Gondolas, Superstructures, and Frames

All 1" or rectangular metal gondola frames with deck, end panels, center panels, vertical slotting, bracketry $3/8$" glass shelves, laminate plastic shelves, binning, trays, lexon shelf-edging strip, snub-nosed brackets, bracket cross bars, faceouts, prongs, hangrods, shelf supports, rubber cushions, levelers, and miscellaneous items necessary to complete the installation.

Division 300—399
Glass Cube Assemblies

All fixtures consisting of $3/16$" polished edges, glass binning, binning dividers, glass cube clip-assembly system, price ticketing, $3/8$" solid lexon shelf dividers. All plastic vertical or horizontal edging strips and center or back support glass or mirrored panels and miscellaneous items necessary to complete installation.

Division 400—499
Freestanding cash-and-wraps, customer service, utility, gift wrap, and customer service counters

All laminate plastic and metal store fixtures, including drawers, doors, shelves within fixtures, access panels, hinges, pulls, locks, hanger and trash bins, binning, trays, dividers, checkledge, drawer slides, levelers, recessed plastic strip, shelf-support clips, prewired duplex, and all miscellaneous items necessary to complete the installation.

Division 500—599
Miscellaneous freestanding custom fixturing

All standard and custom fixturing, including those fixtures designed for specialty merchandising requirements, manufactured in small quantities and not included in other divisions. This includes the refinishing, refurbishing, and relocating of existing fixtures and store equipment. This does not include last-minute items that arrive at the job site installed. No glass is included in this division. Electrical fixtures or hookups that are a part of the fixtures that will be installed at the factory. Any reworking, refinishing, or refurbishing of manufac-turer's fixtures is included in this division. Decorative shaded lamps atop showcase fills will be supplied by owner and hooked up by electrical contractor.

Division 600—699

Metal merchandising racks for hanging merchandise or vendor fixtures

Included are three-way rounds, four way rounds, two-way rounds, and rounds; T-stands, four-way racks, three-way racks, six-way racks, half-circle racks, straight racks, and any other rack configuration as selected by owner.

These items are normally selected, purchased, and delivered to the job site by the owner. The fixture contractor should verify if unpacking, assembly, location is required.

Division 700—709

Perimeter wall decor and casework

All curtain walls, cornices, molding, paneling, jambs, cased openings, doors, wood trim or plastic accessory trim, corner fills special wall fixtures, column enclosures. Eggcrate soffits, illuminated shelves, architectural millwork, decorative wall or overhead treatment at escalators, beams, false beams, illuminated beams, and miscellaneous special trim, millwork, cabinetry to complete wall fixturing and decor. All electrical requirements and equipment that is part of a fixture will arrive at the job site factory installed. Hookup and connection is not part of this division. Cornice lights and other loose strip lights will be installed by the electrical contractor. Special laminate plastic shelves supplied under this division will arrive at the job site with brackets.

All modular and fixed-base platforms, shams, base cabinet with drawers, base cabinet with sliding doors, freestanding base platforms, levelers, modular bunkers, continuous perimeter bunkers, risers, build-ups, laminate plastic and wood shelves, and similar fixtures of production runs. Included are build-ups constructed of wood, laminate plastic, metal, glass, plastic, slotted hardware, electrical hookups where required, and $3/8$" glass shelves. Showcase or center island fixtures, endcaps, wood wing walls, soffits, baffles, special fitting rooms are not included in this division.

Division 800—899

Existing equipment to be modified and reinstalled

(By General Contractor if on perimeter wall; by Freestanding Fixture Contractor if freestanding.)

Division 900—950

All stockroom hardware, hangrod, shelving, dopple decking, handrails, guardrails, stairways, work ledges, baffles, dividers, brackets, and all miscellaneous items necessary to complete the installation.

Division 951—999

Fitting Rooms

Verify with drawings quantity, location, configuration, type, finish, door type, bench or seating, hooks, mirrors, metal finish, hinges, pulls, push plate, knob. latch, levelers, and all miscellaneous items necessary to complete the installation.

Chapter 20

MERCHANDISING SECTIONS

Another responsibility of the store planner is to develop a series of merchandising sections that coordinate with the plan and interior elevations. The merchandising sections indicate what type of hardware, hangrods, casework, shelves, and so on, will be required to support and display the merchandise.

Various types of merchandise will require specific hardware and equipment for proper display. The merchandising sections shown within this chapter are just some of the examples of how different items for sale are featured on walls.

HOW TO READ A MERCHANDISING SECTION

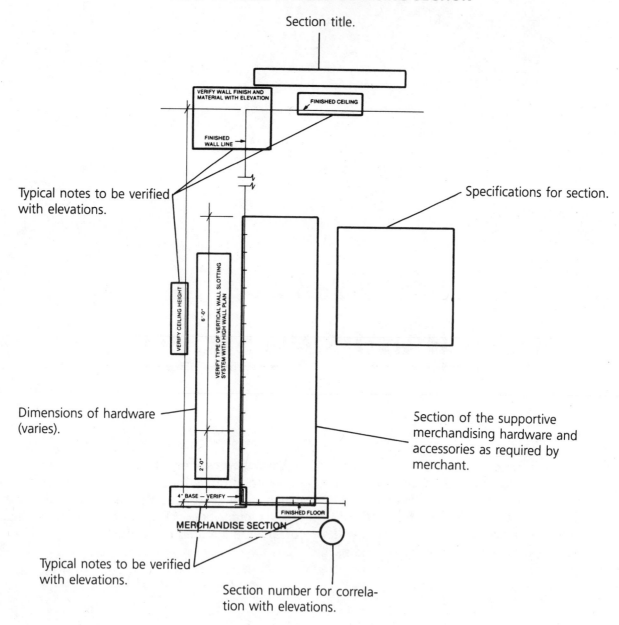

Section title.

VERIFY WALL FINISH AND
MATERIAL WITH ELEVATION

FINISHED CEILING

FINISHED
WALL LINE

Typical notes to be verified
with elevations.

Specifications for section.

VERIFY CEILING HEIGHT

6'-0"

VERIFY TYPE OF VERTICAL WALL SLOTTING
SYSTEM WITH HIGH WALL PLAN

Dimensions of hardware
(varies).

Section of the supportive
merchandising hardware and
accessories as required by
merchant.

2'-0"

4" BASE — VERIFY

FINISHED FLOOR

MERCHANDISE SECTION

Typical notes to be verified
with elevations.

Section number for correlation with elevations.

HOW TO READ AN ELEVATION

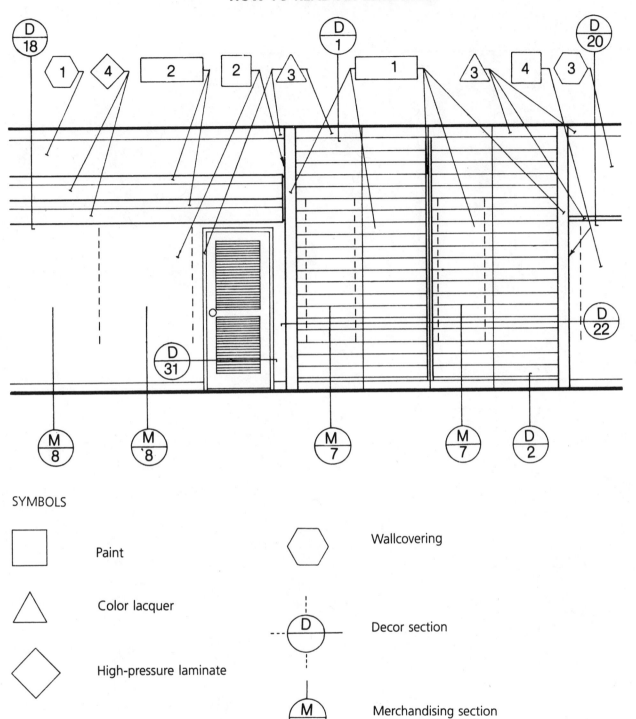

SYMBOLS

☐ Paint

△ Color lacquer

◇ High-pressure laminate

▭ Special finish (indicated)

⬡ Wallcovering

Ⓓ Decor section

Ⓜ Merchandising section

The symbol identifies a finish type even though the number may not be inserted at the time of bidding. The number should correspond with the color schedule list.

HANGING—SINGLE

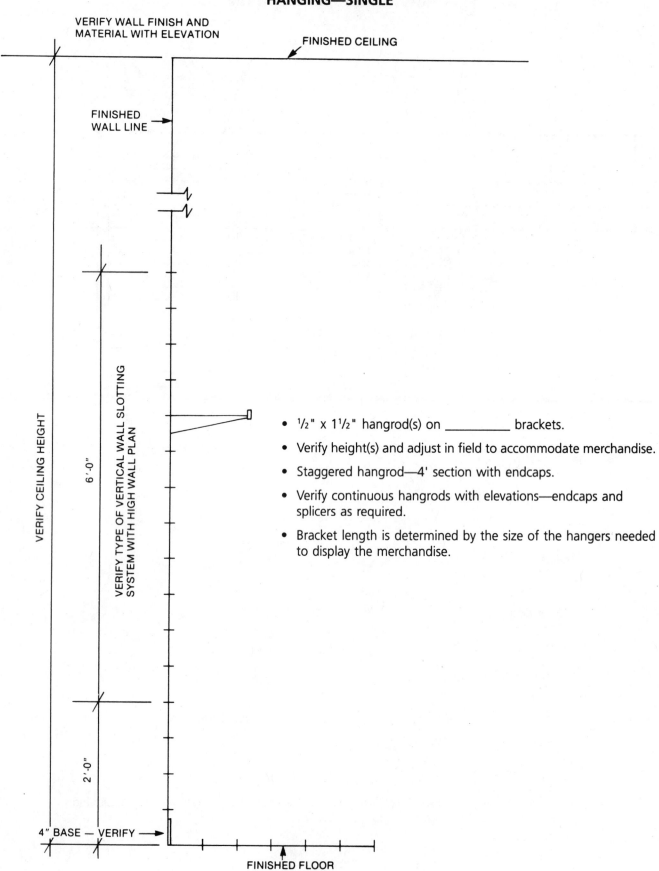

VERIFY WALL FINISH AND
MATERIAL WITH ELEVATION

FINISHED CEILING

FINISHED
WALL LINE

VERIFY CEILING HEIGHT

VERIFY TYPE OF VERTICAL WALL SLOTTING
SYSTEM WITH HIGH WALL PLAN

6'-0"

2'-0"

4" BASE — VERIFY

FINISHED FLOOR

- ½" x 1½" hangrod(s) on _____ brackets.
- Verify height(s) and adjust in field to accommodate merchandise.
- Staggered hangrod—4' section with endcaps.
- Verify continuous hangrods with elevations—endcaps and splicers as required.
- Bracket length is determined by the size of the hangers needed to display the merchandise.

HANGING—DOUBLE

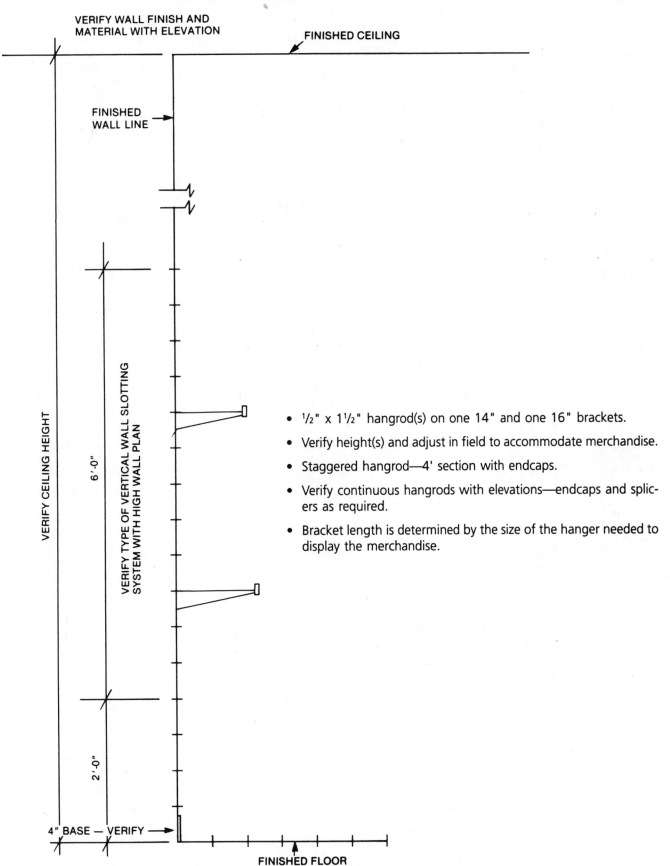

VERIFY WALL FINISH AND
MATERIAL WITH ELEVATION

FINISHED CEILING

FINISHED
WALL LINE

VERIFY CEILING HEIGHT

VERIFY TYPE OF VERTICAL WALL SLOTTING
SYSTEM WITH HIGH WALL PLAN

6'-0"

2'-0"

4" BASE — VERIFY

FINISHED FLOOR

- ½" x 1½" hangrod(s) on one 14" and one 16" brackets.
- Verify height(s) and adjust in field to accommodate merchandise.
- Staggered hangrod—4' section with endcaps.
- Verify continuous hangrods with elevations—endcaps and splicers as required.
- Bracket length is determined by the size of the hanger needed to display the merchandise.

HANGING—TRIPLE: INFANTS/PANTIES/BRAS

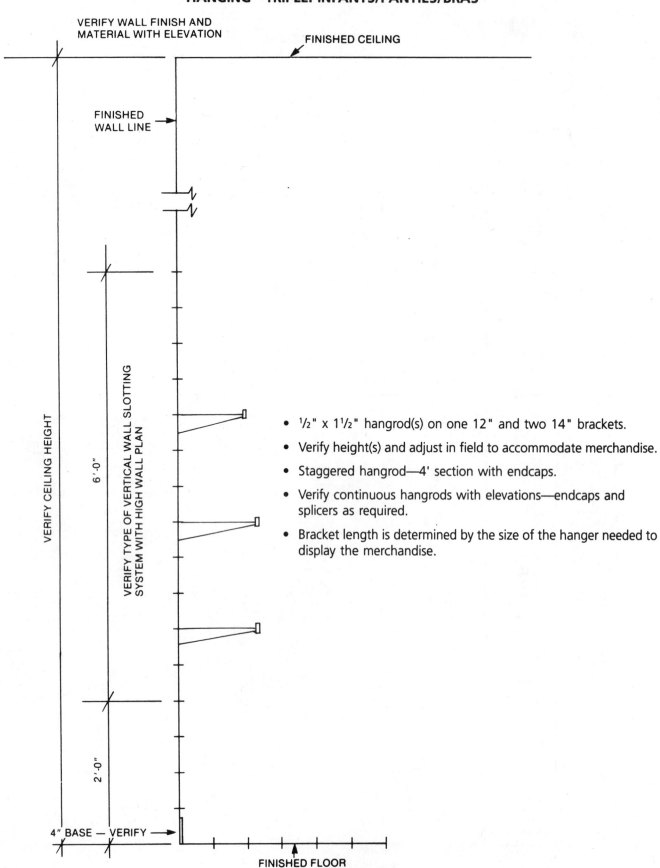

VERIFY WALL FINISH AND
MATERIAL WITH ELEVATION

FINISHED CEILING

FINISHED
WALL LINE

VERIFY CEILING HEIGHT

VERIFY TYPE OF VERTICAL WALL SLOTTING
SYSTEM WITH HIGH WALL PLAN

6'-0"

2'-0"

4" BASE — VERIFY

FINISHED FLOOR

- ½" x 1½" hangrod(s) on one 12" and two 14" brackets.
- Verify height(s) and adjust in field to accommodate merchandise.
- Staggered hangrod—4' section with endcaps.
- Verify continuous hangrods with elevations—endcaps and splicers as required.
- Bracket length is determined by the size of the hanger needed to display the merchandise.

HANGING—SINGLE FACEOUT

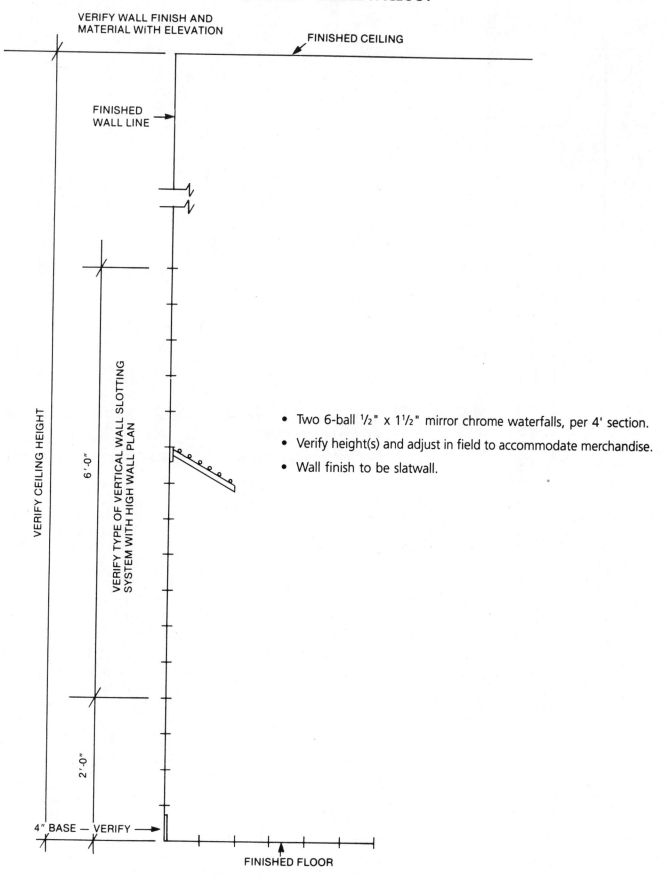

VERIFY WALL FINISH AND
MATERIAL WiTH ELEVATION

FINISHED CEILING

FINISHED
WALL LINE

VERIFY CEILING HEIGHT

6'-0"

VERIFY TYPE OF VERTICAL WALL SLOTTING
SYSTEM WITH HIGH WALL PLAN

2'-0"

4" BASE — VERIFY

FINISHED FLOOR

- Two 6-ball ½" x 1½" mirror chrome waterfalls, per 4' section.
- Verify height(s) and adjust in field to accommodate merchandise.
- Wall finish to be slatwall.

HANGING—SINGLE FACEOUT

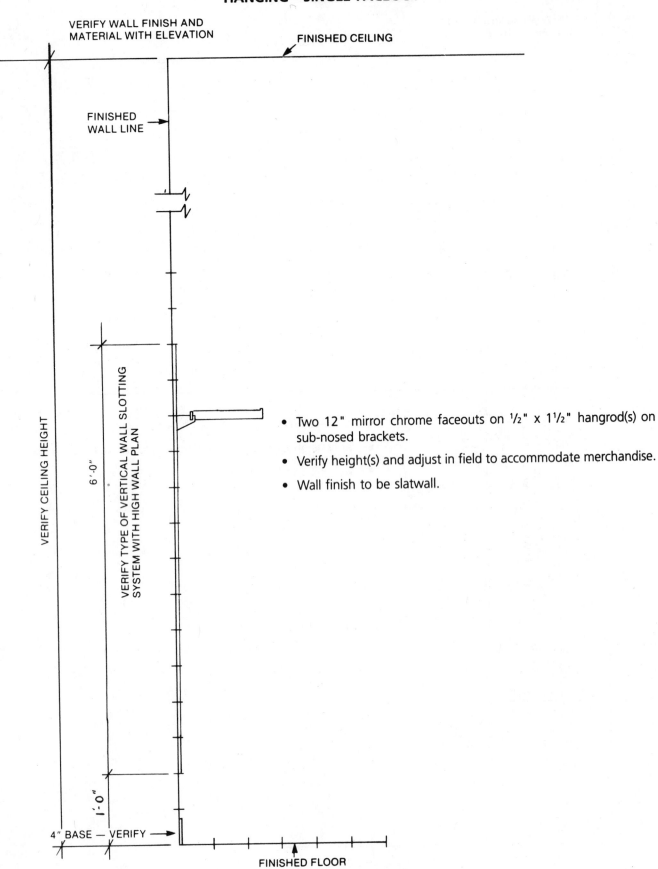

VERIFY WALL FINISH AND
MATERIAL WITH ELEVATION

FINISHED CEILING

FINISHED
WALL LINE

VERIFY CEILING HEIGHT

6'-0"

VERIFY TYPE OF VERTICAL WALL SLOTTING
SYSTEM WITH HIGH WALL PLAN

1'-0"

4" BASE — VERIFY

FINISHED FLOOR

- Two 12" mirror chrome faceouts on $\frac{1}{2}$" x $1\frac{1}{2}$" hangrod(s) on sub-nosed brackets.
- Verify height(s) and adjust in field to accommodate merchandise.
- Wall finish to be slatwall.

HANGING—DOUBLE FACEOUT

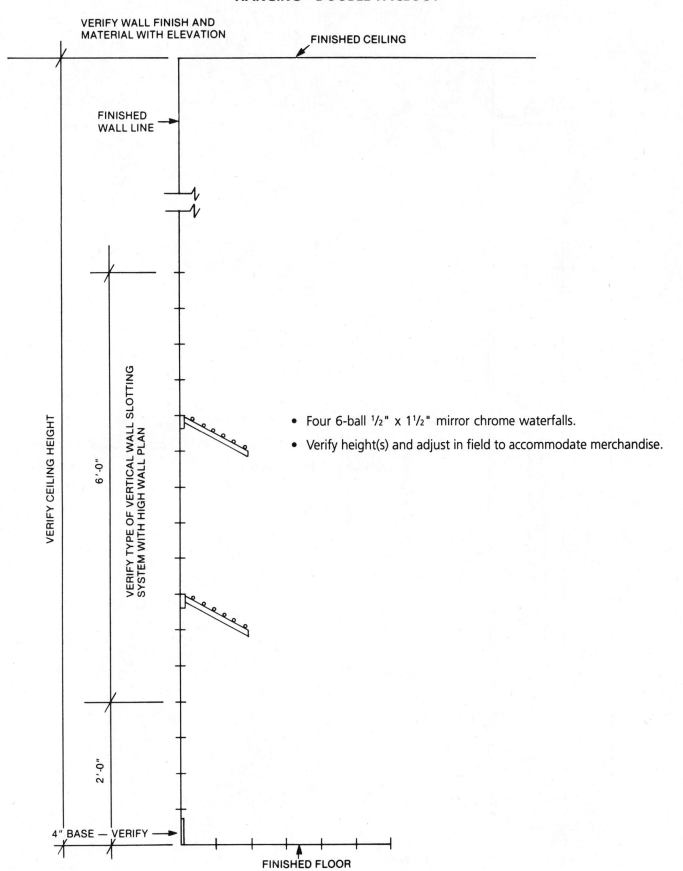

VERIFY WALL FINISH AND
MATERIAL WITH ELEVATION

FINISHED CEILING

FINISHED
WALL LINE

VERIFY CEILING HEIGHT

VERIFY TYPE OF VERTICAL WALL SLOTTING
SYSTEM WITH HIGH WALL PLAN

6'-0"

2'-0"

4" BASE — VERIFY

FINISHED FLOOR

- Four 6-ball ½" x 1½" mirror chrome waterfalls.
- Verify height(s) and adjust in field to accommodate merchandise.

HANGING—DOUBLE FACEOUTS ON SLATWALL

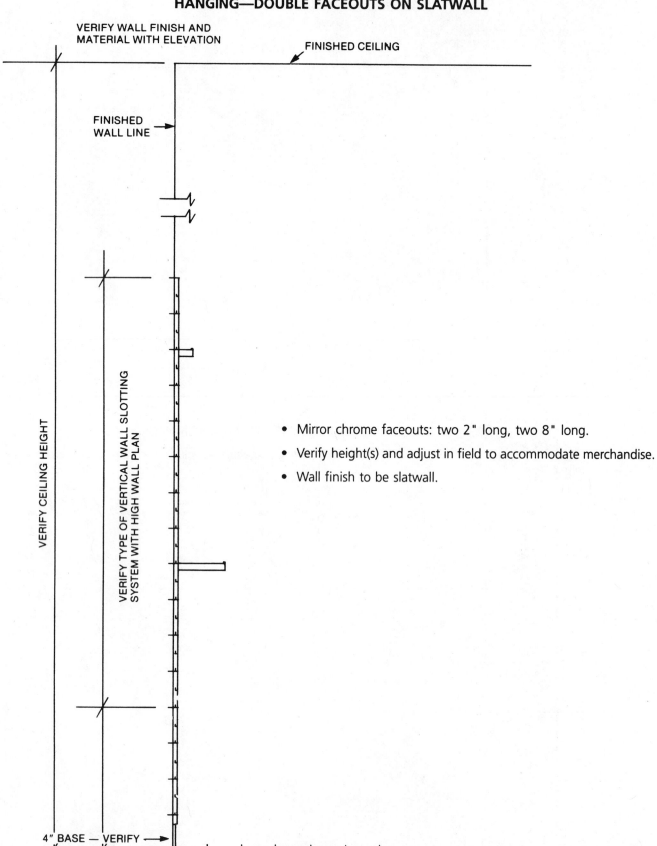

VERIFY WALL FINISH AND
MATERIAL WITH ELEVATION

FINISHED CEILING

FINISHED
WALL LINE

VERIFY CEILING HEIGHT

VERIFY TYPE OF VERTICAL WALL SLOTTING
SYSTEM WITH HIGH WALL PLAN

- Mirror chrome faceouts: two 2" long, two 8" long.
- Verify height(s) and adjust in field to accommodate merchandise.
- Wall finish to be slatwall.

4" BASE — VERIFY

FINISHED FLOOR

HANGING—DOUBLE FACEOUTS—COORDINATES

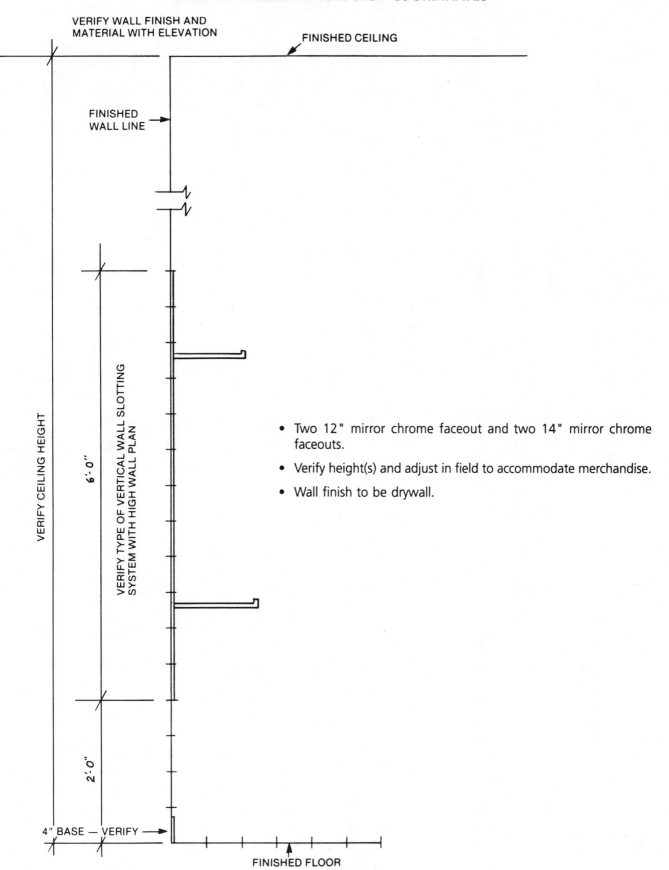

VERIFY WALL FINISH AND
MATERIAL WITH ELEVATION

FINISHED CEILING

FINISHED
WALL LINE

VERIFY CEILING HEIGHT

VERIFY TYPE OF VERTICAL WALL SLOTTING
SYSTEM WITH HIGH WALL PLAN

6'-0"

2'-0"

4" BASE — VERIFY

FINISHED FLOOR

- Two 12" mirror chrome faceout and two 14" mirror chrome faceouts.
- Verify height(s) and adjust in field to accommodate merchandise.
- Wall finish to be drywall.

HANGING—TRIPLE FACEOUT

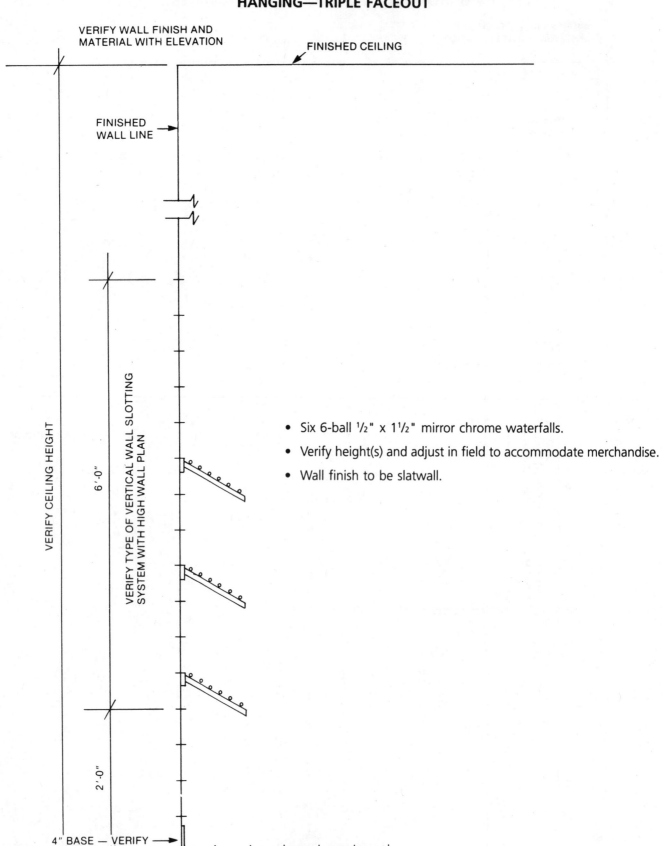

- Six 6-ball ½" x 1½" mirror chrome waterfalls.
- Verify height(s) and adjust in field to accommodate merchandise.
- Wall finish to be slatwall.

HANGING—TRIPLE FACEOUTS—HANDBAGS

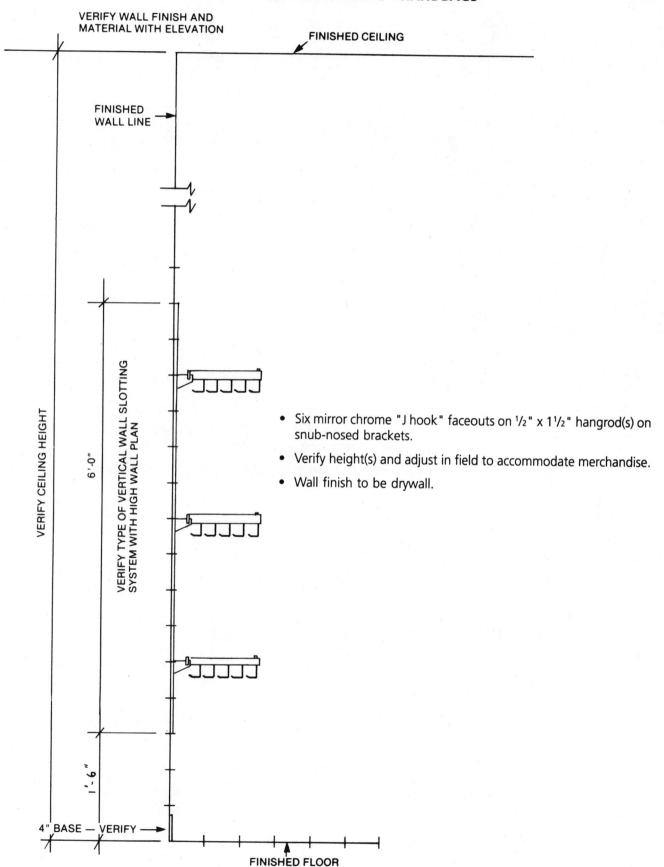

VERIFY WALL FINISH AND
MATERIAL WITH ELEVATION

FINISHED CEILING

FINISHED
WALL LINE

VERIFY CEILING HEIGHT

VERIFY TYPE OF VERTICAL WALL SLOTTING
SYSTEM WITH HIGH WALL PLAN

6'-0"

1'-6"

4" BASE — VERIFY

FINISHED FLOOR

- Six mirror chrome "J hook" faceouts on ½" x 1½" hangrod(s) on snub-nosed brackets.
- Verify height(s) and adjust in field to accommodate merchandise.
- Wall finish to be drywall.

HANGING—TRIPLE FACEOUT

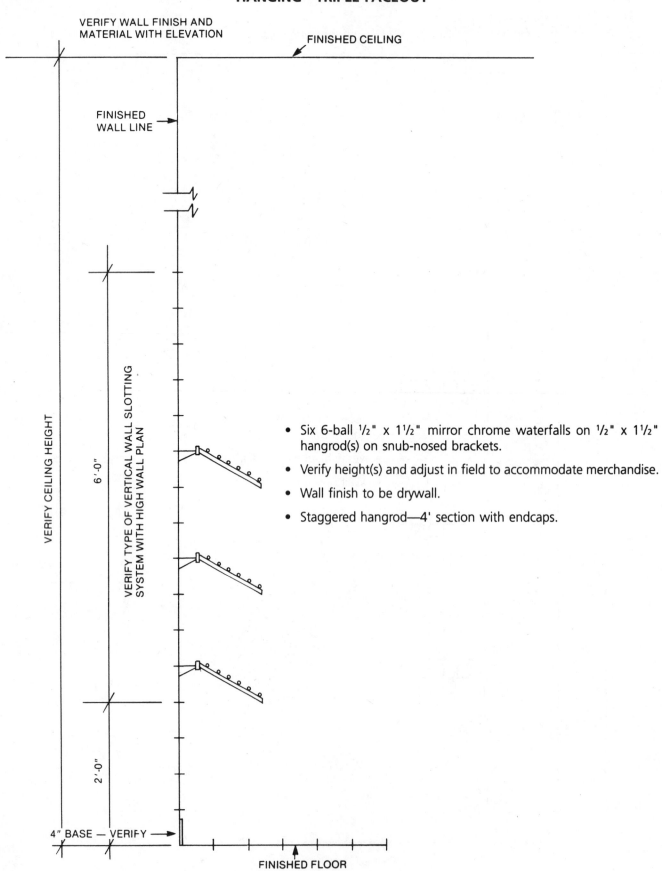

VERIFY WALL FINISH AND
MATERIAL WITH ELEVATION

FINISHED CEILING

FINISHED
WALL LINE

VERIFY CEILING HEIGHT

6'-0"

VERIFY TYPE OF VERTICAL WALL SLOTTING
SYSTEM WITH HIGH WALL PLAN

2'-0"

4" BASE — VERIFY

FINISHED FLOOR

- Six 6-ball $\frac{1}{2}$" x $1\frac{1}{2}$" mirror chrome waterfalls on $\frac{1}{2}$" x $1\frac{1}{2}$" hangrod(s) on snub-nosed brackets.

- Verify height(s) and adjust in field to accommodate merchandise.

- Wall finish to be drywall.

- Staggered hangrod—4' section with endcaps.

HANGING—DOUBLE FACEOUT—HANDBAGS

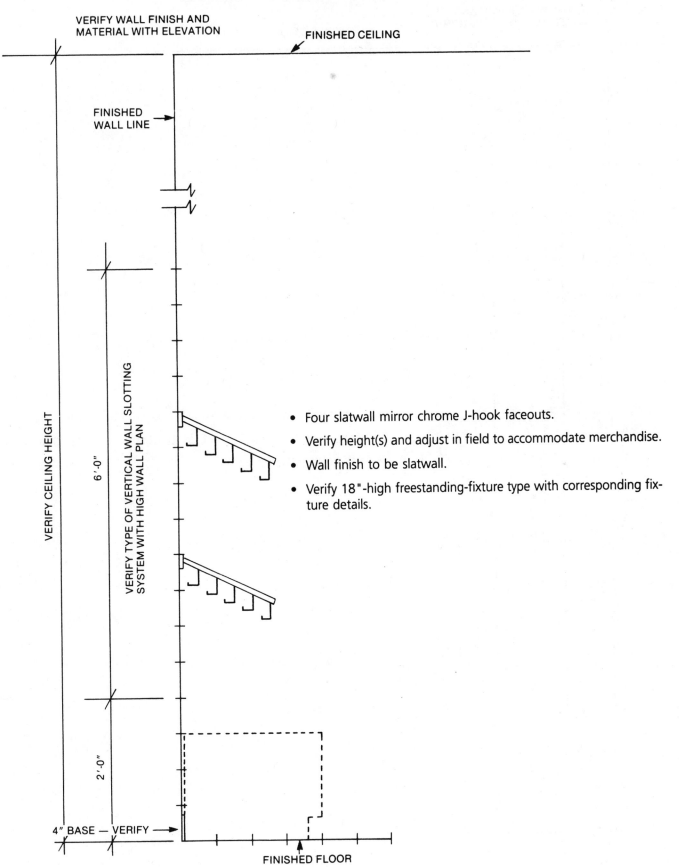

VERIFY WALL FINISH AND
MATERIAL WITH ELEVATION

FINISHED CEILING

FINISHED
WALL LINE

VERIFY CEILING HEIGHT

VERIFY TYPE OF VERTICAL WALL SLOTTING
SYSTEM WITH HIGH WALL PLAN

6'-0"

2'-0"

4" BASE — VERIFY

FINISHED FLOOR

- Four slatwall mirror chrome J-hook faceouts.
- Verify height(s) and adjust in field to accommodate merchandise.
- Wall finish to be slatwall.
- Verify 18"-high freestanding-fixture type with corresponding fixture details.

HANGING—TRIPLE FACEOUT—HANDBAGS

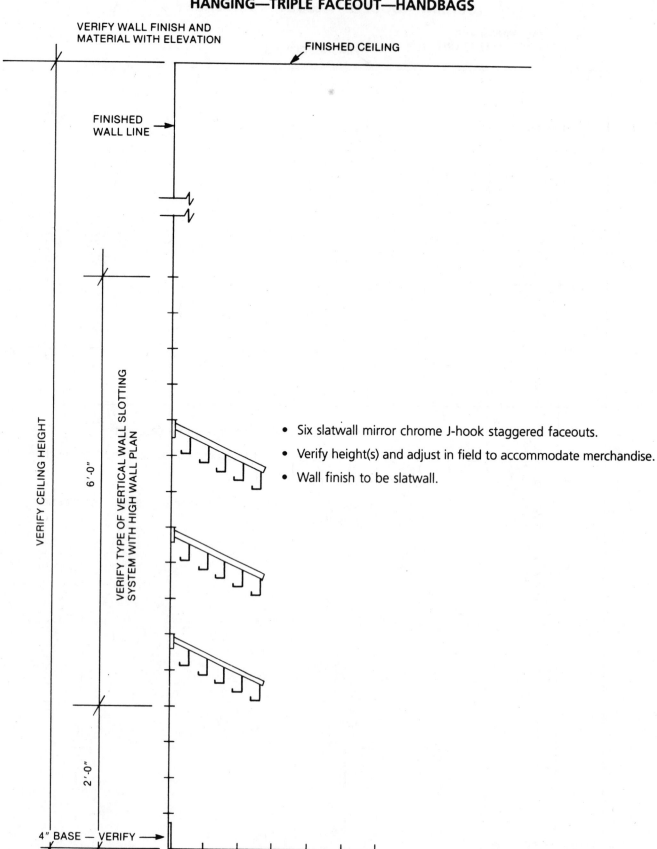

VERIFY WALL FINISH AND
MATERIAL WITH ELEVATION

FINISHED CEILING

FINISHED
WALL LINE

VERIFY CEILING HEIGHT

VERIFY TYPE OF VERTICAL WALL SLOTTING
SYSTEM WITH HIGH WALL PLAN

6'-0"

2'-0"

4" BASE — VERIFY

- Six slatwall mirror chrome J-hook staggered faceouts.
- Verify height(s) and adjust in field to accommodate merchandise.
- Wall finish to be slatwall.

FINISHED FLOOR

SINGLE HANGROD WITH FACEOUT

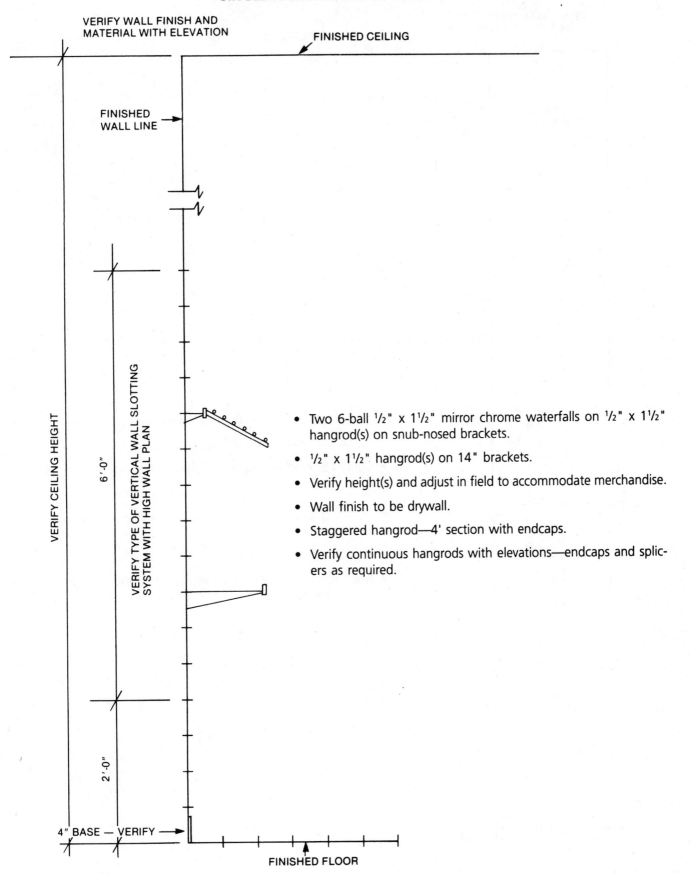

VERIFY WALL FINISH AND MATERIAL WITH ELEVATION

FINISHED CEILING

FINISHED WALL LINE

VERIFY CEILING HEIGHT

VERIFY TYPE OF VERTICAL WALL SLOTTING SYSTEM WITH HIGH WALL PLAN

6'-0"

2'-0"

4" BASE — VERIFY

FINISHED FLOOR

- Two 6-ball ½" x 1½" mirror chrome waterfalls on ½" x 1½" hangrod(s) on snub-nosed brackets.
- ½" x 1½" hangrod(s) on 14" brackets.
- Verify height(s) and adjust in field to accommodate merchandise.
- Wall finish to be drywall.
- Staggered hangrod—4' section with endcaps.
- Verify continuous hangrods with elevations—endcaps and splicers as required.

HANGING—SINGLE HANGROD WITH FACEOUT

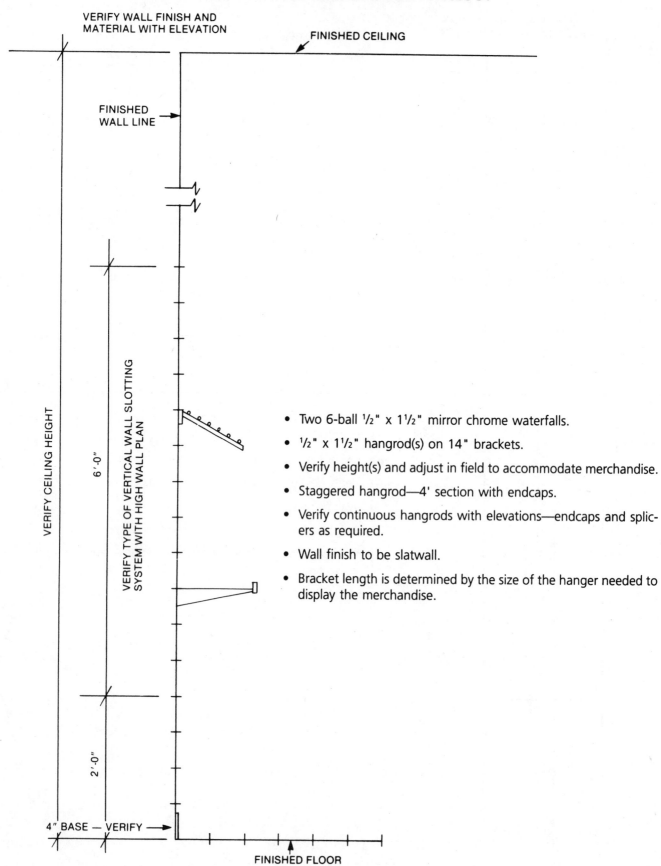

VERIFY WALL FINISH AND
MATERIAL WITH ELEVATION

FINISHED CEILING

FINISHED
WALL LINE

VERIFY CEILING HEIGHT

6'-0"

VERIFY TYPE OF VERTICAL WALL SLOTTING
SYSTEM WITH HIGH WALL PLAN

2'-0"

4" BASE — VERIFY →

FINISHED FLOOR

- Two 6-ball ½" x 1½" mirror chrome waterfalls.
- ½" x 1½" hangrod(s) on 14" brackets.
- Verify height(s) and adjust in field to accommodate merchandise.
- Staggered hangrod—4' section with endcaps.
- Verify continuous hangrods with elevations—endcaps and splicers as required.
- Wall finish to be slatwall.
- Bracket length is determined by the size of the hanger needed to display the merchandise.

SHELF: HANGROD—BRIEFCASE/GARMENT BAGS

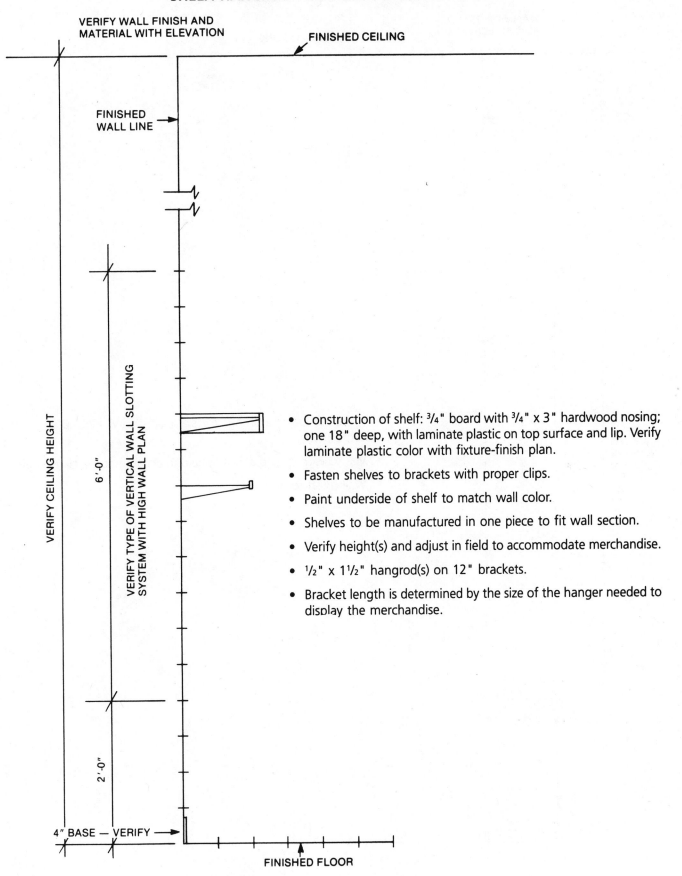

VERIFY WALL FINISH AND
MATERIAL WITH ELEVATION

FINISHED CEILING

FINISHED
WALL LINE

VERIFY CEILING HEIGHT

6'-0"

VERIFY TYPE OF VERTICAL WALL SLOTTING
SYSTEM WITH HIGH WALL PLAN

2'-0"

4" BASE — VERIFY

FINISHED FLOOR

- Construction of shelf: ¾" board with ¾" x 3" hardwood nosing; one 18" deep, with laminate plastic on top surface and lip. Verify laminate plastic color with fixture-finish plan.

- Fasten shelves to brackets with proper clips.

- Paint underside of shelf to match wall color.

- Shelves to be manufactured in one piece to fit wall section.

- Verify height(s) and adjust in field to accommodate merchandise.

- ½" x 1½" hangrod(s) on 12" brackets.

- Bracket length is determined by the size of the hanger needed to display the merchandise.

PRONGS—HOUSEWARES/ACCESSORIES

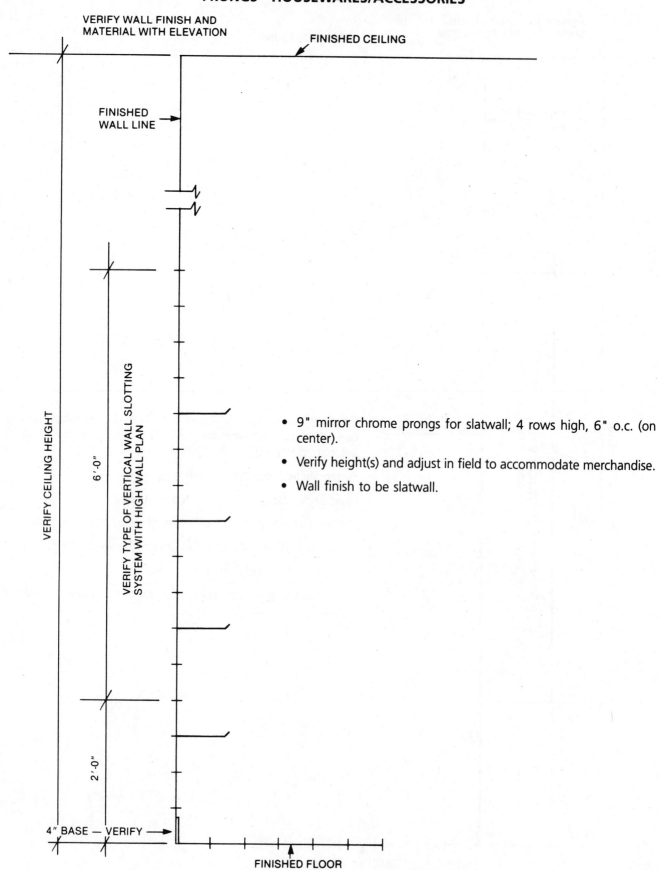

VERIFY WALL FINISH AND
MATERIAL WITH ELEVATION

FINISHED CEILING

FINISHED
WALL LINE

VERIFY CEILING HEIGHT

VERIFY TYPE OF VERTICAL WALL SLOTTING
SYSTEM WITH HIGH WALL PLAN

6'-0"

2'-0"

4" BASE — VERIFY

FINISHED FLOOR

- 9" mirror chrome prongs for slatwall; 4 rows high, 6" o.c. (on center).
- Verify height(s) and adjust in field to accommodate merchandise.
- Wall finish to be slatwall.

PRONGS—BRAS/PACKAGED MERCHANDISE

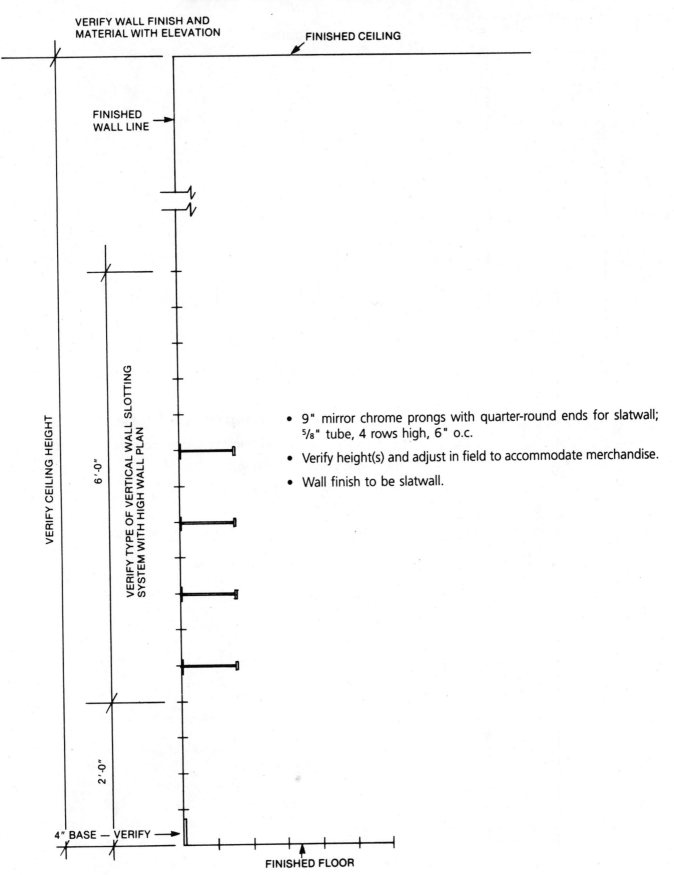

VERIFY WALL FINISH AND
MATERIAL WITH ELEVATION

FINISHED CEILING

FINISHED
WALL LINE

VERIFY CEILING HEIGHT

6'-0"

VERIFY TYPE OF VERTICAL WALL SLOTTING
SYSTEM WITH HIGH WALL PLAN

2'-0"

4" BASE — VERIFY

FINISHED FLOOR

- 9" mirror chrome prongs with quarter-round ends for slatwall; ⁵⁄₈" tube, 4 rows high, 6" o.c.
- Verify height(s) and adjust in field to accommodate merchandise.
- Wall finish to be slatwall.

PRONGS—HOUSEWARES

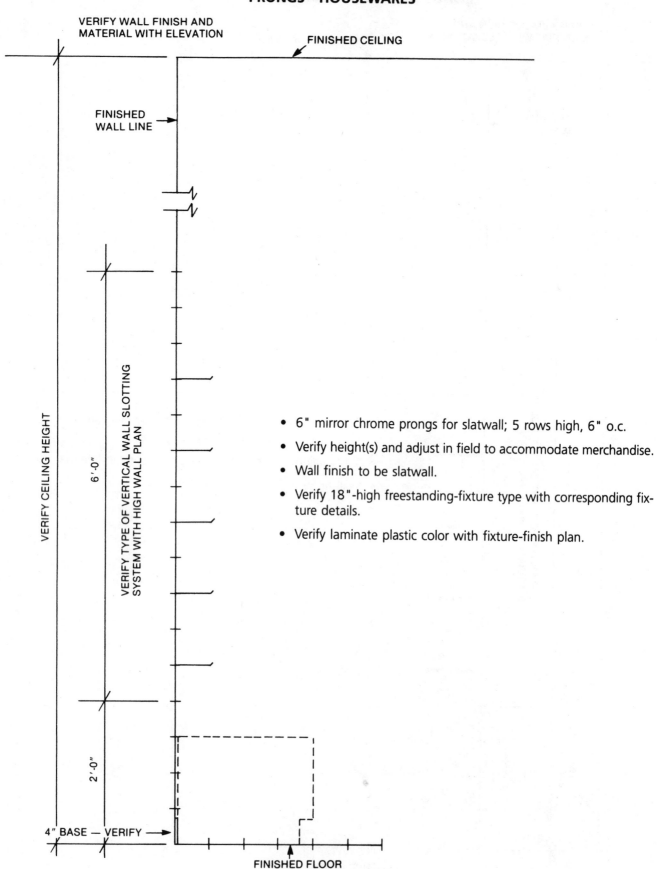

VERIFY WALL FINISH AND
MATERIAL WITH ELEVATION

FINISHED CEILING

FINISHED
WALL LINE

VERIFY CEILING HEIGHT

6'-0"

VERIFY TYPE OF VERTICAL WALL SLOTTING
SYSTEM WITH HIGH WALL PLAN

- 6" mirror chrome prongs for slatwall; 5 rows high, 6" o.c.
- Verify height(s) and adjust in field to accommodate merchandise.
- Wall finish to be slatwall.
- Verify 18"-high freestanding-fixture type with corresponding fixture details.
- Verify laminate plastic color with fixture-finish plan.

2'-0"

4" BASE — VERIFY

FINISHED FLOOR

PRONGS—GADGETS

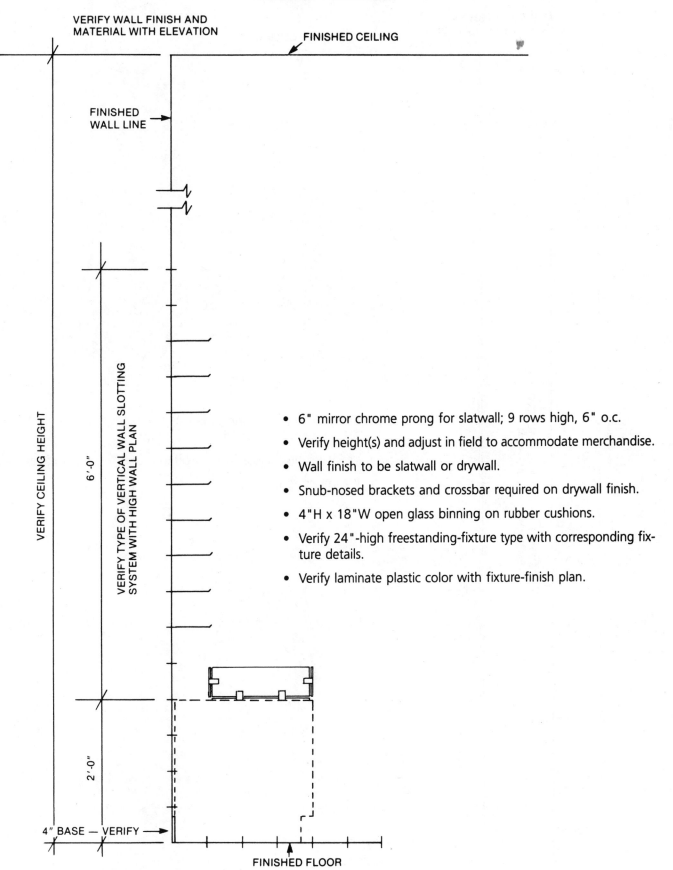

VERIFY WALL FINISH AND
MATERIAL WITH ELEVATION

FINISHED CEILING

FINISHED
WALL LINE

VERIFY CEILING HEIGHT

6'-0"

VERIFY TYPE OF VERTICAL WALL SLOTTING
SYSTEM WITH HIGH WALL PLAN

2'-0"

4" BASE — VERIFY →

FINISHED FLOOR

- 6" mirror chrome prong for slatwall; 9 rows high, 6" o.c.
- Verify height(s) and adjust in field to accommodate merchandise.
- Wall finish to be slatwall or drywall.
- Snub-nosed brackets and crossbar required on drywall finish.
- 4"H x 18"W open glass binning on rubber cushions.
- Verify 24"-high freestanding-fixture type with corresponding fixture details.
- Verify laminate plastic color with fixture-finish plan.

PRONGS—BRAS/PANTIES

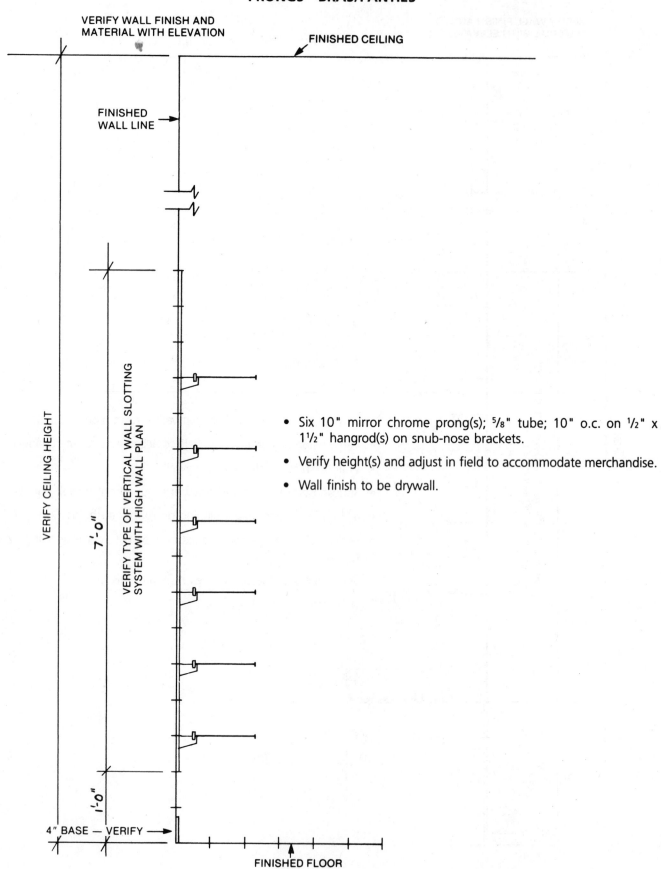

VERIFY WALL FINISH AND
MATERIAL WITH ELEVATION

FINISHED CEILING

FINISHED
WALL LINE

VERIFY CEILING HEIGHT

VERIFY TYPE OF VERTICAL WALL SLOTTING
SYSTEM WITH HIGH WALL PLAN

7'-0"

1'-0"

4" BASE — VERIFY

FINISHED FLOOR

- Six 10" mirror chrome prong(s); $5/8$" tube; 10" o.c. on $1/2$" x $1\frac{1}{2}$" hangrod(s) on snub-nose brackets.
- Verify height(s) and adjust in field to accommodate merchandise.
- Wall finish to be drywall.

SHELF/PRONGS—KNEE HIGHS

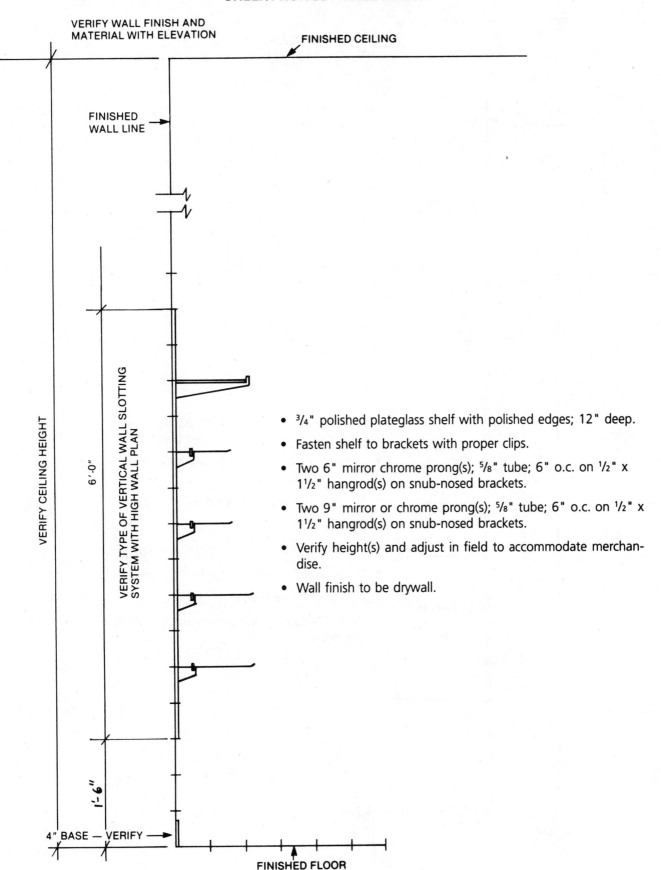

VERIFY WALL FINISH AND
MATERIAL WITH ELEVATION

FINISHED CEILING

FINISHED
WALL LINE

VERIFY CEILING HEIGHT

6'-0"

VERIFY TYPE OF VERTICAL WALL SLOTTING
SYSTEM WITH HIGH WALL PLAN

1'-6"

4" BASE — VERIFY

FINISHED FLOOR

- ¾" polished plateglass shelf with polished edges; 12" deep.
- Fasten shelf to brackets with proper clips.
- Two 6" mirror chrome prong(s); ⅝" tube; 6" o.c. on ½" x 1½" hangrod(s) on snub-nosed brackets.
- Two 9" mirror or chrome prong(s); ⅝" tube; 6" o.c. on ½" x 1½" hangrod(s) on snub-nosed brackets.
- Verify height(s) and adjust in field to accommodate merchandise.
- Wall finish to be drywall.

PRONGS/SHELF—INFANTS

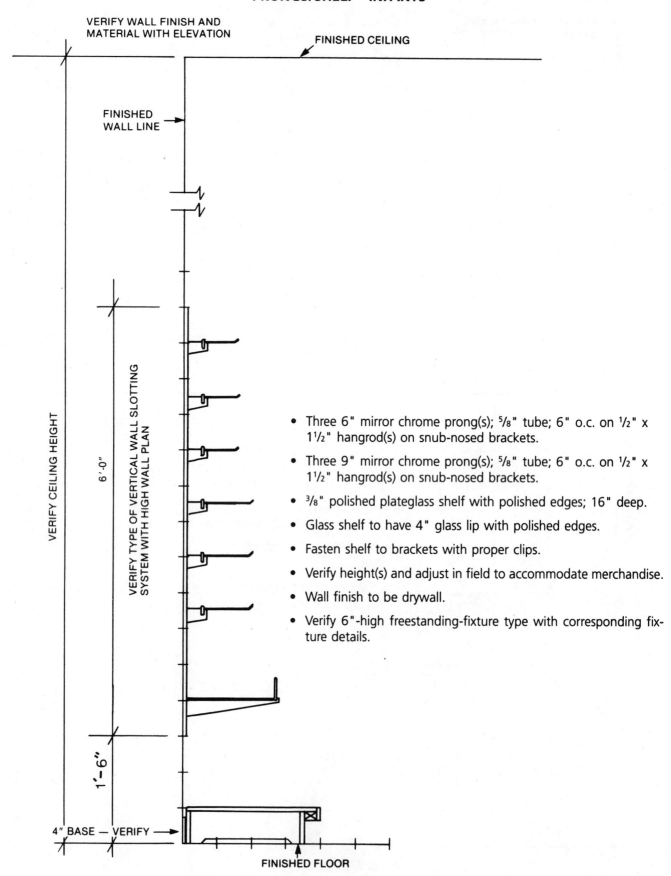

VERIFY WALL FINISH AND
MATERIAL WITH ELEVATION

FINISHED CEILING

FINISHED
WALL LINE

VERIFY CEILING HEIGHT

VERIFY TYPE OF VERTICAL WALL SLOTTING
SYSTEM WITH HIGH WALL PLAN

6'-0"

1'-6"

4" BASE — VERIFY

FINISHED FLOOR

- Three 6" mirror chrome prong(s); $\frac{5}{8}$" tube; 6" o.c. on $\frac{1}{2}$" x 1$\frac{1}{2}$" hangrod(s) on snub-nosed brackets.
- Three 9" mirror chrome prong(s); $\frac{5}{8}$" tube; 6" o.c. on $\frac{1}{2}$" x 1$\frac{1}{2}$" hangrod(s) on snub-nosed brackets.
- $\frac{3}{8}$" polished plateglass shelf with polished edges; 16" deep.
- Glass shelf to have 4" glass lip with polished edges.
- Fasten shelf to brackets with proper clips.
- Verify height(s) and adjust in field to accommodate merchandise.
- Wall finish to be drywall.
- Verify 6"-high freestanding-fixture type with corresponding fixture details.

PRONGS/SHELVES—KITCHEN ACCESSORIES

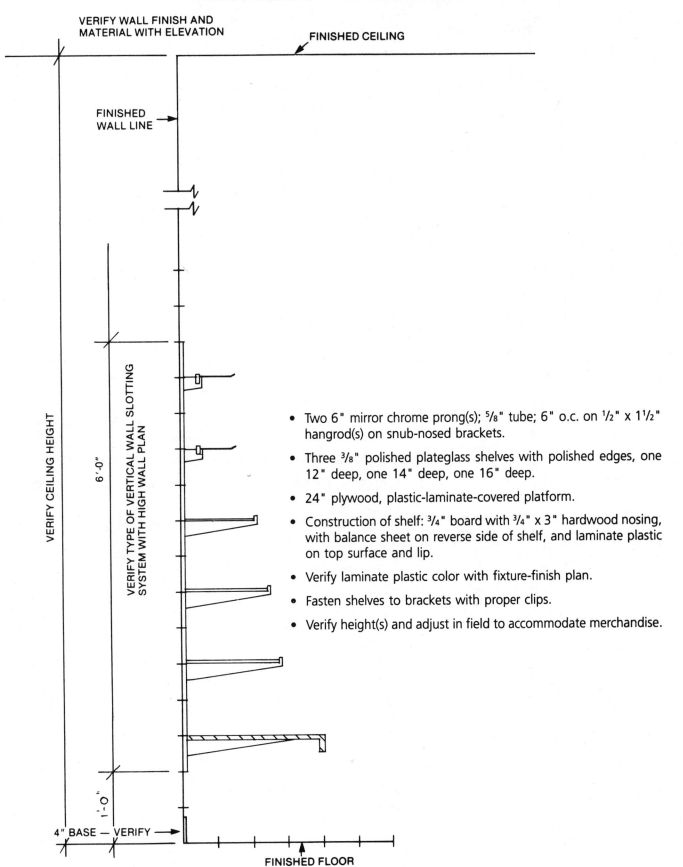

VERIFY WALL FINISH AND
MATERIAL WITH ELEVATION

FINISHED CEILING

FINISHED
WALL LINE

VERIFY CEILING HEIGHT

6'-0"

VERIFY TYPE OF VERTICAL WALL SLOTTING
SYSTEM WITH HIGH WALL PLAN

1'-0"

4" BASE — VERIFY

FINISHED FLOOR

- Two 6" mirror chrome prong(s); ⅝" tube; 6" o.c. on ½" x 1½" hangrod(s) on snub-nosed brackets.

- Three ⅜" polished plateglass shelves with polished edges, one 12" deep, one 14" deep, one 16" deep.

- 24" plywood, plastic-laminate-covered platform.

- Construction of shelf: ¾" board with ¾" x 3" hardwood nosing, with balance sheet on reverse side of shelf, and laminate plastic on top surface and lip.

- Verify laminate plastic color with fixture-finish plan.

- Fasten shelves to brackets with proper clips.

- Verify height(s) and adjust in field to accommodate merchandise.

SHELVES—GIFTS/HOUSEWARES

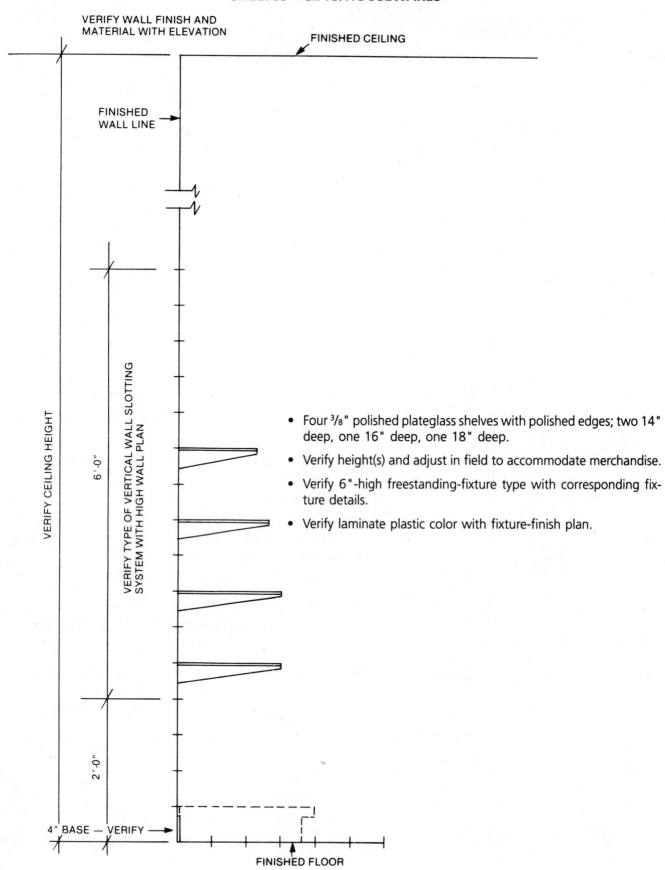

VERIFY WALL FINISH AND
MATERIAL WITH ELEVATION

FINISHED CEILING

FINISHED
WALL LINE

VERIFY CEILING HEIGHT

VERIFY TYPE OF VERTICAL WALL SLOTTING
SYSTEM WITH HIGH WALL PLAN

6'-0"

2'-0"

4" BASE — VERIFY →

FINISHED FLOOR

- Four ³/₈" polished plateglass shelves with polished edges; two 14" deep, one 16" deep, one 18" deep.
- Verify height(s) and adjust in field to accommodate merchandise.
- Verify 6"-high freestanding-fixture type with corresponding fixture details.
- Verify laminate plastic color with fixture-finish plan.

SHELVES—ACCESSORIES/GIFTS

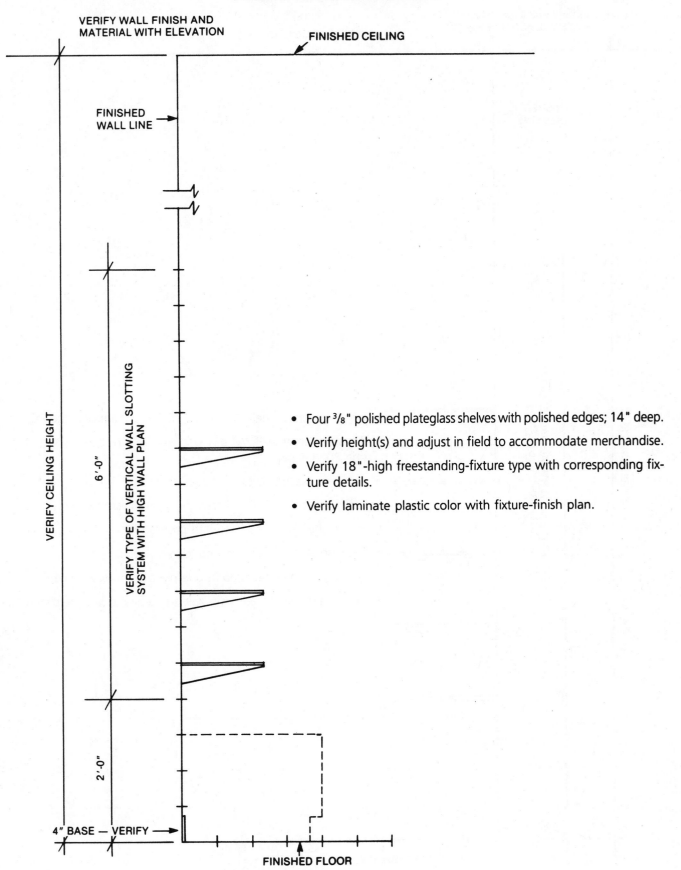

VERIFY WALL FINISH AND
MATERIAL WITH ELEVATION

FINISHED CEILING

FINISHED
WALL LINE

VERIFY CEILING HEIGHT

VERIFY TYPE OF VERTICAL WALL SLOTTING
SYSTEM WITH HIGH WALL PLAN

6'-0"

2'-0"

4" BASE — VERIFY

FINISHED FLOOR

- Four $\frac{3}{8}$" polished plateglass shelves with polished edges; 14" deep.
- Verify height(s) and adjust in field to accommodate merchandise.
- Verify 18"-high freestanding-fixture type with corresponding fixture details.
- Verify laminate plastic color with fixture-finish plan.

SHELVES—DRESS SHIRTS/SWEATERS/GIFTS

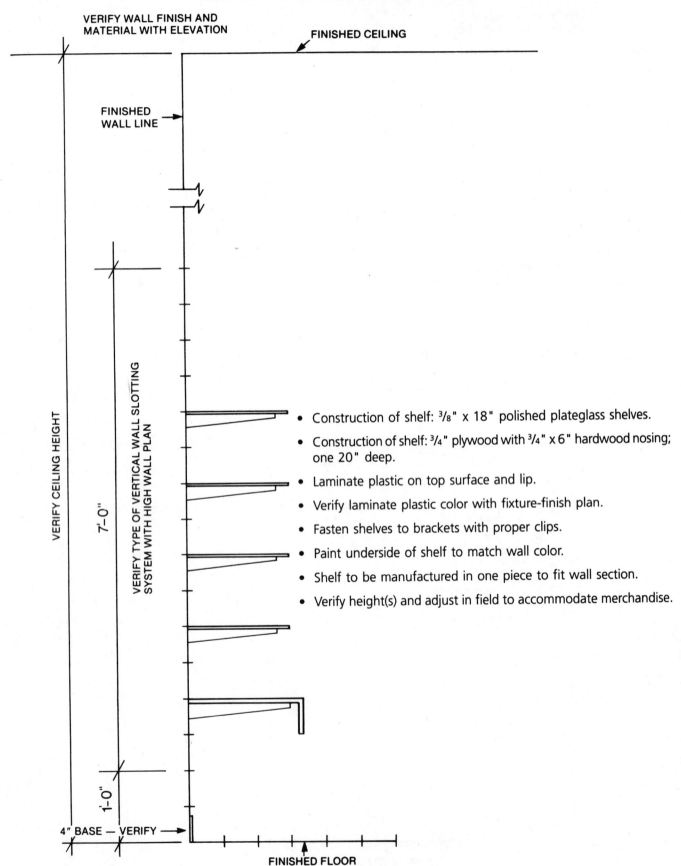

VERIFY WALL FINISH AND
MATERIAL WITH ELEVATION

FINISHED CEILING

FINISHED
WALL LINE

VERIFY CEILING HEIGHT

7'-0"

VERIFY TYPE OF VERTICAL WALL SLOTTING
SYSTEM WITH HIGH WALL PLAN

- Construction of shelf: ³/₈" x 18" polished plateglass shelves.
- Construction of shelf: ³/₄" plywood with ³/₄" x 6" hardwood nosing; one 20" deep.
- Laminate plastic on top surface and lip.
- Verify laminate plastic color with fixture-finish plan.
- Fasten shelves to brackets with proper clips.
- Paint underside of shelf to match wall color.
- Shelf to be manufactured in one piece to fit wall section.
- Verify height(s) and adjust in field to accommodate merchandise.

1'-0"

4" BASE — VERIFY

FINISHED FLOOR

SHELVES—TOWELS

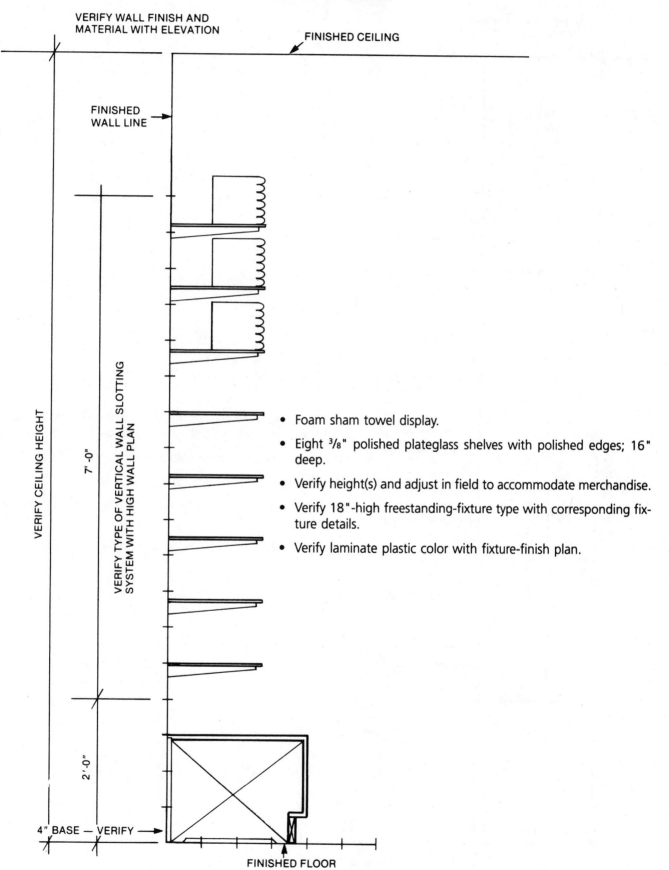

VERIFY WALL FINISH AND
MATERIAL WITH ELEVATION

FINISHED CEILING

FINISHED
WALL LINE

VERIFY CEILING HEIGHT

7'-0"

VERIFY TYPE OF VERTICAL WALL SLOTTING
SYSTEM WITH HIGH WALL PLAN

2'-0"

4" BASE — VERIFY

FINISHED FLOOR

- Foam sham towel display.
- Eight ³/₈" polished plateglass shelves with polished edges; 16" deep.
- Verify height(s) and adjust in field to accommodate merchandise.
- Verify 18"-high freestanding-fixture type with corresponding fixture details.
- Verify laminate plastic color with fixture-finish plan.

SHELVES—HOUSEWARES/GADGETS

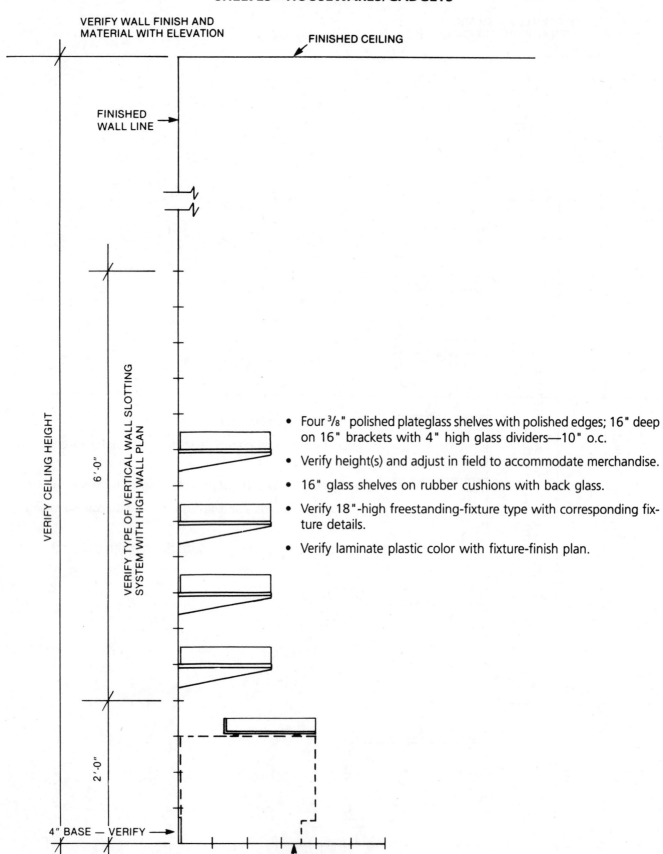

VERIFY WALL FINISH AND
MATERIAL WITH ELEVATION

FINISHED CEILING

FINISHED
WALL LINE

VERIFY CEILING HEIGHT

VERIFY TYPE OF VERTICAL WALL SLOTTING
SYSTEM WITH HIGH WALL PLAN

6'-0"

2'-0"

4" BASE — VERIFY

FINISHED FLOOR

- Four ³⁄₈" polished plateglass shelves with polished edges; 16" deep on 16" brackets with 4" high glass dividers—10" o.c.

- Verify height(s) and adjust in field to accommodate merchandise.

- 16" glass shelves on rubber cushions with back glass.

- Verify 18"-high freestanding-fixture type with corresponding fixture details.

- Verify laminate plastic color with fixture-finish plan.

SHELVES—MEN'S DRESS SHIRTS

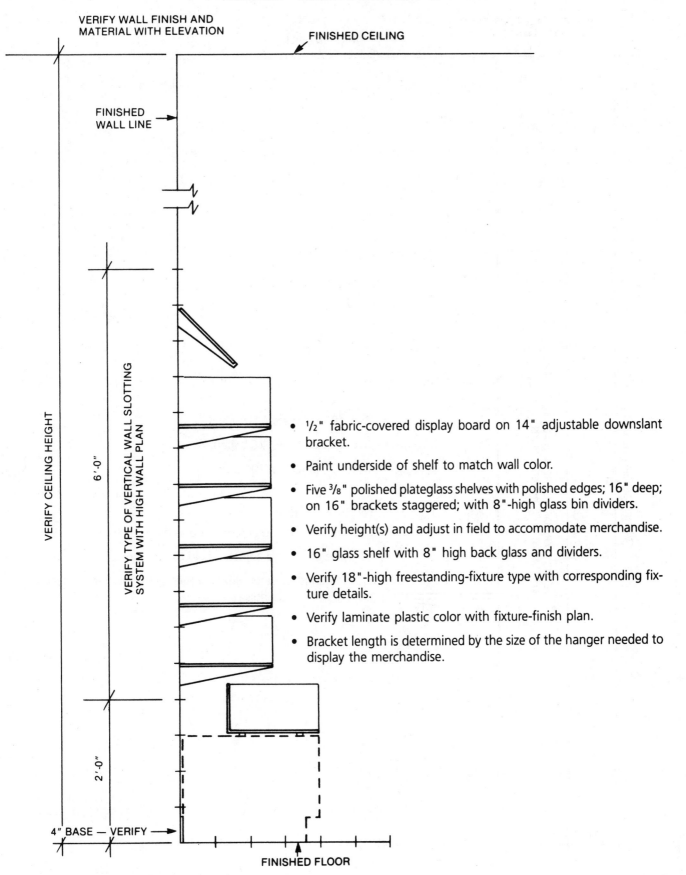

VERIFY WALL FINISH AND
MATERIAL WITH ELEVATION

FINISHED CEILING

FINISHED
WALL LINE

VERIFY CEILING HEIGHT

6'-0"

VERIFY TYPE OF VERTICAL WALL SLOTTING
SYSTEM WITH HIGH WALL PLAN

2'-0"

4" BASE — VERIFY →

FINISHED FLOOR

- ½" fabric-covered display board on 14" adjustable downslant bracket.
- Paint underside of shelf to match wall color.
- Five ³⁄₈" polished plateglass shelves with polished edges; 16" deep; on 16" brackets staggered; with 8"-high glass bin dividers.
- Verify height(s) and adjust in field to accommodate merchandise.
- 16" glass shelf with 8" high back glass and dividers.
- Verify 18"-high freestanding-fixture type with corresponding fixture details.
- Verify laminate plastic color with fixture-finish plan.
- Bracket length is determined by the size of the hanger needed to display the merchandise.

SHELVES—INFANTS/TODDLERS/ACCESSORIES

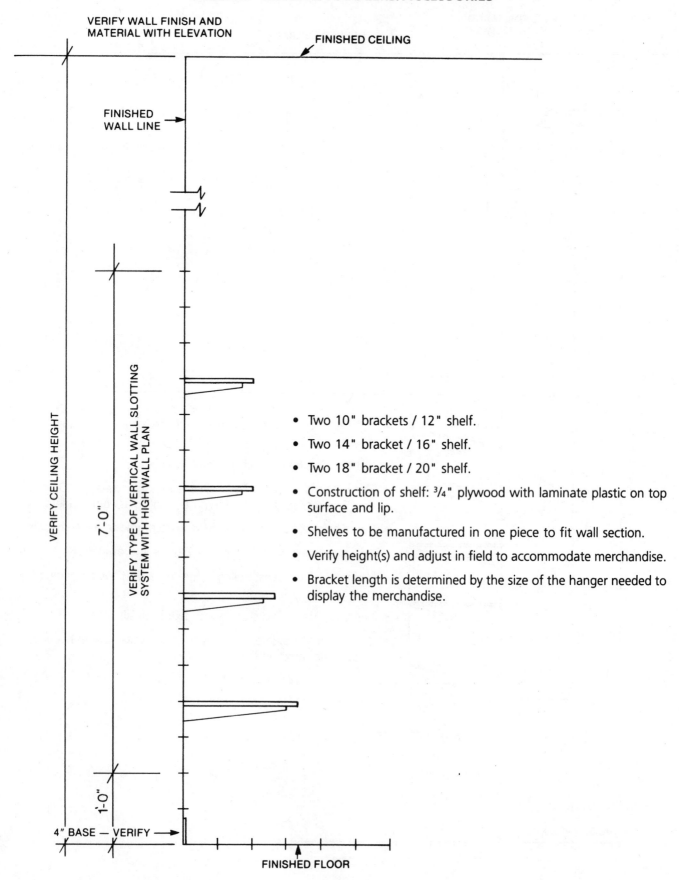

VERIFY WALL FINISH AND
MATERIAL WITH ELEVATION

FINISHED CEILING

FINISHED
WALL LINE

VERIFY CEILING HEIGHT

7'-0"

VERIFY TYPE OF VERTICAL WALL SLOTTING
SYSTEM WITH HIGH WALL PLAN

1'-0"

4" BASE — VERIFY

FINISHED FLOOR

- Two 10" brackets / 12" shelf.
- Two 14" bracket / 16" shelf.
- Two 18" bracket / 20" shelf.
- Construction of shelf: ³/₄" plywood with laminate plastic on top surface and lip.
- Shelves to be manufactured in one piece to fit wall section.
- Verify height(s) and adjust in field to accommodate merchandise.
- Bracket length is determined by the size of the hanger needed to display the merchandise.

SHELVES—JEANS

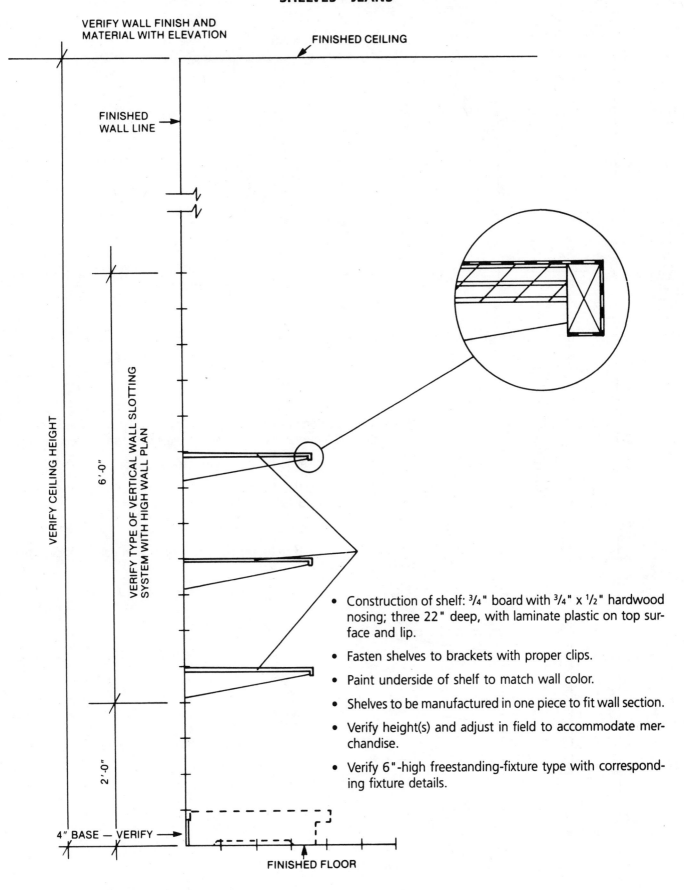

VERIFY WALL FINISH AND
MATERIAL WITH ELEVATION

FINISHED CEILING

FINISHED
WALL LINE

VERIFY CEILING HEIGHT

VERIFY TYPE OF VERTICAL WALL SLOTTING
SYSTEM WITH HIGH WALL PLAN

6'-0"

2'-0"

4" BASE — VERIFY

FINISHED FLOOR

- Construction of shelf: ³⁄₄" board with ³⁄₄" x ¹⁄₂" hardwood nosing; three 22" deep, with laminate plastic on top surface and lip.

- Fasten shelves to brackets with proper clips.

- Paint underside of shelf to match wall color.

- Shelves to be manufactured in one piece to fit wall section.

- Verify height(s) and adjust in field to accommodate merchandise.

- Verify 6"-high freestanding-fixture type with corresponding fixture details.

SHELVES—JEANS

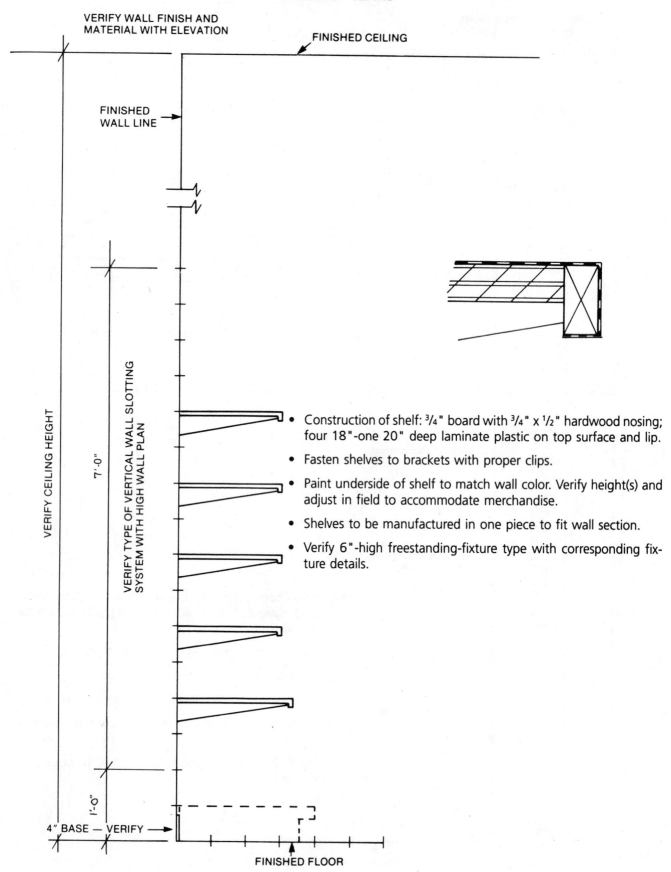

VERIFY WALL FINISH AND
MATERIAL WITH ELEVATION

FINISHED CEILING

FINISHED
WALL LINE

VERIFY CEILING HEIGHT

VERIFY TYPE OF VERTICAL WALL SLOTTING
SYSTEM WITH HIGH WALL PLAN

7'-0"

1'-0"

4" BASE — VERIFY

FINISHED FLOOR

- Construction of shelf: ³/₄" board with ³/₄" x ¹/₂" hardwood nosing; four 18"-one 20" deep laminate plastic on top surface and lip.

- Fasten shelves to brackets with proper clips.

- Paint underside of shelf to match wall color. Verify height(s) and adjust in field to accommodate merchandise.

- Shelves to be manufactured in one piece to fit wall section.

- Verify 6"-high freestanding-fixture type with corresponding fixture details.

SHELVES—TV ELECTRONIC

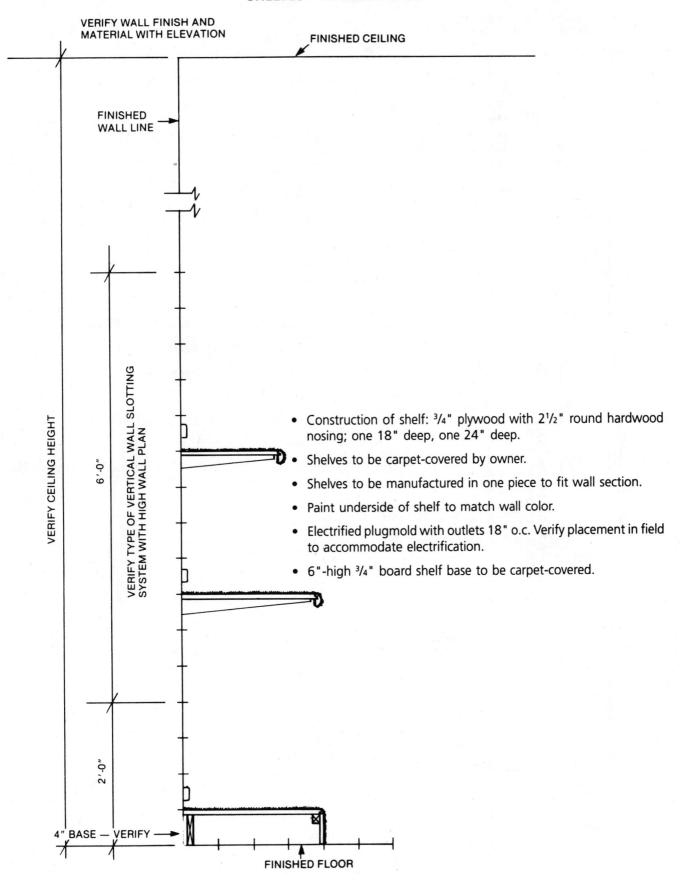

VERIFY WALL FINISH AND MATERIAL WITH ELEVATION

FINISHED CEILING

FINISHED WALL LINE

VERIFY CEILING HEIGHT

VERIFY TYPE OF VERTICAL WALL SLOTTING SYSTEM WITH HIGH WALL PLAN

6'-0"

2'-0"

4" BASE — VERIFY

FINISHED FLOOR

- Construction of shelf: ³/₄" plywood with 2¹/₂" round hardwood nosing; one 18" deep, one 24" deep.
- Shelves to be carpet-covered by owner.
- Shelves to be manufactured in one piece to fit wall section.
- Paint underside of shelf to match wall color.
- Electrified plugmold with outlets 18" o.c. Verify placement in field to accommodate electrification.
- 6"-high ³/₄" board shelf base to be carpet-covered.

SHELVES—SLIPPERS

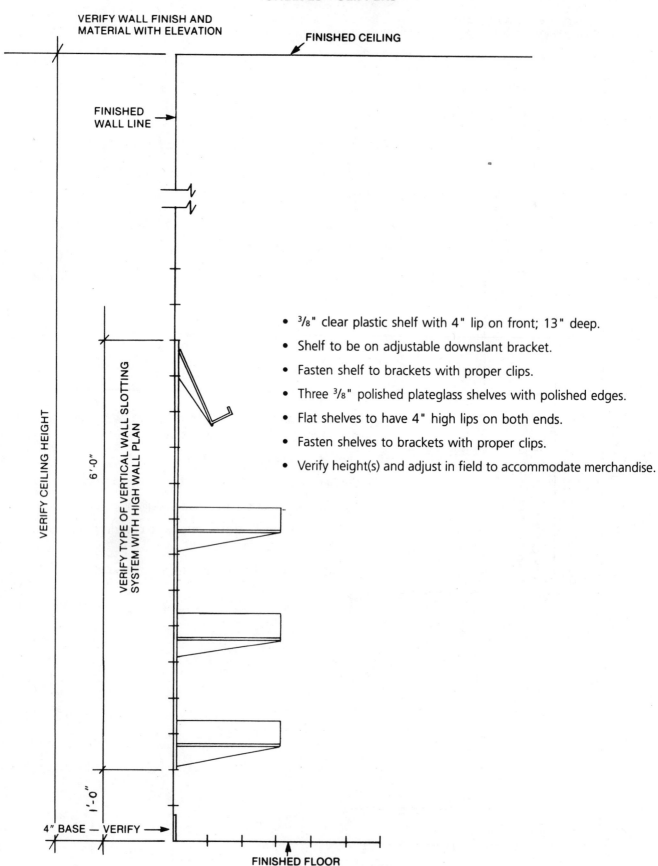

VERIFY WALL FINISH AND
MATERIAL WITH ELEVATION

FINISHED CEILING

FINISHED
WALL LINE

VERIFY CEILING HEIGHT

6'-0"

VERIFY TYPE OF VERTICAL WALL SLOTING
SYSTEM WITH HIGH WALL PLAN

1'-0"

4" BASE — VERIFY

FINISHED FLOOR

- $^{3}/_{8}$" clear plastic shelf with 4" lip on front; 13" deep.
- Shelf to be on adjustable downslant bracket.
- Fasten shelf to brackets with proper clips.
- Three $^{3}/_{8}$" polished plateglass shelves with polished edges.
- Flat shelves to have 4" high lips on both ends.
- Fasten shelves to brackets with proper clips.
- Verify height(s) and adjust in field to accommodate merchandise.

SHELVES—SHOWER ACCESSORIES

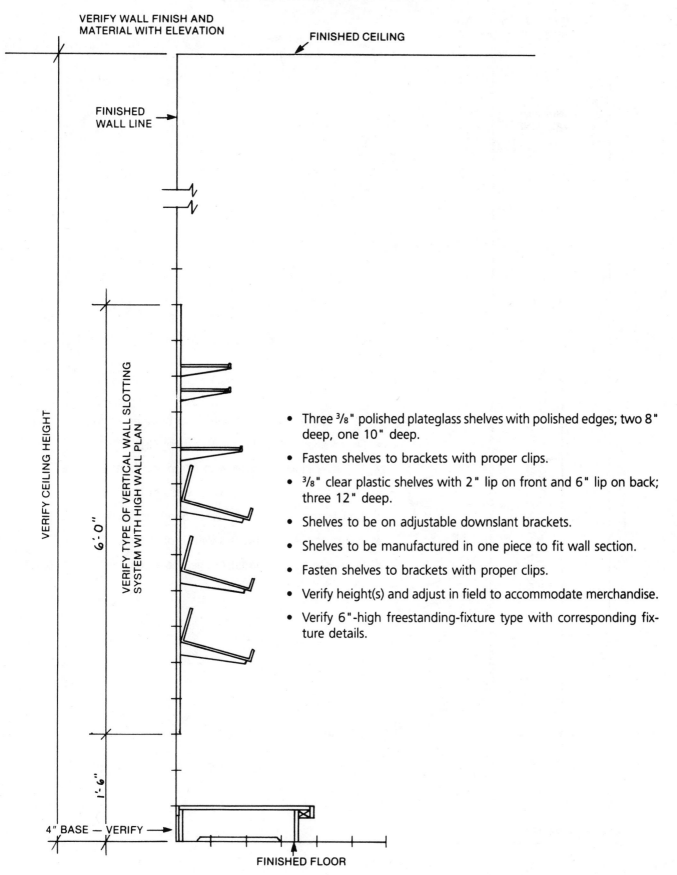

VERIFY WALL FINISH AND
MATERIAL WITH ELEVATION

FINISHED CEILING

FINISHED
WALL LINE

VERIFY CEILING HEIGHT

VERIFY TYPE OF VERTICAL WALL SLOTTING
SYSTEM WITH HIGH WALL PLAN

6'-0"

1'-6"

4" BASE — VERIFY

FINISHED FLOOR

- Three ⅜" polished plateglass shelves with polished edges; two 8" deep, one 10" deep.

- Fasten shelves to brackets with proper clips.

- ⅜" clear plastic shelves with 2" lip on front and 6" lip on back; three 12" deep.

- Shelves to be on adjustable downslant brackets.

- Shelves to be manufactured in one piece to fit wall section.

- Fasten shelves to brackets with proper clips.

- Verify height(s) and adjust in field to accommodate merchandise.

- Verify 6"-high freestanding-fixture type with corresponding fixture details.

SHELVES—INFANTS

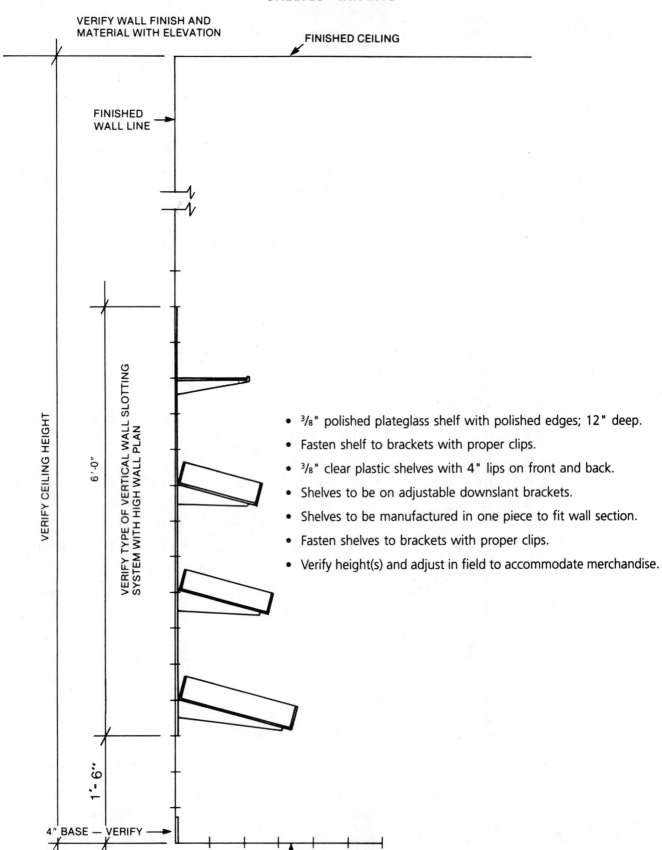

VERIFY WALL FINISH AND
MATERIAL WITH ELEVATION

FINISHED CEILING

FINISHED
WALL LINE

VERIFY CEILING HEIGHT

6'-0"

VERIFY TYPE OF VERTICAL WALL SLOTTING
SYSTEM WITH HIGH WALL PLAN

1'-6"

4" BASE — VERIFY

FINISHED FLOOR

- ³⁄₈" polished plateglass shelf with polished edges; 12" deep.
- Fasten shelf to brackets with proper clips.
- ³⁄₈" clear plastic shelves with 4" lips on front and back.
- Shelves to be on adjustable downslant brackets.
- Shelves to be manufactured in one piece to fit wall section.
- Fasten shelves to brackets with proper clips.
- Verify height(s) and adjust in field to accommodate merchandise.

SHELVES—TABLE TOP

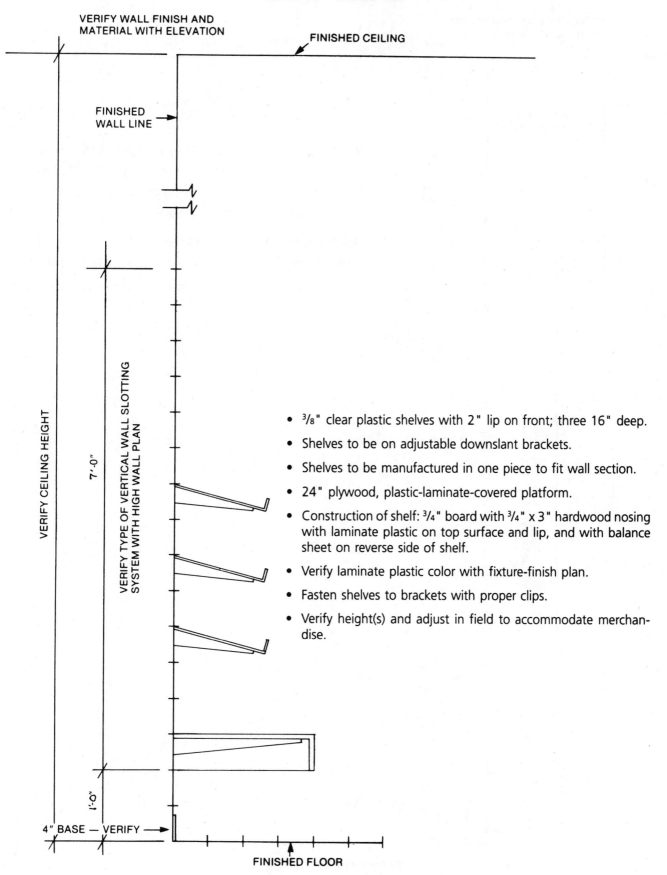

VERIFY WALL FINISH AND
MATERIAL WITH ELEVATION

FINISHED CEILING

FINISHED
WALL LINE

VERIFY CEILING HEIGHT

7'-0"

VERIFY TYPE OF VERTICAL WALL SLOTTING
SYSTEM WITH HIGH WALL PLAN

1'-0"

4" BASE — VERIFY

FINISHED FLOOR

- ³⁄₈" clear plastic shelves with 2" lip on front; three 16" deep.
- Shelves to be on adjustable downslant brackets.
- Shelves to be manufactured in one piece to fit wall section.
- 24" plywood, plastic-laminate-covered platform.
- Construction of shelf: ³⁄₄" board with ³⁄₄" x 3" hardwood nosing with laminate plastic on top surface and lip, and with balance sheet on reverse side of shelf.
- Verify laminate plastic color with fixture-finish plan.
- Fasten shelves to brackets with proper clips.
- Verify height(s) and adjust in field to accommodate merchandise.

SHELVES—COMFORTERS/SPREADS/QUILTS

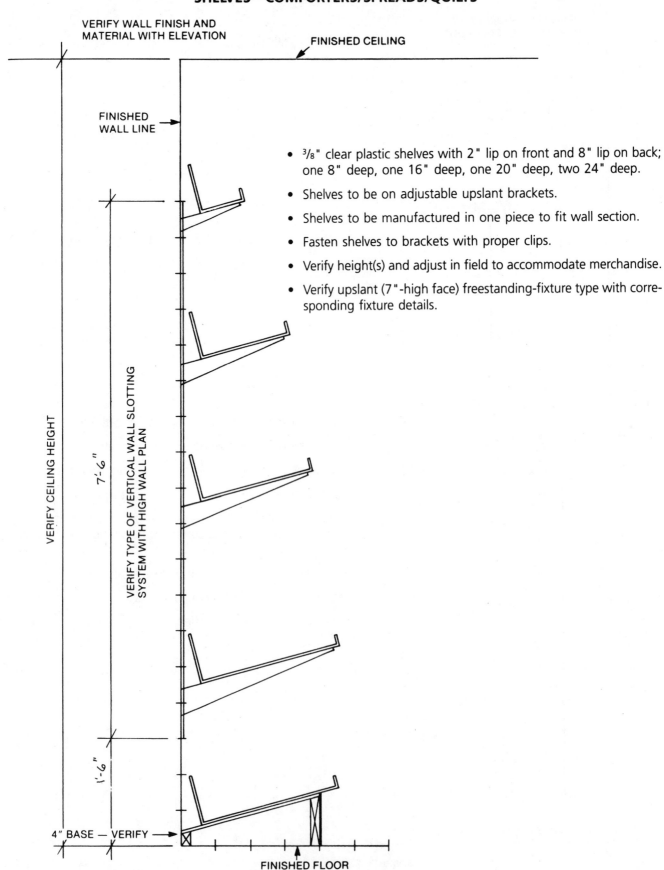

VERIFY WALL FINISH AND
MATERIAL WITH ELEVATION

FINISHED CEILING

FINISHED
WALL LINE

VERIFY CEILING HEIGHT

7'-6"

VERIFY TYPE OF VERTICAL WALL SLOTTING
SYSTEM WITH HIGH WALL PLAN

1'-6"

4" BASE — VERIFY

FINISHED FLOOR

- 3/8" clear plastic shelves with 2" lip on front and 8" lip on back; one 8" deep, one 16" deep, one 20" deep, two 24" deep.
- Shelves to be on adjustable upslant brackets.
- Shelves to be manufactured in one piece to fit wall section.
- Fasten shelves to brackets with proper clips.
- Verify height(s) and adjust in field to accommodate merchandise.
- Verify upslant (7"-high face) freestanding-fixture type with corresponding fixture details.

SHELVES—PILLOWS

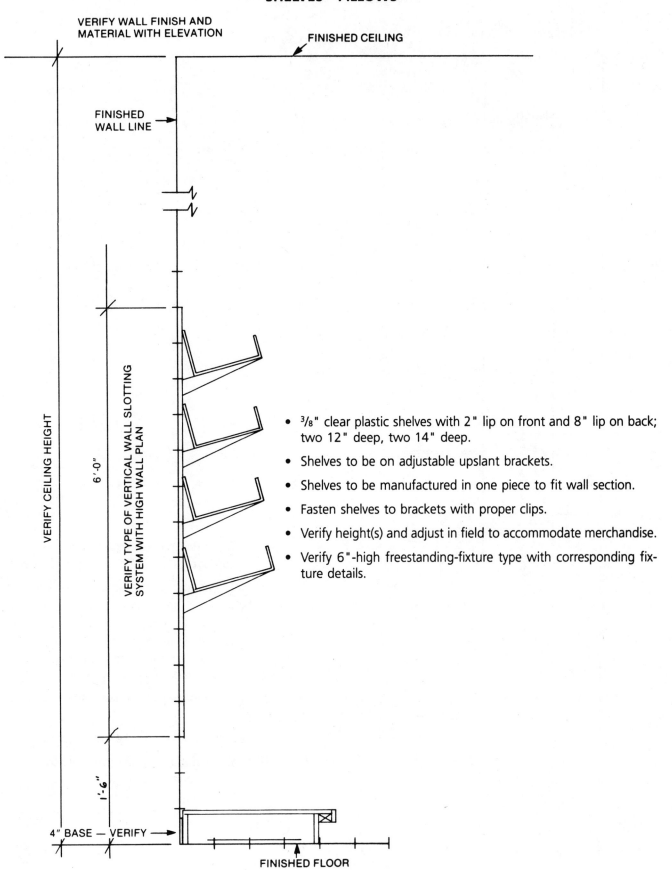

VERIFY WALL FINISH AND
MATERIAL WITH ELEVATION

FINISHED CEILING

FINISHED
WALL LINE

VERIFY CEILING HEIGHT

6'-0"

VERIFY TYPE OF VERTICAL WALL SLOTTING
SYSTEM WITH HIGH WALL PLAN

1'-6"

4" BASE — VERIFY →

FINISHED FLOOR

- $^3/_8$" clear plastic shelves with 2" lip on front and 8" lip on back; two 12" deep, two 14" deep.
- Shelves to be on adjustable upslant brackets.
- Shelves to be manufactured in one piece to fit wall section.
- Fasten shelves to brackets with proper clips.
- Verify height(s) and adjust in field to accommodate merchandise.
- Verify 6"-high freestanding-fixture type with corresponding fixture details.

SHELVES—KITCHEN/LINENS

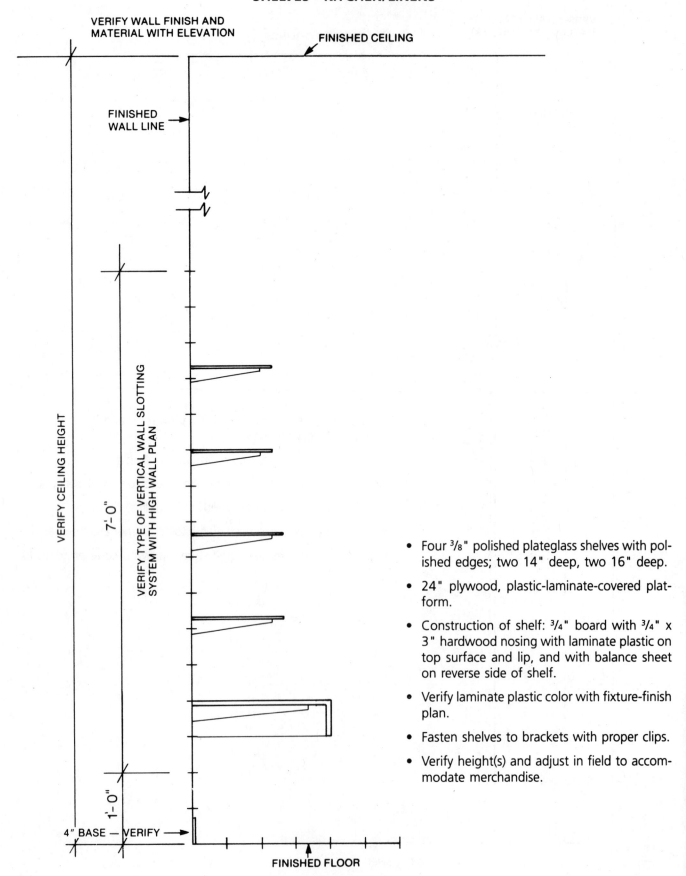

- Four ³⁄₈" polished plateglass shelves with polished edges; two 14" deep, two 16" deep.

- 24" plywood, plastic-laminate-covered platform.

- Construction of shelf: ³⁄₄" board with ³⁄₄" x 3" hardwood nosing with laminate plastic on top surface and lip, and with balance sheet on reverse side of shelf.

- Verify laminate plastic color with fixture-finish plan.

- Fasten shelves to brackets with proper clips.

- Verify height(s) and adjust in field to accommodate merchandise.

SHELVES—LUGGAGE

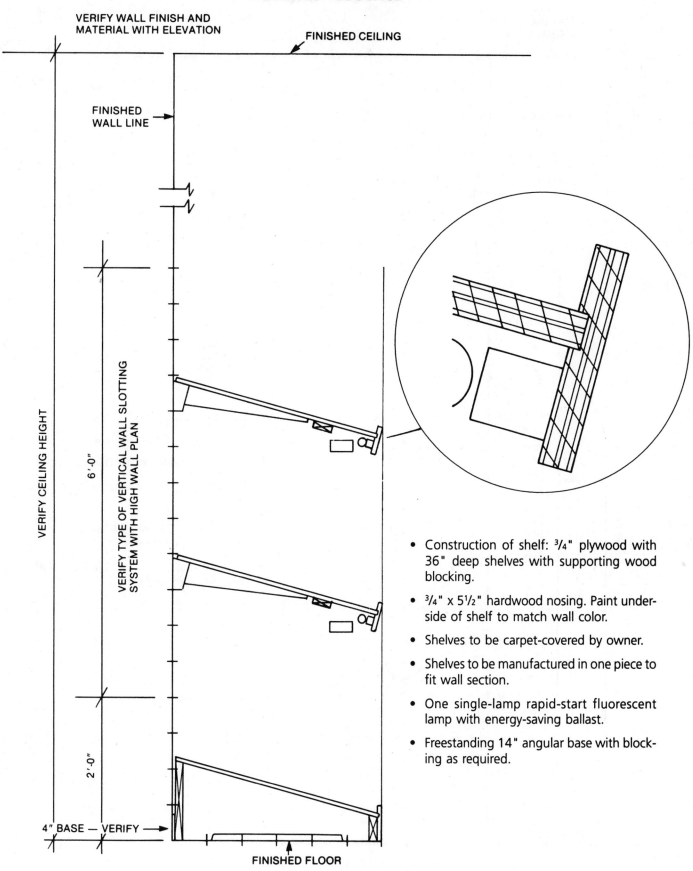

VERIFY WALL FINISH AND
MATERIAL WITH ELEVATION

FINISHED CEILING

FINISHED
WALL LINE

VERIFY CEILING HEIGHT

VERIFY TYPE OF VERTICAL WALL SLOTTING
SYSTEM WITH HIGH WALL PLAN

6'-0"

2'-0"

4" BASE — VERIFY

FINISHED FLOOR

- Construction of shelf: ³⁄₄" plywood with 36" deep shelves with supporting wood blocking.

- ³⁄₄" x 5½" hardwood nosing. Paint underside of shelf to match wall color.

- Shelves to be carpet-covered by owner.

- Shelves to be manufactured in one piece to fit wall section.

- One single-lamp rapid-start fluorescent lamp with energy-saving ballast.

- Freestanding 14" angular base with blocking as required.

SHELVES—PLACEMATS, LINENS

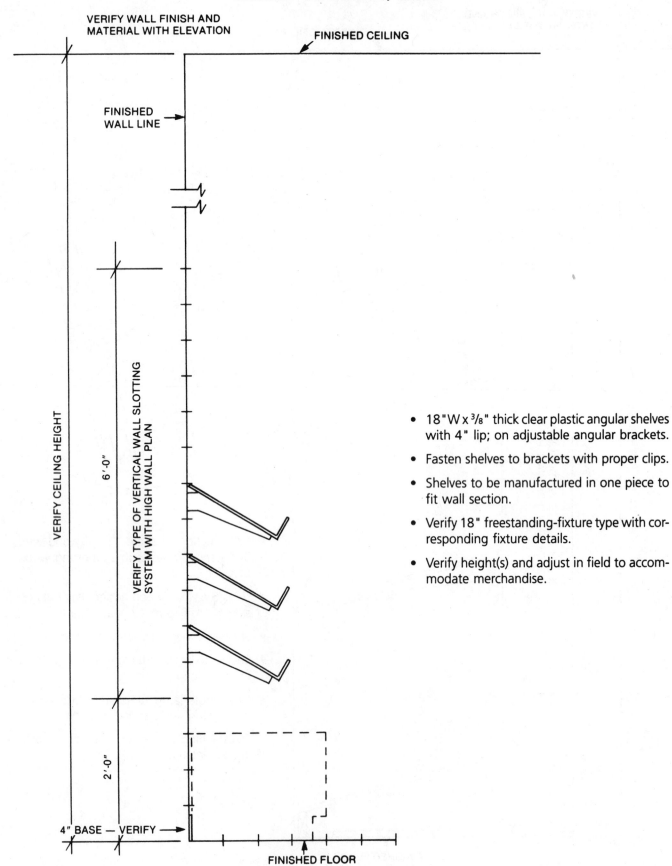

VERIFY WALL FINISH AND
MATERIAL WITH ELEVATION

FINISHED CEILING

FINISHED
WALL LINE

VERIFY CEILING HEIGHT

VERIFY TYPE OF VERTICAL WALL SLOTTING
SYSTEM WITH HIGH WALL PLAN

6'-0"

2'-0"

4" BASE — VERIFY

FINISHED FLOOR

- 18"W x ³⁄₈" thick clear plastic angular shelves with 4" lip; on adjustable angular brackets.

- Fasten shelves to brackets with proper clips.

- Shelves to be manufactured in one piece to fit wall section.

- Verify 18" freestanding-fixture type with corresponding fixture details.

- Verify height(s) and adjust in field to accommodate merchandise.

FIXED ELECTRIFIED SHELVES—CHINA/GIFTS

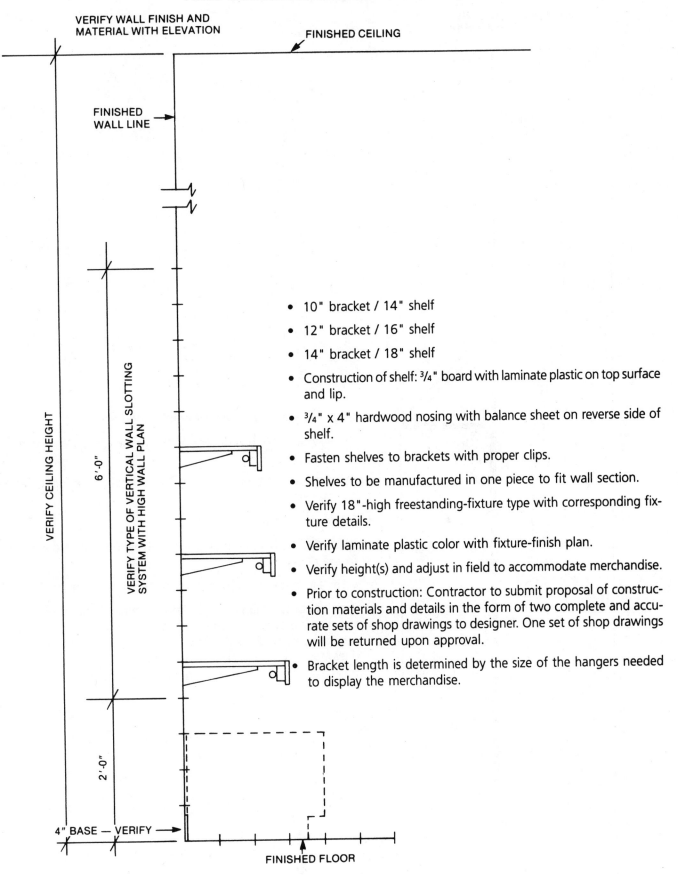

VERIFY WALL FINISH AND
MATERIAL WITH ELEVATION

FINISHED CEILING

FINISHED
WALL LINE

VERIFY CEILING HEIGHT

6'-0"

VERIFY TYPE OF VERTICAL WALL SLOTTING
SYSTEM WITH HIGH WALL PLAN

2'-0"

4" BASE — VERIFY

FINISHED FLOOR

- 10" bracket / 14" shelf
- 12" bracket / 16" shelf
- 14" bracket / 18" shelf
- Construction of shelf: ¾" board with laminate plastic on top surface and lip.
- ¾" x 4" hardwood nosing with balance sheet on reverse side of shelf.
- Fasten shelves to brackets with proper clips.
- Shelves to be manufactured in one piece to fit wall section.
- Verify 18"-high freestanding-fixture type with corresponding fixture details.
- Verify laminate plastic color with fixture-finish plan.
- Verify height(s) and adjust in field to accommodate merchandise.
- Prior to construction: Contractor to submit proposal of construction materials and details in the form of two complete and accurate sets of shop drawings to designer. One set of shop drawings will be returned upon approval.
- Bracket length is determined by the size of the hangers needed to display the merchandise.

CUBES—MEN'S DRESS SHIRTS

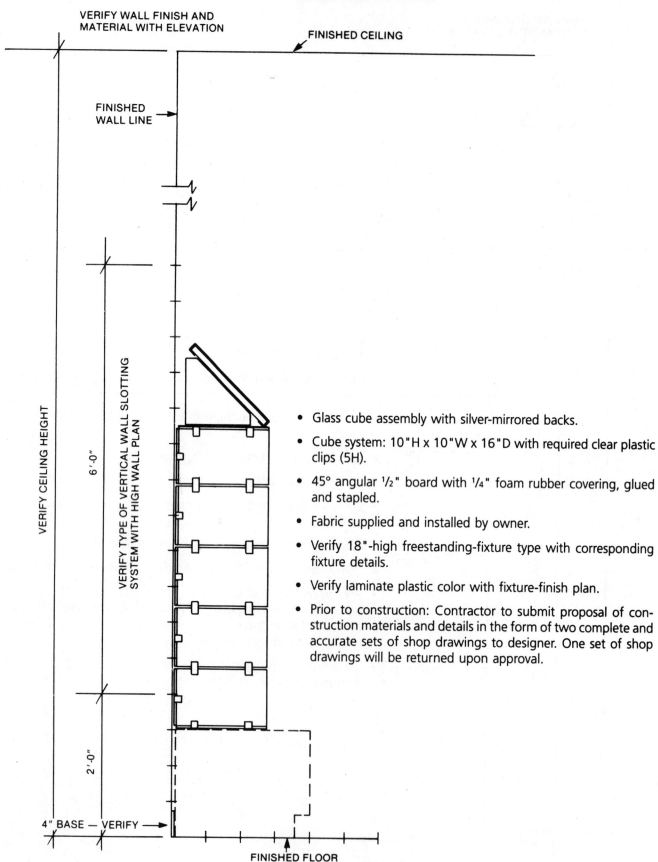

VERIFY WALL FINISH AND
MATERIAL WITH ELEVATION

FINISHED CEILING

FINISHED
WALL LINE

VERIFY CEILING HEIGHT

VERIFY TYPE OF VERTICAL WALL SLOTTING
SYSTEM WITH HIGH WALL PLAN

6'-0"

2'-0"

4" BASE — VERIFY

FINISHED FLOOR

- Glass cube assembly with silver-mirrored backs.
- Cube system: 10"H x 10"W x 16"D with required clear plastic clips (5H).
- 45° angular ½" board with ¼" foam rubber covering, glued and stapled.
- Fabric supplied and installed by owner.
- Verify 18"-high freestanding-fixture type with corresponding fixture details.
- Verify laminate plastic color with fixture-finish plan.
- Prior to construction: Contractor to submit proposal of construction materials and details in the form of two complete and accurate sets of shop drawings to designer. One set of shop drawings will be returned upon approval.

CUBES—SWEATERS

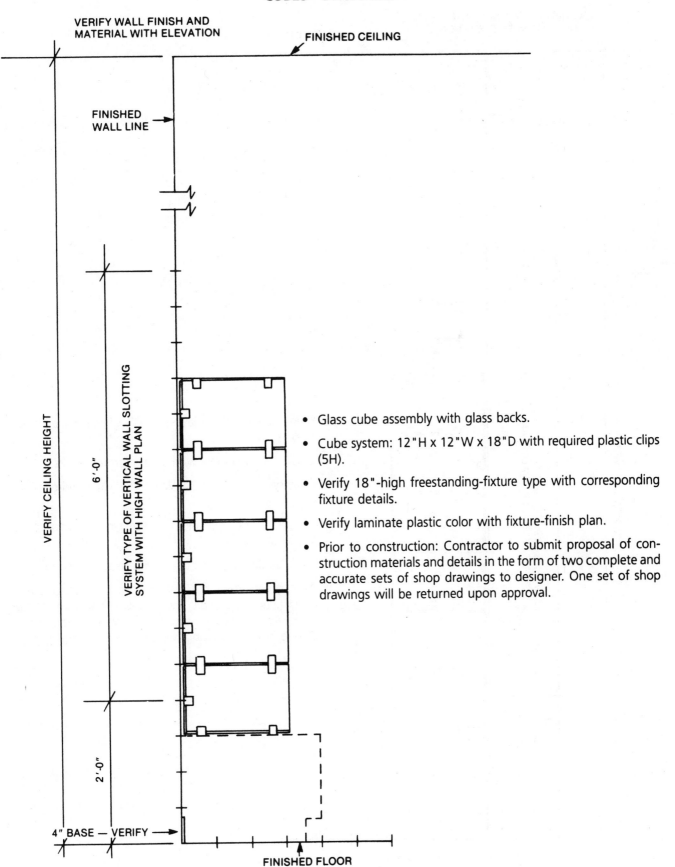

VERIFY WALL FINISH AND
MATERIAL WITH ELEVATION

FINISHED CEILING

FINISHED
WALL LINE

VERIFY CEILING HEIGHT

6'-0"

VERIFY TYPE OF VERTICAL WALL SLOTTING
SYSTEM WITH HIGH WALL PLAN

2'-0"

4" BASE — VERIFY

FINISHED FLOOR

- Glass cube assembly with glass backs.
- Cube system: 12"H x 12"W x 18"D with required plastic clips (5H).
- Verify 18"-high freestanding-fixture type with corresponding fixture details.
- Verify laminate plastic color with fixture-finish plan.
- Prior to construction: Contractor to submit proposal of construction materials and details in the form of two complete and accurate sets of shop drawings to designer. One set of shop drawings will be returned upon approval.

CUBES—TOWELS

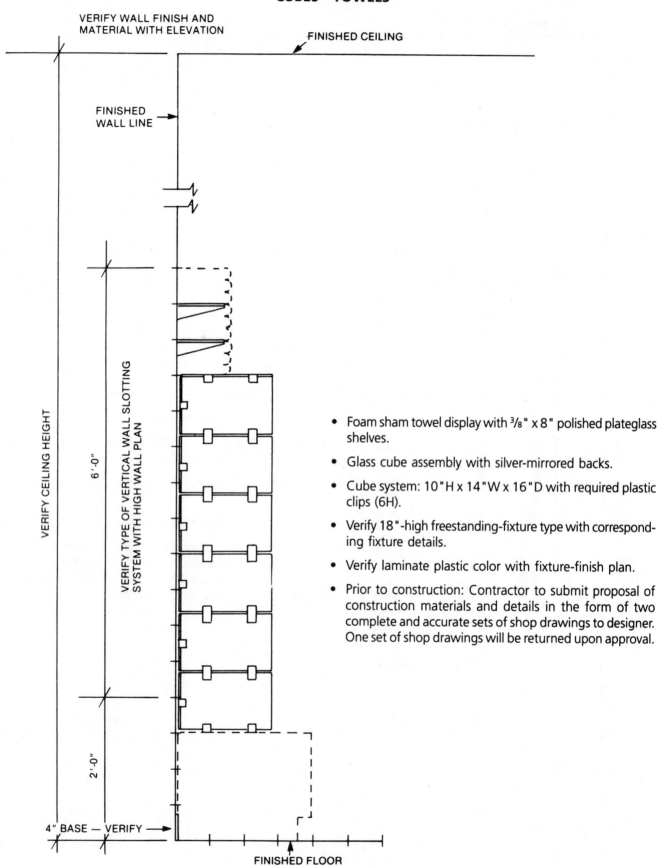

VERIFY WALL FINISH AND
MATERIAL WITH ELEVATION

FINISHED CEILING

FINISHED
WALL LINE

VERIFY CEILING HEIGHT

VERIFY TYPE OF VERTICAL WALL SLOTTING
SYSTEM WITH HIGH WALL PLAN

6'-0"

2'-0"

4" BASE — VERIFY

FINISHED FLOOR

- Foam sham towel display with $\frac{3}{8}$" x 8" polished plateglass shelves.

- Glass cube assembly with silver-mirrored backs.

- Cube system: 10"H x 14"W x 16"D with required plastic clips (6H).

- Verify 18"-high freestanding-fixture type with corresponding fixture details.

- Verify laminate plastic color with fixture-finish plan.

- Prior to construction: Contractor to submit proposal of construction materials and details in the form of two complete and accurate sets of shop drawings to designer. One set of shop drawings will be returned upon approval.

CUBES—TOWELS

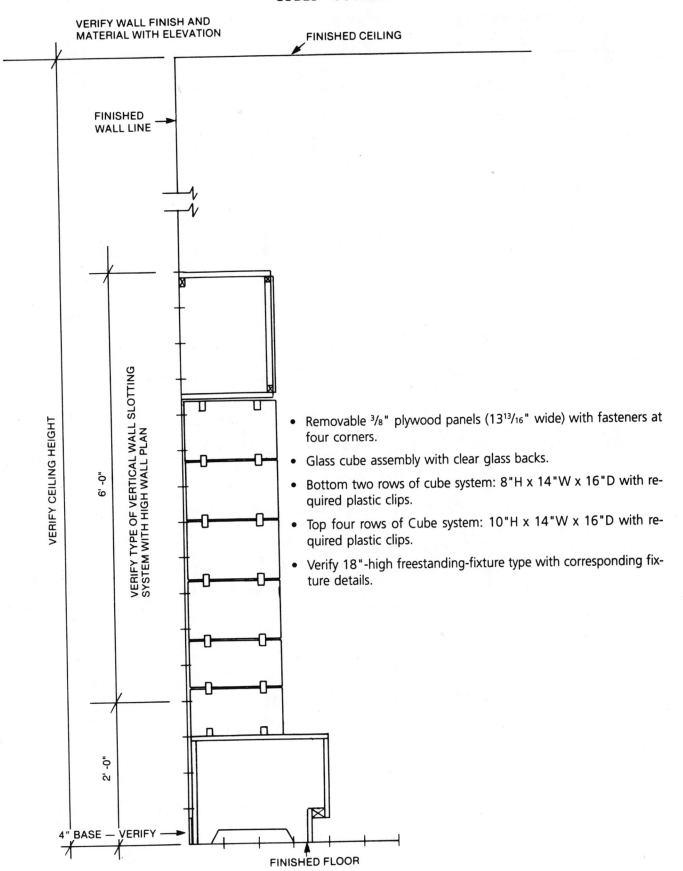

VERIFY WALL FINISH AND MATERIAL WITH ELEVATION

FINISHED CEILING

FINISHED WALL LINE

VERIFY CEILING HEIGHT

VERIFY TYPE OF VERTICAL WALL SLOTTING SYSTEM WITH HIGH WALL PLAN

6'-0"

2'-0"

4" BASE — VERIFY

FINISHED FLOOR

- Removable $^3/_8$" plywood panels ($13^{13}/_{16}$" wide) with fasteners at four corners.
- Glass cube assembly with clear glass backs.
- Bottom two rows of cube system: 8"H x 14"W x 16"D with required plastic clips.
- Top four rows of Cube system: 10"H x 14"W x 16"D with required plastic clips.
- Verify 18"-high freestanding-fixture type with corresponding fixture details.

CUBES—MEN'S FURNISHINGS

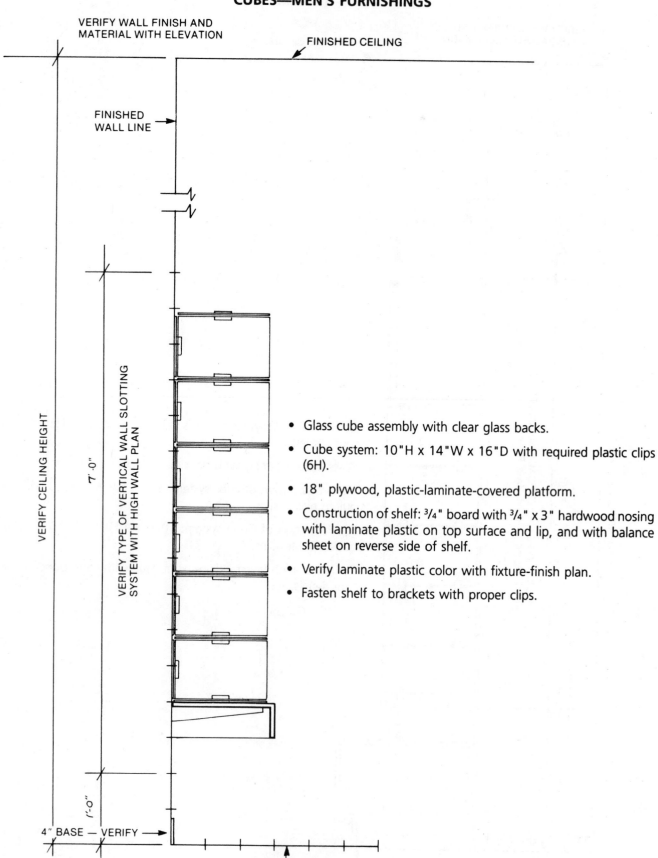

VERIFY WALL FINISH AND
MATERIAL WITH ELEVATION

FINISHED CEILING

FINISHED
WALL LINE

VERIFY CEILING HEIGHT

VERIFY TYPE OF VERTICAL WALL SLOTTING
SYSTEM WITH HIGH WALL PLAN

7'-0"

1'-0"

4" BASE — VERIFY

FINISHED FLOOR

- Glass cube assembly with clear glass backs.
- Cube system: 10"H x 14"W x 16"D with required plastic clips (6H).
- 18" plywood, plastic-laminate-covered platform.
- Construction of shelf: ¾" board with ¾" x 3" hardwood nosing with laminate plastic on top surface and lip, and with balance sheet on reverse side of shelf.
- Verify laminate plastic color with fixture-finish plan.
- Fasten shelf to brackets with proper clips.

SHOWER CURTAINS

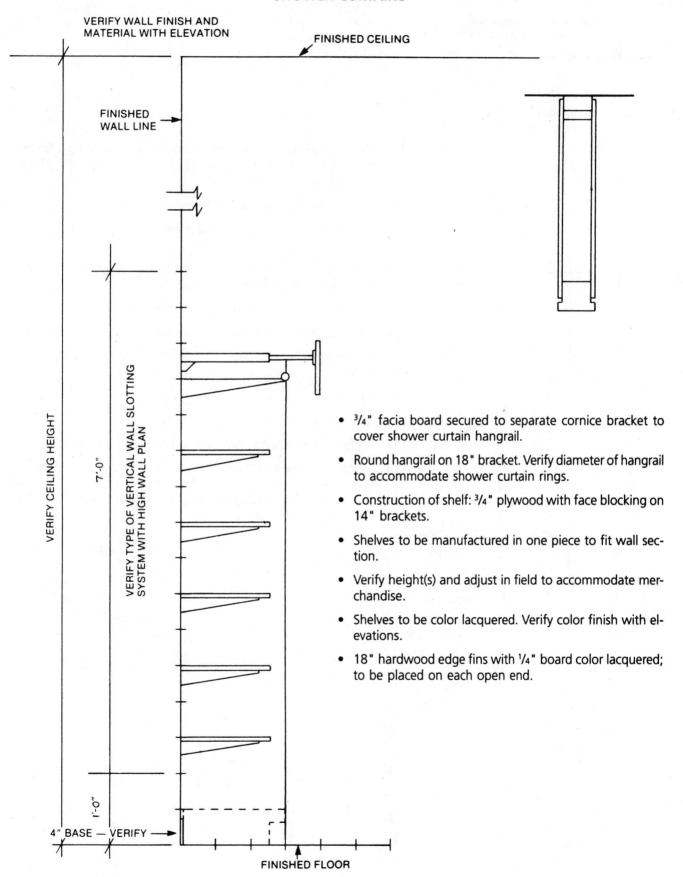

VERIFY WALL FINISH AND
MATERIAL WITH ELEVATION

FINISHED CEILING

FINISHED
WALL LINE

VERIFY CEILING HEIGHT

7'-0"

VERIFY TYPE OF VERTICAL WALL SLOTTING
SYSTEM WITH HIGH WALL PLAN

1'-0"

4" BASE — VERIFY

FINISHED FLOOR

- $\frac{3}{4}$" facia board secured to separate cornice bracket to cover shower curtain hangrail.
- Round hangrail on 18" bracket. Verify diameter of hangrail to accommodate shower curtain rings.
- Construction of shelf: $\frac{3}{4}$" plywood with face blocking on 14" brackets.
- Shelves to be manufactured in one piece to fit wall section.
- Verify height(s) and adjust in field to accommodate merchandise.
- Shelves to be color lacquered. Verify color finish with elevations.
- 18" hardwood edge fins with $\frac{1}{4}$" board color lacquered; to be placed on each open end.

SHOES—MEN'S

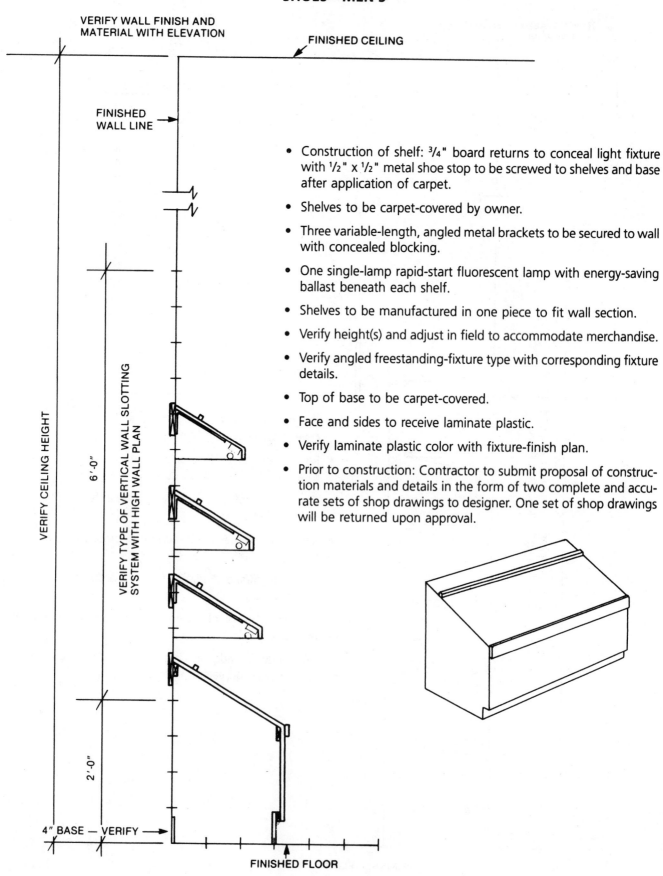

VERIFY WALL FINISH AND
MATERIAL WITH ELEVATION

FINISHED CEILING

FINISHED
WALL LINE

VERIFY CEILING HEIGHT

VERIFY TYPE OF VERTICAL WALL SLOTTING
SYSTEM WITH HIGH WALL PLAN

6'-0"

2'-0"

4" BASE — VERIFY →

FINISHED FLOOR

- Construction of shelf: ¾" board returns to conceal light fixture with ½" x ½" metal shoe stop to be screwed to shelves and base after application of carpet.

- Shelves to be carpet-covered by owner.

- Three variable-length, angled metal brackets to be secured to wall with concealed blocking.

- One single-lamp rapid-start fluorescent lamp with energy-saving ballast beneath each shelf.

- Shelves to be manufactured in one piece to fit wall section.

- Verify height(s) and adjust in field to accommodate merchandise.

- Verify angled freestanding-fixture type with corresponding fixture details.

- Top of base to be carpet-covered.

- Face and sides to receive laminate plastic.

- Verify laminate plastic color with fixture-finish plan.

- Prior to construction: Contractor to submit proposal of construction materials and details in the form of two complete and accurate sets of shop drawings to designer. One set of shop drawings will be returned upon approval.

CURTAINS/DRAPERIES

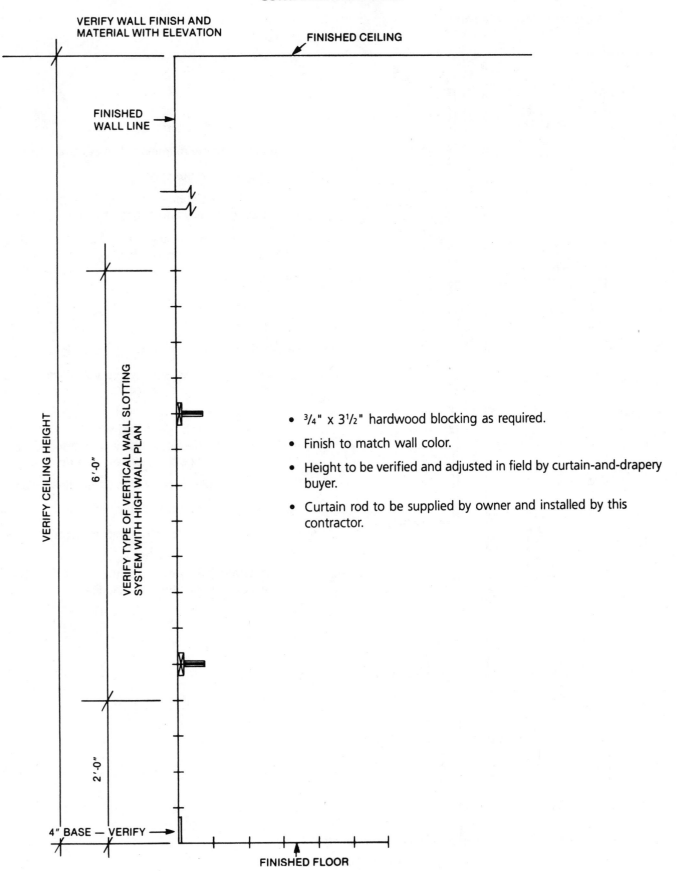

VERIFY WALL FINISH AND
MATERIAL WITH ELEVATION

FINISHED CEILING

FINISHED
WALL LINE

VERIFY CEILING HEIGHT

6'-0"

VERIFY TYPE OF VERTICAL WALL SLOTTING
SYSTEM WITH HIGH WALL PLAN

2'-0"

4" BASE — VERIFY →

FINISHED FLOOR

- ¾" x 3½" hardwood blocking as required.
- Finish to match wall color.
- Height to be verified and adjusted in field by curtain-and-drapery buyer.
- Curtain rod to be supplied by owner and installed by this contractor.

CURTAINS/DRAPERIES

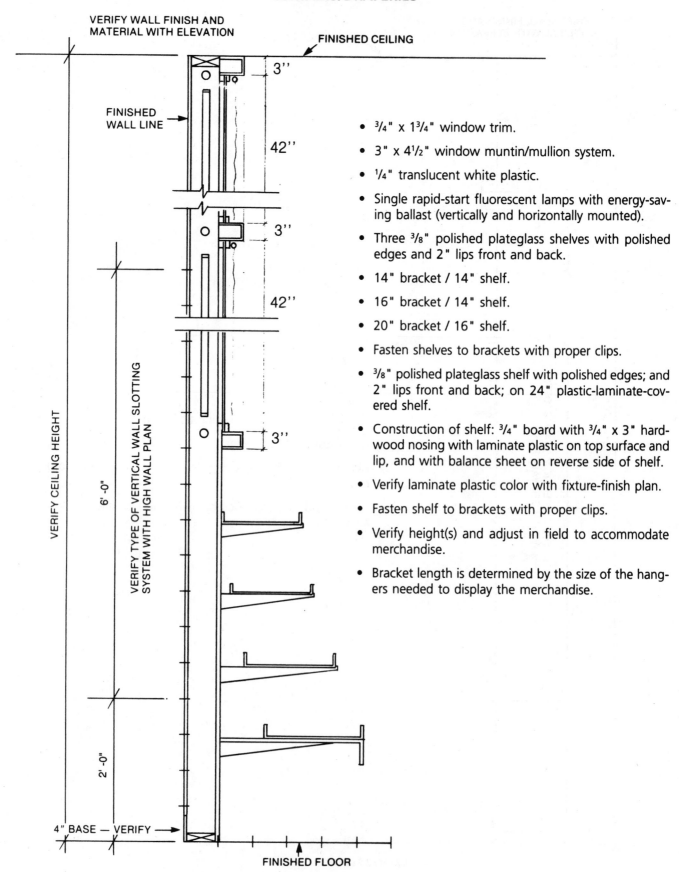

VERIFY WALL FINISH AND
MATERIAL WITH ELEVATION

FINISHED CEILING

FINISHED
WALL LINE

3''

42''

3''

42''

VERIFY CEILING HEIGHT

VERIFY TYPE OF VERTICAL WALL SLOTTING
SYSTEM WITH HIGH WALL PLAN

6'-0"

3''

2'-0"

4" BASE — VERIFY

FINISHED FLOOR

- ³/₄" x 1³/₄" window trim.
- 3" x 4¹/₂" window muntin/mullion system.
- ¹/₄" translucent white plastic.
- Single rapid-start fluorescent lamps with energy-saving ballast (vertically and horizontally mounted).
- Three ³/₈" polished plateglass shelves with polished edges and 2" lips front and back.
- 14" bracket / 14" shelf.
- 16" bracket / 14" shelf.
- 20" bracket / 16" shelf.
- Fasten shelves to brackets with proper clips.
- ³/₈" polished plateglass shelf with polished edges; and 2" lips front and back; on 24" plastic-laminate-covered shelf.
- Construction of shelf: ³/₄" board with ³/₄" x 3" hardwood nosing with laminate plastic on top surface and lip, and with balance sheet on reverse side of shelf.
- Verify laminate plastic color with fixture-finish plan.
- Fasten shelf to brackets with proper clips.
- Verify height(s) and adjust in field to accommodate merchandise.
- Bracket length is determined by the size of the hangers needed to display the merchandise.

CURTAINS/DRAPERIES

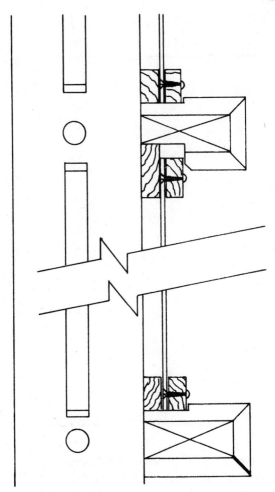

- 3" x 4½" muntin made of ¾" paint-grade wood. Plastic laminate covered.
- Verify laminate plastic color with fixture-finish plan.
- Air space to allow for lift and removal of frame and window.
- Single-lamp rapid-start fluorescent lamps with energy-saving ballast (vertically and horizontally mounted).
- ¼" translucent white plastic screwed from back to front window trim (¾" thick).

Vertical Section—Scale: 3" = 1'0"

¼" holes drilled to allow for insertion of screwdriver, for example, and for lift and removal of window.

Plan section at joint of 2 modules—Scale: 3" = 1'0"

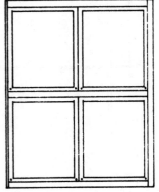

Elevation of one module—
Scale: ¼" x 1'0"

COMFORTER DISPLAYER

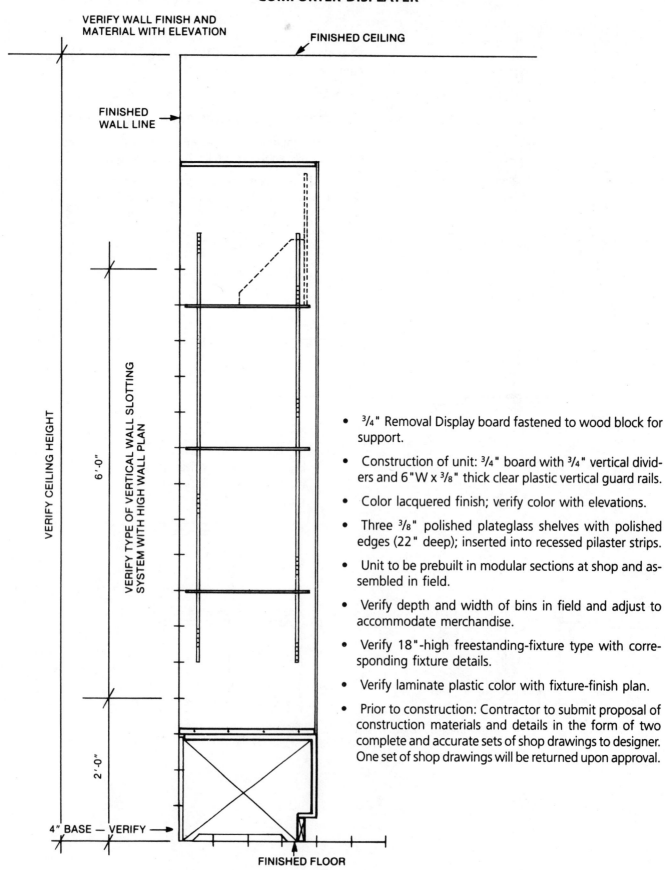

VERIFY WALL FINISH AND
MATERIAL WITH ELEVATION

FINISHED CEILING

FINISHED
WALL LINE

VERIFY CEILING HEIGHT

6'-0"

VERIFY TYPE OF VERTICAL WALL SLOTTING
SYSTEM WITH HIGH WALL PLAN

2'-0"

4" BASE — VERIFY →

FINISHED FLOOR

- ¾" Removal Display board fastened to wood block for support.

- Construction of unit: ¾" board with ¾" vertical dividers and 6"W x ⅜" thick clear plastic vertical guard rails.

- Color lacquered finish; verify color with elevations.

- Three ⅜" polished plateglass shelves with polished edges (22" deep); inserted into recessed pilaster strips.

- Unit to be prebuilt in modular sections at shop and assembled in field.

- Verify depth and width of bins in field and adjust to accommodate merchandise.

- Verify 18"-high freestanding-fixture type with corresponding fixture details.

- Verify laminate plastic color with fixture-finish plan.

- Prior to construction: Contractor to submit proposal of construction materials and details in the form of two complete and accurate sets of shop drawings to designer. One set of shop drawings will be returned upon approval.

PILLOW DISPLAYER

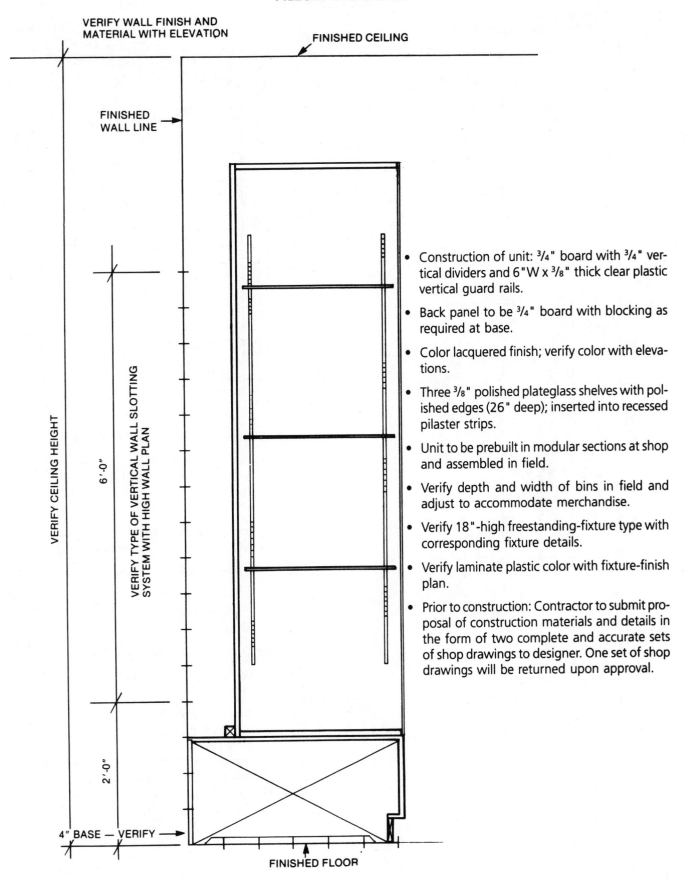

VERIFY WALL FINISH AND
MATERIAL WITH ELEVATION

FINISHED CEILING

FINISHED
WALL LINE

VERIFY CEILING HEIGHT

VERIFY TYPE OF VERTICAL WALL SLOTTING
SYSTEM WITH HIGH WALL PLAN

6'-0"

2'-0"

4" BASE — VERIFY

FINISHED FLOOR

- Construction of unit: ³/₄" board with ³/₄" vertical dividers and 6"W x ³/₈" thick clear plastic vertical guard rails.

- Back panel to be ³/₄" board with blocking as required at base.

- Color lacquered finish; verify color with elevations.

- Three ³/₈" polished plateglass shelves with polished edges (26" deep); inserted into recessed pilaster strips.

- Unit to be prebuilt in modular sections at shop and assembled in field.

- Verify depth and width of bins in field and adjust to accommodate merchandise.

- Verify 18"-high freestanding-fixture type with corresponding fixture details.

- Verify laminate plastic color with fixture-finish plan.

- Prior to construction: Contractor to submit proposal of construction materials and details in the form of two complete and accurate sets of shop drawings to designer. One set of shop drawings will be returned upon approval.

SECURITY DISPLAY CASE

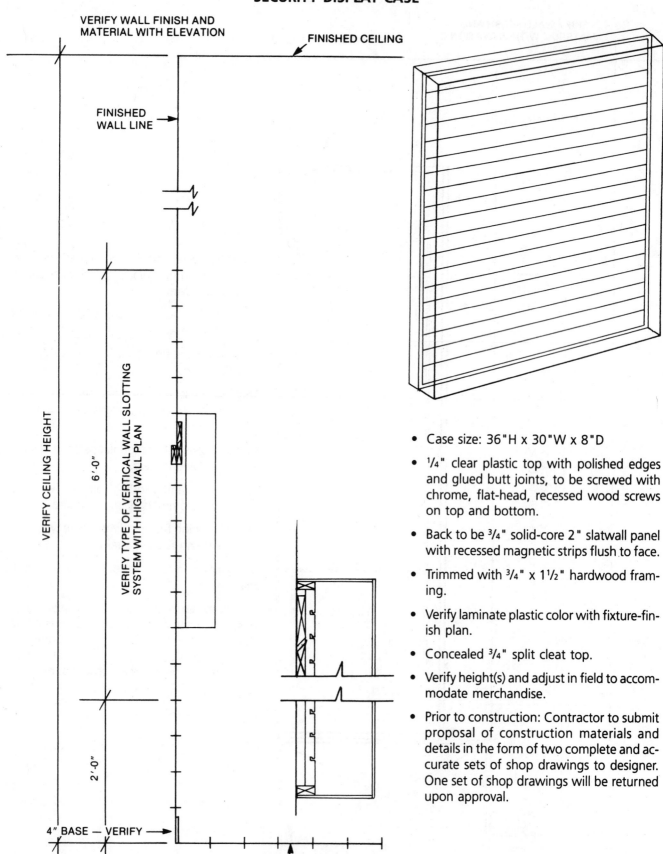

VERIFY WALL FINISH AND
MATERIAL WITH ELEVATION

FINISHED CEILING

FINISHED
WALL LINE

VERIFY CEILING HEIGHT

VERIFY TYPE OF VERTICAL WALL SLOTTING
SYSTEM WITH HIGH WALL PLAN

6'-0"

2'-0"

4" BASE — VERIFY

FINISHED FLOOR

- Case size: 36"H x 30"W x 8"D

- ¼" clear plastic top with polished edges and glued butt joints, to be screwed with chrome, flat-head, recessed wood screws on top and bottom.

- Back to be ¾" solid-core 2" slatwall panel with recessed magnetic strips flush to face.

- Trimmed with ¾" x 1½" hardwood framing.

- Verify laminate plastic color with fixture-finish plan.

- Concealed ¾" split cleat top.

- Verify height(s) and adjust in field to accommodate merchandise.

- Prior to construction: Contractor to submit proposal of construction materials and details in the form of two complete and accurate sets of shop drawings to designer. One set of shop drawings will be returned upon approval.

SHADOW BOX

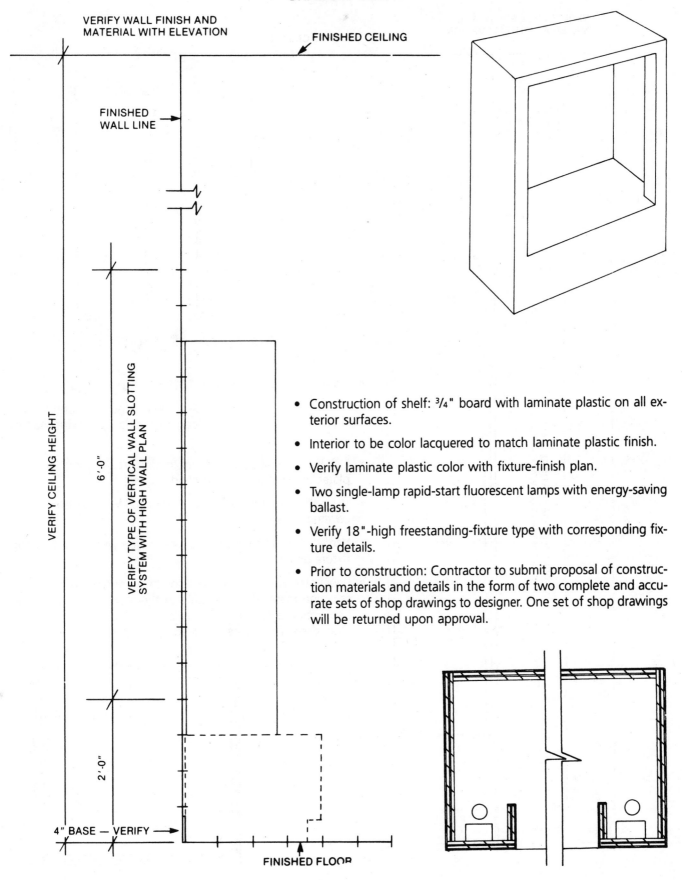

VERIFY WALL FINISH AND
MATERIAL WITH ELEVATION

FINISHED CEILING

FINISHED
WALL LINE

VERIFY CEILING HEIGHT

6'-0"

VERIFY TYPE OF VERTICAL WALL SLOTTING
SYSTEM WITH HIGH WALL PLAN

2'-0"

4" BASE — VERIFY

FINISHED FLOOR

- Construction of shelf: ¾" board with laminate plastic on all exterior surfaces.

- Interior to be color lacquered to match laminate plastic finish.

- Verify laminate plastic color with fixture-finish plan.

- Two single-lamp rapid-start fluorescent lamps with energy-saving ballast.

- Verify 18"-high freestanding-fixture type with corresponding fixture details.

- Prior to construction: Contractor to submit proposal of construction materials and details in the form of two complete and accurate sets of shop drawings to designer. One set of shop drawings will be returned upon approval.

WALL SECURITY CASE

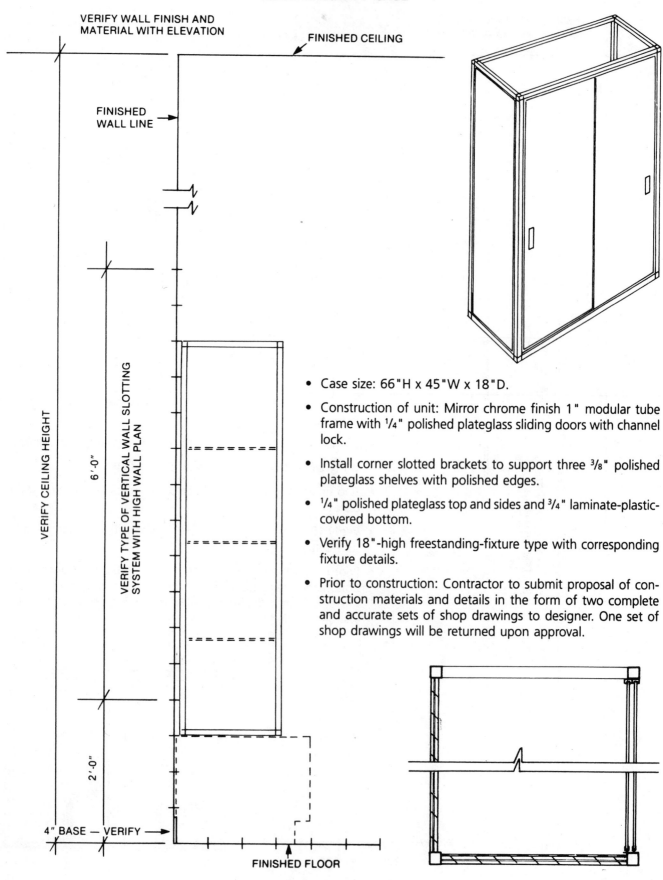

VERIFY WALL FINISH AND
MATERIAL WITH ELEVATION

FINISHED CEILING

FINISHED
WALL LINE

VERIFY CEILING HEIGHT

VERIFY TYPE OF VERTICAL WALL SLOTTING
SYSTEM WITH HIGH WALL PLAN

6'-0"

2'-0"

4" BASE — VERIFY →

FINISHED FLOOR

- Case size: 66"H x 45"W x 18"D.
- Construction of unit: Mirror chrome finish 1" modular tube frame with ¼" polished plateglass sliding doors with channel lock.
- Install corner slotted brackets to support three ⅜" polished plateglass shelves with polished edges.
- ¼" polished plateglass top and sides and ¾" laminate-plastic-covered bottom.
- Verify 18"-high freestanding-fixture type with corresponding fixture details.
- Prior to construction: Contractor to submit proposal of construction materials and details in the form of two complete and accurate sets of shop drawings to designer. One set of shop drawings will be returned upon approval.

WINDOW LIGHT BOX

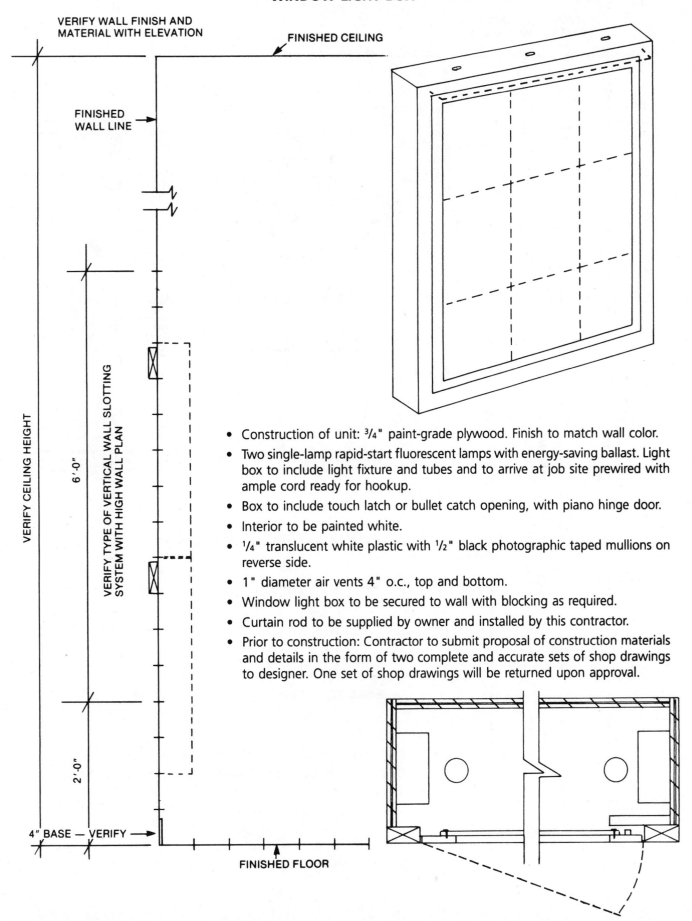

VERIFY WALL FINISH AND
MATERIAL WITH ELEVATION

FINISHED CEILING

FINISHED
WALL LINE

VERIFY CEILING HEIGHT

6'-0"

VERIFY TYPE OF VERTICAL WALL SLOTTING
SYSTEM WITH HIGH WALL PLAN

2'-0"

4" BASE — VERIFY

FINISHED FLOOR

- Construction of unit: ³/₄" paint-grade plywood. Finish to match wall color.
- Two single-lamp rapid-start fluorescent lamps with energy-saving ballast. Light box to include light fixture and tubes and to arrive at job site prewired with ample cord ready for hookup.
- Box to include touch latch or bullet catch opening, with piano hinge door.
- Interior to be painted white.
- ¹/₄" translucent white plastic with ¹/₂" black photographic taped mullions on reverse side.
- 1" diameter air vents 4" o.c., top and bottom.
- Window light box to be secured to wall with blocking as required.
- Curtain rod to be supplied by owner and installed by this contractor.
- Prior to construction: Contractor to submit proposal of construction materials and details in the form of two complete and accurate sets of shop drawings to designer. One set of shop drawings will be returned upon approval.

MERCHANDISING HARDWARE—WOOD STUD

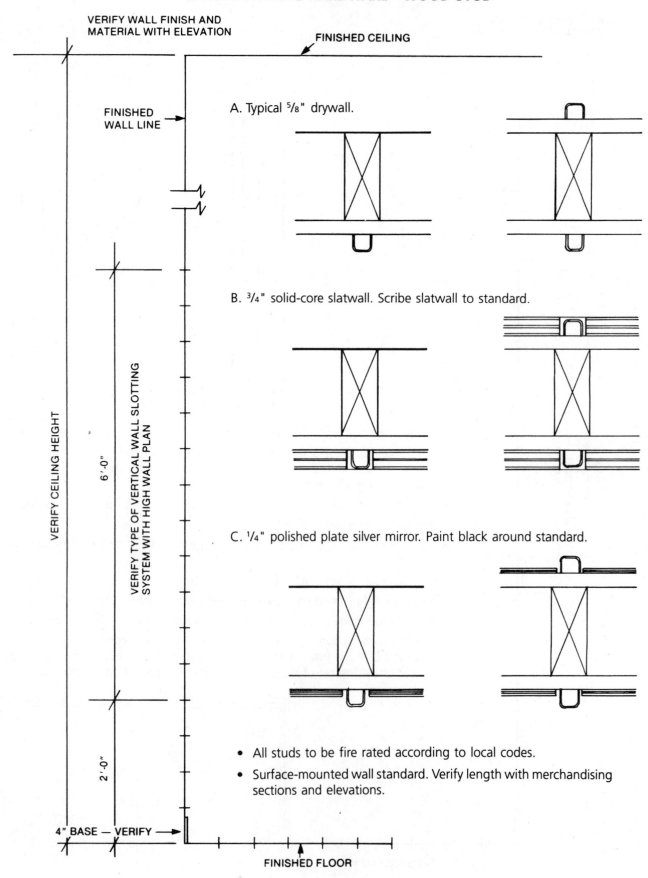

VERIFY WALL FINISH AND
MATERIAL WITH ELEVATION

FINISHED CEILING

FINISHED
WALL LINE

A. Typical ⅝" drywall.

B. ¾" solid-core slatwall. Scribe slatwall to standard.

C. ¼" polished plate silver mirror. Paint black around standard.

VERIFY CEILING HEIGHT

6'-0"

VERIFY TYPE OF VERTICAL WALL SLOTTING
SYSTEM WITH HIGH WALL PLAN

2'-0"

- All studs to be fire rated according to local codes.
- Surface-mounted wall standard. Verify length with merchandising sections and elevations.

4" BASE — VERIFY

FINISHED FLOOR

MERCHANDISING HARDWARE—DISPLAY STUD

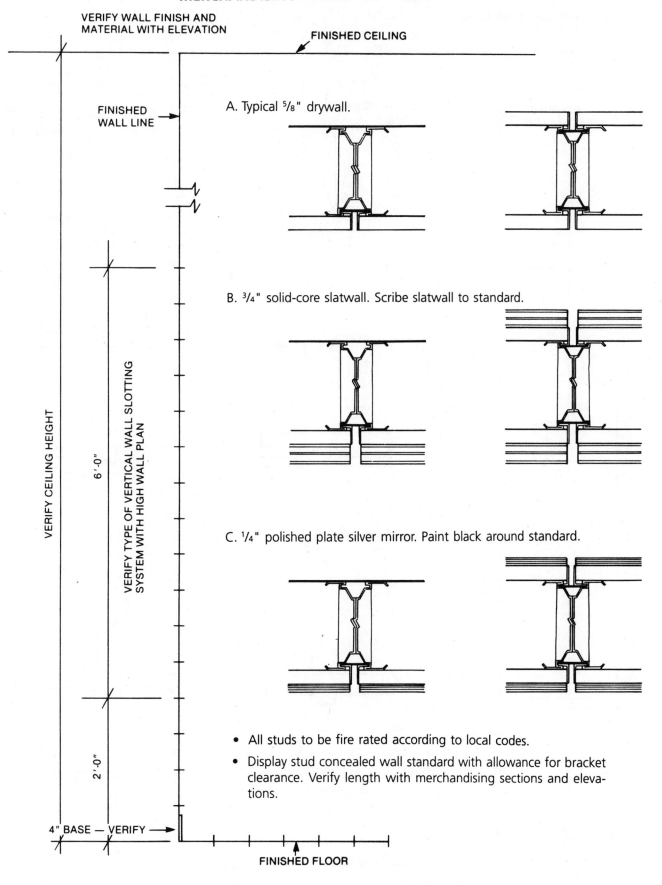

VERIFY WALL FINISH AND
MATERIAL WITH ELEVATION

FINISHED CEILING

FINISHED
WALL LINE

A. Typical ⅝" drywall.

B. ¾" solid-core slatwall. Scribe slatwall to standard.

C. ¼" polished plate silver mirror. Paint black around standard.

VERIFY CEILING HEIGHT

VERIFY TYPE OF VERTICAL WALL SLOTTING
SYSTEM WITH HIGH WALL PLAN

6'-0"

2'-0"

4" BASE — VERIFY

FINISHED FLOOR

- All studs to be fire rated according to local codes.
- Display stud concealed wall standard with allowance for bracket clearance. Verify length with merchandising sections and elevations.

MERCHANDISING HARDWARE—METAL STUD

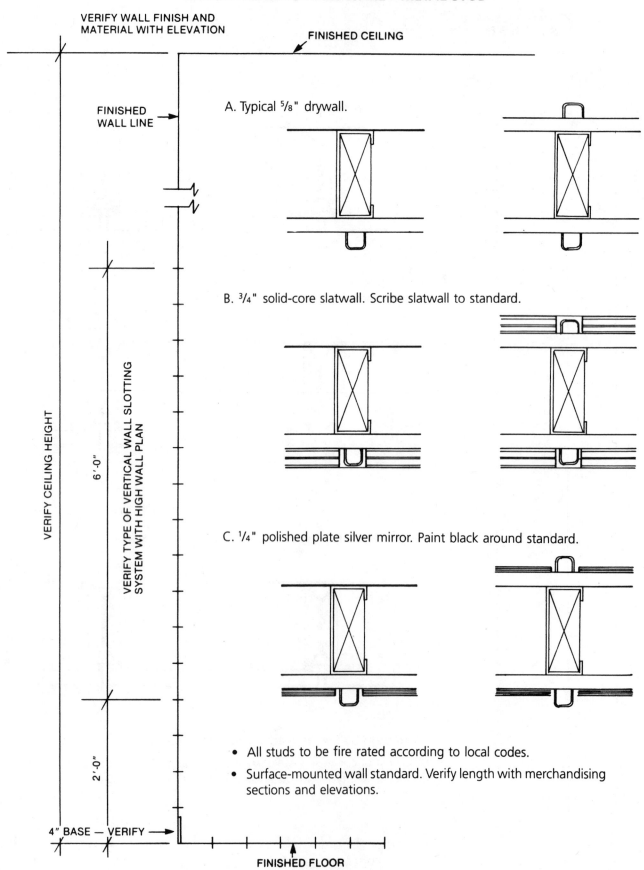

VERIFY WALL FINISH AND
MATERIAL WITH ELEVATION

FINISHED CEILING

FINISHED
WALL LINE

A. Typical ⅝" drywall.

B. ¾" solid-core slatwall. Scribe slatwall to standard.

C. ¼" polished plate silver mirror. Paint black around standard.

VERIFY CEILING HEIGHT

VERIFY TYPE OF VERTICAL WALL SLOTTING
SYSTEM WITH HIGH WALL PLAN

6'-0"

2'-0"

4" BASE — VERIFY

FINISHED FLOOR

- All studs to be fire rated according to local codes.
- Surface-mounted wall standard. Verify length with merchandising sections and elevations.

Chapter 21

DECOR SECTIONS

Another responsibility of the store planner is drawing sections through the decor that appear on the elevations. The decor section will illustrate the shape, size, and materials used to create the design. The decor section will also help the contractor to understand how the item is affixed to the interior walls and how illumination is concealed.

Many times the contractor will fabricate the decor item differently than the planner has illustrated, but the finished appearance will still be the same.

This chapter illustrates the many kinds of decor sections.

HOW TO READ A DECOR SECTION

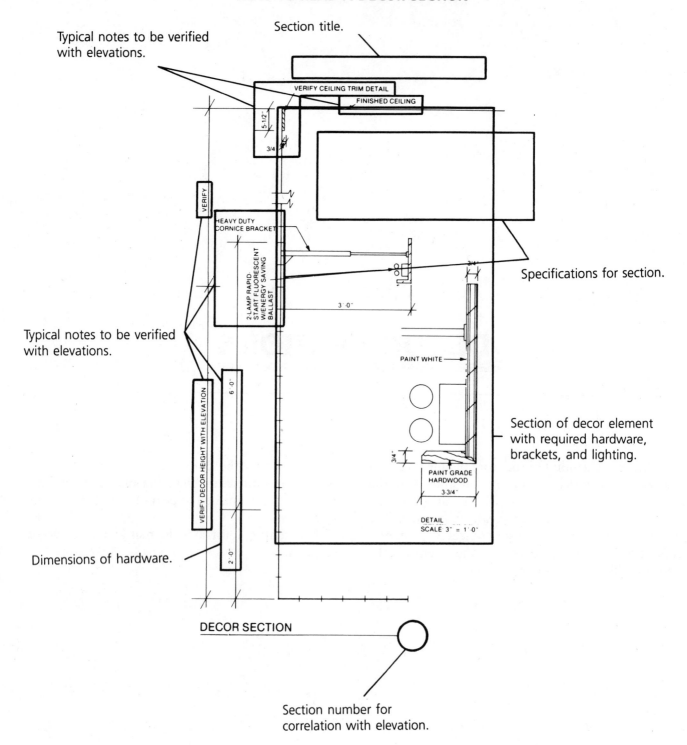

Typical notes to be verified with elevations.

Section title.

VERIFY CEILING TRIM DETAIL

FINISHED CEILING

5-1/2"

3/4

VERIFY

HEAVY DUTY CORNICE BRACKET

2-LAMP RAPID START FLUORESCENT W/ENERGY SAVING BALLAST

Specifications for section.

3'-0"

PAINT WHITE

Typical notes to be verified with elevations.

VERIFY DECOR HEIGHT WITH ELEVATION

6'-0"

Section of decor element with required hardware, brackets, and lighting.

3/4"

PAINT GRADE HARDWOOD

3-3/4"

DETAIL
SCALE 3" = 1'-0"

Dimensions of hardware.

2'-0"

DECOR SECTION

Section number for correlation with elevation.

TYPICAL NOTES TO BE VERIFIED CEILING-TRIM DETAIL

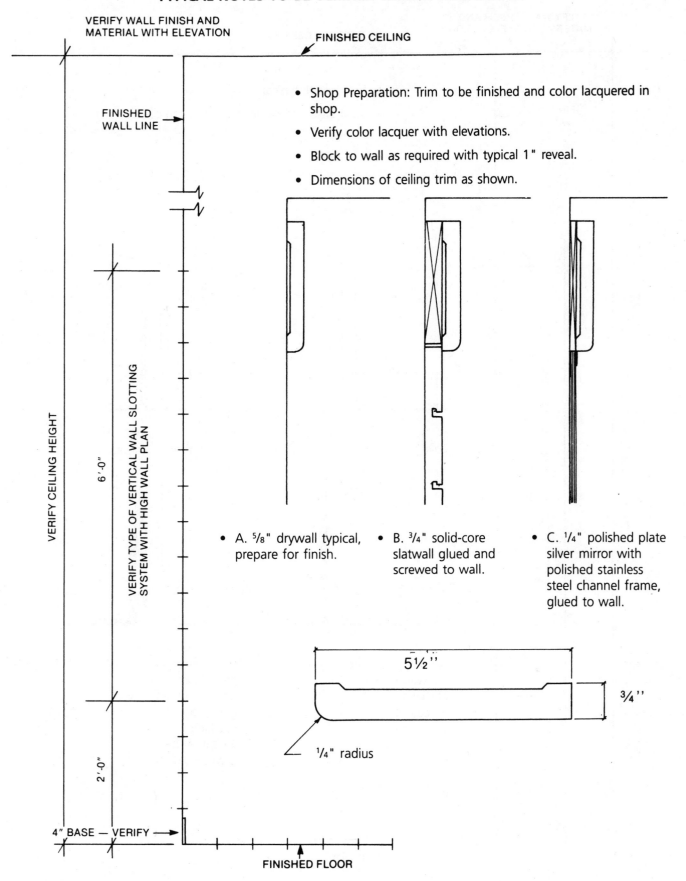

VERIFY WALL FINISH AND MATERIAL WITH ELEVATION

FINISHED CEILING

FINISHED WALL LINE

- Shop Preparation: Trim to be finished and color lacquered in shop.
- Verify color lacquer with elevations.
- Block to wall as required with typical 1" reveal.
- Dimensions of ceiling trim as shown.

VERIFY CEILING HEIGHT

6'-0"

VERIFY TYPE OF VERTICAL WALL SLOTTING SYSTEM WITH HIGH WALL PLAN

- A. ⁵/₈" drywall typical, prepare for finish.
- B. ³/₄" solid-core slatwall glued and screwed to wall.
- C. ¹/₄" polished plate silver mirror with polished stainless steel channel frame, glued to wall.

5½''

¾''

¼" radius

2'-0"

4" BASE — VERIFY

FINISHED FLOOR

BASE DETAIL

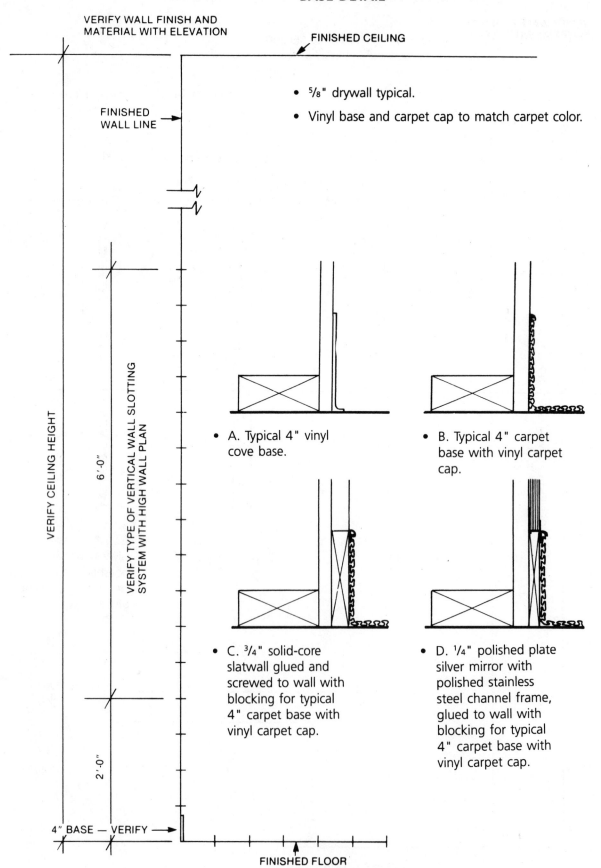

VERIFY WALL FINISH AND
MATERIAL WITH ELEVATION

FINISHED CEILING

FINISHED
WALL LINE

- ⅝" drywall typical.
- Vinyl base and carpet cap to match carpet color.

VERIFY CEILING HEIGHT

VERIFY TYPE OF VERTICAL WALL SLOTTING
SYSTEM WITH HIGH WALL PLAN

6'-0"

2'-0"

- A. Typical 4" vinyl
  cove base.

- B. Typical 4" carpet
  base with vinyl carpet
  cap.

- C. ¾" solid-core
  slatwall glued and
  screwed to wall with
  blocking for typical
  4" carpet base with
  vinyl carpet cap.

- D. ¼" polished plate
  silver mirror with
  polished stainless
  steel channel frame,
  glued to wall with
  blocking for typical
  4" carpet base with
  vinyl carpet cap.

4" BASE — VERIFY

FINISHED FLOOR

FLOORING TRANSITION DETAIL

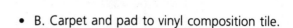

- A. Glue down carpet to vinyl composition tile.

- B. Carpet and pad to vinyl composition tile.

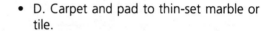

- C. Glue down carpet to thin set marble or tile.

- D. Carpet and pad to thin-set marble or tile.

- E. Glue down carpet to parquet.

- F. Carpet and pad to parquet.

ENDCAP DETAIL

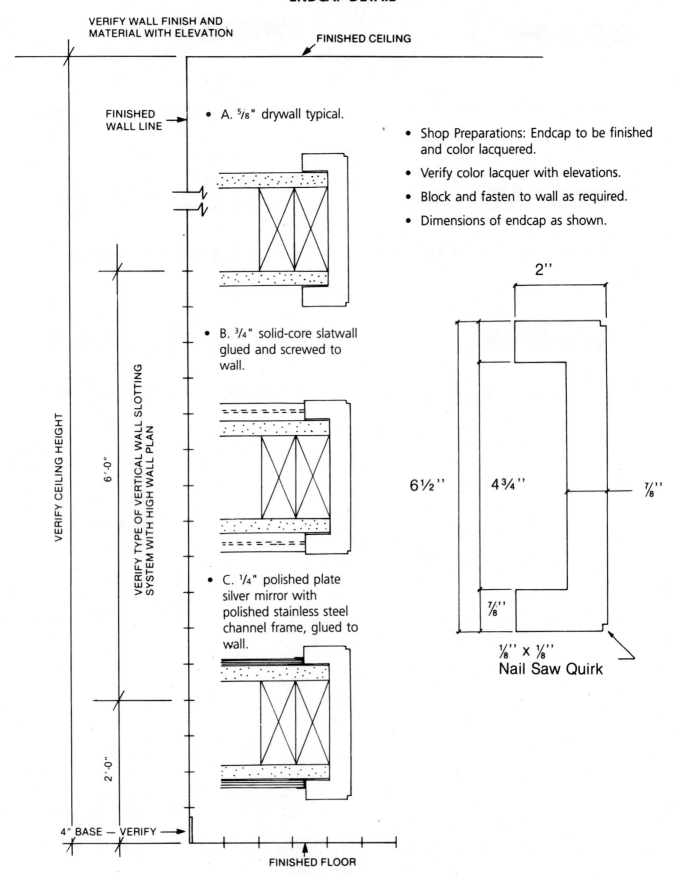

VERIFY WALL FINISH AND
MATERIAL WITH ELEVATION

FINISHED CEILING

FINISHED
WALL LINE

- A. ⅝" drywall typical.

- Shop Preparations: Endcap to be finished and color lacquered.
- Verify color lacquer with elevations.
- Block and fasten to wall as required.
- Dimensions of endcap as shown.

- B. ¾" solid-core slatwall glued and screwed to wall.

- C. ¼" polished plate silver mirror with polished stainless steel channel frame, glued to wall.

VERIFY CEILING HEIGHT

6'-0"

VERIFY TYPE OF VERTICAL WALL SLOTTING SYSTEM WITH HIGH WALL PLAN

2'-0"

4" BASE — VERIFY

FINISHED FLOOR

2"

6½"   4¾"   ⅞"

⅞"

⅞"

⅛" x ⅛"
Nail Saw Quirk

CORNICE BLOCKING DETAIL

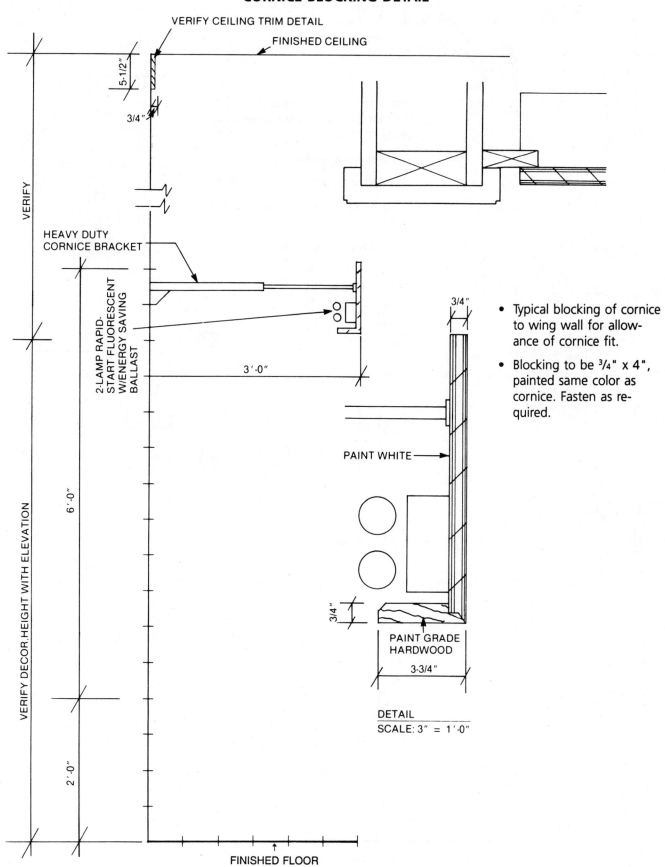

VERIFY CEILING TRIM DETAIL

FINISHED CEILING

5-1/2"

3/4"

VERIFY

HEAVY DUTY
CORNICE BRACKET

2-LAMP RAPID-
START FLUORESCENT
W/ENERGY SAVING
BALLAST

3'-0"

VERIFY DECOR. HEIGHT WITH ELEVATION

6'-0"

2'-0"

FINISHED FLOOR

3/4"

PAINT WHITE

3/4"

PAINT GRADE
HARDWOOD

3-3/4"

DETAIL
SCALE: 3" = 1'-0"

- Typical blocking of cornice to wing wall for allowance of cornice fit.
- Blocking to be ³/₄" x 4", painted same color as cornice. Fasten as required.

FIN DETAIL

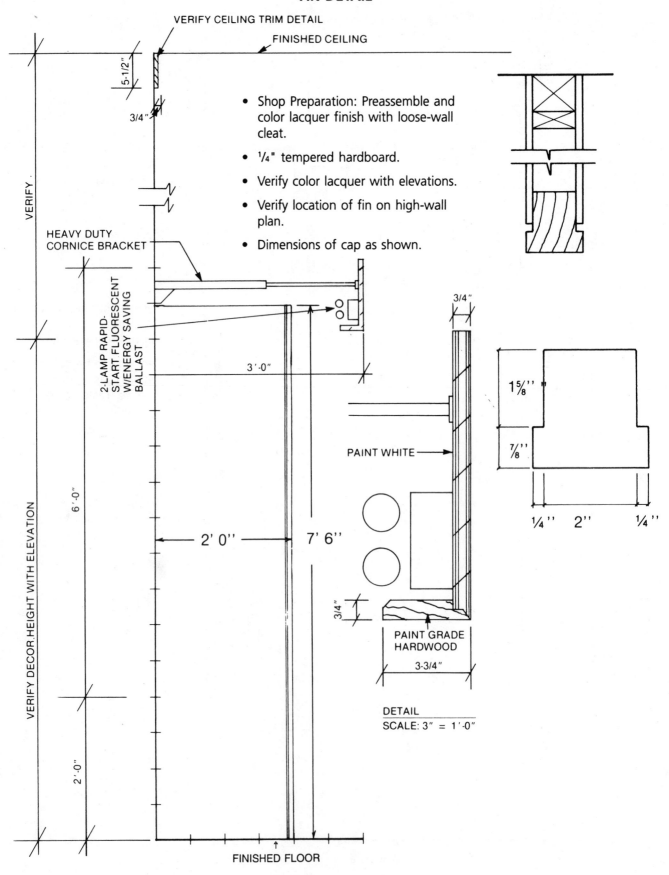

VERIFY CEILING TRIM DETAIL

FINISHED CEILING

5-1/2"

3/4"

- Shop Preparation: Preassemble and color lacquer finish with loose-wall cleat.
- ¼" tempered hardboard.
- Verify color lacquer with elevations.
- Verify location of fin on high-wall plan.
- Dimensions of cap as shown.

VERIFY

HEAVY DUTY CORNICE BRACKET

2-LAMP RAPID-START FLUORESCENT W/ENERGY SAVING BALLAST

3'-0"

3/4"

PAINT WHITE

$1\frac{5}{8}$''

$\frac{7}{8}$''

¼''   2''   ¼''

2' 0''   7' 6''

6'-0"

VERIFY DECOR. HEIGHT WITH ELEVATION

3/4"

PAINT GRADE HARDWOOD

3-3/4"

DETAIL
SCALE: 3" = 1'-0"

2'-0"

FINISHED FLOOR

CORNER FILL DETAIL

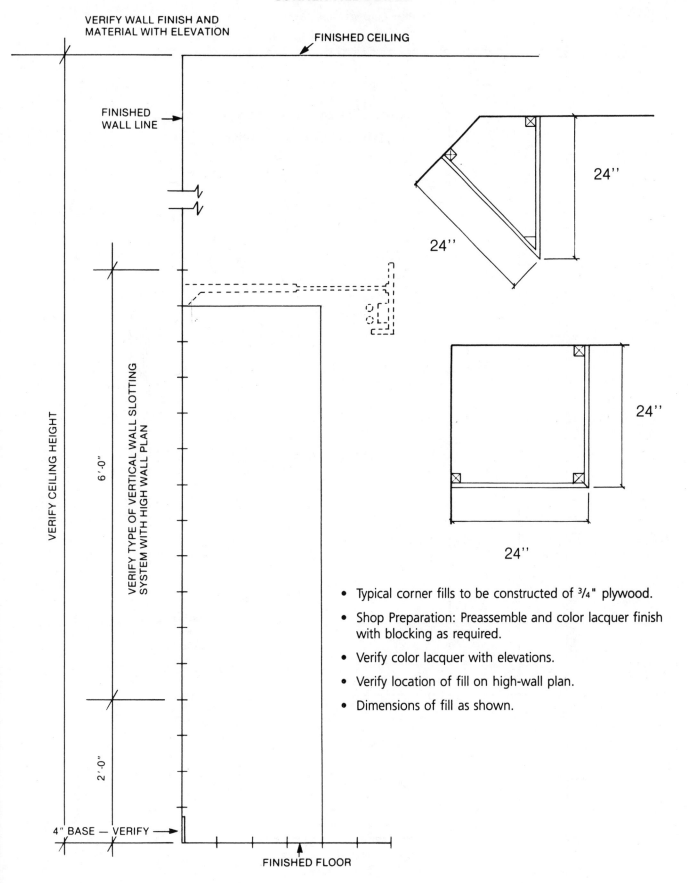

VERIFY WALL FINISH AND
MATERIAL WITH ELEVATION

FINISHED CEILING

FINISHED
WALL LINE

VERIFY CEILING HEIGHT

VERIFY TYPE OF VERTICAL WALL SLOTTING
SYSTEM WITH HIGH WALL PLAN

6'-0"

2'-0"

4" BASE — VERIFY

FINISHED FLOOR

24"

24"

24"

24"

24"

- Typical corner fills to be constructed of ¾" plywood.
- Shop Preparation: Preassemble and color lacquer finish with blocking as required.
- Verify color lacquer with elevations.
- Verify location of fill on high-wall plan.
- Dimensions of fill as shown.

CORNICE

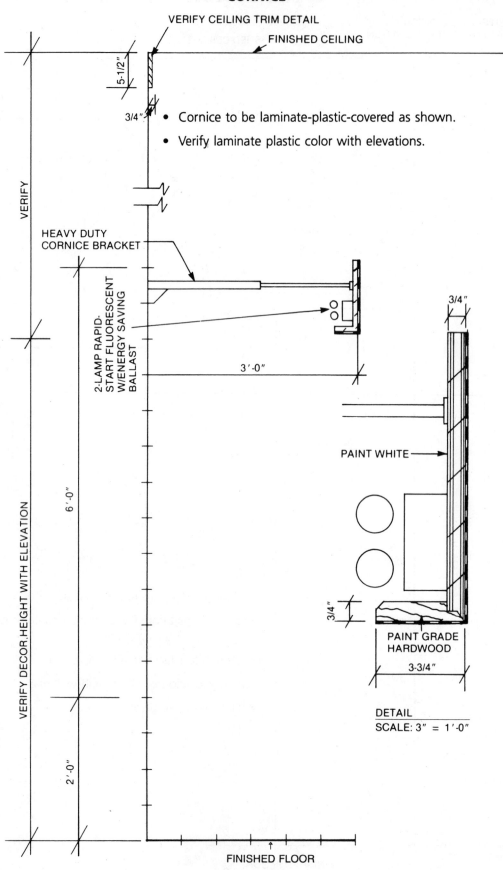

VERIFY CEILING TRIM DETAIL

FINISHED CEILING

5-1/2"

3/4"

- Cornice to be laminate-plastic-covered as shown.
- Verify laminate plastic color with elevations.

VERIFY

HEAVY DUTY
CORNICE BRACKET

2-LAMP RAPID-
START FLUORESCENT
W/ENERGY SAVING
BALLAST

3'-0"

3/4"

PAINT WHITE

VERIFY DECOR. HEIGHT WITH ELEVATION

6'-0"

3/4"

PAINT GRADE
HARDWOOD

3-3/4"

DETAIL
SCALE: 3" = 1'-0"

2'-0"

FINISHED FLOOR

DOUBLE CORNICE

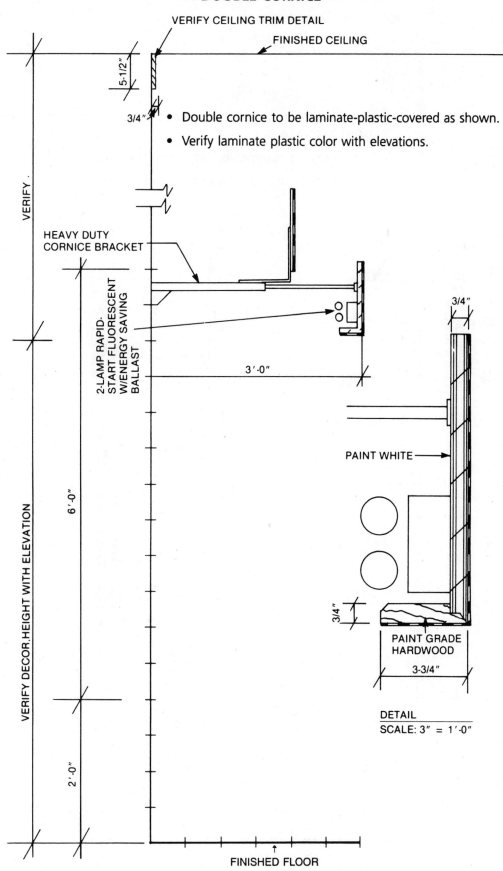

VERIFY CEILING TRIM DETAIL

FINISHED CEILING

5-1/2"

3/4"

- Double cornice to be laminate-plastic-covered as shown.
- Verify laminate plastic color with elevations.

VERIFY

HEAVY DUTY
CORNICE BRACKET

2-LAMP RAPID-
START FLUORESCENT
W/ENERGY SAVING
BALLAST

3/4"

3'-0"

PAINT WHITE

6'-0"

VERIFY DECOR.HEIGHT WITH ELEVATION

3/4"

PAINT GRADE
HARDWOOD

3-3/4"

DETAIL
SCALE: 3" = 1'-0"

2'-0"

FINISHED FLOOR

CORNICE WITH PLEXI MIRROR TRIM

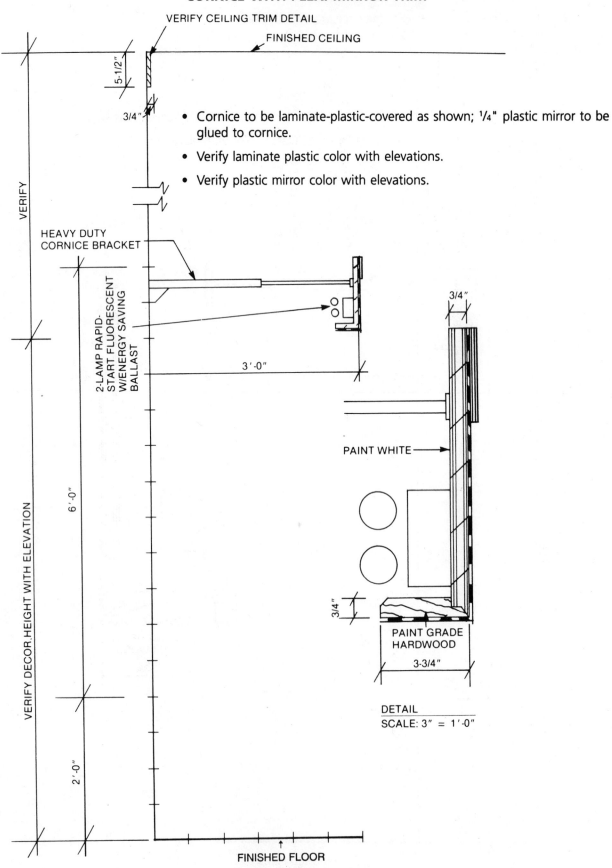

VERIFY CEILING TRIM DETAIL

FINISHED CEILING

5-1/2"

3/4"

- Cornice to be laminate-plastic-covered as shown; ¼" plastic mirror to be glued to cornice.
- Verify laminate plastic color with elevations.
- Verify plastic mirror color with elevations.

VERIFY

HEAVY DUTY
CORNICE BRACKET

2-LAMP RAPID-START FLUORESCENT W/ENERGY SAVING BALLAST

3'-0"

3/4"

PAINT WHITE

6'-0"

VERIFY DECOR. HEIGHT WITH ELEVATION

3/4"

PAINT GRADE
HARDWOOD

3-3/4"

DETAIL
SCALE: 3" = 1'-0"

2'-0"

FINISHED FLOOR

SLATWALL CORNICE

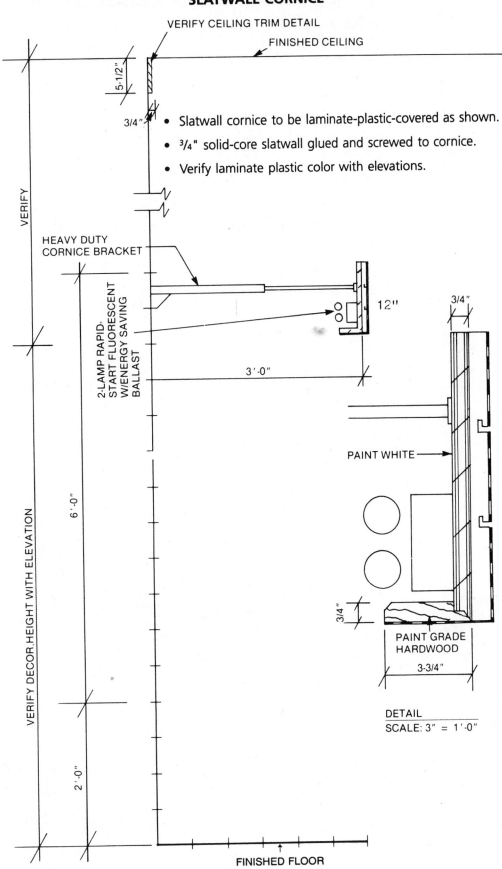

VERIFY CEILING TRIM DETAIL

FINISHED CEILING

5-1/2"

3/4"

- Slatwall cornice to be laminate-plastic-covered as shown.
- ¾" solid-core slatwall glued and screwed to cornice.
- Verify laminate plastic color with elevations.

VERIFY

HEAVY DUTY
CORNICE BRACKET

2-LAMP RAPID-
START FLUORESCENT
W/ENERGY SAVING
BALLAST

12"

3/4"

3'-0"

PAINT WHITE

VERIFY DECOR. HEIGHT WITH ELEVATION

6'-0"

3/4"

PAINT GRADE
HARDWOOD

3-3/4"

2'-0"

DETAIL
SCALE: 3" = 1'-0"

FINISHED FLOOR

SLATWALL CORNICE—MIRROR TRIMS, TOP AND BOTTOM

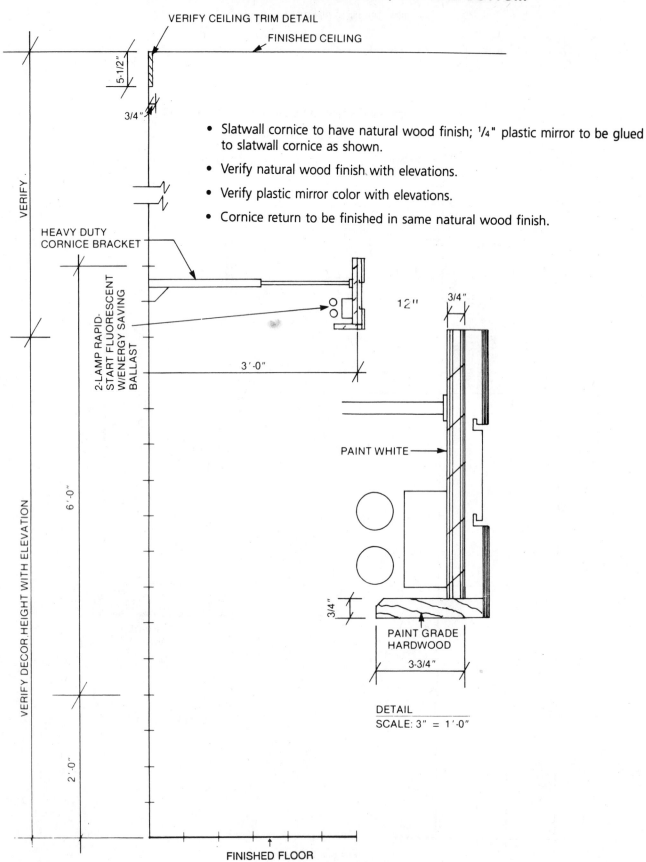

VERIFY CEILING TRIM DETAIL

FINISHED CEILING

5-1/2"

3/4"

VERIFY

- Slatwall cornice to have natural wood finish; ¼" plastic mirror to be glued to slatwall cornice as shown.
- Verify natural wood finish with elevations.
- Verify plastic mirror color with elevations.
- Cornice return to be finished in same natural wood finish.

HEAVY DUTY
CORNICE BRACKET

2-LAMP RAPID-
START FLUORESCENT
W/ENERGY SAVING
BALLAST

12"

3/4"

3'-0"

PAINT WHITE

6'-0"

VERIFY DECOR. HEIGHT WITH ELEVATION

3/4"

PAINT GRADE
HARDWOOD

3-3/4"

DETAIL
SCALE: 3" = 1'-0"

2'-0"

FINISHED FLOOR

CORNICE WITH MOLDING

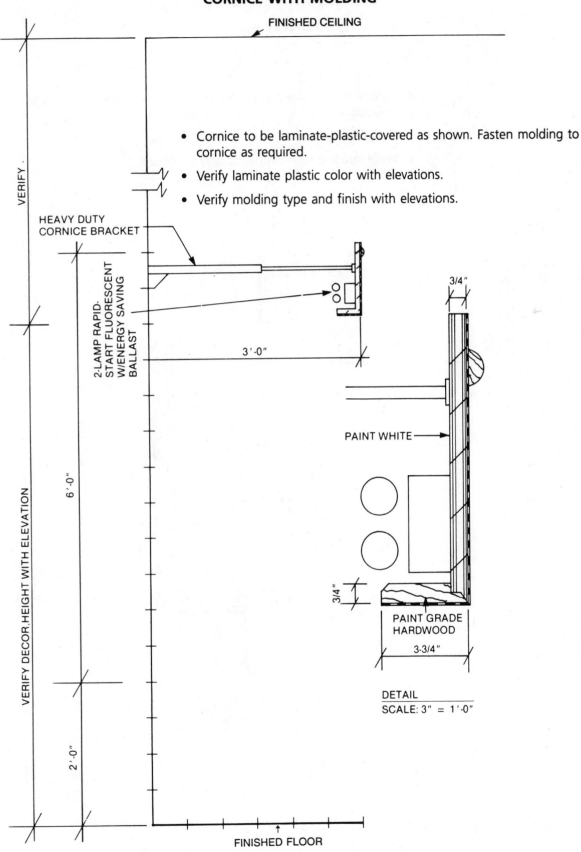

FINISHED CEILING

- Cornice to be laminate-plastic-covered as shown. Fasten molding to cornice as required.
- Verify laminate plastic color with elevations.
- Verify molding type and finish with elevations.

VERIFY

HEAVY DUTY
CORNICE BRACKET

2-LAMP RAPID-
START FLUORESCENT
W/ENERGY SAVING
BALLAST

3'-0"

6'-0"

3/4"

PAINT WHITE

VERIFY DECOR. HEIGHT WITH ELEVATION

3/4"

PAINT GRADE
HARDWOOD

3-3/4"

DETAIL
SCALE: 3" = 1'-0"

2'-0"

FINISHED FLOOR

CORNICE WITH MOLDINGS

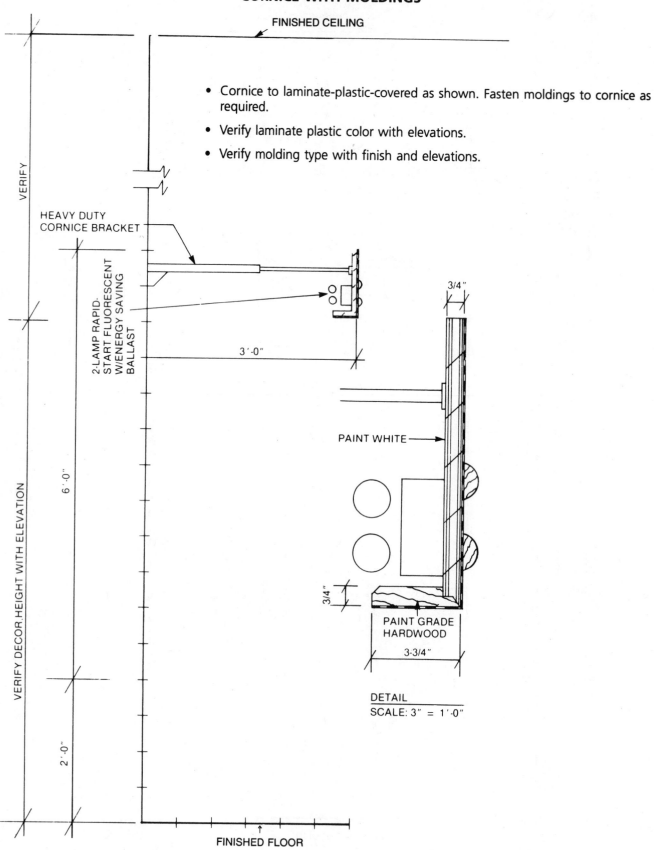

FINISHED CEILING

- Cornice to laminate-plastic-covered as shown. Fasten moldings to cornice as required.
- Verify laminate plastic color with elevations.
- Verify molding type with finish and elevations.

HEAVY DUTY
CORNICE BRACKET

2-LAMP RAPID-
START FLUORESCENT
W/ENERGY SAVING
BALLAST

3'-0"

VERIFY

VERIFY DECOR.HEIGHT WITH ELEVATION

6'-0"

2'-0"

FINISHED FLOOR

3/4"

PAINT WHITE

3/4"

PAINT GRADE
HARDWOOD

3-3/4"

DETAIL
SCALE: 3" = 1'-0"

CORNICE—SILVER MIRROR

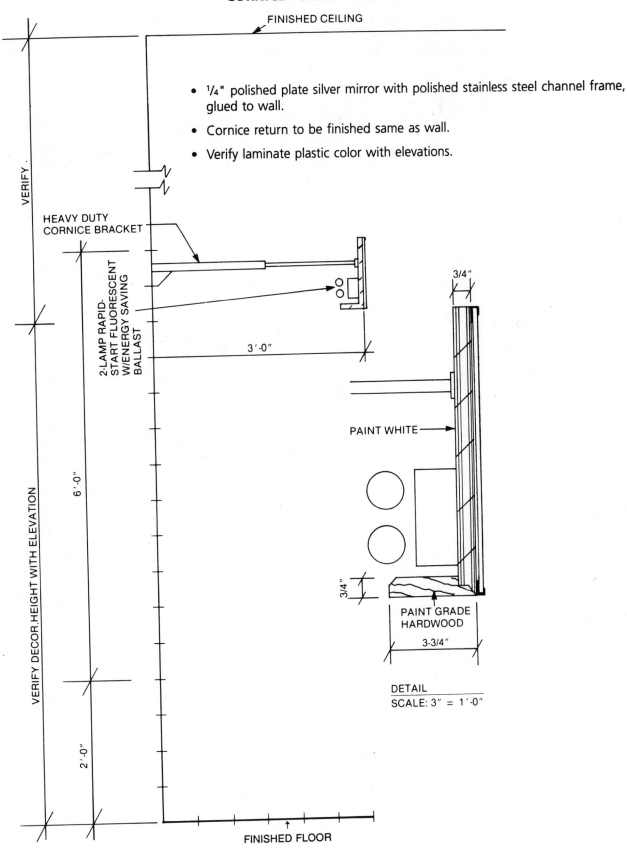

FINISHED CEILING

- ¼" polished plate silver mirror with polished stainless steel channel frame, glued to wall.
- Cornice return to be finished same as wall.
- Verify laminate plastic color with elevations.

VERIFY.

HEAVY DUTY
CORNICE BRACKET

2-LAMP RAPID-
START FLUORESCENT
W/ENERGY SAVING
BALLAST

3'-0"

3/4"

PAINT WHITE

VERIFY DECOR. HEIGHT WITH ELEVATION

6'-0"

2'-0"

3/4"

PAINT GRADE
HARDWOOD

3-3/4"

DETAIL
SCALE: 3" = 1'-0"

FINISHED FLOOR

CORNICE—TUBE

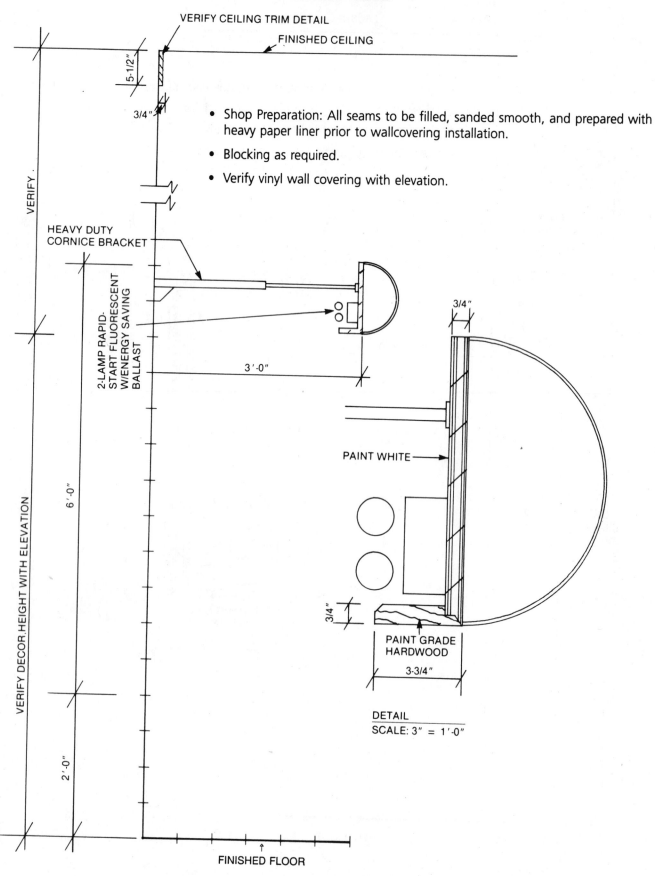

VERIFY CEILING TRIM DETAIL

FINISHED CEILING

5-1/2"

3/4"

VERIFY

- Shop Preparation: All seams to be filled, sanded smooth, and prepared with heavy paper liner prior to wallcovering installation.
- Blocking as required.
- Verify vinyl wall covering with elevation.

HEAVY DUTY
CORNICE BRACKET

2-LAMP RAPID-START FLUORESCENT W/ENERGY SAVING BALLAST

3'-0"

3/4"

PAINT WHITE

6'-0"

VERIFY DECOR. HEIGHT WITH ELEVATION

3/4"

PAINT GRADE HARDWOOD

3-3/4"

DETAIL
SCALE: 3" = 1'-0"

2'-0"

FINISHED FLOOR

DOUBLE CORNICE WITH MOLDINGS

FINISHED CEILING

- Double cornice to be laminate-plastic-covered as shown. Fasten moldings to cornice as required.
- Verify laminate plastic color with elevations.
- Verify molding type and finish with elevations.

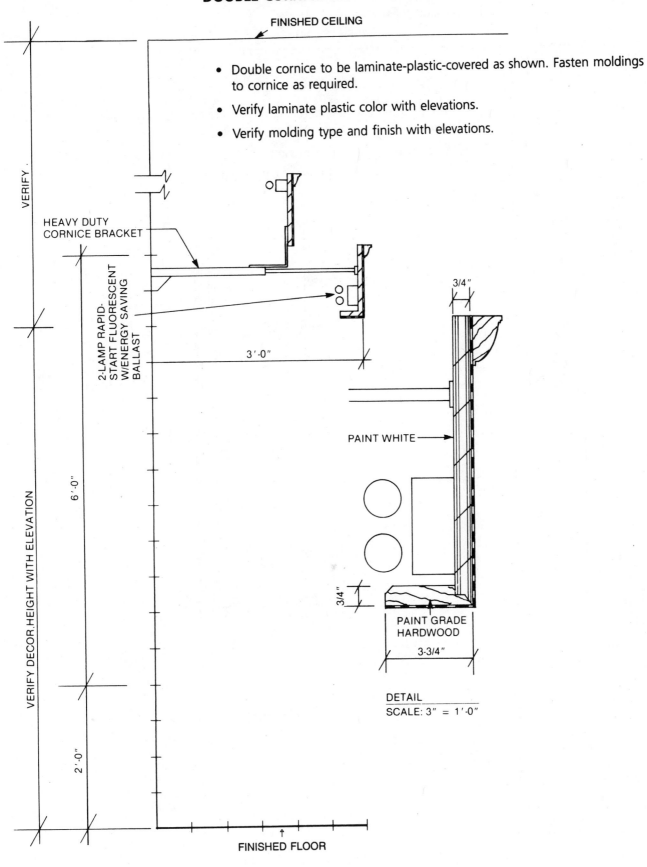

HEAVY DUTY
CORNICE BRACKET

2-LAMP RAPID-START FLUORESCENT W/ENERGY SAVING BALLAST

VERIFY

VERIFY DECOR. HEIGHT WITH ELEVATION

6'-0"

2'-0"

3'-0"

3/4"

3/4"

3-3/4"

PAINT WHITE

PAINT GRADE HARDWOOD

DETAIL
SCALE: 3" = 1'-0"

FINISHED FLOOR

18" CORNICE WITH MOLDINGS, TOP AND BOTTOM

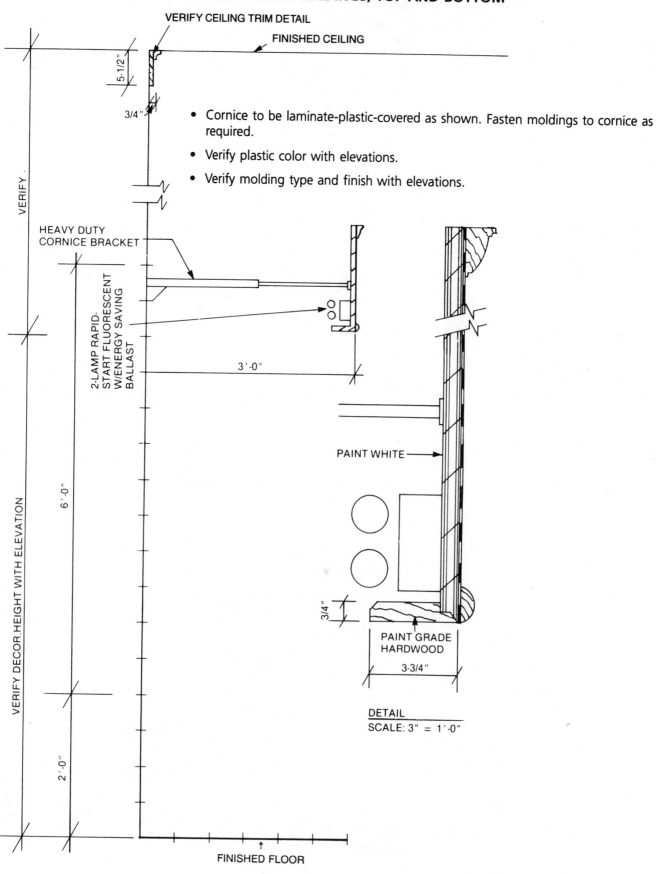

VERIFY CEILING TRIM DETAIL

FINISHED CEILING

5-1/2"

3/4"

- Cornice to be laminate-plastic-covered as shown. Fasten moldings to cornice as required.
- Verify plastic color with elevations.
- Verify molding type and finish with elevations.

VERIFY

HEAVY DUTY
CORNICE BRACKET

2-LAMP RAPID-
START FLUORESCENT
W/ENERGY SAVING
BALLAST

3'-0"

PAINT WHITE

6'-0"

VERIFY DECOR.HEIGHT WITH ELEVATION

3/4"

PAINT GRADE
HARDWOOD

3-3/4"

DETAIL
SCALE: 3" = 1'-0"

2'-0"

FINISHED FLOOR

FREESTANDING CURTAIN WALL DETAIL

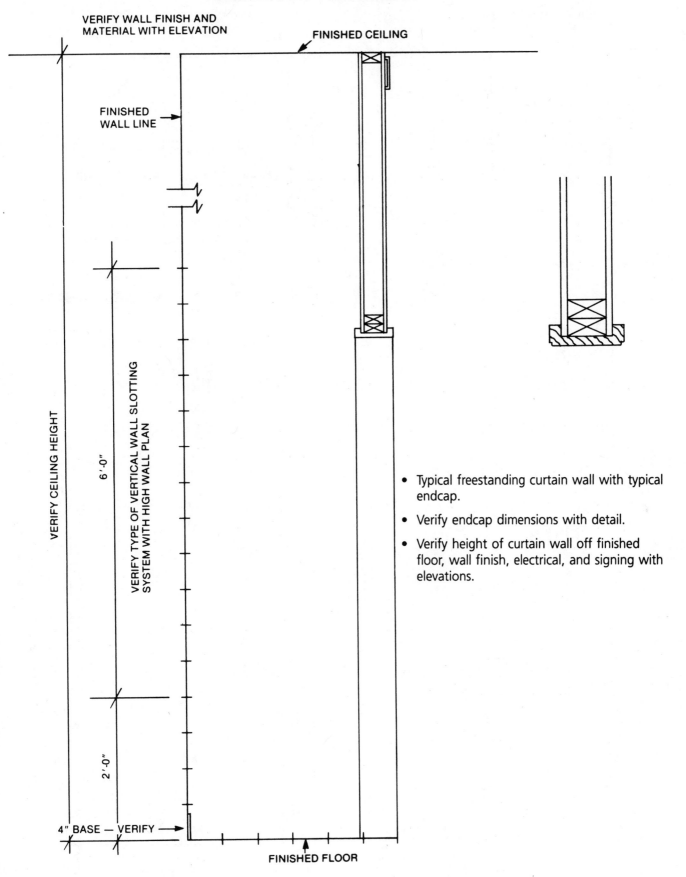

VERIFY WALL FINISH AND
MATERIAL WITH ELEVATION

FINISHED CEILING

FINISHED
WALL LINE

VERIFY CEILING HEIGHT

VERIFY TYPE OF VERTICAL WALL SLOTTING
SYSTEM WITH HIGH WALL PLAN

6'-0"

2'-0"

4" BASE — VERIFY

FINISHED FLOOR

- Typical freestanding curtain wall with typical endcap.
- Verify endcap dimensions with detail.
- Verify height of curtain wall off finished floor, wall finish, electrical, and signing with elevations.

TYPICAL CURTAIN WALL DETAIL

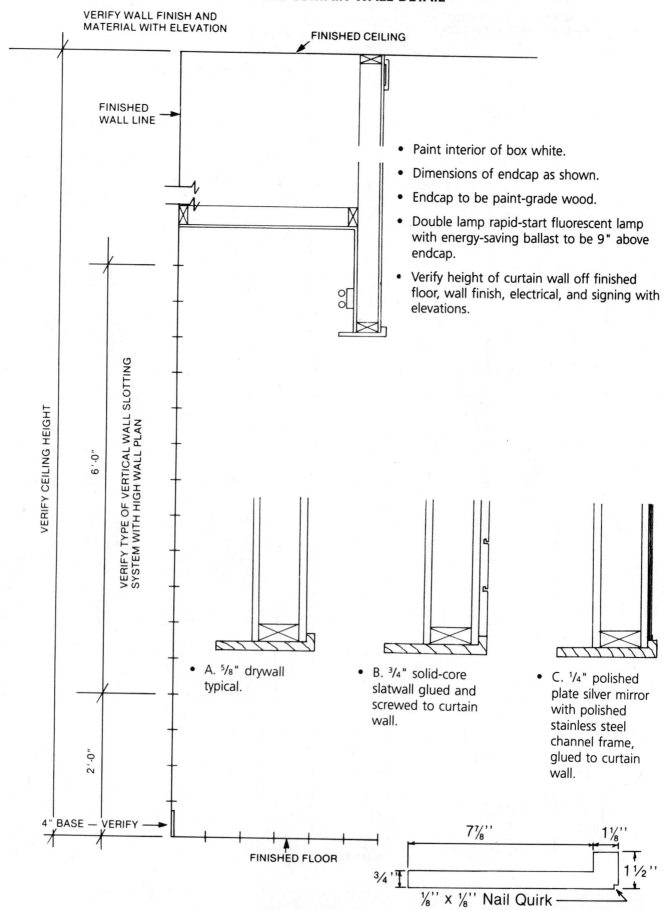

VERIFY WALL FINISH AND
MATERIAL WITH ELEVATION

FINISHED CEILING

FINISHED
WALL LINE

- Paint interior of box white.
- Dimensions of endcap as shown.
- Endcap to be paint-grade wood.
- Double lamp rapid-start fluorescent lamp with energy-saving ballast to be 9" above endcap.
- Verify height of curtain wall off finished floor, wall finish, electrical, and signing with elevations.

VERIFY CEILING HEIGHT

6'-0"

VERIFY TYPE OF VERTICAL WALL SLOTTING
SYSTEM WITH HIGH WALL PLAN

2'-0"

- A. ⅝" drywall typical.

- B. ¾" solid-core slatwall glued and screwed to curtain wall.

- C. ¼" polished plate silver mirror with polished stainless steel channel frame, glued to curtain wall.

4" BASE — VERIFY ►

FINISHED FLOOR

7⅞"   1⅛"

1½"

¾"

⅛" x ⅛" Nail Quirk

18" FASCIA BOARD—SEMICIRCLE, TOP AND BOTTOM

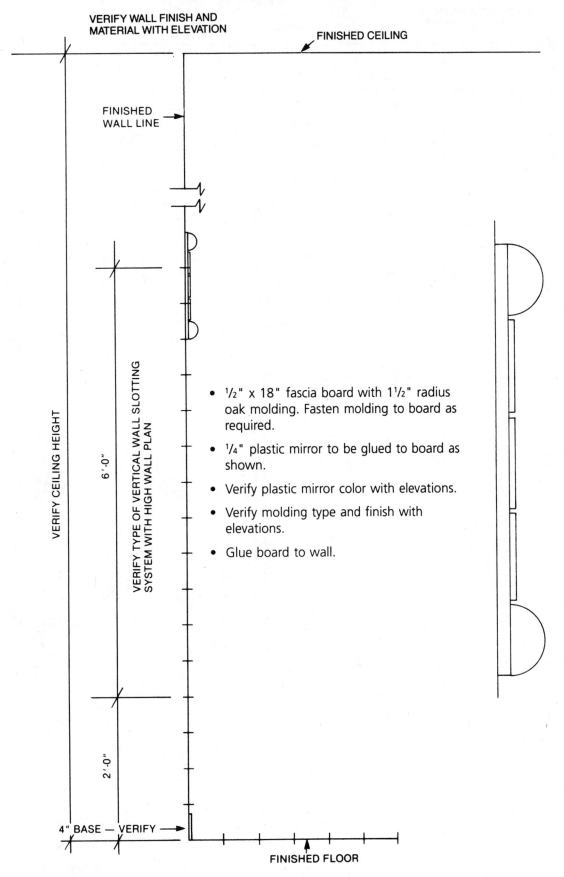

VERIFY WALL FINISH AND
MATERIAL WITH ELEVATION

FINISHED CEILING

FINISHED
WALL LINE

VERIFY CEILING HEIGHT

VERIFY TYPE OF VERTICAL WALL SLOTTING
SYSTEM WITH HIGH WALL PLAN

6'-0"

2'-0"

4" BASE — VERIFY

FINISHED FLOOR

- 1/2" x 18" fascia board with 1½" radius oak molding. Fasten molding to board as required.
- 1/4" plastic mirror to be glued to board as shown.
- Verify plastic mirror color with elevations.
- Verify molding type and finish with elevations.
- Glue board to wall.

SAWTOOTH WALL DETAIL

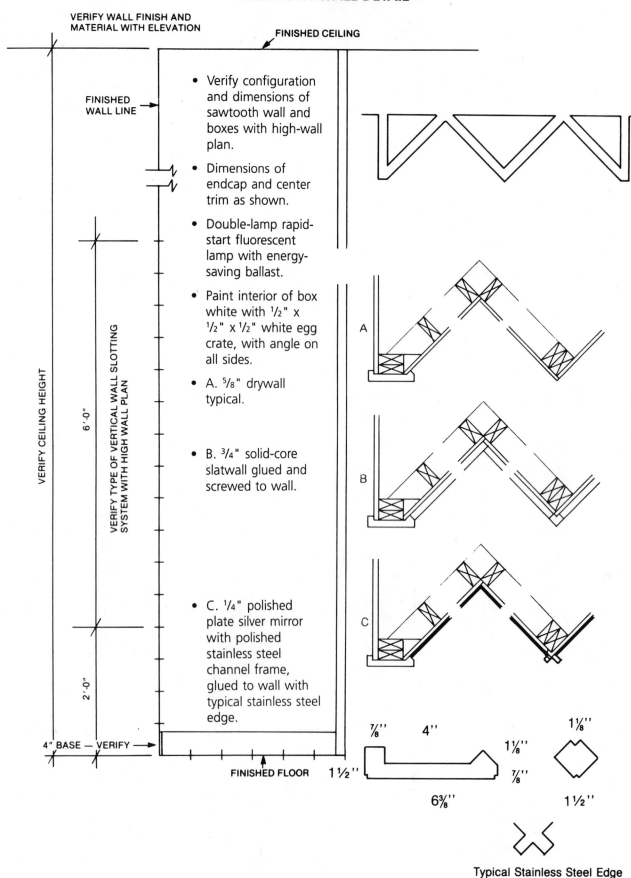

VERIFY WALL FINISH AND
MATERIAL WITH ELEVATION

FINISHED CEILING

FINISHED
WALL LINE

- Verify configuration and dimensions of sawtooth wall and boxes with high-wall plan.

- Dimensions of endcap and center trim as shown.

- Double-lamp rapid-start fluorescent lamp with energy-saving ballast.

- Paint interior of box white with 1/2" x 1/2" x 1/2" white egg crate, with angle on all sides.

- A. 5/8" drywall typical.

- B. 3/4" solid-core slatwall glued and screwed to wall.

- C. 1/4" polished plate silver mirror with polished stainless steel channel frame, glued to wall with typical stainless steel edge.

VERIFY CEILING HEIGHT

VERIFY TYPE OF VERTICAL WALL SLOTTING SYSTEM WITH HIGH WALL PLAN

6'-0"

2'-0"

4" BASE — VERIFY

FINISHED FLOOR

1 1/2"

A

B

C

7/8"   4"   1 1/8"

1 1/8"

7/8"

6 3/8"   1 1/2"

Typical Stainless Steel Edge

SAWTOOTH WALL WITH BOXES DETAIL

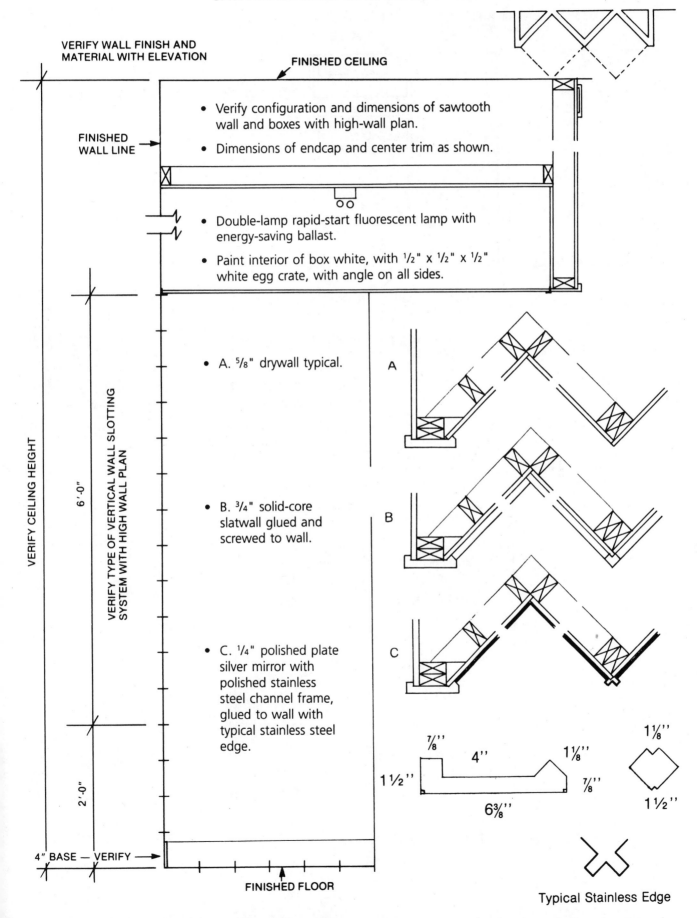

VERIFY WALL FINISH AND
MATERIAL WITH ELEVATION

FINISHED CEILING

FINISHED
WALL LINE

- Verify configuration and dimensions of sawtooth wall and boxes with high-wall plan.
- Dimensions of endcap and center trim as shown.
- Double-lamp rapid-start fluorescent lamp with energy-saving ballast.
- Paint interior of box white, with ½" x ½" x ½" white egg crate, with angle on all sides.

VERIFY CEILING HEIGHT

6'-0"

VERIFY TYPE OF VERTICAL WALL SLOTTING SYSTEM WITH HIGH WALL PLAN

- A. ⅝" drywall typical.

A

- B. ¾" solid-core slatwall glued and screwed to wall.

B

- C. ¼" polished plate silver mirror with polished stainless steel channel frame, glued to wall with typical stainless steel edge.

C

2'-0"

4" BASE — VERIFY

FINISHED FLOOR

⅞"

4"

1⅛"

1½"

⅞"

6⅜"

1⅛"

1½"

Typical Stainless Edge

BAFFLE DETAIL

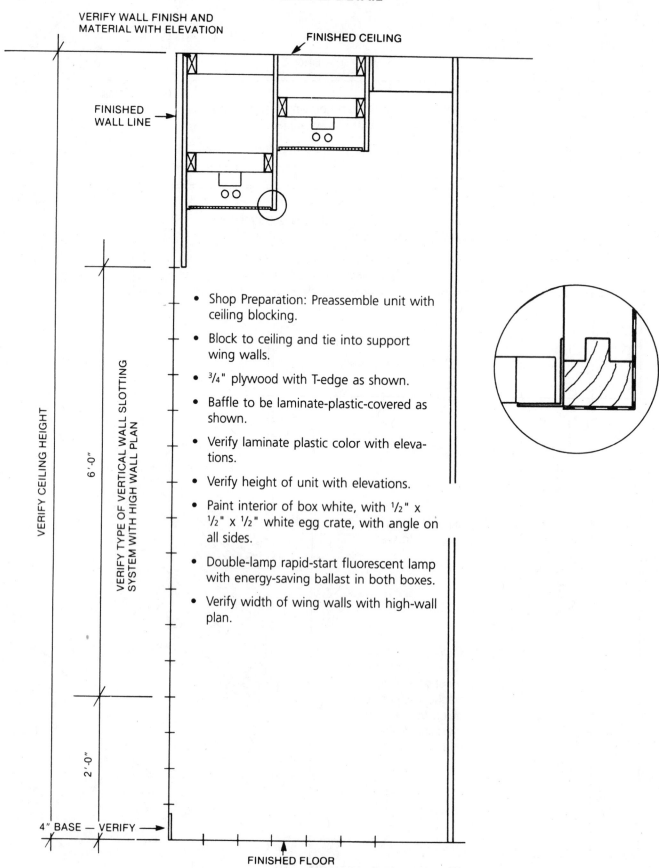

VERIFY WALL FINISH AND
MATERIAL WITH ELEVATION

FINISHED CEILING

FINISHED
WALL LINE

VERIFY CEILING HEIGHT

VERIFY TYPE OF VERTICAL WALL SLOTTING
SYSTEM WITH HIGH WALL PLAN

6'-0"

2'-0"

4" BASE — VERIFY

FINISHED FLOOR

- Shop Preparation: Preassemble unit with ceiling blocking.

- Block to ceiling and tie into support wing walls.

- ³/₄" plywood with T-edge as shown.

- Baffle to be laminate-plastic-covered as shown.

- Verify laminate plastic color with elevations.

- Verify height of unit with elevations.

- Paint interior of box white, with ½" x ½" x ½" white egg crate, with angle on all sides.

- Double-lamp rapid-start fluorescent lamp with energy-saving ballast in both boxes.

- Verify width of wing walls with high-wall plan.

DOOR JAMB DETAIL

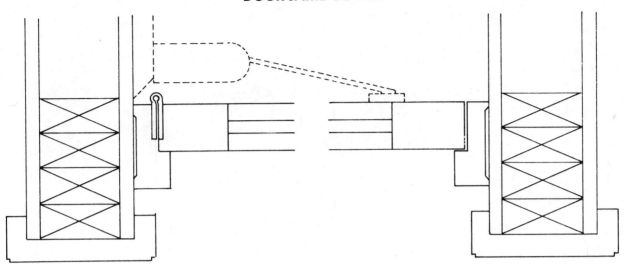

- 5/8" drywall typical.
- Blocking as required.
- Typical endcap as shown.
- 3 hinges required.
- Store-fixture contractor to submit shop drawings for designer's approval.
- Hydraulic door closure and stop as required. All hardware to be brushed stainless steel.
- Door opening to be plumb and square.
- Verify with elevations type of door, door height, door width, transom, swing, lock, push plates, and kick plate.

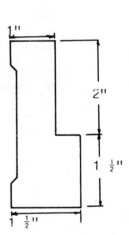

DRYWALL COLUMN—TYPE A

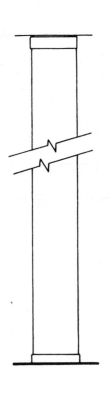

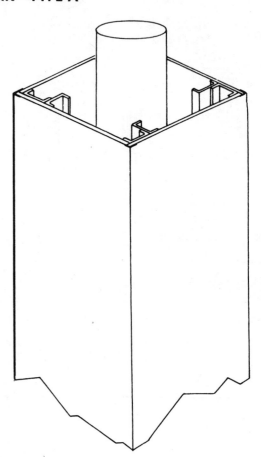

- General contractor to deliver a ⅝" drywall enclosure, plumb and square, with prewired electrical box(es) as shown on power and signal plan.

- Corner, ceiling, and base trims to be included. Corners to be smooth with bead as shown.

- Verify finish on fixture-finish schedule.

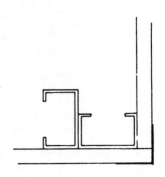

SLATWALL COLUMN—TYPE B

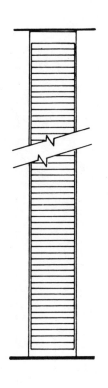

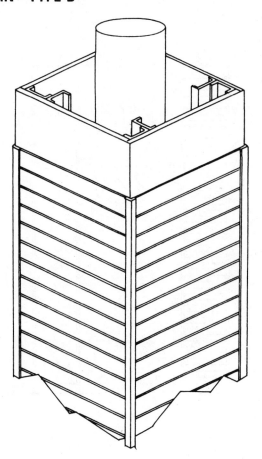

- General contractor to deliver a ⅝" drywall enclosure, plumb and square, with prewired electrical box(es) as shown on power and signal plan.

- Decor contractor to supply and install column enclosure constructed of ¾" solid-core slatwall, prefabricated in shop. Corner, ceiling, and base trims to be included.

- Verify finish on fixture-finish schedule.

- Shim and set with glue.

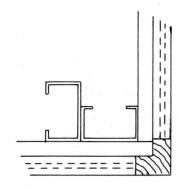

SLATWALL AND MIRROR COLUMN—TYPE C

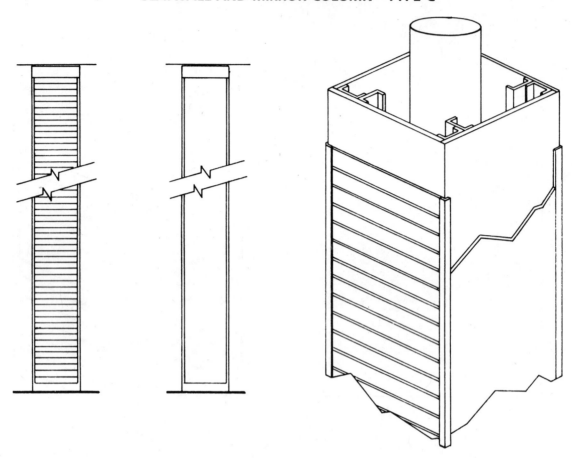

- General contractor to deliver a ⅝" drywall enclosure, plumb and square, with prewired electrical box(es) as shown on power and signal plan.

- Decor contractor to supply and install column enclosure constructed of ¾" solid-core slatwall and ¼" polished plate silver mirror, prefabricated in shop. Corner, ceiling, and base trims to be included.

- Verify finish on fixture-finish schedule.

- Verify placement of mirrors on high-wall plan.

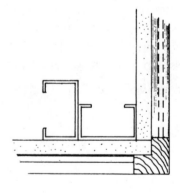

MIRROR COLUMN—TYPE E

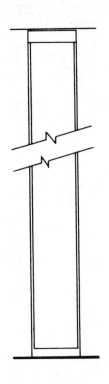

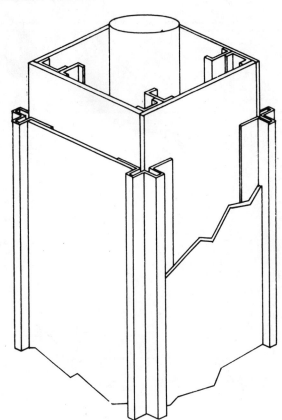

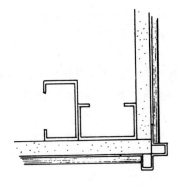

- General contractor to deliver a ⅝" drywall enclosure, plumb and square, with prewired electrical box(es) as shown on power and signal plan.

- Decor contractor to supply and install column enclosure constructed of ¾" solid-core slatwall and ¼" polished plate silver mirror, prefabricated in shop. Corner, ceiling, and base trims to be included.

- No slotting on stainless steel edge.

- Shim and set with glue.

SKYLIGHT DETAIL

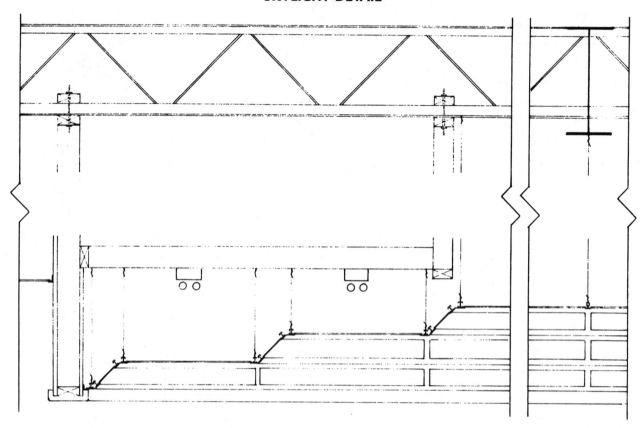

- Verify height of skylight above finished floor.

- Skylight to be constructed of translucent panels and polished brass struts. Opaque surface to be of same struts and cold rolled steel painted standard white.

- Verify inside dimensions and plan for construction of curtain wall.

- Skylight to be prefabricated with final assembly and installation by general contractor.

- Two rows of continuous, overlapping, double-lamp, rapid-start fluorescent lamps with energy-saving ballast.

- Paint interior of box white.

- Contractor to supply shop drawings and correct overall dimensions of skylight area for designer's approval.

Decor Sections 383

TYPICAL OPENINGS

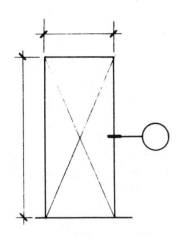

• A. Opening

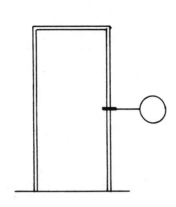

• B. Typical Cased Opening

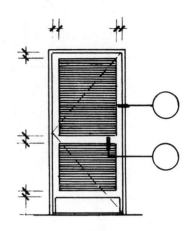

• C. Louver Door

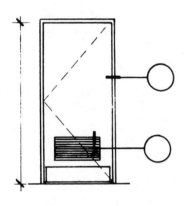

• D. Solid Door (verify grill on door)

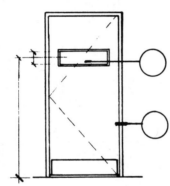

• E. Service Door

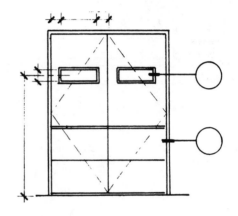

• F. Service Door (pair)

TYPICAL OPENING TREATMENTS

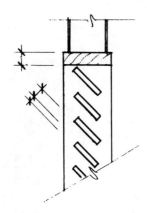

- A. Louver Detail

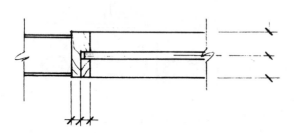

- B. Window Detail

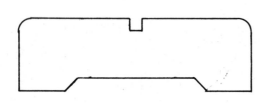

- C. Casing Detail

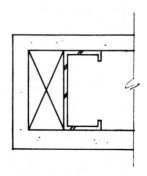

- D. Typical Opening

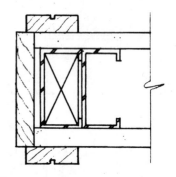

- E. Cased Opening

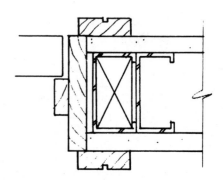

- F. Cased Door Jamb

CEILING DROP DETAIL

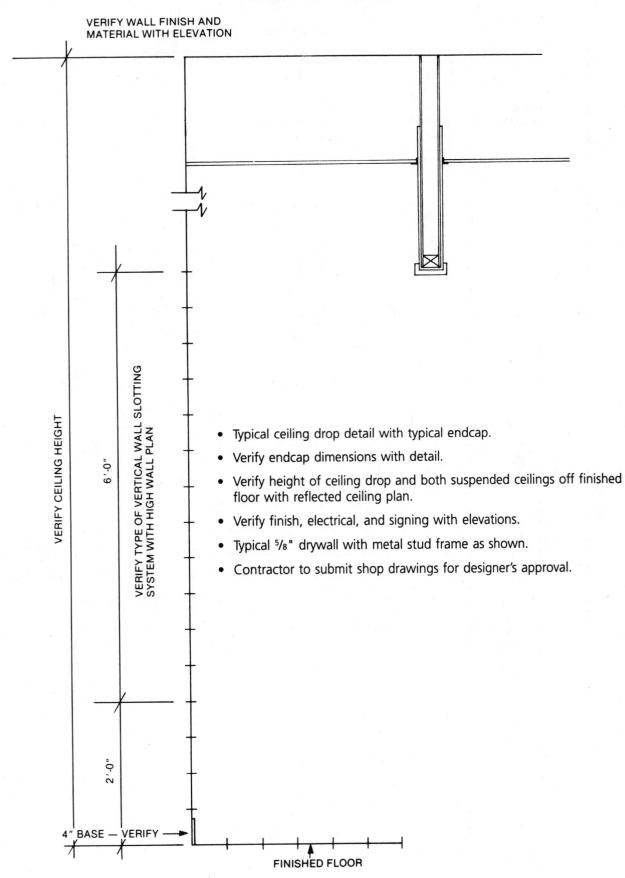

VERIFY WALL FINISH AND
MATERIAL WITH ELEVATION

VERIFY CEILING HEIGHT

VERIFY TYPE OF VERTICAL WALL SLOTTING
SYSTEM WITH HIGH WALL PLAN

6'-0"

2'-0"

4" BASE — VERIFY →

FINISHED FLOOR

- Typical ceiling drop detail with typical endcap.
- Verify endcap dimensions with detail.
- Verify height of ceiling drop and both suspended ceilings off finished floor with reflected ceiling plan.
- Verify finish, electrical, and signing with elevations.
- Typical ⅝" drywall with metal stud frame as shown.
- Contractor to submit shop drawings for designer's approval.

BEAM DETAIL WITH LIGHT

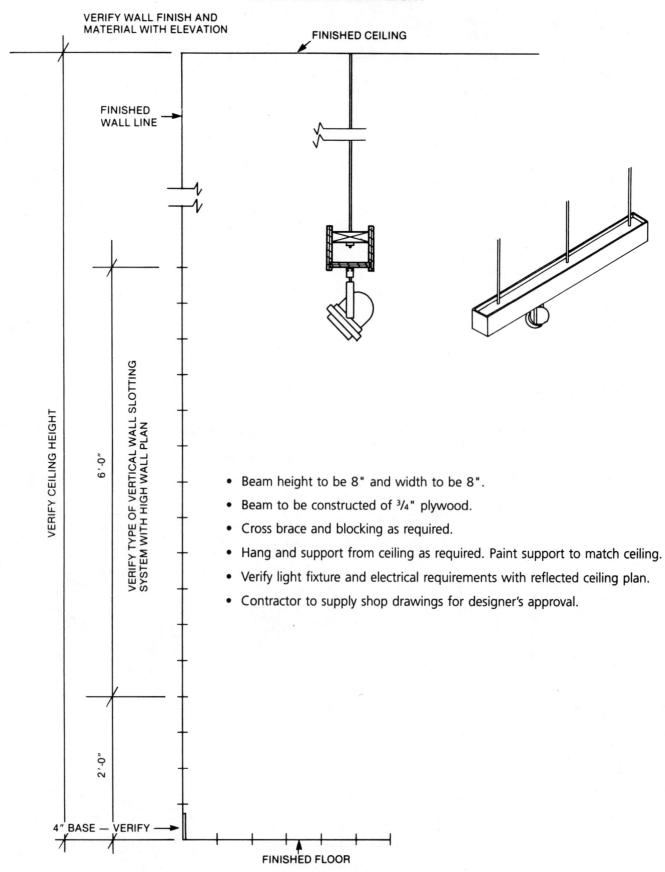

VERIFY WALL FINISH AND
MATERIAL WITH ELEVATION

FINISHED CEILING

FINISHED
WALL LINE

VERIFY CEILING HEIGHT

6'-0"

VERIFY TYPE OF VERTICAL WALL SLOTTING
SYSTEM WITH HIGH WALL PLAN

2'-0"

4" BASE — VERIFY →

FINISHED FLOOR

- Beam height to be 8" and width to be 8".
- Beam to be constructed of 3/4" plywood.
- Cross brace and blocking as required.
- Hang and support from ceiling as required. Paint support to match ceiling.
- Verify light fixture and electrical requirements with reflected ceiling plan.
- Contractor to supply shop drawings for designer's approval.

ILLUMINATED BEAM DETAIL

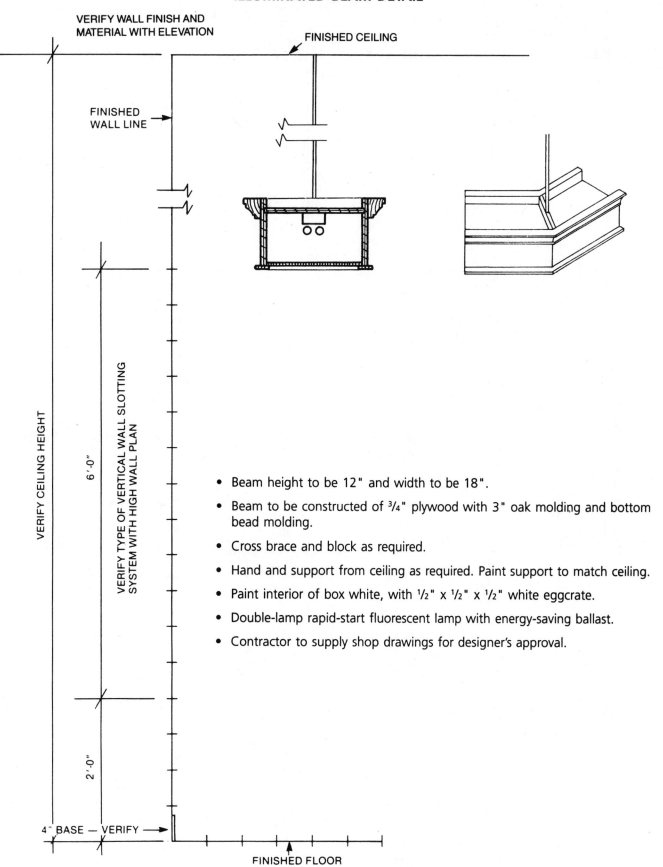

VERIFY WALL FINISH AND
MATERIAL WITH ELEVATION

FINISHED CEILING

FINISHED
WALL LINE

VERIFY CEILING HEIGHT

6'-0"

VERIFY TYPE OF VERTICAL WALL SLOTTING
SYSTEM WITH HIGH WALL PLAN

2'-0"

4" BASE — VERIFY

FINISHED FLOOR

- Beam height to be 12" and width to be 18".
- Beam to be constructed of ¾" plywood with 3" oak molding and bottom bead molding.
- Cross brace and block as required.
- Hand and support from ceiling as required. Paint support to match ceiling.
- Paint interior of box white, with ½" x ½" x ½" white eggcrate.
- Double-lamp rapid-start fluorescent lamp with energy-saving ballast.
- Contractor to supply shop drawings for designer's approval.

ILLUMINATED CEILING DROP

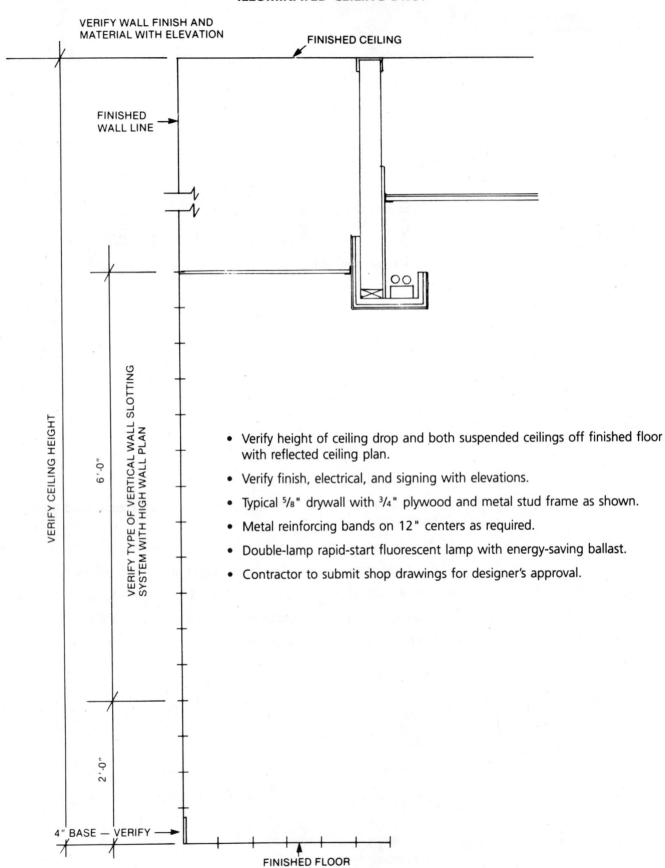

VERIFY WALL FINISH AND
MATERIAL WITH ELEVATION

FINISHED CEILING

FINISHED
WALL LINE

VERIFY CEILING HEIGHT

VERIFY TYPE OF VERTICAL WALL SLOTTING
SYSTEM WITH HIGH WALL PLAN

6'-0"

2'-0"

4" BASE — VERIFY

FINISHED FLOOR

- Verify height of ceiling drop and both suspended ceilings off finished floor with reflected ceiling plan.
- Verify finish, electrical, and signing with elevations.
- Typical ⅝" drywall with ¾" plywood and metal stud frame as shown.
- Metal reinforcing bands on 12" centers as required.
- Double-lamp rapid-start fluorescent lamp with energy-saving ballast.
- Contractor to submit shop drawings for designer's approval.

COFFERED CEILING DETAIL

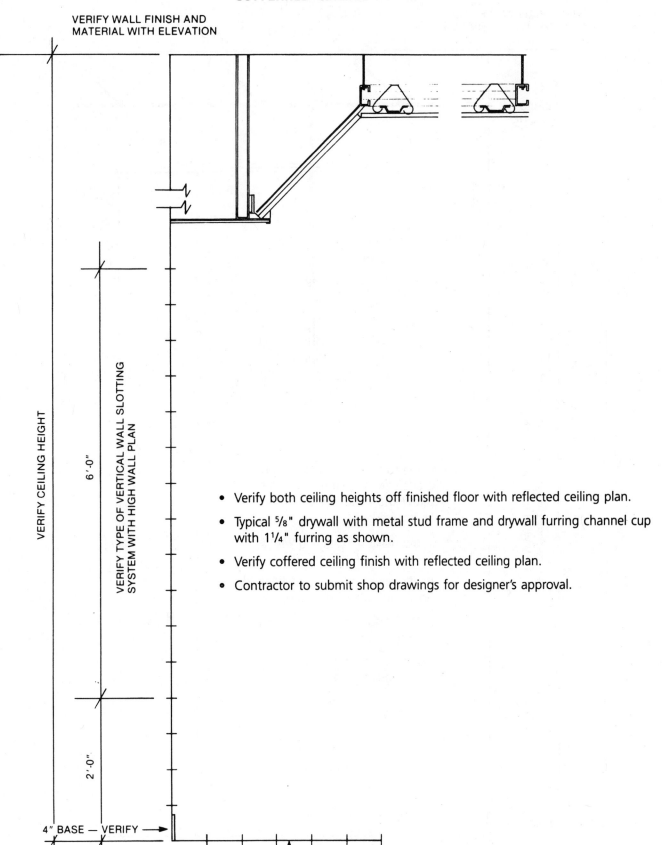

VERIFY WALL FINISH AND
MATERIAL WITH ELEVATION

VERIFY CEILING HEIGHT

6'-0"

VERIFY TYPE OF VERTICAL WALL SLOTTING
SYSTEM WITH HIGH WALL PLAN

2'-0"

4" BASE — VERIFY →

FINISHED FLOOR

- Verify both ceiling heights off finished floor with reflected ceiling plan.
- Typical $5/8$" drywall with metal stud frame and drywall furring channel cup with $1^{1}/_{4}$" furring as shown.
- Verify coffered ceiling finish with reflected ceiling plan.
- Contractor to submit shop drawings for designer's approval.

TYPICAL CEILING BAFFLE

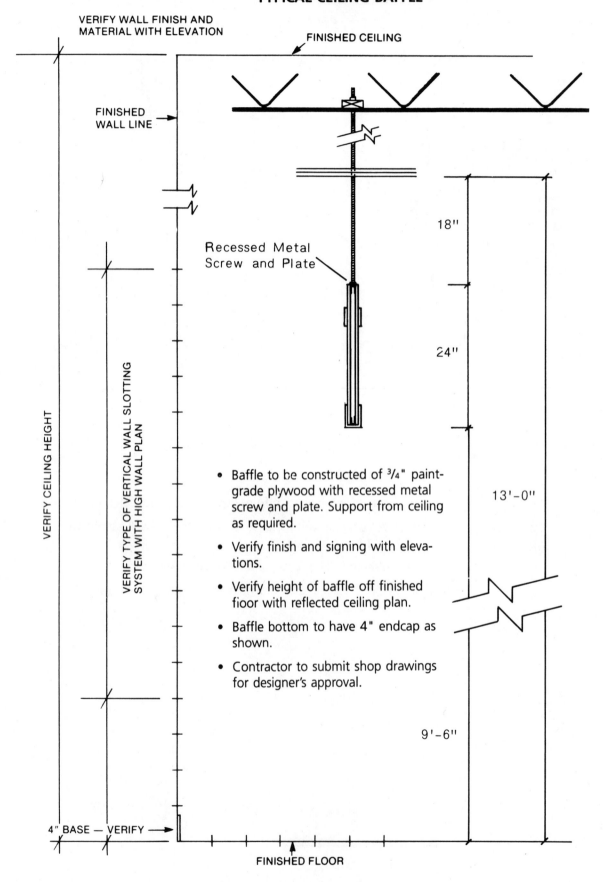

VERIFY WALL FINISH AND
MATERIAL WITH ELEVATION

FINISHED CEILING

FINISHED
WALL LINE

Recessed Metal
Screw and Plate

VERIFY CEILING HEIGHT

VERIFY TYPE OF VERTICAL WALL SLOTTING
SYSTEM WITH HIGH WALL PLAN

18"

24"

13'-0"

9'-6"

- Baffle to be constructed of ¾" paint-grade plywood with recessed metal screw and plate. Support from ceiling as required.

- Verify finish and signing with elevations.

- Verify height of baffle off finished floor with reflected ceiling plan.

- Baffle bottom to have 4" endcap as shown.

- Contractor to submit shop drawings for designer's approval.

4" BASE — VERIFY

FINISHED FLOOR

10" SLATWALL SOFFIT

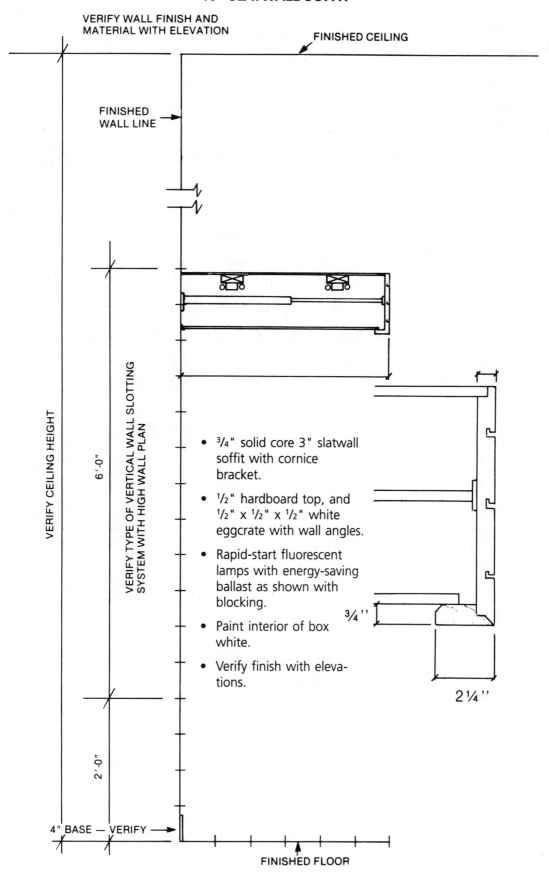

VERIFY WALL FINISH AND
MATERIAL WITH ELEVATION

FINISHED CEILING

FINISHED
WALL LINE

VERIFY CEILING HEIGHT

6'-0"

VERIFY TYPE OF VERTICAL WALL SLOTTING
SYSTEM WITH HIGH WALL PLAN

2'-0"

- ³/₄" solid core 3" slatwall soffit with cornice bracket.

- ¹/₂" hardboard top, and ¹/₂" x ¹/₂" x ¹/₂" white eggcrate with wall angles.

- Rapid-start fluorescent lamps with energy-saving ballast as shown with blocking.

- Paint interior of box white.

- Verify finish with elevations.

³/₄''

2¼''

4" BASE — VERIFY

FINISHED FLOOR

16" SLATWALL SOFFIT

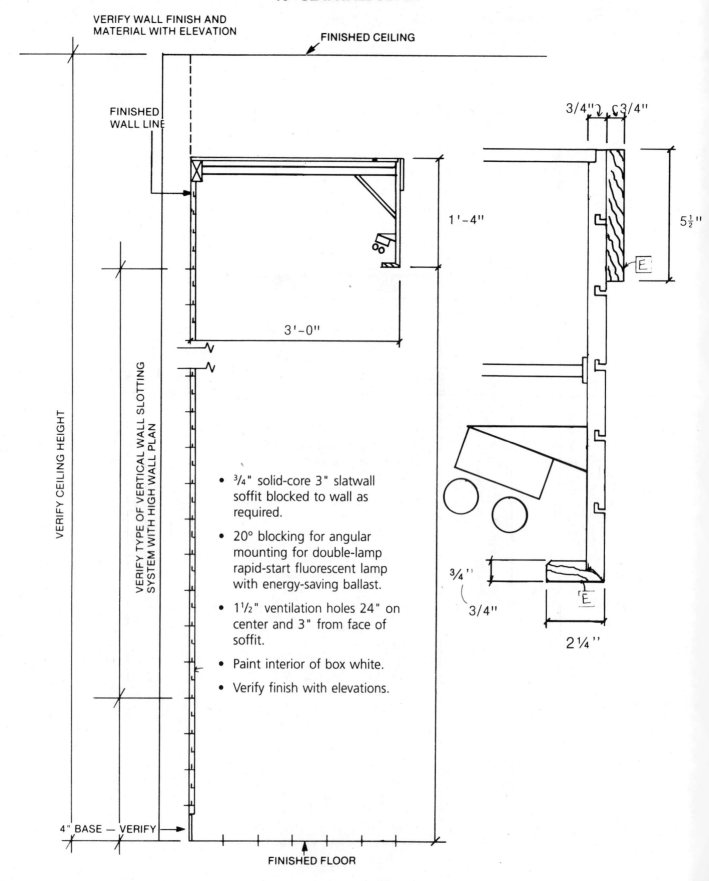

VERIFY WALL FINISH AND
MATERIAL WITH ELEVATION

FINISHED CEILING

FINISHED
WALL LINE

1'–4"

3'–0"

3/4" 3/4"

5½"

E

3/4"

3/4"

E

2¼"

VERIFY CEILING HEIGHT

VERIFY TYPE OF VERTICAL WALL SLOTTING
SYSTEM WITH HIGH WALL PLAN

- ¾" solid-core 3" slatwall soffit blocked to wall as required.

- 20° blocking for angular mounting for double-lamp rapid-start fluorescent lamp with energy-saving ballast.

- 1½" ventilation holes 24" on center and 3" from face of soffit.

- Paint interior of box white.

- Verify finish with elevations.

4" BASE — VERIFY

FINISHED FLOOR

Chapter 22

FREESTANDING FIXTURES

Freestanding fixtures will appear on the Merchandising Plan. They will be keyed with a symbol that will refer them to a fixture-illustration sheet. It is virtually impossible to illustrate every type of freestanding fixture, but within this chapter are illustrated various fixtures that are commonly found in many retail specialty stores.

The purpose of the freestanding-fixture illustration is to identify not only the type of fixture, but also the manner in which it will be constructed. The specifications that accompany the fixture help to explain its accessories and its finishes. These illustrations are to serve only as a guideline and can be changed for individual usage.

FULL-VISION SHOWCASE (TUBE FRAME)

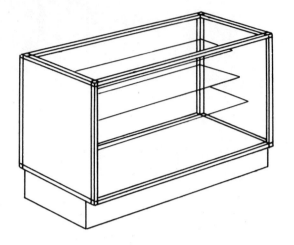

- **Unit Size:** 38"H x 48" or 72"W x 21"D with 8"H x 2¾"D recessed kickbase.

- **Construction of Unit:** Mirror chrome finish 1" modular tube frame and ¾" board with laminate plastic on all surfaces, except kickbase to have brushed-chrome metallic laminate plastic horizontally grained.

- Verify laminate plastic color with fixture-finish plan.

- Verify configuration of showcase island with plan. Kickbase required at showcase line opening.

- 72" showcase *only* to have center slotted post.

- ¼" hardboard doors color-lacquered to match laminate plastic with antijump sliding-door track assembly.

- ¼" polished plate glass with channel required for front and top. Cement top glass on showcase.

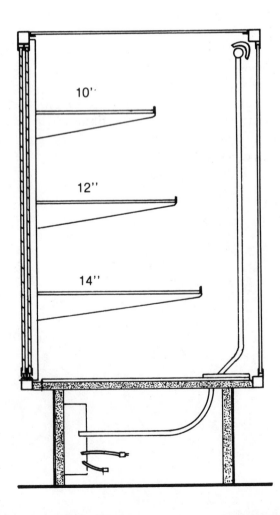

- Prewire showcase with receptacle, 10' power cord, 8" female lead, and fluorescent light rail.

- ⁷⁄₃₂" polished plateglass shelves with polished edges and ¼" clear plastic face clip.

- Removable ¼" upsum board supplied by this contractor and fabric-covered by owner; ¼" x 4" removable plastic mirror with heat-flamed polished edges (loose).

- Side panels of interior to be ¼" polished plate silver mirror with exteriors of panels to be laminate plastic.

- Levelers as required.

- Verify handicap requirement.

- **Prior to Construction:** Contractor to submit proposal of construction materials and details with two complete and accurate sets of shop drawings to designer. One set of shop drawings will be returned upon approval.

ONE-THIRD-VISION SHOWCASE (TUBE FRAME)

- **Unit Size:** 38"H x 48" or 72"W x 21"D with 8"H x 2¾"D recessed kickbase.

- **Construction of Unit:** Mirror chrome finish 1" modular tube frame and ¾" board with laminate plastic on all surfaces, except kickbase to have brushed-chrome metallic laminate plastic horizontally grained.

- **Drawer Construction:** Front to be ¾" board with back and sides of ⅝" solid-core plywood. Bottom to be of ¼" tempered hardboard dadoed into sides and front, glued and nailed. Continuous extruded brushed-aluminum drawer pull (1¾"H x ¾"D) with no. 5 flathead wood screws on 2⅓" centers, with lock if specified, and one set of 17" zinc-plated self-closing drawer slides with bottom nylon levelers. Showcases' and back islands' locks to be keyed alike.

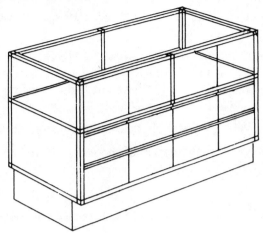

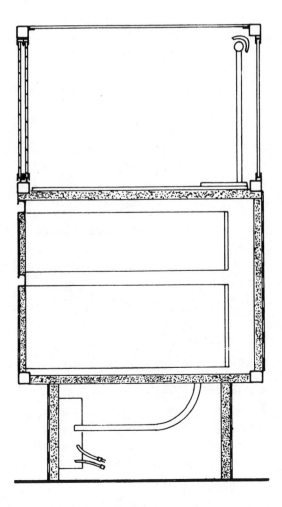

- Verify laminate plastic color with fixture-finish plan.

- Verify configuration of showcase island with plan. Kickbase required at showcase line opening.

- 72" showcase *only* to have center slotted post.

- ¼" hardboard doors color-lacquered to match laminate plastic with antijump sliding-door track assembly.

- ¼" polished plateglass with channel required for front, sides, and top. Cement top glass on showcase.

- Prewire showcase with receptacle, 10' power cord, 8" female lead, and fluorescent light rail.

- Removable ¼" upsum board supplied by this contractor and fabric-covered by owner; ¼" x 4" removable plastic mirror with heat-flamed polished edges (loose).

- ¼" polished plate silver mirror with stainless steel channel on front and sides.

- Levelers as required.

- Verify handicap requirement.

- **Prior to Construction:** Contractor to submit proposal of construction materials and details with two complete and accurate sets of show drawings to designer. One set of shop drawings will be returned upon approval.

OPEN SHOWCASE (TUBE FRAME)

- **Unit Size:** 38"H x 48" or 72"W x 21"D with 8"H x 2¾"D recessed kickbase.

- **Construction of Unit:** Mirror chrome finish 1" modular tube frame and ¾" board with laminate plastic on all surfaces, except kickbase to have brushed-chrome metallic laminate plastic horizontally grained.

- Verify laminate plastic color with fixture-finish plan.

- Verify configuration of showcase island with plan. Kickbase required at showcase line opening.

- 72" showcase *only* to have center slotted post.

- Back panel to be ¾" solid-core 3" slatwall, laminate plastic covered.

- ¼" polished plateglass with channel required for top. Cement top glass on showcase.

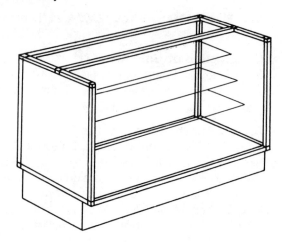

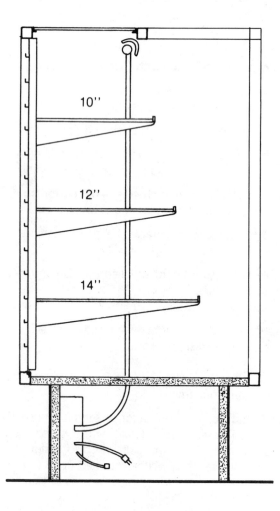

- Prewire showcase with receptacle, 10' power cord, 8" female lead, and fluorescent light rail.

- ⁷/₃₂" polished plateglass shelves with polished edges and ¼" clear plastic face clip.

- Removable ¼" upsum board supplied by this contractor and fabric-covered by owner. 1'3" x 4" removable plastic mirror with heat-flamed polished edges (loose).

- Side panels of interior to be ¼" polished plate silver mirror with exteriors of panels to be laminate plastic.

- Levelers as required.

- Verify handicap requirement.

- **Prior to Construction:** Contractor to submit proposal of construction materials and details with two complete and accurate sets of shop drawings to designer. One set of shop drawings will be returned upon approval.

SHOWCASE FILLS

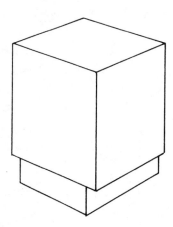

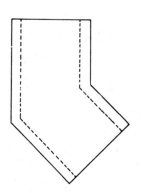

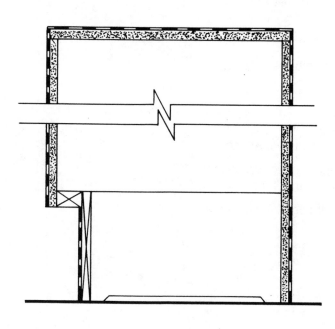

- **Unit Size:** 38"H x 21"D with 8"H x 2³/₄"D recessed kickbase. Width to be variable as shown.

- **Construction of Unit:** ³/₄" board with laminate plastic on all exterior surfaces, except kickbase to have brushed-chrome metallic laminate plastic horizontally grained.

- Verify laminate plastic color with fixture-finish plan.

- Levelers and blocking as required.

- Verify handicap requirement.

- **Prior to Construction:** Contractor to submit proposal of construction materials and details with two complete and accurate sets of shop drawings to designer. One set of shop drawings will be returned upon approval.

8' CASH-AND-WRAP AT SHOWCASE LINE

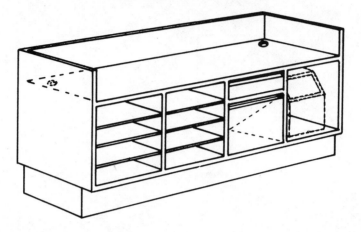

- **Unit Size:** 38"H x 72"W x 21"D with 8"H x 2¾"D recessed kickbase and 1½" rail. Verify counter height with owner.

- **Construction of Unit:** ¾" board with laminate plastic on all exterior surfaces, except kickbase to have brushed-chrome metallic laminate plastic horizontally grained. Color lacquer to match laminate plastic for interior surfaces.

- **Drawer Construction:** Front to be ¾" board with back and sides of ⅝" solid-core plywood. Bottom to be of ¼" tempered hardboard dadoed into sides and font, glued and nailed. Continuous extruded brushed-aluminum drawer pull (1¾"H x ¾"D) with no. 5 flathead wood screws on 2¼" centers, with lock if specified, and one set of 17" zinc-plated self-closing drawer slides with bottom nylon levelers. Drawer front to be 6"H x 18"W.

- Verify laminate plastic color with fixture-finish plan.

- Verify configuration of showcase island with plan. Kickbase required at showcase line opening.

- Two 2" diameter service holes as shown.

- Three ¾" adjustable shelves with tee edges and color lacquer to match the laminate plastic. Recessed pilaster strips for shelves' support and adjustment.

- Locked door to be piano hinged with continuous extruded brushed-aluminum drawer pull and 6" x 6" recessed removable access panel on inside bottom.

- Verify dimensions of receptacle for trash or hangers and of bag size with owner in order to allow for space in unit.

- Levelers and blocking as required.

- Verify handicap requirement.

- **Prior to Construction:** Contractor to submit proposal of construction materials and details with two complete and accurate sets of shop drawings to designer. One set of shop drawings will be returned upon approval.

MUSEUM OR DISPLAY CUBE

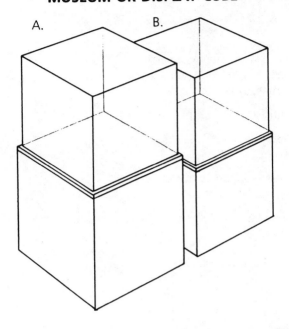

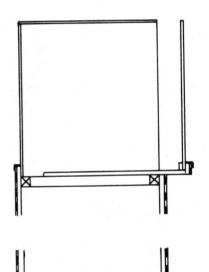

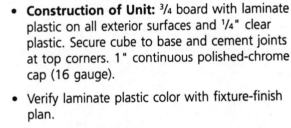

- **Unit Size:** 18"W x 18"D
  Unit A: 48"H
  Unit B: 36"H

- **Construction of Unit:** ¾ board with laminate plastic on all exterior surfaces and ¼" clear plastic. Secure cube to base and cement joints at top corners. 1" continuous polished-chrome cap (16 gauge).

- Verify laminate plastic color with fixture-finish plan.

- Sliding panel and metal trim with lock, 2" lip, and hardwood stop.

- Levelers and blocking as required.

- **Prior to Construction:** Contractor to submit proposal of construction materials and details with two complete and accurate sets of shop drawings to designer. One set of shop drawings will be returned upon approval.

FULL-VISION SHOWCASE

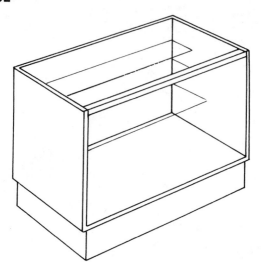

- **Unit Size:** 38"H x 48" or 72"W x 21"D with 8"H x 2¾"D recessed kickbase.

- **Construction of Unit:** ¾" board with laminate plastic on all exterior surfaces, except kickbase to have brushed-chrome metallic laminate plastic horizontally grained.

- Verify laminate plastic color with fixture-finish plan.

- Verify configuration of showcase island with plan. Kickbase required at showcase line opening.

- 72" showcase *only* to have center support with slotted hardware.

- ¼" hardboard doors color-lacquered to match laminate plastic with antijump sliding-door track assembly.

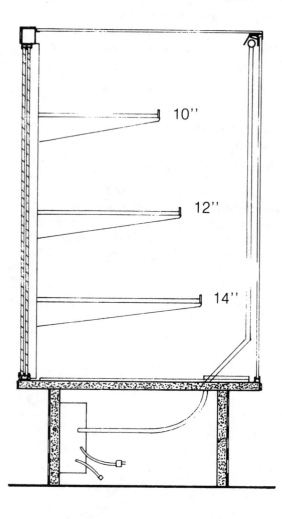

- ¼" polished plateglass with channel required for front and top. Cement top glass on showcase.

- Prewire showcase with receptacle, 10' power cord, 8" female lead, and fluorescent light rail.

- ⁷/₃₂" polished plateglass shelves with polished edges and ¼" clear plastic face clip.

- Removable ¼" upsum board supplied by this contractor and fabric-covered by owner; ¼" x 4" removable plastic mirror with heat-flamed polished edges (loose).

- Side panels of interior to be ¼" polished plate silver mirror with exteriors of panels to be laminate plastic.

- Levelers as required.

- Verify handicap requirement.

- **Prior to Construction:** Contractor to submit proposal of construction materials and details with two complete and accurate sets of shop drawings to designer. One set of shop drawings will be returned upon approval.

ONE-THIRD-VISION SHOWCASE

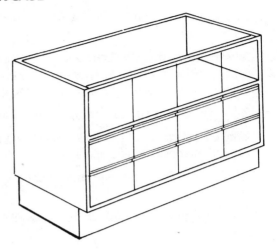

- **Unit Size:** 38"H x 48" or 72"W x 21"D with 8"H x 2¾"D recessed kickbase.

- **Construction of Unit:** ¾ board with laminate plastic on all exterior surfaces, except kickbase to have brushed-chrome metallic laminate plastic horizontally grained.

- **Drawer Construction:** Front to be ¾ board with back and sides of ⅝" solid-core plywood. Bottom to be of ¼" tempered hardboard dadoed into sides and font, glued and nailed. Continuous extruded brushed-aluminum drawer pull (1¾"H x ¾"D) with no. 5 flathead wood screws on 2¼" centers, with lock if specified, and one set of 17" zinc-plated self-closing drawer slides with bottom nylon levelers. Showcases' and back islands' locks to be keyed alike.

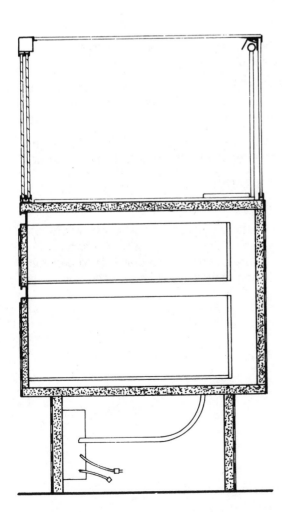

- Verify laminate plastic color with fixture-finish plan.

- Verify configuration of showcase island with plan. Kickbase required at showcase line opening.

- 72" showcase *only* to have center support.

- ¼" hardboard doors color-lacquered to match laminate plastic with antijump sliding-door track assembly.

- ¼" polished plateglass with channel required for front, sides, and top. Cement top glass on showcase.

- Prewire showcase with receptacle, 10' power cord, 8" female lead, and fluorescent light rail.

- Removable ¼" upsum board supplied by this contractor and fabric-covered by owner, ¼" x 4" removable plastic mirror with heat-flamed polished edges (loose).

- ¼" polished plate silver mirror with stainless steel channel on front and sides.

- Levelers as required.

- Verify handicap requirement.

- **Prior to Construction:** Contractor to submit proposal of construction materials and details with two complete and accurate sets of shop drawings to designer. One set of shop drawings will be returned upon approval.

OPEN SHOWCASE

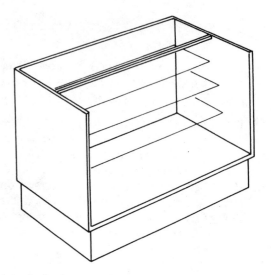

- **Unit Size:** 36"H x 48" or 72"W x 21"D with 8"H x 2¾"D recessed kickbase.

- **Construction of Unit:** ¾" board with laminate plastic on all exterior surfaces, except kickbase to have brushed-chrome metallic laminate plastic horizontally grained.

- Verify laminate plastic color with fixture-finish plan.

- Verify configuration of showcase island with plan. Kickbase required at showcase line opening.

- 72" showcase *only* to have center support with slotted hardware.

- Back panel to be ¾" solid-core 3" slatwall, laminate plastic covered.

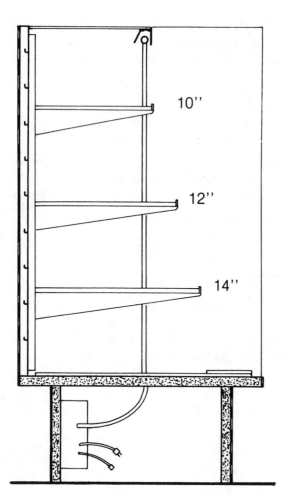

- ¼" polished plateglass with channel required for top. Cement top glass on showcase.

- Prewire showcase with receptacle, 10' power cord, 8" female lead, and fluorescent light rail.

- ⁷⁄₃₂" polished plateglass shelves with polished edges and ¼" clear plastic face clip.

- Removable ¼" upsum board supplied by this contractor and fabric-covered by owner. ¼" x 4" removable plastic mirror with heat-flamed polished edges (loose).

- Side panels of interior to be ¼" polished plate silver mirror with exteriors of panels to be laminate plastic.

- Levelers as required.

- Verify handicap requirement.

- **Prior to Construction:** Contractor to submit proposal of construction materials and details with two complete and accurate sets of shop drawings to designer. One set of shop drawings will be returned upon approval.

3' BACK ISLAND WITH DRAWERS

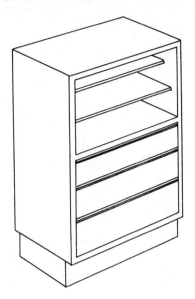

- **Unit Size:** 54"H x 36"W x 18"D with 8"H 2¾"D recessed kickbase and 1½" rail. Counter height to be 38".

- **Construction of Unit:** ¾" board with laminate plastic on all exterior surfaces and counter surface, except kickbase to have brushed-chrome metallic laminate plastic horizontally grained. Color lacquer to match laminate plastic for interior surfaces.

- **Drawer Construction:** Front to be ¾" board with back and sides of ⅝" solid-core plywood. Bottom to be of ¼" tempered hardboard dadoed into sides and front, glued and nailed. Continuous extruded brushed-aluminum drawer pull (1¾"H x ¾" D) with no. 5 flathead wood screws on 2¼" centers, with lock if specified, and one set of 15" zinc-plated self-closing drawer slides with bottom nylon levelers. Top drawers to have locks; if unit is being used in jewelry department, all drawers to have locks. Showcases' and back islands' locks to be keyed alike. Drawer-front heights to be 6", 9", and 12".

- Verify laminate plastic color with fixture-finish plan.

- Verify configuration of back island with plan. Back islands to be constructed so no fills are required for kickbase.

- Two ⅜" x 14" deep polished plateglass shelves with polished edges and proper hardware. Recessed pilaster strips for shelves' support and adjustment.

- Underside of top surface to be painted white with concealed single-lamp slimline fluorescent.

- Levelers and blocking as required.

- Verify handicap requirement.

- **Prior to Construction:** Contractor to submit proposal of construction materials and details with two complete and accurate sets of shop drawings to designer. One set of shop drawings will be returned upon approval.

3' BACK ISLAND WITH DOORS

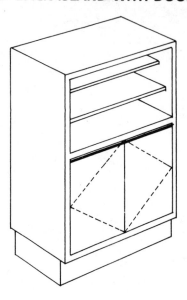

- **Unit Size:** 54"H x 36"W x 18"D with 8"H 2³/₄"D recessed kickbase and 1¹/₂" rail. Counter height to be 38".

- **Construction of Unit:** ³/₄" board with laminate plastic on all exterior surfaces and counter surface, except kickbase to have brushed-chrome metallic laminate plastic horizontally grained. Color lacquer to match laminate plastic for interior surfaces.

- Verify laminate plastic color with fixture-finish plan.

- Verify configuration of back island with plan. Back islands to be constructed so no fills are required for kickbase.

- Two ³/₈" x 14" deep polished plateglass shelves with polished edges and proper hardware. Recessed pilaster strips for shelves' support and adjustment.

- Underside of top surface to be painted white with concealed single-lamp slimline fluorescent.

- Locked doors to be piano hinged with continuous extruded brushed-aluminum drawer pull and 6" x 6" recessed removable access panel on inside bottom.

- Levelers and blocking as required.

- Verify handicap requirement.

- **Prior to Construction:** Contractor to submit proposal of construction materials and details with two complete and accurate sets of shop drawings to designer. One set of shop drawings will be returned upon approval.

3' TRIANGULAR BACK ISLAND

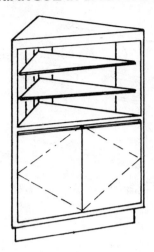

- **Unit Size:** 54"H x 36"W x 36"D with 8"H 2³/₄"D recessed kickbase.

- **Construction of Unit:** ³/₄" board with laminate plastic on all exterior surfaces, except kickbase to have brushed-chrome metallic laminate plastic horizontally grained.

- Verify laminate plastic color with fixture-finish plan.

- Verify configuration of back island with plan. Back islands to be constructed so no fills are required for kickbase.

- ³/₄" polished plateglass shelves with polished edges and proper hardware to set 1" behind front surface as shown.

- Underside of top surface to be painted white with concealed single-lamp slimline fluorescent.

- Locked doors to be piano hinged with continuous extruded brushed-aluminum drawer pull and 6" x 6" recessed removable access panel on inside bottom.

- Levelers and blocking as required.

- Verify handicap requirement.

- **Prior to Construction:** Contractor to submit proposal of construction materials and details with two complete and accurate sets of shop drawings to designer. One set of shop drawings will be returned upon approval.

4' BACK ISLAND WITH DRAWERS

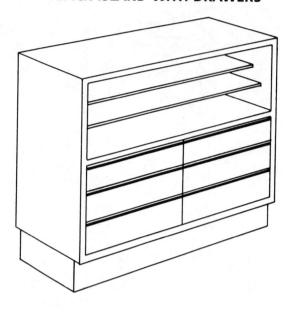

- **Unit Size:** 54"H x 48"W x 18"D with 8"H 2¾"D recessed kickbase and 1½" rail. Counter height to be 38".

- **Construction of Unit:** ¾" board with laminate plastic on all exterior surfaces and counter surface, except kickbase to have brushed-chrome metallic laminate plastic horizontally grained. Color lacquer to match laminate plastic for interior surfaces.

- **Drawer Construction:** Front to be ¾" board with back and sides of ⅝" solid-core plywood. Bottom to be of ¼" tempered hardboard dadoed into sides and front, glued and nailed. Continuous extruded brushed-aluminum drawer pull (1¾"H x ¾" D) with no. 5 flathead wood screws on 2¼" centers, with lock if specified, and one set of 15" zinc-plated self-closing drawer slides with bottom nylon levelers. Top drawers to have locks; if unit is being used in jewelry department, all drawers to have locks. Showcases' and back islands' locks to be keyed alike. Drawer-front heights to be 6", 9", and 12".

- Verify laminate plastic color with fixture-finish plan.

- Verify configuration of back island with plan. Back islands to be constructed so no fills are required for kickbase.

- Two ⅜" x 14" deep polished plateglass shelves with polished edges and proper hardware. Recessed pilaster strips for shelves' support and adjustment.

- Underside of top surface to be painted white with concealed single-lamp slimline fluorescent.

- Levelers and blocking as required.

- Verify handicap requirement.

- **Prior to Construction:** Contractor to submit proposal of construction materials and details with two complete and accurate sets of shop drawings to designer. One set of shop drawings will be returned upon approval.

3' BACK ISLAND WRAP COUNTER

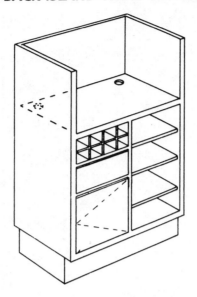

- **Unit Size:** 54"H x 36"W x 24"D with 8"H 2¾"D recessed kickbase and 1½" rail. Counter height to be 38".

- **Construction of Unit:** ¾" board with laminate plastic on all exterior surfaces and counter surface, except kickbase to have brushed-chrome metallic laminate plastic horizontally grained. Color lacquer to match laminate plastic for interior surfaces.

- **Drawer Construction:** Front to be ¾" board with back and sides of ⅝" solid-core plywood. Bottom to be of ¼" tempered hardboard dadoed into sides and front, glued and nailed. Continuous extruded brushed-aluminum drawer pull (1¾"H x ¾" D) with no. 5 flathead wood screws on 2¼" centers, with lock if specified, and one set of 20" zinc-plated self-closing drawer slides with bottom nylon levelers. Top drawers to have locks; if unit is being used in jewelry department, all drawers to have locks. Showcases' and back islands' locks to be keyed alike. Drawer-front heights to be 6".

- Verify laminate plastic color with fixture-finish plan.

- Verify configuration of back island with plan. Back islands to be constructed so no fills are required for kickbase.

- Two 2" diameter service holes as shown.

- Locked door to be piano hinged with continuous extruded brushed-aluminum drawer pull and 6" x 6" recessed removable access panel on inside bottom.

- Three ¾" adjustable shelves with T-edges and color lacquer to match the laminate plastic. Recessed pilaster strips for shelves' support and adjustment.

- Verify size and quantity of filler boxes for charge slips with owner.

- Levelers and blocking as required.

- Verify handicap requirement.

- **Prior to Construction:** Contractor to submit proposal of construction materials and details with two complete and accurate sets of shop drawings to designer. One set of shop drawings will be returned upon approval.

BACK ISLAND FILL

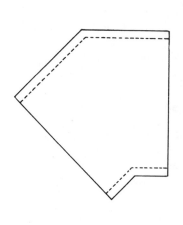

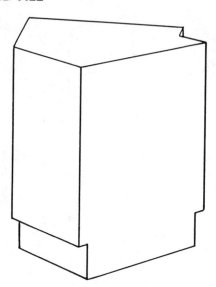

- **Unit Size:** 54"H x 36"D with 8"H 2¾"D recessed kickbase. Width to be variable as shown.

- **Construction of Unit:** ¾" board with laminate plastic on all exterior surfaces, except kickbase to have brushed-chrome metallic laminate plastic horizontally grained.

- Verify laminate plastic color with fixture-finish plan.

- Levelers and blocking as required.

- **Prior to Construction:** Contractor to submit proposal of construction materials and details with two complete and accurate sets of shop drawings to designer. One set of shop drawings will be returned upon approval.

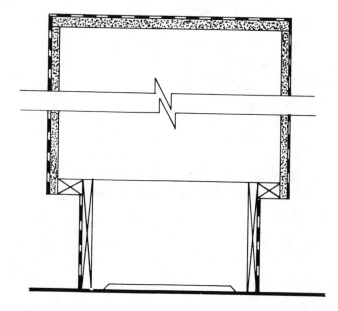

TANDEM WIRING DIAGRAM

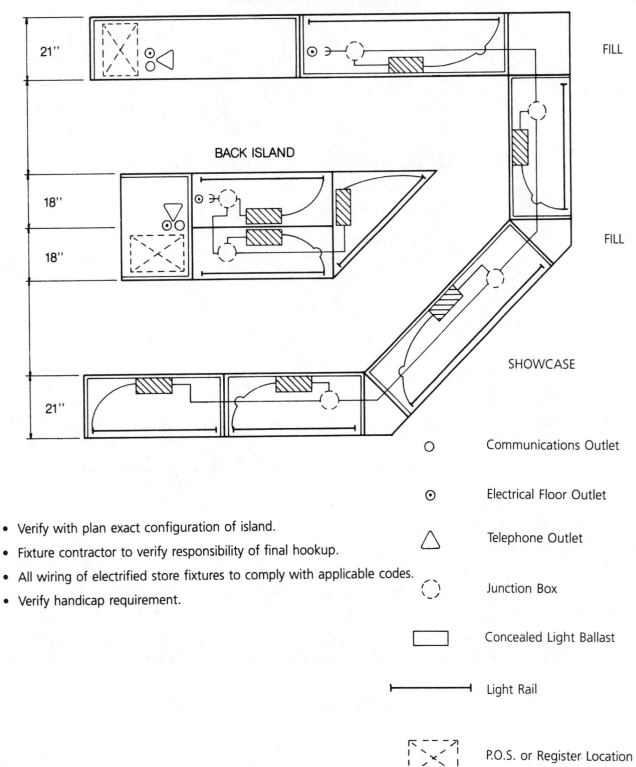

- Verify with plan exact configuration of island.
- Fixture contractor to verify responsibility of final hookup.
- All wiring of electrified store fixtures to comply with applicable codes.
- Verify handicap requirement.

○ Communications Outlet

⊙ Electrical Floor Outlet

△ Telephone Outlet

◌ Junction Box

▭ Concealed Light Ballast

⊢———⊣ Light Rail

⊠ P.O.S. or Register Location

FREESTANDING FITTING ROOM AND MERCHANDISING EXTERIOR WALLS

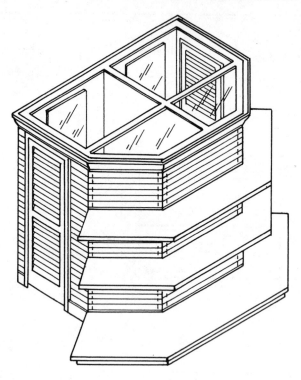

- **Unit Size:** 108"W x 96"D x 96"H

- **Construction of Unit:** Prefabricated shop-made freestanding unit with 36"W x 80"H louvered doors with passage set.

- Two ¼" mirrors 24"W x 60"H with polished edges, siliconed to interior laminate or wood-finished walls.

- One freestanding bench or chair and two coat hooks per fitting room.

- Exterior of unit to be fabricated with ¾" slatwall laminated plastic cover finish with aluminum channel slat inserts.

- Heavy duty standards for self or hardware adjustments.

- Merchandising presentation will determine shelves, hangrods, and faceout hardware.

- Can be modified to accomodate handicap requirements.

- **Prior to Construction:** Contractor to submit proposal of construction materials and details with two complete and accurate sets of shop drawings to designer. One set of shop drawings will be returned upon approval.

FITTING ROOM—FREESTANDING

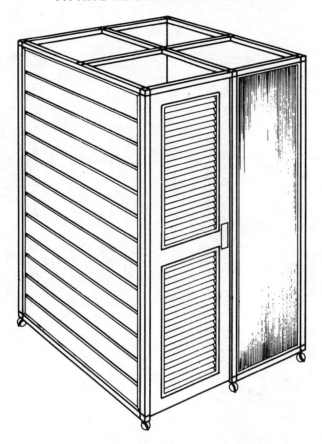

- **Unit Size:** 84"H x 48"W x 48"D

- **Construction of Unit:** Mirror chrome 1" modulartube frame wiht crossbracing as shown. Three panels to be ³/₄" solid-core 6" slatwall; ¹/₄" polished plate silver mirror with stainless channel frame. Full-height paint-grade louver door with required hardware. Door width to be 24". (Note: This unit not recommended for handicapped use.)

- Verify laminate plastic color with fixture-finish plan.

- Two hooks attached to panel as required for fitting room interior.

- Slatwall hardware as specified by owner.

- Five heavy-duty ball casters as required.

- Not required for handicap use.

- **Prior to Construction:** Contractor to submit proposal of construction materials and details with two complete and accurate sets of shop drawings to designer. One set of drawings will be returned upon approval.

FITTING ROOM—WOOD FRAME

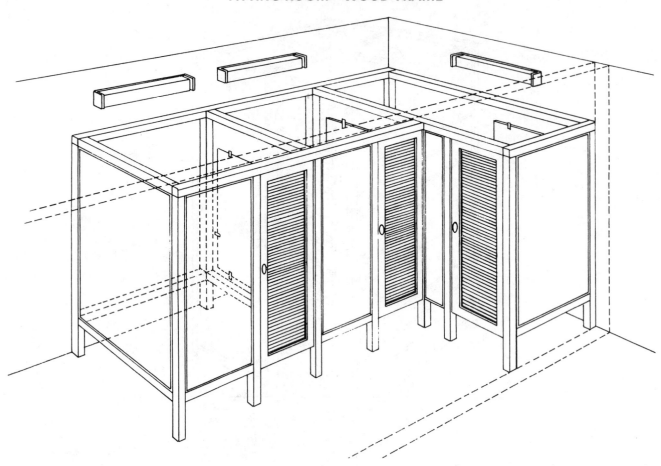

- **Modular Size—Fitting Room:** 96"H x 60"W x 48"D with end fitting room (at right in diagram) to extend 36" for door opening as shown.

- **Construction of Unit:** Post-and-panel construction of 2" hardware frame and ³/₄" board panel vinyl covered, fastened as required.

- Verify vinyl covering, frame, and door finish with fixture-finish plan.

- Full-height paint-grade quality-hardwood louver door with required hardware. Door size to be 80"H x 24"W.

- Prefinish in shop with final assembly on job site.

- Fitting room lights installed by other contractors.

- ¹/₄" polished plateglass silver mirror and two hooks attached to panel as required for each fitting room interior. Mirror to be 60"H x 24"W.

- Optional: ³/₄" plywood bench (16"D with 3" lip), laminate plastic covered. Attach to panel with cleat 18" above finish floor.

- Levelers as required.

- Can be modified for handicap use.

- **Prior to Construction:** Contractor to submit proposal of construction materials and details with two complete and accurate sets of shop drawings to designer. One set of shop drawings will be returned upon approval.

FITTING ROOM—1" TUBE FRAME

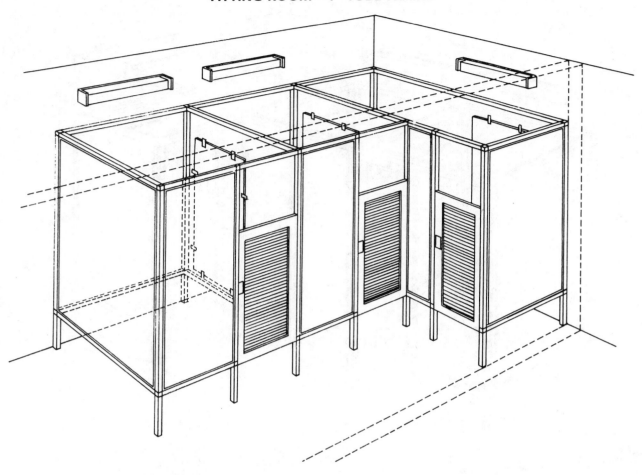

- **Modular Size—Fitting Room:** 96"H x 60"W x 48"D with end fitting room (at right in diagram) to extend 36" for door opening as shown.

- **Construction of Unit:** Post-and-panel construction of 1" modular tube frame and 5/8" plywood panel with plastic laminate on both sides with putty cladding channel.

- Verify laminate plastic color with fixture-finish plan.

- 3/4"-height paint-grade quality-hardwood louver door with required hardware. Door size to be 48"H x 24"W.

- Prefinish in shop with final assembly on job site.

- Fitting room lights installed by other contractors.

- 1/4" polished plateglass silver mirror and two hooks attached to panel as required for each fitting room interior. Mirror to be 60"H x 24"W.

- Optional: 18"H x 46"W x 12"D freestanding bench with top surface laminate plastic covered.

- Levelers as required.

- Can be modified for handicap use.

- **Prior to Construction:** Contractor to submit proposal of construction materials and details with two complete and accurate sets of shop drawings to designer. One set of shop drawings will be returned upon approval.

FITTING ROOM—EXTRUDED ALUMINUM FRAME

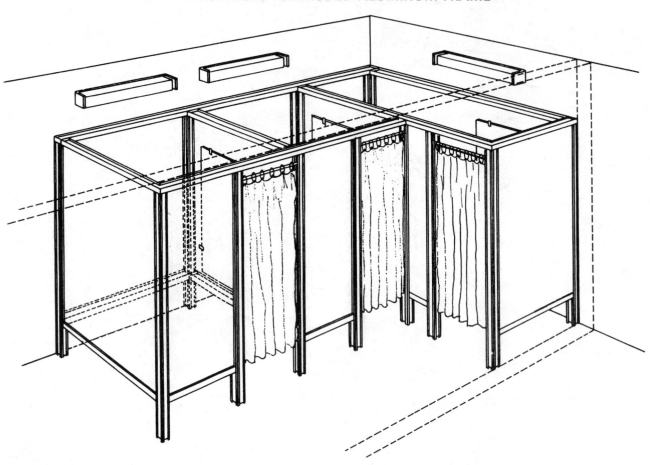

- **Modular Size—Fitting Room:** 96"H x 60"W x 48"D with end fitting room (at right in diagram) to extend 36" for door opening as shown.

- **Construction of Unit:** Post-and-panel construction of 1½" extruded aluminum and ¾" board panel, vinyl covered, fastened as required.

- Verify vinyl covering and frame finish with fixture-finish schedule.

- Install heavy-duty spring-loaded curtain rod with hardware.

- Drapery panel to be two sided with metal hanging rings and grommets, supplied and installed by owner.

- Prefinish in shop with final assembly on job site.

- Fitting room lights installed by other contractors.

- ¼" polished plateglass silver mirror and two hooks attached to panel as required for each fitting room interior. Mirror to be 60"H x 24"W.

- Optional: ¾" plywood bench (16"D with 3" lip), laminate plastic covered. Attach to panel with cleat 18" above finish floor.

- Levelers as required.

- Can be modified for handicap use.

- **Prior to Construction:** Contractor to submit proposal of construction materials and details with two complete and accurate sets of shop drawings to designer. One set of shop drawings will be returned upon approval.

FITTING ROOM—DRYWALL

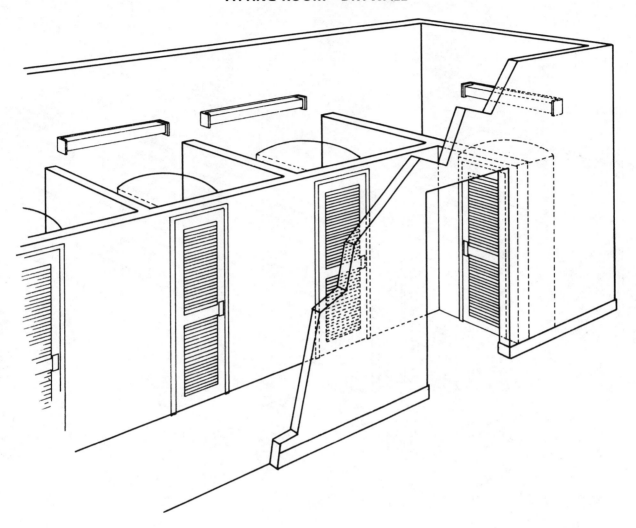

- **Modular Size—Fitting Room:** 96"H x 60"W x 48"D with end fitting room (at right in diagram) to extend 36" for door opening as shown.

- **Construction of Unit:** Construction of 2-by-4 wood or metal studs and ⁵⁄₈" plasterboard.

- Verify vinyl covering, frame, and door finish with fixture-finish plan.

- Full-height paint-grade louver door with required hardware. Door size to be 80"H x 24"W.

- Fitting room lights installed by other contractors.

- ¹⁄₄" polished plateglass silver mirror and two hooks attached to wall as required for each fitting room interior. Mirror to be 60"H x 24"W.

- Optional: ³⁄₄" plywood bench (16"D with 9" lip); laminate plastic covered.

- Can be modified for handicap use.

- **Prior to Construction:** Contractor to submit proposal of construction materials and details with two complete and accurate sets of shop drawings to designer. One set of drawings will be returned upon approval.

FITTING ROOMS—DRYWALL—FREESTANDING

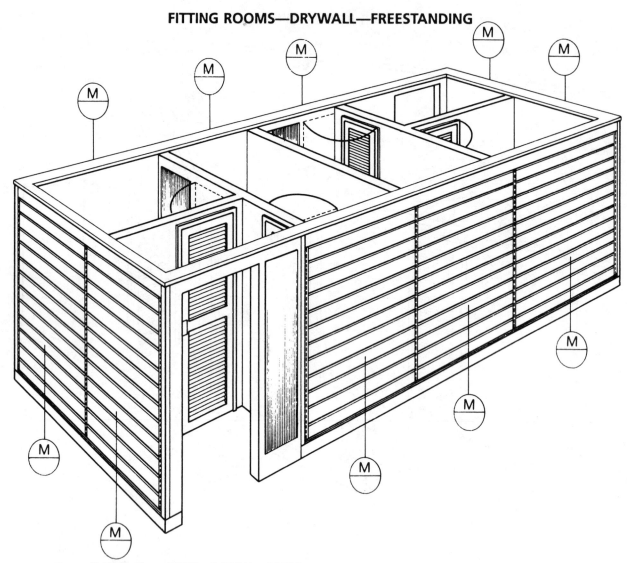

- **Overall Unit Size:** 96"H x 246"W x 102"D

- **Modular Size—Fitting Room:** 96"H x 60"W x 48"D with center fitting rooms to extend 36" for door opening as shown.

- **Construction of Unit:** Construction of 2-by-4 wood or metal studs and ⅝" plasterboard.

- Verify vinyl covering, frame, and door finish with fixture-finish plan.

- Full-height paint-grade louver door with required hardware. Door size to be 80"H x 24"W.

- Verify merchandising requirements with sections.

- ¼" polished plateglass silver mirror and two hooks attached to wall as required for each fitting room interior. Mirror to be 60"H x 24"W.

- Optional: ¾" plywood bench (16"D with 8" lip), laminate plastic covered.

- Can be modified for handicap use.

- **Prior to Construction:** Contractor to submit proposal of construction materials and details with two complete and accurate sets of shop drawings to designer. One set of drawings will be returned upon approval.

FREESTANDING PARTITION WITH FITTING ROOM

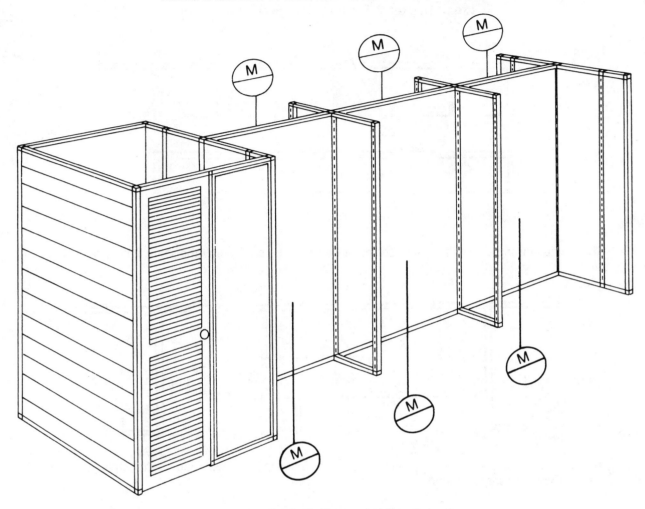

- **Unit Size:** 84"H x 192"W x 48"D with 12" fins every 48" as shown.

- **Construction of Unit:** Mirror chrome finish 1" modular tube frame and ¾" board with laminate plastic on all surfaces. End panel to be ¾" solid-core 6" slatwall; ¼" polished plate silver mirror with stainless channel frame as shown. Full-height paint-grade quality louver door with required hardware. Door to be 24" wide.

- Verify laminate plastic color with fixture-finish plan.

- Two hooks attached to panel as required for fitting room interior.

- Verify merchandising requirements with sections.

- Levelers as required.

- Not recommended for handicap use.

- **Prior to Construction:** Contractor to submit proposal of construction materials and details with two complete and accurate sets of shop drawings to designer. One set of shop drawings will be returned upon approval.

FITTING ROOM LAYOUTS
(See Chapter 2 for handicapped fitting room)

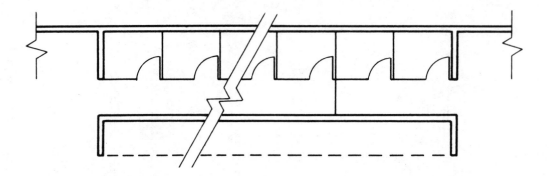

These side entrances allow two adjacent departments to be serviced by the same fitting-room bank.

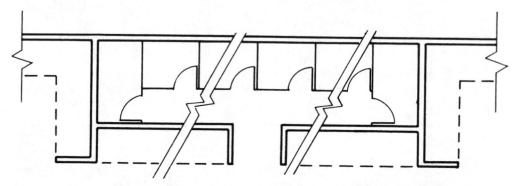

The moveable panel is for flexibility in fitting room demands and shoplifting control. This center entrance allows for spacious fitting rooms at both ends.

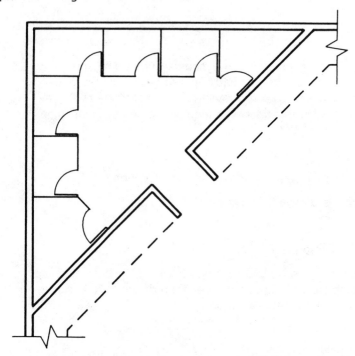

Angular fitting-room banks eliminate a dead corner and provide an alteration fitting area.

6' CASH-AND-WRAP

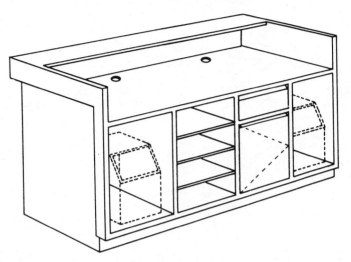

- **Unit Size:** 42"H x 72"W x 30"D with 4"H x 2¾"D recessed kickbase on side shown and 1½" rim. Front rail to be 8" high. Confirm register and/or counter height with owner.

- **Construction of Unit:** ¾" board with laminate plastic on all exterior surfaces. Color lacquer to match laminate plastic for interior surfaces.

- **Drawer Construction:** Front to be ¾" board with back and sides of ⅝" solid-core plywood. Bottom to be of ¼" tempered hardboard dadoed into sides and front, glued and nailed. Continuous extruded brushed-aluminum drawer pull (1¾"H x ¾"D) with no. 5 flathead wood screws on 2¼" centers, with lock if specified, and one set of 20" zinc-plated self-closing drawer slides with bottom nylon levelers. Drawer front to be 6"H x 16"W.

- Verify laminate plastic color with fixture-finish plan.

- Two 2" diameter service holes as shown.

- Duplex outlet at center if code permits.

- Verify dimensions of receptacle for trash or hangers and of bag size with owner in order to allow for space in unit.

- Three ¾" inch adjustable shelves with T-edges and color lacquer to match the laminate plastic. Recessed pilaster strips for shelves' support and adjustment.

- Locked door to be piano hinged with continuous extruded brushed-aluminum drawer pull and 6" x 6" recessed removable access panel on inside bottom.

- Levelers and blocking as required.

- Verify handicap requirements.

- **Prior to Construction:** Contractor to submit proposal of construction materials and details with two complete and accurate sets of shop drawings to designer. One set of shop drawings will be returned upon approval.

8' CASH-AND-WRAP

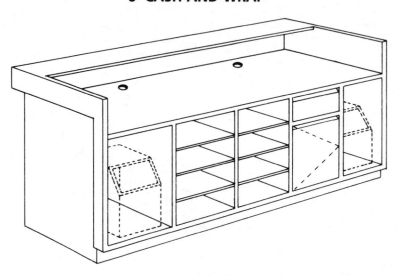

- **Unit Size:** 42"H x 96"W x 30"D with 4"H x 2³/₄"D recessed kickbase on side shown and 1¹/₂" rim. Front rail to be 8" high. Confirm register and/or counter height with owner.

- **Construction of Unit:** ³/₄" board with laminate plastic on all exterior surfaces. Color lacquer to match laminate plastic for interior surfaces.

- **Drawer Construction:** Front to be ³/₄" board with back and sides of ⁵/₈" solid-core plywood. Bottom to be of ¹/₄" tempered hardboard dadoed into sides and front, glued and nailed. Continuous extruded brushed-aluminum drawer pull (1²/₄"H x ³/₄"D) with no. 5 flathead wood screws on 2¹/₄" centers, with lock of specified, and one set of 20" zinc-plated self-closing drawer slides with bottom nylon levelers. Drawer front to be 6"H x 16"W.

- Verify laminate plastic color with fixture-finish plan.

- Two 2" diameter service holes as shown.

- Duplex outlet at center if code permits.

- Verify dimensions of receptacle for trash hangers and of bag size with owner in order to allow for space in unit.

- Two sets of three ³/₄" adjustable shelves with T-edges and color lacquer to match the laminate plastic. Recessed pilaster strips for shelves' support and adjustment.

- Locked door to be piano hinged with continuous extruded brushed-aluminum drawer pull and 6" x 6" recessed removable access panel on inside bottom.

- Levelers and blocking as required.

- Verify handicap requirements.

- **Prior to Construction:** Contractor to submit proposal of construction materials and details with two complete and accurate sets of shop drawings to designer. One set of shop drawings will be returned upon approval.

3' FREESTANDING CASH STAND

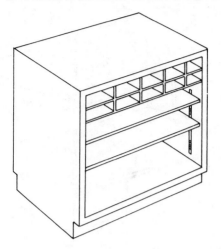

- **Unit Size:** 38"H x 36"W x 30"D with 8"H x 2^3/$_4$"D recessed kickbase on side shown and 1^1/$_2$" rail.

- **Construction of Unit:** ^{3}/$_4$" board with laminate plastic on all exterior surfaces. Color lacquer to match laminate plastic for interior surfaces.

- Verify laminate plastic color with fixture-finish plan.

- Verify size and quantity of filler boxes for charge slips with owner.

- Two ^{3}/$_4$" adjustable shelves with T-edges and color lacquer to match the laminate plastic. Recessed pilaster strips for shelves' support and adjustment.

- Levelers and blocking as required.

- Verify handicap requirements.

- **Prior to Construction:** Contractor to submit proposal of construction materials and details with two complete and accurate sets of shop drawings to designer. One set of shop drawings will be returned upon approval.

CUSTOMER SERVICE TRANSACTION COUNTER (PART A)

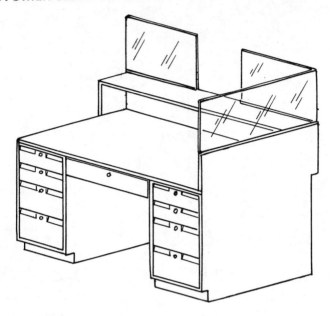

- **Unit Size:** 72"W x 36"D x 42"H

- **Construction of Unit:** ³/₄" board with laminated plastic cover, drawers or shelves required for service activity, ¹/₄" tempered security glass at face and/or return of counter.

- Verify keying requirement.

- Space under customer-service ledge to be designed with pigeon holes for clerk activities.

- Holes with grommets for electrical or point of service, or telephone cords.

- Surface to be neutral color, laminated plastic color.

- Vertical surfaces to be colored laminated plastic cover.

- Verify handicap requirements.

- **Prior to Construction:** Contractor to submit proposal of construction materials and details with two complete and accurate sets of shop drawings to designer. One set of shop drawings will be returned upon approval.

CUSTOMER SERVICE TRANSACTION COUNTER (PART B)

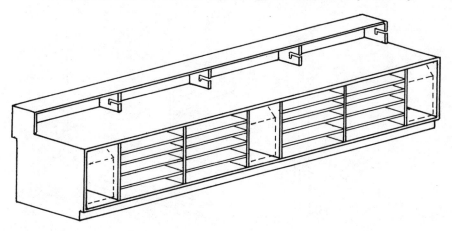

- **Unit Size:** 36"W x 42"H
  Length to adjust to number of employees and size of operation.

- **Construction of Unit:** ¾" board with laminated plastic cover, drawers or shelves required for service activity, ¼" tempered security glass at face and/or return of counter.

- Verify keying requirement.

- Space under customer service ledge to be designed with pigeon holes for clerk activities.

- Holes with grommets for electrical or point of service, or telephone cords.

- Surface to be neutral color, laminated plastic cover.

- Vertical surfaces to be colored laminated plastic cover.

- Store planner to verify operational needs such as credit application, gift wrapping, returns, bill payment, and statement verification.

- Verify handicap requirements.

- **Prior to Construction:** Contractor to submit proposal of construction materials and details with two complete and accurate sets of shop drawings to designer. One set of shop drawings will be returned upon approval.

6' SUPPORT OF CASH-AND-WRAP

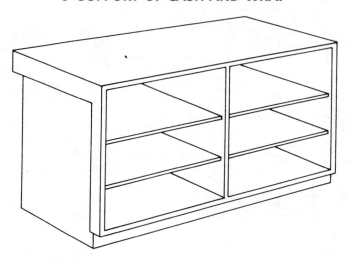

- **Unit Size:** 72"W x 30"D with 4"H x 2¾"D recessed kickbase on side shown and 1½" rim. Front rail to be 8" high. Confirm register and/or counter height with owner.

- **Construction of Unit:** ¾" board with laminate plastic on all exterior surfaces. Color lacquer to match laminate plastic for interior surfaces.

- Verify laminate plastic color with fixture-finish plan.

- Two sets of two ¾" adjustable shelves with T-edges and color lacquer to match the laminate plastic. Recessed pilaster strips for shelves' support and adjustment.

- Levelers and blocking as required.

- Verify handicap requirements.

- **Prior to Construction:** Contractor to submit proposal of construction materials and details with two complete and accurate sets of shop drawings to designer. One set of shop drawings will be returned upon approval.

WALL-MOUNTED CREDIT APPLICATION DESK

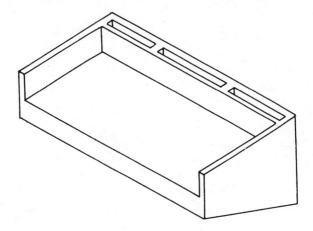

- **Unit Size:** 48"W x 24"D x 12"H
- **Construction of Unit:** Shop-built prefinished laminated plastic cover wall-mounted unit.
- Design and plan size of pigeon holes for forms to stand vertically and be easily seen.
- Provide wood blocking in wall to provide ample mounting of unit.
- Writing surface to be neutral color, laminated plastic cover.
- Vertical surface to be decorative laminated plastic cover.
- Verify handicap requirements.
- **Prior to Construction:** Contractor to submit proposal of construction materials and details with two complete and accurate sets of shop drawings to designer. One set of shop drawings will be returned upon approval.

REMOVABLE-BIN TABLE

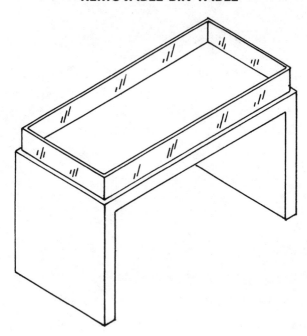

- **Unit Size:** 24"W x 60"D x 30"H

- **Construction of Unit:** Top Unit: Fabricated ³/₈" plexiglas dunk bin with 5" polished edged sides. Glue sides to ³/₈" thick bottom. Bottom Unit: To be built as shown with laminated plastic cover on 2¹/₂" board frame.

- This plexiglas bin unit can also be fabricated to work with any other table size or design.

- Provide levelers.

- **Prior to Construction:** Contractor to submit proposal of construction materials and details with two complete and accurate sets of shop drawings to designer. One set of shop drawings will be returned upon approval.

MULTIPLE REMOVABLE-BIN TABLE

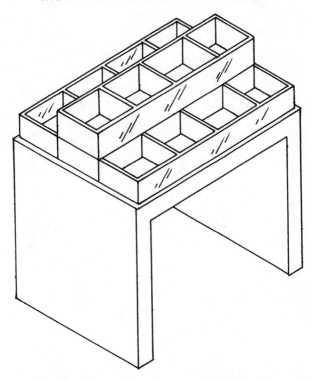

- **Unit Size:** 24"W x 60"D x 30"H

- **Construction of Unit:** Top Unit: Fabricated ³/₈" plexiglas dunk bin with 5" polished edged sides. Glue sides to ³/₈" thick bottom. Bottom Unit: To be built as shown with laminated plastic cover on 2¹/₂" board frame.

- This plexiglas bin unit can also be fabricated to work with any other table size or design.

- Provide levelers.

- **Prior to Construction:** Contractor to submit proposal of construction materials and details with two complete and accurate sets of shop drawings to designer. One set of shop drawings will be returned upon approval.

PARSONS VISUAL MERCHANDISING TABLE

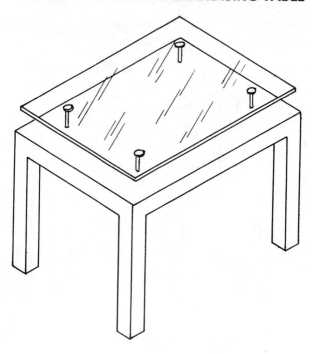

- **Unit Size:** Unit A: 24"W x 24"D x 30"H
  Unit B: 48"W x 24"D x 30"H
  Unit C: 60"W x 30"D x 30"H

- **Construction of Unit:** Prefabricated shop-made laminated plastic cover table with 3" legs and rails.

- Pin set ⅜" tempered polished plateglass 4" above table height. Glass edges to be polished.

- Provide levelers for legs.

- **Prior to Construction:** Contractor to submit proposal of construction materials and details with two complete and accurate sets of shop drawings to designer. One set of shop drawings will be returned upon approval.

NEST TABLES

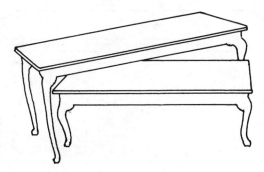

- **Unit Size:** 24" W x 48"D x 30"H
  Nest table to be downsized accordingly.

- **Construction of Unit:** Legs, tops, and edges to be wood, paint, or laminated plastic cover.

- Various types of legs including country, French, colonial, modern, medal wood, plastic, contemporary, and traditional can be used to accentuate department motif.

- Provide levelers.

- **Prior to Construction:** Contractor to submit proposal of construction materials and details with two complete and accurate sets of shop drawings to designer. One set of shop drawings will be returned upon approval.

MERCHANDISING PRESENTATION TABLE

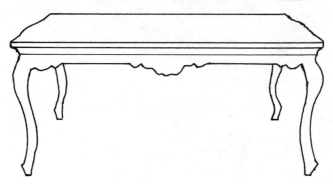

- **Unit Size:** 30"W x 60"D x 30"H

- **Construction of Unit:** Legs, tops, and edges to be wood, paint, or laminated plastic cover.

- Various types of legs including country, French, colonial, modern, medal wood, plastic, contemporary, and traditional can be used to accent department motif.

- Provide levelers.

- **Prior to Construction:** Contractor to submit proposal of construction materials and details with two complete and accurate sets of shop drawings to designer. One set of shop drawings will be returned upon approval.

MERCHANDISING PRESENTATION TABLE

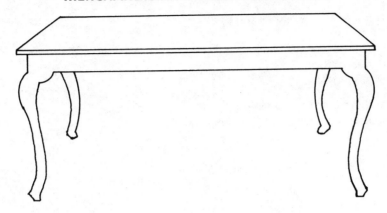

- **Unit Size:** 30"W x 60"D x 30"H

- **Construction of Unit:** Legs, tops, and edges to be wood, paint, or laminated plastic cover.

- Various types of legs including country, French, colonial, modern, medal wood, plastic, contemporary, and traditional can be used to accent department motif.

- Provide levelers.

- **Prior to Construction:** Contractor to submit proposal of construction materials and details with two complete and accurate sets of shop drawings to designer. One set of shop drawings will be returned upon approval.

REVERSIBLE-RIM DRAWERED TABLE

- **Unit Size:** Varies; 8"H x 2¾"D recessed kickbase and 4" rim for reversible top.
  - Unit A: 48"W x 24"D x 30"H
  - Unit B: 48"W x 30"D x 30"H
  - Unit C: 60"W x 30"D x 30"H

- **Construction of Unit:** ¾" board with laminate plastic on all exterior surfaces. Reversible-rim top to be shop fit to table.

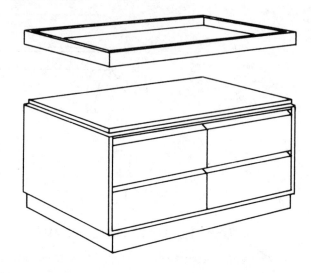

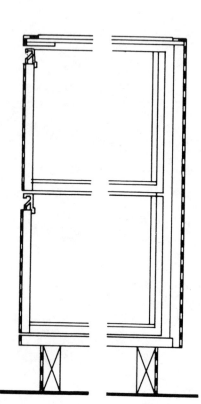

- **Drawer Construction:** Front to be ¾" board, with back and sides of ⅝" solid-core plywood. Bottom to be of ¼" tempered hardboard dadoed into sides and font, glued and nailed. Continuous extruded brushed-aluminum drawer pull (1¾"H x ¾"D) with no. 5 flathead wood screws on 2¼" centers, with lock if specified, and one set of 24" zinc-plated self-closing drawer slides (on Units B and C) with bottom nylon levelers. (Use 20" self-closing drawer slide on 24-inch deep Unit A.)

- Verify laminate plastic color with fixture-finish plan.

- Levelers and blocking as required.

- **Prior to Construction:** Contractor to submit proposal of construction materials and details with two complete and accurate sets of shop drawings to designer. One set of shop drawings will be returned upon approval.

PARSONS TABLE

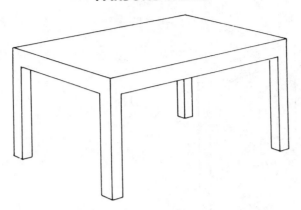

- **Unit Size:** Varies; with 3" rim.
  Unit A: 48"W x 24"D x 30"H
  Unit B: 48"W x 30"D x 30"H
  Unit C: 60"W x 30"D x 30"H

- **Construction of Unit:** ¾" board with laminate plastic on all exterior surfaces with balance sheet on underside of top, 3" hardwood legs.

- Verify laminate plastic color with fixture-finish plan.

- Levelers and blocking as required.

- **Prior to Construction:** Contractor to submit proposal of construction materials and details with two complete and accurate sets of shop drawings to designer. One set of shop drawings will be returned upon approval.

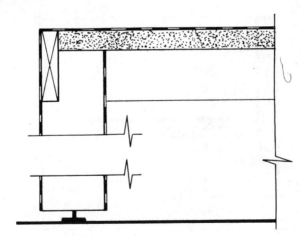

FIXED-RIM PARSONS TABLE

- **Unit Size:** Varies; 4" rim.
  - Unit A: 48"W x 24"D x 30"H
  - Unit B: 48"W x 30"D x 30"H
  - Unit C: 60"W x 30"D x 30"H

- **Construction of Unit:** ³/₄" plywood for table top with balance sheet on underside, 3" hardwood legs. Two 2¹/₂" wood screws as shown. Laminate plastic on all exterior surfaces.

- Verify laminate plastic color with fixture-finish plan.

- Levelers and blocking as required.

- **Prior to Construction:** Contractor to submit proposal of construction materials and details with two complete and accurate sets of shop drawings to designer. One set of shop drawings will be returned upon approval.

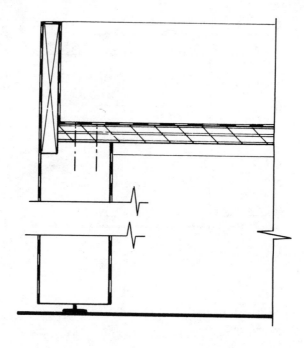

CLOSED-END PARSONS TABLE

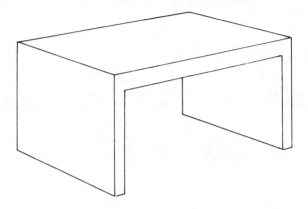

- **Unit Size:** Varies; 3" rim.
  Unit A: 48"W x 24"D x 30"H
  Unit B: 48"W x 30"D x 30"H
  Unit C: 60"W x 30"D x 30"H

- **Construction of Unit:** ³/₄" plywood for table top with balance sheet on underside; ³/₄" board for legs as shown. Laminate plastic on all exterior surfaces.

- Verify laminate plastic color with fixture-finish plan.

- Levelers and blocking as required.

- **Prior to Construction:** Contractor to submit proposal of construction materials and details with two complete and accurate sets of shop drawings to designer. One set of shop drawings will be returned upon approval.

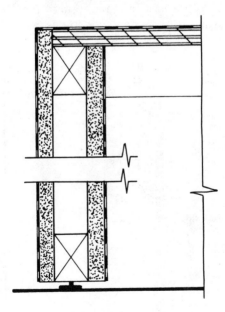

CLOSED-END PARSONS TABLE, CARPET COVERED

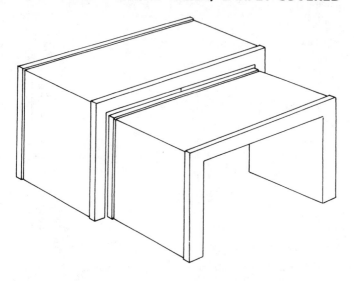

- **Unit Size:** Varies; 4" rim for top.
  Unit A: 30"H x 60"W x 30"D
  Unit B: 24"H x 52"W x 30"D

- **Construction of Unit:** ¾" plywood for table top and ¾" board for legs as shown. Laminate plastic on all exposed surfaces. Carpet to be supplied and installed by owner.

- Verify laminate plastic color with fixture-finish plan.

- Levelers and blocking as required.

- **Prior to Construction:** Contractor to submit proposal of construction materials and details with two complete and accurate sets of shop drawings to designer. One set of shop drawings will be returned upon approval.

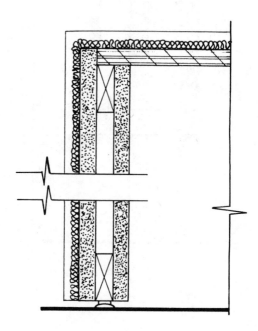

CLOSED-END PARSONS TABLE, CARPET INSERT

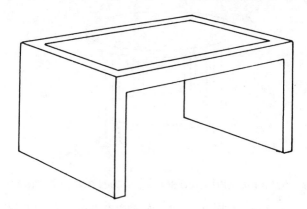

- **Unit Size:** Varies; 3" rim.
  Unit A: 48"W x 24"D x 30"H
  Unit B: 48"W x 30"D x 30"H
  Unit C: 60"W x 30"D x 30"H

- **Construction of Unit:** ³/₄" board with laminate plastic on all exterior surfaces with balance sheet on underside of top.

- Verify laminate plastic color with fixture-finish plan.

- Insert carpet to be supplied and installed by owner. Verify thickness of carpet for insert.

- Levelers and blocking as required.

- **Prior to Construction:** Contractor to submit proposal of construction materials and details with two complete and accurate sets of shop drawings to designer. One set of shop drawings will be returned upon approval.

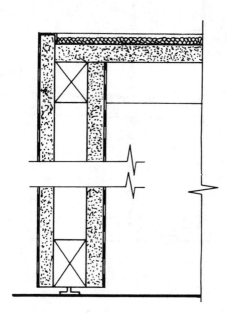

ROUND DISPLAY TABLE

- **Unit Size:** 30"H x 36" diameter, with fixed shelf 6 inches above floor.

- **Construction of Unit:** ³/₄" plywood for table top with balance sheet on underside; 3" hardwood legs. Laminate plastic on all exterior surfaces.

- Verify laminate plastic color with fixture-finish plan.

- Levelers and blocking as required.

- **Prior to Construction:** Contractor to submit proposal of construction materials and details with two complete and accurate sets of shop drawings to designer. One set of shop drawings will be returned upon approval.

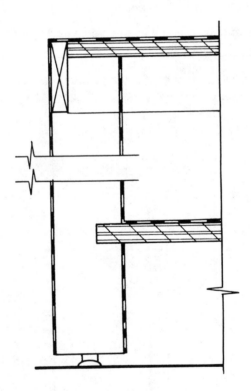

SIT-DOWN DESK

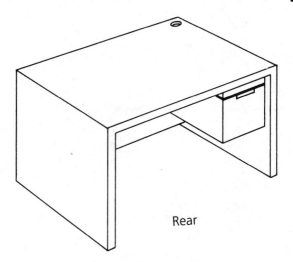

Rear

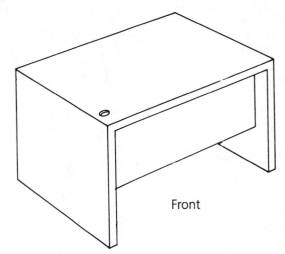

Front

- **Unit Size:** 30"H x 48"W x 30"D with 1½" rim.

- **Construction of Unit:** ¾" board with laminate plastic on all exterior surfaces. Color lacquer to match laminate plastic for interior surfaces.

- **Drawer Construction:** Drawer front to be ¾" board with back and sides of ⅝" solid-core plywood. Bottom to be of ¼" tempered hardboard dadoed into sides and front, glued and nailed. Continuous extruded brushed-aluminum drawer pull (1¾"H x ¾"D) with no. 5 flathead wood screws on 2¼" centers, with lock if specified, and one set of 17" zinc-plated self-closing drawer sides with bottom nylon levelers. Size bottom drawer to fit standard legal-size folder. Pencil drawer front to be 3" in height.

- Verify laminate plastic color with fixture-finish plan.

- One 2" diameter service hole as shown. Modesty panel to be set back 6" from front and bottom of unit.

- Levelers and blocking as required.

- **Prior to Construction:** Contractor to submit proposal of construction materials and details with two complete and accurate sets of shop drawings to designer. One set of shop drawings will be returned upon approval.

STAND-UP DESK

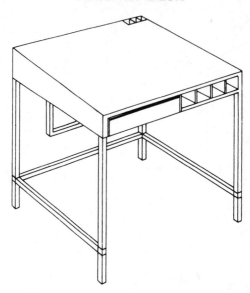

- **Unit Size:** 36"H x 30"D x 42"L with bottom tube and 1½" rail. Verify height with owner.

- **Construction of Unit:** Drawer front to be ¾" board with back and sides of ⅝" solid-core plywood. Bottom to be of ¼" tempered hardboard dadoed into sides and front, glued and nailed. Continuous extruded brushed-aluminum drawer pull (1¾"H x ¾"D) with no. 5 flathead wood screws on 2¼" centers, with lock if specified, and one set of 20" zinc-plated self-closing drawer slides with bottom nylon levelers.

- Verify size and quantity of filler boxes with owner.

- 3" x 3" pencil troughs and hangrod as shown.

- Verify table-top slope with owner.

- Levelers as required.

- **Prior to Construction:** Contractor to submit proposal of construction materials and details with two complete and accurate sets of shop drawings to designer. One set of shop drawings will be returned upon approval.

MILLINERY TABLE

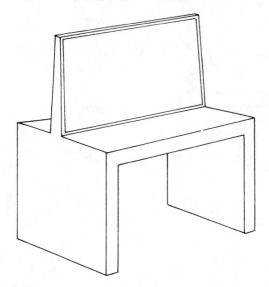

- **Unit Size:** 30"H x 48"W x 30"D with 24"H angled mirror extension and ³/₄" rim. Extension to be 3"D at top and 5"D at base.

- **Construction of Unit:** ³/₄" board with laminate plastic on all exterior surfaces with balance sheet on underside of top. Unit to be assembled so as to leave clean joints between extension and table as shown.

- Verify laminate plastic color with fixture-finish plan.

- ¹/₄" polished plate mirror to be attached to unit as required.

- Levelers and blocking as required.

- **Prior to Construction:** Contractor to submit proposal of construction materials and details with two complete and accurate sets of shop drawings to designer. One set of shop drawings will be returned upon approval.

24" SQUARE ÉTAGÈRE RISER WITH INSERT BASE

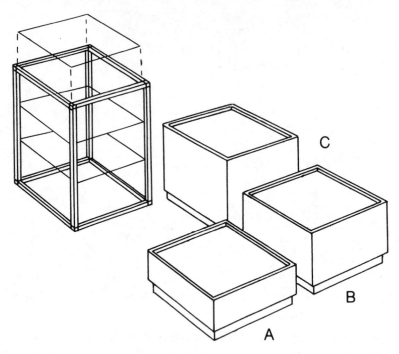

Base

- **Unit Size:** 24"W x 24"D with 4"H x 2³/₄"D recessed kickbase.
  - Unit A: 12"H
  - Unit B: 18"H
  - Unit C: 24"H

- **Construction of Base:** ³/₄" board with laminate plastic on all exterior surfaces. Base to have 1" lip so étagère will set into base.

- Verify laminate plastic color with fixture-finish plan.

- Levelers and blocking as required.

Riser

- **Unit Size:** 36"H x 22"W x 22"D

- **Construction of Riser:** Mirror chrome finish 1" modular tube frame with corner slotting.

- Two ³/₈" polished plateglass shelves with polished edges and proper hardware and glass top as shown.

- **Prior to Construction:** Contractor to submit proposal of construction materials and details with two complete and accurate sets of shop drawings to designer. One set of shop drawings will be returned upon approval.

24" X 48" ÉTAGÈRE RISER WITH DRAWERED BASE

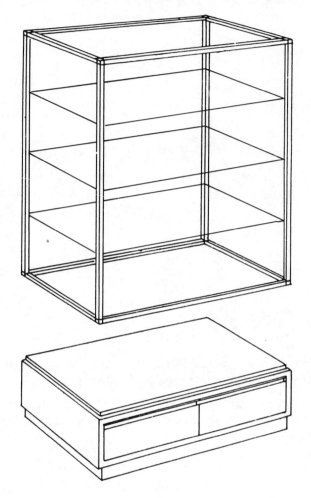

Base

- **Unit Size:** 18"H x 48"W x 24"D with 4"H x 2¾"D recessed kickbase.

- **Construction of Base:** ¾" board with laminate plastic on all exterior surfaces. Étagère to be fit to table.

- **Drawer Construction:** Front to be ¾" board with back and sides of ⅝" solid-core plywood. Bottom to be of ¼" tempered hardboard dadoed into sides and front, glue and nailed. Continuous extruded brushed-aluminum drawer pull (1¾"H x ¾"D) with no. 5 flathead wood screws on 2¼" centers, with lock if specified, and one set of 20" zinc-plated self-closing drawer slides with bottom nylon levelers.

- Verify laminate plastic color with fixture-finish plan.

- Levelers and blocking as required.

Riser

- **Unit Size:** 48"H x 48"W x 24"D

- **Construction of Riser:** Mirror chrome finish 1" modular tube frame with corner slotting.

- Three ⅜" polished plateglass shelves with polished edges and proper hardware.

- **Prior to Construction:** Contractor to submit proposal of construction materials and details with two complete and accurate sets of shop drawings to designer. One set of shop drawings will be returned upon approval.

DISPLAY RISERS

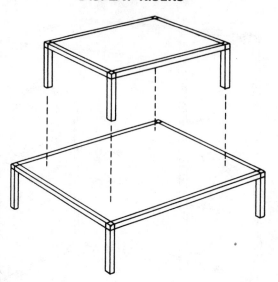

- **Unit Size:** 12" in height.
             Unit A: 42"W x 20"D
             Unit B: 52"W x 30"D

- **Construction of Riser:** Mirror chrome finish 1" modular tube frame with rubber tips on leg bottoms and ¼" polished plateglass inset and flush with top surface.

- **Prior to Construction:** Contractor to submit proposal of construction materials and details with two complete and accurate sets of shop drawings to designer. One set of shop drawings will be returned upon approval.

RUG DISPLAYER

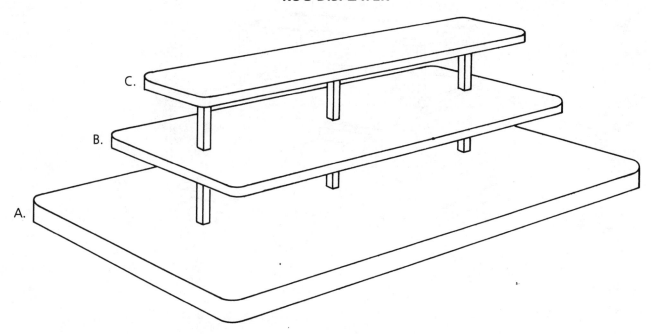

- **Unit Size:** 48"H x 144"W x 72"D with 1½" radius corners.
  Surface A: 6"H x 144"W x 72"D
  Surface B: 27"H x 120"W x 48"D with 3" return.
  Surface C: 48"H x 120"W x 24"D with 3" return.

- **Construction of Unit:** ¾" board with laminate plastic on all exterior surfaces with welded 3" center post and angle brackets as required.

- Posts to be 48" apart and centered on depth of unit.

- Verify laminate plastic color with fixture-finish plan.

- Underside of surfaces B and C to be painted white with concealed single-lamp slimline fluorescent.

- Levelers and blocking as required.

- **Prior to Construction:** Contractor to submit proposal of construction materials and details with two complete and accurate sets of shop drawings to designer. One set of shop drawings will be returned upon approval.

OPEN BASE WITH RISER

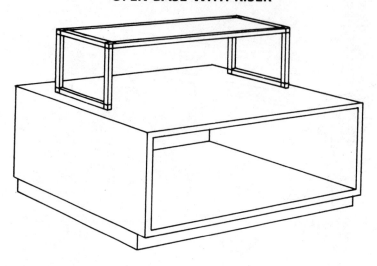

Base

- **Unit Size:** 30"H x 60"W x 48"D with 8"H x 2¾"D recessed kickbase and 1½" rim.

- **Construction of Base:** ¾" board with laminate plastic on all exterior surfaces and on bottom surface. Color lacquer to match laminate plastic for interior surfaces.

- Verify laminate plastic color with fixture-finish plan.

- Levelers and blocking as required.

Riser

- **Unit Size:** 18"H x 42"W x 24"D

- **Construction of Riser:** Mirror chrome finish 1" modular tube frame with nylon gliders and ¼" polished plateglass inset and flush with top surface.

- **Prior to Construction:** Contractor to submit proposal of construction materials and details with two complete and accurate sets of shop drawings to designer. One set of shop drawings will be returned upon approval.

DRAWERED BASE WITH RISERS

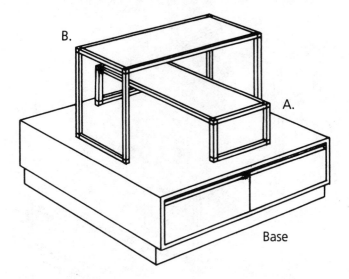

Base

- **Unit Size:** 18"H x 48"W x 48"D with 8"H x 2³/₄"D recessed kickbase.

- **Construction of Base:** ³/₄" board with laminate plastic on all exterior surfaces.

- **Drawer Construction:** Front to be ³/₄" board with back and sides of ⁵/₈" solid-core plywood. Bottom to be of ¹/₄" tempered hardboard dadoed into sides and front, glued and nailed. Continuous extruded brushed-aluminum drawer pull (1³/₄"H x ³/₄"D) with no. 5 flathead wood screws on 2¹/₄" centers, with lock if specified, and one set of 20" zinc-plated self-closing drawer slides with bottom nylon levelers.

- Verify laminate plastic color with fixture-finish plan.

- Levelers and blocking as required.

Risers

- **Unit Size:** 42"W x 18"D
          Unit A: 12"H
          Unit B: 24"H

- **Construction of Riser:** Mirror chrome finish 1" modular tube frame with nylon gliders and ¹/₄" polished plateglass inset and flush with top surface.

- **Prior to Construction:** Contractor to submit proposal of construction materials and details with two complete and accurate sets of shop drawings to designer. One set of shop drawings will be returned upon approval.

DRAWERED BASE WITH STAR RISER

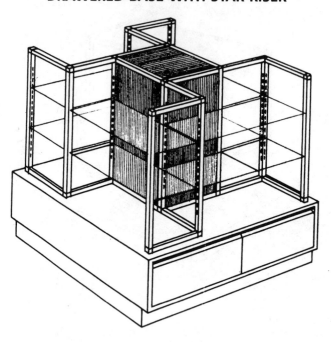

Base

- **Unit Size:** 18"H x 48"W x 48"D with 8"H x 2³/₄"D recessed kickbase.

- **Construction of Base:** ³/₄" board with laminate plastic on all exterior surfaces.

- **Drawer Construction:** Front to be ³/₄" board with back and sides of ⁵/₈" solid-core plywood. Bottom to be of ¹/₄" tempered hardboard dadoed into sides and front, glued and nailed. Continuous extruded brushed-aluminum drawer pull (1³/₄"H x ³/₄"D) with no. 5 flathead wood screws on 2¹/₄" centers, with lock if specified, and one set of 20" zinc-plated self-closing drawer slides with bottom nylon levelers.

- Verify laminate plastic color with fixture-finish plan.

- Levelers and blocking as required.

Riser

- **Unit Size:** 36"H x 42"W x 42"D (overall dimension).

- **Construction of Riser:** Mirror chrome finish 1" modular tube frame with corner slotting.

- Eight ³/₈" x 14" deep shelves of ³/₈" polished plateglass with polished edges and proper hardware.

- ¹/₄" polished plate silver mirror with stainless steel channel on center core as shown by shading. ¹/₄" polished plateglass with channel required for remaining panels.

- **Prior to Construction:** Contractor to submit proposal of construction materials and details with two complete and accurate sets of shop drawings to designer. One set of shop drawings will be returned upon approval.

STAR RISER WITH BASE

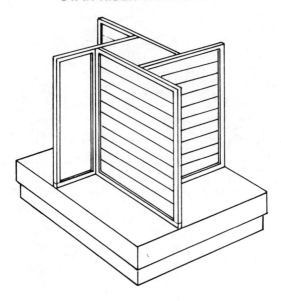

Base

- **Unit Size:** 6"H x 48"W x 48"D with 4"H x 2¾"D recessed kickbase.

- **Construction of Base:** ¾" board with laminate plastic on all exterior surfaces.

- Verify laminate plastic color with fixture-finish plan.

- Levelers and blocking as required.

Riser

- **Unit Size:** 48"H x 48"W x 48"D with 18" set backs for each panel as shown.

- **Construction of Riser:** Mirror chrome finish 1" modular tube frame with ¾" solid-core 3" slatwall inserts, laminate plastic covered.

- **Prior to Construction:** Contractor to submit proposal of construction materials and details with two complete and accurate sets of shop drawings to designer. One set of shop drawings will be returned upon approval.

RISERS WITH BASE

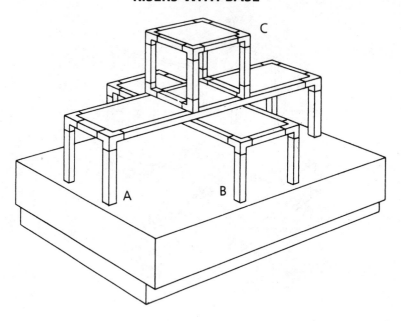

Base

- **Unit Size:** 18" x 72"W x 48"D with 8"H x 2¾"D recessed kickbase.

- **Construction of Base:** ¾" board with laminate plastic on all exterior surfaces.

- Verify laminate plastic color with fixture-finish plan.

- Levelers and blocking as required.

Risers

- **Unit Size:**
  > Unit A: 18"H x 66"W x 24"D
  > Unit B: 12"H x 42"W x 24"D
  > Unit C: 12"H x 24"W x 24"D

- **Construction of Riser:** 1¾" natural white oak verticals and horizontals connected by mirror chrome finish joints as shown with nylon gliders.

- ¼" polished plateglass inset and flush with top surface for all risers.

- **Prior to Construction:** Contractor to submit proposal of construction materials and details with two complete and accurate sets of shop drawings to designer. One set of shop drawings will be returned upon approval.

ONE-WAY TRIPLE ÉTAGÈRE WITH BASE

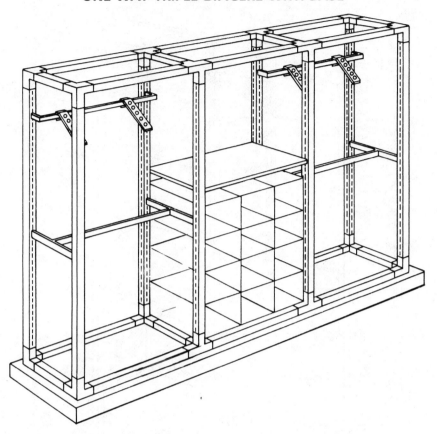

Base

- **Unit Size:** 6"H x 150"W x 30"D

- **Construction of Base:** ³/₄" board with laminate plastic on all exterior surfaces.

- Verify laminate plastic color with fixture-finish plan.

- Levelers and blocking as required.

Étagère

- **Modular Size:** 72"H x 48"W x 24"D

- **Construction of Unit:** 1³/₄" natural white oak verticals and horizontals connected by mirror chrome finish joints as shown with nylon gliders.

- Hardware and/or displays as specified by owner.

- **Prior to Construction:** Contractor to submit proposal of construction materials and details with two complete and accurate sets of shop drawings to designer. One set of shop drawings will be returned upon approval.

- Hardware and Display Requirements: Two H-shaped ¹/₂" x 1¹/₂" hangrods, two 3" U-shaped ¹/₂" x 1¹/₂" hangrods with two waterfalls each, one ³/₄" plywood laminate-plastic-covered shelf and glass-cube assembly.

THREE-WAY TRIPLE ÉTAGÈRE

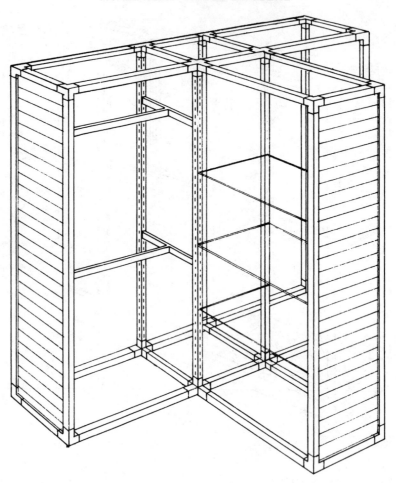

- **Modular Size—Étagère:** 72"H x 48"W x 24"D

- **Construction of Unit:** 1³/₄" natural white oak verticals and horizontals connected by mirror chrome finish joints with slotting as required.

- Hardware and/or displays as specified by owner.

- Levelers as required.

- **Prior to Construction:** Contractor to submit proposal of construction materials and details with two complete and accurate sets of shop drawings to designer. One set of shop drawings will be returned upon approval.

- Hardware and Display Requirements: Four H-shaped ¹/₂" x 1¹/₂" hangrods and three ³/₈" polished plateglass shelves.

10 X 10 X 16 GLASS CUBE ASSEMBLY

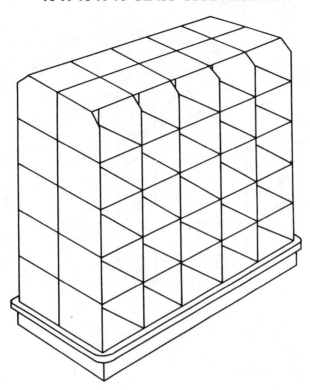

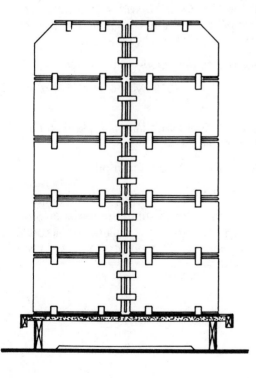

- **Cube Assembly:** 10"H x 10"W x 16"D with 45° beveled top cube and required clear plastic or metal clips (5"H x 5"W x 2"D).

- Verify glass type—annealed or tempered—with owner.

- **Unit Size—Base:** 6"H x 54"W x 36"D with 4"H x 2¾" recessed kickbase and 1½" radius corners.

- **Construction of Base:** ¾" board with laminate plastic on all exterior surfaces with a center support.

- Verify laminate plastic color with fixture-finish plan.

- Levelers and blocking as required.

- **Prior to Construction:** Contractor to submit proposal of construction materials and details with two complete and accurate sets of shop drawings to designer. One set of shop drawings will be returned upon approval.

10 X 10 X 16 GLASS CUBE ASSEMBLY WITH ENDCAP

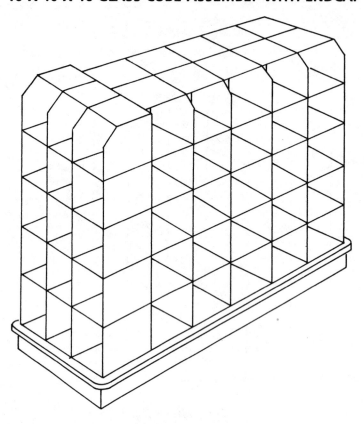

- **Cube Assembly:** 10"H x 10"W x 16"D with 45° beveled top cube and required clear plastic or metal clips (5"H x 5"W x 2"D). Endcap cube to match system (5"H x 1"W x 3"D).

- Verify glass type—annealed or tempered—with owner.

- **Unit Size—Base:** 6"H x 72"W x 36"D with 4"H x 2¾" recessed kickbase and 1½" radius corners.

- **Construction of Base:** ¾" board with laminate plastic on all exterior surfaces with a center support.

- Verify laminate plastic color with fixture-finish plan.

- Levelers and blocking as required.

- **Prior to Construction:** Contractor to submit proposal of construction materials and details with two complete and accurate sets of shop drawings to designer. One set of shop drawings will be returned upon approval.

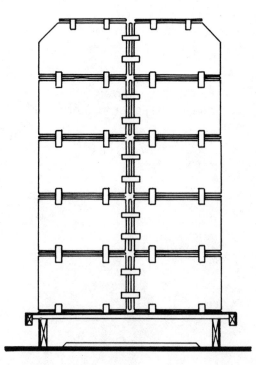

12 X 12 X 12 GLASS CUBE ASSEMBLY

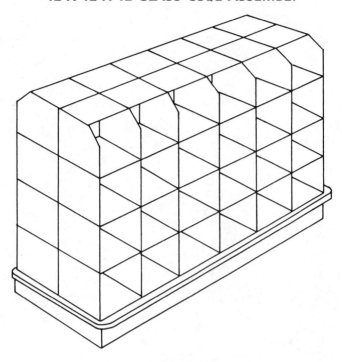

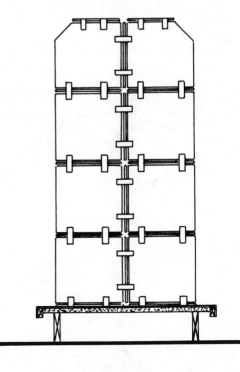

- **Cube Assembly:** 12"H x 12"W x 12"D with 45° beveled top cube and required clear plastic or metal clips (4"H x 6"W x 2"D).

- Verify glass type—annealed or tempered—with owner.

- **Unit Size—Base:** 6"H x 66"W x 30"D with 4"H x 2¾" recessed kickbase and 1½" radius corners.

- **Construction of Base:** ¾" board with laminate plastic on all exterior surfaces with a center support.

- Verify laminate plastic color with fixture-finish plan.

- Levelers and blocking as required.

- **Prior to Construction:** Contractor to submit proposal of construction materials and details with two complete and accurate sets of shop drawings to designer. One set of shop drawings will be returned upon approval.

18 X 18 X 18 GLASS CUBE ASSEMBLY

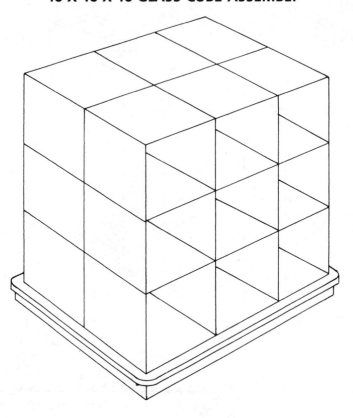

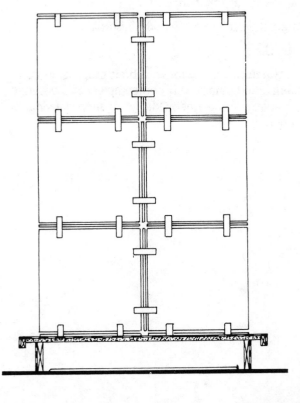

- **Cube Assembly:** 18"H x 18"W x 18"D with required clear plastic or metal clips (3"H x 3"W x 2"D).

- Verify glass type—annealed or tempered—with owner.

- **Unit Size**—Base: 6"H x 60"W x 42"D with 4"H x 2³/₄" recessed kickbase and 1¹/₂" radius corners.

- **Construction of Base:** ³/₄" board with laminate plastic on all exterior surfaces with a center support.

- Verify laminate plastic color with fixture-finish plan.

- Levelers and blocking as required.

- **Prior to Construction:** Contractor to submit proposal of construction materials and details with two complete and accurate sets of shop drawings to designer. One set of shop drawings will be returned upon approval.

17 X 22 X 24 GLASS CUBE ASSEMBLY

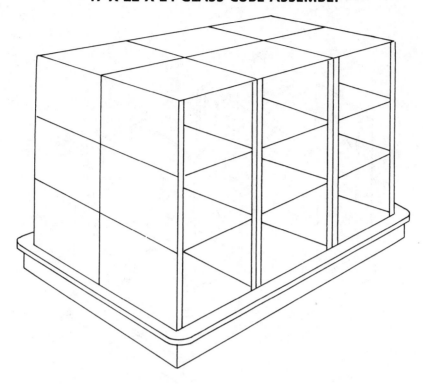

- **Cube Assembly:** 17"H x 22"W x 24"D with required clear plastic or metal clips and 2" rims as shown (3"H x 3"W x 2"D).

- Verify glass type—annealed or tempered—with owner.

- **Unit Size**—Base: 6"H x 72"W x 54"D with 4"H x 2¾" recessed kickbase and 1½" radius corners.

- **Construction of Base:** ¾" board with laminate plastic on all exterior surfaces with a center support.

- Verify laminate plastic color with fixture-finish plan.

- Levelers and blocking as required.

- **Prior to Construction:** Contractor to submit proposal of construction materials and details with two complete and accurate sets of shop drawings to designer. One set of shop drawings will be returned upon approval.

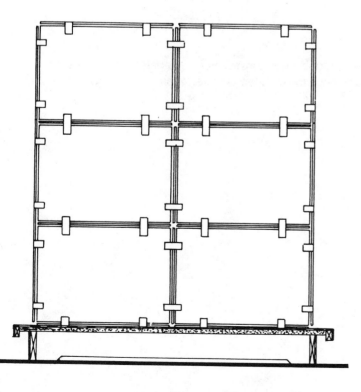

PILLOWS/COMFORTERS/BLANKETS/SPREADS UNIT

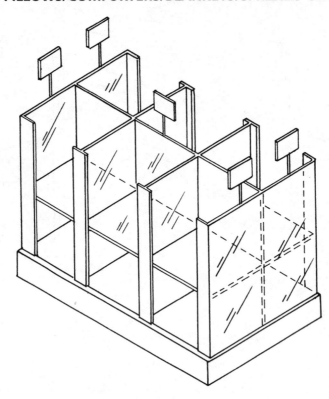

- **Unit Size:** To be verified with size of merchandise.

- **Construction of Unit:** Base: 6" high laminated plastic cover with levelers. Plexiglas unit: Constructed of ½" thick plexiglas with polished edges. Plan and design bins to accommodate exact size of merchandise.

- Plexiglas unit to be glued together using manufacturer's suggested adhesive.

- Plexiglas unit to be set on top of base.

- Chrome sign holders to be signed accordingly.

- **Prior to Construction:** Contractor to submit proposal of construction materials and details with two complete and accurate sets of shop drawings to designer. One set of shop drawings will be returned upon approval.

WIRE-BIN UNIT

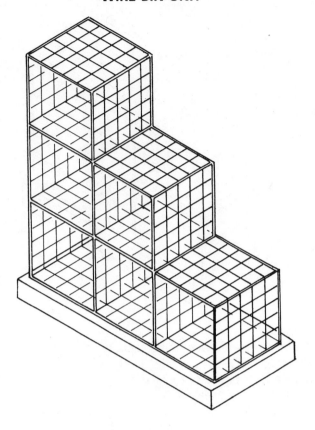

- **Unit Size:** To be determined by size of bins.
  Bin Sizes: 12"W x 12"D x 12"H 18"W x 18"D x 18"H 24"W x 24"D x 24"H

- **Construction of Unit:** Laminated plastic cover with levelers 6" high.

- Wire bins to be stacked to accommodate the merchandise, while creating a visually pleasing unit.

- Anchor bins together with mechanical fastening devices.

- **Prior to Construction:** Contractor to submit proposal of construction materials and details with two complete and accurate sets of shop drawings to designer. One set of shop drawings will be returned upon approval.

TEMPERED GLASS CUBED UNIT

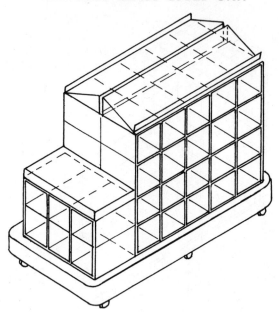

- **Unit Size:** To be determined by merchandising capacity.
  Glass cube sizes: 10'W x 16'D x 10'H—shirts
  Cubes require clear plastic or metal clips
  14'W x 16'D x 14'H—sweaters
  18'W x 18'D x 18'W—other

- **Construction of Unit:** 6" base laminated plastic cover with wheels.

- Assemble glass cubes on base with mechanical glass clip system, including back glass.

- Merchandising shelf to be clear plastic.

- Plexiglas angular displayers can be used on top of cube for visual presentation of merchandise.

- **Prior to Construction:** Contractor to submit proposal of construction materials and details with two complete and accurate sets of shop drawings to designer. One set of shop drawings will be returned upon approval.

HOSIERY FIXTURE

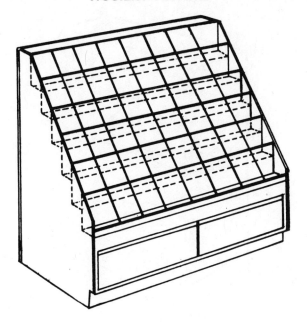

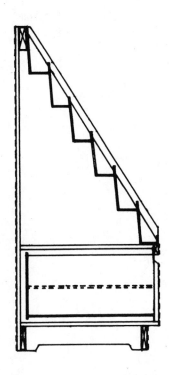

- **Unit Size:** 54"H x 60"W x 24"D with 4"H x 2¾"D recessed kickbase on side shown.

- **Construction of Unit:** ¾" board with laminate plastic on all exterior surfaces with stepped shelves and wire dividers to separate hosiery packets. Minimum front lip on shelves to be 3½".

- **Drawer Construction:** Front to be ¾" board with back and ides of ⅝" solid-core plywood. Bottom to be of ¼" tempered hardboard dadoed into sides and front, glued and nailed. Continuous extruded brushed aluminum drawer pull 1¾"H x ¾"D with no. 5 flathead wood screws on 2¼" centers, with lock if specified, and one set of 20" zinc-plated self-closing drawer slides with bottom nylon levelers. Hosiery packet to stand straight in drawers.

- Verify laminate plastic color with fixture-finish plan.

- Verify with owner size of hosiery packet in order to allow for space in unit.

- Levelers and blocking as required.

- **Prior to Construction:** Contractor to submit proposal of construction materials and details with two complete and accurate sets of shop drawings to designer. One set of shop drawings will be returned upon approval.

HOSIERY UNIT

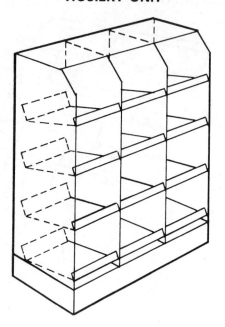

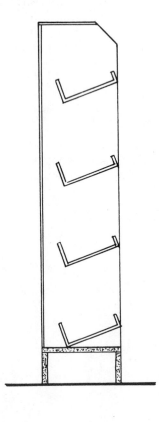

- **Unit Size:** 60"H x 24"W x 13"D

- **Construction of Unit:** $^3/_8$" clear plastic top, sides, and center dividers with $^3/_4$" board laminate plastic 6"H base sized to unit. Back panel to be light bronze or grey plastic.

- Shelves to be 10"W with 4" back and $1^3/_4$" front lip.

- Shelves to be on 20° angle and constructed of $^1/_4$" clear preformed plastic.

- Fasten unit to base with 1" two-way tape as required.

- Verify laminate plastic color with fixture-finish plan.

- Levelers and blocking as required.

- **Prior to Construction:** Contractor to submit proposal of construction materials and details with two complete and accurate sets of shop drawings to designer. One set of shop drawings will be returned upon approval.

PERIMETER PLATFORM

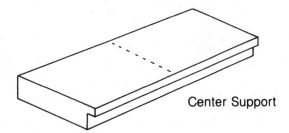

Center Support

- **Unit Size:** 6"H x 24"D with 4"H x 2¾"D recessed kickbase. Width of unit to be as shown on merchandising plan. Leave ½" tolerance.

- **Construction of Unit:** ¾" board with laminate plastic on all exterior surfaces.

- Verify laminate plastic color with fixture-finish plan.

- Levelers and blocking as required.

- **Prior to Construction:** Contractor to submit proposal of construction materials and details with two complete and accurate sets of shop drawings to designer. One set of shop drawings will be returned upon approval.

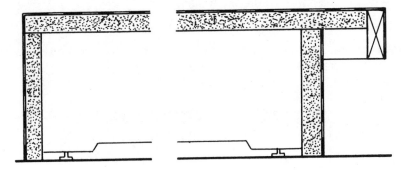

18" PERIMETER BASE

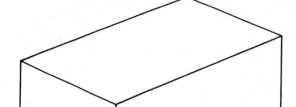

- **Unit Size:** 18"H x 24"D with 4"H x 2¾"D recessed kickbase. Width of unit to be as shown on merchandising plan. Leave ½" tolerance.

- **Construction of Unit:** ¾" board with laminate plastic on all exterior surfaces.

- Verify laminate plastic color with fixture-finish plan.

- Levelers and blocking as required.

- **Prior to Construction:** Contractor to submit proposal of construction materials and details with two complete and accurate sets of shop drawings to designer. One set of shop drawings will be returned upon approval.

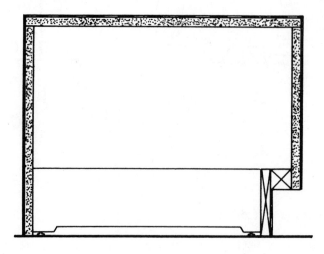

18" PERIMETER DRAWERED BASE

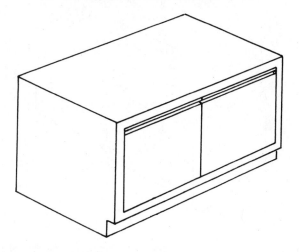

- **Unit Size:** 18"H x 24"D with 4"H x 2¾"D recessed kickbase. Width of unit to be as shown as merchandising plan. Leave ½" tolerance.

- **Construction of Unit:** ¾" board with laminate plastic on all exterior surfaces.

- **Drawer Construction:** Front to be ¾" board with back and sides of ⅝" solid-core plywood. Bottom to be of ¼" tempered hardboard dadoed into sides and front, glued and nailed. Continuous extruded brushed-aluminum drawer pull (1¾"H x ¾"D) with no. 5 flathead wood screws on 2¼" centers, with lock if specified, and one set of 20" zinc-plated self-closing drawer slides with bottom nylon levelers.

- Verify laminate plastic color with fixture-finish plan.

- Levelers and blocking as required.

- **Prior to Construction:** Contractor to submit proposal of construction materials and details with two complete and accurate sets of shop drawings to designer. One set of shop drawings will be returned upon approval.

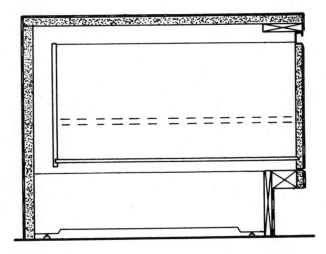

18" PERIMETER SLIDING-DOOR BASE

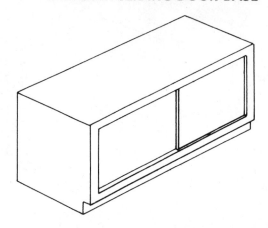

- **Unit Size:** 18"H x 24"D with 4"H x 2¾"D recessed kickbase. Width of unit to be as shown on merchandising plan. Leave ½" tolerance.

- **Construction of Unit:** ¾" board with laminate plastic on all exterior surfaces.

- Verify laminate plastic color with fixture-finish plan.

- ¼" hardboard doors color lacquered to match laminate plastic with antijump sliding-door track assembly.

- Levelers and blocking as required.

- **Prior to Construction:** Contractor to submit proposal of construction materials and details with two complete and accurate sets of shop drawings to designer. One set of shop drawings will be returned upon approval.

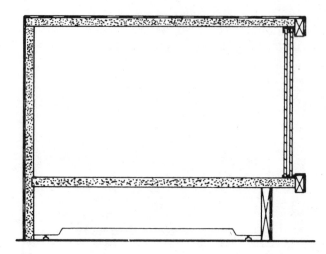

DISPLAY PLATFORM—HEXAGONAL

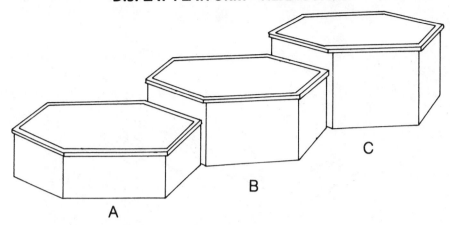

- **Unit Size:** Dimensions as taken from the merchandising plan, unless otherwise noted.
  Unit A: 12"H
  Unit B: 18"H
  Unit C: 24"H

- **Construction of Unit:** ¾" board with ⅝"D x 1½"W natural white oak with clear sealer.

- Carpet insert for top and sides to be supplied and installed by owner.

- Levelers and blocking as required.

- **Prior to Construction:** Contractor to submit proposal of construction materials and details with two complete and accurate sets of shop drawings to designer. One set of shop drawings will be returned upon approval.

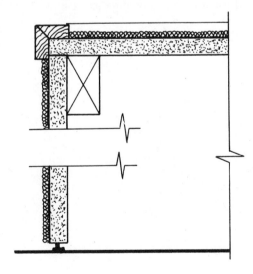

FREESTANDING VISUAL MERCHANDISING DISPLAY PLATFORM

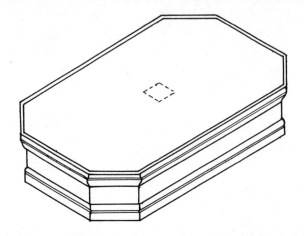

- **Unit Size:** Unit A: 30"W x 48"D x 12"H
  Unit B: 36"W x 60"D x 12"H
  Unit C: 42"W x 72"D x 12"H

- **Construction of Unit:** ³/₄" board with applied painted molding and trim.

- Provide access panel for electrical feed.

- Cover top with the same carpet as surrounding area.

- Provide levelers.

- **Prior to Construction:** Contractor to submit proposal of construction materials and details with two complete and accurate sets of shop drawings to designer. One set of shop drawings will be returned upon approval.

DISPLAY CUBES

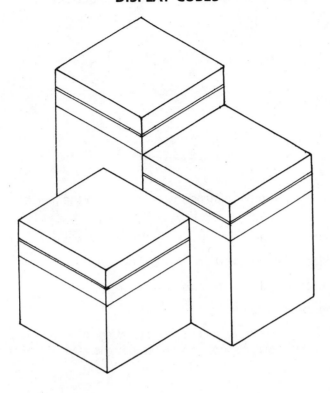

- **Unit Size:** Unit A: 18"W x 18"D x 24"H
                  Unit B: 18"W x 18"D x 30"H
                  Unit C: 18"W x 18"D x 36"H

- **Construction of Unit:** ³/₄" board with corner blocking and levelers.

- Laminated plastic cover board with decorative accent band.

- Provide levelers.

- **Prior to Construction:** Contractor to submit proposal of construction materials and details with two complete and accurate sets of shop drawings to designer. One set of shop drawings will be returned upon approval.

DISPLAY PLATFORM—HALF HEXAGONAL

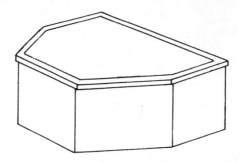

- **Unit Size:** 24" in height with other dimensions as taken from the merchandising plan, unless otherwise noted.

- **Construction of Unit:** ¾" board with ⅝"D x 1½"W natural white oak with clear sealer.

- Carpet for top and sides to be supplied and installed by owner.

- Verify laminate plastic color with fixture-finish plan.

- Levelers and blocking as required.

- **Prior to Construction:** Contractor to submit proposal of construction materials and details with two complete and accurate sets of shop drawings to designer. One set of shop drawings will be returned upon approval.

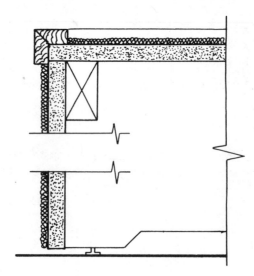

DISPLAY PLATFORM—CUBE

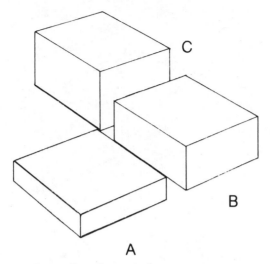

- **Unit Size:** 36"W x 36"D unless otherwise noted.
    Unit A: 12"H
    Unit B: 18"H
    Unit C: 24"H

- **Construction of Unit:** ³/₄" board with laminate plastic on all exterior surfaces.

- Verify laminate plastic color with fixture-finish plan.

- Levelers and blocking as required.

- **Prior to Construction:** Contractor to submit proposal of construction materials and details with two complete and accurate sets of shop drawings to designer. One set of shop drawings will be returned upon approval.

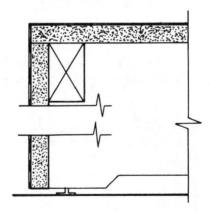

DISPLAY CUBES WITH MIRRORED TOP

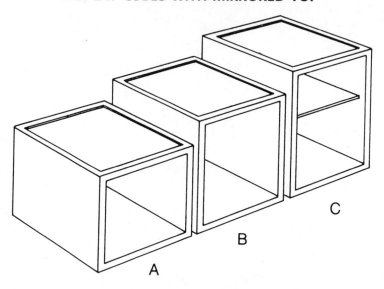

- **Unit Size:** 24"W x 24"D with 1½" x ¾"D rim.
  Unit A: 24"H
  Unit B: 30"H
  Unit C: 36"H

- **Construction of Unit:** ¾" board with laminate plastic on all exterior surfaces. Color lacquer to match laminate plastic for interior surfaces.

- Verify laminate plastic color with fixture-finish plan.

- ¼" polished plateglass mirror inset and flush with top surface.

- Levelers and blocking as required.

- ¼" adjustable polished plateglass shelf for unit C.

- **Prior to Construction:** Contractor to submit proposal of construction materials and details with two complete and accurate sets of shop drawings to designer. One set of shop drawings will be returned upon approval.

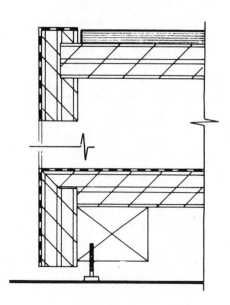

CURTAIN AND BEDSPREAD DISPLAY

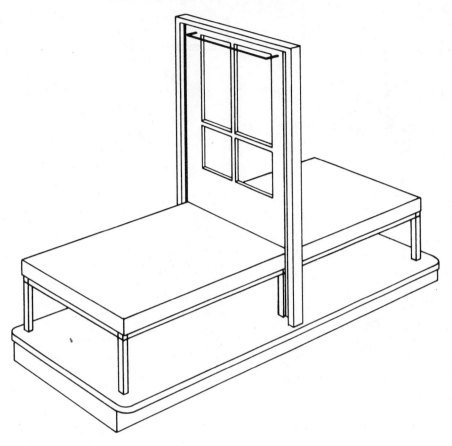

Base

- **Unit Size:** 6"H x 108"W x 48"D with 4"H x 2¾"D recessed kickbase and 1½" radius corners. Connected frame to be 84" in height.

- **Construction of Base:** ¾" board with laminate plastic on all exterior surfaces with 1½" x 3½" frame with ¾" paint-grade birch dadoed into frame. Frame to be laminate plastic covered with insert plywood to be matching color lacquer.

- Verify laminate plastic color with fixture-finish plan.

- Window mullions to be 1½" wide and 3" off top and sides of frame.

- Curtain rod supplied by owner and installed by this contractor.

- Levelers and blocking as required.

Risers

- **Unit Size:** 18"H x 48"W x 39"D

- **Construction of Riser:** Mirror chrome finish 1" modular tube frame with recessed ¾" board and 4" foam pad.

- **Prior to Construction:** Contractor to submit proposal of construction materials and details with two complete and accurate sets of shop drawings to designer. One set of shop drawings will be returned upon approval.

DEMONSTRATION UNIT

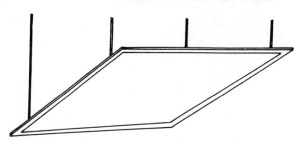

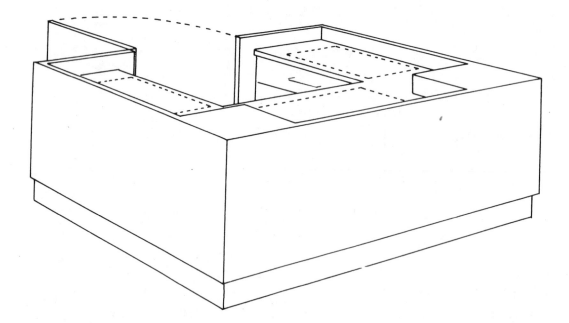

- **Unit Size:** 42"H x 96"W x 96"D with 1½" rim. Counter height to be 36" and depth to be 24".

- **Construction of Unit:** ¾" board with laminate plastic on all exterior surfaces.

- Verify laminate plastic color with fixture-finish plan.

- Verify sink, electrical cooking surface, and refrigeration requirements with owner.

- Doors to be piano hinged with continuous extruded brushed-aluminum drawer pull and three ¾" adjustable shelves with T-edges and color lacquer to match the laminate plastic. Entrance door to exclude drawer pull, and opening to be 24" wide.

- Two 12"W x 12"D display surfaces to be flush with top as shown.

- Angled mirror to be ¼" polished plate silver mirror with stainless steel channel on all sides (60"W x 36"D). Hang and support from ceiling as required. paint supports to match ceiling color.

- Levelers and blocking as required.

- **Prior to Construction:** Contractor to submit proposal of construction materials and details with two complete and accurate sets of shop drawings to designer. One set of shop drawings will be returned upon approval.

RECEIVING TABLE

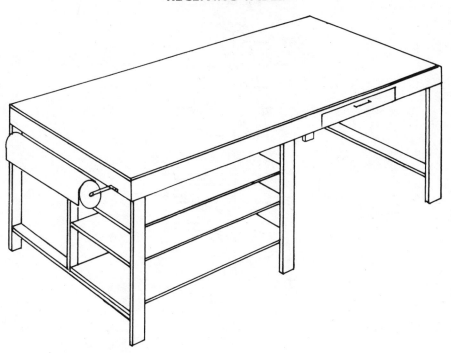

- **Unit Size:** 36"X x 96"W x 48"D
- **Construction of Unit:** 2" by 4" construction with ³/₄" board for counter surface covered with ¹/₄" tempered hardboard.
- Clear sealer for finish.
- Three ³/₄" plywood shelves supported as required.
- One wrapping-paper holder and drawer as shown. Verify sizes with owner.
- Verify handicap requirements.
- Levelers and blocking as required.

MUG TREE

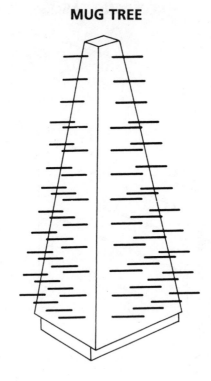

- **Unit Size:** Base 24"W x 24"D with 8"H x 2¾"D recessed kickbase. Height to be 72" with top block 6 inches square.

- **Construction of Unit:** ¾" board with color lacquer to match laminate plastic for exterior surfaces: 10" x ½" diameter dowel rods to be natural and fastened perpendicular to surface (up slant).

- Verify laminate plastic color with fixture-finish plan.

- Verify mug size with owner. Add 1½" clearance to determine dowel spacing.

- Levelers and blocking as required.

- **Prior to Construction:** Contractor to submit proposal of construction materials and details with two complete and accurate sets of shop drawings to designer. One set of shop drawings will be returned upon approval.

FREESTANDING MERCHANDISING TRIPLE MIRROR

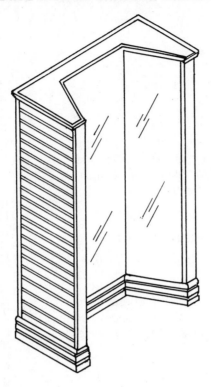

- **Unit Size:** 48"W x 30"D x 84"H

- **Construction of Unit:** Fabricated from ¾" board and slatwall with metal inserts, ¼" polished plate mirror base and crown trim to be decorative molding. Wood and laminated plastic finish to match.

- Verify type of optional faceout hardware required for merchandise presentation.

- Provide levelers.

- **Prior to Construction:** Contractor to submit proposal of construction materials and details with two complete and accurate sets of shop drawings to designer. One set of shop drawings will be returned upon approval.

ADJUSTABLE TRIPLE MIRROR—WOOD FRAME

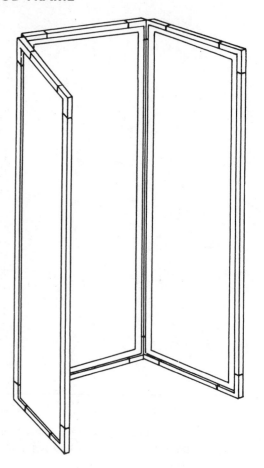

- **Unit Size:** 80" in height with other dimensions as shown in diagram.

- **Construction of Unit:** 1³/₄" natural white oak verticals and horizontals connected by mirror chrome finish joints and ³/₄" board with laminate plastic on all exposed surfaces.

- Verify laminate plastic color with fixture-finish plan.

- ¹/₄" polished plateglass silver mirror secured to board with glue and stainless channel frame.

- Levelers as required.

- **Prior to Construction:** Contractor to submit proposal of construction materials and details with two complete and accurate sets of shop drawings to designer. One set of shop drawings will be returned upon approval.

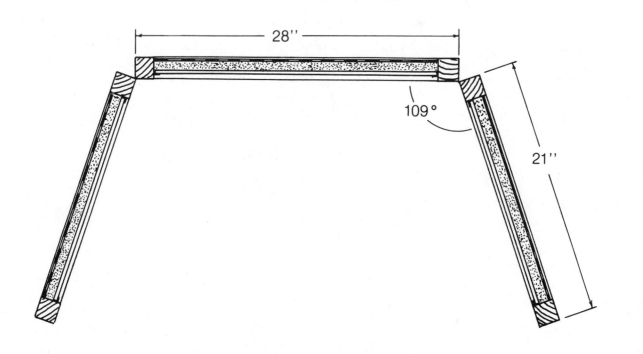

FIXED TRIPLE MIRROR—TUBE FRAME

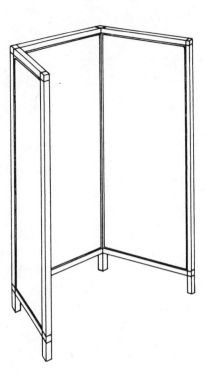

- **Unit Size:** 80" in height with bottom tube 6" in height. Other dimensions as shown in diagram.

- **Construction of Unit:** Mirror chrome finish 1" modular tube frame and ³/₄" board with laminate plastic on all surfaces, except mirrored surface.

- Verify laminate plastic color with fixture-finish plan.

- ¹/₄" polished plateglass silver mirror secured to board with glue and stainless channel frame.

- Levelers as required.

- **Prior to Construction:** Contractor to submit proposal of construction materials and details with two complete and accurate sets of shop drawings to designer. One set of shop drawings will be returned upon approval.

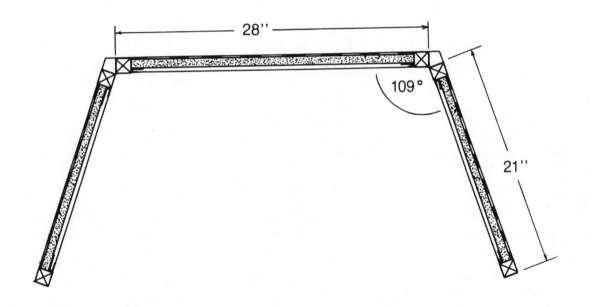

FEATURE DISPLAY PEDESTAL

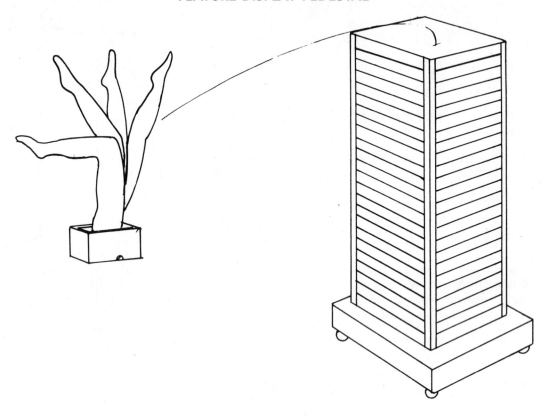

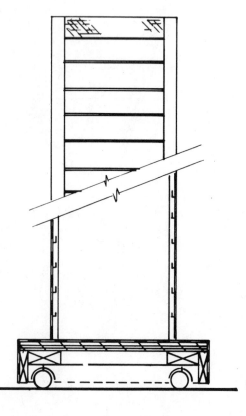

- One ⅛" clear plastic 6-leg unit with white plastic base.

- Heights to be adjusted in field to accommodate merchandise.

Base

- **Unit Size:** 6"H x 24"W x 24"D with 4"H x 2¾"D recessed kickbase.

- **Construction of Base:** ¾" board with laminate plastic on all exterior surfaces with four 2½" heavy-duty ball casters.

Pedestal

- **Unit Size:** 46"H x 16"W x 16"D

- **Construction of Pedestal:** ¾" solid-core 3" slatwall and 1½" trim with laminate plastic on all exterior surfaces. Top band of slatwall to be bronze plastic mirror.

- Verify laminate plastic color with fixture-finish plan.

- Slatwall hardware and displays as specified by owner.

- Block as required.

- **Prior to Construction:** Contractor to submit proposal of construction materials and details with two complete and accurate sets of shop drawings to designer. One set of shop drawings will be returned upon approval.

FEATURE DISPLAY PEDESTAL—HATS

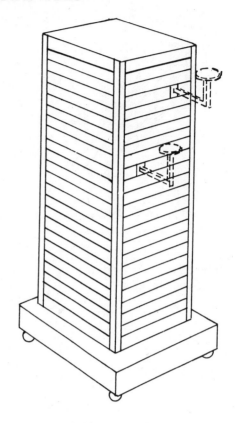

- Eight mirror chrome finish slatwall hat accessories of ¼" tube with top foam pad.

- Heights to be adjusted in field to accommodate merchandise.

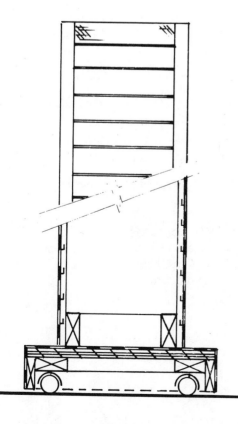

Base

- **Unit Size:** 6"H x 24"W x 24"D with 4"H x 2¾"D recessed kickbase.

- **Construction of Base:** ¾" board with laminate plastic on all exterior surfaces with four 2½" heavy duty ball casters.

Pedestal

- **Unit Size:** 48"H x 16"W x 16"D

- **Construction of Pedestal:** ¾" solid-core 3" slatwall and 1½" trim with laminate plastic on all exterior surfaces. Top band of slatwall to be bronze plastic mirror.

- Verify laminate plastic color with fixture-finish plan.

- Slatwall hardware and displays as specified by owner.

- Blocking as required.

- **Prior to Construction:** Contractor to submit proposal of construction materials and details with two complete and accurate sets of shop drawings to designer. One set of shop drawings will be returned upon approval.

FEATURE DISPLAY PEDESTAL—CLUTCH BAGS

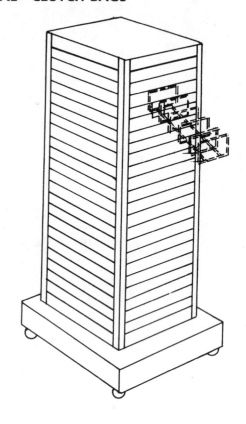

- Four mirror chrome finish slatwall clutch bag holders of ¼" tube as shown.

- Heights to be adjusted in field to accommodate merchandise.

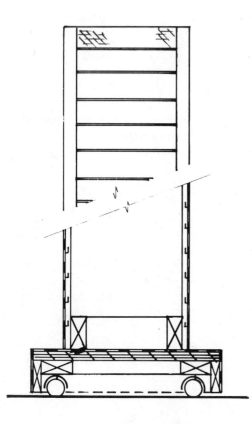

Base

- **Unit Size:** 6"H x 24"W x 24"D with 4"H x 2¾"D recessed kickbase.

- **Construction of Base:** ¾" board with laminate plastic on all exterior surfaces with four 2½" heavy-duty ball casters.

Pedestal

- **Unit Size:** 48"H x 16"W x 16"D

- **Construction of Pedestal:** ¾" solid-core 3" slatwall and 1½" trim with laminate plastic on all exterior surfaces. Top band of slatwall to be bronze plastic mirror.

- Verify laminate plastic color with fixture-finish plan.

- Slatwall hardware and displays as specified by owner.

- Blocking as required.

- **Prior to Construction:** Contractor to submit proposal of construction materials and details with two complete and accurate sets of shop drawings to designer. One set of shop drawings will be returned upon approval.

FEATURE DISPLAY PEDESTAL—ACCESSORIES

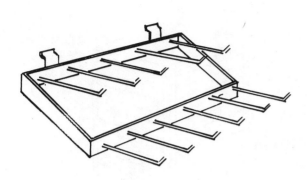

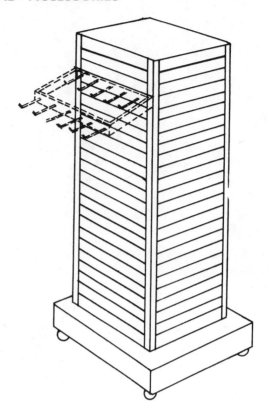

- Four mirror chrome finish slatwall belt or tie accessories with ¼" prongs as shown.

- Heights to be adjusted in field to accommodate merchandise.

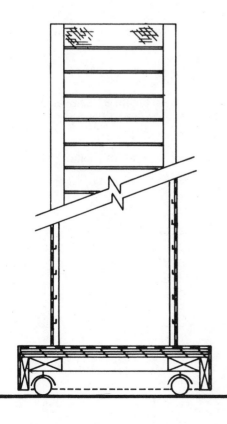

Base

- **Unit Size:** 6"H x 24"W x 24"D with 4"H x 2¾"D recessed kickbase.

- **Construction of Base:** ¾" board with laminate plastic on all exterior surfaces with four 2½" heavy-duty ball casters.

Pedestal

- **Unit Size:** 48"H x 16"W x 16"D

- **Construction of Pedestal:** ¾" solid-core 3" slatwall and 1½" trim with laminate plastic on all exterior surfaces. Top band of slatwall to be bronze plastic mirror.

- Verify laminate plastic color with fixture-finish plan.

- Slatwall hardware and displays as specified by owner.

- Blocking as required.

- **Prior to Construction:** Contractor to submit proposal of construction materials and details with two complete and accurate sets of shop drawings to designer. One set of shop drawings will be returned upon approval.

FEATURE DISPLAY PEDESTAL—WATERFALLS

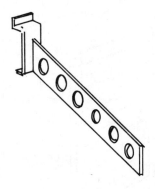

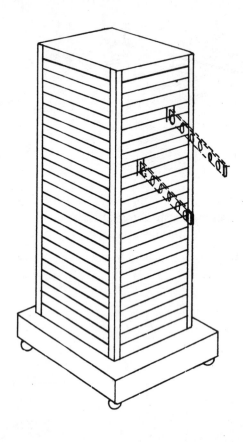

- Eight ¼" x 1½" size 1" diameter hole mirror chrome finish slatwall waterfalls.

- Heights to be adjusted in field to accommodate merchandise.

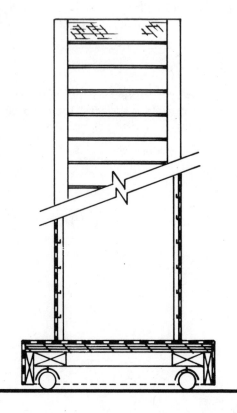

Base

- **Unit Size:** 6"H x 24"W x 24"D with 4"H x 2¾"D recessed kickbase.

- **Construction of Base:** ¾" board with laminate plastic on all exterior surfaces with four 2½" heavy duty ball casters.

Pedestal

- **Unit Size:** 48"H x 16"W x 16"D

- **Construction of Pedestal:** ¾" solid-core 3" slatwall and 1½" trim with laminate plastic on all exterior surfaces. Top band of slatwall to be bronze plastic mirror.

- Verify laminate plastic color with fixture-finish plan.

- Slatwall hardware and displays as specified by owner.

- Blocking as required.

- **Prior to Construction:** Contractor to submit proposal of construction materials and details with two complete and accurate sets of shop drawings to designer. One set of shop drawings will be returned upon approval.

FEATURE DISPLAY PEDESTAL—FACEOUTS, WATERFALLS

- Six ½" x 1½" 6-cube mirror chrome finish slatwall waterfalls.

- Heights to be adjusted in field to accommodate merchandise.

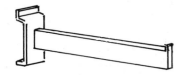

- Seven ½" x 1½" x 12" mirror chrome finish slatwall faceouts.

- Heights to be adjusted in field to accommodate merchandise.

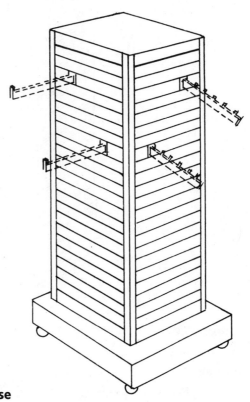

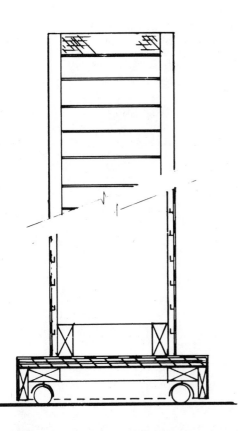

Base

- **Unit Size:** 6"H x 24"W x 24"D with 4"H x 2¾"D recessed kickbase.

- **Construction of Base:** ¾" board with laminate plastic on all exterior surfaces with four 2½" heavy-duty ball casters.

Pedestal

- **Unit Size:** 48"H x 16"W x 16"D

- **Construction of Pedestal:** ¾" solid-core 3" slatwall and 1½" trim with laminate plastic on all exterior surfaces. Top band of slatwall to be bronze plastic mirror.

- Verify laminate plastic color with fixture-finish plan.

- Slatwall hardware and displays as specified by owner.

- Blocking as required.

- **Prior to Construction:** Contractor to submit proposal of construction materials and details with two complete and accurate sets of shop drawings to designer. One set of shop drawings will be returned upon approval.

SLATWALL TOWER

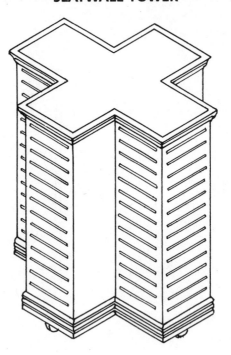

- **Unit Size:** Width, depth, and height of unit to be determined by merchandise type.

- **Construction of Unit:** Fabricated from ³/₄" board and slatwall with metal inserts. Top and bottom trim molding to match laminated plastic cover color.

- Verify merchandising faceout hardware requirements.

- Install heavy-duty wheels.

- Recommended height not to exceed 54".

- **Prior to Construction:** Contractor to submit proposal of construction materials and details with two complete and accurate sets of shop drawings to designer. One set of shop drawings will be returned upon approval.

SLATWALL TOWER WITH BASE

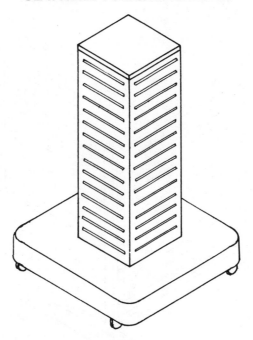

- **Unit Size:** Width, depth, and height of unit to be determined by merchandise type. Sample shows tower 24"W x 24"D x 48"H; base 48"W x 48"D x 6"H.

- **Construction of Unit:** Fabricated from ¾" board and slatwall with metal inserts. Top and bottom trim molding to match laminated plastic cover color.

- Verify merchandising faceout hardware requirements.

- Install heavy-duty wheels.

- Recommended height not to exceed 54".

- Fix tower to base.

- **Prior to Construction:** Contractor to submit proposal of construction materials and details with two complete and accurate sets of shop drawings to designer. One set of shop drawings will be returned upon approval.

SLATWALL GONDOLA

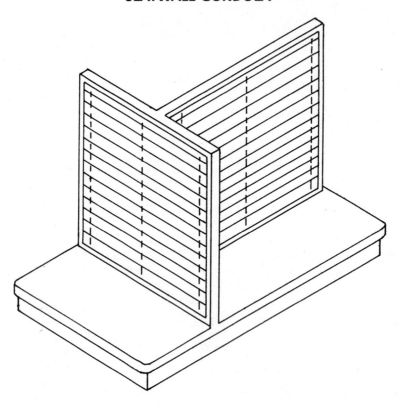

- **Unit Size:** Unit A: 30"W x 66"L x 42"H
  Unit B: 36"W x 72"L x 42"H

- **Construction of Unit:** Fabricated from ³/₄" cover board and slatwall with metal inserts. Recessed adjustable standards using wheels or levelers.

- Provide 4" kickbase on 1¹/₂" thick deck.

- Cap and trim to be ³/₄" x 1¹/₂" wide.

- Slatwall to be neutral in color. Base, trim, and edging to be decorative in color.

- **Prior to Construction:** Contractor to submit proposal of construction materials and details with two complete and accurate sets of shop drawings to designer. One set of shop drawings will be returned upon approval.

SPECIALTY SHOP CASEWORK

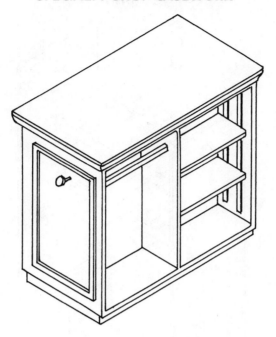

- **Unit Size:** 46"W x 72"D x 42"H

- **Construction of Unit:** Fabricated from ¾" wood veneer board with decorative moldings.

- Included in this unit are adjustable wood or glass hangrods. Hooks or prongs at end of unit for displays.

- Color of wood finish to be compatible with or accentuate shop decor.

- This unit is on heavy-duty wheels.

- Top of unit to be used for visual merchandising.

- **Prior to Construction:** Contractor to submit proposal of construction materials and details with two complete and accurate sets of shop drawings to designer. One set of shop drawings will be returned upon approval.

PEG UNIT

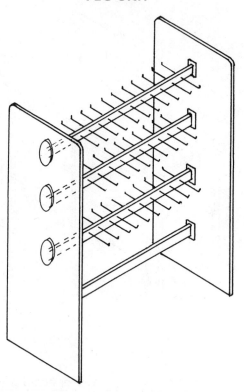

- **Unit Size:** 24" or 30"W x 48" or 60"D x 42" or 48"H

- **Construction of Unit:** Fabricated from ½" thick polished plexiglas with rectangular chrome cross bars and decorative fasteners.

- Prong type: Length and size to be determined by type of merchandise-presentation format.

- This unit is recommended for use on carpet flooring only.

- Recommended for hanging materials.

- **Prior to Construction:** Contractor to submit proposal of construction materials and details with two complete and accurate sets of shop drawings to designer. One set of shop drawings will be returned upon approval.

SLATWALL GONDOLA

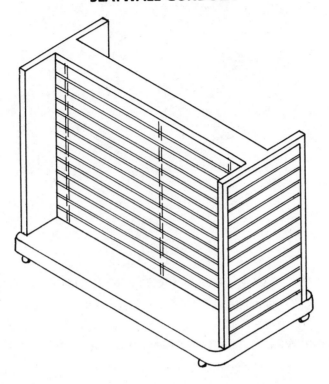

- **Unit Size:** Unit A: 18"W x 60"L x 42"H
    Unit B: 24"W x 60"L x 42"H
    Unit C: 30"W x 60"L x 42"H

- **Construction of Unit:** Fabricated from ³/₄" laminated plastic cover board and slatwall with metal inserts. Recessed adjustable standards using wheels or levelers.

- Provide 4" kickbase on 1¹/₂" thick deck.

- Cap and trim to be ³/₄" x 1¹/₂" wide.

- Slatwall to be neutral in color. Base, trim, and edging to be decorative in color.

- **Prior to Construction:** Contractor to submit proposal of construction materials and details with two complete and accurate sets of shop drawings to designer. One set of shop drawings will be returned upon approval.

JEANS/SHIRTS/OR SWEATER UNIT

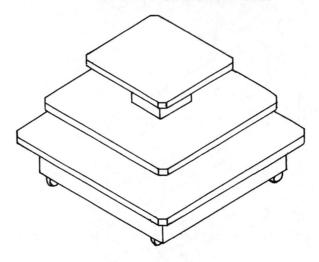

- **Unit Size:** To be determined by merchandise-presentation format.
- **Construction of Unit:** ³/₄" laminated plastic cover board with 1½" edge trim and heavy duty wheels.
- Unit to be designed to create tiered effect for viewing of merchandise.
- Space between shelves to be determined by the height of merchandise to be stacked.
- Height of unit not to exceed 3' 6".
- **Prior to Construction:** Contractor to submit proposal of construction materials and details with two complete and accurate sets of shop drawings to designer. One set of shop drawings will be returned upon approval.

JEANS/SHIRTS/OR SWEATER UNIT

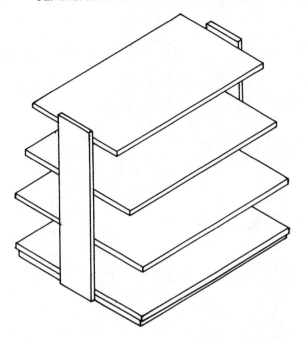

- **Unit Size:** 36"W x 60"L x 42"H
- **Construction of Unit:** Constructed out of 1½" laminated plastic cover board with edge trim.
- Blocking under shelving required for support.
- Shelves arranged for tiered effect of merchandising.
- 4" kickbase with recessed wheels.
- Height of shelves to be determined by stacking of merchandise.
- **Prior to Construction:** Contractor to submit proposal of construction materials and details with two complete and accurate sets of shop drawings to designer. One set of shop drawings will be returned upon approval.

STEPPED GRID DISPLAYER

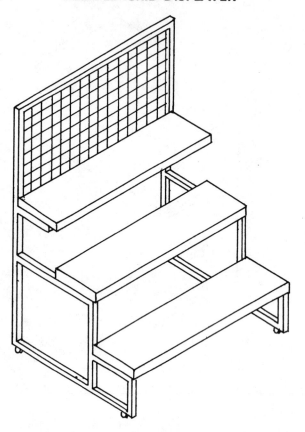

- **Unit Size:** 30"W x 48"D x 42"H

- **Construction of Unit:** Prefabricated 1" metal frame with chrome or powder coat finish. 1½" fixed laminated plastic covered shelves.

- Used for displaying shoes, socks, or any folded merchandise.

- Provide levelers.

- **Prior to Construction:** Contractor to submit proposal of construction materials and details with two complete and accurate sets of shop drawings to designer. One set of shop drawings will be returned upon approval.

GONDOLA—9" PRONGS

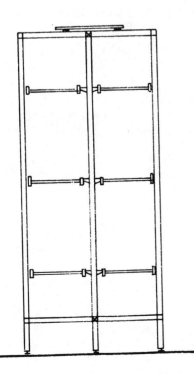

- **Unit Size:** 54"H x 60"W x 24"D

- **Construction of Unit:** Mirror chrome finish 1" modular tube frame; $1/4$" clear plastic ends and center panel with putty cladding channel.

- Three rows of 9" mirror chrome finish prongs with quarter-round ends on $1/2$" x $1\frac{1}{2}$" hangrod and snubnosed bracket. Heights to be adjusted in field to accommodate merchandise.

- $3/4$" polished plateglass shelf (16"D) for unit top as shown.

- Levelers as required.

- **Prior to Construction:** Contractor to submit proposal of construction materials and details with two complete and accurate sets of shop drawings to designer. One set of shop drawings will be returned upon approval.

GONDOLA—DOUBLE 10", 12", 14" GLASS SHELVES

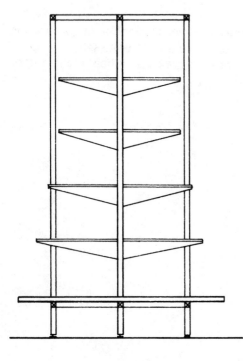

- **Unit Size:** 54"H x 60"W x 24"D

- **Construction of Unit:** Mirror chrome finish 1" modular tube frame; 18 x 1¼" laminate plastic deck with putty rubber bumper and 1½" radius front corners; ¾" solid-core 3" slatwall end panels; laminate plastic covered, ¼" plastic center panel with putty cladding channel.

- Verify laminate plastic color with fixture-finish plan.

- Four 10", two 12", and two 14" by ³⁄₈" polished plateglass shelves with polished edges and proper hardware. Heights to be adjusted in field to accommodate merchandise.

- ³⁄₈" polished plateglass shelf (16"D) for unit top as shown.

- Levelers as required.

- **Prior to Construction:** Contractor to submit proposal of construction materials and details with two complete and accurate sets of shop drawings to designer. One set of shop drawings will be returned upon approval.

GONDOLA—6" PRONGS AND DOUBLE 16" GLASS SHELVES

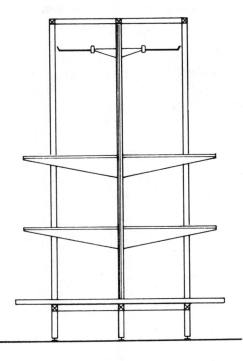

- **Unit Size:** 54"H x 60"W x 24"D
- **Construction of Unit:** Mirror chrome finish 1" modular tube frame; 18" x 1¼" laminate plastic deck with putty rubber bumper and 1½" radius front corners; ¼" plastic ends and center panels with putty cladding channel.
- Verify laminate plastic color with fixture-finish plan.
- One row of 6" mirror chrome finish prongs on ½" x 1½" hangrod and snubnosed bracket.
- Four 16", ⅜" polished plateglass shelves with polished edges and proper hardware. Heights to be adjusted in field to accommodate merchandise.
- Levelers as required.
- **Prior to Construction:** Contractor to submit proposal of construction materials and details with two complete and accurate sets of shop drawings to designer. One set of shop drawings will be returned upon approval.

GONDOLA—16" GLASS SHELVES

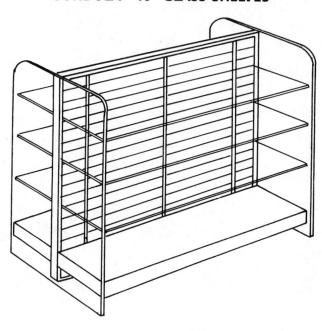

- **Unit Size:** 54"H x 60"W x 36"D with 3" radius top corners as shown.

- **Construction of Unit:** ³/₄" board with ³/₄" solid-core slatwall glued and screwed to board and laminate plastic covered; 2¹/₂" x 1" frame as shown. End panels to be ¹/₂" plastic and fastened to center frame as required. Unit to include standard slotted hardware as shown.

- Verify laminate plastic color with fixture-finish plan.

- Six 16", ³/₈" polished plateglass shelves with polished edges and proper hardware. Heights to be adjusted in field to accommodate merchandise.

- Two ³/₄" plywood shelves to be laminate plastic covered with end returns.

- Levelers as required.

- **Prior to Construction:** Contractor to submit proposal of construction materials and details with two complete and accurate sets of shop drawings to designer. One set of shop drawings will be returned upon approval.

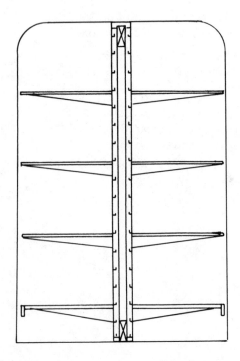

SHEET FIXTURE

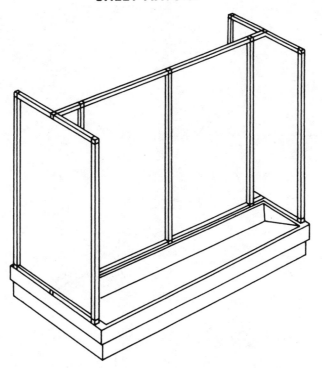

Base

- **Unit Size:** 8"H x 60"W x 30"D with 4"H x 2¾"D recessed kickbase and recessed surface as shown.

- **Construction of Base:** ¾" board with laminate plastic on all exterior surfaces.

- Verify laminate plastic color with fixture-finish plan.

- Levelers and blocking as required.

Riser

- **Unit Size:** 48"H x 60"W x 24"D

- **Construction of Riser:** Mirror chrome finish 1" modular tube frame with ¼" bronze plastic end panels and ¾" board center panel, laminate plastic covered.

- ¼" clear preformed plastic shelves (10"H x 10"D) with 2" front lip. Fasten shelves to 7 x 7 angle with 15° angled hardware as required; four shelves per side.

- **Prior to Construction:** Contractor to submit proposal of construction materials and details with two complete and accurate sets of shop drawings to designer. One set of shop drawings will be returned upon approval.

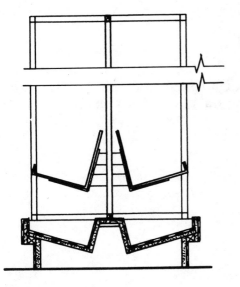

T—STANDS

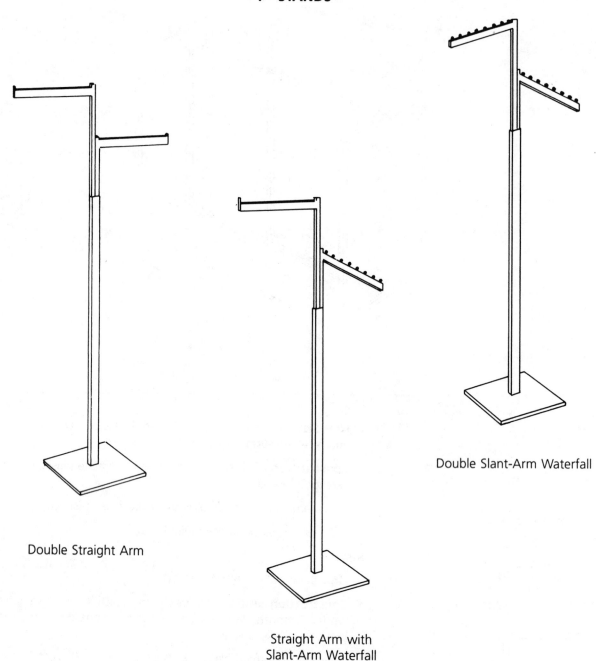

Double Straight Arm

Straight Arm with
Slant-Arm Waterfall

Double Slant-Arm Waterfall

The use of straight or slant arms, or the combination of the two, is dependent upon the type of merchandise one wishes to display. These racks are most effective when displaying feature merchandise within a given area. T-stands are most commonly used on aisle lines or at points of sale.

TIE/BELT RACKS

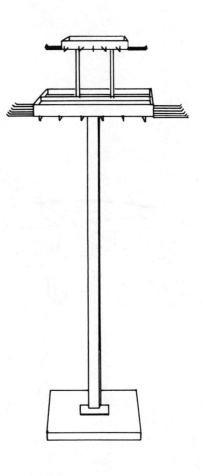

4-Sided Double-Tier Rack

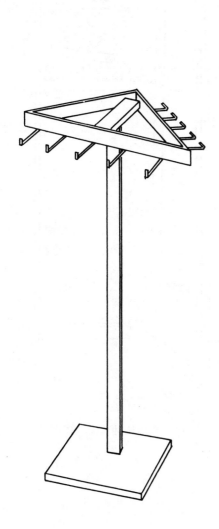

3-Sided Single-Tier Rack

As with most accessory racks, tie and belt racks are available in several shapes and sizes. The triangular rack is commonly used when displaying smaller quantities. In larger departments where the inventory is much greater, the 4-sided double-tier rack will prove most efficient in neatly displaying the merchandise. For maximum visibility, tie and belt racks should be located near points of sale or in central areas of a given department.

ROUND RACKS

3-Tier Adjustable Round Rack

Continuous Round Rack

Round racks are the most widely used fixtures in apparel display because they can accommodate such a high quantity of merchandise. They are available with fixed or adjustable heights and in 36" or 42" diameters.

MOVABLE GRID MERCHANDISER

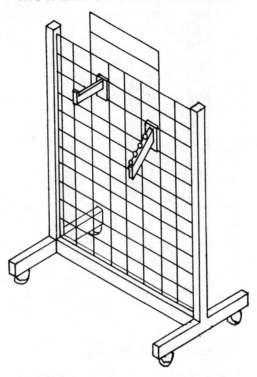

- **Unit Size:** Size of unit to be predetermined by manufacturer.
- **Construction of Unit:** The height, length, and width of unit can vary depending on the configuration of merchandise-presentation format and the stability of the unit.
- Verify grid type and size and coordinate with faceout hardware.
- Verify wheels, castors, or levelers.
- **Prior to Construction:** Contractor to submit proposal of construction materials and details with two complete and accurate sets of shop drawings to designer. One set of shop drawings will be returned upon approval.

MOVABLE GRID MERCHANDISER

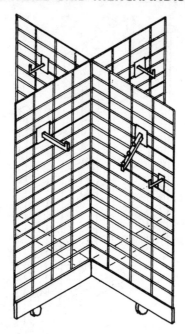

- **Unit Size:** Size of unit to be predetermined by manufacturer.
- **Construction of Unit:** The height, length, and width of unit can vary depending on the configuration of merchandise-presentation format and the stability of the unit.
- Verify grid type and size and coordinate with faceout hardware.
- Verify wheels, castors, or levelers.
- **Prior to Construction:** Contractor to submit proposal of construction materials and details with two complete and accurate sets of shop drawings to designer. One set of shop drawings will be returned upon approval.

MOVABLE GRID MERCHANDISER

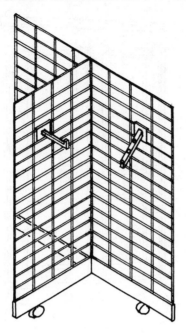

- **Unit Size:** Size of unit to be predetermined by manufacturer.
- **Construction of Unit:** The height, length, and width of unit can vary depending on the configuration of merchandise-presentation format and the stability of the unit.
- Verify grid type and size and coordinate with faceout hardware.
- Verify wheels, castors, or levelers.
- **Prior to Construction:** Contractor to submit proposal of construction materials and details with two complete and accurate sets of shop drawings to designer. One set of shop drawings will be returned upon approval.

ARMOIR

- **Unit Size:** Various.

- **Construction of Unit:** Existing.

- Existing old decorative casework can be incorporated in any retail selling environment.

- Condition, size, and exterior finish can be used as is or can be refinished.

- Interior of cabinet should be fitted with new hardware, lights, and wallcoverings or paint.

- **Prior to Construction:** Contractor to submit proposal of construction materials and details with two complete and accurate sets of shop drawings to designer. One set of shop drawings will be returned upon approval.

ÉTAGÈRE

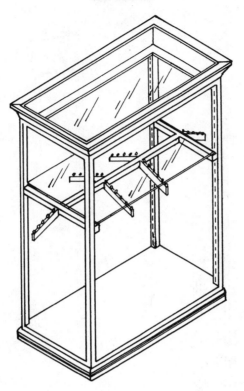

- **Unit Size:** Unit A: 24"W x 48"D x 84"H
  Unit B: 30"W x 60"D x 84"H

- **Construction of Unit:** Vertical wood uprights with recessed adjustable standards attached to base and cap.

- Adjustable hangrods, faceout, and glass shelves can be incorporated.

- The use of this fixture can be on the selling floor or placed against a perimeter wall.

- Wood finish should complement decor of department.

- **Prior to Construction:** Contractor to submit proposal of construction materials and details with two complete and accurate sets of shop drawings to designer. One set of shop drawings will be returned upon approval.

ÉTAGÈRES

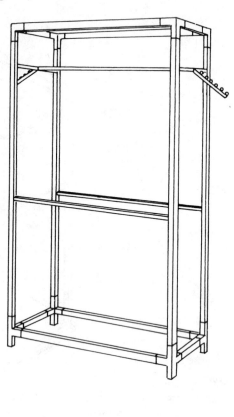

Hanging Étagère

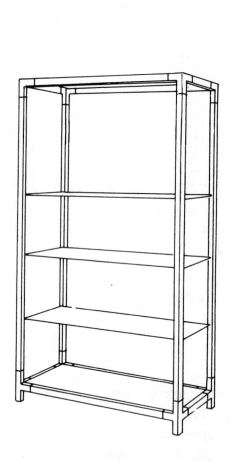

Shelved Étagère

Étagères can be designed to display any type of merchandise. For flat merchandise, glass shelves are incorporated into the fixture. For hanging merchandise, crossbar and faceout systems are available. Although étagères are found throughout a store, a popular and practical application is to use them to visually divide two departments without building a wall.

ADJUSTABLE HANDBAG RACKS

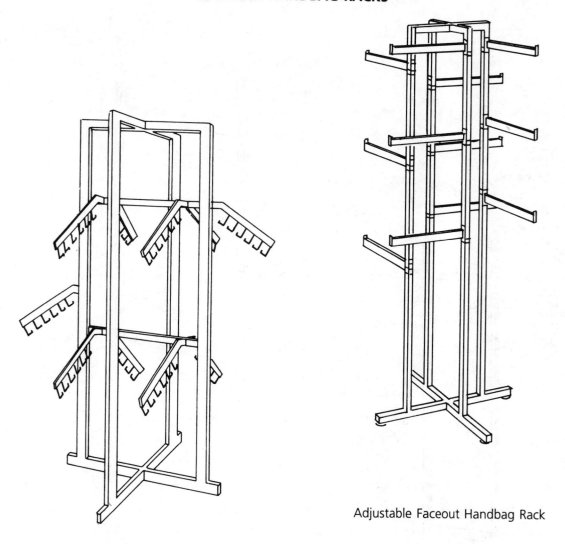

Adjustable Faceout Handbag Rack

Adjustable J-Hook Handbag Rack

A major advantage of these fixtures is that they help display maximum inventory with a minimum space. The heights of the faceouts can be adjusted to accommodate the merchandise.

4-WAY AND 6-WAY ADJUSTABLE RACKS

4-Way Adjustable Rack

5-Way Adjustable Rack

These adjustable display fixtures help bring attention to a grouping or classification of related merchandise; 4-way and 6-way racks are most often found in the coordinates section of a department.

4-WAY RACKS

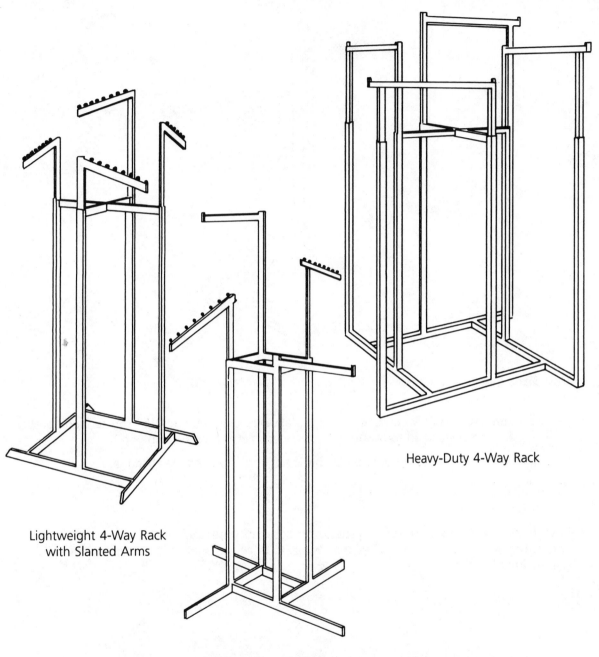

Heavy-Duty 4-Way Rack

Lightweight 4-Way Rack
with Slanted Arms

Lightweight 4-Way Rack
with Combination Straight
and Slated Arms

These fixtures are effectively used to display merchandise to its optimum. The heights of the arms can be adjusted to accommodate any size merchandise.

CUSTOM T-STAND

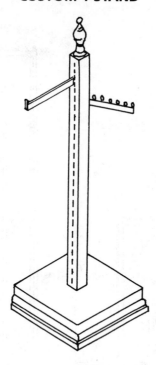

- **Unit Size:** Base 18"W x 18"D
  Height: 72"H

- **Construction of Unit:** 6" wood base with decorative molding. Vertical 2½" square wood post with recessed metal standard for adjustability and decorative wood turning.

- Waterfall or straight faceout to be used for presentation of hanging merchandise.

- Verify if weighted base is required.

- Provide levelers.

- **Prior to Construction:** Contractor to submit proposal of construction materials and details with two complete and accurate sets of shop drawings to designer. One set of shop drawings will be returned upon approval.

STOCKROOM SHELVING UNITS

- **Unit Size:** Unit A: 18"L x 48"W x 96"H
  Unit B: 24"L x 48"W x 96"H

- **Construction of Unit:** Prefabricated stockroom shelving units by various manufacturers. To consist of vertical adjustable uprights with X crossbrace for support. Base and top to be permanently installed.

- Integrated shelves adjust to height of merchandise.

- This type of unit can be set in tandem.

- **Prior to Construction:** Contractor to submit proposal of construction materials and details with two complete and accurate sets of shop drawings to designer. One set of shop drawings will be returned upon approval.

STOCKROOM SHELVING UNITS

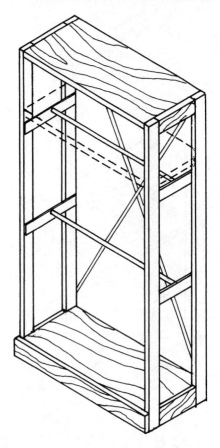

- **Unit Size:** Unit A: 18"L x 48"W x 96"H
  Unit B: 24"L x 48"W x 96"H

- **Construction of Unit:** Prefabricated stockroom shelving units by various manufacturers. To consist of vertical adjustable uprights with X crossbrace for support. Base and top to be permanently installed.

- Integrated hangrods adjust to height of merchandise.

- This type of unit can be set in tandem.

- **Prior to Construction:** Contractor to submit proposal of construction materials and details with two complete and accurate sets of shop drawings to designer. One set of shop drawings will be returned upon approval.

VISUAL MERCHANDISING SHELF

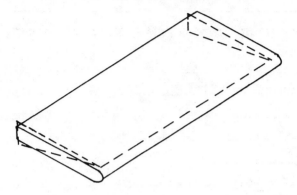

- **Unit Size:** To be determined by the spacing of wall hardware and application. The width is typically 16" to 18"; the length is typically 48" to 72"; and the thickness is 2½".

- **Construction of Unit:** Design shelf to set on top of two brackets that mechanically fasten to wall hardware.

- The finish can be wood or laminated plastic cover.

- This type of shelf is used within a department to bring attention to display of merchandise.

- **Prior to Construction:** Contractor to submit proposal of construction materials and details with two complete and accurate sets of shop drawings to designer. One set of shop drawings will be returned upon approval.

CHROME RACK SPECIFICATION GUIDELINES

1. Size of Tubing   _____ x _____
2. Gauge of Rack Steel Tubing (16 Ga.)   _____
3. Gauge of Steel Rods   _____
4. Gauge of Extenders (16 Ga.)   _____
5. Gauge of Base Stock   _____
6. Finish of Raw Tubing (Polished)   _____
7. Type of Finish (Polished Mirror Chrome)   _____
8. Type of Spring and Button Mechanism and Spacing   _____
9. Type of Mechanical Fittings (Mfg.)   _____
10. Type of Spring-Load Mechanism   _____
11. Type of ElectroPlating on Plastic or Metal Caps   _____
12. Type of Stretchers   _____
13. Type of Spotwelds, Grinding, and Finishing   _____
14. Lengths of Extenders (Hangrods or Arms)   _____
15. Lengths of Waterfall and Spacing of Pins   _____
16. Metal Lugs Welded into Tube Gauge   _____
17. Type of Screw, Thread, and Head Type   _____
    Allen _____   Phillips _____   Straight _____
18. Type and Manufacturer of Bolts   _____
19. Type of Leveler   _____
20. Type of Ball Caster   _____
21. Type of Set Screws   _____
22. Type of Clamp or Arm   _____
23. Thickness of Glass Top   _____
24. Type of Rubber Pads to Rest Glass on   _____
25. Adjustable Heights from   _____" to _____"
26. Type of Sign Fitting   _____
27. Thickness of Plastic Accessories   _____
28. Metal or Plastic Caps   _____

This guideline will help you compare the quality of the racks you are considering as you make your final selection.

Chapter 23

SEQUENTIAL PHASING OF A PROJECT AND PROJECT BUDGETING

Phasing

The proper phasing of a project is especially important when stores, undergoing remodeling, remain open for business. Merchants and customers are often considerably inconvenienced during such periods, and planners must insist on cooperation among the trades so work flows smoothly and expeditiously.

Tidy work habits help. A good cleaning is generally needed daily and is absolutely essential before a subcontractor begins a new phase.

Phasing is a term generally used to describe the "overlapping" of trades, materials, and installations in any store area. After a project is begun at an established point, it moves progressively through the space to be processed until all work is complete.

Obviously, the phased schedule must coincide with the merchant's stated completion timetables. Planners should make sure that all work is ordered and installed on time in the right sequence so no extra time is needed or, even worse, so no completed work need be torn out and redone because a phase was inadvertently skipped. The phasing schedule

may require simultaneous startups in more than one store area or level.

In any event, each contractor should be expected to build, fabricate, and install to the full extent directed by drawings and specifications.

In reviewing the phasing schedule, contractors should be on the alert for all of the following:

1. Demolition/removal requirements
2. Configuration of new drywall lines and aisles
3. Placement of supportive wall-merchandising systems
4. Electrical, ceiling, perimeter, and floor requirements
5. Perimeter decor and cornice lines
6. Cutting and patching required for floors, walls, and so on
7. Patching and repairing of wall finishes needed
8. Ceiling system repairs called for
9. HVAC requirements
10. Stock-shelving needs
11. Plumbing work
12. Fire protection and sprinkler systems
13. Paint and wallcoverings

14. Flooring
15. Installation of freestanding equipment

Project Construction and Fixturing Budget

From the beginning of the project it is important that close records and an accounting of all expenditures for services be kept by both the merchant and the store planner. Items such as the square footage of the building, the store planner's compensation, the architect's compensation along with the extra costs, and all reimbursables should be closely monitored.

Other construction and fixturing budgets that refer to general contracts for both construction and interior perimeter work, along with freestanding fixtures, should be used to compare bids prior to the awarding of contracts. These schedules give both the merchant and the store planner a quick and handy reference point.

Store Name _____
Store No./Location _____
Completion Date _____
Job Telephone _____
Job FAX _____

Store Planner _____
Address _____
City, State _____
Telephone _____
FAX _____

PROJECT CONSTRUCTION AND FIXTURING BUDGET	Job # _____ Date _____ Sheet _____			
	SQUARE FOOTAGE	% OF TOTAL		
Building—Gross				
Actual selling space				
Nonselling space				
CATEGORIES				

STORE PLANNER	DATE	COST/SQ. FT	EXTRA COST	TOTAL	
Date Design Contract Awarded					
Start of Drawings					
Completion of Drawings					
Negotiated Fee					
Reimbursables					
Blueprinting/Photo Transfers					
Extra Fees					

Store Name _____
Store No./Location _____
Completion Date _____
Job Telephone _____
Job FAX _____

Store Planner _____
Address _____
City, State _____
Telephone _____
FAX _____

PROJECT CONSTRUCTION AND FIXTURING BUDGET	Job # _____	Date _____
	Sheet _____	

ARCHITECT	DATE	COST/SQ. FT	EXTRA COST	TOTAL COST	
Contract Awarded					
Start of Drawings					
Completion of Drawings					
Negotiated Fee					
Reimbursables					
Blueprinting/Photo Transfers					
Extra Fees					

Store Name _____
Store No./Location _____
Completion Date _____
Job Telephone _____
Job FAX _____

Store Planner _____
Address _____
City, State _____
Telephone _____
FAX _____

PROJECT CONSTRUCTION AND FIXTURING BUDGET	Job # _____ Date _____ Sheet _____				
GENERAL CONTRACTOR A	DATE				
Bid Date					
Award Date					
Starting Date of Construction					
Completion Date of Construction					
GENERAL CONTRACTOR B	DATE				
Bid Date					
Award Date					
Starting Date of Construction					
Completion Date of Construction					

Store Name _____

Store No./Location _____

Completion Date _____

Job Telephone _____

Job FAX _____

Store Planner _____

Address _____

City, State _____

Telephone _____

FAX _____

PROJECT CONSTRUCTION AND FIXTURING BUDGET	Job # _____ Date _____ Sheet _____				
PERIMETER DECOR CONTRACTOR A	DATE				
Bid Date					
Award Date					
Manufacturing Starting Date					
Installation Completion Date					
PERIMETER DECOR CONTRACTOR B	DATE				
Bid Date					
Award Date					
Manufacturing Starting Date					
Installation Completion Date					

Store Name _____
Store No./Location _____
Completion Date _____
Job Telephone _____
Job FAX _____

Store Planner _____
Address _____
City, State _____
Telephone _____
FAX _____

PROJECT CONSTRUCTION AND FIXTURING BUDGET	Job # _____ Date _____				
	Sheet _____				
FREESTANDING FIXTURE CONTRACTOR A	DATE				
Bid Date					
Award Date					
Manufacturing Starting Date					
Delivery Date					
Installation Completion Date					
FREESTANDING FIXTURE CONTRACTOR B	DATE				
Bid Date					
Award Date					
Manufacturing Starting Date					
Delivery Date					
Installation Completion Date					

Store Name _____
Store No./Location _____
Completion Date _____
Job Telephone _____
Job FAX _____

Store Planner _____
Address _____
City, State _____
Telephone _____
FAX _____

PROJECT CONSTRUCTION AND FIXTURING BUDGET	Job # _____ Date _____ Sheet _____				
FREESTANDING GARMENT RACK CONTRACTOR A	DATE				
Bid Date					
Award Date					
Manufacturing Starting Date					
Delivery Date					
Installation Completion Date					
FREESTANDING GARMENT RACK CONTRACTOR B	DATE				
Bid Date					
Award Date					
Manufacturing Starting Date					
Delivery Date					
Installation Completion Date					

Chapter 24

GENERAL REQUIREMENT SCHEDULE

The purpose of the General Requirement Schedule is to help the merchant and the store planner review every category of either job responsibility or service. This schedule will also serve as a convenient checklist to insure that each item has been discussed and not overlooked. By using these schedules the planner can keep track of order dates, categories, square-footage cost, estimated cost, extra cost, actual cost, and any additional notations. Nothing is more aggravating to the client (or to the planner) than not being able to readily answer simple questions about these subjects and having to fumble through files and stray papers to locate the information. These schedules assure reduced planner frustration and time-wasting scrambling. The various forms and schedules within this section will help the user keep track of timing, cost, stages of the project, responsibilities, descriptions, and so on. These schedules should be used from the predesign of any project to the store opening.

Store Name _____
Store No./Location _____
Completion Date _____
Job Telephone _____
Job FAX _____

Store Planner _____
Address _____
City, State _____
Telephone _____
FAX _____

GENERAL REQUIREMENT SCHEDULE

Job # _____   Date _____
Sheet _____

DATE	CATEGORY	SQ. FT.	ESTIMATED COST	EXTRA COST	ACTUAL COST	NOTES
	PREDESIGN GENERAL REQUIREMENTS					
	• Building permits					
	• Driveway permits					
	• Inspections					
	• Builder's risk insurance					
	• Owner's protective insurance					
	• Performance bond insurance					
	• Workman's comp. liability insurance					
	• Project development					
	• General survey					
	• Professional survey					
	• Demolition					
	• Excavation					
	• Soil test					

Store Name _____
Store No./Location _____
Completion Date _____
Job Telephone _____
Job FAX _____

Store Planner _____
Address _____
City, State _____
Telephone _____
FAX _____

GENERAL REQUIREMENT SCHEDULE	Job # _____ Date _____ Sheet _____				

DATE	CATEGORY	SQ. FT.	ESTIMATED COST	EXTRA COST	ACTUAL COST	NOTES
	PREDESIGN (cont.)					
	• Equipment rental					
	• Daily cleaning					
	• Construction office					
	• Presite preparation					
	• Soil drainage					
	• Grading					
	• Staking					
	• Piling					
	• Moisture protection					
	• Miscellaneous removal					
	• Developing building outline					
	• Locating all passages and utilities					
	• Approval of building wall plan					

Store Name _____
Store No./Location _____
Completion Date _____
Job Telephone _____
Job FAX _____

Store Planner _____
Address _____
City, State _____
Telephone _____
FAX _____

| GENERAL REQUIREMENT SCHEDULE | Job # _____ Date _____ |
| | Sheet _____ |

DATE	CATEGORY	SQ. FT.	ESTIMATED COST	EXTRA COST	ACTUAL COST	NOTES
	DESIGN PHASE					
	• Sample color and material palettes					
	• Developing floor plans					
	• Developing schedules					
	• Developing merchandising plans					
	• Developing fixture plans					
	• Developing floor electrical plans					
	• Developing ceiling electrical plans					
	• Completion of wall and backdrop					
	• Completion of freestanding fixtures					
	• Final review of design and backdrop					
	• Final review of freestanding fixtures					
	• Final review of building and selling					
	• Blueprinting					

Store Name _____

Store No./Location _____

Completion Date _____

Job Telephone _____

Job FAX _____

Store Planner _____

Address _____

City, State _____

Telephone _____

FAX _____

GENERAL REQUIREMENT SCHEDULE		Job # _____ Date _____			
		Sheet _____			

DATE	CATEGORY	SQ. FT.	ESTIMATED COST	EXTRA COST	ACTUAL COST	NOTES
	DESIGN PHASE (cont.)					
	• Completion of drawings and specifications					

Store Name _____
Store No./Location _____
Completion Date _____
Job Telephone _____
Job FAX _____

Store Planner _____
Address _____
City, State _____
Telephone _____
FAX _____

| GENERAL REQUIREMENT SCHEDULE | Job # _____ Date _____ Sheet _____ | | | | | |

DATE	CATEGORY	SQ. FT.	ESTIMATED COST	EXTRA COST	ACTUAL COST	NOTES
	POSTDESIGN GENERAL REQUIREMENTS					
	• Date project ready for bid					
	• Bid dates					
	• Review of bids					
	• Award construction bid					
	• Award backdrop bid					
	• Award freestanding bid					
	• Check shop drawings (first review)					
	• Check shop drawings (second review)					
	• Start of construction					
	• Precast slabs					
	• Installation of footings					
	• Ballast stone					
	• Concrete slab installation					

Store Name _____

Store No./Location _____

Completion Date _____

Job Telephone _____

Job FAX _____

Store Planner _____

Address _____

City, State _____

Telephone _____

FAX _____

GENERAL REQUIREMENT SCHEDULE

Job # _____   Date _____

Sheet _____

DATE	CATEGORY	SQ. FT.	ESTIMATED COST	EXTRA COST	ACTUAL COST	NOTES
	POSTDESIGN (cont.)					
	• Concrete testing					
	• Concrete topping					
	• Compactor pads					
	• Dock pads					
	• Dock levelers					
	• Elevators					
	• Escalators					
	• Conveyor systems					

Store Name _____

Store No./Location _____

Completion Date _____

Job Telephone _____

Job FAX _____

Store Planner _____

Address _____

City, State _____

Telephone _____

FAX _____

GENERAL REQUIREMENT SCHEDULE						Job # _____ Date _____ Sheet _____

DATE	CATEGORY	SQ. FT.	ESTIMATED COST	EXTRA COST	ACTUAL COST	NOTES
	TEMPORARY SERVICES REQUIRED					
	• Road					
	• Electrical					
	• Heat					
	• Water					
	• Toilets					
	• Barricades					
	• Fences					
	• Inspections					
	• Dumpster rental					
	• Dumpster unloading					

Store Name _____
Store No./Location _____
Completion Date _____
Job Telephone _____
Job FAX _____

Store Planner _____
Address _____
City, State _____
Telephone _____
FAX _____

GENERAL REQUIREMENT SCHEDULE

Job # _____   Date _____

Sheet _____

DATE	CATEGORY	SQ. FT.	ESTIMATED COST	EXTRA COST	ACTUAL COST	NOTES
	STEEL Supervisor:					
	• Structural steel design					
	• Structural steel bid					
	• Structural steel award					
	• Structural steel erection					
	• Structural steel inspection					
	• Bar joists					
	• Roof decking					
	• Flashing					
	• Roofing					
	• Installation of roof					
	• Roof drains					
	• Build-ups					
	• Sheet metal					

Store Name _____
Store No./Location _____
Completion Date _____
Job Telephone _____
Job FAX _____

Store Planner _____
Address _____
City, State _____
Telephone _____
FAX _____

GENERAL REQUIREMENT SCHEDULE		Job # _____		Date _____		
				Sheet _____		
DATE	CATEGORY	SQ. FT.	ESTIMATED COST	EXTRA COST	ACTUAL COST	NOTES
	STEEL (cont.) Supervisor:					
	• Canopies					
	• Decorative metal					
	• Smoke relief					
	• Dock shelters					

Store Name _____

Store No./Location _____

Completion Date _____

Job Telephone _____

Job FAX _____

Store Planner _____

Address _____

City, State _____

Telephone _____

FAX _____

GENERAL REQUIREMENT SCHEDULE

Job # _____   Date _____

Sheet _____

DATE	CATEGORY	SQ. FT.	ESTIMATED COST	EXTRA COST	ACTUAL COST	NOTES
	CEILING Supervisor:					
	• Ceiling design					
	• Repairs to existing ceiling					
	• Installation of new ceiling					

Store Name _____

Store No./Location _____

Completion Date _____

Job Telephone _____

Job FAX _____

Store Planner _____

Address _____

City, State _____

Telephone _____

FAX _____

GENERAL REQUIREMENT SCHEDULE	Job # _____ Date _____ Sheet _____					
DATE	CATEGORY	SQ. FT.	ESTIMATED COST	EXTRA COST	ACTUAL COST	NOTES
	ELECTRICAL Supervisor:					
	• Ceiling-wiring diagram					
	• Installation of ceiling wiring					
	• Floor-wiring diagram					
	• Installation of floor wiring					
	• Removal of existing fixtures					
	• Installation of ceiling fixtures					
	• Installation of floor fixtures					
	• Microprocessor					
	• Point-of-sale wiring					
	• Switchgear					
	• Panels					
	• Low voltage					
	• Installation of cornice lighting					

Store Name _____

Store No./Location _____

Completion Date _____

Job Telephone _____

Job FAX _____

Store Planner _____

Address _____

City, State _____

Telephone _____

FAX _____

	GENERAL REQUIREMENT SCHEDULE		Job # _____ Date _____ Sheet _____			
DATE	CATEGORY	SQ. FT.	ESTIMATED COST	EXTRA COST	ACTUAL COST	NOTES
	ELECTRICAL (cont.) Supervisor:					
	• Installation of stockroom lighting					
	• Installation of alteration room lighting					
	• Bulb cost					
	• Lamp cost					
	• Plugmold					
	• Television system					
	• Telephone system					
	• Special systems design					

Store Name _____
Store No./Location _____
Completion Date _____
Job Telephone _____
Job FAX _____

Store Planner _____
Address _____
City, State _____
Telephone _____
FAX _____

GENERAL REQUIREMENT SCHEDULE	Job # _____ Date _____ Sheet _____

DATE	CATEGORY	SQ. FT.	ESTIMATED COST	EXTRA COST	ACTUAL COST	NOTES
	PLUMBING Supervisor:					
	• Sprinkler-design layout					
	• Sprinkler system					
	• Installation of new sprinklers					
	• Relocation and drop of existing sprinklers					
	• Process plumbing					
	• Pipe coverings					
	• Vanities					
	• Toilet partitions					
	• Drinking fountains					
	• Toilet accessories					

Store Name _____
Store No./Location _____
Completion Date _____
Job Telephone _____
Job FAX _____

Store Planner _____
Address _____
City, State _____
Telephone _____
FAX _____

GENERAL REQUIREMENT SCHEDULE			Job # _____	Date _____		
				Sheet _____		
DATE	CATEGORY	SQ. FT.	ESTIMATED COST	EXTRA COST	ACTUAL COST	NOTES
	HVAC Supervisor:					
	• HVAC design and layout					
	• Process heating					
	• Ventilation					
	• Compressors					
	• Duct work					
	• Wrapping of duct work					
	• Insulation					
	• Location of rooftop units					
	• Installation					

Store Name _____

Store No./Location _____

Completion Date _____

Job Telephone _____

Job FAX _____

Store Planner _____

Address _____

City, State _____

Telephone _____

FAX _____

GENERAL REQUIREMENT SCHEDULE			Job # _____		Date _____	
				Sheet _____		
DATE	CATEGORY	SQ. FT.	ESTIMATED COST	EXTRA COST	ACTUAL COST	NOTES
	MASONRY Supervisor:					
	• Blocking to grade					
	• Installation of block wall					
	• Installation of exterior wall finish					
	• Sample stones or panels					
	• Dock shelters					

Store Name _____

Store No./Location _____

Completion Date _____

Job Telephone _____

Job FAX _____

Store Planner _____

Address _____

City, State _____

Telephone _____

FAX _____

GENERAL REQUIREMENT SCHEDULE

Job # _____   Date _____

Sheet _____

DATE	CATEGORY	SQ. FT.	ESTIMATED COST	EXTRA COST	ACTUAL COST	NOTES
	CARPENTRY Supervisor:					
	• Frame and close openings					
	• Installation of partition walls and blocking					
	• Installation of backdrop					
	• Installation of millwork					
	• Installation of building hardware					
	• Installation of wood doors					
	• Installation of wall insulation					
	• Field check of actual dimensions					

Store Name _____
Store No./Location _____
Completion Date _____
Job Telephone _____
Job FAX _____

Store Planner _____
Address _____
City, State _____
Telephone _____
FAX _____

GENERAL REQUIREMENT SCHEDULE			Job # _____	Date _____		
				Sheet _____		
DATE	CATEGORY	SQ. FT.	ESTIMATED COST	EXTRA COST	ACTUAL COST	NOTES
	PAINT AND WALLCOVERING Supervisor:					
	• Additional wall preparation of repair					
	• Print/Paint					
	• Wallcovering A					
	• Wallcovering B					
	• Wallcovering C					
	• Wallcovering A installation					
	• Wallcovering B installation					
	• Wallcovering C installation					
	• Scaffolding					
	• Extra work required					

Store Name _____

Store No./Location _____

Completion Date _____

Job Telephone _____

Job FAX _____

Store Planner _____

Address _____

City, State _____

Telephone _____

FAX _____

GENERAL REQUIREMENT SCHEDULE

Job # _____   Date _____

Sheet _____

DATE	CATEGORY	SQ. FT.	ESTIMATED COST	EXTRA COST	ACTUAL COST	NOTES
	FLOORING Supervisor:					
	• Existing carpet removal					
	• Carpet					
	• Carpet installation					
	• Existing hard-floor removal					
	• Floor sealer					
	• Resilient flooring					
	• Marble flooring					
	• Wood flooring					
	• Terrazzo flooring					
	• Ceramic tile flooring					
	• Vinyl base					
	• Protection					
	• Cleanup					

Store Name _____
Store No./Location _____
Completion Date _____
Job Telephone _____
Job FAX _____

Store Planner _____
Address _____
City, State _____
Telephone _____
FAX _____

GENERAL REQUIREMENT SCHEDULE   Job # _____   Date _____

Sheet _____

DATE	CATEGORY	SQ. FT.	ESTIMATED COST	EXTRA COST	ACTUAL COST	NOTES
	ENTRANCES AND GLAZING Supervisor:					
	• Overhead receiving doors					
	• Overhead mall doors					
	• Sliding anodized aluminum mall doors					
	• Exterior anodized aluminum doors and closures					
	• Steel doors and frames					
	• Vestibules					
	• Fire doors					
	• Steel or aluminum sashes					
	• Weather stripping					
	• Caulking					
	• Window cleaning					
	• Entrance glazing layout and design					
	• Entrance glazing bid date					

Store Name _____

Store No./Location _____

Completion Date _____

Job Telephone _____

Job FAX _____

Store Planner _____

Address _____

City, State _____

Telephone _____

FAX _____

GENERAL REQUIREMENT SCHEDULE

Job # _____   Date _____

Sheet _____

DATE	CATEGORY	SQ. FT.	ESTIMATED COST	EXTRA COST	ACTUAL COST	NOTES
	NONSELLING EQUIPMENT					
	• Office equipment—furniture and desks					
	• Office equipment—employee lockers					
	• Office equipment—freight					
	• Office equipment installation					
	• Point-of-sale equipment					
	• Computers					
	• CRT terminals					
	• Telephone room					
	• Lounge seating and tables					
	• Time clock					
	• Paging system					
	• Music system					
	• Marking systems					

Store Name _____
Store No./Location _____
Completion Date _____
Job Telephone _____
Job FAX _____

Store Planner _____
Address _____
City, State _____
Telephone _____
FAX _____

GENERAL REQUIREMENT SCHEDULE   Job # _____ Date _____
Sheet _____

DATE	CATEGORY	SQ. FT.	ESTIMATED COST	EXTRA COST	ACTUAL COST	NOTES
	NONSELLING EQUIPMENT (cont.)					
	• Compactor					
	• Fire extinguishers and maintenance					
	• Stockroom shelving					
	• Nonselling fixtures					

Store Name _____

Store No./Location _____

Completion Date _____

Job Telephone _____

Job FAX _____

Store Planner _____

Address _____

City, State _____

Telephone _____

FAX _____

GENERAL REQUIREMENT SCHEDULE

Job # _____   Date _____

Sheet _____

DATE	CATEGORY	SQ. FT.	ESTIMATED COST	EXTRA COST	ACTUAL COST	NOTES
	RESTAURANT Supervisor:					
	• Food-service design					
	• Food-preparation equipment					
	• Food-preparation machines and hookup					
	• Food-preparation electrical hookup					
	• Dining room furniture					
	• Installation					

Store Name _____
Store No./Location _____
Completion Date _____
Job Telephone _____
Job FAX _____

Store Planner _____
Address _____
City, State _____
Telephone _____
FAX _____

GENERAL REQUIREMENT SCHEDULE		Job # _____	Date _____			
			Sheet _____			
DATE	CATEGORY	SQ. FT.	ESTIMATED COST	EXTRA COST	ACTUAL COST	NOTES
	PREOPENING GENERAL REQUIREMENTS					
	• Special construction					
	• Signage					
	• Telephones					
	• Paving					
	• Landscaping					
	• General cleanup					
	• Final cleanup					
	• Special services					
	• Security staff					
	• Punchlist					
	• Job photographs					
	• Store promotions					
	STORE OPENING					

Store Name _____

Store No./Location _____

Completion Date _____

Job Telephone _____

Job FAX _____

Store Planner _____

Address _____

City, State _____

Telephone _____

FAX _____

CONSTRUCTION SCHEDULE

Job # _____   Date _____

Sheet _____

RESPONSIBLE PARTY*	STAGE OF PROJECT	JAN	FEB	MAR	APR	MAY	JUN	JUL	AUG	SEP	OCT	NOV	DEC	

* O   Owner
  SP Store planner
   A   Architect
   E   Engineer
   C   Contractor

Store Name _____
Store No./Location _____
Completion Date _____
Job Telephone _____
Job FAX _____

Store Planner _____
Address _____
City, State _____
Telephone _____
FAX _____

DOOR AND OPENING SCHEDULE

Job # _____   Date _____

Sheet _____

DOOR/ OPENING #	TYPE*	ROOM #	LOCATION	SIZE	FINISH	NOTES

*A—Opening
 B—Cased opening
 C—Louver door
 D—Solid door
 E—Service door
 F—Service door (pair)

Store Name _____

Store No./Location _____

Completion Date _____

Job Telephone _____

Job FAX _____

Store Planner _____

Address _____

City, State _____

Telephone _____

FAX _____

BUILDING HARDWARE SCHEDULE

Job # _____   Date _____

Sheet _____

SUPPLIER	PART #	QUAN.	DESCRIPTION	SIZE	FINISH	UNIT COST	TOTAL

Store Name _____

Store No./Location _____

Completion Date _____

Job Telephone _____

Job FAX _____

Store Planner _____

Address _____

City, State _____

Telephone _____

FAX _____

MERCHANDISING HARDWARE SCHEDULE

Job # _____   Date _____

Sheet _____

SUPPLIER	PART #	QUAN.	DESCRIPTION	SIZE	FINISH	UNIT COST	TOTAL

Store Name _____

Store No./Location _____

Completion Date _____

Job Telephone _____

Job FAX _____

Store Planner _____

Address _____

City, State _____

Telephone _____

FAX _____

PERIMETER DECOR SCHEDULE

Job # _____ Date _____

Sheet _____

DEPT.	DEC. #	DECOR INCLUDED	DECOR NOT INCLUDED	PRICE/ LIN. FT.	INSTALLED PRICE	REMARKS	

Store Name _____

Store No./Location _____

Completion Date _____

Job Telephone _____

Job FAX _____

Store Planner _____

Address _____

City, State _____

Telephone _____

FAX _____

ROOM FINISH SCHEDULE

Job # _____   Date _____

Sheet _____

ROOM #	FLOOR	BASE	CEILING HEIGHT	WALLS	NOTES

Store Name _____

Store No./Location _____

Completion Date _____

Job Telephone _____

Job FAX _____

Store Planner _____

Address _____

City, State _____

Telephone _____

FAX _____

FREESTANDING FIXTURE SCHEDULE

Job # _____   Date _____

Sheet _____

DEPT.	FIX. #	DESCRIPTION	CONT.	LENGTH	QUAN.	UNIT PRICE	INSTALLED PRICE	REMARKS

Store Name _____
Store No./Location _____
Completion Date _____
Job Telephone _____
Job FAX _____

Store Planner _____
Address _____
City, State _____
Telephone _____
FAX _____

HARDWARE SCHEDULE			Job # _____ Date _____		
			Sheet _____		

NUMBER OF
  PIECES

LOOSE	ATTACH.	DESCRIPTION	UNIT COST	TOTAL	

Store Name _____

Store No./Location _____

Completion Date _____

Job Telephone _____

Job FAX _____

Store Planner _____

Address _____

City, State _____

Telephone _____

FAX _____

CUTTING BILL SCHEDULE

Job # _____ Date _____

Sheet _____

NO.	PER UNIT	AMT.	THICK	WIDTH	LENGTH	UNIT MATERIAL	DESCRIPTION	COST	TOTAL	

Store Name _____
Store No./Location _____
Completion Date _____
Job Telephone _____
Job FAX _____

Store Planner _____
Address _____
City, State _____
Telephone _____
FAX _____

STORE-FIXTURE FINISH SCHEDULE

Job # _____   Date _____

Sheet _____

		FINISH DESCRIPTION	
Exterior			
Interior Display			
Interior storage			
Top			
Edge Band			
Drawer Fronts			
Base			
Doors			

Chapter 25

PLANNING FOR SECURITY

Security Awareness

The ability of store planners to design retail stores with maximum security requires knowledge, talent, and imagination beyond that necessary to merely sell merchandise. The major challenge of designing for security is to project goods so they *can* be sold.

The lack of a well-conceived security plan—reviewed and approved by store management—is an open invitation to theft. Too often, security measures are overlooked or neglected in the store-planning process.

Planners who are fully aware of the most common shoplifting problems know how people act and react in the retailing environment. They also know how to design space and recommend measures that help foil theft. The sound approach is to be presenting merchandise for honest customers in as relaxed a fashion as possible, yet taking necessary precautions to minimize shoplifting.

Professional shoplifters will case retail stores to learn the security systems that are in use and the periods that have the most lax security. They will return when the timing is best, using their tools of the trade.

Whereas the professional thief is seldom caught, the amateur who is unaware of the security measures in effect is often apprehended. Shoplifters, posing as casual browsers not needing service, wait for the moment when they are unobserved. Sales personnel must be trained to observe everyone nearby, especially those who appear suspicious.

Retailers should develop effective guidelines for security in every corner of the store. They should also keep current with the latest and best techniques for eliminating or reducing pilferage, whether it involves outsiders or store personnel. Even with the best alarm systems, uniformed guards, convex and two-way mirrors, closed-circuit cameras, and fitting-room warning signs, shoplifters are still determined to "beat the system."

Plan Early

To achieve maximum security, store owners and managers will want to inform store planners early in the game as to the degree of security desired and how they want to observe customers and staff. The layout of walls and the placement of fixtures and control points should all be discussed so places such as entrances, exits, fitting rooms, stockrooms, and areas used for receiving and cash transactions give little or no concealment to people with ulterior motives.

Designing for maximum security can be fairly simple when realistic approaches are taken. In complex situations where a planner clearly lacks the knowledge to prepare an adequate security plan, the guidance of a professional consultant may be needed.

Selling and nonselling areas in each department must be examined for security risks. Fixture layouts and heights, wall layouts and heights, and the extent of security coverages must also be considered.

Whether an open, core, or cluster plan is used as the merchandising concept, freestanding fixtures that rise above eye level (54") should be avoided. High fixtures require more staff vigilance to keep a department secure.

Transaction Areas

Cash-transaction areas should be centrally located so they control entrances into fitting-room areas and should have clear views of one or more departments or classifications. Transaction areas at a showcase line or wrap counter in ready-to-wear sections should be made to look as if customers are to be served from just one side of the counter.

Most merchants try to keep wrap areas at floor level, but some elevate them for improved visibility. Many ready-to-wear departments have dual counters, one for the transaction, the other for wrapping.

Other Security Areas

There are several locations (or conditions) that must be considered in any retail store security plan:

1. Entrances
The size of openings to stores varies, of course, depending on the type of store and square footage. Entrances, show windows, and traffic aisles are used to help direct customers as they approach merchandise areas. Exactly what merchandise will be placed at the store opening and how it is to be presented are also prime security considerations.

Retailers with ample space are likely to rely on aisles to "invite" customers in but will use freestanding fixtures with acrylic backs to display classifications of value that are near entrances. Some retailers use see-through glass panels from floor to ceiling to give clear visibility into the store and, at the same time, cut security expenses. When goods are placed at the front line of a store, additional security provisions of some kind are needed.

Professional shoplifters, who always seem to be well-versed in the most common types of security devices, will case many stores and target those that are least protected.

2. Wall Configurations
Dividing walls and stockrooms should never create isolated or obscure pockets convenient for shoplifting. A dividing wall can be used when merchandising spaces for more than one department are needed. Locks may be required on doors to stockrooms. When a dividing wall is placed at the department line, a second control point will be needed to service the department on the other side of the wall.

When the height of merchandise creates a visibility problem, the merchandise is better protected when placed at perimeter walls. The walls act as a focal point and force customers to turn their backs to the aisles and elevate their arms to select and inspect the classifications.

3. Fitting Rooms
Positioning, viewing visibility, and monitoring are keys to good fitting-room security. Salespeople serving clothing departments should have clear vision from cash-and-wrap counters into fitting-room areas. Fitting rooms should have just one entrance since two entrance points allow customers to go in at one entrance, conceal merchandise, and exit from the other—ideal for teams of sneak thieves and their diversionary tactics.

4. Showcase Merchandising Line
Most showcase merchandise is of higher monetary value. The best showcases are those designed to discourage tampering. Items displayed on top of a showcase should be of lesser value. Smaller items, of course, are most easily removed and concealed.

When presenting better merchandise from showcases, salespeople should pay careful attention to all customers and avoid distractions. The glass tops of a showcase should always be cemented or mechanically anchored so they cannot be lifted. When the value of items warrants, shatter-proof and tamper-proof glass is in order.

When back islands are used in conjunction with showcases, the cases should be keyed alike, except for those that carry more valuable items.

5. Receiving and Nonselling Areas

Enough cannot be said about the immeasurable amount of merchandise pilfered from store premises by employees. A trusted management representative should always be present whenever receiving doors are opened or when trash is being removed. Every measure must be considered to assure proper security control. Almost any owner of a store can recount a litany of painful experiences involving theft by "trusted" employees.

6. Display Projection

Any unprotected interior display section is a target for shoplifters. Even large bulky items need safeguarding in display areas. All of this presents an ongoing challenge—both to the salespeople and the shoplifter. Good judgment must be used to safeguard all displays that the public can touch.

Display-Inventory Control

All large retail stores should have a system that accounts for the whereabouts of items collected from various departments for use in displays. Such a system requires entries of every item borrowed and every item returned. If the system is to work, all borrowed "props" are due to be returned just as soon as the displays are dismantled.

Crime Deterrents

Experts in the security field have produced a wide array of devices and techniques to thwart or reduce pilferage. Most devices are effective to certain limits, even if they only serve as deterrents to crime. The conflict for merchants is that vigorous measures tend to detract from the desired pleasantness of shopping. Naturally, when customers feel they are being treated with suspicion, they are less inclined to buy.

Few merchants need to be reminded that store personnel must be well educated on the subject of security and constantly reminded of its crucial importance. This staff education should include guidance on how to recognize potential shoplifters when their images appear in mirrors and on cameras and door-monitoring systems.

Security Booths

Booths with two-way mirrors, created as observation stations for security personnel, should be designed so their placement and purpose are worked into the design and not obvious. The interiors of such booths should not be lighted since two-way mirrors can reveal the shadows of the person inside. The benefits of staffed security booths must be studied carefully to determine if their extra cost is warranted in helping to apprehend shoplifters who might otherwise go unobserved. The added operational costs can, in time, outweigh the cost of alternate security systems.

Signs and Notices

Signs are often used to remind customers of the consequences of stealing. The messages must be strong enough to discourage thieves, yet not so bold as to offend legitimate customers. Paradoxically, signs may also temp some people to take the chance of pilfering, no matter how the sign is worded. Some daring thief will take the stated consequences as nothing but a challenge. However, in most cases, signs are considered a cheap deterrent to shoplifting.

Summary

Store planners should design a store with fixtures that do not obstruct the full vision of a department. Fixtures should not be over 54" high; otherwise sales personnel will lose contact with shoppers. Under such conditions, garments can be dropped into a bag placed beneath a rack, taken off showcases and counters and slipped into a bag draped over an arm, placed under a coat or large bag for concealment, or stuffed into an oversized piece of clothing.

The most elaborate security plan will never guarantee the safety of every piece of merchandise in the store; even locked glass cases can be broken. Yet, carefully planning every aspect of security tailored to the particular store's circumstances is one of the store planner's chief responsibilities.

Chapter 26

COLOR AND MATERIAL SPECIFICATIONS

Creating with Colors

The importance of astute color selection in the store-design process cannot be overemphasized. The interior color palette should serve as more than just a flattering backdrop for presenting merchandise; the overall coloring, including textures and finishes, conveys the "personality" of a retail environment. In choosing colors, planners must first carefully consider the type of merchandise to be presented and the space it will define, taking into account the decor of immediately adjoining departments and those across the aisles.

Another important influence on color choices is the lighting, as viewed from the standpoint of both types and amounts. A single color, under fluorescent lighting, will be perceived as different in value and tone from the same one viewed under incandescent illumination. The light-reflecting qualities, for instance, of semigloss and enamel paints are better than that of flat paints.

When a department is located in the rear corner of a store, for example, the area can be brightened by using paint and wallcoverings in light tones. Accents or special finishes above the cornice can attract attention to a department that might otherwise be lost from the customer's view.

Trends in Color

What is the trend in color today? Ask ten planners and you may get ten different answers. Viewing color trends in retailing is like watching a passing parade. That is why colors, as well as textures and patterns, must be carefully chosen for longevity, not just for immediate fads.

Everyone plans for today, of course, but experienced planners consider tomorrow to be just as important. Suppose the store being designed will not be revamped for another seven or ten years. How will the color scheme be viewed at the end of that time? Will it be an unmistakable reminder of an outdated era?

Interior decor in retailing has gone through a fairly rapid series of transitions in the last 20 years. Some of the biggest judgmental mistakes in this period have had to do with opting for a color or texture that was "trendy" at the time but that actually distracted from the salability of goods as time went on. When energy costs were low, for example, retailers would sometimes paint high ceilings with dark colors to create the illusion that the ceiling was lower. This meant that lighting levels had be increased since dark colors absorb more light and reflect less light.

Then came bright, garish colors that took credit for high shock value but distracted from the merchandise. Next were overscaled wallcoverings with reflective backgrounds that conflicted with the patterns and colors of merchandising. For a time, many used bold painted graphics to redo an interior inexpensively, only to discover that such graphics soon became dated. Then the more bland neutral tones came into vogue.

There is a critical need to be a visionary in the store-planning business because store planners with accurate views of the future are most likely to have a greater success rate when it comes to creating designs that last.

Store Planners and Color Choices

Some planners have a history of trying to dictate color choices. That is a good reason for merchants with strong likes and dislikes in color to make their feelings known early. Store planners are expected to recommend carpet colors, wall colors, texture types and patterns, along with price ranges, carpet face weights, and so on; but in the end, it is the merchants who pay the bill, and their views must be taken fully into account.

The good store planners are always looking for unifying factors that tie design concepts together. At a certain point, planners must stop to consider how well the color schemes blend from the standpoint of overall balance. Is one color shouting too loudly? Is another too subdued for the kind of identification the department should have? Do all the colors work well together?

Colors must be clearly defined on the interior elevation. Each texture, wallcovering, wood finish, laminate, and paint on the elevation is identified, using a symbol system.

The desired personality of the store will not always be uniformly reflected in the color palette. Neutral or jewel-tone colors will appear lighter in large scale. Darker colors and accents will bring extra definition and attention to detail.

It is important to note that many customers have difficulty differentiating colors within a large space, and proper sinage may have the key role in differentiation of departments.

Each year, new interiors are proposed for thousands of new and remodeled stores. Many of the stores are under common ownership, but located in various parts of the country. Store planners are faced with decisions such as whether to replicate one plan for all stores or to customize according to the need of the geographical location. Obviously, many times, the plans will have to be individually tailored to suit temperature, environmental, and lifestyle differences from one area to another.

Neutral Color

Neutral tones, such as off-whites, light taupes, grays, and beige tones, are now in fashion and are excellent candidates as backgrounds for displaying most types of sportswear, ready-to-wear clothing, hard lines, small electronics, and giftware. These colors generally are less distracting, less likely to be in conflict with the merchandise on display, and safer bets as backgrounds for merchandise subject to seasonal change. Neutrals used above the cornice line can help create illusions of greater space.

Not only do neutral walls make more flattering backgrounds for merchandise, they are also easier to illuminate. The neutral backgrounds of today are quite understated. Neutral colors, when used in conjunction with textured vinyl wallcoverings and finishes, often take on different effects.

The lighter tones of neutral colors are best used below the cornice line behind ready-to-wear items. Deeper tones, however, can create a dynamic background for reflective merchandise such as crystal, silver, and china. Light pastel shades (the so-called "feminine" colors) are effective behind women's ready-to-wear, lingerie, or cosmetics. Earthtones or grays create a sophisticated look for men's sportswear or for housewares. Bolder accents of semigloss primary colors, applied to cornices with special trim, can help define a children's department. At least for today!

Naturally, there is a wide variety of textures from which to choose in complementing colors used elsewhere: vinyls, grasscloths, woven fabrics, glossy materials, and many others. Laminate plastics, as an example, when coordinated well with carpet colors, can be used to complement merchandise and to focus attention on the fixture design as well. Remember, too, that aisle material must be carefully chosen to complement the color scheme and give a unified, coordinated look to designs.

The Role of Cornice Areas

A single laminated cornice with an accent of silver pleximirror might identify a fashion department, whereas a half-round tube cornice might best define an adjacent department. Natural wood cornices with bronze trim could be used to add a feeling of sophistication. These are just a few examples.

Textured vinyl wallcoverings can be very attractive and add visual excitement; but a moiré (water-like) pattern would not be appropriate for a men's clothing department, nor would a dark color be acceptable for lingerie.

When choosing wallcoverings, ask the following questions:

- In what department is the material to be applied?
- Does a light or heavy texture/pattern read better from a distance?
- Does the color coordinate with the rest of the department?

Remember, the wall area above the cornice is the most visible to customers from a distance. When colors, textures, and patterns are used wisely as visual tools, these vital wall sections can be most effective in luring customers to new areas of a store, encouraging extra sales.

Accent Backgrounds

Accent backgrounds can also be used to bring attention to a section or particular merchandise classification—plain color breaks up a long, bland wall; a wood veneer slatwall brings attention to featured merchandise; a textured or suede vinyl wallcovering adds sophistication to a grouping.

Accent colors, which should always be chosen and applied with caution, must be used to accent, not overwhelm. In choosing any color tones for paint or texture, avoid those that are not generally popular, that distract, and that adversely affect the overall appearance of the department and merchandise.

Deep accent colors do not present some goods to their best advantage. Pastel and jewel tones can be used to introduce a particular mood or create a special ambiance within a space. Rich, subtle heather tones can play an important role in subliminal selling.

The thoroughness and sensibleness of early planning for colors and textures will have much to do with a store's success in making a sound return on its investments.

Color in Carpeting

Carpeting is often the most important element in developing a color palette. Everything specified, it seems (paints, wallcoverings, laminates, special finishes, etc.), are derived from or related in some way to the color of the carpeting.

When choosing carpets, the following must be considered:

1. Classification of department and carpet budget
2. Type of merchandise being sold
3. All other colors and textures planned or already in use

The color of the carpeting, as with everything, should reflect the image of the department in which it is installed, for example, mauve or beige in women's, gray or taupe in men's. Tweed carpets can be placed most anywhere in the store.

Border carpet can help accentuate and identify a department—the border is confined to the aisle line; the balance of the department will have a second carpet. High-traffic areas, of course, require carpets of high density and wearability.

After optional carpet samples are chosen, it is a good idea to send larger versions of the samples to clients so they can get the clearest possible idea of its actual appearance. (A 12- by 18-inch sample can look considerably different from a 2-inch square in a sample book.) How merchants respond should be a key in decisions about the toning and values of the carpet selected.

The basic colors of paint, laminates, wallcoverings, and wood finishes all must blend in a complementary way. When possible, recommend several alternates in each category.

Remember Image

When presenting color palettes to clients during design presentation, the planner should take into account the image that clients want to present. Merchants put their trust in the store planner's ability as a color coordinator to suggest the materials that will properly reinforce the basic design concept. A design presentation that is well thought out will help to get early agreement on formalizing the concept. Remember, too, in most every case, merchants will have the final say about what colors and textures are to be used.

Color Palettes and Material Books

Color palettes are an important part of a planner's design presentation. Color chips of paint, laminate plastic, wallcoverings, carpets, hard floorcovering samples, wood finishes, special finishes, and so on, are affixed to a neutral heavy-stock illustration board. The samples should be neatly arranged in a manner that groups each area of materials together. The store name and department name should be neatly printed on the board for quick identification. The reverse side of the color palette should have cost information for each one of the materials.

The forms that are provided in this chapter have paint, laminate, wallcoverings, floorcoverings, special finishes, furniture, lighting, accessories, and signage that will be used to produce color books.

Color books are not produced until the color palette has been approved by the client. In most cases, the planner will produce a minimum of seven color books. After the project has been awarded, color books will be distributed to the owner, the perimeter decor contractor, the free-standing fixture contractor, the painting contractor, the landlord, and the designer, as well as one for the permanent file. An index should be provided in the book with all the purchasing information and costs. All wallcoverings should have an accompanying letter from the manufacturer that states its fire rating. The color books should be identically assembled and placed in binders. The cover face of the binder should identify the project and the store planner.

COLOR PALETTE

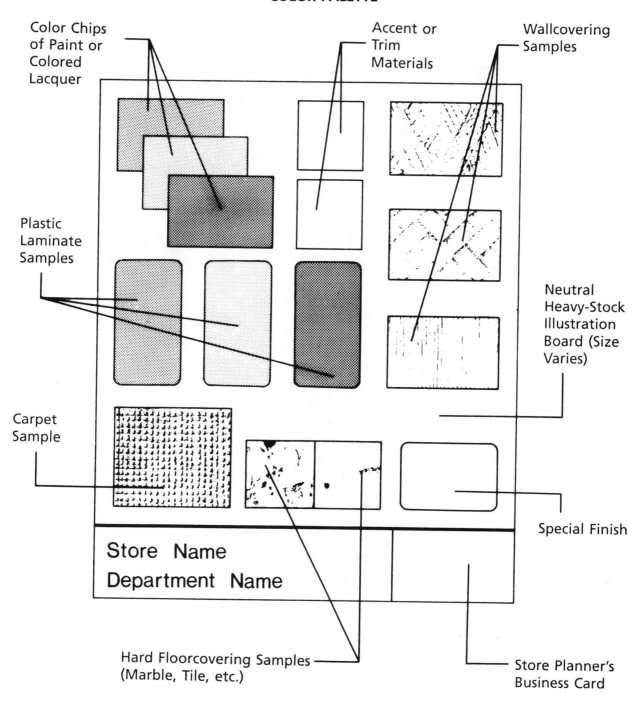

Color Chips
of Paint or
Colored
Lacquer

Accent or
Trim
Materials

Wallcovering
Samples

Plastic
Laminate
Samples

Neutral
Heavy-Stock
Illustration
Board (Size
Varies)

Carpet
Sample

Store Name
Department Name

Special Finish

Hard Floorcovering Samples
(Marble, Tile, etc.)

Store Planner's
Business Card

Store Name _____

Store #/Location _____

Store Planner _____

MATERIALS & FIXTURE SPECIFICATIONS

Contents	Abbreviation
Paint	P
Wood Finishes	WF
Wallcovering	WC
Plastic Laminate	PL
Colored Lacquer	CL
Carpet	C
Ceramic Tile	CT
Wood Flooring	WF
Vinyl Tile	VT
Vinyl Base	VB
Special Finishes	SF
Upholstery	U
Seating	S
Shoe Stool	SS
Accent Furniture	AF
Accent Lamp	AL
Accent Mirror	AM
Planter	P
Mannequin	M
Signage	Sign

MATERIAL SPECIFICATION

MATERIAL _____Paint_____

Store Name/# _____
Address _____
City, State, ZIP _____
Telephone # _____
FAX # _____
Date _____

Store Planner _____
Address _____
City, State, ZIP _____
Telephone # _____
Fax # _____
Sheet _____ of _____

Project # _____

Reference No. P-1	Reference No. P-2	Reference No. P-3
Vendor:	Vendor:	Vendor:
Address:	Address:	Address:
City, State, ZIP:	City, State, ZIP:	City, State, ZIP:
Contact/Telephone Number:	Contact/Telephone Number:	Contact/Telephone Number:
Order Info:	Order Info:	Order Info:
P.O. #	P.O. #	P.O. #
Quantity:	Quantity:	Quantity:
Remarks:	Remarks:	Remarks:
Place Sample Here	Place Sample Here	Place Sample Here

MATERIAL SPECIFICATION

MATERIAL___ Wood Finishes ___

Store Name/# _____
Address _____
City, State, ZIP _____
Telephone # _____
FAX # _____
Date _____

Store Planner _____
Address _____
City, State, ZIP _____
Telephone # _____
Fax # _____
Sheet _____ of _____

Project # _____

Reference No. WD-1	Reference No. WD-2	Reference No. WD-3
Vendor:	Vendor:	Vendor:
Address:	Address:	Address:
City, State, ZIP:	City, State, ZIP:	City, State, ZIP:
Contact/Telephone Number:	Contact/Telephone Number:	Contact/Telephone Number:
Order Info:	Order Info:	Order Info:
P.O. #	P.O. #	P.O. #
Quantity:	Quantity:	Quantity:
Remarks:	Remarks:	Remarks:
Place Sample Here	Place Sample Here	Place Sample Here

MATERIAL SPECIFICATION

MATERIAL___ Wallcovering ___

Store Name/# _____
Address _____
City, State, ZIP _____
Telephone # _____
FAX # _____
Date _____

Store Planner _____
Address _____
City, State, ZIP _____
Telephone # _____
Fax # _____
Sheet _____ of _____

Project # _____

Reference No. WC-1	Reference No. WC-2	Reference No. WC-3
Vendor:	Vendor:	Vendor:
Address:	Address:	Address:
City, State, ZIP:	City, State, ZIP:	City, State, ZIP:
Contact/Telephone Number:	Contact/Telephone Number:	Contact/Telephone Number:
Order Info:	Order Info:	Order Info:
P.O. #	P.O. #	P.O. #
Quantity:	Quantity:	Quantity:
Remarks:	Remarks:	Remarks:
Place Sample Here	Place Sample Here	Place Sample Here

MATERIAL SPECIFICATION

MATERIAL____Plastic Laminate____

Store Name/# _____
Address _____
City, State, ZIP _____
Telephone # _____
FAX # _____
Date _____

Store Planner _____
Address _____
City, State, ZIP _____
Telephone # _____
Fax # _____
Sheet _____ of _____

Project # _____

Reference No. PL-1	Reference No. PL-2	Reference No. PL-3
Vendor:	Vendor:	Vendor:
Address:	Address:	Address:
City, State, ZIP:	City, State, ZIP:	City, State, ZIP:
Contact/Telephone Number:	Contact/Telephone Number:	Contact/Telephone Number:
Order Info:	Order Info:	Order Info:
P.O. #	P.O. #	P.O. #
Quantity:	Quantity:	Quantity:
Remarks:	Remarks:	Remarks:
Place Sample Here	Place Sample Here	Place Sample Here

MATERIAL SPECIFICATION

MATERIAL   Colored Lacquer

Store Name/# _____
Address _____
City, State, ZIP _____
Telephone # _____
FAX # _____
Date _____

Store Planner _____
Address _____
City, State, ZIP _____
Telephone # _____
Fax # _____
Sheet _____ of _____

Project # _____

Reference No. CL-1	Reference No. CL-2	Reference No. CL-3
Vendor:	Vendor:	Vendor:
Address:	Address:	Address:
City, State, ZIP:	City, State, ZIP:	City, State, ZIP:
Contact/Telephone Number:	Contact/Telephone Number:	Contact/Telephone Number:
Order Info:	Order Info:	Order Info:
P.O. #	P.O. #	P.O. #
Quantity:	Quantity:	Quantity:
Remarks:	Remarks:	Remarks:
Place Sample Here	Place Sample Here	Place Sample Here

MATERIAL SPECIFICATION

MATERIAL   Carpet

Store Name/# _____
Address _____
City, State, ZIP _____
Telephone # _____
FAX # _____
Date _____

Store Planner _____
Address _____
City, State, ZIP _____
Telephone # _____
Fax # _____
Sheet _____ of _____

Project # _____

Reference No. C-1	Reference No. C-2	Reference No. C-3
Vendor:	Vendor:	Vendor:
Address:	Address:	Address:
City, State, ZIP:	City, State, ZIP:	City, State, ZIP:
Contact/Telephone Number:	Contact/Telephone Number:	Contact/Telephone Number:
Order Info:	Order Info:	Order Info:
P.O. #	P.O. #	P.O. #
Quantity:	Quantity:	Quantity:
Remarks:	Remarks:	Remarks:
Place Sample Here	Place Sample Here	Place Sample Here

MATERIAL SPECIFICATION

MATERIAL ___Ceramic Tile___

Store Name/# _____
Address _____
City, State, ZIP _____
Telephone # _____
FAX # _____
Date _____

Store Planner _____
Address _____
City, State, ZIP _____
Telephone # _____
Fax # _____
Sheet _____ of _____

Project # _____

Reference No. CT-1	Reference No. CT-2	Reference No. CT-3
Vendor:	Vendor:	Vendor:
Address:	Address:	Address:
City, State, ZIP:	City, State, ZIP:	City, State, ZIP:
Contact/Telephone Number:	Contact/Telephone Number:	Contact/Telephone Number:
Order Info:	Order Info:	Order Info:
P.O. #	P.O. #	P.O. #
Quantity:	Quantity:	Quantity:
Remarks:	Remarks:	Remarks:
Place Sample Here	Place Sample Here	Place Sample Here

MATERIAL SPECIFICATION

MATERIAL___ Wood Flooring___

Store Name/# _____
Address _____
City, State, ZIP _____
Telephone # _____
FAX # _____
Date _____

Store Planner _____
Address _____
City, State, ZIP _____
Telephone # _____
Fax # _____
Sheet _____ of _____

Project # _____

Reference No. W-1	Reference No. W-2	Reference No. W-3
Vendor:	Vendor:	Vendor:
Address:	Address:	Address:
City, State, ZIP:	City, State, ZIP:	City, State, ZIP:
Contact/Telephone Number:	Contact/Telephone Number:	Contact/Telephone Number:
Order Info:	Order Info:	Order Info:
P.O. #	P.O. #	P.O. #
Quantity:	Quantity:	Quantity:
Remarks:	Remarks:	Remarks:
Place Sample Here	Place Sample Here	Place Sample Here

MATERIAL SPECIFICATION

MATERIAL _____ Vinyl Tile _____

Store Name/# _____
Address _____
City, State, ZIP _____
Telephone # _____
FAX # _____
Date _____

Store Planner _____
Address _____
City, State, ZIP _____
Telephone # _____
Fax # _____
Sheet _____ of _____

Project # _____

Reference No. VT-1	Reference No. VT-2	Reference No. VT-3
Vendor:	Vendor:	Vendor:
Address:	Address:	Address:
City, State, ZIP:	City, State, ZIP:	City, State, ZIP:
Contact/Telephone Number:	Contact/Telephone Number:	Contact/Telephone Number:
Order Info:	Order Info:	Order Info:
P.O. #	P.O. #	P.O. #
Quantity:	Quantity:	Quantity:
Remarks:	Remarks:	Remarks:
Place Sample Here	Place Sample Here	Place Sample Here

MATERIAL SPECIFICATION

MATERIAL_____Vinyl Base_____

Store Name/# _____
Address _____
City, State, ZIP _____
Telephone # _____
FAX # _____
Date _____

Store Planner _____
Address _____
City, State, ZIP _____
Telephone # _____
Fax # _____
Sheet _____ of _____

Project # _____

Reference No. VB-1	Reference No. VB-2	Reference No. VB-3
Vendor:	Vendor:	Vendor:
Address:	Address:	Address:
City, State, ZIP:	City, State, ZIP:	City, State, ZIP:
Contact/Telephone Number:	Contact/Telephone Number:	Contact/Telephone Number:
Order Info:	Order Info:	Order Info:
P.O. #	P.O. #	P.O. #
Quantity:	Quantity:	Quantity:
Remarks:	Remarks:	Remarks:
Place Sample Here	Place Sample Here	Place Sample Here

MATERIAL SPECIFICATION   **MATERIAL** <u>Special Finishes</u>

Store Name/# _____   Store Planner _____
Address _____   Address _____
City, State, ZIP _____   City, State, ZIP _____
Telephone # _____   Telephone # _____
FAX # _____   Fax # _____
Date _____   Sheet _____ of _____

Project # _____

Reference No. SF-1	Reference No. SF-2	Reference No. SF-3
Vendor:	Vendor:	Vendor:
Address:	Address:	Address:
City, State, ZIP:	City, State, ZIP:	City, State, ZIP:
Contact/Telephone Number:	Contact/Telephone Number:	Contact/Telephone Number:
Order Info:	Order Info:	Order Info:
P.O. #	P.O. #	P.O. #
Quantity:	Quantity:	Quantity:
Remarks:	Remarks:	Remarks:
Place Sample Here	Place Sample Here	Place Sample Here

MATERIAL SPECIFICATION   MATERIAL _____ Upholstery _____

Store Name/# _____   Store Planner _____
Address _____   Address _____
City, State, ZIP _____   City, State, ZIP _____
Telephone # _____   Telephone # _____
FAX # _____   Fax # _____
Date _____   Sheet _____ of _____

Project # _____

Reference No. UP-1	Reference No. UP-2	Reference No. UP-3
Vendor:	Vendor:	Vendor:
Address:	Address:	Address:
City, State, ZIP:	City, State, ZIP:	City, State, ZIP:
Contact/Telephone Number:	Contact/Telephone Number:	Contact/Telephone Number:
Order Info:	Order Info:	Order Info:
P.O. #	P.O. #	P.O. #
Quantity:	Quantity:	Quantity:
Remarks:	Remarks:	Remarks:
Place Sample Here	Place Sample Here	Place Sample Here

FIXTURE SPECIFICATION   FIXTURE____ Seating ____

Store Name/# _____	Store Planner _____
Address _____	Address _____
City, State, ZIP _____	City, State, ZIP _____
Telephone # _____	Telephone # _____
FAX # _____	Fax # _____
Date _____	Sheet _____ of _____

Project # _____

Photograph/Drawing:		Reference No.
		Manufacturer:
		Address:
		City, State, ZIP:
		Contact:
		Telephone:
Place Picture of Chair Here		Chair Style and #:
		Finish:
		Quantity:
		Price/F.O.B. Job Site:
		Tag for Department:
		Date to Be at Store:
		Remarks:
		Fabric Color:
Place Fabric Sample Here		Fabric Style and #:
		Remarks:

FIXTURE SPECIFICATION

FIXTURE   Shoe Stool

Store Name/# _____   Store Planner _____
Address _____   Address _____
City, State, ZIP _____   City, State, ZIP _____
Telephone # _____   Telephone # _____
FAX # _____   Fax # _____
Date _____   Sheet _____ of _____

Project # _____

Photograph/Drawing:		Reference No.
		Manufacturer:
		Address:
		City, State, ZIP:
		Contact:
		Telephone:
Place Picture of Shoe Stool Here		Chair Style and #:
		Finish:
		Quantity:
		Price/F.O.B. Job Site:
		Tag for Department:
		Date to Be at Store:
		Remarks:
		Fabric Color:
		Fabric Style and #:
Place Fabric Sample Here		
		Remarks:

FIXTURE SPECIFICATION

FIXTURE <u>Accent Furniture</u>

Store Name/# _____
Address _____
City, State, ZIP _____
Telephone # _____
FAX # _____
Date _____

Store Planner _____
Address _____
City, State, ZIP _____
Telephone # _____
Fax # _____
Sheet _____ of _____

Project # _____

Photograph/Drawing:	Reference No.
	Manufacturer:
	Address:
	City, State, ZIP:
	Contact:
	Telephone:
	Item Style and #:
Place Picture of Furniture Here	Finish:
	Quantity:
	Price/F.O.B. Job Site:
	Tag for Department:
	Date to Be at Store:
	Remarks:
Place Fabric Sample Here	Fabric Color:
	Fabric Style and #:
	Remarks:

FIXTURE SPECIFICATION

FIXTURE _____ <u>Signage</u> _____

Store Name/# _____
Address _____
City, State, ZIP _____
Telephone # _____
FAX # _____
Date _____

Store Planner _____
Address _____
City, State, ZIP _____
Telephone # _____
Fax # _____
Sheet _____ of _____

Project # _____

ABCDEFGHIJKLMNOPQRSTUVWXYZ
abcdefghijklmnopqrstuvwxyz
1234567890

Location:

Elevation Numbers:

Quantity:

Sign Wording:

Letter Style:

Letter Height/Thickness:

Center Line of Sign from Finished Floor:

Face Material/Finish Color:

Return Color of Signage:

Installation/Mounting Procedure:

Manufacturer/Source:

Telephone:

Fax:

Special Notes:

FIXTURE SPECIFICATION

FIXTURE____ <u>Accent Lamp</u>

Store Name/# _____	Store Planner _____
Address _____	Address _____
City, State, ZIP _____	City, State, ZIP _____
Telephone # _____	Telephone # _____
FAX # _____	Fax # _____
Date _____	Sheet _____ of _____

Project # _____

Photograph/Drawing:	Reference No.
	Manufacturer:
	Address:
	City, State, ZIP:
	Contact:
	Telephone:
	Lamp Style and #:
Place Picture of Lamp Here	Finish:
	Quantity:
	Price/F.O.B. Job Site:
	Tag for Department:
	Date to Be at Store:
	Remarks:
	Manufacturer:
	Address:
	City, State, ZIP:
	Contact:
	Telephone:
	Lamp Style and #:
	Finish:
	Quantity:
Place Picture of Lamp Here	Price/F.O.B. Job Site:
	Tag for Department:
	Date to Be at Store:
	Remarks:

FIXTURE SPECIFICATION

FIXTURE __Accent Mirror__

Store Name/# _____
Address _____
City, State, ZIP _____
Telephone # _____
FAX # _____
Date _____

Store Planner _____
Address _____
City, State, ZIP _____
Telephone # _____
Fax # _____
Sheet _____ of _____

Project # _____

Photograph/Drawing:	Reference No.
	Manufacturer:
	Address:
	City, State, ZIP:
	Contact:
	Telephone:
	Mirror Style and #:
	Finish:
	Quantity:
Place Picture of Mirror Here	
	Price/F.O.B. Job Site:
	Tag for Department:
	Date to Be at Store:
	Remarks:
	Manufacturer:
	Address:
	City, State, ZIP:
	Contact:
	Telephone:
	Mirror Style and #:
	Finish:
	Quantity:
Place Picture of Mirror Here	
	Price/F.O.B. Job Site:
	Tag for Department:
	Date to Be at Store:
	Remarks:

FIXTURE SPECIFICATION

FIXTURE ___Planter___

Store Name/# _____
Address _____
City, State, ZIP _____
Telephone # _____
FAX # _____
Date _____

Store Planner _____
Address _____
City, State, ZIP _____
Telephone # _____
Fax # _____
Sheet _____ of _____

Project # _____

Photograph/Drawing:	Reference No.
	Manufacturer:
	Address:
	City, State, ZIP:
	Contact:
	Telephone:
	Planter Style and #:
	Finish:
Place Picture of Planter Here	Quantity:
	Price/F.O.B. Job Site:
	Tag for Department:
	Date to Be at Store:
	Remarks:
	Manufacturer:
	Address:
	City, State, ZIP:
	Contact:
	Telephone:
	Planter Style and #:
	Finish:
Place Picture of Planter Here	Quantity:
	Price/F.O.B. Job Site:
	Tag for Department:
	Date to Be at Store:
	Remarks:

FIXTURE SPECIFICATION

FIXTURE___Mannequin___

Store Name/# _____
Address _____
City, State, ZIP _____
Telephone # _____
FAX # _____
Date _____

Store Planner _____
Address _____
City, State, ZIP _____
Telephone # _____
Fax # _____
Sheet _____ of _____

Project # _____

Photograph/Drawing:	Reference No.
	Manufacturer:
	Address:
	City, State, ZIP:
	Contact:
	Telephone:
Place Picture of Mannequin Here	Mannequin Style and #:
	Finish:
	Quantity:
	Price/F.O.B. Job Site:
	Tag for Department:
	Date to Be at Store:
	Remarks:
	Manufacturer:
	Address:
	City, State, ZIP:
	Contact:
	Telephone:
	Mannequin Style and #:
Place Picture of Mannequin Here	Finish:
	Quantity:
	Price/F.O.B. Job Site:
	Tag for Department:
	Date to Be at Store:
	Remarks:

Chapter 27

STORE RENOVATIONS

Why Remodel?

Retailing, like most industries, is in a continuous state of flux. The high cost of new construction is forcing retail companies of all sizes to remodel older stores. Owners of obsolete buildings are finding ways to convert them to profitable space. Many local and national chains that recognize the need to update their facilities periodically have initiated long-range programs to do so every few years.

Merchants are always on the lookout for other more modest ways to economize, such as converting nonproductive areas like stockrooms to additional selling space and eliminating or reducing the size of the least profitable departments.

Merchants want to feel that remodeling will achieve the best possible return on investment. The whole purpose is to improve profitability by increasing sales per square foot and doing it at the lowest possible figure without compromising appearance and image. Another purpose is to maintain the existing sales base while attracting new customers.

Retailers and store planners strive to project the actual costs of modernization, but there are so many variables, including store types, store sizes, and the diversity of store conditions, that it is difficult to accurately pinpoint final costs.

Types of Remodeling

In making the concerted effort required to remodel a store, existing conditions first need to be surveyed and analyzed, the scope of work clearly established, and all limitations clearly identified. The implications of each of these factors will impact on the total estimated cost.

There are three basic types of remodeling:

1. Cosmetic remodeling
2. Minor remodeling
3. Major remodeling

Cosmetic remodeling involves paint, carpeting, and other decorative accents to give the interior a fresh appearance. *Minor remodeling* may include removing or adding walls to accommodate new departmental merchandise and eliminating or expanding departments on a single floor or in a portion of the store. It is a minor remodeling, for example, when a percentage of equipment is replaced or when wall construction, lighting, painting, flooring, and fixturing are affected by budget and scope of work. *Major remodeling* involves reconfiguration of walled departments and reclassification of adjacencies and new store equipment and decor.

In all three categories of remodeling, the planner must work within a predetermined range of costs, based on the type of store (e.g., specialty, discount, budget, and department). The extent of renovation can vary substantially with the type of store, the image desired, and the servicing required. A substantial portion of capital expenses will go to construction, decor, and fixtures.

Stores that cater to fashion and home environment markets—also specialty department stores—tend to update often. Other stores usually remodel as needs dictate.

This question always arises in the redesigning of a store: What is included in the way of construction and decor? Separate budgets must be calculated to establish bottom-line figures for the finished project: one for construction and one for decor and fixturing.

It is difficult to remodel any store without making lease-hold improvements to the building or property. Existing leases, landlord obligations, and tax credits or allowances are all considerations in any remodeling project. The planner must evaluate the scope of work and budget to assure that a sound return on investment is likely and that the most efficient cost-saving measures are applied in the selection of materials and usage of materials.

Handicap requirement must be reviewed and updated.

Supportive Systems

At the outset of the remodeling, conditions of all supportive systems must be examined, including ceilings, aisle materials, carpets, walls, supportive wall-merchandising systems, freestanding fixtures, and lighting. Each supportive system designed to induce impulse purchases, of course, has an average lifetime. Any additional years of service that exceed the manufacturer's claims are, in effect, cost savings.

In planning a store remodeling, these are typical questions that arise:

1. Will ceiling and perimeter lighting require adjustment?
2. Will new ceiling pads be necessary?
3. How many existing walls with supportive hard-ware will be reused?
4. Will aisles change?
5. What areas will require new carpeting, decor, fixturing?
6. Which fixtures will be reused?
7. Will existing hardware be reused, or must a new system be introduced?
8. What is reworkable and nonreworkable, given the new scope of work?
9. What, if any, fixtures will the owner purchase directly?
10. Will renovation take place during shopping periods?
11. What work will the landlord undertake?
12. What work will the general contractor assume?
13. What work will be performed by the perimeter and decor contractors?
14. What work will be performed by in-house personnel?
15. For what work will an outside store planner/consultant be responsible?

Boosting Sales

The relocation of departments, the square footages assigned, and the adjacency plan all play key roles in whether the sales-and-profit picture is improved by the changes, just as eliminating an unproductive sales department can spark a new or expanded department to produce a greater sales volume.

In many cases, when a building that houses merchandise of one type and quality level is vacated, a new merchant comes along who recognizes demands for a new type, price range, or image. In essence, many stores abandon an unprofitable operation only to find later that someone else has developed a new concept more in tune with what the customers now are looking for, including merchandise.

In remodeling a store, it is essential to be able to answer the following question in a convincing and precise manner: When, where, and how will the remodeling increase sales, profits, and return on investment? Keep in mind that within ten years, the design and merchandising presentation may well take on an obsolete look. The overriding reason for remodeling is to boost sales—by reallocating space, expanding and shrinking departments as needed, and making fruitful cosmetic changes.

Competition has a way of monitoring retail stores within a given trading area to determine how much impact remodeling actually has influenced sales.

Some merchants are willing to neglect the appearance of their stores and put off remodeling in hopes that their customers will remain loyal. The smart merchant regularly evaluates overall physical conditions, inside and out, makes changes when the timing is right, and improves support systems to spur and attract new customers.

Store planners need to assist merchants in determining their needs and in developing concepts that help generate new traffic and improve the appearance of the store. Stores should be attractively designed to enhance merchandise, yet the customers should not be left feeling that they are paying the overhead for an excessively decorated store.

The extent of remodeling will depend largely on the ability of store planners to ingeniously stretch the available budget dollars while not compromising too greatly on quality and appearance. Even though remodeling can be expensive, there is no fail-safe way to guarantee a sales increase. Merchants should help guide store planners by stressing the marketing of merchandise, rather than store design.

In remodeling large stores with single or multiple levels, the work may be performed in stages. If all phases are well coordinated, the retail facility should be able to enjoy a smooth transition with no interruption in business.

Chapter 28

CONTRACTOR PREQUALIFICATIONS

Before plans, elevations, and details are completed, planners and clients must concern themselves with the qualifications of the general and fixture contractors who will be bidding on the project.

Usually, clients will have the names of contracting companies with whom they have had prior experience or that have been recommended to them, but they will still want the planner to suggest names of contractors whom the planner feels are qualified.

Planners should allow enough time to become well acquainted with the work of all contractors in the bidding. Fixture contractors are specialists whose operations can vary widely in terms of task capabilities, quality, and manpower, factors that must be carefully weighed against the scope and budget of the project. Planners should look at the credentials of each bidding contractor closely.

Many contractors restrict themselves to certain types of work in which they specialize. Contractors generally fall into one of these categories:

1. General Contractors
2. Design/Build Contractors
3. Perimeter/Freestanding Fixtures Contractors

4. Drop-Shipped Perimeter-Decor General Contractor

Prequalifying Contractors

Answers to the following queries will be valuable to store planners when reporting to clients on the credentials of contractors:

1. What is the quality of their employee supervision?
2. What types of retail establishments do they seem to serve well or serve poorly?
3. What are their areas of specialization?
4. Are they fully knowledgeable about store fixturing?
5. What special capabilities does the company have?
6. Does their management seem to communicate well with subordinates at all levels?
7. How many employees do they have?
8. What is the background and experience of the field supervisors?
9. Is their shop flexible enough to handle phases

that are taken out of sequence and delivery dates that are earlier than originally ordered?

10. Is their production process smooth?
11. Do they have sufficient quality-control checkpoints?
12. What is the square footage of their production space?
13. What geographical area do they adequately serve?
14. What projects have they completed recently?
15. How satisfactory were these projects to their owners?
16. What jobs best represent their finished product?
17. What are their procedures for estimating the time required for processing?
18. Is their estimating department competent to handle the size of the client's job?
19. What can be learned about the contractor's integrity?
20. Do they have a good reputation for competence among their peers?
21. Do they communicate understandably with planners?
22. Are they flexible in handling change orders over the phone?
23. How is the morale of the company?
24. Are their shop employees capable of quality craftsmanship?
25. Are their wage scales competitive?
26. Are they a union or nonunion shop?
27. Do they have upcoming contracts that could overtax their capacity if they were to be awarded the project?
28. Are their plant operations geared to high productivity?
29. Are employee grievances handled promptly so as not to interfere with productivity?
30. How well do they ship, handle, box, blanket wrap, preassemble, and assemble the finished product?
31. Are their finished products delivered and installed to the specifications of their customers/ planner?
32. Are electrified store fixtures fully inspected prior to use by the customer?
33. Are fixture damages noted and clearly explained on shipping orders?
34. Do they have frequent callbacks for repair or service to equipment?
35. Are callbacks treated promptly?
36. Are customer claims of unsatisfactory performance settled promptly and fairly?
37. What guaranties, bonds, warranties, and other security do they offer?

Trade Cooperation

All contractors should be encouraged to work together so all project phases are completed in harmony. Each "trade" should do its best to coordinate its phase (or phases) with the others so extra labor is not required. All work must be coordinated with the design schedule under the direction of jobsite supervisors or the general contractor.

Contractors are responsible for paying for damages caused by their crew prior to the punchlist inspection and for the protection of the work previously completed at the site by other contractors.

Remember: Owners have the right to award separate contracts for work or materials not covered in the terms of the basic contract. Such outside purchases might be for customized store equipment or carpeting, for example.

Contractor's Insurance

Owners sometimes require contractors to carry special insurance coverage, the specifics of which must be spelled out clearly to the contractors by the owners. If no existing form is available for collecting the relevant information, answers to these questions will help:

1. What are the contractors' liabilities while the building is being renovated or constructed?
2. Will contractors be responsible for obtaining their own required coverage, or will the contractors be added or additionally named insureds to existing policies held by the owner?
3. Should the general contractor be responsible for providing extended coverage to subcontractors? on job-site equipment? on completed work while other work continues?
4. If public liability insurance is required of the contractor, what provisions should be included?
5. What should the limits of coverage be in terms of dollar (or face) value?
6. What should the limits of bodily injury coverage be?
7. What period should "completed operation" insurance cover? (Length of project)

8. If vehicles are to be used, exactly what type of bodily injury and property damage coverage should be required?

9. What workers' compensation insurance is called for to meet requirements of the state(s) in which the project(s) is sited?

10. How much time should be allowed for contractors to submit proof of insurance to the owner?

11. What provisions for indemnification are required by state law for out-of-state projects? by the owner?

12. Is an early completion date so critical that a greater chance of property damage and personal injury exists?

13. Can the cost of the additional coverage necessarily be justified by the risk potential?

14. Do the contractors and landlord have excess insurance coverage (additional coverage beyond the limits of the primary policy)?

15. How will the owner be notified if insurance is dropped for premium nonpayment or if a carrier is substituted?

Chapter 29

INVITATION-TO-BID GUIDELINES

The Cover Letter

A document known as the *Invitation to Bid* and the general guidelines attached inform contractors of the contract provisions that must be honored if the contractor is to qualify. Before bid requirements are discussed, it is important to examine the contents of the covering letter mailed with the Invitation to Bid. The letter should include the following:

1. The full name of the project
2. The address and location of the installation
3. The square footage of the project
4. The scope of work required
5. The name of the planner who prepared the bid documents
6. The telephone numbers and addresses of those to reach should questions arise
7. Bid date
8. The time and place where bids are to be sent
9. The projected starting and completion dates of the project

The Bid Document

Now, to the bid document itself. The Invitation to Bid, among other things, reminds contractors that the bid must include the estimated costs for materials, labor, and services necessary to successfully execute all portions of the project covered by the bid. The bid invitation also states the rules regarding opening, reviewing, and awarding of bids; all responsibilities the owner wishes to assume; plus a thorough explanation of all schedules and timeframes within which contractors are expected to work.

An enclosed *decor* (or *fixture*) *agreement* states the dates of the agreement between clients and subcontractors; gives anticipated completion dates; and covers allowances, contingencies, permits, taxes, and fees directly related to fixtures and decor.

Typical Provisions

The following is a list of typical provisions found in the more common type bid documents and contracts. Those provisions pertaining to work arrangements may include statements such as:

1. Overtime must be authorized by owner.
2. An accounting of hours worked must be submitted by the contractor as part of the standard documentation required.
3. Authorizations for excess costs due to unforeseen field conditions or overtime require a separate payment agreement. (Such unforeseen delays can be due to strikes, vandalism, natural catastrophes, etc.)
4. Requests for extensions of deadlines should be made by the contractor in writing.
5. Clients are expected to grant contractors additional "workdays lost" when there is sufficient cause.
6. Before payments are dispersed to contractors, clients should ask the planner to compare the status of work to the payment schedule.
7. It is the contractor's responsibility to itemize all services performed.
8. Ten percent of all remaining jobs should be held up until the planner has completed an inspection of the punchlist and is satisfied that the itemized schedule conforms to the work actually performed.

Examples of statements that may be included relative to provisions that pertain to the quality of materials and workmanship are:

1. Warranties should promise that the finished products will be up to industry standards, will perform in the manner intended, and will be free of defects.
2. Contractors should be held responsible for correcting failures, without cost to the client, for the period of one year.
3. Contractors should be obligated to furnish fixtures and do all installation work in accordance with the drawings.
4. Contractors are expected to recognize and correct problems within the labor force that could affect the quality of materials and workmanship.

Miscellaneous provisions that may be appropriate to cover in the list of agreements exchanged are:

1. The client has the right to inspect the manufacturing facility where fixtures are being made and the amount of work completed when the percentage of work shown on invoices as completed appears to be higher than the actual work performed.
2. Terms regarding defaults, arbitration procedures, and work termination should be clearly spelled out.
3. The contractor must list all subcontractors and subtrades to be retained.
4. In accordance with local and state laws, the contractor must provide for workers' compensation, employers' liability, and public liability insurance for property damage or bodily injury, with amounts of coverage stated. Additional coverages, such as those for vandalism, water damage, and fire, should also be included.
5. The owner may request a performance bond that is equal to the sum contracted.
6. When the contractor is an independent agent and not an agent of the owner, the fact should be stated.
7. The signed contract cannot be transferred or restructured and must comply with all applicable laws and codes.
8. Notarized lien waivers are to be provided to the owner for each payment received.

When all of the stated provisions have been carefully reviewed and approved, the signatures of the owners and contractors (verified by witnesses) are required in order to initiate the contract.

(CAVEAT: None of the information in this "Invitation-to-Bid Guidelines" section should be construed as professional legal advice or to replace such counsel. The statements are offered merely as general lay guidelines for the preparation of bid document and contracts. Laws governing these matters vary from state to state and municipality to municipality. Consult attorneys in these matters as necessary.)

Sample Forms

Invitation to Bid and Proposal Forms

Date

Company Name

Address

City, State, ZIP

Dear Contractors:

You are hereby invited to bid on one or more contracts for the following project:

_____(Store Name)_____

_____(Location)_____

Bids will be accepted for these contracts:

1. **General Construction** consists of demolition and removal, new drywall, metal studs, ceiling, wallcovering, field painting, perimeter casework, decor, signage, and items specified in the bidding documents and on proposal form "GC."
2. **Freestanding Fixture** consists of removal or modification of existing fixtures, furnishing and installation of new freestanding fixtures, and associated items as specified in the bidding documents and on proposal form "FSF."
3. **Floorcovering** consists of removal and replacement of floorcovering and base, including carpet, tile, resilient and/or wood flooring, carpet case, vinyl base, and all preparation as specified in the bidding documents and on proposal form "FC."

Enclosed are bid documents for the aforementioned project.

The project manual of standard drawings, details, formats, proposals, and titles consists of:

Cover sheet
Perspectives
Demolition of existing wall plan
Merchandising plan
Fixture-finish schedule and color key plan
New high-wall key plan
Existing electrical ceiling plan
New electrical ceiling plan
New floorcovering/Power-and-signal plan
Perimeter strip elevations
Fitting room details
Stockroom shelving plan
Specifications and general notes
Cover letter and Invitation to Bid
List of qualified bidders
Color and materials list/sources
General contractor proposal form
Legend of store fixture
Index of merchandising sections
Merchandising sections

Decor sections and typical details
Freestanding fixtures

Please use the above list to verify the contents of the bid package. Please contact the planners if additional copies are needed. The contractor will be held responsible for notifying the planner of any discrepancies and/or omissions of the bid documents. The documents, including this letter, are to become part of the bid proposal.

Please provide a separate cost (including taxes, delivery, and installation) for each section of proposal forms enclosed. All bidders will be notified of any addendum or modifications as per owner's request. Bids are due in the following office on:

Date _____ Time _____

To the Attention of _____(Store Planner)_____

Address _____City _____ State _____ ZIP _____

FAX number _____

_____(Client's name)_____

_____(Project name)_____

Please mark the outside of envelopes with bidder's name and words "Interior Renovation." Telephone bids are acceptable on (Date) _____ (Time) _____ only, with a confirming telegram and written proposal in the office of (Store Planner's Name) no later than _____(Date)_____ _____(Time)_____.

NOTE: Discrepancies between telephone bids and written bids will result in disqualification. Any bids received after the date and time specified may be disqualified.

The private opening of bids will be conducted by _____(Store Planner's Name)_____. Bids will be reviewed by _____(Store Planner's Name)_____ and store owner and will be awarded the week of _____(Date)_____. The owner is not obligated to accept the lowest bid and reserves the right to reject any and all bids. Field work for said project will commence immediately following the bid award, the week of _____(Date)_____, with completion date set for _____(Date)_____. All contractors will be notified of any change in schedule.

Proposal Forms—Two copies of the appropriate proposal form shall be submitted with each bid. All items of information should be provided (alternates, separate prices, unit prices, etc.). Forms shall be submitted in sealed envelopes, marked in accordance with the instructions to the bidder.

Bid Security—All bidders shall submit bid security, in the form of a certified check or bid bond, in the amount of 10 percent of the total bid.*

Performance Bond—Successful bidders will be required to obtain a performance bond and labor and material payment bond in the amount of 100 percent of the contract amount.

On-site Inspection—All bidders are required to attend a prebid on-site inspection at a time determined by the owner. The owner has the right to waive the prebid inspection.

Any questions regarding the project should be referred to the job captain _____(Name)_____ _____(Planning Firm)_____.

*Note: This step may not always be required.

Telephone ( )_____FAX ( )_____, Monday through Friday

between _____A.M. and _____P.M.

Sincerely,

_____ (Store Planner's Name) _____

Proposal Form "GC" (General Contract)

TO: _____ FOR: _____

SUBMITTED BY:

_____DATE_____19_____

NAME OF BIDDER

_____

ADDRESS/PHONE/FAX

We, the undersigned BIDDER, having familiarized ourselves with the site, the local conditions affecting the cost of the Project, and the Bidding and Contract Documents, including Addendum Nos. _____, for the construction of the above referenced Project as prepared by the firm of _____ (Store Planning Firm)_____ _____(City)_____(State)_____, do hereby propose to provide and furnish all labor, materials, tools, equipment, utility and transportation serves, scaffolding, insurance, supervision, and all other services and facilities necessary, as required by said Contract Documents, to complete all work as hereinafter designated, for the sum of money enumerated, the said amount, constituting the Base Bid.

The following Contract Documents constitute the basis of our proposal for the work:

    DRAWINGS: SHEET NOS.: _____(Insert appropriate sheet nos.)

    Project Manual, Dated _____ for

_____ (Store Planning Firm) _____

    Project No._____

BID SECURITY: Enclosed with this Bid is Bid Security in the amount of 10 percent of the Base Bid in accordance with the requirements of the Instructions to Bidders if requested by OWNER.

COMPLETION TIME: If awarded the Contract, the undersigned agrees to complete all work within _____ consecutive working days from the date of notice to proceed.

BASE BID: All prices quoted represent the entire cost of the project in accordance with the bidding documents, and we acknowledge that no subsequent claim will be honored for any increase in wage scales, material prices, cost, or any other rates affecting the construction industry and/or this project.

The undersigned agrees to perform all work set forth in the bidding documents for the sum of:

_____ DOLLARS ($_____)

ALTERNATE PRICES:

If the OWNER elects to delete portions of the work or to perform with his own forces or under separate contracts with others, the following amounts can be deducted from our Base Bid:

ALTERNATE GC-1

For detailing all field-applied vinyl wallcovering and all field painting, deduct from the Base Bid the sum of:

_____ DOLLARS ($ _____)

ALTERNATE GC-2

For deleting all ³⁄₈-inch thick glass shelves on perimeter walls, deduct from the Base Bid the sum of:

_____ DOLLARS ($ _____)

ALTERNATE GC-3

For deleting all perimeter casework, as itemized in Division 700 of the "Legend of Store Fixtures," deduct from the Base Bid the sum of:

_____ DOLLARS ($ _____)

ALTERNATE GC-4

For deleting all perimeter cornice, decor, and millwork, deduct from the Base Bid the sum of:

_____ DOLLARS ($ _____)

ALTERNATE GC-5

For deleting the perimeter signage package, deduct from the Base Bid the sum of:

_____ DOLLARS ($ _____)

ALTERNATE GC-6

For deleting fitting rooms, deduct from the Base Bid the sum of:

_____ DOLLARS ($ _____)

ALTERNATE GC-7

For deleting all new showcase, fills, delivery, and installation, deduct from the Base Bid the sum of:

_____ DOLLARS ($ _____)

In submitting this proposal, it is hereby understood that the OWNER reserves the unrestricted privilege of rejecting any or all Bids, or parts of Bids, and to waive any informalities in Bidding. It is also understood that if the OWNER elects to delete any alternate Bid, it is the successful BIDDER's responsibility to supply take off and quantity.

It is agreed that this proposal shall be irrevocable for a period of sixty (60) days after the specified date for receiving Bids.

FIRM NAME _____

BY _____

TITLE _____

DATE _____

State whether a:

Corporation	( )
Partnership	( )
Sole Proprietorship	( )
Limited Liability Company	( )

_____
                    Witness

DATE _____

OFFICIAL ADDRESS

_____

_____

_____

Telephone Number _____

FAX _____

Proposal Form "FC" (Floorcovering Contract)

TO: _____ FOR: _____

SUBMITTED BY:

_____DATE_____19_____

NAME OF BIDDER

_____

ADDRESS/PHONE/FAX

We, the undersigned BIDDER, having familiarized ourselves with the site, the local conditions affecting the cost of the Project, and the Bidding and Contract Documents, including Addendum Nos. _____, for the construction of the above referenced Project as prepared by the firm of _____(Store Planning Firm)_____ _____(City)_____ (State)_____, do hereby propose to provide and furnish all labor, materials, tools, equipment, utility and transportation serves, scaffolding, insurance, supervision, and all other services and facilities necessary, as required by said Contract Documents, to complete all work as hereinafter designated, for the sum of money enumerated, the said amount, constituting the Base Bid.

The following Contract Documents constitute the basis of our proposal for the work:

DRAWINGS: SHEET NOS.: _____(Insert appropriate sheet nos.)

Project Manual, Dated _____ for

_____(Store Planning Firm)_____

Project No._____

BID SECURITY: Enclosed with this Bid is Bid Security in the amount of ten percent (10%) of the Base Bid in accordance with the requirements of the Instruction to Bidders if requested by OWNER.

COMPLETION TIME: If awarded the Contract, the undersigned agrees to complete all work within _____ consecutive working days from the date of notice to proceed.

BASE BID: All prices quoted represent the entire cost of the project in accordance with the bidding documents, and we acknowledge that no subsequent claim will be honored for any increase in wage scales, material prices, cost, or any other rates affecting the construction industry and/or this project.

The undersigned agrees to perform all work set forth in the bidding documents for the sum of:

_____ DOLLARS ($ _____)

ALTERNATE PRICES:

The following alternates, unit prices, and quantities form the basis of our Base Bid. If the OWNER elects to delete certain floorcoverings, the following amounts may be deleted from our Base Bid:

ALTERNATE FC-1

The unit price for removing and legally disposing of existing carpeting, as shown on plans, is $ per square yard, based on   sq. yds. for a total cost of $.

ALTERNATE FC-2

The unit price for removing and legally disposing of existing carpeting, as shown on plans, is $ per square yard, based on   sq. yds. for a total cost of $.

ALTERNATE FC-3

The unit prices for storing, delivering, and installing new carpet base (to be purchased directly by the OWNER) are as follows for various types of carpet:

CARPET TYPE	QUANTITY (sq. yds.) (Including 10% excess)	COST/ SQ. YD.	TOTAL COST
A. C-1	sq. yds. $		$
B. C-2	sq. yds. $		$
C. C-3	sq. yds. $		$
D. C-4	sq. yds. $		$
E. C-5	sq. yds. $		$

Total cost of new carpeting installation $_____

All material costs are included in the above except for the cost of carpet material itself.

ALTERNATE FC-4

The following quantities of various types of flooring materials form the basis of our proposal. All quantities include 10 percent excess for waste, plus two unopened cartons (or 5 percent excess area) for OWNER's maintenance purposes:

TYPE OF FLOORING	QUANTITY (sq. ft.)	COST/SQ. FT.	TOTAL COST
Wood Parquet	sq. ft.	$	$
Vinyl Composition Tile	sq. ft.	$	$
Marble Tile	sq. ft.	$	$
Quarry Tile	sq. ft.	$	$

Ceramic Tile _____ sq. ft. $ _____ $ _____

Terrazzo _____ sq. ft. $ _____ $ _____

Total cost of new flooring installation $ _____

In submitting this proposal, it is hereby understood that the OWNER reserves the unrestricted privilege of rejecting any or all Bids, or parts of Bids, and to waive any informalities in Bidding.

It is agreed that this proposal shall be irrevocable for a period of sixty (60) days after the specified date for receiving Bids.

FIRM NAME _____

BY _____

TITLE _____

DATE _____

State whether a:

Corporation   ( )

Partnership   ( )

Sole Proprietorship   ( )

Limited Liability Company   ( )

_____
Witness

DATE _____

OFFICIAL ADDRESS

_____

_____

_____

Telephone Number _____

FAX _____

Proposal Form "FSF" (Freestanding Fixture Contract)

TO: _____   FOR: _____

SUBMITTED BY:

_____ DATE _____ 19 _____

NAME OF BIDDER

_____

ADDRESS/PHONE/FAX

We, the undersigned BIDDER, having familiarized ourselves with the site, the local conditions affecting the cost of the Project, and the Bidding and Contract Documents, including Addendum Nos. _____, for the construction of the above referenced Project as prepared by the firm of _____ (Store Planning Firm) _____ (City) _____ (State) _____, do hereby propose to provide and furnish all labor, materials, tools, equipment, utility and transportation serves, scaffolding, insurance, supervision, and all other services and facilities necessary, as required by said Contract Documents, to complete all work as hereinafter designated, for the sum of money enumerated, the said amount, constituting the Base Bid.

The following Contract Documents constitute the basis of our proposal for the work:

DRAWINGS: SHEET NOS.: _____(Insert appropriate sheet nos.)

Project Manual, Dated _____ for

_____ (Store Planning Firm) _____

Project No._____

BID SECURITY: Enclosed with this Bid is Bid Security in the amount of ten percent (10%) of the Base Bid in accordance with the requirements of the instructions to Bidders.

COMPLETION TIME: If awarded the Contract, the undersigned agrees to complete all work within _____consecutive working days from the date of notice to proceed.

UNIT PRICES: We have submitted all unit prices itemized on the separate freestanding fixture list.

Our hourly rate for unloading, unpacking, assembling, and setting up OWNER-furnished merchandising units is $_____ per hour per man.

In submitting this proposal, it is hereby understood that the OWNER reserves the unrestricted privilege of rejecting any or all Bids, or parts of Bids, and to waive any information in Bidding.

It is agreed that this proposal shall be irrevocable for a period of sixty (60) days after the specified date for receiving Bids.

FIRM NAME _____

BY _____

TITLE _____

DATE _____

State whether a:

Corporation ( )

Partnership ( )

Sole Proprietorship ( )

Limited Liability Company ( )

_____
                Witness

DATE _____

OFFICIAL ADDRESS

_____

_____

_____

Telephone Number _____

FAX _____

Chapter 30

SHOP DRAWINGS: KEY TO QUALITY CONSTRUCTION

Once contracts for perimeter and freestanding fixture construction have been awarded, the successful bidders must produce shop drawings for approval by the planner's office before construction can begin. In the process, the planner must be satisfied that all fixture designs are appropriate for the uses to which they will be put.

Each drawing must be examined and reexamined by the fixture contractor's job captain or checker and again reviewed very carefully by the planner's job captain or checker.

If a drawing is to be complete, it must indicate exact measurements and note all types of board finishes, trims, hardware, fittings, and accessories required.

All changes made in the design and construction must be shown. If a checker at a store-planning firm insists on unusual production or engineering methods, the fixture contractor should be expected to alert the principal planner when additional costs will be incurred or as to how money can be saved. There are times when checkers call for unnecessary changes in construction. Revisions requested by planners must be accompanied by detailed notes, dated and

initialed, that indicate the exact construction methods desired. Planners must make a habit of returning corrected and approved drawings to the fixture manufacturer immediately after approval so late deliveries can be prevented.

Proper Identification

Aside from showing clearly how designs are to be implemented, drawings should show a number of items of identification. These include the customer's name, store number, store address, planner's name, fixture job number, date, name of the person making the drawing, the number of pages in sequence, delivery dates, and the initials of the checkers. The numbers on drawings must correspond with the work order numbers.

Each drawing has an assigned job number, whether for a single fixture or an assembly of fixtures. When more than one drawing is necessary to show fabrication techniques and assembly instructions, each drawing must display the same job number, but with a dash and second number added to note each drawing's place in the sequence. When changes in details are made, revision numbers are shown in the triangle found in the title block. The same triangle and number must appear at the point on the drawing where the detail has been changed. Changes and new entries on such sequential drawings should be indicated on the first sheet.

Dimensions and Measurements

The detail dimensions should tell the exact measurements and sizes of each piece of material used. All measurements must correspond with the plan, elevations, and sections of the fixture. It is also important to include full dimensions of any accessories that will be applied to the fixtures. When mistakes are found, obviously the dimensions must be refigured.

There is no need for duplication of measurements or other data on the same plan, section, or detail. Mistaken calculations cost money in time when extra checking and redrafting are required. Most shop drawings are dimensioned in numerical and fractional measurements, including those for tolerances.

The locations of glue, screw holes, and applications of metal and plastic are indicated. Dimensions under 100 inches should be described in inches; those greater than 100 inches should be shown in feet and inches. Uniform procedures prevent confusion.

Cross Sections

Small isometric scale drawings in the upper right- or left-hand corner can give an overview that shows shapes and sizes of fixtures and front, rear, and side elevations. Such drawings have scaled cross sections, for both plans and elevations, to show the types of construction in profile.

Sometimes the scale of cross sections will differ: either half-scale/full size or quarter-scale/full size, for instance. Symbols representing plywood, solid wood, glass, metal, and laminates are indicated only at joints. It is not necessary to carry cross-hatching throughout the drawing.

Electrified Fixtures

When fixtures are electrified, drawings should show the type, location, and usage of each fixture; electrical concealment and hookup instructions; and the precise requirements for plugs, pigtail connections, and lengths of cord (check local codes). Each electrical fixture should be listed by type, metal finish, lamp color, and ballast type (ballasts can either be of the self-contained or remote type). All necessary accessories, such as wire molds, switches, and cover plates, should be covered as well. The drawings should provide the fixture manufacturer with a cutting or billing list that gives the type and sizes of all materials, noting any conditions that will make extra lead time necessary.

Hardware Specifics

All items to be manufactured by a metal shop that are not buyouts (bought outside) will require working drawings. Such drawings should show the direction of the grain (usually the full length, unless otherwise specified by the planner) and give the width of extension-drawer slides (detailing of slides can be omitted), and the exact size of all sliding-door hardware. If the hardware specifications are changed, for reasons such as unavailability or change in style or measurement, the measurements must match those of the new hardware.

If the planner approves, buyers should try to use slides, tracks, pulls, and other hardware items that are commonly available. It is important to list and show all of the types of hardware planned since items such as rails, sliding door accessories, and tracks provide the working (mechanical) functions of the system.

All doors selected should be warp-proof. The material type and application should be given for sliding doors. If high-pressure laminate is affixed to the exterior of the door, the same laminate (called a "balance sheet") must be applied to the opposite (inside) surface.

Drawers must be durable enough to last as long as the fixture. The sides, backs, and fronts of drawers must be a minimum of $1/2$" to $5/8$" in width. Drawer bottoms usually are $1/4$" or $3/8$" thick to prevent sagging. Most drawers are four-sided boxes. The drawer fronts must be designed to exactly fit the inside drawer opening.

The Comprehensive Work Order

These items of information should be included if the work order is to be a document that fully serves its function:

Company Name
Company Address
City, State, Zip Code

Telephone Number—Office
Telephone Number—Manufacturing
FAX Numbers
Date Order Received
Customer Order Number
Planner's Name and Job Number
Delivery Date Requested
Bank Order (or Projected Delivery Date)
Date of Invoicing
Address for Billing Purposes
Shipping Address
Attention to (name and title; company name; city, state, zip code, telephone number)
Name of Company Sold to
Attention to (field supervisor's name)
Ship to (complete address)
Date Shipped
Number of Units Shipped (cartons, crates, etc.)
Gross Weight
Shipping (Waybill) Number
Terms of Shipment (prepaid, freight, collect)
How Items Will Be Shipped (in-house carrier, common carrier, etc.)
Buyer's Name
Salesperson's Name
Customer's Name
Detailed Description of Merchandise

Quantity Ordered
Quantity Shipped
Part (or Unit) Number
Unit Price
Quantity Back-ordered to Be Shipped
Dollar Volume of Shipment

Note: Upon receipt of a shipment at the destination, any damage noted should immediately be recorded on the work order (or shipping order), together with the authorization number for returning merchandise for reworking, the terms of returns, the amount of all handling charges, required general terms, and any service charges incurred.

Shop Drawings/Illustrations

A store planner must be familiar with all the typical joints that are used in building store fixtures. The knowledge of assembly is important in helping to control the cost of the fixture. There are 29 examples of illustrated store fixtures that indicate how the fixtures are assembled. Each contractor may build the fixture differently, depending on the equipment used to mill and fabricate the finished fixture. However, the overall appearance and strength of the fixture should be the same.

TYPICAL WOOD JOINTS

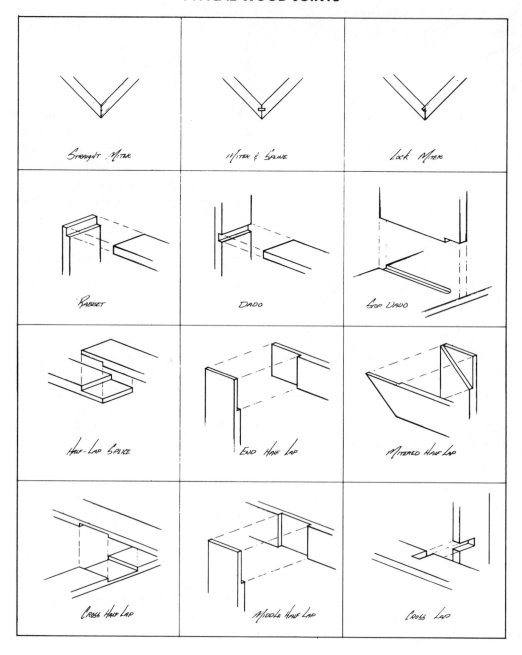

TYPICAL DRAWER

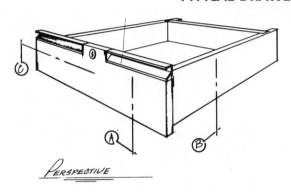

Perspective

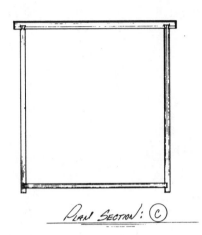

Plan Section: Ⓒ

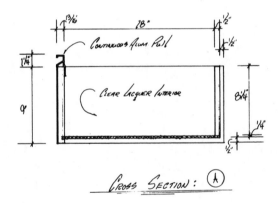

Cross Section: Ⓐ

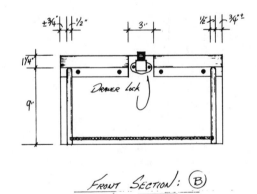

Front Section: Ⓑ

TYPICAL CORNICE

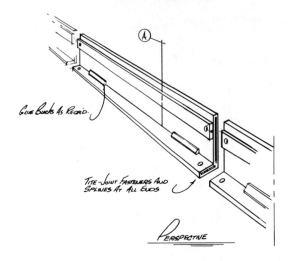

Glue Bucks As Reqrd.

Tite-Joint Fasteners And
Splines At All Ends

Perspective

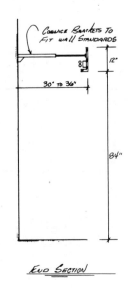

Cornice Brackets To
Fit Wall Standards

12"

30" to 36"

84"

End Section

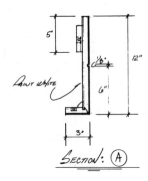

5"

½"⌀

12"

Paint White

6"

3"

Section: (A)

PERIMETER PLATFORM

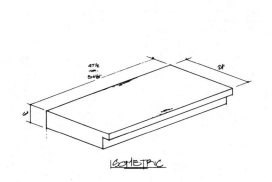

ISOMETRIC

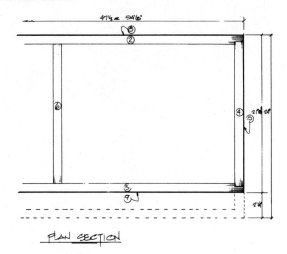

PLAN SECTION

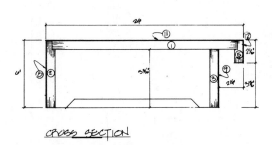

CROSS SECTION

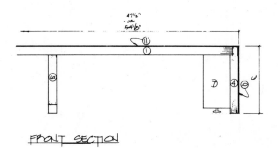

FRONT SECTION

PERIMETER DRAWERED BASE

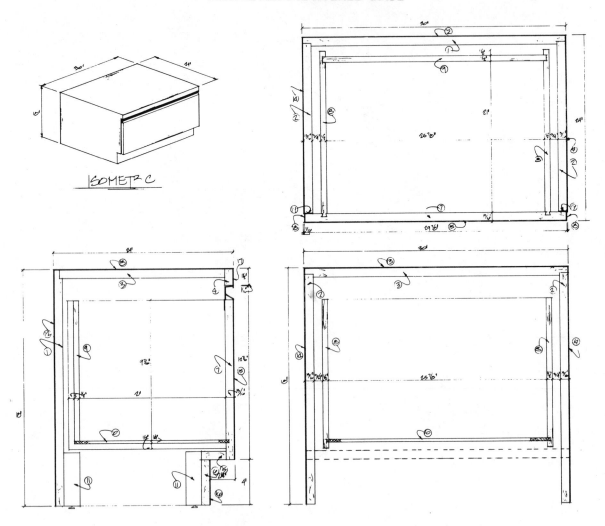

ISOMETRIC

PERIMETER BASE

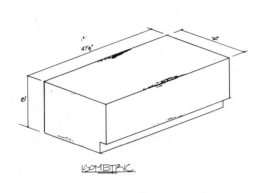

ISOMETRIC

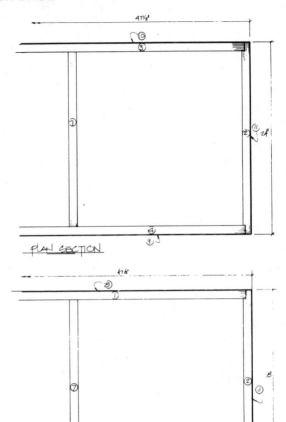

PLAN SECTION

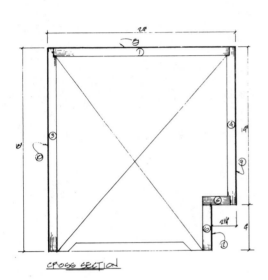

CROSS SECTION

FRONT SECTION

BASE FOR GLASS CUBES

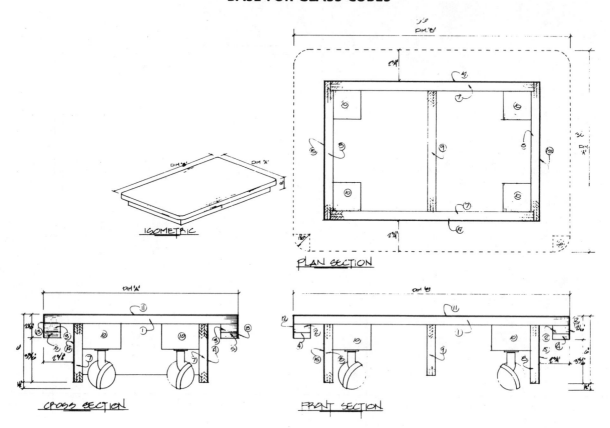

ISOMETRIC

PLAN SECTION

CROSS SECTION

FRONT SECTION

OPEN BASE

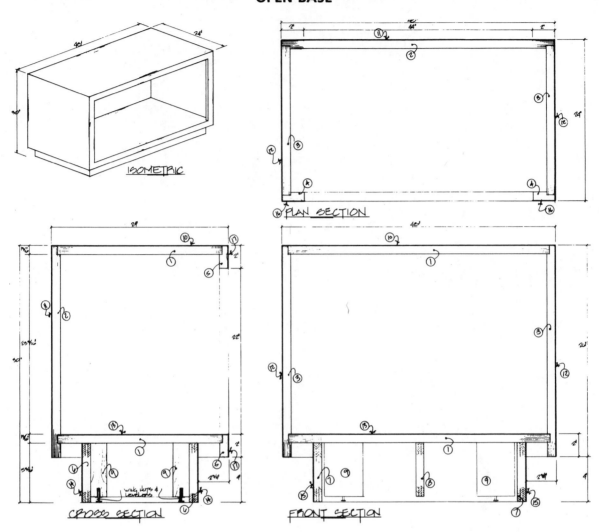

ISOMETRIC

PLAN SECTION

CROSS SECTION

FRONT SECTION

HEXAGONAL DISPLAY BASE

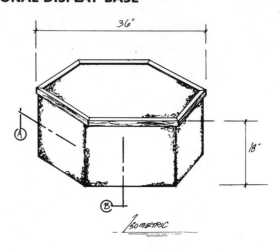

36"

18"

A

B

Isometric

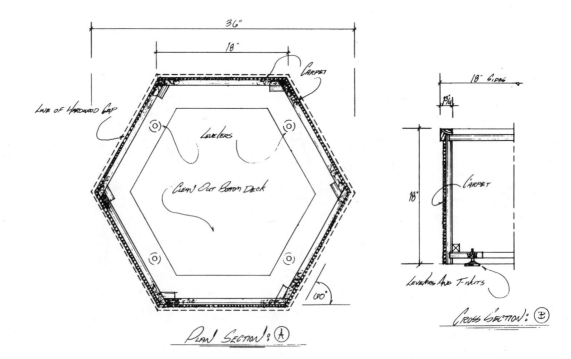

36"

18"

Carpet

Line of Hardwood Cap

Levelers

Clean Out Bottom Deck

90°

Plan Section: (A)

18" Sides

1¾"

18"

Carpet

Levelers And T-nuts

Cross Section: (B)

DISPLAY CUBE—PLASTIC LAMINATE

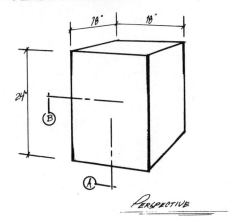

Perspective

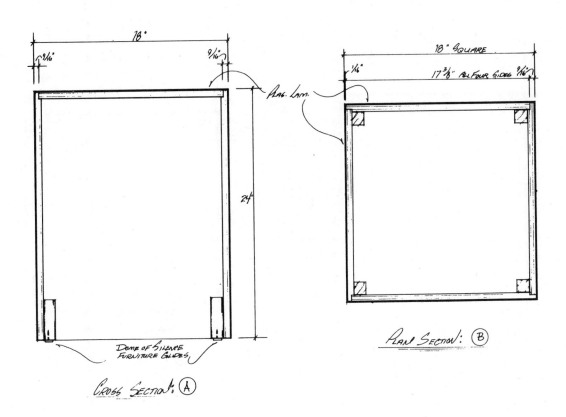

Cross Section: (A)

Plan Section: (B)

DISPLAY CUBE—CARPET COVERED

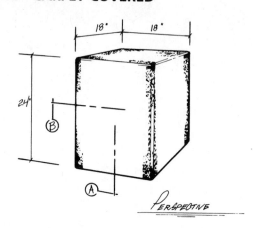

PERSPECTIVE

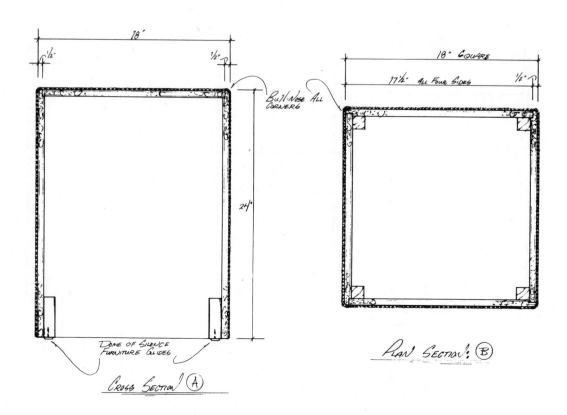

Bull-Nose All Corners

Dome of Silence Furniture Glides

CROSS SECTION (A)

18" SQUARE

17½" ALL FOUR SIDES

PLAN SECTION: (B)

DISPLAY CUBE—WOOD FINISH

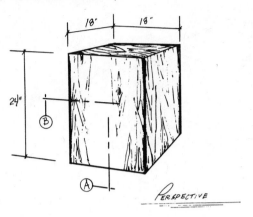

18"   18"

24"

Ⓑ

Ⓐ

Perspective

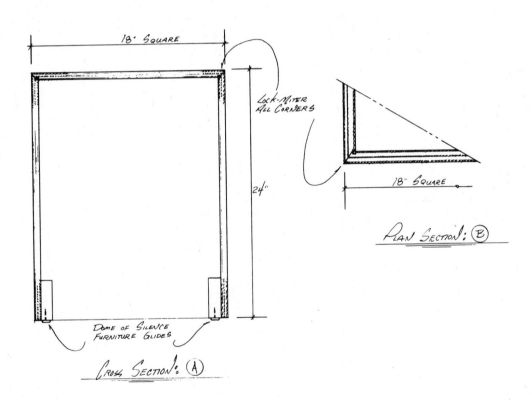

18" Square

Lock-Miter
All Corners

24"

18" Square

Plan Section: Ⓑ

Dome of Silence
Furniture Glides

Cross Section: Ⓐ

DISPLAY CUBE—MIRRORED TOP

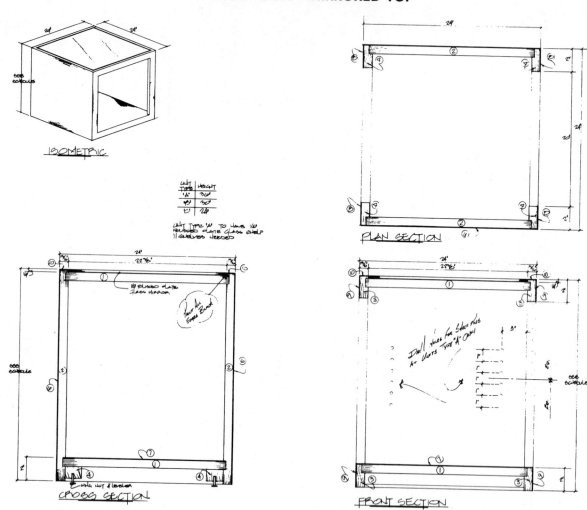

MUSEUM OR DISPLAY CUBE

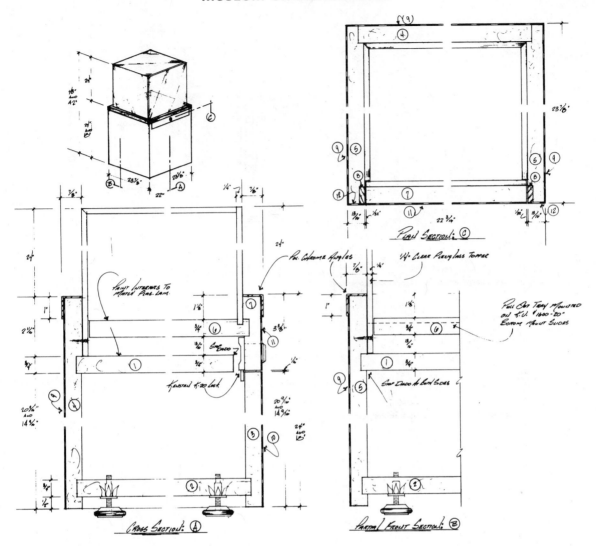

PLAN SECTION: C

CROSS SECTION: A

PARTIAL FRONT SECTION: B

TRIPLE DISPLAY CUBES—MIRRORED TOP

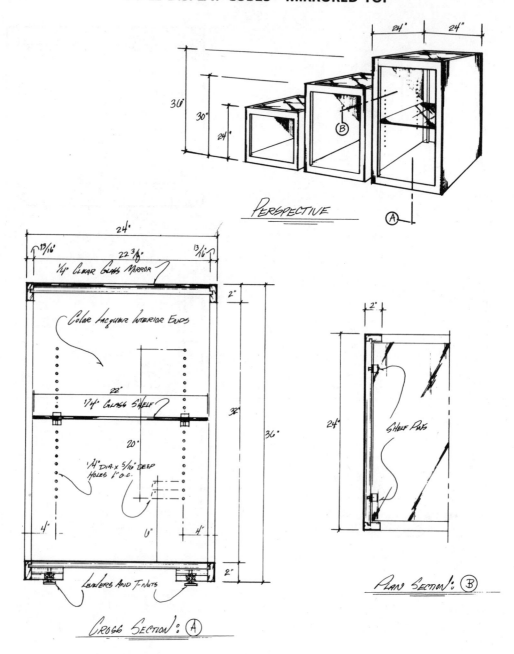

PERSPECTIVE

24"

1/4" CLEAR GLASS MIRROR

Color Lacquer Interior Ends

22"

1/4" GLASS SHELF

20"

1/4" DIA. x 5/16" DEEP HOLES 1" O.C.

4"   0"   4"

LEVELERS AND T-NUTS

CROSS SECTION: (A)

SHELF PINS

PLAN SECTION: (B)

FEATURE DISPLAY PEDESTAL

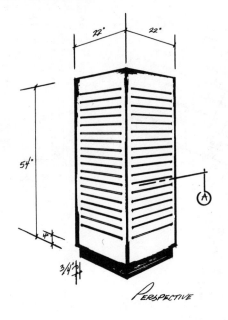

Perspective

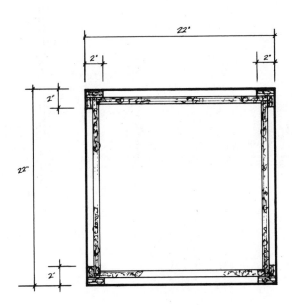

Plan Section: A

Plas. Lam. Applied over 3/4" Slatwall (3" o.c.) After Unit is Assembled. Slats may Be Cleaned Out By Using Slots in Slatwall As Guides For Router Bit, Eliminating Any Vertical or Horizontal Laminate Seams.

HOSIERY FIXTURE

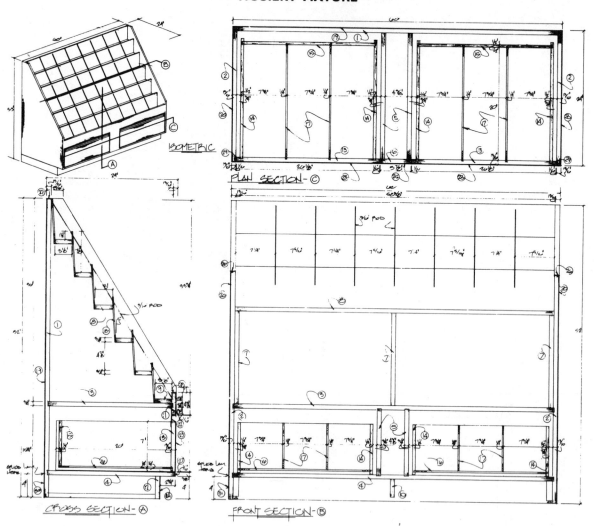

ISOMETRIC

PLAN SECTION-C

CROSS SECTION-A

FRONT SECTION-B

PARSONS TABLE

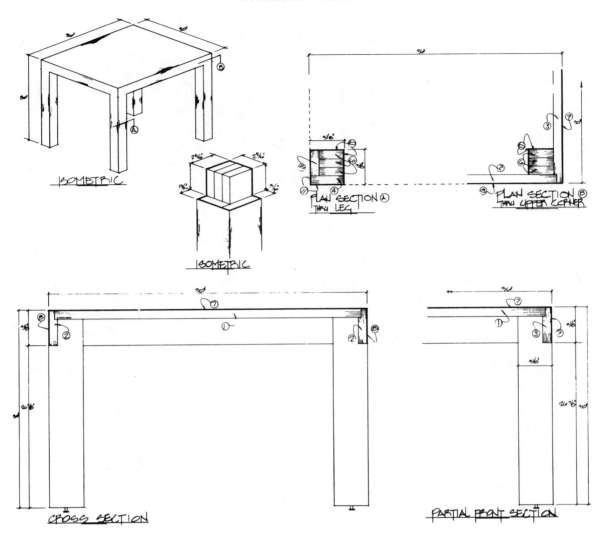

ISOMETRIC

ISOMETRIC

PLAN SECTION Ⓐ
THRU LEG

PLAN SECTION Ⓑ
THRU UPPER CORNER

CROSS SECTION

PARTIAL FRONT SECTION

FIXED-RIM, CLOSED-END PARSONS TABLE

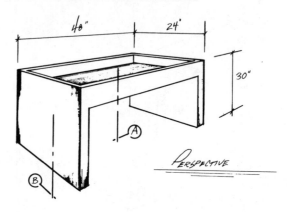

Perspective

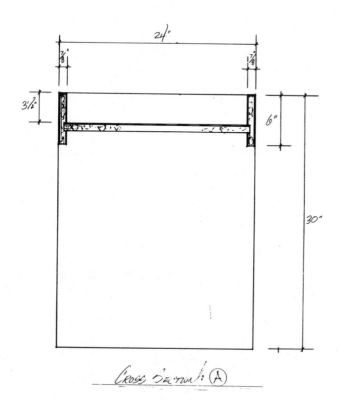

Cross Section: (A)

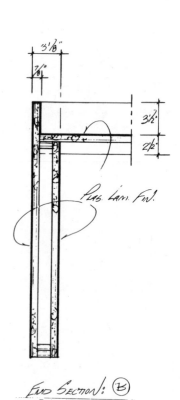

Plas. Lam. Fin.

End Section: (B)

REVERSIBLE RIM, DRAWERED TABLE

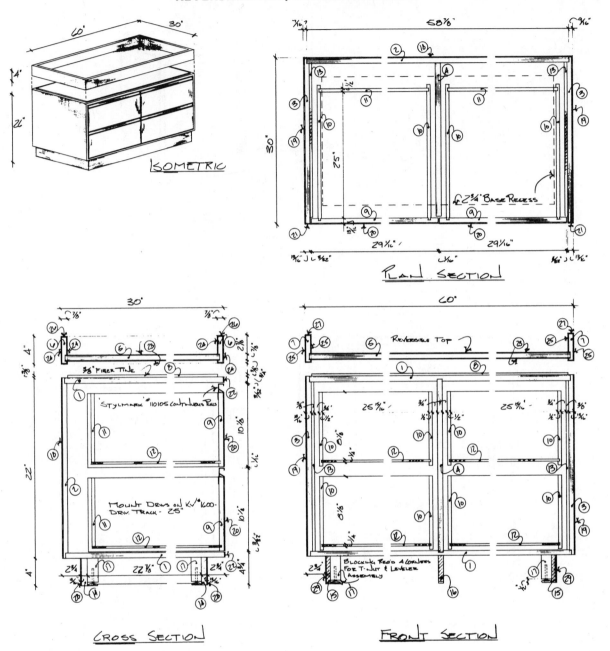

HINGED-DOOR TABLE

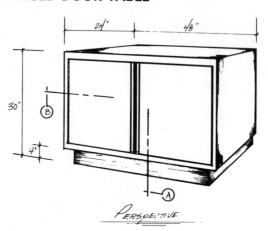

PERSPECTIVE

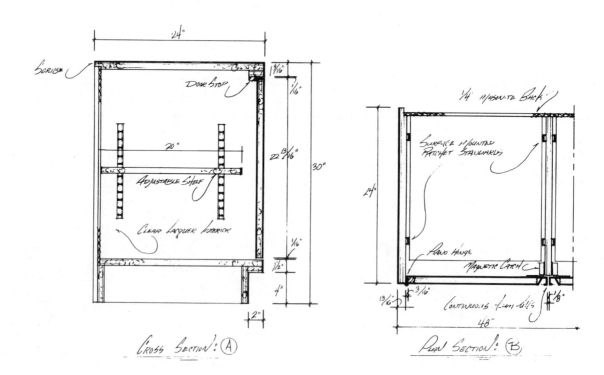

CROSS SECTION: (A)

PLAN SECTION: (B)

SLIDING-DOOR TABLE

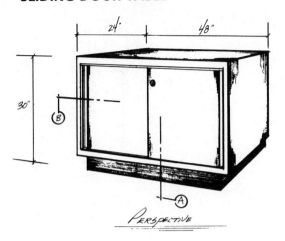

PERSPECTIVE

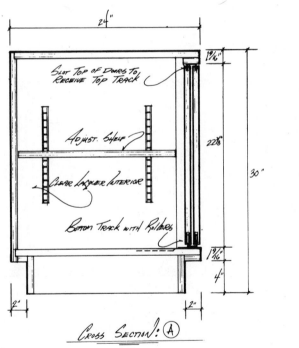

Slot Top of Doors to
Receive Top Track

Adjust. Shelf

Clear Lacquer Interior

Bottom Track with Rollers

24"

1 9/16"

22 7/8"

30"

1 9/16"

4"

2"   2"

Cross Section: Ⓐ

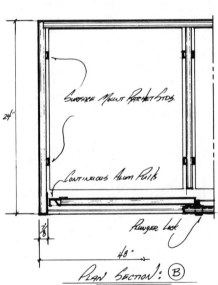

Surface Mount Ratchet Stds.

Continuous Alum Pulls

Plunger Lock

24"

7/8"

48"

Plan Section: Ⓑ

DRAWERED TABLE

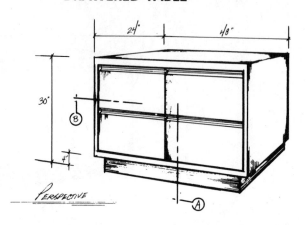

PERSPECTIVE

DRAWERS MAY BE MOUNTED ON
SELF CLOSING, OR FULL EXTENSION
SIDE MOUNT SLIDES.

CONTINUOUS PULLS MAY BE SELECTED
FROM A WIDE VARIETY OF FINISHES IF AN
ALUMINUM PULL IS USED.

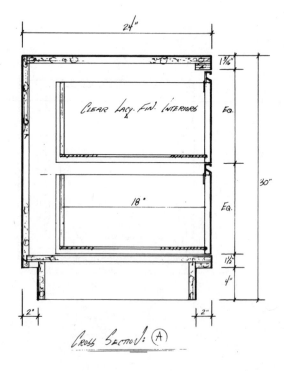

CLEAR LACQ. FIN. INTERIORS

18"

CROSS SECTION: (A)

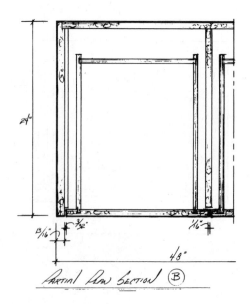

PARTIAL PLAN SECTION (B)

BACK ISLAND WITH DRAWERS

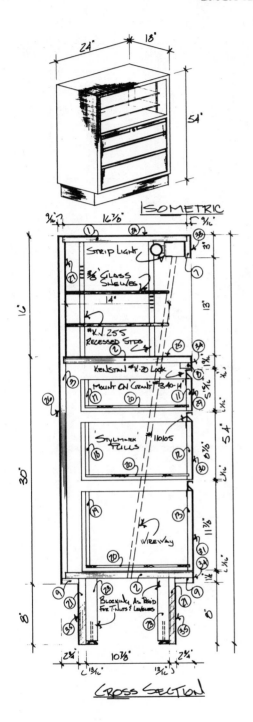

ISOMETRIC

CROSS SECTION

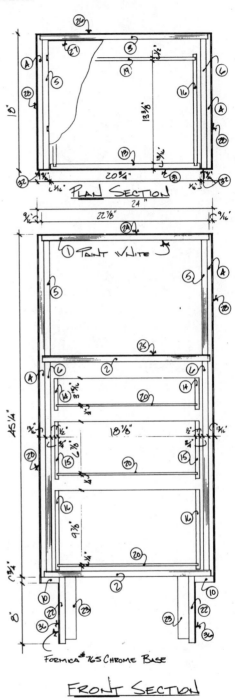

PLAN SECTION

FRONT SECTION

FORMICA # 765 CHROME BASE

BACK ISLAND WRAP COUNTER

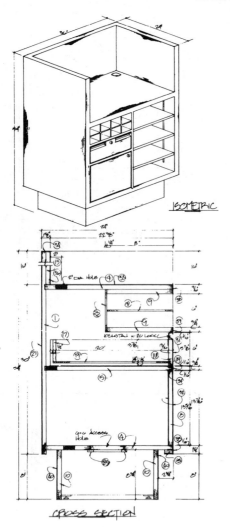

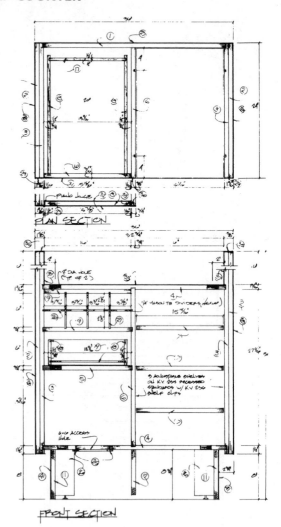

TWO-THIRDS VISION SHOWCASE

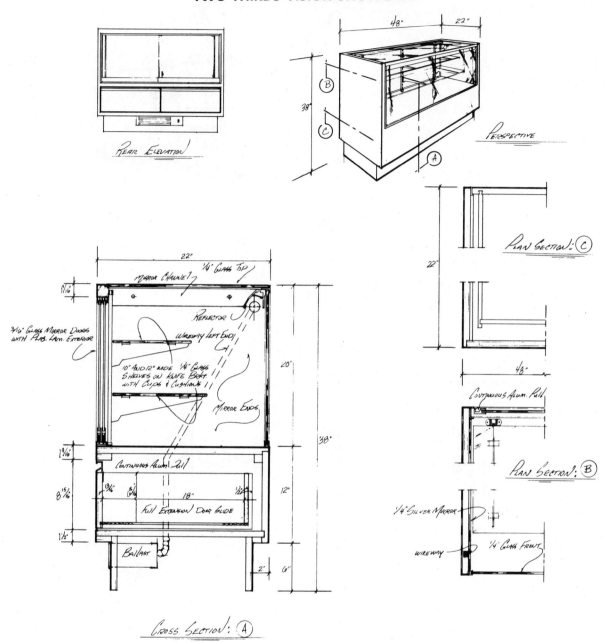

REAR ELEVATION

PERSPECTIVE

PLAN SECTION: C

PLAN SECTION: B

CROSS SECTION: A

FULL-VISION SHOWCASE

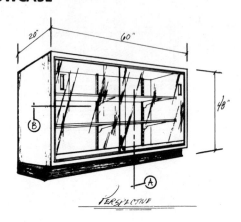

PERSPECTIVE

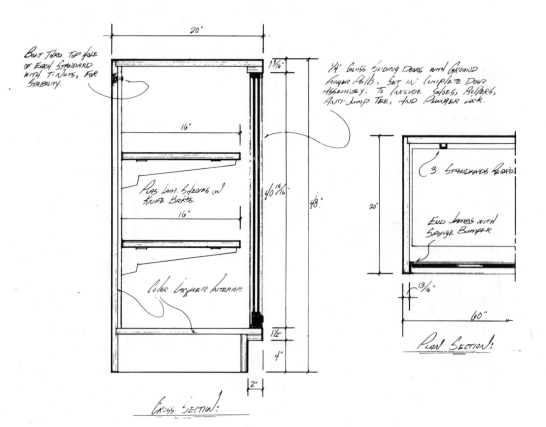

BOLT THRU TOP HOLE OF EACH STANDARD WITH T-NUTS, FOR STABILITY.

¼" GLASS SLIDING DOORS WITH GROUND FINGER PULLS, SET IN COMPLETE DOOR ASSEMBLY. TO INCLUDE SHOES, ROLLERS, ANTI-JUMP TEE, AND PLUNGER LOCK.

PLAS. LAM. SHELVES ON KNIFE BRKTS.

COLOR LACQUER INTERIOR

CROSS SECTION

3 STANDARDS REQ'D

END JAMBS WITH SPONGE BUMPER

PLAN SECTION

THREE-WAY MIRROR

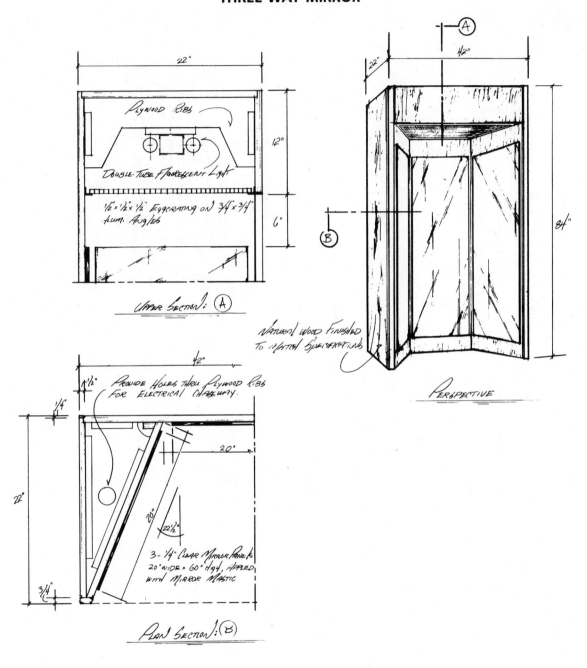

PLYWOOD RIBS

DOUBLE-TUBE FLUORESCENT LIGHT

½" x ½" x ½" EGGCRATING ON ¾" x ¾" ALUM. ANGLES

12"

6"

22"

UPPER SECTION: Ⓐ

Ⓐ

22"   42"

84"

PERSPECTIVE

NATURAL WOOD FINISHED TO MATCH SPECIFICATIONS

Ⓑ

42"

PROVIDE HOLES THRU PLYWOOD RIBS FOR ELECTRICAL CHASEWAY.

1 ½"

¼"

20"

22"

20"

20"

22½°

3 - ¼" CLEAR MIRROR PANELS 20" WIDE x 60" HIGH, APPLIED WITH MIRROR MASTIC

¾"

PLAN SECTION: Ⓑ

SECURITY CASE

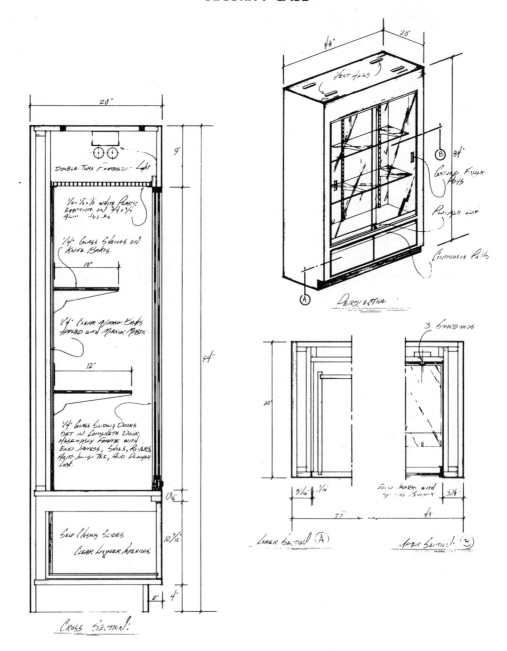

Chapter 31

JOB MEETINGS: MINUTES AND REPORTS

The purpose of job meetings is to discuss and review a project. The owner should open the first job meeting by familiarizing each contractor and trade represented at the meeting with production-schedule completion dates. Since the project will be completed in phases, it is imperative that the exact starting and completion dates be clearly understood and honored. Job meetings are also a good time to review all security policies that will be in force during the construction periods.

The following are examples of operational procedures that should be discussed at job meetings:

1. Time of working hours
2. The sign-in and sign-out sheet procedures for entering and exiting the building
3. The locations of all designated entrances and exits used by contractors and trades
4. Inspections of toolboxes, lunchboxes, bags, and boxes planned by security department as workmen exit the store
5. Security procedures for contractors, subcontractors, and trades making purchases at lunch time or after working hours

6. Policies regarding the touching of merchandise by workmen during working hours
7. Designated areas for smoking and eating
8. Designated areas for safeguarding coats and outerwear worn into the store
9. Assigned locations and times for lunch
10. Procedures for leaving the building
11. Procedures for accidents, whether they involve people or sections of the building

The minutes of each job meeting should include the date and time of that meeting, should give the status of job progress to date, should recap discussions of topics held over from previous meetings, and should give the date and time of the next meeting.

Progress reports should state the exact conditions of the project as they existed at the time of the meeting and any refinements made during each project stage. Contractors should be asked to discuss their respective work procedures.

A loose-leaf binder should be maintained that contains all minutes and job reports. Copies of the minutes should be supplied to each job supervisor and all others attending the meetings.

| Store Name _____ |
| Store No./Location _____ |
| Completion Date _____ |
| Job Telephone _____ |
| Job FAX _____ |

| Store Planner _____ |
| Address _____ |
| City, State _____ |
| Telephone _____ |
| FAX _____ |

JOB MEETING MINUTES

Job # _____   Date _____

Sheet _____

Project Name	Date
_____	_____
Meeting Place	Time
_____	_____
Owner's Rep.	Meeting #
_____	_____
Store Planner's Rep.	Next Meeting
_____	_____

Gen. Contractor's Rep.

IN ATTENDANCE (NAME)	COMPANY NAME	TELEPHONE

Store Name _____
Store No./Location _____
Completion Date _____
Job Telephone _____
Job FAX _____

Store Planner _____
Address _____
City, State _____
Telephone _____
FAX _____

JOB MEETING MINUTES

Job # _____   Date _____

Sheet _____

Purpose/Subject of Meeting:

General Notes

Work-in-Progress Report

Store Name _____

Store No./Location _____

Completion Date _____

Job Telephone _____

Job FAX _____

Store Planner _____

Address _____

City, State _____

Telephone _____

FAX _____

JOB MEETING MINUTES   Job # _____   Date _____

Sheet _____

Continuing and Additional Work Report

Changes to Original Contract

_____

Name of Store Planner's Rep.

Copies Sent to

Chapter 32

MANUFACTURING STORE-FIXTURE BUDGET

In order to plan, merchandise, and design a store, it is necessary that the store planner review with the client every facet of the building's interior. This will not only help clarify the client's preferences, but will also help establish a list of products that will finish out the interior while, at the same time, helping to estimate the store-fixture budget.

Within the course of any project, it will be necessary for many of the team members to prepare various estimated budgets to which they will adhere as closely as possible. It is the store planner's job to live within the budget and avoid cost overruns.

The Purpose of Estimating

The general contractor will build the interior walls or decor. Every unit in the store, including the freestanding fixtures and decor work, will be estimated using a system to project direct cost. The main purpose of an estimate is not only to make a decision on the type of fixturing or mechanical system, but also to establish a level of quality to which the planner must adhere. If the system chosen is unavailable, an equal substitute of the same quality should be used. The estimated store-fixture budget will include quantities and take-offs of materials. This will include the unit requirements of any type of wall system, decor, merchandising hardware system, decor, brackets, shelves, freestanding fixtures, and so on. The quantity is listed in columns that are considered a take-off or unit requirement schedule. With each system selected, there will be a material and labor factor included in the cost of the selected products.

In the eyes of a veteran store planner, an estimated store-fixture budget helps to break out labor hours, manufacturing time, material costs, brokerage of material, any subcontracting fees required, and sales tax. Labor rates for the manufacturing or installation of the item will be predetermined by the manufacturer.

Other Considerations

The factory direct cost rate and the factory overhead rate are also part of the process that keeps manufacturers in business. In the case of a store-fixture contractor, the exact materials, the labor costs, and the lowest possible direct rate should be applied in order to keep a wood mill in operation. Also included is the direct overhead expense.

Many times, a job might be taken at the lowest rate of cost and is extended over a one-year period for a breakeven point. No store-fixture manufacturing company or store planner can operate for a long period of time if a project just covers costs. If the project covers costs and expenses but leaves no profits this results in the highest direct cost.

Estimating Methods

There are many methods that a store-fixture contractor may use in scheduling of manufacturing to allow direct cost. The estimate helps each contractor break down the number of production hours that are required to manufacture or deliver a finished product. Many times, in operating a manufacturing business, management may project and lay out a six-month period estimating the number of production hours, along with the direct labor hours for operating, and assign those hours to various months for minimum and maximum production periods in order to insure delivery. In some cases, when a contract is not issued to a manufacturer of store equipment, they may have the liberty to proceed ahead of schedule, filling the production period within that month with the available man hours. Of course, the owner is responsible for authorizing manufacturing of store equipment within a contract. In other cases, if a manufacturer has taken on a workload that requires more production hours than the workers are capable of, overtime is a consideration, as is farming out components. Naturally, any work farmed out must be completed with the expected quality and appearance.

Scheduling Problems

At times, if a store-fixture manufacturer goes ahead of schedule, it can cause problems such as a shortage in the availability of material, double handling of products, cramped working conditions, high interest rates, delayed income, and frayed nerves. Being behind schedule can also cause problems, such as unestimated production overtime, liquidation damages, loss of customers, holdback of payments, and even establishing a questionable reputation.

Manufacturer's Representative

The various store-fixture contractors are the store planner's direct contact with the manufacturing companies and use sales calls to introduce the store planner to new products and/or services. It is the job of the manufacturer's representative to inform the store planner of the progress that has been made in the development of any specialized store equipment item and any features that might express technologies or progressive growth within a company.

When any manufacturer of store equipment loses a job to a competitor, it is the representative's responsibility to find the reason, for example, if the bid for the product or service was too high or, in the case of a low bid, why it was disqualified. If the latter is the case, there is the possibility that some items were inadvertently left out. This information helps the manufacturer to project market conditions or competitive trends in pricing. On the original contract for the products, the planner will clearly specify the breakdown and any change orders that may have occurred with invoicing. A breakdown further explains the original contract cost and additional change order cost. A production schedule helps the manufacturer pinpoint the delivery of raw products to the factory for manufacturing. It will also help pinpoint door deliveries to the finished project location. It is important that any contingencies—including do's, don'ts, ifs, ands, or buts—be clearly stated.

Engineer's Report

The purpose of the engineer's report is to keep management abreast of the entire project and process as it is being coordinated internally within production and manufacturing prior to shipping. The weekly detailed progress report will bring to the attention of the manager any problems that will affect the production or delivery schedule of the finished products to the job site. Many times it will be necessary for several field inspections of the project in order to assure that the schedule aligns with the project. Each store-fixturing manufacturing operation must have a set of firm but flexible rules by which to operate the business in order to insure the timely delivery of products, while at the same time maintaining product guidelines and procedures.

Miscellaneous Forms

A Store-Fixturing Manufacturer
Any Street
Any Place

ESTIMATE RECAP

	COST	SALE	EST. PROFIT
PLANT MAN HOURS			
PLANT LABOR			
PLANT OVERHEAD			
MANUFACTURING MATERIAL			
BROKERAGE			
INSTALLATION			
MISC _____			
TOTAL COST—SALE & PROFIT			
SALES TAX			
TOTAL CONTRACT AMOUNT			

ADDITIONAL INFORMATION

_____

_____

_____

_____

_____

_____

_____

_____

A Store-Fixturing Manufacturer
Any Street
Any Place

JOB CHECK LIST

1. Date Bid _____ Money _____

2. Date Awarded _____

3. Date Received Architectural Plans _____

4. Date Architectural Plans _____

5. Date Complete Specifications _____

6. Date Schedule Letter Sent _____

7. Date Schedule Letter Answered _____

8. Date EST/Detailer Job Communication _____

9. Date Shop Drawings Started _____

10. Date Shop Drawings Finished _____

11. Hardware Samples _____

12. Date Plastic Laminate Ordered _____

13. Date Hardware Ordered _____

14. Date Plywood Ordered _____

15. Date Solid Stock Ordered _____

16. Date Job Field Checked _____

17. Shop Orders Written   25% _____   50% _____   100% _____

JOB NUMBER_____

ADDITIONAL INFORMATION

_____

_____

_____

_____

_____

_____

**A Store-Fixturing Manufacturer
Any Street
Any Place**

CHECKLIST—DETAILERS

1. Elevation _____ Plan Section _____ Section _____

2. Height _____ Width _____ Depth _____

3. Scribe Detail _____

4. Quantity _____

5. Room Location _____

6. Details _____

7. Access to Building _____ Room _____

8. Cabinet Break _____ K.D. _____

9. Plywood Specifications _____ Solid Stock Specs _____

10. Hardware Quantities _____ Location_____ Type _____

11. Plastic Laminate Color and No._____ Finish _____

12. Top View Showing Splices, Joints_____

13. Millwork D4s (show finished surfaces) _____ Joinery_____

14. Loose Shipment for Assembly on Job _____

ADDITIONAL INFORMATION

_____

_____

_____

_____

_____

_____

_____

_____

A Store-Fixturing Manufacturer
Any Street
Any Place

Telephone Number

RE: Production Schedule

Job: _____

No: _____

Eng: _____

Dear Client:

Your job _____ has been assigned factory No. _____. For better service and communications, the following engineer, (Mr./Ms.) _____, has been assigned to follow your job from start to finish. If there are any questions, correspondence, delivery, or complaints, please contact him/her directly.

In an attempt to further increase our service and efficiency, we request the following information:

1. Address and location of job site: _____

2. Field phone/FAX: _____

3. Job superintendent: _____

4. Door delivery date: _____

5. Date first millwork delivery: _____

6. Date last millwork delivery: _____

7. Scheduled completion date: _____

8. Estimate date to field dimension: _____

9. Hardware supplier and address: _____

10. Sink cutouts will be done by us only if sink rims are sent to us prior to our delivery. Please have supplier send rims as soon as possible.

11. Door grilles cut out and installed at door factory only. If *specifications require* a Store-Fixturing Manufacturer to install door grilles, give supplier's name and address.

IMPORTANT: To prevent delivery delay, we must have the above information before we have the approved shop drawings. If we do not receive this data, we must assign a delivery date to the job for our own production schedule, and this might not coincide with your expected delivery date.

ADDITIONAL INFORMATION

_____

_____

_____

Appendix 1

THE ROLE OF THE ARCHITECT

S. R. Frolichstein, AIA, Chicago, IL

The architect's role in store planning includes dealing with code requirements, structural design, and the coordination of the HVAC (heating, ventilating, air-conditioning) systems, electrical design, and the plumbing and sprinkler work required for a building.

Many of today's store planners are registered architects, and the trend is a growing one. One reason for this trend is that an architect's certification often is required on drawings prepared for construction.

By virtue of their education (usually a five- or six-year college degree) and experience (usually three or more years of working for a registered architect), registered architects are full-fledged design professionals. By passing comprehensive exams, they are registered to practice in one or many states.

The Store-Planning Team

The complexity and requirements of a project always dictate the makeup of the store-planning team. On the pages that follow, a visual demonstration is provided of how this makeup varies to suit a set of typical circumstances.

Diagram A illustrates a situation in which the client is an experienced retailer with construction background. The client takes the lead by hiring the necessary design professionals. If the space is clearly defined, meets code, and has all required utility services running to the space, a store planner may be the only outside consultant necessary. If the project becomes sufficiently complex, the services of an electrical engineer will be required to plan the lighting, power, and circuiting. A mechanical engineer may be added to the team to plan the HVAC requirements, plumbing, and sprinkler work. If structural changes are being made, if an addition is being built, or if the building is being newly constructed, an architect and probably a structural engineer will be added. If the retailer's work goes beyond the building, the services of a civil engineer, landscape architect, and traffic planner may be needed.

In this example, each consultant works for and is paid by the retailer. However, the entire group works together as a team, communicates regularly, and has the common goal of designing the best retail space to meet the client's aesthetic and budgetary demands.

649

A.

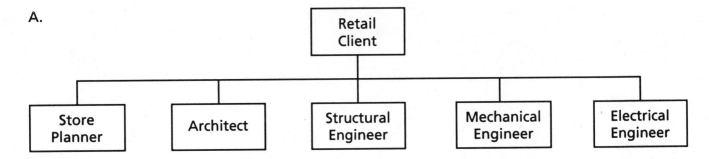

Diagram B differs from A in that it assumes the client has engaged one of the professionals, the store planner. Because of the complexity of the job, the store planner, acting as the prime contractor, may add an architect and several consulting engineers as consultants. In addition to the store planner's fees for direct work, proposals must be secured from the other supporting design professionals. This fee will also be included in the total bill. It is normal, in these circumstances, for the lead consultant to mark up the fees presented by the other professionals by 10 to 25 percent.

The preceding diagrams can, and should, be changed to suit the existing circumstances. Usually the lead consultant is the one who has landed the job, but it may be the architect who hires the store planner or, less commonly, one of the other consultants.

Stages of Work as Defined by the American Institute of Architects (AIA) Contract

The AIA Contract subdivides a construction job into five phases. When each phase is fully reviewed at completion, the problem of space that is not designed to suit the client's needs can often be avoided.

If each phase meets with the approval of the client before the next is begun, there is less chance of expensive mistakes that fail to meet the client's needs.

1. **Program and Schematic Design** The Program is written, starting with rough sketches and flow diagrams, to define the scope of work, and problems are stated. At the end of this phase, the rough floor plan is completed, and a budget for the work is established.

2. **Final Design** The finished plan, with notes, is completed. The entrances and exits to the store are defined. The lighting and other mechanical equipment are investigated. The walls and all store fixtures are drawn in. Checks are made to assure that the space meets all zoning ordinances and code and lease requirements. Finishes in the whole space are discussed. The drawing and outline specification are reviewed with the client. The budget is verified.

3. **Documents** The documents phase represents approximately 50 percent of the work. Working drawings and specifications are done. During and at the end of the phase, drawings and specifications should be reviewed carefully by the

B.

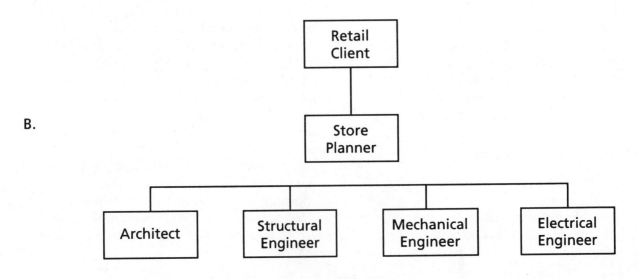

client. Again the budget is discussed. (It is advisable to have the client review and approve the drawings at 50 percent, 90 percent, and 100 percent completion.)

4. Bidding Phase Drawings are distributed to various contractors. Work may be competitively bid or negotiated with individual contractors. The work also can be handled with a general contractor who distributes all the subcontract work, or the client may choose to engage different contractors for each phase. The latter method requires more work by the client. At the end of the bidding phase, the price quotations are assembled and analyzed by the planner. In order to establish proper fees, the entire scope of work must be understood.

5. Construction Phase At the beginning of the job, the architect must determine how much of his work is included in this phase. The architect should visit the site periodically to answer contractors' questions and communicate any changes. The architect administers contract documents, checks all shop and fixture drawings, and makes regular scheduled visits to the site; in effect, he "runs the job" for the client.

In any good retail plan, the building's shell, access, parking, landscaping, and signing must all be considered collectively, whether the building is a freestanding retail store, rehabilitated space, or part of a new department store.

When the Services of an Architect Are Not Required

An architect's services are not required when: (1) the landlord (ore retail client) has established the outside perimeter walls of the new retail space (whether a freestanding building or part of a shopping center), (2) when the utility services to the space are defined, and (3) when others are taking care of the code requirements. In these circumstances, the store planner is the only design professional who needs to be involved.

Remodelings and Alterations

Often, completion of the store planner's function will require adding the services of an architect or other design consultantss. The following are some of the conditions in which additional consultants will likely be required:

1. Structural changes are being made to an existing building.

2. An addition to the building is being built.

3. Because of the nature of its use or for reasons of added population, the space must be altered to meet zoning ordinances or building codes. Alterations may be required, for example, when industrial or store space is being converted to retail space. If additions, relocations, or altering are required to meet codes, an architect should be employed. If anything in the plan alters the use in such a way that weight affects an additional structure, a structural engineer or architect should be added to the team.

4. When there are questions as to the structural integrity or the weather-tightness of the building, an architect, civil engineer, structural engineer, roof consultant, or possibly a soil engineer or testing laboratory may be called in to investigate. Obviously, if cracks in a floor slab or wall are in question or if there is a water leak in the building, these problems should be solved before a new interior is constructed.

5. Store planners are often capable of doing a lighting plan and fixture schedule. However, the circuiting of the fixtures may require the services of an electrical engineer.

6. When the lighting load is changed and power is added for additional equipment and the population of the space may be changed because of use, the HVAC systems must be altered or redesigned. In this case, the services of an experienced mechanical engineer are required.

7. When toilets must be altered or relocated or when additional sinks must be added to the space, a mechanical engineer is often used to design these areas in order to satisfy building requirements and codes.

8. Sprinklers are used in most new retail spaces. Sprinklers are often required by code; but even if they are not required, the insurance rates for most stores make sprinklers a sensible addition. In coordinating the work, especially the location of light fixtures, duct work, and diffusers, the spacing, location, and appearance of sprinkler heads must be

considered in the planning. The installation of sprinklers must be coordinated by en engineer or sprinkler contractor with a qualified engineering staff.

New Construction

In a project built from the ground up, the store planner will often be part of the design team. When a retailer needs a new freestanding building or a department store attached to a shopping center, the work must be well coordinated among all members of the design team. Obviously, the team's goal must be to develop the best retail space that can be designed within the project's objectives and budget.

The tasks involved in a major department store project are frequently quite extensive and could require a team of design professionals such as the following:

1. Store planner
2. Architect
3. Civil engineer
4. Soil and material laboratory
5. Traffic planner
6. Structural engineer
7. Electrical engineer
8. HVAC engineer
9. Plumbing and sprinkler contractor
10. Roof consultant
11. Specification writer
12. Cost consultant

Depending upon the size and scope of a project, other design consultants could be added or deleted as required.

Appendix 2

VISUAL MERCHANDISING ROLE IN STORE PLANNING

Tom. V. Natalini, SVM

Several years ago, the term *Visual Merchandising Director* was nonexistent. This unique individual represents and a giant step above the Display Director, who now reports to the Visual Merchandising Director or Vice President. In a number of corporations, the store-planning staff reports to the Visual Director. However, most Visual Directors and Store Planning Directors report to the Director of Stores and/or the Chief Executive Officer. In this case, there is a strong partnership, with all working toward a common goal, the result being a highly energized store projecting the right plan, design, and presentation.

Responsibilities of the Visual Merchandising Director

- Designing store image (in conjunction with management's direction)
- Store planning (in some companies)
- Display staff
- Budgets
- Retail markets (home furnishings, men's and boy's, young world, and ready-to-wear)
- Visual markets (domestic, European, and oriental)
- Management meetings
- Sales promotion meetings
- Buyers' meetings
- Review of visual deficiencies through store visits
- Review of store-planning projects (new store and renovations) for placement of visual presentations
- Maintain current and future trend presentations
- Total store presentation of merchandise on fixtures, as well as displays and shop concepts.
- Attaining advance notice of fashion trends from buyers
- Meeting with merchandise managers and divisional merchandise managers concerning shop requests

Part of the Visual Merchandising Director's role is maintaining close contact with Buyers, Divisional Merchandise Managers, General Merchandise Managers, and Divisional Sales Managers. The Visual person attends all meetings regarding merchandise to be presented on freestanding fixtures as well as perimeter presentation. This person is also responsible for the selection of merchandise to be presented in shops, forward display areas, and windows. He or she is responsible for the selection of fixtures, presentation techniques on fixtures, placement of fixtures, and the planning of areas for major display locations within each unit store. This responsibility is then translated to the Planning and Store Design office for new stores and renovations. The Visual person must administer the techniques of presentation incorporating the common sense merchandising theories. The same disciplines used to create an exciting window must be incorporated into the interior of each unit. Windows are no longer on the outside of a store; they have moved into the interior. By creating Visual Merchandising Guidelines, each unit will, as a whole, represent the same store image to the customer. This Visual statement, unit to unit, will in turn result in additional sales.

In close relationship with the Director of Stores, Visual Merchandising Directors plan future departmental moves, keeping in mind the natural adjacencies of each department, with the ultimate intention of moving the customer easily from one family of business to another. The Visual Merchandising Director's responsibilities also include the placement of accent lighting and, in some cases, the general overhead-light scheme.

The Visual Merchandising Director's Role in New Store and Renovation Construction

- Selection of proper fixturing for each department
- Planning areas for highlight presentations and selecting mannequins
- Selection of counter-top fixtures and perimeter presentation units
- Creation of an opening theme that will project to the store image to the customer
- Working closely with the store planner and designer to create the proper ambiance for merchandise through current department color trends
- Participating in all color reviews with store planning for new store and renovation construction

In conclusion, the Visual Merchandising Director is the final link between the store and the customer.

Appendix 3

GUIDELINES CONCERNING BIDDING, AWARDING OF CONTRACTS, MANUFACTURING, INSTALLATION, AND JOB COMPLETION

Capitol Interiors, Inc.

The following is our concept for guidelines concerning bidding, awarding of contracts, manufacturing, installation, and job completion.

Bidding

1. All bidders should be qualified as to their ability to perform the work, their quality, and their financial stability. Many of the large department store chains have a contractor/manufacturer prequalification form that is submitted on an annual basis.

2. Prior to submitting bid documents to the various bidders, it is suggested that the anticipated bidders be notified by mail or telephone of the following information:
- Scope of work: A brief description of the project (new or renovation) and what portion the bidder is requested to bid (total job, pe-

rimeters only, showcases and back islands, loose fixtures, etc.)
- Date bid documents will be available.
- Bidding period: On a 50,000-square-foot or larger new store, the normal bid period should be 3 to 4 weeks; on a renovation, 5 to 6 weeks.
- Start of installation date and project completion date: The designer should be aware of the availability of materials being used in the design concept. Many laminates, special-design metal work, fabrics, veneers, and so on, are long-lead items taking 8 to 10 weeks for availability. This can affect both the start and completion of a project.

  (The above will save money and time for both the owner and contractor/manufacturer.)

3. The bond ability of the prospective bidder should be known.

On Award of Contract

1. A meeting should be held with the successful bidder(s) to review the scope of work in the respective contracts, to assure that all items are covered, and to determine the installation schedule and timing.

2. Contract should include, in addition to the contract sum, the hourly rate, including overhead and profit. For the various tradespeople, it should include percentage of overhead and profit for materials. This is necessary to accommodate field change orders.

3. There should be a designation of the owner's representative who will be the only person to authorize a change in the field. This is necessary as many merchandise managers are not too familiar with drawings and request changes in the field. With one person responsible, these changes can be kept to a minimum.

4. It should be the contractor's responsibility to submit a schedule showing date shop drawings will go out for approval. The turnaround time for designer approval should not exceed five (5) working days.

5. Change orders from owners and/or designers.

Request should be approved on a firm cost rather than time and material.

New Stores vs. Renovation

On bidding a new store, the bid documents should reflect all the scope-of-work and design intent. However, on renovations, we recommend a prebid walkthrough at the job site consisting of the bidders, design office representative, and owner's representative. This is necessary to review the scope of work, receiving facilities, staging areas, various stages or zones of working, delays of time from one zone to the next, and so on. This walkthrough should be within one week from issue of bid documents.

Cost Savings

Without changing design and merchandising intent, there are many times when the contractor/manufacturer can make suggestions in material or construction. Example: 1/2" tempered glass 48" x 96" will cost 25% more in one piece rather than 2 lites 24" x 96". This savings is the amount of manpower necessary to install the glass. There is a great variance in costs of laminates from manufacturer to manufacturer. The selection of this material can affect the cost of the project.

Appendix 4

THE PROJECT MANUAL/PROJECT SPECIFICATIONS

Warren J. Kostak, ARA, CSI, Kostak Associates

Background

The Project Manual is the compilation of written documents that describe the legal, contractual, and technological requirements of a construction project. Traditionally, all elements of the construction that could not be described adequately by graphic means were relegated to a body of written work known as the project specifications. Prior to the sixties, the project "spec book" tended to be a loosely organized catch-all of information that generally reflected the ideas of individual designers or the office practice of a design or architectural firm. During the sixties and seventies, through the cooperation of private organizations and professional societies, tremendous progress was made toward developing a standard format for construction specifications. The objective was to reduce the confusion and gray areas of the design-and-construction process so that designers and builders could communicate more effectively and improve the end result of their combined efforts.

Today, many governmental agencies and most private design and engineering firms involved in building construction utilize written construction documents organized around what is known as the C.S.I. Format. Developed by The Construction Specifications Institute in 1963, the C.S.I. Format has emerged as the industry standard for the organization of construction specifications in the United States. The C.S.I. Format organizes the Project Manual into four distinct areas of information: (1) Bidding Requirements, (2) Contract Forms, (3) Conditions of the Contract, and (4) Technological Specifications (16 divisions).

"Soft" Data

The first three groups of information describe the legal, contractual, and nontechnological aspects of a construction project. These can be thought of as the "soft" items of a project—those that do not describe any physical construction elements. Several professional societies, including the American Institute of Architects (AIA) and the American Society of Interior Designers (ASID), publish standardized documents that can be used to describe these soft items in the Project Manual. Specifiers generally agree that it is prudent to use these standard documents because they assist in the organization of the

Project Manual and are widely accepted by the construction industry.

Bidding Requirements

The bidding requirements contain information to assist the prospective bidders in preparing and submitting a bid. This information usually consists of the invitation to bid; instructions to bidders; and a bid, or proposal, form. The invitation to bid provides basic data about the project, such as location, owner, designer, person to receive bids, description of work, and bid security requirements. The instructions to bidders provides more detailed information about the project and lists the requirements that must be followed during the bidding process. Standard forms of instructions to bidders are available from various professional organizations. These standard forms are usually modified by "supplementary" instructions that describe the detailed requirements of the specific project under consideration. The bid form is generally written in the format of a letter from the bidder to the owner. Blank spaces are left throughout the form so that the bidder can insert information on prices, quantities, time schedules, and other specific information required by the owner. The objective of the bid form is to insure that all the bidders provide the same information so that the bids can be compared on an equal basis.

Contract Forms

The contract or construction agreement between the owner and the contractor may take several forms, among which are the stipulated sum, the cost-plus fee, and the unit-price contract. The stipulated-sum contract is most generally used for competitively bid work. Its primary advantage is that the total cost of the construction is known before construction begins. The cost-plus contract is one in which the contractor is paid for the actual cost of labor and materials plus a fee. The fee covers certain items of the contractor's overhead as well as his profit. The unit-price contract is based upon estimated quantities of specific units of work (labor and materials) and a fixed price per unit.

The construction agreement may also be some combination of the aforementioned forms. The most common is the stipulated-sum agreement with certain unit prices specified at the time the agreement is executed. The unit-price provisions then give the owner some flexibility during the construction process. If, for example, the owner desires to change

certain elements of the construction, he may do so with confidence if he has predetermined unit prices that cover the items of work under consideration. He knows in advance what the approximate cost of these changes will be, and he can make his decision accordingly.

As with bidding requirements, many professional societies and trade organizations have developed standardized forms of agreement covering the types of contracts. These forms should be used whenever possible; their use over the years has tested their adequacy and has reduced misunderstandings sometimes inherent in the process of construction.

Conditions of the Contract

The final, and perhaps most complex, area of soft information—the conditions of the contract—are usually divided into two parts: (1) the general conditions and (2) the supplementary conditions. The general conditions describe the duties and responsibilities of the parties entering into the construction contract and detail how the contract will be administered. While generally not a signatory to the contract, the designer is often called upon to administer the contract during construction and must be thoroughly familiar with the conditions of the contract. Standard, published general conditions should be used wherever possible to avoid misinterpretation and reduce unnecessary liability on the part of the designer or specifier.

The standard general conditions usually have to be modified to suit each individual project. These modifications are known as the supplementary conditions and consist of changing, adding, or deleting information contained in the standard general conditions. Examples of conditions usually requiring modifications are progress payments to the contractor, types of insurance required and dollar limits for each type, stipulations regarding changes in the construction, and additional compensation for charges.

"Hard" Data

The remaining portions of the Project Manual address the technological aspects of the physical construction, as opposed to the legal-contractual aspects discussed. It describes the type and quality of materials used, as well as their method of installation and, in some instances, the desired end result. These specifications are organized in a sixteen-division C.S.I. format with each division encompassing one broad area of construction technology. The only exception to this is division one—general requirements—which describes administrative procedures that relate to some, or all, of the subsequent divisions.

The general outline, or format, for the entire Project Manual would appear as follows:

(SOFT DATA)

Division 0—Bidding Requirements
　　　　　　Contract Forms
　　　　　　Conditions of the Contract

(HARD DATA)

Division 1— General Requirements (administrative)
Division 2— Sitework
Division 3— Concrete
Division 4— Masonry
Division 5— Metals
Division 6— Wood and Plastics
Division 7— Thermal and Moisture Protection
Division 8— Doors and Windows
Division 9— Finishes
Division 10— Specialties
Division 11— Equipment
Division 12— Furnishings
Division 13— Special Construction
Division 14— Conveying Systems
Division 15— Mechanical
Division 16— Electrical

When specifying for retail store construction, the designer/specifier is usually working within the confines of an existing building shell or leased tenant space. Because of that fact, many of the technological divisions of the Project Manual would not be required (i.e., sitework, concrete, masonry, etc.). Most commonly used for interior projects would be Division 0, Division 1, Division 6, Division 8, Division 9, and Division 12.

Specification Production and Automation

By using standardized formats and published forms in the Project Manual, the designer/specifier simplifies the preparation of the construction documents, improves communication and understanding between participants, and creates options for automated production of specifications.

Since the early seventies, private companies have offered computerized specification services, based on the 16-division format, to the design industry. These services provide even the smallest firm the speed and accuracy of automated specification systems without the capital investment required for computer hardware. In the past, these services have been geared to general building construction and not to interior design as a specific market. Along with the increasing sophistication of these systems, however, the search for new markets is inevitable. The future will undoubtedly see more automated specification "packages" for specialty areas of design, including contract furnishings and interiors. The design firms that utilize standardized forms, formats, and specifications will be in the best position to take advantage of these developments, and hence, will be able to maintain their edge in the increasingly competitive arena of interior design.

Appendix 5

AIA CONTRACT DOCUMENTATION FOR STORE PLANNING AND CONSTRUCTION

Richard B. Cook, FAIA, Stowell Cook Frolichstein, Inc., Architects

The Agreement

The consultants hired by the Client to perform the refixturing of an existing store or the fixturing of a new store typically include a Store Planner and an Architect. The Store Planner or the Architect will generally have a direct contract with the Client. If the project involves safety, health, or welfare (i.e., any structural or mechanical revisions), chances are the state-licensed architect will indeed be the professional sealing the drawings. In a number of cases, this issue determines who will sign the original contract with the Client. In most cases, this contract will be with the Architect of record since he or she must be licensed to practice in the state where the project is sited.

The proposed agreement will be either one of the standard documents of the AIA (American Institute of Architects) or one prepared by the Consultant or Client. Large businesses generally prepare their own contracts in-house, using corporate attorneys.

For most projects, the Store Planner and Architect form a mutually supportive association. This cooperative effort can commence as informally as a hand shake or as formally as the signing of a detailed AIA joint-venture agreement. Typically, a simple letter form is used whereby one of the parties sets forth the scope of the other party's responsibilities, compensation, and so on, and that addressee signs off under "Approved" or similar heading at the bottom of the proposal.

This agreement, then, becomes the contract between the Store Planner and the Architect and generally spells out key terms, such as monetary consideration, duration of the project, insurance requirements, documents required, and schedule. Once the Store Planner and the Architect, who should review the proposed agreement together with the Client, finalize the contract, it becomes an enforceable agreement in which both, through their mutual association, are bound. Whether that form of agreement between the Architect and the Store Planner takes the form of a joint venture or an informal association, each is inseparable from the other, and they both are bound by the same agreement.

The first step of the project is obtaining the written contract agreed upon by the Client, the Architect, and Store Planner, who is sometimes called the "Consultant." This contract frames the relationship that spans the life of the project.

The Timing of the Store Planner's and the Architect's Initial Involvement

Generally the Store Planner or the Architect makes the initial client contact and establishes the relationship; however, in a growing number of cases, they are working in tandem to secure the client's commission. Once the contract between the Architect and the Store Planner has been executed and is in place (whether it be a letter agreement, a joint venture, or an association), the project is underway. The involvement of both the Store Planner and the Architect should be clearly spelled out in their agreement. This specifically includes the precise work each will undertake, the compensation, and the extent of their time and the duration of the project itself. A schedule should be prepared between the Architect and the Store Planner to set project deadlines. When, as an Architect, I have worked with Store Planners, the initial planning and general store layout or refixturing of the store was performed by the Store Planner. Occasionally, if a new building were involved, the Architect would set certain required parameters of the store. The layout of the store's merchandise plan rests on the building and its parameters and is subject to variation and change throughout the development of the project. Only after the Architect has established the initial building parameters of life-safety concerns, such as stair locations, exits, mechanical distribution, and building structure and materials, can store planning proceed. The Architect should establish the code review to determine ADA (Americans with Disabilities Act) requirements and the various ordinance restrictions of the county or city where the project is located. The Store Planner formulates casework locations, aisle arrangements, and so on. The overall initial timing of the project in the design phase is important to ensure that the project proceeds into the contract-document, bidding, and construction phases on schedule.

Normally, the Store Planner is responsible for the fixturing and fitting of the merchandise shown by drawings—whether they be sketches, perspectives, or design layout plans—as well as the specifications that are eventually needed for the colors of the fabrics, materials, elevations, and more. The Architect provides the usual consultants—structural, mechanical, electrical, plumbing—as well as special consultants, such as elevator and fire-protection consultants, that might be required in order to facilitate the easy building of the project.

Generally working through a project with a Client, the Store Planner and the Architect, if they are both outsourced, attend meetings jointly to meet the Client and discuss their concerns about the building, as well as the layout of the fixturing and furniture. These services continue throughout the project, design, contract-document, and construction phases. Under a normal contract relationship, the Store Planner would prepare in the design phase (after the initial flow diagrams of the plan layout of the departments) all elevations, complete with color of the store's interior and fixturing.

The Architect, during the design phase (after the initial code review and drawing up of the parameters of the building), would also establish the design of the facility, working in cooperation with the Store Planner to determine the merchandise space required. In conjunction with this determination, stairs and exits are located. The design of the facility basically follows the AIA Contract Guidelines in which the proposed architectural treatment is shown and the plan and colored-material selections are made; and often, the Store Planner, as well as the Architect, provides a budget for the anticipated work. These AIA Contract Guidelines are enumerated in AIA B141, "Owner Architect Agreement."

From the design phase, the Store Planner and Architect move into the contract-document phase, preparing the working drawings and the specifications for project bids. The working drawings are separated into those areas for which the Store Planner and the Architect each have responsibility. The Store Planner is usually charged with designating all the materials and finishes, as well as specifications for the fixtures and fittings. The Architect provides similar documentation—referring to mechanical, electrical, structural, and other engineers, or perhaps completing them in his or her own offices—as well as the architectural treatments of the building. These contract documents form the basis for the bidding process from which the contracts for general construction and for the outfitting of the store will be awarded.

Frequently, Architect and Store Planner are required to provide an estimate of construction costs for the work anticipated under the contract documents. During the bidding phase, Store Planner and Architect work jointly to answer contractor's and manufacturer's questions regarding the contract documents they (Store Planner and Architect) have prepared. Those queries are answered in writing by both parties, and both parties generally attend the bid opening. Bids are received by Architect and Store Planner together, and a contract will be written for the general construction work by the Architect or the Owner. A separate contract is generally drafted for the fixtures and fittings.

During the construction phase, Store Planner and Architect visit the site to scrutinize the quality of work. At no time do they individually warrant or guarantee the quality of any contractor's work, nor are they involved with supervising the project's on-site safety since professional liability insurance precludes such participation.

During the course of the project, the frequency of Consultant, Store Planner, or Architect job-site visits is determined by the stage of the project's completion and the Owner's desires. Generally, the Store Planner inspects the later stages of the project, while the Architect visits throughout the entire project. Structural consultants usually visit the site only for concrete pours, and mechanical engineers usually visit during the project's later stages. Shop-drawing review, answering contractor's questions, and providing the supplemental drawings proceed throughout the construction phase jointly by the Store Planner and the Architect.

At the project's completion, both the Store Planner and the Architect participate in a comprehensive "punching out" of the building. This final phase includes checking the project for workmanship and certifying that the directives of the contract documents have been accomplished. Generally, the Architect will provide a document stating the project is substantially complete. This document should not be confused with an occupancy permit, which is secured from the local municipality.

AIA Documents

Standardized AIA documents have been used in this profession since the latter part of the nineteenth century. These documents have been regularly revised to reflect the current state of the law with regard to architectural and construction issues. The popularity of these documents continues to this day. The lead document, AIA A201, "General Conditions of the Contract for Construction," sets the tone and tenor of all the related documents. AIA documents are divided into a number of subgroups that have different architectural objectives (note: there is no E series):

A Series—Owner/Contractor Documents

B Series—Owner/Architect Documents
C Series—Architect/Consultant Documents
D Series—Architect/Industry Documents
F Series—Compensation Guidelines
G Series—Architect Office and Project Documents

Over the years, the AIA has developed a large "family" of related documents in which all documents work together so an AIA B141, "Agreement between Architect and Owner," works in conjunction with AIA A201, "General Conditions of the Contract for Construction." These documents take on added importance since they are intended to be modified by supplemental conditions for the AIA General Conditions and have portions deleted and others added freely. A511, "Guide for Supplementary Conditions," is used to add or delete portions of A201 to tailor the construction contract to the particular needs of the project.

Part of the appeal of using the AIA documents is that they are prepared by general practitioners in the field of architecture and not by attorneys prone to use confusing "legalese." These Architects meet on a quarterly basis to write and review new documents, depending on the cycle of those documents themselves. Once a new A201 has been established, all other related documents are updated on the same ten-year cycle.

The family of AIA Documents has grown over the years as the professions of Architecture and related design fields have become more complex to meet with societal needs. These newer arrivals include:

A171—Standard Form of Owner/Contractor Agreement for Furniture, Furnishings, and Equipment
A177—Abbreviated Owner/Contractor Agreement for Furniture, Furnishings, and Equipment
A191—Standard Form of Agreement between Owner and Design/Builder
A491—Standard Form of Agreement between Design/Builder and Contractor
B171—Standard Form of Agreement for Interior Design Services
B177—Abbreviated Form of Agreement for Interior Design Services
B901—Standard Form of Agreement between Design/Builder and Architect
C141—Standard Form of Agreement between Architect and Consultant
C142—Abbreviated Form of Agreement between Architect and Consultant

C727—Standard Form of Agreement between Architect and Consultant for Special Services
C801—Joint Venture Agreement

Many documents come in abbreviated form for small projects including general construction and construction management. All are described in great detail in the AIA Documents Synopsis.

Contract modifications are achieved by the adoption of supplemental conditions that supersede general conditions or by the actual modification of the contract itself. In all cases, the contract has a binding arbitration clause (to resolve any disputes that could affect the parties) that can either be retained or struck, depending on the desires of the Owner and Consultant. Nonbinding mediation is currently the dispute-resolution method of choice.

Generally, the Owner and the Space Planner will work on the specifications together with the Architect using the AIA's "General Conditions" and the "Supplementary General Conditions" that alter certain General Conditions. These agreements are usually reviewed by the Client's in-house attorneys with insurance requirements coming directly from the Client. In AIA Form A511, "Guide for Supplementary Conditions," insurance requirements for contracts are clearly spelled out as to insurance requirements, coverage minimums, and time limits.

Appendix 6

SPECIFICATIONS FOR THE MANUFACTURE OF STORE FIXTURES

National Association of Store Fixture Manufacturers

Section I

General Conditions

A. Definitions
   1. The *Contract Documents* consist of (1) the agreement, (2) the general conditions of the contract, (3) the supplementary general conditions, (4) the drawings, specifications, and *scope of the work*, including all modifications, thereof incorporated in the documents before their execution. These form the *Contract*.
   2. The *Owner*, the *Contractor*, and the *Architect* are those mentioned as such in the agreement. They are treated throughout the contract documents as if each were of the singular number and masculine gender. The term *Architect* shall refer to architects, store architects, store designers, or designers.
   3. The term *Subcontractor* as employed herein, includes only those having a direct contract with the contractor, and it includes one who furnishes material worked to a special design according to the plans or specifications of this work, but does not include one who merely furnishes material not so worked.
   4. The term *Work* of the Contractor or Subcontractor includes labor or materials or both *in accordance with the scope of the work*.

B. Quality of Work
   1. Qualifications of Workmanship:
      a. All work must be performed by a contractor equipped and experienced to do work equal in all respects to the best standards for fabricating, finishing, and installing fine-quality cabinet and fixture work.
      b. Only mechanics who are sufficiently qualified as skilled in cabinet and fixture work to produce a first-class product shall be employed in the fabricating, finishing, and installation of the units included in this contract. The contractor must show evidence of thorough experience in this field to the complete satisfaction of the owner and the architect.

c. All fixtures shall be made and finished at the shop of the contractor and assembled in single and complete units to the greatest extent that the requirements of delivery and installation in the building will permit. Large pieces requiring sectional construction shall have their several parts accurately fitted and aligned with each other in the shop before shipment. They shall be provided with ample hidden means of fastening to render the work substantial, rigid, and permanently secured in the building.

2. Guarantee

The contractor guarantees that all materials and workmanship shall be of the quality specified and shown and that any defect due to the use of improper workmanship or material discovered and made known to him within one year from the date the installation is substantially completed shall be repaired or replaced by him without additional expense to the owner. The owner shall give notice of observed defects with reasonable promptness.

C. Special Features of the Contract and Its Execution

1. General:

   a. Written notice shall be deemed to have been duly served if delivered in person to the individual or to a member of the firm or to an officer of the corporation for whom it is intended, or if delivered at or sent by registered mail to the last business address known to him who gives the notice.

   b. All the limits stated in the contract documents are of the essence to the contract.

   c. The law of the place of building shall govern the construction of this contract.

2. Subcontracting:

Subcontracting various phases of work is basic to the construction industry. However, subcontracting any portion of the work does not relieve the contractor of his responsibility for labor, material, or quality. Should the contractor elect to subcontract any phase of his work before proceeding, he must notify the architect or owner of his intentions.

3. Contract Changes:

   a. The owner, without invalidating the contract, may order extra work or make changes by altering, adding to, or deducting from the work, the contract sum being adjusted accordingly.

   b. All directions causing changes in the type of work, additions or subtractions of work, and changes in measurement shall be confirmed in writing to the contractor before the work is done. Directions that do not affect the work itself or the cost of doing the work but are offered in the normal progress of the job shall be confirmed in writing upon request.

   c. When an approved shop drawing or a change ordered or required in the field (not due to an error by the contractor) reflects a credit or extra, the contractor shall notify the architect after the return of the shop drawing or after the request for change in the field.

   d. Approval for such credit or extra must be obtained from the owner's representative before the manufacture of said item or field change. Absence of response for 10 days after receipt by the architect of the request for the amount of the extra or the credit shall constitute approval.

4. Delivery:

   a. The architect shall furnish the contractor a building schedule and a sequential installation schedule. The contractor, insofar as is practicable, will schedule his work to conform to this schedule. *Any variation from this schedule shall be forwarded to the contractor immediately.*

   b. Delivery of cabinet and fixture work and commencement of installation at the job site shall be at the time established by the architect. However, no cabinet work shall be permitted in the building before the building is completely enclosed, plaster is dry, and all overhead painting and ceiling work of others is finished and the scaffolding removed.

   If the conditions in (a) and (b) are not met, the owner's representative shall agree to an extension of the contractor's completion date or shall order the contractor to proceed with delivery at the job site and shall waive the owner's right of redress in the event of defects resulting from swelling or shrinkage of solid lumber or plywood, the reaction of moisture on finishes or other attributable to building conditions.

5. Storage:

The contractor will agree to store, handle, and insure completed fixtures that cannot be delivered to the job site through no fault of his own for a period not exceeding 30 days after the scheduled delivery date. The cost of the storage, handling, and insurance shall be borne by the owner thereafter. Invoices will be rendered in accordance with the terms of the contract and payments shall be due as stipulated therein.

6. Delays:

If the contractor is delayed at any time in the progress of the work by any act or neglect of the owner or the architect; or of any employee of either; or by any other contractor employed by the owner; or by changes ordered in the work; or by strikes, lockouts, fire, unusual delay in transportation, unavoidable casualties or any causes beyond the contractor's control; or by delay authorized by the architect pending arbitration; or by any other cause that the architect shall decide to justify a delay, the contractor shall give notification in writing and the time of completion shall be extended for such reasonable period as agreed upon by the parties involved.

7. Inspection:

The architect or his representative shall have access to all work at either the contractor's or the owner's premises.

8. Patents:

The contractor shall protect and save harmless the owner from loss or damage caused by suit or infringement of patents used in the manufacture of the fixtures, unless the architect has specified a particular process or product leading to infringement. It shall be the responsibility of the contractor to notify the architect promptly of infringements of which he becomes aware.

9. Name Plates:

Name plates of any type will be allowed on this work unless prohibited by the owner.

10. Owner's Right to Terminate Contract:

a. The owner may terminate the contract if: (1) the contractor should be adjudged a bankrupt, (2) he should have a general assignment for creditor's benefit, (3) a receiver should be appointed because of an alleged insolvency, (4) he should repeatedly fail to supply enough workmen or materials for the proper execution of the contract, *provided there are workmen available in the local area of this installation, and that the owner, architect, and contractor agree that additional workmen are needed,* (5) he should fail to pay *proper claims* by subcontractors for material or labor, (6) he should disregard laws, ordinances or the architect's instructions *provided the architect's instructions are in accord with the contract,* (7) he should be guilty of any other substantial violation of the contract.

b. In such cases, the owner, on certificate of the architect that sufficient cause exists and 7 days after receipt by the contractor of written notice, may, without prejudice to any other right or remedy, terminate the employment of the contractor and take possession of the premises and of all materials, and finish the work in a reasonable manner. In such case, the contractor shall not be entitled to receive any further payment, *other than approved payments,* until the work is finished.

c. A reasonable cost to the owner for finishing the work shall be deducted from the balance due to the contractor on the contract. Expenses incurred by the owner shall be certified by the architect and written proof of such expenditures shall be submitted to the contractor.

11. Contractor's Right to Stop Work or Terminate Contract:

a. If the work should be stopped under an order of any court or other public authority for a period of 30 days, through no act or fault of the contractor or of anyone employed by him, then the contractor may, upon 7 days' written notice to the owner and the architect, terminate this contract and recover from the owner payment for all work executed and any proven loss sustained upon any plant or materials and reasonable profit and damages.

b. If the architect fails to issue any certificate for payment, through no fault of the contractor, within 10 days after the contractor's formal request for payment, or if the owner should fail to pay to the contractor, within 15 days of its maturity and presentation, any sum certified by the architect or awarded by arbitrators, then the contractor may, upon 7 days' written notice to the owner and the architect, stop the work or terminate this contract as set out in the preceding paragraph.

12. Arbitration:

a. All disputes, claims or questions under this contract shall be submitted to arbitration in accordance with the provisions, then obtaining, in the standard form of arbitration procedure of the American Institute of Architects. This agreement shall be specifically enforceable under the prevailing arbitration law. Judgment upon the award rendered may be entered in the highest court of the forum, state or federal, having jurisdiction. The decision of the arbitrators shall be a condition precedent to any right of legal action that either party may have against the other.

b. Notice of the demand for arbitration of a dispute shall be filed in writing with the architect and the other party of the contract. If the arbitration is an appeal from the architect's decision, a demand thereof shall be made within 10 days of its receipt. In any other case, the demand for arbitration shall be made within a reasonable time after the dispute has arisen. In no case, however, shall a demand be made by the owner later than 30 days after completion of the work and by the contractor 10 days after the time of final payment.

13. Assignment:

Neither party to the contract shall assign the contract or sublet it as a whole without the written consent of the other, nor shall the contractor assign any moneys due or to become due to him hereunder without the previous written consent of the owner.

14. Substitutions and Changes:

Substitution of materials or changes of details may be made by the contractor with the approval of the owner's representative.

D. Drawings, Specifications, and Samples

1. General:

a. The drawings and specifications are complementary, and the requirements of one shall be as binding as if required by both.

b. Figure dimensions shall take precedence over scale measurements, detail drawings over general drawings, and drawings of later date over those of earlier date.

c. Addenda specifications shall take precedence over original specifications and earlier adenda thereto.

d. Specifications, instructions to bidder *and scope of the work* shall take precedence over drawings where any conflict exists.

e. The contractor shall not execute any part of the work requiring supplementary details or approved shop drawings until he has received such details or approved shop drawings.

2. Furnishing Drawings and Specifications:

The architect will furnish to the contractor free of charge a sufficient number of copies of drawings and specifications necessary for the proper execution of the work.

3. Shop Drawings:

a. The contractor shall prepare shop drawings as required in the execution of his work and shall submit these to the architect for approval or modifications as requested.

b. Sheet dimensions shall not exceed 42 x 72 inches.

c. Drawings or units of dissimilar design or character shall not be placed in the same sheet.

d. The numbering system shall be singular and consecutive.

e. Show drawings shall contain all information necessary for fabrication. Two sets of shop drawings or a single sepia shall be sent to the architect for his approval. The architect will retain one set and return the second set with his corrections and written approval; or he will return the sepia with his corrections and written approval, and the contractor will send him a corrected print.

4. Samples:

   The architect will furnish to the contractor samples of materials and of painted or natural wood finishes. The contractor shall then submit for approval a reasonable number of samples, matching in grain, color, and size, those furnished by the architect.

E. Installation

1. General:

   a. All installation work shall be done by the contractor under the direction of his supervisor whose skill, techniques, and knowledge are such that he can direct the installation in accordance with the true intent and meaning of the drawings and specifications.

   b. All cabinetwork shall be installed by mechanics experienced in this type of work. It shall be set, scribed plumb, square, and level, and be secured in position as indicated on drawings and approved shop details.

   c. Extreme care shall be exercised to avoid damaging finished surfaces during handling and erecting of the cabinetwork.

      After installation the contractor shall touch up all finished surfaces where marred or damaged.

2. Field Measurements:

   a. The contractor shall secure such field measurements at the job site as may be required for his work as early as possible after contracts are awarded. If the state of completion of the building is such as to delay the taking of field measurements, the general building contractor shall provide a detailed plan showing all required measurements.

   b. If any discrepancies exist between the architect's drawings and the field dimensions, the contractor shall report same in writing to the architect and shall not proceed with the portion of the work in question until discrepancies are clarified.

   c. The contractor shall call to the owner's representative's attention any changes required because of job conditions and shall get written approval before making these changes.

3. Cooperation with Other Contractors:

   The contractor shall cooperate with other contractors working on the job to coordinate properly his work with theirs.

4. Cutting and Fitting:

   The contractor shall do all cutting and fitting as required in his work to receive properly other contractor's work. Any cutting and fitting necessitated through the neglect of others or that could not have been reasonably assumed at the time of bidding must be approved by the owner's representative before execution of the work, and the contractor shall be reimbursed for this work.

5. Supervision:

   The contractor shall keep a competent superintendent, satisfactory to the owner's representative, on the job at all times during the progress of the work.

6. Permits and Regulations:

   a. Permits or licenses of a temporary nature necessary for the execution of the work shall be secured and paid for by the owner.

   b. The contractor shall give all notices and comply with all laws, ordinances, rules, or regulations bearing on the conduct of the work.

   c. It shall be the responsibility of the architect to ensure that his plans and specifications conform with the local requirements. If the contractor observes that the drawings and specifications are in variance with the local regulations, he shall promptly notify the architect.

7. Building Services:

   The owner shall furnish to the contractor free of charge freight elevator service, hoists, electric power, adequate light, heat, water, and toilet facilities as per agreed installation schedule. Contractor shall be responsible that units are of a proper size to fit freight elevator.

8. Removal of Debris:

   The contractor shall at all times keep the premises free from accumulations of waste materials or rubbish caused by his employees at work. At the completion of the work, he shall remove all his rubbish from and about the building and all his tools, scaffolding, and surplus materials and shall leave his work "broom clean."

9. Protection of Work and Property:

The contractor shall maintain reasonable protection to safeguard his work from damage and to protect the owner's property from injury or loss arising in connection with this contract.

F. Financial Responsibilities

1. Insurance:

a. The contractor shall carry workmen's compensation insurance as required by law. He shall carry public liability insurance in an amount not less than $500,000.00 for injury to any one person and not less than $1,000,000.00 for any accident involving two or more persons. He shall carry property damage insurance in a minimum amount of $2,000,000.00.

The contractor shall furnish certificates of insurance or evidence of such insurance to the owner upon request.

b. The owner will provide extended coverage insurance on the structure in which this contract is to be performed. This insurance policy will cover items of the material and work stored or installed on the premises whether the property of the owner or of the contractor.

c. The owner shall be responsible for and at his option maintain such insurance as will protect him from his contingent liability for damages for personal injuries, including death, that may arise from operations under this contract.

d. The title passing from contractor to owner and all insurance coverage responsibilities shall take place when the fixtures, materials, and work are delivered to the premises.

2. Performance Bond:

The owner shall have the right prior to the signing of the contract to require the contractor to furnish bonds covering the faithful performance of the contract in such form as the owner may prescribe and with such sureties as he may approve. The cost of these bonds will be paid by the owner.

3. Liens:

a. Neither the final payment nor any part of the retained percentage shall become due until the contractor, if required, shall deliver to the owner a complete release of all liens arising out of this contract, or receipts in full in lieu thereof and, if required in either case, an affidavit that, so far as he has knowledge or information, the releases and receipts include all the labor and material for which a lien could be filed; but the contractor may, if any subcontractor refuses to furnish a release or receipt in full, furnish a bond satisfactory to the owner, to indemnify him against any lien.

b. If any lien remains unsatisfied after all payments are made, the contractor shall refund to the owner all moneys that the latter may be compelled to pay in discharging such a lien, including all costs and a reasonable fee to an attorney.

4. Payments:

a. The contractor shall submit for approval to the architect a request for payment at the first of each month for work and materials in process. Five percent of this amount will be held back until the completion of the job. The request must be accompanied by a waiver of lien and, when paid, is not to be construed as acceptance of the work or indication of the value of the work performed.

b. Final payment shall be made within 10 days after acceptance of the work or within 30 days of substantial completion. If the work is not accepted within 20 days after substantial completion, the owner shall pay to the contractor the total amount outstanding including the five percent held back and shall withhold only an amount equal to the fair value of correction and touch-up deemed necessary.

5. Cash Allowances:

a. The contractor shall include in the contract sum all allowances named in the contract documents and shall cause the work so covered to be done by such contractors and for such sums as the architect may direct, the contract sum being adjusted in conformity therewith.

b. The contractor declares that the contract sum includes such sums for expenses and profit on account of case allowance as he deems proper. No demand for expenses or profit other than those included in the contract sum shall be allowed.

   c. The contractor shall not be required to employ for any such work persons against whom he has a reasonable objection.

6. Overtime:

   a. Overtime may be requested by the architect. The owner shall bear all direct costs of overtime both in the factory and on the job.

   b. Should any controversy arise as to responsibilities when the schedule is not maintained, the architect shall be the sole arbitrator.

7. Taxes:

All state and local taxes are not included in the contract price. If requested by the owner, the contractor will add the stipulated amount to the contract and pay the taxes to the proper authorities.

Section II

Cabinet and Wall Materials and Fixture Construction

A. Purpose

This section specifies acceptable wood and wood-based materials; laminates of wood, wood fiber, plastic, and other materials; fixture construction and manufacturing requirements; and methods of assigning or ascertaining quality standards in the manufacture of store fixtures, store perimeters, and associated architectural structures. A variety of alternative materials and procedures in manufacturing are presented to provide flexibility to the architect, store planner, designer, and manufacturer. Materials, processes, and construction, specified by paragraph in the contract documents, shall be adhered to without modification unless changes are agreed upon by the architect and the fixture manufacturer.

B. Scope

This specification applies to all wood and related materials used in fixtures, store perimeters, and interiors of buildings, which are manufactured and supplied by the fixture industry. It shall apply to all purchased materials used in fabrication of fixtures. It provides physical requirements, test values and procedures, tolerances, workmanship, and quality values for the ben-

efit of the fixture manufacturer and the architect.

The fixture contractor shall furnish all labor, materials, manufacturing facilities, services, and transportation required to manufacture and install completely all items of cabinet work and fixtures indicated in the contract documents. Fixtures not installed will also comply with specifications for materials and construction.

C. Identification of Fixtures

Every fixture and all removable parts of fixtures and wall materials shall be plainly numbered on an unexposed portion to correspond with the number of the fixture shown on the architect's or manufacturer's plans.

D. Wood

1. General:

   a. All wood, wood-base, wood-composite, and wood-fibrous materials shall be in compliance with the following paragraphs. Materials not specified shall be permitted in fixtures if equivalent in appearance and performance for the intended use and approved by the architect.

   b. Where equivalent materials are permitted, equivalence shall imply equal or better than the specified materials in appearance and performance.

   c. All domestic wood species used shall be identified by common commercial names for the species or groups of species desired as listed at the end of this article. Common names for imported woods shall be interpreted as the name in most common usage and in compliance with any rulings made by the Federal Trade Commission.

   d. Wood moisture content of all wood materials shall be in conformance with the requirements and/or specifications for the material and the service conditions. All lumber from which wood parts and fixtures are made shall have a moisture content of 5 to 12 percent.

E. Wood—Lumber, Solid, Edge-Glued, Finger-Jointed, Laminated

1. Definitions:

   a. Wood: solid, lumber—A part or piece of wood in unmodified form made from one piece of timber that is not increased in dimension by gluing or other forms of fastening.

b. Wood: solid, edge-glued—A part made of two or more pieces of wood edge-glued to increase the width dimension of lumber or parts.

c. Wood: finger-jointed—A part made of two or more pieces of wood joined together end to end by fingers and glued to increase the length dimension of the lumber.

d. Wood: solid, laminated—A part made of two or more pieces of wood joined by gluing, with the grain of the adjacent layers parallel, to increase the thickness dimension of the lumber or parts.

2. Wood: Solid, Lumber
All hardwood and cypress lumber purchased for use in the manufacture of wood fixtures and parts shall comply with the National Hardwood Lumber Association's rules for measurement and inspection (grades) of lumber.

All softwood lumber purchased for use in the manufacture of wood fixtures and parts shall comply with grading rules and specifications applicable to the particular species of lumber.

The moisture content of all lumber shall be between 5 and 12 percent with all other wood parts and wood materials not over 10 percent.

All imported softwood and hardwood lumber or parts purchased for use in the manufacture of fixtures shall comply with the established grades for the species or shall comply with grades established between the buyer and seller.

3. Wood: Solid, Edge-Glued
Edge-glued wood parts made from lumber cuttings shall comply with quality and grade requirements of the contract. The adhesives and gluing operations shall meet the standard or superior requirements specified under paragraph J.6. Fixture Manufacturing: Glues and Gluing.

4. Wood: Finger-Jointed
Finger-jointed wood parts shall have a minimum of five fingers on each piece per inch of thickness. The adhesives, machining, and gluing operations must be of superior quality as specified under paragraph

J.6. Fixture Manufacturing: Glues and Gluing.

5. Wood: Solid, Laminated
Wood parts prepared for laminating shall be free of decay, knot holes, large knots over 1½ inches in diameter, warp, and splits. All other defects or character marks may be placed in the interior of the laminates so they do not appear on the exposed surfaces after final machining.

F. Wood—Plywood, Softwood, Hardwood, and Decorative Plywood

1. Definitions:
Plywood is a flat or curved wood construction made of two or more layers of veneer separated by a core with grain directions at approximately right angles to the adjacent layer in the assembly. Plywood is usually identified by the material applied on the face; that is, birch plywood has a birch face veneer.

a. Three-ply plywood consists of a face veneer, core, and back. Generally all plies are veneer; however, the core may be of wood or wood-base materials or other composition products.

b. Five-ply, seven-ply, and so on, plywood construction consists of (1) faces that are the exposed plies, (2) cross bands, two or more plies, that are directly under the faces with grain direction, when made of veneer, at right angles to the faces, (3) a core of veneer, edge-glued lumber, particle board, or other material with grain direction, when present, at right angles to the adjacent cross bands.

c. Balanced plywood construction consists of equal plies of veneer or other material on both sides of the core. The plies on both sides of the center line are balanced with the same or like material, thickness, and direction of grain on opposite sides of the core. The core can vary in thickness and material to meet the architect's needs.

d. Symmetrically balanced plywood construction consists of equal amounts of the same material in each grain direction at right angles to the face and parallel with the face, that is, 1/28, 1/14, 1/28, or 1/40, 1/20, 1/20, 1/20, 1/40.

2. Softwood Plywood or Construction and Industrial Plywood:
The Voluntary Product Standard PS1-74, or the latest revision for Construction and Industrial use, shall be used by store fixture manufacturers in their procurement of plywood. Construction and Industrial plywood is classified by exposure capability and grade into two types, Interior and Exterior.

The selection of the types, grades, and surface requirements of the plywood, depending on location in the fixtures and service conditions intended for the fixtures, must be carefully made from the variety of options available in PS1-74.

A "Certificate of Inspection" shall be obtained with each plywood shipment. Each plywood panel so certified shall bear the stamp of assurance that the plywood meets the specification requirements.

3. Hardwood and Decorative Plywood:
Hardwood plywood purchased for use in store fixtures shall comply with the National Bureau of Standards Voluntary Product Standard PS51-71 or the latest revision for hardwood and decorative plywood.

PS51-71 covers the principal types, grades, and constructions of plywood made primarily with hardwood veneer faces. Specified are: face veneer species and grades; requirements for lumber, particleboard, medium density fiberboard, and veneer cores; the type of glue bond desired; and other requirements for quality plywood.

a. Hardwood plywood for exposed surfaces shall be Type II, unless otherwise specified, water-resistant glue bonds, premium to good grade veneer, faces of tight-cut veneer, and in compliance with hardwood plywood tests. For unexposed or interior surfaces, the lower grades of plywood may be used as specified on the manufacturer's or architect's plans.

b. A statement of compliance with PS51-71 or latest revision may be specified or required with each purchase. Each plywood panel in the conformance shall be labeled and bear the name and address of the producer or distributor.

G. Wood-Base and Wood Composites: Particle Board, Hardboard, Medium-Density Fiberboard, Insulation Board, Waferboard, and Ply-Strand Board

1. General:
All wood-base and wood-composition materials of particles, flakes, fibers, and fibrous bundles bonded with varying amounts and kinds of adherents shall be in compliance with the following paragraphs. Materials not specified shall be permitted in fixtures if equivalent or better in appearance and performance for the intended use and approved by the architect.

2. Definitions:
a. Particle boards are either homogenous or layered boards made from specially cut flakes, splinters, shavings, and other particles or combinations of particles bonded together with a thermosetting synthetic resin. Particle board densities may range from 30 to 60 pounds per cubic foot.

b. Hardboard is a panel manufactured primarily from interfelted lignocellulose (wood) fibers that are consolidated under heat and pressure in a hot press to a density of 31 pounds or greater. Other materials may be added to improve certain properties, such as stiffness, hardness, finishing properties, and resistance to abrasion and moisture, as well as to increase strength, durability, and utility.

c. Medium-density fiberboard (MDF) is a dry formed panel product manufactured from wood lignocellulose fibers combined with a synthetic resin or other suitable binder. The panels are compressed in a hot press to a density of 31 to 50 pounds per cubic foot. The binder and other materials may be added during manufacture to improve certain properties.

d. Insulation board is a low-density fiberboard formed from a wet-pulping process. The panels have a density of 2 to 30 pounds per cubic foot. Normally no binder is added to the fibrous mat. As the name implies, panels are used primarily for thermal and acoustical insulation.

e. Waferboards and ply-strand boards are specifically manufactured to improve durability and strength.

3. Particle Board:
   a. Particle boards shall comply with ANSI A 208.1-1979 or latest revision thereof for mat-formed wood particle board. Extruded particle board when specified for plywood core material shall conform to the general requirements of the above commercial standards.
   b. Particle boards used in fixtures shall have a minimum density of 37 pounds per cubic foot.
   c. Particle board surfaces shall not have indentations greater than $1/100$ inch as measured by $1/100$-inch radius anvil or stylus. Surface irregularities shall not telegraph through a $1/40$ inch or thicker face veneer or surface overlay.
   d. The moisture content of particle board panels at time of shipment shall not be in excess of 10 percent.

4. Hardboard:
   a. Hardboard shall comply with Voluntary Product Standards PS 58-73 or the latest revision prepared by the American Hardboard Association and known as Basic Hardboard. Other Voluntary Product Standards using hardboard are Prefinished Hardboard Paneling PS 59-73 and Hardboard Siding PS 60-73. Basic hardboards are classified as Tempered, Standard, Service-tempered, Service, and Industrialite.
   b. The moisture content of hardboards should range between 4 and 8 percent. Purchase orders should specify the class, surface requirements, and thickness-variation tolerance for each classification of hardboard.

5. Medium-Density Fiberboard:
   Medium-density fiberboard shall conform to the ANSI A 208.2-1980 and latest revisions thereof. The moisture content of medium-density fiberboard panels should range between 4 and 8 percent.

6. Insulation Board:
   Insulation board purchased and used in fixtures shall conform to the Insulation Board Standard of the U.S. Department of Commerce.

H. Decorative Plastic Laminates and Overlays
   1. General:
      Plastic laminates, resin-impregnated paper laminates, postforming plastic, conformable plastic fibers, paper and paper-base overlays, natural and synthetic fiber sheets, and similar decorative and protective materials shall be in compliance with the following paragraphs. Materials not specified shall be permitted if equivalent or better in appearance properties and performance for the intended use and approved by the architect.
   2. Definitions:
      a. High-pressure laminates are thermosetting resin-impregnated rigid-surfacing materials usually made of multilayers of resin-impregnated paper laminates and a protective plastic film.
      b. Postforming plastic laminates are thermosetting resin-impregnated paper laminates containing crepe filler stock to permit postforming with heat and pressure.
      c. Vertical surface-type laminates are designed specifically for vertical applications where appearance, durability, and resistance to heat and stains are required. This type should be used only in accordance with the laminate manufacturer's recommendations.
      d. Conformable plastic films are flexible plastic sheets made to conform to the contours and shape of flat and molded-core materials.
      e. Overlays are sheets of paper, resin-impregnated fiber, or plastic film with or without thin veneer designed to form an opaque film over the substrate.
   3. High-Pressure Laminates:
      a. High-pressure laminates shall conform to National Electric Manufacturers Association (NEMA) standards LD3-1980 or latest revision thereof and shall have been demonstrated to pass NEMA tests for plastic laminates.
      b. High-pressure laminates shall be uniform in color, uniform in gloss and texture, and without blisters, wrinkles, racks, dents, heat marks, and other imperfections that impair their appearance and serviceability.
      c. High-pressure laminates for both horizontal and vertical applications shall have a minimum thickness of .050 inch and shall have a thickness tolerance not

exceeding plus/minus .005 inch. An additional .001 inch tolerance is allowed for each additional $1/32$ inch of thickness. Laminates for only vertical-surface use may have a minimum thickness of $1/32$ (.031) inch.

4. Postforming Plastic Laminates:
   a. Postforming plastic laminates shall comply with NEMA standards LD3-1980 or latest revisions thereof.
   b. Postforming laminates shall be able to conform under heat and pressure to the radius of curvature of a countertop or edge without cracking or breaking.

5. Conformable Films:
   Conformable plastic films may be specified to the same decorative and performance requirements as the NEMA standards for high-pressure laminates.

6. Fire-Rated Type Laminate:
   A fire-rated laminate is similar to a general purpose laminate or a vertical-surface laminate. In addition, due to its special design and construction, it provides lower fire hazard characteristics of flamespread, fuel contributed, and/or smoke developed. These laminates should comply with NEMA Standard LD3-1980.

7. Overlays:
   a. Overlays shall mask the grain, checks, patches, or sound defects of particle board, plywood, or lumber. Overlaid plywood shall comply with the specification for overlaid plywood as contained in the Commercial Standard CS 45-60 or latest revision thereof.
   b. Overlayment for particle board may be a cellulose fiber sheet containing a minimum of 20 percent melamine or phenol-formaldehyde resin. The impregnated sheet shall not be less than .12 inch thick and shall weigh not less than 65 pounds per 1,000 square feet. The bond between the overlay and the particle board shall be equal in performance to the bond between particles within the board.
   c. All other overlays shall comply with the product specifications.

I. Moisture Content
   1. General:
      All lumber used in fixtures shall have a moisture content of 5 to 12 percent. Hardboard and medium-density fiberboard should have 4 to 8 percent moisture content. All other wood materials manufactured shall be dried to within 4 to 10 percent moisture content.

      All purchase orders for wood materials, wood-base materials, precut or partly fabricated wood parts, dimension stock, and other wood fixture products shall specify that the materials must have a moisture content as specified above. Any shipment or part of the shipment exceeding the above designated moisture content is cause for rejection of all or part of the order.

   2. Method of Determining Moisture Content:
      Moisture content shall be measured by the oven-dry method from samples taken from the shipment or by moisture meters that have been calibrated and checked with oven-dry moisture content determinations. Wood and wood-base materials that have resins or chemicals that alter moisture readings (fire-resistant treated wood, particle board, hardboard, etc.) shall have moisture content determined by the oven-dry method.

   3. Storage of Wood and Wood-Base Materials:
      Lumber, plywood, particle board, hardboard, and other wood-base materials and the completed fixtures shall be stored where the atmospheric conditions will maintain the moisture content of the wood material and the fixtures within the limits of 4 to 10 percent.

J. Fixture Manufacturing
   1. General:
      All wood fixtures, perimeters, and interiors manufactured shall comply with the following:

      All materials specified must be the highest of their respective kinds for the purposes intended. Each exposed material must be expertly selected and compatible in color, grain, and character.

      All items manufactured shall be of cabinetwork construction, shall be accurately machined, and shall have joints properly fitted.

   2. Exposed Wood Parts:
      a. All solid wood and plywood transparent finished surfaces exposed to view after installation and the interiors of open cases and glass-door cases shall be

clear or character marked and selected for color, grain, attractive, and decorative features. Species used shall be specified by their common commercial names (see end of article). The wood shall be free of checks, cross-grain, splits, holes, and other features specified that would impair appearance and service.

b. Exposed wood parts for opaque finishes shall normally be diffuse porous, fine-textured hardwood of species such as red maple, sweet gum, black gum, tupelo, yellow poplar, or magnolia that have a species average of at least 0.40 specific gravity on an oven-dry basis (see Density Class in table at end of article). Surfaces to be finished shall be sound and free from all defects that will show in any way through an opaque finish.

c. Accessible exposed wood parts, normally hidden but partly exposed during use of the fixture shall be similar in quality to that mentioned in the two preceding paragraphs, 2a and 2b, except for color, grain, and other wood characteristics that do not impair serviceability. These parts may be made of a wide variety of species and materials such as particle board and medium-density fiberboard.

3. Unexposed Wood Parts:
   a. Unexposed wood parts shall be hardwoods or softwoods or wood composites with a minimum species average of 0.36 specific gravity on an oven-dry basis such as red maple, sweet gum, black gum, magnolia, yellow poplar, Douglas fir, southern pine, or tamarack.
   b. Parts shall be free from rot, knot holes, and splits. Such defects that do not seriously impair strength, interfere with fastening, or lower quality in any other way will be permitted.

4. Machining and Joinery:
   a. All wood parts shall be machined accurately to the dimensions and tolerances called for in the contract documents. Precision or machining shall be such to insure proper function and appearance. Exposed end-to-side grain, mitred, and similar joints shall form the desired angle precisely and shall mate with no percep-

tible glueline thickness or variation in thickness.

b. Knife marks, torn grain, and other machining imperfections that will not be completely removed in sanding shall not be permitted on any exposed surfaces.

c. Sanding of machined parts preparatory to finishing shall e done in accordance with Section III, paragraph B of these specifications.

d. Joinery details shown on shop drawings by the fixture manufacturers shall establish the type of construction desired. Mortise-and-tenon and dowel joints subject to stress shall be reinforced with screws, nails, bolts, angle iron, or glued corner blocks as shown on shop drawings. The fixture manufacturer's shop standards for tight, strong, and durable joints shall conform to high-quality joinery.

e. Joint detail, as shown on the working drawings, shall be accurately machined so that mating parts to receive glue shall have proper clearance on all sides (approximately .002 to .005 inch) at the time of assembly.

f. Dry joints shall not be used except in fixtures designed for easy disassembly. The method of assembly of large perimeters and long parts for fixtures shall be shown on the shop drawing.

g. In dowel joints, only spirally grooved, noncompressed dowels shall be used. Dowel diameters shall be measured to fit the bored hole.

h. Mortises, tenons, clamp nails, lock mitres, and other methods of joinery, as shown on shop drawings, may be used. Joints may be reinforced with glue blocks, screws, nails, staples, or bolts as specified.

5. Decorative Plastic Laminates:
   a. Decorative plastic laminates shall be bonded to a core made of veneer, lumber, plywood, or wood or wood-fiber composites. A backing sheet of laminate .020 in thickness or the same thickness as the face shall be used to balance the assembly and reduce the warping tendency. Plasterboard, gypsum board, plaster, and similar materials shall not be

used as core material because their internal bond strength is not sufficient for this service.

   b. Machining, gluing, assembly and fabrication of laminates to core materials, and assembly of laminated panels in fixtures shall follow recommendations of manufacturers and the NEMA Standard LD3-1980.

6. Glues and Gluing:

   a. All adhesives used in manufacturing shall conform to the adhesive manufacturer's recommendations.

   b. Adhesives used in plywood shall be urea-formaldehyde, phenol-formaldehyde, melamine, and resorcinol-formaldehyde.

   c. Adhesives used in laminating thick structural parts requiring high strength shall be urea-formaldehyde or resorcinol-formaldehyde. Laminates of small posts, legs, and other parts not subjected to high-strength requirements may use hot or cold animal glue or polyvinyl acetate resin emulsions.

   d. Adhesives used in edge-to-edge gluing of such items as tops, core stock, shelving, and so on, shall be urea-formaldehyde, animal glue, polyvinyl acetate resin emulsions, or resorcinol-formaldehyde. Adhesives used in bonding plastic laminates shall be contact cements, hot-melts, and urea-formaldehyde.

   e. Adhesives used for assembly of parts, such as with dowels, splines, mortise and tenons, and so on, shall be polyvinyl acetate resin emulsions or animal glue. When rapid adhesive-curing techniques are available, urea-formaldehyde or resorcinol-formaldehyde adhesives may be used.

   f. Gluing procedures specified herein shall be adequate to insure a glue bond shear strength equal to or greater than the materials being joined. Shear tests shall show 75 percent or greater wood failure.

     (1) Pressures used in gluing with rigid platens shall be for softwoods 100 to 150 pounds per square inch (psi); for hardwoods 150 to 200 psi. When nonrigid platens are used, pressures shall be a minimum of 50 psi.

     (2) Pressures shall be maintained until the adhesive is solidified or cured and adequate strength has developed to permit handling without disturbing the bond.

     (3) Adhesives selected for dissimilar materials, such as plastic laminates and particle board, shall be those recommended by the manufacturers of both the materials and the adhesives.

     (4) Plastic laminates bonded to underlayment with urea-fomaldehyde shall be considered a superior procedure, whereas contact-cement bonds are a standard procedure.

     (5) Plastic components may be bonded to wood and other materials with epoxy-type adhesives or adhesives specified for the particular components.

   g. Contact cements and hot-melt adhesives may be used in nonstructural parts of fixtures to add on decorative laminates, films, and edge-banding materials.

   h. All adhesives shall be adequately bonded to mating surfaces before being subjected to machining or other forms of stress.

7. Edge Banding—Veneer, Core Edge Bands, Edge Molding:

   a. Definitions:

     (1) Veneer edge bands are strips of veneer, plastic, resin-impregnated paper, or similar materials that are bonded to the plywood ends and sides to obscure the components in the plywood construction.

     (2) Core edge bands are clear, solid wood strips that are bonded to the sides and ends of the core and form a part of the core.

     (3) Edge molding is considered strips of wood, metal, plastic, or composition materials attached to the ends and sides of panels to obscure the plywood components, to form a protective border, and, when designed, to increase the edge thickness of the panel.

   b. Veneer edge bands shall be a minimum of $1/40$ inch thick, full panel length or width, and wide enough to cover the edges and ends of the panel. The color and grain should blend with the faces.

(1) Prior to application of edge bands, the panel edges shall be machined smooth and the panel size cut to the dimensions required.

(2) Bonds between edge bands and panel edges shall be without gaps or delamination and shall be glued with hot-melt, contact cement, urea-formaldehyde, or other synthetic resins.

(3) After curing the adhesive, the bands shall be trimmed, without chipping, tearing, or stripping, to the panel thickness, width, and length.

c. Core edge bands shall be used as specified by contract documents to permit better quality surfaces after shaping panel edges, to provide stronger fastenings, and to improve surface appearance. For shaped edges, the core band shall be at least $1/4$ inch under the cross band to obscure the core material. For improved screw holding strength, core bands shall be wide enough to accommodate the intended fastening and shall be at least $1/2$ inch wide on either edge.

(1) Edge strips shall be fastened to the core with adhesives used in the core assembly or with several types of compatible natural and synthetic adhesive. Machined surfaces shall be smooth and straight so no gaps show in the core stock.

(2) Joints for the core bands may be V-shaped, small tongue and groove, or a straight, smooth flat edge-to-edge joint.

(3) The moisture content of the core bands shall be within plus or minus 2 percent of the moisture content of the core stock.

(4) The quality of the edge strips shall be straight and clear.

d. Edge moldings shall be of the species, type of materials, size, shape, and other details as specified in the contract documents. The color, grain, and design characteristics shall blend with the panel faces.

(1) Prior to application of edge mold-

ings, the panel shall be cut to the size required so that after moldings are added the size shall be machinable to the finished size. Tolerances for the finished size shall be specified.

(2) Joints for the edge moldings may be V-shaped, small tongue and groove, or a straight, smooth edge-to-edge joint.

(3) Edge moldings shall be fastened with superior fastenings of metal, plastic, cement, and/or adhesives. All fastenings shall develop sufficient strength to adhere the molding in a superior manner as indicated in the Glues and Gluing portion of this specification.

K. Fixture Assembly

1. General:

a. All fixtures shall be assembled by skilled cabinetmakers under expert supervision. Workmanship shall be uniformly of the best possible quality of cabinetmaking, and assemblies shall be handcrafted to the necessary degree to achieve the accuracy of fitting and finishing characteristic of high-quality cabinetwork.

b. All cabinetmaking, assembly, and finishing shall be done in the contractor's factory unless otherwise required, which shall be adequately equipped to accomplish a high-quality job. All components shall be factory assembled as completely as transportation and field installation will permit.

2. Fastenings:

a. In assembly, all parts shall be joined and fastened in a manner to provide a structurally sound unit that will retain its rigidity and serviceability for the period of its intended use. Fastenings and fastening techniques will be such that they are inconspicuous and in no way impair the appearance of the fixture.

b. Acceptable adhesives for assembly are hot and cold animal glue, polyvinyl acetate resin emulsions, and thermosetting synthetic resins that are formulated with gap-filling properties.

(1) Assembly glues shall be used in strict accordance with manufacturer's recommendations.

(2) Excess glue and squeeze-out shall be

carefully cleaned from all joints and surfaces.

  c. Screws and bolts shall be the usual type of mechanical fastenings and shall be used in preference to nails or staples except for attaching certain edge moldings, dust panels, case backs, and similar components that do not contribute to rigidity or structural strength.

    (1) Wherever possible, lead holes shall be bored for screw fastenings. Countersink holes shall be bored for all countersunk screws.

    (2) Screws shall not be hammer driven.

    (3) Care shall be exercised not to over-tighten screws.

    (4) Screws shall be of adequate size and used in sufficient numbers to insure a permanently secure fastening.

  d. Nails shall be used only where there is no other suitable means of fastening or applying pressure for glued assemblies.

    (1) Exposed-face nailing shall not be used except where there is no other possible means of attachment or of applying gluing pressure. Face nails will be countersunk and puttied to match the face wood.

    (2) Splitting of any parts as a result of nailing will not be acceptable.

L. Fire-Resistant Components

  1. Materials:

All wood materials requiring fire resistance or fire-retarding compliance with national, state, and local codes and specified by the architect must be fire-retardant pressure treated.

The fire-retardant treating wood material must comply with Federal Specification SS-A-118 or latest revision thereof.

The treated material received by the fixture manufacturer shall have 5 to 10 percent moisture content.

  2. Flame-Spread Rating:

Architects may specify a flame-spread rating of Class C or III, which is a rating of 75 to 200 by the ASTM, E84, 25-foot-tunnel test. Most $1/4$ inch and thicker hardwood plywood and many other wood materials have a flame-spread rating of Class C or III. The model building codes may require a Class A or I flame-spread rating of 0 to 25 for some stores and other places of public assembly. Hardwood plywood and other wood materials are available with Class A or Class B flame-spread ratings and should be used where required.

  3. Certification:

Adequate certification by Underwriters Laboratory or an acceptable certifying agency must accompany the fire-resistant materials used by the fixture manufacturer. The certification is the responsibility of the supplier of the fire-resistant materials.

SECTION III

Wood Finishing

A. Terminology for Finishing

For clarification, certain items used in this section are here defined:

  1. Fine-textured woods and diffuse porous woods—woods such as maple, beech, birch, gum, basswood, yellow poplar, sycamore, and cherry, having small pores.

  2. Coarse-textured woods and ring porous woods—woods such as oak, walnut, Honduras mahogany, African mahogany, Philippine lauan, ash, and elm, having large, visible, open pores.

  3. Oil stain—a transparent solution of dye powders soluble in aromatic hydrocarbons. Normally dry to recoat in 2 to 4 hours. Need sealers over them that do not dissolve the stain and create bleeding. Shellac is normally used. Have poor color stability.

  4. Water stain—transparent solution of water soluble dry powders. Causes raised grain and requires longer drying before sanding and coating. Good color stability.

  5. N.G.R. (non-grain-raising) stain—a transparent solution of water-stain powders, in solvents other than water, that does not swell the wood fibers and create raised grain. Good color stability. Dries very rapidly. Recoat in 10 minutes.

  6. Organo-metallic stain—a transparent solution of organic dyes dissolved in organic solvents. A type of N.G.R. stain. Gives best color stability of soluble dye stains. Dries very fast. Can be recoated in 10 minutes. A superior quality stain.

  7. Sap stain—Dye colors selected to blend sapwood into heartwood. Also used to darken

light colored woods to resemble heartwood of species used in face veneers. Usually N.G.R.-type stains.

8. Pigmented wiping stain—a thin mixture of varnish resin, with added specially ground color pigments of natural earth type. Must be kept agitated or settling occurs. Dries in 4 hours or more at moderate room temperature. Good color stability.

9. Washcoat—a thin solution of a coating. A lacquer washcoat is normally a 4 to 6 percent solids solution of a lacquer sealer. A shellac washcoat is normally the equivalent of a ½ pound cut of shellac (see definition 25). Primary purposes of washcoats are: (1) to stiffen raised grain fibers and allow clean sanding, (2) to form a sealing layer between stain and succeeding coatings of finish, and (3) to allow cleaner, easier filler wiping.

10. Lacquer sealer—a quick drying lacquer, so formulated as to provide quick dry and good holdout of succeeding coats, and often containing sanding agents, such as zinc stearate, to allow dry sanding of sealer. Requires constant stirring to avoid separation of ingredients. Usually contains 10 to 20 percent solids at spray consistency. One full wet coat (see definition 24) deposits approximately ½ to ¾ mil of dry film thickness.

11. Vinyl lacquer sealer—a lacquer-base sealer with vinyl resins forming part of the solids. Better adhesion, toughness, and flexibility than standard lacquer sealers. A superior quality coating.

12. Lacquer—nitrocellulose dissolved in several organic solvents. Other solids in the form of liquified resins blended into nitrocellulose to impart flexibility, hardness, adhesion, resistance to contaminants, and other properties desired. Can be supplied as a superior quality coating.

13. Water-white lacquer—a transparent lacquer having no apparent color, normally used over light-colored surfaces. Usually contains approximately 20 to 25 percent solids at spray consistency. One full wet coat deposits approximately 1 mil of dry film thickness.

14. Clear lacquer—a transparent lacquer, unpigmented, but having some natural color, usually a light amber. Normally used over surfaces where slight darkening by topcoats

is allowable. Usually contains approximately 20 to 25 percent solids at spray consistency. One full wet coat deposits approximately 1 mil of dry film thickness.

15. Flat lacquer—a clear or water-white lacquer to which clear flatting agents have been added to diffuse light reflection from the surface of the dried film causing a reduction in gloss.

16. Gloss—usually applied to lacquer. Gloss is also variable in other topcoat materials. It is an indication of gloss by a meter reading of light reflection from film surfaces.

17. Hot lacquer—a lacquer formulated for spraying at elevated temperatures, usually 160°F. Normally contains 27 to 35 percent or greater solids content. Produces in two sprayed coats the equivalent of three coats of normal cold-sprayed lacquer. Normally produces 1½ mils or greater of dry film thickness in one sprayed coat.

18. Lacquer enamel—a clear lacquer to which has been added coloring pigments, bulking pigments, and others. Forms an opaque film. Requires constant agitation to prevent color changes due to settling out of pigments. Usually contains 25 to 35 percent or greater solids content at spray consistency. One full wet coat deposits approximately 1 to 2 mils or greater of dry film thickness.

19. Cellulose-acetate-butyrate—a coating similar to lacquer with nitrocellulose replaced by cellulose-acetate-butyrate. Excellent cold check resistant. Nonyellowing and nonsoftening when in contact with imitation leathers, synthetic rubber, and other synthetic materials. Good color stability and mar resistant. A superior quality coating.

20. Alkyd-urea synthetic varnish—a catalyzed synthetic varnish requiring heat to harden the film. Solids content usually 35 to 50 percent. Lacquer solvents and synthetic rubber materials have no effect. Very check resistant and mar resistant. A really superior quality coating.

21. Polyester coatings—a combination of a synthetic resin and a chemical monomer, usually styrene with a catalyst and an activator. Difficult to apply except as a flow-coat on flat surfaces. Film durability and resistance nearly equal high-pressure plastic laminates.

22. Vinyl-amino coatings—a catalyzed vinyl

coating similar to alkyd-urea varnish. Highly resistant to solvents, acids, and other contaminants.

23. Polyurethanes—a two-component synthetic finish with limited pot-life. A high-gloss, tough, flexible, mar-resistant finish. Adheres well to stained wood but not so well over fillers or glazes. A costly, highly durable film.

24. Full wet coat—a coat of finishing material applied in such a manner as to exhibit an all-over wet appearance (as contrasted to a dry or sandy spray). Usually considered to be near the maximum amount that can be applied on a vertical surface without sags or runs.

25. Cut (of shellac)—a number of pounds of resin added to each gallon of solvent. Liquid shellac is often supplied as a "4 lb. cut." Equal parts of a "4 lb. cut" of shellac and alcohol produce the accepted equivalent of a "2 lb. cut." One part of a "4 lb. cut" of shellac to seven parts of alcohol produces the accepted equivalent of a "1/2 lb. cut."

26. Uniforming—application of colored finishing materials to wood surfaces, finished or unfinished, to minimize variations in color or intensity of color. Usually performed where different woods are used in the same construction or to even up the color of all units in a group. Major use is on transparent and toned finishes.

27. Lacquer undercoater—a heavily pigmented lacquer enamel. Formulated to provide filling, sealing, and coloring. Can normally be sanded without lubricant. Usually air dries in 1 hour or more.

28. Toner—thin lacquer containing specially ground chemical and earth pigments. Thin applications have low hiding power. Dries rapidly. Can be recoated in 15 minutes or longer.

29. Wood filler—a mixture of oils, resins, color pigments, bulking pigments, and other ingredients. Usually thinned for spray application with VM&P. Naptha or varsol at following rates: for walnut, Honduras mahogany, ash, and similar woods, 10 to 12 pounds filler/gallon VM&P Naptha. Primary purpose to fill and color vessels of pores of the wood and provide a level surface for succeeding coats. Formulated to air dry in 4 hours or more.

30. Glaze—a finely ground pigment in a vehicle with suitable binder to blend with various coatings. Usually applied after sealer to highlight grain and figure and to amplify character of the wood surface.

31. Shading stain—a thin topcoating, usually lacquer, containing stains. Usually applied after sealer to blend woods and form a more unified color. Also used to tint or darken edges, trim, corners, and borders.

32. Orange peel—a roughness of sprayed surface, resembling the surface of an orange, caused by lack of flow of sprayed finish droplets.

33. Edge enamel—a pigmented opaque coating usually prepared for use on edges of particle board and medium-density fiber board.

34. Synthetic—coating resins prepared artificially or chemically rather than occurring naturally.

35. Water base coatings—resins suspended as droplets surrounded by a film of water as a vehicle. When the water evaporates, the resins coalesce to form a continuous resin film.

B. General Requirements

1. All wood cabinets and fixtures shall be finished by the manufacturer or contractor to enhance their appearance and serviceability. Where requirements are modified to meet special conditions, deviations will be made by the contractor using application methods, workmanship, and materials equal or superior to those specified by the architect.

2. All woodwork shall be finished with protective coatings on exposed surfaces and visible interiors in the contractor's plant whenever possible.

3. Samples:

   Finished samples shall be submitted in duplicate by the contractor when requested by the architect. After approval, one sample of each finish shall be retained by the architect, and the signed duplicate shall be returned to the contractor.

   Colors and coatings shall be as specified and as indicated on drawings or color schedules. All transparent color coatings shall allow for natural wood color variations. All opaque finishes shall match specified color coatings and approved samples of finishes.

4. Materials:

   a. All finishes and components shall conform to the latest available A.S.T.M. specifications for test methods.

b. Exposed protective coatings shall be resistant to mild acids (perspiration), mild alkalis (soap solutions), and mild solvents (alcohol).

c. Protective coatings for interior wood finishing shall be classified as Standard Quality or Superior Quality.

(1) Standard quality coating materials shall meet the minimum requirements of (1) a 10-cycle cold-check test, (2) a 2-pound test, (3) a water-resistance test, and (4) a crosshatch test.

(2) Superior quality coating materials shall meet the minimum requirements of (1) a 20-cycle cold-check test, (2) a 4-pound print test, (3) a test for water and alcohol resistance, (4) a crosshatch test, and (5) a test for mild acids and bases.

5. Workmanship:

a. All workmanship shall be done by skilled, trained, and qualified craftspeople. The contractor shall have a complete finishing department, comprising one or more spray booths with power driven exhaust, adequate spray guns, and other facilities necessary to permit application of Standard Quality or Superior Quality finishing.

b. Unless otherwise specified herein, all materials shall be applied in strict accordance with the directions of the finishing material manufacturer.

c. Doors and other components unsecured, that are free to warp, shall be given a sufficient number of coats of finishing materials on opposite sides and edges to equalize moisture gain or loss and thus minimize warpage.

d. Completed cabinets and woodwork shall not show runs, bubbles, brush marks, orange peel, or other detrimental surface conditions.

C. Preparation for Finishing

1. Sanding:

All wood surfaces shall be sanded smooth prior to finishing.

All sanding shall be parallel to the grain of the wood.

On all exterior or exposed surfaces, a grit size of 4/0 (150) or finer shall be used. Spot or partial sanding with coarser or finer grit will not be acceptable.

All wood surfaces shall be kept free from dust, dirt, oil, adhesives, or other substances that would interfere with finish adhesion or absorption. Surfaces sanded more than 2 days prior to finishing shall be given a light resanding with 6/0 (220) or finer grit abrasive. All knife-edge corners shall be carefully eased with 6/0 (220) or finer abrasive paper.

2. Repair of Defects:

Sand-through of veneer or overlays at edges, corners, or other areas shall not be allowed except for opaque finishes. Dents, scratches, and similar blemishes shall be removed by swelling with heat and moisture followed by drying and sanding prior to finishing.

All surface glue deposits, burnished spots, and handling marks shall be removed before finishing. Veneer splits or checks shall be repaired with inlays and sanded to avoid detection at a viewing distance of 2 feet.

3. Glue Sizing:

Glue sizing will not be required, except on exterior surfaces or ropey or spiral-grained woods. Glue sizing may be required, however, when staining and coating methods are used that do not develop a uniformity of color within the natural range of color acceptability of the wood used.

D. Bleaching of Exposed Wood Surfaces

Bleaching will be required only when necessary to obtain the desired colors or color uniformity.

1. Materials:

Two types of bleaching solutions may be used: (1) a two-solution bleach comprised of sodium hydroxide (caustic soda activator) and hydrogen peroxide and applied as two separate materials or mixed in the proper proportions and applied as one solution; or (2) a one-solution bleach consisting of hydrogen peroxide (usually 35 percent) and an activator plus a self-neutralizer. After bleaching with solutions containing caustic soda, neutralize the caustic with a 5 to 10 percent solution of acetic acid (or white vinegar) by a wet application of the wood surface. Again, wet the bleached surfaces with water and sponge dry with a clean acetate sponge.

2. Process:

Bleach all exposed surfaces when specified. Apply the bleach in a uniform wet coating. Allow time (30 minutes to 2 hours) for the bleaching action. Dry until the wood surface has returned to approximately its original moisture content or the whiteness desired.

Neutralize caustic soda with a wet film of a 5 to 10 percent solution of acetic acid.

Wash thoroughly with clean water, and wipe wood surfaces with a sponge that is rinsed often in fresh clean water. Tests for alkalinity may be made since bleach residue may affect subsequent coats, using pHydrion paper of 7.5 to 9.0 pH range or using a tincture of phenolthalein. Several pieces of pH paper placed on a moistened bleached surface or several drops of phenolthalein on the dry bleached surface will change to pink or red color, momentarily, when the surface contains a basic residue. All bleached surfaces shall be dried to 6 to 10 percent moisture content. After drying, lightly smooth-sand bleached surfaces using 6/0 (220 grit) or finer abrasive paper.

3. Finish bleached sanded surfaces according to Section E.

E. Transparent Finishes for Exposed Wood Surfaces

Criterion for determining the quality of a finish shall be its durability in service. A durable finish shall be high in (1) check resistance, (2) resistance to abrasion, (3) resistance to contaminates and solvents, (4) color retention, (5) adhesion, (6) toughness, (7) hardness, (8) flexibility, and (9) similar methods of measuring serviceability.

1. Unstained Natural Finish for Exposed Wood Surfaces:

a. Natural finish for coarse-textured woods—A sap stain such as the sapwood of walnut, may be required to darken the white wood.

(1) Apply washcoat of lacquer, synthetic varnish, or other synthetic coatings, compatible with the topcoat. Dry and sand lightly with 7/0 (240) grit opencoat abrasive paper.

(2) Apply wood filler over all open-grained wood. Wood filler contains pigments that normally are lighter or darker than the surrounding wood. Filler shall be allowed to "flash off" until a flat or dull appearance is noted. At this point, surfaces shall be pad wiped by machine or by hand, with downward pressure across the grain, pushing excess filler into the press.

This initial padding shall be followed with a clean wipe across the grain to remove excess filler. After this operation, lightly wipe parallel to the grain with a clean cloth to remove all crosswipe marks. Excess filler in corners, carvings, or similar depressions shall be brushed out or picked out cleanly. Dry filler thoroughly before sealing.

(3) Apply full wet coat of lacquer sealer, synthetic varnish sealer, or other synthetic coatings. Dry to sand.

(4) Lightly sand out all roughness with 7/0 (240 grit) opencoat abrasive paper. Dust off thoroughly with air jet.

(5) Apply shading (colored) lacquer or compatible synthetic materials if necessary to obtain uniformity of color or to blend color and to obtain amplification of wood grain.

(6) Apply full wet coat of water-white lacquer, synthetic varnish, or other synthetic coating.

(7) Scuff lightly with 8/0 (280 grit) opencoat abrasive paper if necessary to remove any roughness present. Dust off with air jet.

(8) Apply second full wet coat of water-white lacquer, synthetic varnish, or other synthetic coatings. Dry thoroughly. (In any finish schedule, if hot lacquers (at 30 to 35 percent solids) are used as the topcoats, two hot-sprayed coats shall be considered sufficient to replace three coats of normal cold-spray lacquer (20 percent solids).)

(9) Rub and/or polish, if required, following procedure in G.

b. Natural finish for fine-textured woods—

Natural finish is generally applied to fine-textured diffuse porous species.

Except for omitting steps 1 and 2—washcoat and filler—the procedure is the same as that for paragraph E.1.a., "Natural finish for coarse-textured woods," of this section. Follow exact procedure (3) through (9).

2. Stained Finish for Exposed Wood Surfaces:
a. Stained finish for coarse-textured woods—
(1) Apply one coat of stain (N.G.R., water, or pigmented wiping). A sap stain may be required to change the white sapwood to the heartwood color.
   (a) If N.G.R. stain is used, dry thoroughly (5 to 10 minutes of force dry), and apply even washcoat of coatings compatible with topcoat. Scuff-sand lightly when dry with 7/0 (240 grit) opencoat abrasive paper.
   (b) If water stain is used, dry 2 hours at room temperature or dry 15 minutes in drying oven at 130° to 140°F. Apply even washcoat of coatings compatible with topcoat. Sand lightly with 7/0 (240 grit) opencoat abrasive paper.
   (c) If pigmented wiping stain is used, wipe evenly and cleanly, removing accumulations in crevices, inside corners, and so on by dry brush or wiping. Dry according to manufacturer's direction.
(2) Apply washcoat of lacquer synthetic varnish or other synthetic coatings. Dry and sand lightly with 7/0 (240 grit) opencoat abrasive paper.
(3) Apply wood filler of appropriate color following procedure shown under E.1.a., step (2). Dry thoroughly.
(4) Apply one full coat lacquer sealer, vinyl sealer, or synthetic sealer. Dry thoroughly.
(5) Sand sealer lightly with 7/0 paper to remove all roughness, and dust off with air jet.
(6) Apply shading, glazing, highlighting,

or distressing materials and operations where specified.
(7) Apply one full wet coat clear lacquer synthetic varnish or other synthetics. (Water-white may be specified but is not essential for dark stained finishes.) Dry completely.
(8) Apply second full wet film to topcoating. Dry materials completely.
(9) Rub and/or polish, if necessary, following procedure in G.
b. Stained finish for fine-textured, diffuse porous woods—
(1) Follow procedure under E.2.a., except filler and washcoat may be omitted. For some diffuse porous woods, a washcoat, followed by a very low solids content filler or glaze application, will slightly color small pores and bring out the grain of the wood.

3. Toner Finish for Exposed Wood Surfaces: When bleaching is not practical, or a uniforming color background is desired, toner finish may be used that allows wood grain to show through the finish.
a. Toner finish for coarse-textured woods—
(1) Spray one or more, as required, light uniform coats of toner over all surfaces. Avoid excessive buildup of coating at overlaps of spray pattern to avoid streaks. Natural grain pattern of the wood shall not be obscured by toner application. Dry completely.
(2) Apply low solids content water-white lacquer or synthetic washcoat evenly over all exposed surfaces. Dry completely. Scuff-sand lightly to remove roughness with 8/0 (280 grit) opencoat abrasive paper. Dust off thoroughly with air jet.
(3) Apply wood filler to correct color and consistency, and complete schedule outlined under E.1.a., starting with step (2), the filling operation.
b. Toner finish for fine-textured woods—
(1) Spray one or more, as required, very light coats of low pigment content

and very low solids content toner. The amount of solids in the toner and the thin coating should create a uniform color without closing the small, fine pores of the wood.

(2) Spray a thin washcoat, a very light coat, without closing the fine wood pores. Dry.

(3) Sand very lightly, only if necessary to remove nibs, with 280 or finer grit paper. Avoid cutthrough, which removes toner. If toner is removed and color is not uniform, touch up with toner and washcoat.

(4) Apply a very thin, fine ground filler-glaze or pigment stain over the toned surface. Wipe in circular pattern to deposit coloring materials in small pores. Follow by wiping with clean, soft cloths and brushing with fine bristle brush, parallel with the grain. Deposits of filler-glaze in corners shall be removed by brushing or wiping.

(5) Continue with sealers and topcoats as specified in E.1.a.

F. Special Wood Finishes

Variations from paragraph E, "Transparent Finishes for Exposed Wood Surfaces," may be made by fixture manufacturer and the architect using the schedule in this section.

1. Close-to-the-Grain Wood Finishes:
   a. Rubbed-oil effect finish—
   Finishes having a rubbed-oil effect shall be protected with coatings that meet the requirements of a standard quality or superior quality finish.

   (1) Apply stain colors compatible with oils, or if color is incorporated in the oils, use a uniforming touch-up or sap staining on portions of surface to attain uniformity of color.

   (2) On open-grain, coarse-textured woods, a pigmented stain may be applied if required for specified color, wiping clean with the grain. Dry overnight or 1 hour at 140°F.

   (3) Apply a sealer, dry, and light sand with 7/0 (240 grit) opencoat abrasive paper.

   (4) Apply two coats of flat lacquer or the equivalent of other film coating materials. Dry each coat overnight, or dry in an oven 1 hour at 140°F. Sand between coats with 8/0 paper. After final coat, sanding is not necessary. Rub with steel wool, 5/0 grade, to remove nibs if surface is not smooth.

2. Special Effects Finishes:
   a. Special character finishes, such as multicolor, spatter, pearlescent, crackle, wrinkle, or others, shall be made in accordance with printed directions of the finish material manufacturer.
   b. Silk-screen designs, leather or imitation leather, embossing, and other decorative systems shall be applied and protected with at least one application of coatings.

G. Rubbing and Polishing

For each wood material used and each finishing schedule used, the rubbing-and-polishing methods for the coatings shall be selected from the following systems. The fixture manufacturer and architect shall specify which areas (tops, sides, etc.) will be rubbed and/or polished.

1. No Rubbing and Polishing:
   Unexposed interior areas, drawer sides, interiors shelving, and similar parts shall not require any rubbing or polishing, other than removal by fine abrasive paper, of any roughness created by the material or finishing process used.

2. Flat Off-the-Gun Finish Surfaces:
   No rubbing with abrasive. Minute roughness removed with 3/0 or finer steel wool.

3. Steel Wool—Dull Stain:
   A 3/0 and 4/0 steel wool shall be used, parallel to the grain of the wood, to remove roughness and create an overall dull satin sheen in those areas specified; 4/0 steel wool will create a slightly higher luster than 3/0 steel wood.

4. Dull Satin:
   Machine or hand sand with 320 grit silicon carbide abrasive paper, using a nonblooming lubricant. All rubbing shall be done parallel to the grain of the wood. Follow with an even rub in long continuous strokes with 4/0 steel wool or 400 grit paper. All lubricant and rubbing slush shall be removed. Surface shall be clean and dry before waxing.

5. Period Satin:
   Machine or hand sand with 320, 360, or 400 grit silicon carbide abrasive paper, using a nonblooming lubricant, until all orange peel and other irregularities in surface film are removed. Follow this by hand rubbing with 3-F pumice using a soft felt pad in long continuous strokes. All residual pumice and rubbing slush shall be removed. Dry completely before waxing.

6. High-Sheen Satin:
   Machine or hand sand with 360 or 400 grit silicon carbide abrasive paper, using a nonblooming lubricant, to remove all surface film irregularities. Follow with 4-F pumice by machine or hand, with soft felt rubbing pads. If a higher sheen is desired, small amounts of rottenstone shall be added to the 4-F pumice.

7. High Luster:
   Machine or hand sand surface, parallel to the grain, with 500 grit silicon carbide abrasive paper, using a nonblooming lubricant. Follow with a final sanding with 600 grit silicon carbide abrasive paper to create an all-over fine scratch pattern. Irregularities in flat surfaces missed by these two operations shall be rubbed by hand with soft felt pad, using 4-F pumice. Clean the surface so that no abrasive particles or pumice remain. Apply rubbing compound and rub with rotary pad to an all-over even sheen. clean off all compound, and then polish lightly with rotary buffer and a clean lamb's wool pad. Care should be exercised in both the compounding and polishing operations to prevent burning or softening of finish by frictional heat of the buffer pad.

H. Pigmented Opaque Finishes for Exposed Wood Finishes
   1. Painted Finish for Coarse-Textured Wood Surfaces:
      Particle board, fiber board, and related materials with rough unfilled surfaces may be finished similarly.
      a. Apply pigmented primer or undercoat compatible with finish. Dry then lightly sand with 280 grit abrasive.
      b. Apply paste wood filler according to directions for filling under E.1.a. (2). Dry thoroughly.
      c. Apply full set coat of approved undercoating enamel primer. This undercoater shall be of a proper ground color with relation to the aforesaid finish coat. Dry.
      d. Sand all undercoated surfaces with 5/0 or finer opencoat abrasive paper to complete removal of all roughness.
      e. Apply full wet coat of pigmented lacquer or synthetic enamel. Dry thoroughly and scuff-sand with 7/0 (240 grit) or finer opencoat abrasive paper to remove accumulated roughness. Dust off completely with air jet.
      f. Apply second coat. Dry completely.
   2. Painted Finish for Fine-Textured Wood Surfaces or Unfilled Particle Board or Fiber Board:
      Follow procedure outlined for coarse-textured woods (H.1.), but eliminate step b, the filling operation.

I. Finish for Unexposed Areas
   1. Unexposed Drawer Surfaces:
      Apply one coat of lacquer sealer on all inside surfaces of drawers. Skips, in corners or elsewhere, shall not be allowed.
      When dry, hand sand with 6/0 opencoat abrasive paper to remove roughness. Dust thoroughly with air jet.
   2. Accessible Interior Parts (Shelves, Partitions, etc.):
      Apply one coat lacquer sealer; dry. Remove any roughness by scuff-sanding with 6/0 opencoat abrasive paper.

J. Field Painting
   Large panels and other items that cannot be satisfactorily finish painted in the shop may be painted in the field when specified by the architect.
   1. All such items shall be factory primed in a manner appropriate to the selected finish coat.
   2. Finish painting in the field shall conform to the appropriate preceding paragraphs.

SECTION IV

Metal Work and Hardware

A. General
   1. All metal work and hardware shall comply with design and performance requirements indicated by the architect. In general, the architect will assume prime responsibility

for aesthetic aspects, structural design, and functional requirements. The fixture manufacturer assumes responsibility for workmanship and performance while in compliance with the structural design requirements. In the event that the design structural requirements are inadequate, it is the responsibility of the architect to initiate corrective action and confer with the fixture manufacturer.

2. All metal work and hardware items shall be new material and shall meet highest standards of workmanship. Unless otherwise indicated, all metal work and hardware shall be the best available for the intended use.

3. Deviations from specifications are allowed only by prior approval and written consent of the architect.

4. Where equivalent or substitute materials are permitted, it is required that equivalence shall pertain to appearance, manufacture, workmanship, performance, and strength. In instances where alternate or substitute materials or methods are deemed advantageous by the contractor, bids shall be made on the original specifications, and suggested alternatives shall be an amendment to the specification and shall be clearly separated from the original specification. All deviations, alternatives, and substitutions shall be identified, and the effect on performance, strength, appearance, manufacture, and workmanship shall be noted and any increase or decrease in the amount bid will be given in order to aid the architect in his decision to approve or reject the deviations.

5. No metal framing or tubing shall contain sections less than 18 gauge (.048 in.) unless approved by the architect.

6. All materials, manufacturing practices, and products shall meet the standards of the American Society for Testing Materials or other specified standards. Part 1 Steel Piping, Tubing, and Fittings, Part 2 Ferrous Castings Specifications, Part 7 Die Cast Metals, Aluminum, and Magnesium Alloys, and Part 8 Non-Ferrous Metals Specifications of ASTM Standards shall be an integral part of specifications herein as indicated.

7. Where published standards allow a choice not specified by the architect, the contractor or fixture manufacturer shall evaluate the alternate and submit the evaluation and choice to the architect for approval.

B. Samples
1. The contractor or fixture manufacturer shall submit permanently labeled samples in duplicate when and if required by the architect. Following approval for design, color, size, and surface finish, the architect shall retain one sample of each item and return the duplicate to the contractor with written affirmation.

2. All designs, colors, materials, and finishes shall be as specified herein and/or as indicated on drawings or schedules. Where manufacturers' catalog numbers are indicated, these shall be construed to establish color, finish, design, and minimum standards of material, workmanship, quality, and performance in lieu of samples. Equivalent items when proposed by the contractor must have written approval by the architect.

3. All metal items and materials used by the contractor shall in every respect match approved samples.

C. Workmanship
1. All workmanship shall meet highest commercial standards and comply with ASTM and other cited specifications where applicable. Custom metal work shall be performed only by skilled individuals under expert supervision in properly equipped shops.

2. Slotted members shall be of the dimensions indicated by the contract documents. Slots shall be punched cleanly and accurately, free of rough edges or burrs. Concavity, distortion, and dimensional tolerance shall not exceed .012 inch. Accessories accommodated by slotted members must be completely and easily interchangeable and must lock positively and rigidly in place.

3. Exposed surfaces shall be uniform in appearance throughout any area carrying a specified color and finish.

4. Brushed finishes at miters, joints, or changes in directions shall be clearly defined. No other joints on these surfaces shall be visible.

5. Bends and angles shall be as sharp as the type and thickness of material will reasonably permit.

6. All metal work subject to possible contact

688   **Retail Store Planning & Design Manual**

with the person or merchandise shall be free of burrs, sharp edges, and other damaging or injurious irregularities.

7. Visible metal work shall be free of weld lines, die marks, flashing, blow holes, imperfect joints, or defects that detract from appearance or performance.

8. Insofar as possible, all mechanical fastening shall be concealed. Screws and rivets on exposed areas are permitted only by approval of the architect. Load-bearing threaded fasteners shall engage a thread length at least equal to half the major diameter in steel or equal to the major diameter in nonferrous material. In no case shall less than $2^1/2$ threads be engaged, except for sheet metal screws subject to negligible tensile loads.

9. Dimensional tolerances shall be plus or minus .012 inch unless otherwise stated, except that for framing members, dimensions of length, and angular tolerances shall be such that there shall be no interference with intended alignment, appearance, or function. Tolerances for sections and straightness shall be those given in appropriate published standards ASTM A450, A268, B221, and A511.

10. All finished materials shall be carefully wrapped and protected from damage during transport or installation.

11. Metal drawer guides, sliding door hardware, and other rolling, sliding, hinged, or tracked metal moving parts shall operate smoothly and easily, without apparent sagging. Catches and stops shall be positive in operation. Suitable bumpers will be provided to cushion moving parts at limits of travel.

12. Drawers more than 8 inches high and/or 20 inches wide shall be mounted on ball or roller bearings.

13. Leveling devices of not less than 1 inch adjustable travel shall be provided on all legs and supports.

D. Welding

1. All arc, resistance, and induction welding, brazing, and soldering shall be done by qualified operators using suitable materials and practices as recognized by the American Welding Society. Fusion welds shall be sound and uniform, continuous when exposed, the weld metal being thoroughly fused on all surfaces and edges without undercutting or overlap. Weld or filler metal shall project at least $1/32$ inch above butt joints before grinding or filing. Filler joints shall have a fusion bead width equal to no less than the thickness of one of the welded base materials; brazed or soldered filler metal shall have a radius equal to such thickness.

2. Arc welding of stainless steel and aluminum shall normally employ inert gas shielding.

3. Welds that are exposed or form bearing or contact surfaces shall be ground or filed flush with surrounding areas. Depressions are not permitted on exposed or on rolling contact areas. Fillers with organic binders are permitted under painted surfaces, but must be rigid and thoroughly adhered to the base metal.

4. On exposed areas, welds shall be blended and polished to match exactly the appearance and color of the adjacent surfaces unless an opaque organic or metallic coating is to be applied to the surface. If an opaque coating is to be applied, the final surface must be uniform in color and finish across the weld or braze and surrounding area. In all cases, exposed welded joints must be rendered smooth and not noticeable to the eye in the finished product.

E. Stainless Steel

1. All stainless steel items shall meet applicable standards of ASTM and AISI with respect to analysis, manufacture, finish, properties, and tolerances.

2. Corrosion-resistant or stainless steel shall mean type AISI 302 (SAE 30302 and ASTM 511). For welded stainless steel not to be subsequently annealed, a carbon content of .08 percent shall not be exceeded, unless the reduced corrosion resistance is expressly permitted by the designer or architect. When the designer or architect does require special items and special effects AISI 430 steels shall be permitted.

3. The designation "stainless steel" shall imply that clad constructions are not permitted.

4. Exposed stainless steel surfaces shall be ground and polished equal to at least a No. 7 finish as defined by ASTM specification A167, when no surface finish is specified.

Other surface finishes may be specified such as (1) a No. 4 dull finish; (2) a No. 6 satin finish made by brushing the No. 4 finish using a medium abrasive; or (3) a No. 8 mirror finish, the most reflective finish commonly produced. The No. 8 finish is made by polishing with successively finer abrasives then buffing, with a very fine buffing compound. The surface is free of grit lines caused by preliminary grinding operations. For these special effects, samples may be required for approval.

F. Carbon Steel
1. In general, carbon steel members shall be cold-rolled strip meeting ASTM specification A109. Pickled hot-rolled shapes may be used for concealed and inconspicuous members as approved by the architect.
2. Carbon steel surfaces to receive exposed finishes or electroplating shall be manufactured from strip with a No. 3 best bright finish as defined in ASTM A109. If to be ground and buffed before electroplating, a No. 2 bright finish is permitted.
3. Surfaces to be coated with opaque organic finishes may normally employ a No. 1 dull finish. Surfaces shall be degreased and phosphatized before painting.
4. Material for flat blanking, such as brackets, shall be used in the No.1 full hard temper. Material for rolling and forming shall employ the hardest commercial temper that will permit the necessary bends without surface cracking.
5. All carbon steel members shall be covered by a rust and corrosion-resistant coating, either metallic or organic, and shall be guaranteed against rust for a period of 1 year from installation.

G. Aluminum
1. Aluminum materials and their treatments shall comply with standards of ASTM or the Aluminum Association. Extruded shapes shall be as specified in ASTM B221 and B235. Sheet and plate shall conform to ASTM specification B209. Cast aluminum shall follow ASTM specifications B26, B85, or B108.
2. Aluminum alloy AA 6061 (ASTM GS 11A) temper T4 or AA 6063 (ASTM GS 10A) temper T5 shall be implied in all specifications calling for aluminum, the latter being specified for anodic surface treatments. F temper as fabricated or annealed material may be used for non-load-bearing and other approved parts.
3. Anodized coatings on aluminum shall be in accordance with Federal Specifications MIL-8625 and shall match color and finish of samples approved by the architect.
4. Dyed anodized coatings shall be sealed in 1 percent nickel acetate bath for 20 minutes at 190°F.
5. Mechanical, chemical, or electrolytic surface treatments of aluminum parts shall in general follow practices endorsed by the Aluminum Association, which will lead to the intended levels of performance and appearance.

H. Zinc Alloy
1. Zinc-based alloys for die casting shall meet ASTM specifications B240 and B327. The term "zinc-based alloy" shall imply ASTM alloy AC41A.
2. Zinc coatings on ferrous materials other than those electrodeposited shall adhere to ASTM standards A123, A93, and A163.

I. Copper Allloys
1. Nickel silver or nickel bronze shall imply a copper alloy containing 17 to 29 percent nickel with 10 to 18 percent zinc and 62 percent copper as described in Federal Specifications FF-H-106a.
Nickel brass or German silver shall imply copper alloys containing over 10 percent zinc, with nickel in amounts sufficient to give white color.
2. The general term "bronze" shall be applied to copper-base alloys containing additional elements other than zinc and in amounts sufficient to be predominate over zinc in the alloy.
a. Commercial bronze shall imply copper-zinc alloys containing at least 90 percent copper.
b. Brass shall imply copper-zinc alloys containing at least 70 percent copper.
3. Copper alloy materials shall comply with applicable ASTM standards. Alloy samples shall be submitted to the architect for color approval. Reference is made to ASTM B151, B248, B249, B251, B122, and B124.

J. Miscellaneous Metals and Alloys
1. Bronze, brass, magnesium, monel, chrome,

and other alloys shall conform to appropriate specifications of ASTM.

2. Fabrication, finishes, and practices outlined in ASTM standards and the Metal Handbook of the American Society of Metals shall be used as a general guide with these materials.

3. Finishes acceptable for various metals are described in the following examples:

    a. Mirror Chrome; M-21 Smooth Specular—Achieved by cutting with aluminum oxide or silicon carbide compounds, starting with relatively coarse grits and finishing with 320 grits using a peripheral wheel speed of 6000 fpm. Follow by buffing with aluminum oxide buffing compound using a peripheral wheel speed of 7000 fpm. The surface desired is a mirror reflectivity, free of grit lines caused by preliminary grinding operations and also free of all foreign materials.

    b. Satin Chrome; M-31 Fine Satin—Achieved by wheel or belt polishing with aluminum oxide or silicon carbide abrasives of 180 to 240 grit, using a peripheral wheel speed of 6000 fpm.

    c. Mirror Bronze; M-21 Smooth Specular—Achieved by cutting with aluminum oxide or silicon carbide compounds, starting with relatively coarse grits and finishing with 320 grits using a peripheral wheel speed of 6000 fpm. Follow by buffing with aluminum oxide buffing compounds using a peripheral wheel speed of 7000 fpm. The surface desired is a mirror reflectivity, free of grit lines caused by preliminary grinding operations and also free of all foreign materials. The finished material will then receive two protective coats of lacquer with interim drying, and such lacquer coating shall be free of all foreign material.

    d. Satin Bronze; M-31 Fine Stain—Achieved by wheel or belt polishing with aluminum oxide or silicon carbide abrasives of 180 to 240 grit, using a peripheral wheel speed of 6000 fpm. The finished material will then receive two protective coats of lacquer, and such

lacquer coating shall be free of all foreign material.

    e. Mirror Brass; M-21 Smooth Specular—Achieved by cutting with aluminum oxide or silicon carbide compounds, starting with relatively coarse grits and finishing with 320 grits using a peripheral wheel speed of 6000 fpm. Follow by buffing with aluminum oxide buffing compounds using a peripheral wheel speed of 7000 fpm. The surface desired is a mirror reflectivity, free of grit lines caused by preliminary grinding operations and also free of all foreign materials. The finished material will then receive two protective coats of lacquer with interim drying, and such lacquer coating shall be free of all foreign materials.

    f. Satin Brass; M-31 Stain—Achieved by wheel or belt polishing with aluminum oxide or silicon carbide abrasives of 180 to 240 grit, using a peripheral wheel speed of 6000 fpm. The finished material will then receive two protective coats of lacquer, and such lacquer coating shall be free of all foreign materials.

K. Electrodeposited Coating (Platings)

1. All electrodeposited coatings shall conform with the specifications and practices adopted or endorsed by the American Electroplaters' Society, The American Standards Association, and/or ASTM, A164, A165.

2. Electrodeposited coatings on significant surfaces exposed to sight or wear shall be at least equal to grades GS, LS, RS, NS, OS, and TS as defined in appropriate ASTM and ASA standards as follows:

Type FS, Nickel and Chromium on Steel ASTM A166:
Copper plus Nickel, min. thickness	0.00120 inch
Final nickel, min. thickness	0.00060 inch
Chromium (if required), min. thickness	0.00001 inch

Type OS, Cadmium on Steel ASTM A165
Cadmium, min. thickness	0.0003 inch

Type LS, Zinc on Steel ASTM A164:
Zinc, min. thickness	0.0005 inch

Type FC, Nickel and Chromium on Copper-based alloys ASTM B141:
Nickel, min. thickness	0.00050 inch
Chromium (if required), min. thickness	0.00001 inch

Type FZ, Nickel, and Chromium on Zinc-based alloys ASTM B142:
Copper plus nickel, min. thickness	0.00120 inch

Copper, min. thickness   0.00020 inch
Final nickel, min. thickness   0.00050 inch
Chromium (if required), min. thickness 0.00001 inch
Copper-based coatings on various base materials:
Copper-based coating, min. thickness   0.00120 inch

3. Preparation of specific base materials for electrocoating shall be in accordance with ASTM standards B183 for carbon steel, B252 for zinc-based alloys, B253 for aluminum alloys, B281 for copper-based alloys, B254 for stainless steels, and B320 for cast iron.

4. General cleaning of metals prior to electroplating shall follow ASTM B322, B183, B242, B252, B253, B254, B281.

5. Electrodeposited coatings exposing copper-based alloys, nickel, or other materials subject to tarnish or color change shall be protected by suitably formulated transparent organic coating.

6. Color and surface finish after plating shall be uniform and identical to specific samples approved by the architect. Welds, imperfections, and blemishes visible at a distance of two feet shall not be permitted.

7. Electrodeposited coatings shall show no evidence of corrosion after 32 hours salt spray as described in Federal Specification QQ-M-151 and FF-H-111a.

L. Organic and Synthetic Coatings

1. All metal surfaces including electroplated coatings, susceptible to oxidation, corrosion or other discoloration and deterioration, shall be protected by a coating. Such coating shall show no evidence of failure after 32 hours of salt spray as described in Federal Specification QQ-M-151.

2. All finishes shall be best quality. Application and handling of such finishes shall be in strict compliance with the finish manufacturer's written directions, under expert supervision. Samples must be submitted to the architect for approval, along with a written statement of finish performance as determined by manufacturer's tests.

3. Before any finish is applied, surfaces must be properly cleaned and prepared, free of defects or irregularities detrimental to the final appearance and performance of the finish. All metal surfaces shall be carefully inspected for uniformly good cleaning and shall be properly degreased, phosphatized, and rinsed. No sludge or surface film shall be evident on drying. Chromic acid seal and rinse and base coats shall be used as required by the architect.

4. Finishes must be applied in a manner that yields a smooth, uniform, and continuous coating, free of surface defects, runs, sags, or bubbles.

5. Coatings must display excellent adhesion throughout and be free from appreciable color change. Dry color samples after a period of 2 months shall be indistinguishable from freshly prepared samples when compared at a distance of 2 feet.

6. In general, total dry film thickness for finishes shall be not less than 1.5 mils.

M. Strength and Rigidity

1. Load-bearing members and accessories shall imply all items expected to exhibit mechanical resistance to external loads or forces. Non-load-bearing members will, in general, be decorative rather than structural in nature; but they are required to possess sufficient mechanical strength to resist minor accidental loads and retain original shape.

2. All metal work shall be manufactured and assembled in a manner that will guarantee adequate strength for the intended purpose. A reasonable safety margin for probable service overloads, accidental or otherwise, shall be provided, although this shall not be construed to include negligent abuse.

3. The manufacture of standards, uprights, brackets, hangrods, drawer slides, shelves, and similar material purchased by the contractor or made by the contractor shall clearly comply with accepted industry requirements. Manufacturers shall have printed in their catalogs the descriptions and limitations of the metal fixtures and parts.

4. All metal frame and structural units shall, in addition to adequate strength, exhibit a high degree of rigidity in service. Distortion impairing the operation or fit of moving members will not be permitted. In general, metal work shall be sufficiently rigid to eliminate perceptible sagging, distortion, or deflection in the intended service.

SECTION V

Glass, Glazing, and Mirrors

A. Purpose

This section covers the requirements for glass, glazing, and mirrors. It is intended to identify these requirements and the materials that are acceptable.

B. Scope

1. The contractor shall furnish all glass and mirror materials complying to these requirements or as indicated in the contract documents.

2. The contractor shall furnish all labor required for complete glazing of all items as indicated in the contract documents.

C. Materials

1. General:

a. All glazing and mirror materials shall comply with the applicable existing standards and/or specifications stated in this section. In the absence of applicable standards or specifications, the materials shall be of the best quality available.

b. Glass terminology and standards shall be as set forth in the Federal Specification DD-G-451D dated April 25, 1977, or later revisions thereof. All glass used in fixture work shall comply to this standard.

c. Mirrors used in fixtures shall comply with Federal Specification DD-M-00411 or later revisions and amendments thereof.

2. Glass Classification for Intended Use:

a. Type I: Primary glass (float or sheet)

Primary glass has three specifications:

CLASS 1 Transparent glass

CLASS 2 Heat absorbing and light reducing

CLASS 3 Light reducing, tinted

CLASS 1: Transparent glass has six quality standards in conformance with Federal Specification DD-G-451D.

Quality 1. Mirror select quality. Intended for silvering for mirror applications and is seldom used for glazing.

Quality 2. Mirror quality. Intended for mirror applications.

Quality 3. Glazing select quality. Intended for uses where superior glazing quality is required for windows, doors, furniture, and fixtures.

Quality 4. Glazing A quality. Intended for selected glazing.

Quality 5. Glazing B quality. Intended for general glazing and other uses.

Quality 6. Greenhouse quality. Intended for greenhouse glazing or similar applications where quality is unimportant.

CLASSES 2 and 3: Heat absorbing and light reducing. Quality 3, 4, and 5 may be specified where reduction of solar heat is required or for reducing the amount of visible light transmission for use in applications where glare is a problem.

b. Type II: Rolled glass, flat

CLASS 1 Translucent

CLASS 2 Heat absorbing

CLASS 3 Light reducing, tinted

There are three forms in Classes 1, 2, and 3.

1. Wired, polished on both sides

2. Wired and figured

3. Figured

Rolled glass may be specified as translucent, heat absorbing, light reducing, tinted, decorative, and wired mesh.

Type II glasses are intended for use in:

1. Fixtures where design and esthetics are major considerations

2. Fire retardation

3. Security and safety

4. Sky lights, pattern, or form

5. Fixtures where heat and light are major factors

It should be investigated whether federal and local laws apply regarding Type I and Type II glasses before a contract is accepted.

3. Mirror Glass:

Mirrors shall be made with Type I, primary glass (float or sheet), Class 1, transparent, quality q1 mirror select or q2 mirror as specified in Federal Specification DD-G-451D or latest revisions thereof.

4. Mirrors:

    a. Mirrors, unless otherwise specified, shall be 1/8"-3/16"-1/4"-inch (nominal).

    b. The mirror shall consist of the glass specified herein coated with multiple layers of silver on one surface. The silver shall be protected by a metallic copper film, which in turn shall be protected by a suitable organic coating. The detailed requirements shall be as follows in DD-M-00411a.

SECTION VI

Electrical Work

A. General

1. The fixture manufacturer shall furnish all electrical material and work that is an integral part of fixtures he manufactures and installs.

2. Insofar as possible, all items shall be completely installed and prewired in the store-fixture manufacturing plant, with wires terminating in a junction or ballast box located as specified in drawings.

3. Final connections to source of supply and interconnection between fixtures will be done by others.

4. Electrical materials, equipment, and workmanship shall conform to the National Electrical Code, the State Electrical Code, the City Electrical Code, and all codes of the National Board of Fire Underwriters and of state and local bodies having jurisdiction.

5. Insofar as possible, all wiring, boxes, conduits, and cable shall be concealed.

B. Materials

1. All fixtures shall be new and shall be listed and approved by Underwriters Laboratories.

2. Lamps will be provided by others. The fixture manufacturer will furnish a complete schedule of lamps required as part of his work. This list must be submitted prior to delivery of fixtures, as specified by the architect.

3. All electrical fixtures shall have a factory-applied protective coating. Exposed surfaces shall be free of scratches and other blemishes that detract from appearance. Exterior finishes and materials shall be as selected by the architect.

4. Fluorescent lighting shall be rapid-starting and free of stroboscopic effects. Ballast shall be high-power factor type, self-contained in fixtures, wherever possible.

5. The fixture manufacturer shall furnish all fluorescent, slimline, or incandescent fixtures in connection with perimeter valance and/or core fixturing and fitting-room lights. These shall be installed by others.

6. Continuous strip lighting shall imply lamp spacing not to exceed 6 inches.

7. Showcase reflectors, as specified in the contract documents, shall be furnished by the fixture manufacturer.

    a. Outlets at the ends of reflectors shall accommodate regular BX or flexible cable.

    b. Lamp sockets will be spaced for the longest possible lamps to provide continuous light without dark spots.

8. Fluorescent or slimline light strips, as specified in the contract documents, shall be furnished complete with sockets, channels, couplings, covers and guards, wiring, conduits, ballasts, ballast boxes, utility boxes, and when specified, reflectors.

    a. Channels, covers, and ends shall be heavy gauge steel with white baked-enamel finish.

    b. Strip lighting shall have self-contained, rapid-starting high-power factor ballasts.

9. Cutouts shall be provided by the fixture manufacturer for wire mold that cannot be installed in the shop.
In this case, the wire molds will be provided by the fixture manufacturer but installed by others.

10. The fixture manufacturer shall not provide connectors, jumpers, and pigtails required in connection with electrical work on the owner's premises.

All electrical work on the owner's premises shall be done by others.

SECTION VII

Decorator Materials

A. Applied by Contractor

1. Wallpaper, rugs, and similar decoratory materials that can reasonably be factory applied will be installed by the contractor. Materials to be applied in shop by contrac-

tor should be supplied by contractor to better control delivery and quantity.

2. Installation of decorator materials will be of highest quality workmanship.

  a. Surfaces to receive such materials will be smooth, flat, and without imperfections that will be visible in the completed fixture.

  b. Materials will be affixed in the most appropriate manner to provide the best obtainable service.

B. Applied by Others

  1. Decorator materials that must be applied in the field shall be furnished and installed by others.

  2. When such materials are to be field installed, surfaces to receive these materials will be appropriately prepared by the contractor.

NAMES AND CHARACTERISTICS OF COMMON FIXTURE WOODS

Hardwoods

Common Commercial Name	Official Common Name[1]	Botanical Name[1]	Density Class[2]	Texture[3]	Grain[4]
Alder	red alder	*Alnus rubra*	Low	Fine	Uniform
White ash	blue ash	*Fraxinus quadrangulata*	Intermediate	Coarse	Nonuniform
	green ash	*Fraxinus Pennsylvanica*	Intermediate	Coarse	Nonuniform
	white ash	*Fraxinus americana*	Intermediate	Coarse	Nonuniform
Basswood	American basswood	*Tilia americana*	Low	Fine	Uniform
Beech	American beech	*Fagus grandifolia*	High	Fine	Uniform
Butternut	white walnut	*Juglans cinerea*	Low	Intermediate	Intermediate
Yellow birch	yellow birch	*Betula alleghaniensis*	High	Fine	Uniform
	sweet birch	*Betula lenta*	High	Fine	Uniform
White birch	paper birch	*Betula payrifera*	Intermediate	Fine	Uniform
Buckeye	Ohio buckeye	*Aesculus glabra*	Low	Fine	Uniform
	yellow buckeye	*Aesculus Octandra*	Low	Fine	Uniform
Cherry	black cherry	*Prunus serotina*	Intermediate	Fine	Uniform
Hard elm	rock elm	*Ulmus thomasii*	High	Intermediate	Intermediate
Soft elm	American elm	*Ulmus americana*	Intermediate	Coarse	Nonuniform
	slippery elm	*Ulmus rubra*	Intermediate	Coarse	Nonuniform
Tupelo gum	swamp tupelo	*Nyssa sylvatica var. biflora*	Intermediate	Fine	Uniform
	black tupelo (black gum)	*Nyssa sylvatica*	Intermediate	Fine	Uniform
	water tupelo	*Nyssa aquatica*	Intermediate	Fine	Uniform
Red gum	sweet gum	*Liquidambar styraciflua*	Intermediate	Fine	Uniform
Hackberry	hackberry	*Celtis occidentalis*	Intermediate	Coarse	Nonuniform
Magnolia	cucumber tree	*Magnolia acuminata*	Intermediate	Fine	Uniform
Hard maple	sugar maple	*Acer saccharum*	High	Fine	Uniform
Soft maple	red maple	*Acer rubrum*	Intermediate	Fine	Uniform
	silver maple	*Acer saccharinum*	Intermediate	Fine	Uniform
Red oak	black oak	*Quercus velutina*	High	Coarse	Nonuniform
	cherrybark oak	*Quercus falcata var. pagodaefolia*	High	Coarse	Nonuniform
	northern red oak	*Quercus rubra*	High	Coarse	Nonuniform
	scarlet oak	*Quercus coccinea*	High	Coarse	Nonuniform
	shumard oak	*Quercus shumardii*	High	Coarse	Nonuniform
	southern red oak	*Quercus falcata*	High	Coarse	Nonuniform
	willow oak	*Quercus phellos*	High	Coarse	Nonuniform
White Oak	bur oak	*Quercus macrocarpa*	High	Coarse	Nonuniform
	chestnut oak	*Quercus Prinus*	High	Coarse	Nonuniform
	swamp chestnut oak	*Quercus michauxii*	High	Coarse	Nonuniform
	swamp white oak	*Quercus bicolor*	High	Coarse	Nonuniform
	white oak	*Quercus alba*	High	Coarse	Nonuniform
Pecan	bitternut hickory	*Carya cordiformis*	High	Intermediate	Intermediate
	water hickory	*Carya aquatica*	High	Intermediate	Intermediate
	pecan	*Carya illinoensis*	High	Intermediate	Intermediate
Poplar	yellow poplar	*Lirodendron tulipifera*	Low	Fine	Uniform
Sycamore	American sycamore	*Platanus occidentalis*	Intermediate	Fine	Uniform
Walnut	black walnut	*Juglans nigra*	Intermediate	Coarse	Intermediate

SOFTWOODS

Common Commercial Name	Official Common Name	Botanical Name	Density Class	Texture	Grain
Cedar	eastern red cedar	*Juniperus virginiana*	Low	Fine	Uniform
Cypress	bald cypress	*Taxodium distichum*	Low	Fine	Uniform
Fir	Douglas fir	*Pseudotsuga menziesii*	Intermediate	Fine	Contrasty
Hemlock	western hemlock	*Tsuga heterophylla*	Low	Fine	Intermediate

Common Commercial Name	Official Common Name[1]	Botanical Name[1]	Density Class[2]	Texture[3]	Grain[4]
Larch	western larch	*Larix occidentalis*	Intermediate	Fine	Contrasty
Soft pine	sugar pine	*Pinus lambertiana*	Low	Fine	Uniform
	western white pine	*Pinus monticola*	Low	Fine	Uniform
	eastern white pine	*Pinus strobus*	Low	Fine	Uniform
Ponderosa pine	ponderosa pine	*Pinus ponderosa*	Low	Fine	Intermediate
Southern yellow pine	Loblolly pine	*Pinus taeda*	Intermediate	Fine	Contrasty
	longleaf pine	*Pinus palustris*	High	Fine	Contrasty
	shortleaf pine	*Pinus echinata*	Intermediate	Fine	Contrasty
	slash pine	*Pinus elliottii*	High	Fine	Contrasty
Redwood	redwood	*Sequoia sempervirens*	Low	Fine	Intermediate
Spruce	Sitka spruce	*Picea sitchensis*	Low	Fine	uniform

IMPORTED TROPICAL WOOD[5]

Common Commercial Name	Official Common Name[1]	Botanical Name[1]	Density Class[2]	Texture[3]	Grain[4]
Andiroba	cedro macho	*Carapa spp.*[6]	Intermediate	Coarse	Uniform
Avodire	avodire	*Turraeanthus spp.*	Intermediate	Intermediate	Uniform
Banak	virola	*Virola spp.*	Intermediate	Intermediate	Uniform
Cativo	cativo	*Prioria copaifera*	Low	Coarse	Uniform
Cedro	cedro	*Cedrela spp.*	Low	Coarse	Uniform
Lauans	Philippine mahogany	*Shorea spp.*	Low	Coarse	Uniform
	Parashorea spp.		Low	Coarse	Uniform
	Penacme spp.		Low	Coarse	Uniform
Limba	korina	*Terminolia superba*	Low to Intermediate	Coarse	Uniform
Mahogany	American mahogany	*Swietenia spp.*	Intermediate	Coarse	Uniform
	African mahogany	*Khaya spp.*	Intermediate	Coarse	Uniform
Obeche	obeche	*Triplochiton scleroxylon*	Low	Intermediate	Intermediate
Primavera	primavera	*Cybistax spp.*	Low to Intermediate	Coarse	Irregular
Ramin	ramin	*Gonystylus spp.*	High	Fine	Uniform
Rosewood	Brazilian rosewood jacaranda	*Dalbergia nigra*	High	Intermediate	Uniform
	Indian rosewood	*Dalbergia latifolia*	High	Intermediate	Uniform
Sapele	sapele	*Entandrophragma cylindricum*	Intermediate to High	Intermediate	Uniform
Teak	teak	*Tectona grandis*	High	Intermediate	Uniform
Walnut, tropical	walnut	*Jugians spp.*	High	Coarse	Uniform

[1] From *North American Trees*, 1976, 3rd Edition, by Richard J. Preston, Publ. by The Iowa State University Press and Forest Products Lab. Report No. 125.

[2] *Low density* implies specific gravity based on oven-dry weight and volume below 0.50; *Intermediate density* implies specific gravity of 0.50–0.59; *High density* implies specific gravity of 0.60 or higher.

[3] Texture refers to size of cellular elements.

[4] Grain refers to the variability of texture or density within growth ring or annular ring pattern.

[5] From "Properties of Imported Tropical Woods" by Francis Kukachka, USDA, Forest Service, Forest Products Laboratory, Research Paper, FPL 125, March 1970.

[6] Species.

Appendix 7

THE FIVE "F'S" OF SELECTING GARMENT RACKS

Joel Alperson, Omaha Fixtures Manufacturing

Through display fixturing, retailers have the opportunity to reinforce their market identity, and maximize the volume of goods they can sell. As a result, garment racks should be viewed as both functional and visual tools.

Form

Traditionally, the most popular fixtures have been the round rack, two-arm and four-arm costumers, double-rail, and tri-circle racks. While far from new, these fixtures mark the boundary of basic rack design. (Illustration 1.)

The round rack can merchandise relatively large quantities of garments in an endless circle of sizes and colors. The primary disadvantage of this fixture is that the customer only sees the shoulder of each garment. Unlike the round rack, the four-arm and two-arm racks allow the garments at the ends of the rack arms to be seen in full view. On the other hand, these racks work best merchandising only one garment size per arm.

The double-rail rack and tri-level round racks are something of a compromise between the racks with arms and the round rack. While the double-rail and tri-level racks present the customer with several garments in full view, they can also hold a large volume of merchandise.

Over the years, however, retailers have sought more distinctive fixturing. The retail market ultimately turned to more innovative designs.

Garment racks have now evolved to a point where design is limited only by the designer's imagination. Freestanding display units are often made of wire grid, slatwall, and metal tubing of various shapes and sizes. Fixturing may also combine wood, glass, and a limitless variety of other materials.

Fit

While garment rack construction methods are not as varied as garment rack design, they are no less critical to the success of the fixture. A rack that has many assembled parts might not be ideal in cases where the fixture must be moved a lot and subjected to heavy duty use.

Retailers can minimize the number of parts in a fixture by welding or permanently connecting as

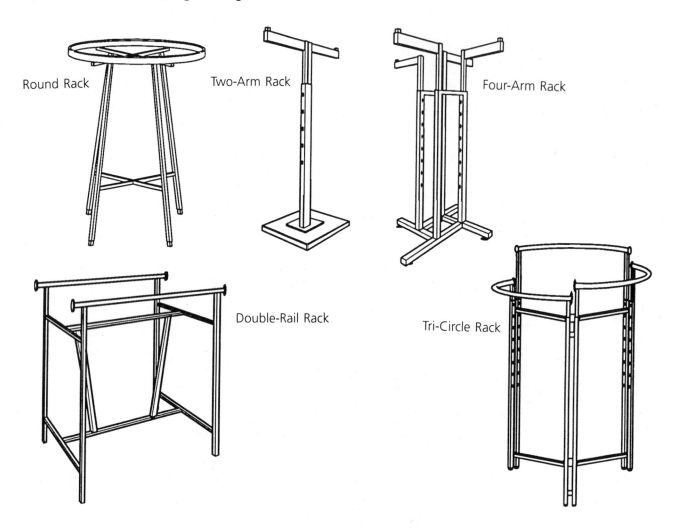

Round Rack

Two-Arm Rack

Four-Arm Rack

Double-Rail Rack

Tri-Circle Rack

Illustration 1.

many pieces as possible. Permanent connections not only minimize the number of parts that can be lost or broken, but they lessen the chance that the fixture will loosen over time. Loose or wobbly fixtures can leave the customer with a poor impression of the entire store. (Illustration 2.)

Function

The number of garments a fixture will hold per square foot directly affects the number of garments retailers can sell at any given time. Floor fixtures should be considered not from a side view, but from a top view. When these racks are full, is there nonmerchandised space within or around the fixtures? Consider the round rack for example. Fully merchandised, its center space is empty, and the aisles around it are not perfectly straight. While seemingly insignificant on an individual basis, multiplied by the number of racks in a store or department, the

space gained by using more efficient racks can be significant and surprising.

Finish

The finishes available for garment racks have broadened considerably over the years. Twenty years ago, the only commonly used finishes were chrome and a few wet painted colors. Today, powdercoated, brushed, textured, clear coated, and even rusted finishes are all part of what make garment racks far more distinctive than ever before. Produced in sufficient quantity, finishes can even be customized to meet a retailer's specific needs.

Fabrication

Finally, there is the question of where to have fixtures fabricated. Over the last 15 years import quality has improved to the point where excellent

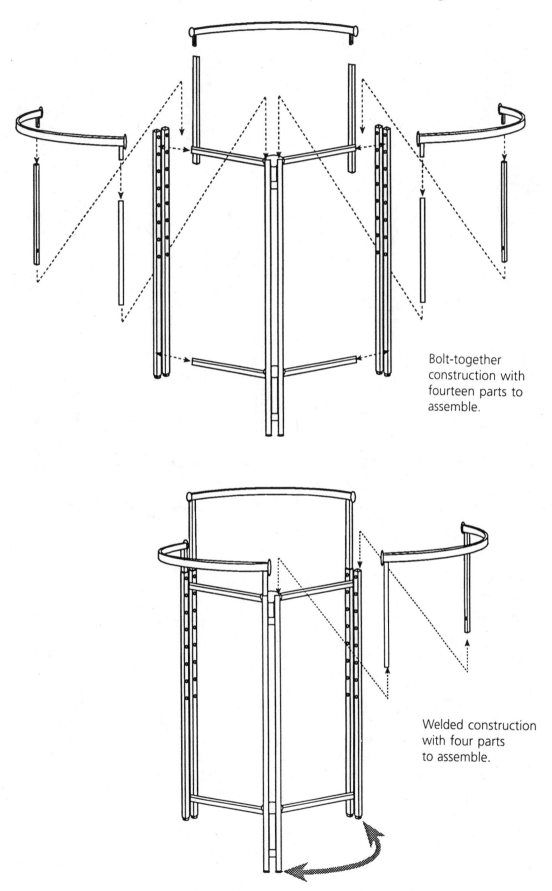

Bolt-together
construction with
fourteen parts to
assemble.

Welded construction
with four parts
to assemble.

Illustration 2.

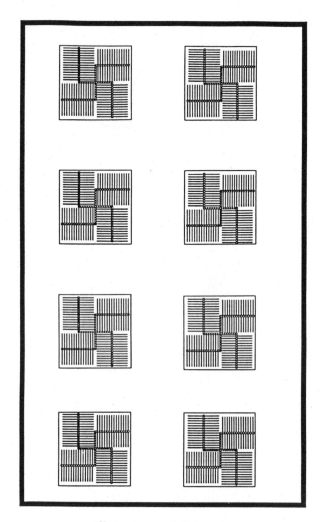

Efficient use of floor space.

Grey area shows loss of usable floor space.

products can be had at very attractive prices. Just as with American made products, however, not all factories are alike. A product's country of origin doesn't necessarily indicate that product's level of quality. Generally speaking, and only generally speaking, it is probably best to leave the cutting edge fixtures to the U.S. and European manufacturers for now. These are often special materials and fabrication techniques with which an overseas factory may not have enough experience.

If a retailer really wants to see whether a fixture is going to work for him or not, he should try to see it in somebody else's store. Even seeing a different fixture made by the same manufacturer can help in determining that manufacturer's production expertise.

To summarize, the retailer should know whether the fixtures he has are conveying his retail message effectively (form and finish). He should know whether they are space efficient (function), whether they are constructed to meet his long term needs (fit and fabrication), and whether they offer a reasonable payback (all of the above). If the racks pass these tests, the retailer will know his fixtures are improving his store's appearance, and ultimately his bottom line.

Appendix 8

HIGH-PRESSURE DECORATIVE LAMINATE AND SOLID SURFACING IN THE RETAIL/DISPLAY INDUSTRY

David Embry, Director of Design, Wilsonart/Gibraltar

High-Pressure Decorative Laminate

High-pressure decorative laminate is a paper product created of layers of resin-impregnated papers pressed under high heat. The process creates a surfacing material that possesses many characteristics of plastic (e.g., durability, low maintenance), as well as the good looks and variety of decorative options associated with printed paper.

How Is It Made?

Alpha-cellulose decorative paper, printed with either a solid color or pattern, is impregnated with melamine resin, then layered over kraft paper that has been impregnated with phenolic resins. Melamine resins provide strength and durability, while phenolic resins lend flexibility to the finished product.

The layers of paper are then placed in an industrial press under very high heat and pressure, for about an hour.

Types

There are several popular types of HPDL commonly used in commercial and residential applications.

• **General Purpose/Grade Laminate:** the most commonly used and thickest (0.050" nominal thickness) of the conventional laminates. General Purpose Laminate is used for countertops and work surfaces where normal wear and durability are needed.

• **Vertical Grade Laminate:** the thinnest laminate (0.030" nominal thickness), designed specifically for use on cabinetry and casework where the wear- and impact-resistance of General Purpose Laminate is not necessary.

• **Postforming Grade Laminate:** the most flexible of the laminate types, engineered for bending on a simple radius. Postforming Grade Laminate (0.042" nominal thickness) is most frequently seen

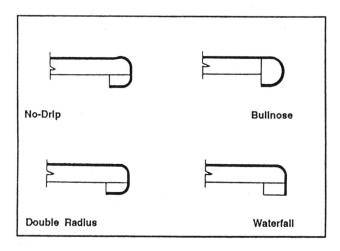

Postformed edge treatments.

on countertops, work surfaces, and cabinetry with rounded- or curved-edge treatments and/or curved or wrapped backsplashes.

Postforming Grade Laminate is enjoying great popularity now with the need to reduce incidence of sharp edges on work or display surfaces.

Other types or thicknesses of laminate are also available to meet special needs, including ultra-thin laminates, for wrapping extremely tight radii, and phenolic-core laminates of up to 1 inch in thickness.

Sizes

High-pressure decorative laminate comes in a wide range of sheet sizes to meet a variety of needs. Widths available include 30, 36, 48, 60 and 72 inches; lengths range from 60 to 144 inches. Laminates may also be "cut to size" by special order.

Colors and Patterns

Decorative laminate is available in literally hundreds of colors and patterns, including solid colors, faux woodgrains and stones, and abstract and computer-generated designs.

The development of photography and computer design has made it possible to recreate or reinterpret stones and woodgrains more realistically than ever. Gone are the days when laminate was seen as a cheap-looking surfacing alternative. New richer patterns, brighter more intense colors, and a wide range of hues and shades make laminate desirable wherever design flexibility is wanted.

Performance Options

Because of the widespread use of decorative laminate in commercial institutions and facilities, laminate manufacturers have developed several specialty-performance options to meet market demand:

• **Fire-Rated Laminates** provide extra flame- and smoke-spread protection in areas where code makes these demands.

• **Heavy-Wear Laminates** offer additional protection against repeated impact and/or scratching. These durable laminates are particularly popular in high-traffic areas and areas where machinery or other equipment often comes in contact with surfaces.

• **Chemical-Resistant Laminates**, originally designed to meet the needs of laboratories and healthcare facilities, are frequently seen today at cosmetic counters, hair and nail salons, and other retail areas where chemicals may be dispensed. Some chemical-resistant laminates are also resistant to buildup of bacteria.

Finishes

The development of a wide range of textured finishes has contributed to the growing popularity of decorative laminates in the retail industry.

Matte and gloss finishes are the most popular options. Finishes may reproduce realistic textures, such as the graining of wood or the nubbiness of fabric. Other options include grid, slate, and pebbled textures.

Finishes can be used to create a variety of interesting effects in the retail environment.

• Columns, walls, or fixtures clad in a woodgrain laminate with a woodgrain finish can provide the look of fine veneer with considerably improved durability.

• Using different finishes on the same color and/or in the same vicinity offers dimensional variety.

• Beaded finishes resist fingerprinting and provide improved scratch-resistance.

• Mirror gloss finishes offer reflectivity but should be used in low-traffic areas or on vertical surfaces to reduce possibility of scratches and smudges.

Related Materials

Several "specialty" laminates offer additional design flexibility and opportunities in the retail environment:

• **Custom laminates** can be cut and decorated prior to the laminating process, thus sealing special designs beneath the wear overlay of the laminate.

Two popular custom laminates include screen printing and seamless inlay. In screen printing, multicolor logos or other artwork are screen-printed on the decorative paper, then layered over kraft paper and pressed.

Seamless inlay enables the designer to incorporate two different laminate patterns for an inlay effect. A design is laser-cut out of the decorative top paper, then layered over a second decorative sheet, allowing the design to show through. The two decorative layers are then combined with the kraft paper core and laminated normally.

Both custom-laminate options allow designers to specify custom designs more cost-effectively and without the problems of peeling or cracking paint or seam lines that gather grime.

• **Colorthrough laminates** are made using multiple layers of decorative paper, without the kraft paper core. This eliminates the core paper "brown line" so often seen in laminate applications.

Because color runs straight through the laminate sheet, colorthrough laminate can be layered to create pinstriped or monolithic designs on fixtures.

Colorthrough laminate has been widely used for signage by laser-cutting through one layer of colorthrough laminate to expose a second, contrasting layer. Currently, only solid colors are available in colorthrough laminate.

• **Pearlescent laminates** feature a dimensional, multicolored effect, created by incorporating potassium aluminum silicate (PAS), a naturally occurring mineral, into the laminate and eliminating the wear overlay used in conventional laminate. These glossy, holographic laminates are recommended for vertical surfaces only, due to slightly reduced wear resistance.

Used for walls, columns, fixtures, and freestand-

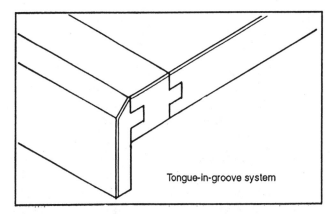

Tongue-in-groove system

Additional accent strips can be added to the deck of the work surface to extend the design. Molding pieces are pieced together using a tongue-in-groove system that ensures a tight fit.

ing displays, pearlescent laminates add drama and intensity to otherwise ordinary spaces.

• **Decorative metal with laminate backing:** Some manufacturers now offer decorative metals—solid brass and anodized aluminum—with a "phenolic core" or kraft paper backer. This backer provides improved workability and impact resistance.

• **Decorative laminate moldings:** A variety of moldings clad in decorative laminate are now available, making it easier and more cost-effective to specify custom-edge treatments on fixtures and displays.

Bevel moldings offer two faces for customization: contrasting striping or single-color monolithic. Moldings eliminate the "brown line" and provide a dimensional thickness to tops, creating the impression of more expensive materials.

Solid Surfacing

Technically speaking, solid surfacing is a homogeneous blend of polyester and/or acrylic resins with mineral fillers. Formulas vary by brand, but the product characteristics are essentially the same: it is durable, repairable, easily workable, and performs well in commercial installations.

Unique Characteristics

Solid surfacing is one of the most versatile, high-performance design media on the market, with many characteristics that make it ideal for retail environments.

First, it requires no substrate and, therefore, avoids the problems other surfacing materials face when a substrate is required.

Individual sheets and complementary accessories, such as sinks, backsplashes, and edge moldings, can be bonded together and finished, forming a nearly invisible joint that is resistant to the problems that plague grout lines and seams: moisture, bacterial growth, and dirt accumulation.

This ability to bond pieces invisibly also contributes to the unique look of solid surfacing, which appears to be fine, quarried granite or marble but is infinitely more workable than natural stone.

Skilled woodworkers find that solid surfacing can be worked much like wood. Special router bits and blades can be used to carve and etch the material to create unusual effects. Contrasting colors and patterns can be pieced together and bonded to create seamless designs.

Solid surfacing is also repairable. Minor scratches and nicks, even burns, can be buffed or sanded out with common abrasive pads or fine sandpaper. More serious damage can be repaired by removing the damaged area and bonding in new material.

Solid surfacing, because of this repairability, can be continually renewed, making it, essentially, "ageless." A countertop today can be refabricated into signage 20 years from now. Solid surfacing is nonporous, making it impervious to mold and mildew, and nonsupportive to the growth of fungus and bacteria.

Performance Benefits

As solid surfacing manufacturers explore new uses for their products, greater emphasis is being placed on product performance; for example, higher quality solid surfacing products carry a Class 1 fire rating. Some manufacturers have attained National Sanitation Foundation NSF-Class 51 rating for food-splash zone; others have achieved the more rigorous rating for food contact also.

Product benefits are being more clearly and definitively communicated through compliance with regulations set by Underwriters Laboratories, National Sanitation Foundation (NSF), Canadian Standards Association (CSA), British Standards Institute (BSI), Japanese Industrial Standards (JIS), and the all-encompassing International Standards Organization ISO-9002 series standards. Compliance with these standards provides the architect and designer quality assurance as they consider solid surfacing for a given application.

Color and Design Options

While more than half of all installations of solid surfacing use some variation on white or almond, the development of speckled, granite effects and more trend-aware colorways continues. In the past five years, every solid surfacing manufacturer has more than doubled its product offerings, bringing in richer, deeper colors and patterns, as well as a broader range of neutrals.

Recently, sophisticated color-matching technology has led to better ability to match colors, not only from sheet to sheet, but batch to batch. This same technology enables some manufacturers of both solid surfacing and decorative laminate to cross-match colors between the two media.

Product Offerings

Solid surfacing comes in standard sheets or panels, typically available in thicknesses of $3/4$, $1/2$, and $1/4$ inch to accommodate a wide range of surface needs, as well as dimensional and functional requirements. Widths range from 30 inches to 36 inches, and lengths from 60 inches to 144 inches.

The ability to bond accessories to sheets has led to development of these correlating products, also made of solid surfacing:

- Kitchen sinks and vanity bowls
- Bathroom and shower accessories
- Tub- and shower-surround kits
- Prefabricated moldings, edge treatments, backsplashes, and window sills
- Decorative hardware for cabinetry

Custom products using solid surfacing now include:
- Intricate artwork
- Moldings, railings, and wainscoting
- Furniture and furniture components
- Prefabricated inlay design tiles
- Light fixtures

Environmental Impact

Solid surfacing is an entirely reusable material. While there is no formal program for reclamation of the material—the long life span of the product and the fact that it has been available for only about 20 years have not made this necessary—recycling of outdated work surfaces is certainly a possibility.

The ability to produce a color-consistent material makes it possible for fabricators to use leftovers from one job to complete another—a significant reduction in waste. Matching strip products also contribute to this waste reduction, because fabricators are not forced to order full sheets of contrasting material when creating decorative edge treatments, backsplashes, and window sills.

Other uses for waste material include manufacture of trophies, signage, decorative hardware, cutlery handles, clocks, furniture components, decorative tiles, flooring tiles, moldings, and window sills.

A range of product characteristics make solid surfacing a good choice for "clean" environments. Not only do the nonporous surface and inconspicuous hard seams prohibit bacterial growth, but the material itself does not contaminate the environment or contribute to poor indoor air quality.

Uses for Decorative Laminate and Solid Surfacing in the Retail/Display Industry

Decorative laminate has long been one of the workhorses of the retail industry. Durability, low-cost installation and replacement, easy maintenance, and a wide range of design choices make it ideal for high-traffic, high-drama areas. Solid surfacing, on the other hand, is a relative newcomer in the industry. However, its unique characteristics make it ideal for certain installations.

Some of the applications for both products include:

• **Countertops:** Decorative laminate in work areas and sales areas alike is one of the most commonly used and sensible options for work surfaces, whether seen or unseen by customers. Use of heavy-wear laminates on exchange counters, for example, improves durability. Chemical-resistant laminates in areas where staining is possible—cosmetic counters, salons, food display—is recommended.

Solid surfacing is ideal for work surfaces anywhere. Easy maintenance and repairability shrug off most problems it will encounter.

• **Casework and fixtures:** Again, decorative laminate provides a cost-effective, low-maintenance surface with a wide range of design options. HPDL can also be changed out regularly, to create a variety of effects without the high cost of replacement.

Pearlescent laminates used on fixtures look different from every view and should be used in high-drama areas.

Again, chemical-resistant laminates are ideal for salons and cosmetic fixtures.

Heavy-wear laminates are recommended wherever repeated impact from shopping carts, wheelchairs, and other equipment is expected.

• **Displays:** Displays, like casework, are ideal for decorative laminate. Durable, easy to clean and maintain, inexpensive to replace or recover, laminate-clad displays can word hard and look good.

Specialty laminates, such as pearlescent or colorthrough laminate or decorative metals with laminate backers, are particularly well-suited to displays because of the extra drama and color they can add to a space.

• **Signage:** Decorative laminates, which can be screen-printed or etched, can be used for signage. Custom laminates, screen-printed prior to lamination, provide more durable signage. Colorthrough laminate can be layered and engraved to create multicolor, dimensional effects.

Solid surfacing is also ideal for signage. Lettering can be carved and/or inlayed into the surface for a carved-stone look. Braille characters can be etched into or out of the surface also.

• **Restrooms and changing rooms:** These have perhaps the most obvious uses for decorative laminate, which can be used on benches, partitions, doors, and, of course, countertops.

Laminate is both durable and easy to maintain, and updates are affordable when necessary. When the look demands higher-end, more elegant materials, consider solid surfacing, which offers many advantages over natural stone: repairability, no staining, chips and scratches buffed away. Solid surfacing can also be used for toilet partitions, mirror frames, and other detailing.

• **Columns/Cladding:** Most laminates can be wrapped around columns or used to clad walls, partitions, and other decorative or functional structures within a retail space. Postforming grade laminates should be specified when tight wraps are necessary.

Columns and other architectural details can be created entirely out of solid surfacing, which can be shaped and carved much like wood. Repairability and lasting good looks make the initial investment in solid surfacing pay off in the long term.

• **Elevator cabs:** Using decorative laminate inside elevator cabs can extend decorative themes into the elevators. The easy maintenance and durability make laminate a better option than wood or other soft materials, especially in high-traffic zones.

Consider heavy-wear laminates in areas where elevators are continuously used by large crowds or in freight or equipment elevators.

Consider solid surfacing also in high-traffic areas, where repairability may be an important advantage.

Final Considerations

Recent developments in the world of surfacing have enabled designers to use a variety of materials as both functional and decorative design media.

In retail environments, laminate can take the place of more fragile or expensive materials, while providing the level of good looks required in a visual environment. The lower cost of laminate often permits specifiers to create more interesting effects on a tight budget. Use of trendy colors and designs is easier when the cost of replacement, later, is more affordable.

Solid surfacing, although more expensive than laminate, provides myriad advantages and performance characteristics that only add to its good looks and workability. It also offers a range of benefits, including easy maintenance and repairability, not available from other high-end surfacing options.

For more information about the wide range of decorative laminate products now available for use in retail environments, contact manufacturers through their local representatives.

David Embry is director of design for Wilsonart, manufacturer of Wilsonart Decorative Laminates and Gilbraltar Solid Surfacing. For information on Wilsonart products, call 1-800-433-3222, or write Wilsonart, 600 General Bruce Drive, P.O. Box 6110, Temple, TX 76503-6110.

INCLUSION OF QUALITY STANDARDS AS A MEANS OF MEASUREMENT FROM FIXTURE DESIGN TO FABRICATION

Charles T. Cady, Chairman of the Board, American Woodcraft, Inc., and President, CEO, Strata Design, Inc.

The last 30 years of woodwork manufacturing in the United States can be characterized by continual change. A generation of woodworkers have grown up drawing more and more materials and equipment from resources devoted to developing process manufacturing. Changes seen in the last five years have accelerated at an almost exponential rate and permeated all aspects of woodworking. Development of Standard Practice in manufacturing has begun in many parts of the woodworking industry. The result is that woodworking firms can better develop wood as a natural, renewable resource into high-quality, high-technology products and components for use in the 1990s.

As specific areas of wood manufacturing developed standards, quality and consistency of product made improvements in related wood disciplines more achievable. *Rough milling* of logs was more predictable and usable. *Dimension milling* then developed a set of defined standards. Lumber of specific size and girth and of specific quality and appearance can be purchased.

Defined process standards in wood manufacture have resulted in significant cost savings with increased quality levels for the end user. *Veneering* is a fine example. Costs were controlled and lowered by specifically controlling grain pattern, using thin slicings from rough-milled or dimensioned lumber. These slicings are arranged and joined in a specific and controlled manner to achieve specific, repeatable visual effects.

Panel Manufacturing has developed quantifiable standards as a result of developments in the previously described lumber specialties. Substrates with specific measurable characteristics have evolved during the last ten years. Standard Manufacturing Practice has allowed such characteristics as screw-holding ability (x, y, and z planes), resin content (urea versus nonurea), and fire rating to be named and easily defined when writing quality specifications for store fixtures.

The ability of specifiers to communicate expectations of quality levels to the supplier by including definitions of quality of the wood materials and of wood finishing have resulted in progress being made to produce better fixtures at controllable costs. Without the development of Standard Manufacturing Practices in the wood and related industries (metal, glass, plastics, paint, etc.), rapid quality standards progress would not have been possible! Woodworkers have the luxury of adopting an almost complete set of quality standards for the component parts of store fixtures. This luxury always improves product and decision making:

1. Quality specifications can be revised to accommodate new ideas in a regularly used fixture.
2. Quality specifications can be used to measure product quality and consistency.
3. Adherence to quality specifications by a manufacturer can be used as a means of "post-qualification" of the manufacturer for future orders.

The challenge now is to move forward in the development of quality standards based on Standard Practice in the manufacture of cabinets and fixtures themselves. How does the purchaser get the needed and wanted fixtures delivered with product consistency and quality? The answer is to develop and subscribe to a means of quantifying quality that is better than ever before. But to the purchaser, the process issues that contribute to quality seem extremely remote from their responsibilities. And in an era of limited resources (time), this is true. Therefore, purchasing executives should look for quality standard definitions that are already in use. Definitions should be chosen that can be communicated and understood equally by the purchaser's management team and by the manufacturing supplier. But again, how to find the definitions? How to be sure the right "spec" is written? Continual cost pressures, shorter lead times, and fewer experienced specifiers on the purchaser's staff raise the significance of these questions exponentially.

Identification and utilization of fixture manufacturers that are already managing or controlling their manufacturing process will go a long way in assuring a good fixture-purchase outcome. It is very likely that a longer-term relationship can develop with a manufacturer that is continually committed to improving the "process." Such manufacturer qualification and utilization is incumbent upon the purchaser, or "Caveat Emptor"!

The purchaser can identify "process thinking" by the fixture manufacturer at various points in a developing resource relationship. Standardization of materials, parts dimensions, joinery techniques, and finish systems can be seen when visiting the engineering departments of a quality-oriented manufacturer before the first prototype is even contemplated. Shop-drawing output is a leading indicator of standard woodwork and finishing practices. Electrical and electronics cabling standards can now be found in certain woodwork firms, thus providing more value to the purchaser. The common ground for the purchaser and the manufacturer, working with a set of standard practices, is the defined quality that each party can identify in the wanted product. Successful quality assurance programs cannot exist cost effectively without acknowledgment of the value of Standard Practices.

Quality Standards criteria are drawn up over a period of years. Such criteria are continually evolving as the pace of technology accelerates. As technology accelerates, the manufacturing process must change with greater speed. Extensive research is performed each year by the National Association of Store Fixture Manufacturers (NASFM) and the Architectural Woodwork Institute (AWI), using data and in-depth interviews with their member firms. The product criteria must be looked at more frequently if the purchaser wants to achieve and maintain the best products in the marketplace. NASFM and AWI provide the driving force among woodwork manufacturers that strive for excellence. Discussion papers and technical reports on a variety of woodwork subjects are available from both national organizations. Rely on these sources—develop relationships with "process thinking" manufacturers—to help your firm conclude what the right questions are and the appropriate answers for your fixturing needs.

Appendix 10

CONDUCTING AN EXISTING-STORE-CONDITION SURVEY AND FIXTURE INVENTORY

Kenneth R. Zajac, AIA

Introduction

Before a design on a store makeover begins, a survey of the store must be performed. This survey should include an inventory of existing fixtures and furniture, locations of fixed architectural elements, mechanical features such as sprinkler heads and ceiling diffusers, and photographs that document these conditions. Information gathered in this survey will be used to evaluate what furniture can be reused and whether fixed architectural components will conflict with the new design.

Several tools will be required to efficiently perform the survey, including a sketch pad, clipboard, various pens or pencils, colored markers, tape measure, camera with flash, plenty of film, and some type of shoulder bag or fanny pack to carry all of these items and still keep both hands free for writing, and so on.

Survey of Existing Conditions

The first step in conducting a store survey is to obtain existing plans for the store. A set of floor plans and elevations will be an essential tool in recording existing conditions in the store. Plans can be obtained by several methods. The owner, landlord, building engineer, or operations manager may have a set of plans in the store or filed off-site at a corporate headquarters. The architect or store planner of record, if known and still in business, may have the originals on file. Another possible source would be the local building department where plans, either blueprint or on microfilm, may be on file because a building permit had been obtained for the work. If the building has some historical or architectural significance, plans may even be archived at a local historical society, museum, or university.

If plans are not available, then a sketch plan will be necessary to assist in recording the required information. To construct a basic plan of the store to be surveyed, walk the perimeter and note departmental dividing walls, windows, mall entrances, and so on. If there are lay-in ceilings, the standard-size tiles of either two feet or four feet will provide modules for determining the overall size of the building. The ceiling tiles can be counted from column to column and a typical bay size can be established. Most buildings are built on typical structural bays like 30 feet by 30 feet. Other fixed components, such as stairs, elevators, washrooms, fitting rooms, and offices, can be similarly spotted. Walls and door openings can be located by tape measure.

By methodically recording the architectural features of a space, a detailed sketch plan will evolve that can be used to survey the store. Not all buildings will lay out so easily as described, but by establishing some major landmarks within the space and subdividing the plan into smaller areas, a plan from which to work will still develop.

With an existing plan of the store or space, the survey can now begin. A starting point must be determined in order to document all conditions in the store in a thorough manner. A logical place would be at a mall entrance or primary circulation aisle. The surveyor should work in either a clockwise or a counterclockwise rotation along the perimeter walls of a department and photograph continuous views of the walls, documenting all hardware, displays, and so on. A photo-record should be made of each department, showing any freestanding elements such as changing rooms or cashwraps. At the same time, notes should be made of where any electrical, telephone, or computer lines may enter into the cashwraps, showcases, or back islands. This information will help in determining whether relocation of these fixtures is possible in the remodeling. The plan should also record any architectural features that may impact the new design, including detailed moldings, built-in displays, projecting walls, and recessed wall standards, if there are any, as relocation of these components may require partial demolition of the walls in which they are installed. Records should be made of any electrical outlets in walls as their location also may impact the new design work.

A separate reflected ceiling plan can also be constructed by counting ceiling tiles. Close attention should be paid to light fixtures, sprinkler heads, ceiling diffusers, exit signs, and other fixed ceiling elements such as soffits, skylights, recessed lights, and coffered ceilings.

All of these components will determine where new walls or other features may be built. A limited budget may not permit reworking of the structural, mechanical, or electrical systems to accommodate new walls, and special attention should be given to incorporating these existing elements in the new

design. However, if the structural, mechanical, or electrical components are to be relocated, than a licensed architect or engineer will need to be consulted.

Additional information that should be included in the survey is typical ceiling heights and existing floor finishes. All of the information recorded will assist in the preparation of drawings for the new work, such as plans, elevations, sections, reflected ceiling plans, and details.

Fixture Survey

The other half of a store survey is to inventory all loose fixtures, built-in fixtures, and furniture in each department. This information, when assembled in a final form, will be essential for the store designer and the store representatives to determine which fixtures can be reused, allocation of fixtures to each department, if additional fixtures will need to be purchased for the new design, or if fixtures will be discarded. An attached master checklist (See Exhibit A) is one suggested way to inventory all fixtures in each department. Most computer software spreadsheet programs will allow for creation of some type of working checklist. Different conditions or design criteria may require altering this format.

Pertinent information to be recorded on these forms includes the type of fixture, quantities of each fixture, finishes, overall dimensions, and an assessment as to whether the fixture can be refurbished for reuse, or is damaged and unusable or considered obsolete. A sketch may also be required to describe some fixtures.

A photograph of each type of fixture will assist all involved in the project in understanding the myriad fixtures that are used in modern store design. In order to accurately record each fixture type, an identifier number should be placed in the photograph. This will eliminate confusion later when all of the photographs are being organized and matched with the departments in which they are located. The photograph number can also be referenced in the completed inventory form.

Some operations managers may require that each fixture be tagged individually for internal inventory control. Various adhesive tags, available in numerous colors at office supply stores, can be used for this purpose. The store manager should be consulted for any preference for location of these tags on the fixtures.

The information obtained through the fixture

survey can then be translated into a final form, such as the example shown for typical Women's and Men's departments in Exhibit B. If required, the total fixture count for each department should be included. The completed survey forms and photographs should be compiled into some type of binder for each reference. Several binders will probably be required for distribution to the store manager, operations manager, or other key personnel on the design/remodeling team.

The completion of an existing-store-condition survey and fixture inventory will be essential in determining what built-in features or fixtures either will be reused in the new design or do not meet the program requirements for the store remodel. By taking a systematic approach, a concise survey of a store can be accomplished in a limited amount of time.

EXHIBIT A

Fixture Inventory

Store: _____
Location: _____

Department Name: _____   Floor: _____

A-1 Loose Fixtures/Racks   Color Code: _____

	Qty.	Sketch/Photo #	Reuse
Racks (Chrome)	_____	_____	Y/N
T-Stands	_____	_____	Y/N
4-Way	_____	_____	Y/N
Round 36"	_____	_____	Y/N
Round 42"	_____	_____	Y/N
3-Way Round	_____	_____	Y/N
Others	_____	_____	Y/N
_____	_____	_____	Y/N
_____	_____	_____	Y/N
_____	_____	_____	Y/N
_____	_____	_____	Y/N
_____	_____	_____	Y/N
_____	_____	_____	Y/N
_____	_____	_____	Y/N

Notes:

_____

_____

_____

_____

_____

_____

A-2 Special Fixtures

Vendor Shop Fixtures (Name or Merch. I.D. #)	**Qty.**	**L**	**H**	**W**	Color Code: _____ **Sketch/Photo #**	**Reuse**
_____	__	__	__	__	__	Y/N
_____	__	__	__	__	__	Y/N
_____	__	__	__	__	__	Y/N
_____	__	__	__	__	__	Y/N
_____	__	__	__	__	__	Y/N

Custom Features Description	**Qty.**	**L**	**H**	**W**	Color Code: _____ **Sketch/Photo #**	**Reuse**
_____	__	__	__	__	__	Y/N
_____	__	__	__	__	__	Y/N
_____	__	__	__	__	__	Y/N
_____	__	__	__	__	__	Y/N
_____	__	__	__	__	__	Y/N

Notes:

_____

_____

_____

A-3 Gondolas

Description	**Qty.**	**L**	**H**	**W**	Color Code: _____ **Sketch/Photo #**	**Reuse**
_____	__	__	__	__	__	Y/N
_____	__	__	__	__	__	Y/N
_____	__	__	__	__	__	Y/N
_____	__	__	__	__	__	Y/N
_____	__	__	__	__	__	Y/N

Notes:

_____

_____

_____

A-4 Glass Cubes W/Base

Color Code: _____

Description	Qty.	L	H	W	Sketch/Photo #	Reuse
_____	____	____	____	____	_____	Y/N
_____	____	____	____	____	_____	Y/N
_____	____	____	____	____	_____	Y/N
_____	____	____	____	____	_____	Y/N
_____	____	____	____	____	_____	Y/N

Notes:

_____

_____

_____

A-5 High-Pressure Lamiante Cubes

Color Code: _____

Description	Qty.	L	H	W	Sketch/Photo #	Reuse
_____	____	____	____	____	_____	Y/N
_____	____	____	____	____	_____	Y/N
_____	____	____	____	____	_____	Y/N
_____	____	____	____	____	_____	Y/N
_____	____	____	____	____	_____	Y/N

Notes:

_____

_____

_____

A-6 Misc. Custom Fixtures

Color Code: _____

Description	Qty.	L	H	W	Sketch/Photo #	Reuse
_____	____	____	____	____	_____	Y/N
_____	____	____	____	____	_____	Y/N
_____	____	____	____	____	_____	Y/N
_____	____	____	____	____	_____	Y/N
_____	____	____	____	____	_____	Y/N

Notes:

_____

_____

A-7 3-Way Mirrors

Color Code: _____

Description	Qty.	L	H	W	Sketch/Photo #	Reuse
_____	___	___	___	___	_____	Y/N
_____	___	___	___	___	_____	Y/N
_____	___	___	___	___	_____	Y/N
_____	___	___	___	___	_____	Y/N
_____	___	___	___	___	_____	Y/N

Notes:

_____

_____

_____

A-8 Tables

Color Code: _____

Description	Qty.	L	H	W	Sketch/Photo #	Reuse
_____	___	___	___	___	_____	Y/N
_____	___	___	___	___	_____	Y/N
_____	___	___	___	___	_____	Y/N
_____	___	___	___	___	_____	Y/N
_____	___	___	___	___	_____	Y/N

Notes:

_____

_____

_____

B-1 Cash Wraps

Color Code: _____

Description	Qty.	L	H	W	Sketch/Photo #	Reuse
_____	___	___	___	___	_____	Y/N
_____	___	___	___	___	_____	Y/N
_____	___	___	___	___	_____	Y/N
_____	___	___	___	___	_____	Y/N
_____	___	___	___	___	_____	Y/N

Notes:

_____

_____

_____

C-1 Showcases

Full-Vision

Color Code: _____

	Qty.	L	H	W	Sketch/Photo #	Reuse
_____	___	___	___	___	____	Y/N
_____	___	___	___	___	____	Y/N
_____	___	___	___	___	____	Y/N
_____	___	___	___	___	____	Y/N
_____	___	___	___	___	____	Y/N

Notes:

_____

_____

_____

$^1/_2$-Vision

	Qty.	L	H	W	Sketch/Photo #	Reuse
_____	___	___	___	___	____	Y/N
_____	___	___	___	___	____	Y/N
_____	___	___	___	___	____	Y/N
_____	___	___	___	___	____	Y/N
_____	___	___	___	___	____	Y/N

Notes:

_____

_____

_____

$^2/_3$-Vision

	Qty.	L	H	W	Sketch/Photo #	Reuse
_____	___	___	___	___	____	Y/N
_____	___	___	___	___	____	Y/N
_____	___	___	___	___	____	Y/N
_____	___	___	___	___	____	Y/N
_____	___	___	___	___	____	Y/N

Notes:

_____

_____

_____

C-2 Back Islands
Full-Vision

	Qty.	L	H	W	Color Code: _____ Sketch/Photo #	Reuse
_____	____	____	____	____	____	Y/N
_____	____	____	____	____	____	Y/N
_____	____	____	____	____	____	Y/N
_____	____	____	____	____	____	Y/N
_____	____	____	____	____	____	Y/N

Notes:

_____

_____

_____

D-1 Wall Hardware
Type

Type	Size/Length	Sketch/Photo #	Color Code: None Reuse
Oval Hangrod	_____	____	Y/N
Rec. Handrods	_____	____	Y/N
Surf. Mtd. Std.	_____	____	Y/N
12" H.R. Bkts.	_____	____	Y/N
14" H.R. Bkts.	_____	____	Y/N
16" H.R. Bkts.	_____	____	Y/N
18" H.R. Bkts.	_____	____	Y/N
Snub-Nosed Bkt.	_____	____	Y/N
Adj. Bkt.	_____	____	Y/N
Straight Faceout	_____	____	Y/N
Waterfall Faceouts	_____	____	Y/N
Prongs	_____	____	Y/N
Prong W/End	_____	____	Y/N
Cornice Bkts.	_____	____	Y/N
Cross Bars	_____	____	Y/N
Pull Outs	_____	____	Y/N
Slatwall H.W.	_____	____	Y/N
Other			
_____	_____	____	Y/N
_____	_____	____	Y/N
_____	_____	____	Y/N
_____	_____	____	Y/N
_____	_____	____	Y/N
_____	_____	____	Y/N
_____	_____	____	Y/N

Notes:

_____

_____

_____

D-2 Wall Hardware (cont.)

¹/₄" Glass Shelves	Width/Length	Sketch/Photo #	Color Code: None Reuse
_____	_____	____	Y/N
_____	_____	____	Y/N
_____	_____	____	Y/N
_____	_____	____	Y/N
_____	_____	____	Y/N
_____	_____	____	Y/N
_____	_____	____	Y/N

Notes:

_____

_____

_____

D-3 Accent Shelves

Description	Width/Length	Sketch/Photo #	Color Code: None Reuse
_____	_____	____	Y/N
_____	_____	____	Y/N
_____	_____	____	Y/N
_____	_____	____	Y/N
_____	_____	____	Y/N
_____	_____	____	Y/N
_____	_____	____	Y/N
_____	_____	____	Y/N
_____	_____	____	Y/N

Notes:

_____

_____

_____

E-Fitting Rooms

Description	Mirror Size	Qty.	Color Code: _____	
			Sketch/Photo #	Reuse
_____	_____	___	_____	Y/N
_____	_____	___	_____	Y/N
_____	_____	___	_____	Y/N
_____	_____	___	_____	Y/N

Notes:

_____

_____

_____

F-1 Fitting Room Customer Seating

Description	Finish	Seat	Qty.	Color Code: _____	
				Sketch/Photo #	Reuse
Metal/Wood_____	____	____	____	____	Y/N
Metal/Wood_____	____	____	____	____	Y/N
Metal/Wood_____	____	____	____	____	Y/N
Metal/Wood_____	____	____	____	____	Y/N

Notes:

_____

_____

_____

F-2 Decorative Furniture and Antiques

Description	Finish	Qty.	Sketch/Photo #	Color Code: _____
				Reuse
_____	____	___	____	Y/N
_____	____	___	____	Y/N
_____	____	___	____	Y/N
_____	____	___	____	Y/N
_____	____	___	____	Y/N

Notes:

_____

_____

_____

F-3 Visual Mer. Fur. Pieces

Color Code: _____

Description/Size	Finish	Qty.	Sketch/Photo #	Reuse
_____	_____	_____	_____	Y/N
_____	_____	_____	_____	Y/N
_____	_____	_____	_____	Y/N
_____	_____	_____	_____	Y/N
_____	_____	_____	_____	Y/N
_____	_____	_____	_____	Y/N
_____	_____	_____	_____	Y/N
_____	_____	_____	_____	Y/N

Other

_____	_____	_____	_____	Y/N
_____	_____	_____	_____	Y/N
_____	_____	_____	_____	Y/N
_____	_____	_____	_____	Y/N
_____	_____	_____	_____	Y/N
_____	_____	_____	_____	Y/N
_____	_____	_____	_____	Y/N

Notes:

_____

_____

_____

Stockroom Fixtures

Color Code: _____

Description Qty.	L	H	W	Sketch/Photo #	Reuse
_____	____	___	___	_____	Y/N
_____	____	___	___	_____	Y/N
_____	____	___	___	_____	Y/N
_____	____	___	___	_____	Y/N
_____	____	___	___	_____	Y/N
_____	____	___	___	_____	Y/N
_____	____	___	___	_____	Y/N
_____	____	___	___	_____	Y/N
_____	____	___	___	_____	Y/N

Notes:

_____

_____

_____

EXHIBIT B

ABC Store Chicago, IL   **Fixture Survey Inventory**

Department: Men's

Loose Fixtures/Racks

Description	Photo #	Qty.	Dimensions	Reuse
4-Way—chrome	N/A	34	42" x 42"	Y
4-Way w/high bar—chrome	50	2	42" x 42"	N
Round—chrome	N/A	12	36" Dia.	Y
Gondola hanging rack—chrome	9	9	60' Long	Y
Belt rack—chrome	52	2	24" x 24"	N
Tie rack—chrome	53	7	21" x 21"	N
Glass/chrome shelving unit	58	1	37" x 37" x 58 1/2" H	N

Misc. Vendor Fixtures

Description	Photo #	Qty.	Dimensions	Reuse
Vendor table	54	3	24" x 48" x 30" H	Y
Shirt gondola—2 tier—wood	55	2	48" x 48" x 30" H	N
			30" x 30" x 43" H	
Jeans gondola—3 tier—H.P. laminate	56	1	38" x 59" x 41" H	N
Levis gondola—3 tier—H.P. laminate	59	3	57" x 39" x 42"H	Y
Jeans shelving units—H.P. laminate	60	2	29" x 17" x 84" H	N
Jockey gondola—chrome/plexiglass	61	4	62 1/2" x 20" x 52 1/2"H	Y
Sock slatwall gondola	62	2	54" x 32" x 56" H	Y
Shirt gondola—wood/glass cubes	63	5	67" x 34 1/2" x 54" H	Y
Sweater gondola—wood/glass	64	2	44 1/2" x 28" x 48" H	N
Misc. gondola	65	1	60" x 36" x 52" H	N
Sunglasses stand	66	1	14" x 14" x 69" H	Y
Pants gondola—3 tier (w/casters)	67	1	69" x 31" x 35" H	Y
Pants shelving unit—6 tier—modular	69	5	40 1/2" x 16" x 75 1/2"H	Y

Tables/Cubes

Description	Photo #	Qty.	Dimensions	Reuse
H.P. laminate cubes	N/A	1	30" x 30" x 12" H	Y
Wood nesting tables	54a	1	33" x 58" x 30 1/2" H	Y
			24" x 48" x 24" H	
Tables	57	5	60" x 48" x 30" H	Y
Tables (round display)—particle board	N/A	3	36" Dia.	Y

Glass/Plexiglass Cubes W/Base

Description	Photo #	Qty.	Dimensions	Reuse
Glass cubes w/H.P. Laminate base (2 x 4 x 2 modules)	68	1	28" x 32" x 52" H	Y

Showcases

Description	Photo #	Qty.	Dimensions	Reuse
2/3 Glass	69a/69b	2	2 @ 89" Long	Y

Remarks

1. Relaminate all cubes. Color to be selected.

Department: Women's (Coats, Sportswear, Dresses, Petites, Large Sizes, Designer, & Swimwear)

Loose Fixtures/Racks

Description	Photo #	Qty.	Dimensions	Reuse
T-Stands (waterfall)—chrome	N/A	18	12" x 36"	Y
4-Way—chrome	N/A	99	42" x 42"	Y
4-Way w/high bar—chrome	8	10	42" x 42"	Y
6-Way—chrome	N/A	4	60" Long	Y
Round—chrome	N/A	42	36" Dia.	Y
Gondola hanging rack—chrome	9	12	60" Long	N

Misc. Vendor Fixtures

Tubular metal shelving unit	12	2	28" x 72"	Y

Tables/Cubes

H.P. laminate Cubes	N/A	2	30" x 30" x 12" H	Y

Remarks

1. Most gondola racks have severe wear at the chrome finish; replacement is recommended.
2. Relaminate all cubes. Color to be selected.

Appendix 11

RENOVATION OF EXISTING STORE WHILE IN OPERATION

Construction Services of Bristol

Construction Services of Bristol, Inc., as General Contractor, builds a finished product from the designer's concept of the customer's requirements. Whether the project is a new building or the renovation of an existing building, preliminary work begins with the project manager's review of architectural plans and specifications, invitations to bid on subcontracted work, on-site review of field conditions, development of a job-completion schedule, and the organization and submittal of the project-cost bid.

Once the contract is awarded, the project manager reviews the project takeoff, plans and specifications, schedule, and subcontractor list with the job superintendent. Al this point, the project moves onto the job site where all construction phases are coordinated and supervised by the job superintendent. The superintendent's responsibilities include job-site layout, quality control, general contractor's manpower and subcontractor scheduling, interpretation of architectural plans and specifications, security, job safety, and public relations.

Each project has its own personality and challenge that require a specific approach to its construction. An 80,000-sq.-ft. renovation of a retail department store on two floors, for example, had to be accomplished without interrupting normal business operations, and also by an established completion date.

During the initial review of this project, the project manager developed a bar chart between start and completion dates to get a perspective of time involved for manpower, subcontractor, and material delivery requirements. This bar chart was fine tuned into a grid of the floor plan to more accurately coordinate work. Because a new suspended acoustical ceiling, a new HVAC, new lighting, and new carpet and tile were specified, a night work shift had to be added to the normal day working hours. Then the work involved was categorized and applied to the appropriate trade, and subcontractors were invited to bid on the project. The estimator coordinated and compiled winning bids into a total job-cost bid to the customer (or customer's representative).

After the customer awarded the general contract, a subcontractor's list was handed over to the job superintendent, in addition to the job schedule and a review of the project. The job superintendent sets up a field office on the job site and becomes familiar with job conditions, working dimensions, and access to work areas. Concurrently, the project manager confirms delivery dates on long-lead items (millwork, wallcovering, carpet, and tile) with subcontractors to be sure that the dates fit within the job schedule.

These dates are reconfirmed and updated at each weekly job meeting and are compared with actual field conditions to more accurately schedule installation. The general contractor, owner, architect, and all subcontractors currently involved with the project during the week are present at the job meeting, which covers job progress, questions regarding plans and specifications, change orders, and job procedure, in addition to material delivery dates.

On this 80,000-sq.-ft. project, millwork items (perimeter decor valances, loose fixtures, showcases) were long-lead items that had to be delivered on time to insure a smooth transition of merchandise display. Because these items are custom fabricated from an individual design, the contractor must draft shop drawings for approval, order material (slatwall, for example, which is also custom made), then fabricate the items in a craftsmanlike manner that reflects the quality and style required by the project designer. The period prior to fabrication, then, can take up to 12 weeks, underscoring the need for early and consistent contact with the fixture contractor(s). This 80,000-sq.-ft. project included approximately 1,600 linear feet of perimeter decor, which phased in as the final step with the orderly turnover of each department because communication was maintained with the fixture contractor from the initial award of the general contract to the delivery day on the job site.

Months before the slatwall and chrome waterfall hangers started arriving, however, the job superintendent was starting up crews installing a fire-retardant polyethylene curtain along the interior perimeter of the project from floor to ceiling to separate a five-foot-wide work space from the public. The curtain was devised to serve two purposes: (1) dust protection and (2) visual barrier.

Once the polyethylene curtain was in place, the existing gypsum board walls were demolished to conform to the more efficient design specified. The resulting dust was contained behind the curtain, even as merchandise sales were transacted on the main floor, and the customers were also protected from demolition hazards. The visual barrier also worked,

during the rough-framing/drywall phases of construction, to hide the unsightly conditions until the final coat of taping compound was applied to the gypsum board joints. After the walls were painted, the polyethylene curtain was taken down, area by area, and the perimeter decor was installed in public view.

A tile aisle that directed traffic flow through the main areas on this 80,000-sq.-ft. renovation project was also installed during normal working hours, although the layout had to be done off hours. The tile installation was performed by roping off sections approximately 50 feet long on the main floor in areas chosen through the job superintendent's observation in consultation with department managers regarding best time of day or week to do the work in that particular area. The tile was cut away from the installation area, allowing the laying of the tile to remain quiet and interesting to passersby.

Jackhammering and sawcutting of concrete floors, installation of the acoustical suspended ceiling, HVAC work, fire protection, light fixtures (650 recessed and spotlighting fixtures), carpeting, and a skylight in the existing escalator well were scheduled for the night shift. Because all these phases occurred over or on the main floor area, and business could not be interrupted, the work had to be done when the store was closed. The layout on this project required relocating all cash register terminals. The jackhammering needed to cut new chases in the concrete floors would have been too noisy to do during normal working hours. In addition, floor fixtures and showcases could be moved out and back in place without interrupting business. All conduit was installed and a quick-setting cement was dry by the store's opening the next day.

Similar to all other phases, the acoustical suspended ceiling, fire protection, lighting, and HVAC followed the floor-plan schedule devised to coordinate the availability of departments to minimize disruption. The ceiling was started according to this schedule—not sooner or later. As a result, the fire protection, lighting, HVAC, and the merchandise departments could depend on accurate dates to plan their work routine.

Each night, at the beginning of the shift, a crew moved all existing floor fixtures that would be in the path of a rolling staging and covered the remaining merchandise with polyethylene. The carpenters, electricians, and pipefitters proceeded to install their own work above without damaging or dirtying merchandise. As the work moved through an area, fixtures were replaced; the polyethylene was removed; and the area was cleaned and ready for the store opening in the morning.

The carpet installation required the most floor space in the main selling area on both levels. In comparison to the ceiling installation, all floor fixtures and showcases had to be removed from the grid areas and greater areas had to be obtained to make the installation productive. As a result, the carpet installation was also completed during the night work shift, in a separate phase after the ceiling work was completed. The carpet base could be installed during normal working hours because the areas involved were at the perimeter of the sales floor and the area was involved only for short periods (15 to 20 minutes) as the tradespeople progressed along the wall.

Any work performed in the escalator well also had to be done during the night shift or during the two hours before the store opened in the morning. A prefabricated, artificially lighted skylight was specified for this project to brighten the escalator well, without cutting into the roof. The escalators could not be shut down during normal working hours, so a suspended staging system was devised and left in place until all trades completed their work on the skylight. The mirrors were also installed off this staging for safety considerations; but the remaining wall decor (wallcovering, plastic laminate, and painting) was installed from ladders and floor-mounted stagings that were assembled and broken down each night or prior to the store's opening in the morning.

Pinpoint scheduling, subcontractor coordination and cooperation, and constantly updated communication among the general contractor, the customer, designer, subcontractors, and store personnel on this renovation project were the key elements in completing on time without interrupting sales volume. When department managers were told they could expect work to begin in their area on a certain day, they organized their schedule to accommodate the change and informed their sales personnel. Subcontractors worked with each other and organized material deliveries to be sure the transition from one phase to the next was orderly and on time. Any and all questions from store personnel regarding noise, temperature comfort levels, decor, or procedure were answered as soon as possible, either directly or through their department managers by the job superintendent. This practice meant the store personnel were informed and involved regarding major renovations to their environment, reinforcing the positive attitude necessary to maintain sales volume. It also meant that stock was relocated efficiently when the new loose fixtures arrived to replace the existing fixtures during the final phase of construction, because by this time everyone involved could trust that the date proposed for a move was when that move would take place, even though sometimes tradespeople were working frantically during the final hours to make sure the schedules were adhered to.

By the completion date, the 80,000-sq.ft. store had a new appearance in which sales volume could expand; the store personnel gained a new, more efficient environment to stimulate sales; and the owner maintained a consistent sales volume while the project was going on in the midst of a busy retail merchandise operation.

	A	B	C	D	E	F	G
1	D-4 I-5 DW-7 C-9 S-5 E-9 PD-15 P-10 H-5	D-4 I-5 DW-8 C-9 S-5 E-9 PD-15 P-11 H-5	D-2 I-5 DW-5 C-10 S-5 E-10 PD-16 P-11 H-5	D-1 I-5 DW-9 C-11 S-5 E-10 PD-16 P-6 H-5	D-1 I-5 DW-3 C-12 S-5 E-12 PD-17 P-16 H-5	D-1 I-5 DW-2 C-12 S-5 E-13 PD-17 P-6 H-5	S-4 H-4 I-4 C-14 E-13 P-16
2	D-3 I-5 DW-7 C-9 S-5 E-9 PD-19 P-10 H-5	DW-7 E-9 S-5 H-6 I-6 C-9	S-5 H-5 I-5 C-10 E-10	S-4 H-4 I-4 C-11 E-12	S-4 H-4 I-4 C-12 E-12	S-4 H-4 I-4 C-12 E-13	D-9 I-4 DW-13 C-14 S-4 E-13 PD-22 P-16 H-4
3	D-2 I-6 DW-6 C-9 S-6 E-9 PD-19 P-9 H-6	S-6 H-6 I-6 C-10 E-10	S-6 H-6 I-6 C-10 E-10	S-4 E-12 H-4 I-4 C-11	S-4 H-4 I-4 C-12 E-12	S-4 H-4 I-4 C-13 E-13	D-9 I-4 DW-13 C-9 S-4 E-13 PD-22 P-15 H-4
4	D-2 I-3 DW-6 C-9 S-6 E-9 PD-13 P-9 H-6	S-6 H-6 I-6 C-10 E-10	S-6 H-6 I-6 C-10 E-10	S-3 E-11 H-3 I-3 C-11	S-3 H-3 I-3 C-12 E-12	S-3 H-3 I-3 C-13 E-14	D-8 I-2 DW-12 C-13 S-21 E-14 PD-21 H-2 P-15
5	D-1 I-3 DW-5 C-9 S-3 E-9 PD-13 P-8 H-3	S-3 H-3 I-3 C-10 E-10	S-3 H-3 I-3 C-11 E-11	S-2 H-2 I-2 C-11 E-11	S-2 H-2 I-2 C-12 E-11	S-2 H-2 I-2 C-13 E-14	D-7 I-2 DW-11 C-13 S-2 E-14 PD-21 P-14 H-2
6	D-1 I-3 DW-5 C-9 S-3 E-9 PD-12 P-8 H-3	D-5 I-3 DW-8 C-10 S-3 E-10 PD-18 E-10 H-3 P-12	D-5 I-3 DW-9 C-11 S-3 E-11 PD-18 P-12 H-3	S-2 P-12 H-2 I-2 C-11 E-11	D-6 I-2 DW-9 C-12 S-2 E-11 PD-19 P-13 H-2	D-6 I-2 DW-10 C-13 S-2 E-14 PD-19 P-13 H-2	D-7 I-2 DW-10 C-13 S-2 E-14 PD-20 P-14 H-2

MALL ENTRANCE

PHASE AND PROJECT WORK, WEEKS 1 THRU 14

D   —   Demolition

DW —   Drywall

S   —   Sprinkler

PD —   Perimeter Decor

H   —   HVAC

I   —   Insulation

C   —   Ceiling

E   —   Electrical

P   —   Paint and Wallcover

Appendix 12

THE ROLE OF COMPUTER-AIDED DESIGN IN STORE PLANNING

Hughes W. Thompson, Jr., AIA, Connell & Thompson: Architects

History

Computer-aided design (CAD) is having an increasingly significant role in the process of store planning, design, construction, and management. Since the advent of relatively inexpensive personal-computer-based CAD systems in the early 1980s, the use of such systems among store planners, designers, architects, and engineers has risen steadily. Today, the majority of professionals in these fields use CAD systems for at least some portion of their work.

Benefits of CAD

CAD systems can be thought of as "drawing processors" that process graphical documents in the same way that word processing programs process text documents and spreadsheet programs process numerical documents. The major benefits of CAD systems are the same as those of more familiar computer applications:

1. The computer can speed up the process of creating the document by allowing elements to be easily

copied, relocated, or deleted. Common tasks such as dimensioning or spellchecking can be automated, thus increasing accuracy. The same tools that aid in the creation of a document can be used to easily modify it at any time.

2. Perfect copies can be made of the document or of a portion of the document. The copies can be used for the development of similar documents by the creator or by others. Documents can be transferred to different applications or even to entirely different computer systems. Once an element of a document is created, it can be used over and over again in many different contexts.

This chapter will discuss the many ways in which computer-aided design is being used in the store-planning and construction process. Applications of CAD in the planning and design process will be reviewed, followed by an explanation of the role of CAD in the production of construction documents. Next, the idea of "intelligent drawings" will be discussed, with a review of its applications in store planning. Finally, a case study of an expansion program for a national chain will discuss the use of CAD systems in the real world.

Design Process

Many designers and architects who use CAD systems for the majority of their work still return to the traditional pencil and tracing paper at the earliest stages of the design process. Freehand sketching is the most immediate and familiar method for getting their ideas on paper. Many feel that the precision demanded by the CAD system is an unnecessary hindrance to design. As designers become more comfortable in drawing on a computer, they find it less inhibiting and tend to use it for more and more tasks.

Use of CAD systems for conceptual design also depends on the task at hand. In studying the design of a display fixture with a wide variety of possible forms, most designers might prefer to start with a series of freehand sketches. On the other hand, in laying out a group of fixtures of a fixed size in a defined area, the precision of the CAD system is of great benefit in fitting the pieces of the puzzle together. Elements can be easily moved around and rearranged on the screen, and a multitude of alternate plans can be quickly developed.

Design Drawings

No matter how the initial design work is done, the design is at some point transferred into the computer. This corresponds to the creation of the initial "hard-line" drawings in manual drafting. The context of the design is normally drawn first. In the case of a renovation, this may come from actual field surveys or lease drawings provided by a landlord. If the building in which the store is located was designed on a CAD system, it is possible for the building architect to supply existing conditions drawings to the store planner in electronic form. While conditions still should be field verified, starting with a CAD drawing of the space can save a great deal of redrafting.

If the design incorporates manufactured items such as store fixtures, the drawings of these fixtures may also be available on CAD. In the architectural field, manufacturers of windows, furniture, appliances, and other building elements are making CAD drawings of their products available to designers so that they can be incorporated directly into their designs. As the use of CAD becomes more common in the store-planning field, this practice will become common for the manufacturers of display fixtures as well. Design information can also be transferred in the opposite direction: A store planner's design drawings for custom display fixtures can be transferred to a manufacturer in electronic form. The manufacturer can then develop shop drawings directly from the design drawings without redrafting of the basic elements.

Presentation Drawings

A primary purpose for the development of design drawings is presentation to the client for decision-making purposes. The client will often want to see alternative schemes for the store design. After initial review by the client, the design will be studied further; the design will be changed and presented again. The use of CAD makes this process much faster and easier. Most of the basic elements of the various alternative schemes may remain the same. With the CAD system, it is simple to make a copy of one scheme and modify only the elements that are different. The same drawing that is plotted at large scale for a presentation can be reduced and faxed to the client for immediate feedback. Important elements of the design can be printed at an enlarged scale for closer study. Sometimes an independent store planner may be working with in-house design staff who also use CAD. In this case, design drawings can be exchanged electronically by modem or on disk.

The ease of modifying CAD drawings encourages greater development of alternative designs and greater refinement of the final design. CAD allows more time for the preliminary design process because the drawings developed can be translated directly and relatively quickly into construction documents.

Three-Dimensional Visualization and Animation

CAD is often associated with dramatic three-dimensional renderings of buildings and realistic animated "walk-throughs" of spaces that only exist in the designer's imagination. However, the majority of work done on CAD systems is the same type of two-dimensional drawing produced by most manual drafting. Three-dimensional CAD drafting involves a fundamentally different approach. Two-dimen-

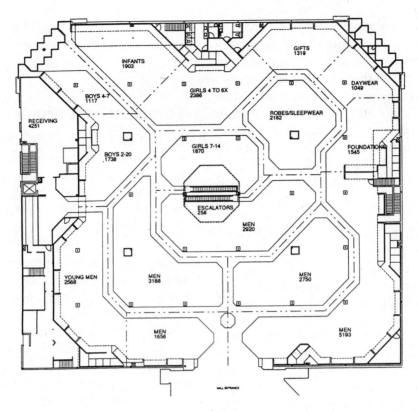

A merchandising plan for a department store. The boundary of each department is linked to the department label, and the square footage is automatically calculated. As the plan is modified during the design process, the distribution of space among departments can be easily tracked.

Three-dimensional view of a storefront, generated from a two-dimensional merchandising plan. Each display fixture is drawn as a simple three-dimensional block. The drawing has sufficient detail to allow the client to make decisions on the size of the openings, the placement of fixtures, and so on.

sional drawings are very abstract representations of the real world. Only those elements necessary to the purpose of the drawing are shown. Three-dimensional drawings, on the other hand, attempt to create models of the real elements they represent. They are created from solids and surfaces, rather than from lines. Every important surface on the object or in the space must be accurately drawn in its correct position in three dimensions.

Special CAD programs have been developed for three-dimensional work. Some major programs combine two-dimensional drafting, three-dimensional modeling, and rendering capabilities. In these programs, two-dimensional drawings can be translated into three-dimensional models relatively easily. Elements such as furniture have both two- and three-dimensional counterparts and can be translated back and forth. Once the three-dimensional model has been developed, it can be viewed from any angle, and a series of views can be printed out. The initial "wire-frame" model can be made more realistic by using increasingly sophisticated tools. Rendering programs can emulate the effect of lighting on the model, creating shades, shadows, and highlights. The effect of various types and locations of lights can be studied. So-called "photorealistic" rendering programs allow great control over surface treatments. The effect of reflective surfaces, rough textures, and pre-

cise color matches can all be represented. A series of views of the model can be combined in sequence to create the effect of a walk through the actual space.

Construction Documents

In the CAD design and drafting process, a smaller proportion of the overall time is spent in the construction documents phase. This is because much of the work done during the design phase can be easily translated into construction drawings. It is during this phase that the greatest benefits of automation can be applied. Standard details, title blocks, notes, and schedules previously developed by the designer can be easily modified for use in the new design. As in the design phase, the designer can take advantage of "symbol libraries" of commonly used elements that can be inserted into the drawing. Because of the precision of CAD drafting, dimensions can be automatically calculated and inserted by the computer. Since all or part of the drawing can be copied and reused, a floor plan may be drawn once and will become the basis for the demolition, merchandising, and reflected ceiling plans as well as the electrical, lighting, sprinkler, and mechanical plans developed by the consulting engineers.

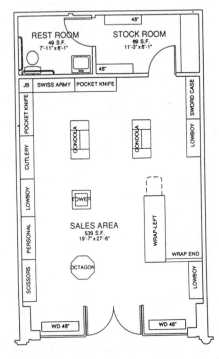

FIXTURE SCHEDULE						
ID	FIXTURE TYPE	PRODUCTS	WIDTH	DEPTH	HEIGHT	QUANTITY
AL	WRAP-LEFT		7'-0"	2'-3"	3'-10"	1
AP	WRAP END		4'-0"	4"	3'-10"	1
C	GONDOLA	VARIOUS	4'-0"	2'-0"	4'-6"	2
DG	WD 48"	WINDOW DISPLAY	4'-0"	1'-0"	8"	2
E	TOWER	VARIOUS	2'-0"	2'-0"	4'-6"	1
F	POCKET KNIFE	POCKET KNIVES	4'-6"	1'-6"	7'-0"	2
F	SWISS ARMY	SWISS ARMY KNIVES	4'-6"	1'-6"	7'-0"	1
GS	SCISSORS	SCISSORS	4'-6"	1'-6"	7'-0"	1
H	CUTLERY	KITCHEN KNIVES	4'-6"	1'-6"	7'-0"	1
JB	JB	CORNER BASE	1'-6"	1'-6"	4"	1
K	PERSONAL	PERSONAL CARE	4'-6"	1'-6"	7'-0"	1
L	LOWBOY	VARIOUS	4'-0"	1'-6"	1'-6"	3
MS	SWORD CASE	SWORDS	4'-6"	1'-6"	7'-0"	1
O	OCTAGON	VARIOUS	2'-6"	2'-6"	7'-4"	1
						19

An intelligent fixture plan in which is stored data about each display fixture in the drawing. The schedule is generated automatically from the stored data.

Intelligent Drawings

So-called "intelligent" drawings incorporate data as well as graphical elements in the drawing file. Most of the data is hidden from view but can be manipulated and extracted by the CAD user: A drawing of a display fixture on a plan may include a visible item number. Hidden within a label is additional data about the fixture including its dimensions, manufacturer, finish, and so on. As the fixtures are copied around the drawing, the data is copied as well and modified if required. Once this intelligent fixture plan is developed, a complete fixture inventory for the store can be developed, broken down by type, manufacturer, or department. The computer can be asked to find and highlight all of the fixtures of a given type. By simply picking a fixture on the plan, the CAD user can view all of the relevant information about the item.

Almost any type of information incorporated into a drawing can be tracked in an intelligent way. During the design phase, the area of each department can be automatically calculated, and a space inventory of the store can be developed as needed. In the construction documents phase, data on doors, lighting fixtures, finishes, and equipment can be built into the drawing and extracted into schedules. Takeoffs of materials can be generated for cost-estimating purposes. After construction is complete, the intelligent drawings should be maintained and updated as the store changes. They thus become important facilities-management tools for the client.

Example Application of CAD

The following case illustrates how CAD techniques are used extensively on a major expansion program for a national retail client. The program involves specialty stores in shopping malls throughout the country, including both new locations and renovations of existing stores. The client's store planner developed a new prototype store design and fixture designs for this expansion program. As each location becomes available, the space is field-verified by a local representative, and the existing conditions are entered into the CAD system. The next step is to adapt the prototype store to the space available. All of this design work is done on the computer. Standard drawings of all of the various fixture types

were developed. These are copied and move around the space to develop the merchandising plan. If there is a previous store of similar size and proportions, this may be copied and modified as required. The fixture plan is then sent to the client for approval and is modified based upon the client's comments. If the store plan is unusual, three-dimensional views are developed to assist the client in assessing how the space will best be merchandised. These views are taken from both the outside and inside of the store.

After the merchandising plan is approved by the client, the plan is developed into a formal preliminary design submission for client and landlord approval. The floor plan is copied, and a reflected ceiling plan is developed from it. The storefront and interior elevations are adapted from the most similar previous design. Standard signage and storefront details are added. Intelligent drawing techniques are used to automatically develop finish and fixture schedules from information in the drawing. These are sent to suppliers of display fixtures, lighting fixtures, and carpeting who execute orders for the store.

After client and landlord approval of the preliminary design, the plans are developed into construction drawings. Additional standard details are added and modified as required. Extensive standard notes are edited and added to the drawings. The floor plan is transferred on disk to the engineers who develop mechanical, electrical, and sprinkler plans, adding their own standard details and notes. The drawings are then assembled and sent out for final landlord approval, bidding, permitting, and construction. Any modifications or clarification sketches required are made in the original drawing files. The relevant portion of the drawing is then plotted out as a sketch. At the end of construction, the as-built drawings are turned over to the client on disk.

Although each store is different, a great many elements of the design and construction package are the same from store to store. The standard notes and details are constantly being refined as lessons are learned from the construction and operation of each new store. The use of CAD systems helps to assure quality control by accurately transferring the updated information into the package for the new store.

Appendix 13

THE EDUCATIONAL BENEFITS OF STORE-PLANNING COURSES

Patricia A. Martin, Former Member Design Faculty,

Northern Illinois University, DeKalb, IL

Why should courses in store planning be included in an interior design curriculum at a university? How do they help to achieve overall interior design education objectives? What benefits would store-planning courses provide students who intend to become or are interested in becoming store planners? What facets of store planning are not emphasized in other areas of design instruction that, if taught, could enrich design students' knowledge and understanding of the field as a whole?

Many educational institutions in the United States that have interior design curriculums do not teach courses in store planning/design, and even fewer have curriculums specifically geared to that design specialization. Some schools occasionally do incorporate store-design projects to provide some variety to the types of environments they have their students consider. Perhaps more schools and universities would offer special courses if they knew the beneficial outcomes.

Curricular Benefits Flow from Clearly Defined Educational Objectives

When interior design professors at Northern Illinois University initiated two store-planning courses within the curriculum ten years ago, in conjunction with the Institute of Store Planners and their student design competition, their objectives were to:

- Inaugurate realistic projects for students in order to strengthen the professional focus of the program.
- Exhibit the use of a clear problem-solving process beginning with an elaborate problem statement (program) and continuing through concept development into final details.
- Provide an opportunity to deal with complex design elements whose varying sizes, shapes, and combinations are not common.
- Provide enriching extracurricular activities

and field trips to learn about the technical aspects.

- Provide an understanding and concern for various lighting approaches for their efficiency and effectiveness.
- Create an awareness of store planning design as a career choice.
- Provide the benefit of experience in a specified field without having to make a commitment to it.

The association with the Institute of Store Planners caused faculty to consider how they might provide for and/or reinforce these objectives and take action to implement them. The addition of store planning has prompted:

1. Course sequence changes
2. Course content changes
3. Course additions
4. An increase in extracurricular learning experiences such as field trips, guest speakers on aesthetic and technical topics, and attendance at professional meetings.

The previously offered furniture design course, for example, was changed to meet the detailing needs of case goods and fixturing. The placement within the curriculum was altered as well, so that it could play a more supportive role in the students' education. As the association progressed and the work of the students was evaluated, it became obvious that the junior-level perspective/rendering course should be divided into two courses to increase the professionalism of the students' visualizing skills. A simpler, proportional method of perspective is now presented to the students, which allows them to understand the three-dimensional drawing approach more easily and produces more visually pleasing results. It too was garnered from the association with store planners.

A course was also developed to focus in on different design specializations on a rotating basis, such as a bank or restaurant design. It was now seen that each could serve as an emphasis for one of the overall program objectives.

While the faculty had always provided extracurricular learning experiences prior to introducing store planning, those now offered to the students heightened faculty awareness to their inherent value. Schools have subsequently offered more of these learning experiences for student enrichment. This

was accomplished with the assistance of graduate school funding or through the generosity of firms with whom the program had an on-going relationship.

Faculty Benefits

The faculty involved on a regular basis have also benefited from the association with store planners. Besides the obvious deepening on one's understanding of the design field, the association has provided new professional learning opportunities, such as sabbatical studies or trips for professional lecture engagements, that have, in turn, influenced the content incorporated into courses. The store planners have also graciously shared drawings of all types—both presentation and working drawings for university resource files. These files provide illustrative material for lectures and serve as a learning aid for students. All these additions and alterations have assisted the faculty in providing sound learning opportunities for students and the impetus for refining educational objectives in the future.

Major Benefits for Students

To elevate the benefits that store-planning courses have for students, informal survey interviews were conducted with students who had graduated in the past ten years from Northern Illinois University. The data showed that the value of two store-planning courses were as follows:

- Understood the design process more fully as a problem-solving methodology.
- Valued acquaintance with outside-related sources.
- Realized the importance of considering and incorporating human factors into the design process if an effective solution is to be developed.
- Valued highly the insights they took from the various types of critiques incorporated into the courses.
- Valued the emphasis that was placed on sound drafting and detailing knowledge.

Former students now in a wide array of design positions mentioned these responses repeatedly during their interviews. However, graduates whose employment involved store planning-responsibilities also added two additional benefits:

- Knowledge of basic theoretical store-planning concepts.

- Knowledge of specific sources and terminology related to store planning design.

A Further Analysis of Store-Planning Course Benefits

The design program'a curriculum stresses problem solving from the first residential design course all the way through the final interior design and architectural courses. With each course, the methodology base is expanded or varied so that students will leave the program with an understanding of the various mental tools and procedures that can be used. By the time students take the first store-planning course, they have already been taught two distinct problem-solving approaches. Perhaps the emphasis graduates placed on the value of the store-planning courses' design methodology stems from the fact that they brought a readiness to appreciate its worth. Or, perhaps the clarity and comprehension of the total design process involved in the store-planning courses enhanced their prior knowledge. In the programming phases, students are required to analyze merchandising requirements by using problem-solving matrices, such as affinity and cross-impact matrices, tools for the resolution of merchandising adjacencies within or between departments. Information from these and other methodologies are then utilized to develop strict criteria for an effective solution.

Benefits of Marketing Education

The program benefits the **marketing education students** while they are in school by:

- Helping them to develop marketable skills that lead to successful employment immediately upon graduation.
- Providing an occupational orientation to the business world and the American economic system through a combination of classroom instruction and directed experiences.
- Making them aware of their own potential for success.
- Providing greater opportunities for advancement and job satisfaction.
- Making them aware of the importance of additional education and training to develop full potential.

The program benefits the employee by:

- Increasing job satisfaction.
- Preparing them for better job opportunities and advancement.
- Improving customer relations.
- Increasing the opportunity for financial gain.

The program benefits the employer and the owner of business by:

- Offering instruction in the operations phases of their business.
- Reducing turnover of personnel.
- Providing better trained personnel.
- Decreasing training costs.
- Assisting them to better serve the public and to operate more profitably.

The program benefits the consumer by:

- Increasing efficiency in marketing.
- Providing well-trained salespeople who help customer satisfaction.

It immediately becomes apparent, therefore, that several large groups of citizens have a direct interest, and a still larger group an indirect interest, in marketing education. These groups are composed of all those persons who produce for marketing, all those who benefit from marketing, and all those who engage in marketing.

Getting Involved in Marketing Education

Many business people, educators, business firms, educational institutions, trade associations, and other agencies are participating in the marketing education program. Examples of their contributions include providing scholarships and endowments, participating directly in the educational activities, and supporting and publicizing the program. Further needs and additional opportunities for participation in, and support of, the program include:

1. Encouraging initiation of and providing assistance in the organization and development of new programs.
2. Supporting present programs and working for their improvement and expansion.
3. Participating in the development of local and state plans by communicating the concerns of youth and adults of the community.

4. Serving on advisory committees.
5. Increasing public understanding of the value of marketing education.
6. Supporting the marketing education program, by encouraging adequate financial support by local and state governments and by business organizations and foundations.
7. Encouraging qualified people to enter the field as instructional personnel.
8. Serving as a teacher in the marketing education program either on a full-time or part-time basis.

If you are interested in getting more information about marketing education or its companion student organization, contact one or more of the following:

1. (Your) State Supervisor of Marketing Education, State Department of Vocational Education
2. Marketing & Distributive Education, Program Specialist U.S. Department of Education, Washington, DC 20202
3. Distributive Education Clubs of America, 1908 Association Drive, Reston, VA, 22091
4. Your local educational agencies.

Appendix 14

THE EDUCATION OF AN INTERIOR DESIGNER

William T. Brown, Professor Emeritus, Northern Illinois University, DeKalb, IL

People who wish to design interiors for an occupation generally have an unreal image of what being an interior designer means, and they encounter frustrating, even conflicting, educational alternatives. No one type of school or curriculum is standardized and presently provides an ideal education. For that matter, no one type of interior design professional exists. Many professionals, who are card-carrying members of one of the many professional societies, are decorators. Some are licensed architects; some are store planners; and innumerable others are specialists of one type or another within an ill-defined interior design profession. Therefore, a great diversity of people qualify to be called "interior designer" whose training or education has little in common.

People seeking entry into the interior design profession can choose between four-year degree-granting universities, technical training schools, and community colleges. At a university where they can get both bachelor's and master's degrees, they will find programs housed within Schools of Architecture, Design, or Home Economics (often recently given a more attractive name like School of Human Ecol-

ogy). Curriculums in the three schools are very different. All of them require some liberal arts, but architectural curriculums are singlemindedly focused on making every course contribute to the architectural education in a very direct manner. Curriculums in Art and Home Economics are not so tightly focused and must be examined individually to determine how many courses do not apply at all or apply only vaguely. Often, five or more courses have little or no relevance because curricular control resides in an Art or Home Economics department that is intent upon serving those faculty rather than the interior design students. However, even with this waste, potential interior designers may find far more in-depth study of interiors in those schools rather than in schools of Architecture. In the curriculums in Architecture, the emphasis has traditionally been placed on building structure and the mechanical aspects, rather than on the interiors. Interior designers, even those characterized as architects, have historically been treated as second-class citizens by the architectural community. Schools of Architecture, in general, continue to place interior design far down on their priority list. Nevertheless, their quality control for removing those of marginal ability and the AIA licensing has given much respectability to their graduates.

Professional trade schools in interior design tend to have funding difficulties, are narrowly focused, and are generally short in time span. Most of them aim at a specific area of technical training. They are not degree-granting institutions. But, one must remember that the interior design profession does not require degrees for entry. Most offices are influenced by prior experience and a design portfolio.

Community colleges have small full-time faculties and large part-time faculties. The educational time span is short, and nearly everyone who wishes to study is admitted. The part-time faculty has difficulty in establishing continuity and quality control.

While it is entirely possible for a person to gain an education through the apprenticeship system in a design office, few could be accommodated, and most productive offices cannot disrupt the work of highly paid professionals to teach. In the long run, it has proved to be too costly for the office. The expense of maintaining a large professional faculty, dedicated to excellence in teaching and curriculum development on an outgoing basis, is the primary reason that universities and a very few heavily endowed private professional schools offer the best choice for a place to receive an interior design education. People can be trained as specialists rather quickly, but university degrees require four or five years of course work because they have responsibility for offering an opportunity to go beyond training to provide a philosophic and aesthetic base. They also help to develop experience in design methods for solving the problems in design that often have no one correct answer, but rather a number of alternatives. Aesthetic and sociological choices must be made according to beliefs and values. Education includes a formulating of values, and it takes time.

Academic institutions now serve as a place for a person to gain prerequisite skills prior to employment in a design office. We, in a sense, do preliminary screening and weed out those who are unsuitable. We see an academic education as a necessary preliminary to practical experience in a series of design offices. Only then will the designer become totally tempered and mature. It is doubtful that the education is ever really complete.

Interior design study in some schools is primarily technical training. At a university where the degree is housed within a Department of Art, we intend that it be an education. Toward that end, a minimum of twenty-five professors, all of whom are specialists in particular disciplines and have a broad diversity of critical opinions, are used to challenge and stimulate critical thinking. We begin the student's curricular experiences with courses that are weighted toward providing prerequisite drawing skills, technological understanding, and analytic investigative techniques. We then gradually increase assignment complexity and the opportunity for open-ended, hypothetical, even meditative and uncertain ideas to emerge in the studio solutions, and elicit philosophic debate between students and faculty during critiques.

Interior design education begins with studio courses in freehand drawing, drafting, detailing, and perspective and rendering that form a base for the visualization of ideas. We have found that designers lack thinking ability when their visualization skills are poor. Our courses in architecture provide rudimentary knowledge in building structure and the mechanical aspects. Basic design and color courses develop sensitivity to space, form, proportion, texture, and color. Fire codes, space standard, and lighting fundamentals continue to furnish technical information.

We recognize that the students in these essentially technical courses produce exercises short on originality. They reflect training more than education. Students who are determined and work hard generally do well at becoming technicians. Some students resist development beyond this stage. These people have value to a design office; in fact they are found there in large numbers. They are good at visualization, enjoy solving technical problems, and are often good at program analysis. They can produce capable plans and working drawings, yet they lack the critical knowledge and values necessary to the comprehensive problem-solving designer who should lead the profession into the twenty first century.

Many people who wish to enter the profession do not wish to make working drawings and have little interest in the technical aspects. They do not wish to become complex functional or aesthetic problemsolvers. They prefer to develop concepts verbally or in nontechnical sketch form, leaving others to figure out how their idea might be built. They focus on furnishings, wallcoverings, textiles, carpet, color, pattern, texture, and so on, and are intensely interested in interior ambience. We encourage these students to seek an education at a two-year community college. It is not that these issues are unimportant; it is merely that we do not wish to limit ourselves to the aspects that are primarily decorative. In fact, we deemphazise this part of the education.

During the later stages of a student's education, we progressively increase the number of studio assignments that allow a student to create a solution in which the aesthetics are arbitrary and to submit the choice to critical debate and defend it. Formalism, symbolism, functionalism, period motifs, eternal archetypes, and other issues are debated in these critiques. Architectural and interior design criticism has developed uncertainty and raised questions concerning validity of theoretic positions in the minds of students whose counterparts of the 60s would have followed modernism faithfully. To question and debate these issues, a person must be educated beyond interior technology. Knowledge from literature, music, art, architecture, and furniture history provide a basis that is further enriched with more input from sociology, psychology, statistics, philosophy, and other liberal arts disciplines. An interior designer is only, in part, a technician. The more difficult role is that of aesthetic philosopher and problem-solving decision maker. It is this developmental level that is most difficult to attain.

Universities find four and five years to be a minimal period in which to explore these issues. Schools of Design and Schools of Architecture realize their graduates are lacking experience in the practical matters of business, communication, team work, and administration. But academic institutions cannot do all of these things in four or five years, and we lack the appropriate setting. We believe that design offices are the best place for teaching these things.

At most universities, classroom activities do not mirror professional practice. They are, by choice, more idealistic, exploratory, and hypothetical. However, we recognize the importance of having students closely interact with practicing professionals. Speakers from a variety of design offices are invited to lecture, and field trips are organized. Each year, the Chicago Chapter of the Institute of Store Planners presents a design problem, critiques the student proposals, and evaluates the final drawings. Also, a great number of studio design programs are based on actual inprogress work of faculty or others in the design community.

Those who are entering the interior design profession, and those who are in one of the stages within the profession and who seek change, must ask themselves in what capacity they wish to serve: decorator/designer, technical interior specialist, or comprehensive interior designer. They must ask themselves honestly in which classification they fall by experience, training, and education. They must decide in which category they are temperamentally, intectually, and artistically suited to succeed. They must how much time and effort they are willing to devote to their career objectives in which type of school to enroll, and to which particular school within that type.

The initial choice of school limits the alternatives of how a person will progress within the interior profession. Architects generally are continuing to view interiors as secondary concerns. For those architects who do not, all alternatives are open. Those who graduate from Design Schools or interior design departments within Art Schools can move to the top of the profession quickly after they achieve the comprehensive designer stage. Unfortunately, many of them remain as technicians. The choice is made by the individual. All educational alternatives are imperfect, and the profession is ill-defined. But for those who make the correct choice for themselves, it will be exciting and rewarding.

Appendix 15

VISUAL MARKETING AND STORE DESIGN MARKETS

The Visual Marketing & Store Design Show

The Visual Marketing & Store Design Show is an established semi-annual marketplace and the pre-eminent showcase for visual merchandising, store planning, store design, store fixturing, point of purchase, display, and design. Twice a year, in May and December, more than 5,000 leading national and international marketers attend the Show in New York City. Attendees include representatives from department and specialty stores; malls; hotel and restaurant chains; advertising agencies; home fashions manufacturers and architecture and interior design firms; discounters; and the home furnishings, video/electronic, apparel, gift, and stationery industries.

As the retail capital of the United States and as home to countless industries serving retail, New York City has long been recognized as the premier marketplace for visual marketing and store design resources. Consequently, for the past 50 years, New York City has been home to the industry's semi-annual market. In 1993, George Little Management, Inc., (GLM) assumed production and management of the Show, which is now sponsored by NADI™ (National Association of Display Industries) and

cosponsored by *VM+SD* (Visual Merchandising and Store Design) magazine, and endorsed by ISP (Institute of Store Planners).

The latest and the best the industry has to offer is exhibited at New York City's Jacob K. Javits Convention Center (spring), Passenger Ship Terminal Piers (fall), and local showrooms. Each market runs four days, and more than 175 exhibitors display their products in a variety of booth configurations and sizes in exhibit space that exceeds 30,000 square feet. Identifying a real opportunity for synergy among shows, in 1994, GLM held The Visual Marketing & Store Design Show in May to coincide with the following GLM shows: the National Stationery Show®, International Contemporary Furniture Fair® (ICFF), and Surtex®. Teaming The Visual Marketing & Store Design Show with proven GLM shows promised exhibitors increased numbers of attendees—upwards of 40,000—new markets, and international attention.

NADI is an association comprised of retailers, suppliers, and allied disciplines dedicated to fostering the growth of the visual merchandising and store design industries. For association information, contact NADI, 355 Lexington Avenue, New York, NY 10017, (212) 661-4261, FAX (212) 370-9047.

A comprehensive and targeted advertising, direct mail, and telemarketing strategy is employed to generate attendee awareness before each Show. An aggressive publicity program promotes the Show. National and international media coverage is extensive before, during, and after the Show. Attendee and exhibitor information is available by contacting GLM, Ten Bank Street, Suite 1200, White Plains, NY 10606-1954, 1-800-272-SHOW, FAX (914) 948-6180.

Since 1993, the Show has also included a critical educational element. An extensive two-day seminar program that focuses on current design trends and issues related to the visual design industry are offered by The Planning and Visual Education Partnership (PAVE). PAVE is a creative nonprofit alliance of the ISP, NADI, S.V.M. (Society of Visual Merchandisers), and *VM+SD*. Its objective is to educate and motivate retail management, visual merchandisers, store planners, architects, specifiers, manufacturers, and students. PAVE seeks to encourage interaction among these related constituencies through progressive seminars, with proceeds dedicated to financial aid and targeted internships for qualified students.

The seminar series provides a critical educational forum and is also a valuable contribution to the personal and professional growth of participants new to the industry. Such prominent industry specialists as Gordon Thompson of Nike Shoes, Alan Questrom of Federated, Robert Mettler of Sears, David Nichols of Mercantile, Ed Pettersen of Kinney, David Rockwell of the Rockwell Group, Philip Miller of Saks Fifth Avenue, and James Mansour of James Mansour, Ltd., are engaged as speakers to share their knowledge, experience, and insights.

The PAVE Seminar Programs are held for two hours on each of two days during The Visual Marketing & Store Design Show with a reduced seminar fee for students with valid identification. In the fall of each year, PAVE also affords students the opportunity to compete in the annual PAVE Student Design Competition for three cash prizes awarded in each of two categories: for two-year-program students and for four-year-program students. The winners are announced at The Visual Marketing & Store Design Show in December, and special displays, showcasing finalists' entries, are presented at the show. For more information about PAVE programs, contact PAVE, c/o GLM, Ten Bank Street, Suite 1200, White Plains, NY 10606-1954, (914) 421-3200, FAX (914) 948-6180.

The entrances and lobbies of the Show, the PAVE Seminar space, and displays exhibiting the PAVE Student Design Competition finalists' entries are designed with exhibitors products to stimulate excitement in the execution of creative visions.

The producers of the Show provide an "Open Call" for new designers to apply for exhibit space at the show, the purpose of which is both to generate excitement in the marketplace and to support and promote new designers. This complimentary exhibit space is made available to up to 10 designers whose product entries demonstrate creativity and originality and are appropriate to the marketplace. Product entries include innovative designs, ideas, trends, shapes, colors, textures, finishes, lacquers, forms, furniture, light fixtures, props, and decorative and display materials. For "Open Call" information and applications, contact GLM, Ten Bank Street, Suite 1200, White Plains, NY 10606-1954, (914) 421-3200, FAX (914) 948-6180.

The Visual Marketing & Store Design Show has received industry acclaim and support of its commitment to vitalizing the marketplace by creating an expanded range of exhibitors and targeting a broad retail audience. The special features of The Visual Marketing & Store Design Show impress and inspire industry-related corporations by offering visual merchandisers an energizing environment of creative exhibitors, stimulating showrooms, and visionary speakers and by providing quality training and financial support to aspiring students.

Appendix 16

THE INSTITUTE OF STORE PLANNERS

What is the Institute of Store Planners?

I.S.P. is a profesional association of over 1100 members in the categories of professional, associate, trade, student, educational, visual merchandising, media, and international associate. 1996 will be the I.S.P.'s 35th Anniversary Year.

I.S.P. is *the* recognized organization of professional store planners and designers dedicated to excellence in the development of retail environments. Its members have a direct and positive effect on retail performance by serving as the creative link between the retailer and customer; and by establishing and maintaining the highest professinal standards and practices.

The Institute of Store Planners (ISP) is a professional association of interior retail store planning and design specialists founded in 1961. With headquarters just outside New York City, ISP now has over 1,100 members internationally, with 13 chapters throughout the United States and one overseas. Membership of the Institute consists of professional store planners and designers, associate store planners, visual merchandisers, students, and educators, as well as contractors and suppliers to the industry.

ISP is an association of professionals whose mission is:

- To promote excellence in store planning and design.
- To establish and maintain standards of practice and professional ethics.
- To promote the store planning and design profession as a distinct discipline.
- To contribute to public health, safety, and welfare through creative retail environments.
- To provide growth opportunities within the profession.
- To educate and encourage new entrants to the profession.
- To promote the benefit of professional store planning and design to the client, to the public, and, to the design community.

Why Are Retailers Turning to ISP Members?

To succeed in the tough and competitive retail business, retailers need stores designed to make a profit from the first day. Yet merchandising is changing. Every day seems to bring new products, trends, markets, and techniques. To design up-to-date facilities, more owners are turning to specialists in the field of retail interiors. ISP members design interiors with the operator's objectives in mind: to increase sales, reduce risk, build well and rapidly, and surpass the competition.

In the past, some shops were designed by building designers or interior planners, specializing in office or residential work. While expert in their own fields, these designers were often not experienced in planning retail environments, including merchandising, security, maintenance, lighting, leasing factors, and fixture systems. Without experience in merchandise presentation, they often created stores that got disappointing results.

ISP members have shown thousands of retailers how to save time, money, and effort; they offer a smooth development of quality facilities of which all can be proud.

What Are the Qualifications for Membership in ISP?

Individuals can qualify for membership in one of eight categories:

• **Professional Member:** An individual who meets the following requirements:

1. An individual engaged on a full-time basis in the profession of store planning for a minimum of eight years, and shall be professionally competent in five or more of the following areas of endeavor in store planning:
   • planning
   • design
   • architecture
   • fixture design
   • merchandising
   • lighting
   • color and material selection
   • specificatin writing
   • project administration
   as certified by two sponsors, who are professional members in good standing of ISP.
2. same as above, with a minimum of six years experience for any applicant presenting a four year degree in architecture, interior design, or engineering from an accredited college or university.
3. same as above, with a minimum of four years experience for any applicant presenting a college degree and either NCIDQ or NCARB certification.

• **Associate Member:** An individual engaged on a full-time basis in the profession of store planning who does not meet the qualifications required for Professional membership.

• **International Associate Member:** An individual residing and/or working in a country other than the USA or Canada who meets one of the following criteria:
   — Is a Registered Architect
   — Is in business as a designer or decorator
   — Is employed full time in the planning and/or design office of a retail organization or a shoplifting contractor

• **Visual Merchandising Member:** An individual engaged on a full-time basis in the profession of visual merchandising for retail stores who does not meet the qualifications for Professional membership.

• **Educational Member:** A department head or full-time professor instructor in store planning, architecture, or interior design in a university, college, or design or technical school.

• **Student Member:** A store-planning, interior design, and/or architectural student presently enrolled on a full-/or part-time basis in a university, college, or design or technical school who is interested in pursuing a career in nonresidential design.

• **Trade Member:** An individual representing a company that provides products and/or services to the store-planning profession.

• **Media Member:** An individual editor or writer of architecture, design, or visual arts publications active in the store-planning field.

Where are the ISP Chapters located and how do I get involved?

Specifically, What Does ISP Have to Offer?

Chapter Meetings

ISP Chapter meetings are held monthly and provide exposure to local, national, and international trends in store planning through presentations and tours by other design professionals and contractors. The meetings provide a chance for store-planning and design specialists to meet with their peers and to explore specific issues relating to the profession. ISP strongly encourages involvement and individual participation in the Chapter activities. For information on the Chapter nearest you, including plans and dates for future meetings, contact ISP International Executive Office, 25 North Broadway, Tarrytown, NY, 10591, TEL (914) 332-1806, FAX (914) 332-1541.

Design Competitions

To recognize and encourage excellence in store-planning design, the Institute holds two international design competitions annually. One is for completed store projects and is open to all members. The other is for students enrolled in college-level design courses. The winning entries of both competitions are published in nationally recognized store design magazines, displayed at national trade shows, and awarded prizes at major industry events.

Educational Support

To encourage quality new entrants into the profession, the Institute cooperates with various universities and technical colleges by providing from its membership, lecturers, critics, and judges for interior design courses specializing in store planning. An active ISP National Education Committee is working to promote a standard curriculum for students of store planning.

Licensing and Professional Support

ISP is a member of the National Council For Interior Design Qualification. NCIDQ is the orga-nization responsible for developing and administering the examination required for professional membership in any of the participating design organizations or in any state or Canadian province with a licensing statute. The examination tests for knowledge and technical skills required to be a practicing interior designer. ISP serves as a forum for store planners to address the licensing issue and assists members in preparing for qualifying exams.

ISP promotes recognition of the store-planning profession by actively participating in local and national store-planning events and by authoring articles for national industry publications on store-planning issues. Seminars are offered on store planning and design. ISP participates in several international trade shows and conferences.

Publications

ISP publishes a *Quarterly Newsletter* to keep members up-to-date on local, national, and international ISP activities. Various other papers, notices, and newsletters are published by the individual chapters.

A *Directory of Store Planners & Consultants* is available free of charge to retailers or anyone needing help in finding a store planning/design firm in a specific geographic area or with experience in a specific type of project.

An *Employment Referral Service* is available to the membership and to retailers seeking qualified store planners.

A *Membership Directory* is available all members. A mailing list of ISP members is available for purchase.

CODE OF ETHICS FOR PROFESSIONAL AND ASSOCIATE MEMBERS OF ISP

A member shall not accept any compensation for his services other than from his client or employer.

A member shall not render professional services without compensation.

A member shall not knowingly compete with another member on a basis of professional charges, or use donations as a device for obtaining professional advantage.

A member shall not offer his services in a competition except as provided by such competition codes as it Institute may establish.

A member who has been retained as a Professional Advisor in a competition shall not accept employment as a Designer/Planner for that project.

A member who also represents a manufacturing concern shall refrain from promoting same at meetings, shall not use the name of the Institute of Store Planners or its initials in conjunction with/or as an endorsement for said manufacturing concern.

A member shall not knowingly injure falsely or maliciously, the professional reputation/ prospects, or practice of another member of the profession.

A member shall not divide fees except with professionals related to the Store Planning Field and with those regularly employed or known to be associated with his office.

A member, when advertising, shall not use self-laudatory, exaggerated, or misleading publicity.

A member shall not solicit, not permit others to solicit in his name, advertisements or other support toward the cost of any publication presenting his work.

A member shall at no time act in a manner detrimental to the best interest of the profession.

A member shall not imply that his membership constitutes any approval or endorsement by the Institute of Store Planners of his professional services.

Appendix 17

AMERICAN SOCIETY OF INTERIOR DESIGNERS

ASID represents more than 20,000 practicing interior designers. Of those designers, 4,000 practice residential design; 6,400 practice contract design; and 9,600 practice a combination of residential and contract design. Most of them specify the products and services used in their design work, and more than 70 percent of ASID professional designers own or manage their design firms.

ASID interior designers specialize in a wide range of areas. In the commercial sector, our members provide services to the corporate, health care, institutional, hospitality and retail environments. In the residential hospitality and retail environments. In the residential field, our members provide services ranging from space planning or designing a home office to customizing a home to meet specific client needs.

Professional members of ASID satisfy rigorous acceptance standards: They must have a combination of accredited design education and/or full-time work experience, and pass the two-day National Council for Interior Design Qualification (NCIDQ) examination.

Allied Members practice interior design and are working towards completion of the requirements for ASID Professional membership. Successful completion of the NCIDQ exam plus other qualifications entitles Allied Members to advance to Professional membership.

Student Chapter Membership is available to students enrolled in an interior design program where an ASID student chapter exists.

Student Corresponding Membership is available to students in interior design programs in an area not served by an ASID student chapter.

Industry Foundation (IF) Membership is open to suppliers of the interior design industry. Membership provides interaction between interior designers and the interior furnishings industry that supplies services and manufactured products. IF members include manufacturers and their representatives, related trade associations and market centers.

Education: A commitment to education began when ASID founded the Foundation for Interior Design Education Research (FIDER), now an independent agency which accredits interior design programs at 200 colleges and universities. Students receive valuable professional and leadership training skills through ASID membership. Members of the National Student Council govern student programs, such as Student Connection and Career Options Fair held annually during the ASID National Conference. The quarterly student news-letter, ACCESS, keeps students informed about issues related to entering the field of interior design.

More than 150 courses, offering Continuing Education Units (CEU's), are available through local chapters and at the ASID National Conference. They provide knowledge of new techniques, products, important issues and business management. More than 100 of these approved professional development courses are offered for design professionals throughout the year. The STEP (self-testing exercises for pre-professionals are also offered to help ASID members prepare for the NCIDQ exam.

Chapter Services: While ASID is a national association, it also provides services at the local level through 49 chapters that span North America. These chapters are the focal point for the designer's involvement in the society and its programs. Chapters activities provide support for individual practice, education, community service projects, marketing and industry relations.

Marketing and Communications: The marketing and communications programs promote interior design services of ASID members. Specific marketing and media relations tactics have been implemented to enhance consumer awareness. In support of these efforts, ASID communicates current professional news to major media publications and ASID members. Consumers interested in interior design services can call ASID's toll-free referral service, (800) 775-ASID. ASID's client/designer selection service will match client's needs with the appropriate professional interior designer in their area.

Brochures and other pieces are available to help members in their marketing efforts. ASID members receive a bimonthly magazine, The ASID Report, that provides each member with hands-on information to improve their design practice. Student members receive a student newsletter three times a year.

Government and Public Affairs: The Government and Public Affairs Department monitors issues influencing the interior design practice—environmental safety laws, building and fire codes, universal design regulations, historic preservation and state registration of designers. ASID's Code of Ethics provides guidelines for professional practice with clients, suppliers, and colleagues. To date, more than $2 million has been provided by ASID to support title registration efforts. Licensing is already law in 17 states or jurisdictions and with lobbying efforts the number of states will continue to grow.

ASID is a member of the National Legislative Coalition for Interior Designers, which is made up of all the major interior design organizations to promote the major interior designer's right to practice. Public service activities are undertaken by more than 75% of ASID's chapters to help improve the quality of life for those in their communities.

Membership Programs and Resources: The ASID Membership Department is designed to provide assistance to members and to promote association membership and its benefits to all qualified individuals. ASID offers group life, health and professional liability insurance. Other programs include overnight mail and telephone service discounts, ASID contracts and business forms, ASID Yellow Pages advertising, and ASID MasterCard.

ASID Industry Foundation: The ASID Industry Foundation (IF) offers a forum that unites the professional designer with manufacturers of design-related products and services. IF members build relationships with design practioners that lead to improved products and services, business practices, design education and communication. Industry Foundation publishes an annual directory and product bulletins sponsored by member companies. Industry Annex Workshops, which educate interior designers about trends and technological development in the industry, are offered at the ASID National Conference.

The American Society of Interior Designers is the oldest and largest professional organization for interior designers. ASID was established in 1975, resulting from a merger of two interior design associations that had been formed in 1931. With more than 30,500 members, ASID establishes a common identity for professionals and businesses in the field of interior design. Our members include 20,000 interior design practitioners, 7,000 students and 3,500 manufacturers and representatives of products and services for interior design. ASID promotes professionalism in interior design services and products for the home and workplace.

ASID provides education for design practitioners that helps businesses conform to environmental and safety standards. Education prepares designers to create accessible spaces for persons with disabilities. ASID designers receive the most current information on appropriate materials, technology, building codes, government regulations, flammability standards, design psychology, and product performance. With this knowledge, ASID designers protect the safety and welfare of people in interior environments.

Appendix 18

METRIC CONVERSION FACTORS

Customary to Metric

Metric to Customary

Length

1 in.	= 25.4 mm
1 ft	= 0.3048 m
	= 304.8 mm
1 yd	= 0.9144 m
1 mi	= 1.609344 km

1mm	= 0.039 370 in.
1m	= 1.093 61 yd
	= 3.280 84 ft
1 km	= 0.621 371 mi

Area

1 sq. in.	= 645.16 mm²
1 sq. ft	= 0.092 903 m²
1 sq. yd	= 0.836 127 m²
1 acre	= 0.404 686 ha
	= 4046.86 m²
1 sq. mi	= 2.589 99 km²

1 mm2	= 0.001 55 sq. in.
1 m2	= 1.195 99 sq. yd
	= 10.7639 sq. ft
1 ha	= 2.471 05 acre
1 km2	= 0.386 102 sq. mi

Volume, Capacity, Section Modulus

1 fl. oz	= 29.573 53 mL
1 pint	= 0.473 176 L
1 gal	= 3.785 412 L
1 cu. in.	= 16 387.1 mm³
	(or mL)

1 mL	= 0.061 024 cu. in.
	= 0.033 814 fl. oz
1 L	= 0.035 315 cu. ft
	= 0.264 172 gal
	= 2.113 378 pint

| **Customary to Metric** | | **Metric to Customary** |

Volume, Capacity, Section Modulus

1 cu. ft	= 0.028 317 m³			
	= 28.3168 L	1 mm³	= 61.0237 x 10^{-6} cu. in.
1 cu. yd	= 0.764 555 m³	1 m³	= 1.307 95 cu. yd
			= 35.3147 cu. ft

INDEX

ABOUT THE AUTHOR

Michael Lopez, President and CEO of Michael Lopez Designs, Inc. of McHenry, Illinois, is a specialist in the field of store merchandising, planning, design, lighting, and construction, with over 30 years' experience. His associations include: The National Retail Federation, the American Society of Interior Designers (ASID), and past president of the Midwest Chapter of the Institute of Store Planners (ISP). All of these affiliations emphasize the professional involvement and education of Michael Lopez in the retail industry.

Mr. Lopez's apprenticeship background, from fixture manufacturers to major national department and specialty store conglomerates, culminated with Michael Lopez Designs, Inc., incorporating in 1978. He brings his experience in guiding retail management by applying and tailoring store planning philosophy and visual merchandising techniques to increase sales. He has established a national reputation for developing profit-making retail facilities.

Inquiries and comments can be sent to

MICHAEL LOPEZ DESIGNS, INC.
P.O. Box 1690
McHenry, Illinois 60051-1690
(815) 385-1600
FAX: (815) 385-1610